# DAVE STONE

# NEW

# HOME

# MARKETING

**REAL ESTATE EDUCATION COMPANY**
a division of Dearborn Financial Publishing, Inc.

Executive Editor: Kathleen A. Welton
Project Editor: Chris Christensen, Ellen Allen
Copy Editor: Dale Boroviak
Design: Edwin Harris

Published by Real Estate Education Company
a division of Dearborn Financial Publishing, Inc.

Printed in the United States of America

90  91  10  9  8  7  6  5  4  3  2

Library of Congress Cataloging-in-Publication Data

Stone, Dave.
  New home marketing.

  Bibliography: p.
  Includes index.
  1. Dwellings—Marketing.   2. House selling.
3. Real estate business.   I. Title.
HD1390.5.S76  1988        333.33'068'8        88-23015
ISBN 0-88462-114-6

This book is dedicated to the most important person in my life, who has supported and assisted me for more than 40 years, and whose faith in me has been a renewing source of strength throughout my career. Without her love and unselfish patience in allowing me to pursue my research, business activities and extensive travels, I would never have had the inspiration or motivation to complete this work!

*To my loving wife: Iva Dell*

# Contents

## 9    Customer Satisfaction and a Quality Delivery System    471

## 10    Managing and Monitoring the Marketing Functions    491

# Preface

*New Home Marketing* is a book I have long wanted to write. The first outline and sketchy draft was begun in 1978 and then placed on the shelf because of commitments to clients and other business interests. A few years ago, it came off the shelf with my sincere intention to finish the work within 12 months. In actuality, it has taken more than five years to assemble, write and edit this manual. My clients and associates have played major roles in helping me to produce the book. Every marketing assignment provided an additional opportunity to research and test marketing principles that were ultimately incorporated into the text. The checklists, examples, forms and systems have been summarized, verified and modified many times as we attempted to meet specific sales and marketing opportunities or issues.

I am very grateful for the support given to me by my friends in the industry. They have unselfishly shared experiences and knowledge with me; many of the articles, case histories and exhibits were provided by these marketing professionals. In fact, the quantity of information given to me far exceeded the limitations of this volume, so I have, of necessity, been selective in choosing the final examples. The individuals and companies who have been part of my research efforts are identified in the appendix. However, I would be remiss if I did not acknowledge a few people who were key advisors to me throughout the long process of assembling and writing this book. To each of the following, I extend my personal appreciation for the advice and knowledge they have shared with me to make this book a reality:

Lee Anderson, Project Management Co, Minneapolis, MN
William E. Becker, Becker & Associates, Teaneck, NJ
Richard Bryan, The Ryland Group, Columbia, MD
Karen Butera, Karen Butera, Inc., Palo Alto, CA
Randy Chamberlain, Habitat, Inc. Tempe, AZ
Steve Critchfield, Critchfield, Inc., Wichita, KS
Fred Dumser, The Ryland Group, Columbia, MD
Richard Elkman, Group II Advertising, Philadephia, PA
George Fulton, Fulton Research Co., Fairfax, VA

Lester Goodman, Goodman & Hixon, Inc., Irvine, CA
Pete Halter, Secured Communities, Inc., Atlanta, GA
Jim Hale, Fonville-Morisey, Realtors, Raleigh, NC
Tom Johnson, The Weigand Company, Wichita, KS
Nicki Joy, Nicki Joy and Associates, Brookville, MD
David Olson, The Olson Marketing Group, Denver, CO
Marc Putman, Development Directions, Inc., Rochester, MN
Tom Richey, Richey Resources, Inc., Houston TX
Gary Ryness, The Ryness Company, Danville, CA
Michael Scotko, Scotko Sign & Display Co., Gibbsboro, NJ
John Sims, Weichert New Homes and Land, Inc., Morristown, NJ
David Wolfe, Wolfe Resources, Annapolis, MD

Recognizing that my readers represent a universe of differing backgrounds and needs, I have attempted to cover the subject from several perspectives. While the primary approach is that of a marketing director who is part of a team including a professional staff of on-site new home sales specialists, I also provide practical guidelines for managing marketing functions for the small-volume builder without benefit of a marketing assistant or sales manager. Equally important is the growing role of the broker-oriented new home sales organizations that service the sales and marketing needs of multiple clients in their areas of influence. In this country, real estate brokers sell more new houses than all builder-controlled in-house sales operations, either by directly managing marketing efforts or serving as cooperative agents. An increasing number of progressive real estate brokerage companies are establishing new home sales divisions staffed with professional marketers and full-time builder sales specialists. Then there are the roles of the housing consultants, researchers, merchandisers, advertisers, sales managers and strategizers. They provide the subcontracting support needed by those at the marketing helm. Many of them have contributed to the information in this manual. Our mutual efforts will, I hope, be beneficial to all readers.

You will note that the book contains several dominant themes that are woven into each chapter. One theme is the absolute need for valid research. One cannot effectively build a marketing plan without having first laid a solid foundation on which it can rest securely. The marketing manager who attempts to make decisions without first having surveyed the marketplace is risking failure. Another underlying message I have tried to impart is the need for flexible strategies that can adjust to changing conditions and fluctuating markets. Establishing game plans that minimize risk while increasing market potential is the best way to insure survival. I have also greatly emphasized the need for superior performers on the sales line. It is a waste of advertising dollars to bring prospects to a new housing community to have them meet with representatives who do not know how to qualify, demonstrate and close!

Finding cost-efficient methods of attracting prospective buyers has also been one of the main principles of this book. Too often, marketing experts are prone to investing substantial dollars in newspapers and other expensive media before they have profiled customers and evaluated the most efficient ways of reaching them. I believe that lead-generating programs must include self-prospecting efforts by salespeople and cooperating brokers. Cultivating referrals is one of the least expensive means of maintaining momentum, but it usually receives only minor attention by those plotting basic marketing campaigns. Equitable marketing plans always incorporate efficient prospecting strategies that begin with the lead-generating responsibilities of front-line sales personnel!

Finally, it will be obvious to my readers that I have strong convictions about the importance of the on-site marketing environment. The objectives of packaging and presentation must be defined before those of prospecting and promotion. We always deal with an emotionally charged decision process influenced by everything that customers see, hear and feel! Sales are lost whenever the sales environment is not adequately prepared for communicating values to well-profiled prospects. This does not mean you must always have furnished models—or any kind of models! It means that value-building messages must be visually and verbally dramatized in an environment that permits maximum emotional participation by customers. I sincerely believe that if we invest planning time and dollars in the presentation elements (including adequately training sales personnel) we can realize more sales at a lower cost per prospect!

Dave Stone

# 1: 'Who's in Charge?'

As we open this guidebook for housing marketers, the first question we must ask is:

*"Who should be in charge of the marketing disciplines?"*

We are constantly amazed to discover how fragmented are the marketing operations of most building companies. Sales and marketing are often mysterious elements of the business plan that are relegated to a group of sorcerers known as sales agents and advertising agencies. Many production-oriented builders assume that merely constructing a reasonably good housing product will assure sales success. For these companies, marketing managers, sales agents and consultants are relatively unimportant in the scheme of things. Many players in the housing industry lack a clear understanding of marketing and its multifaceted disciplines.

Effective marketing means much more than promoting and selling new real estate properties. Marketing encompasses almost every aspect of a residential development company's operations from land acquisition to product design and, ultimately, to the satisfaction of the residents. Marketing is the interpretive discipline that must relate all business decisions to their potential impact on consumer's acceptance or rejection of the product. It encompasses all of the following functions to create a successful new residential development:

- land acquisition feasibility research
- land planning
- product design and mix
- pricing strategies for every home and homesite
- flexible financing alternatives
- equity release programs
- planning construction sequences and marketing phases
- selection of plans and models to be featured
- designing on-site marketing facilities
- selection and management of sales personnel
- cooperative broker relationships
- marketing budgets and pro formas

- sales training and orientation
- advertising and promotion for target markets
- public relations and publicity
- resident relationships
- quality delivery systems
- sales processing system
- consumer research

These broad categories require checklists that must be evaluated and monitored if the marketing responsibilities are to be adequately covered.

The primary reason for so many unsuccessful housing ventures and so many builders who fail to attain the profitability they envision is the failure to follow sound marketing principles in the development of new housing environments. What to build, how to price it, what features to include in each design, how to reach the profiled prospects and what salespeople to recruit are marketing functions that critically influence the economic future of the enterprise.

In small developer/builder companies it is not uncommon to have the owner elect to maintain direct control over all marketing functions including sales management. This frequently results from a sincere belief that assignment of these functions to anyone else would increase the financial risks of the enterprise. Concern for overhead, economic necessity involved in all aspects of land acquisition through design stages to final sales and closings, and a strong control need characterize most builders who maintain total involvement in their marketing operations. Since financial success depends on effective marketing, it is logical that the principals in any building company remain deeply involved in the major decisions that influence public acceptance of their housing environments.

However, a big difference exists between assuming the responsibilities for managing the marketing functions and fully understanding the ingredients required for marketing success. The principal's background and personal experience dictate how perceptively he or she will respond to the challenges and opportunities of developing a workable marketing strategy. Only a small percentage of developers and builders in the United States enter the profession from a sales and marketing background.

Most of them enter from either the construction trades or related businesses. There are many more professionally educated builders today than in previous generations. A number of the clients of The Stone Institute entered the industry with degrees in business administration, finance or construction. Their education gives them a much broader appreciation of the relationships among the disciplines of construction, finance, marketing and administration. Despite the increase of well-educated business managers entering this rapidly changing field, the small-volume builders from the construction trades and the do-it-yourself owners are still the backbone of the housing industry.

Regardless of the building company's size, the marketing roles are too complex to be trusted solely to the judgment of one individual. Even a small-volume builder needs advice from real estate agents, marketing consultants, designers, financiers and friendly competitors. Even if one has the knowledge and ability to develop practical marketing formulas, it is sound business insurance to involve others whose disciplines can validate or challenge proposed decisions before they are executed. Many builders make the classic mistake of following their own "gut" instincts without benefit of adequate research, competitive indexing or the advice of experienced marketers. The results are frequently disastrous! The casebooks are full of horror stories about free-wheeling builders and investors who started housing projects that were never completed, companies that filed bankruptcy because the products they designed could not be sold for a profit, lenders who take back unfinished or unsold homes they never intended owning and land sellers forced to repossess developed sites because of mortgage defaults. Not all of these failures were directly related to poor marketing. Some were just business incompetence, others fraudulently conceived. Others were victims of unexpected reverses in local market conditions that even the experts might not have foreseen. But most failures in the housing industry can be directly or indirectly traced to decisions that were made without having sound marketing strategies in place. Avoiding losses and enhancing the financial potential of the venture should be primary motives for seeking and responding to advice from those who understand and can interpret the marketing scene.

Small-volume builders are typically those who produce less than 20 to 25 homes a year. Obviously, a low-volume builder has the challenge of trying to keep overhead costs in line with limited production. There is seldom room for a full-time marketing director in that size company unless an investment is being made to expand the business to greater volume in subsequent years. The builder-manager will, of necessity, be his or her own marketing director unless an outside brokerage organization is employed to assume that function. Real estate brokers play a very important role in the representation of modest-sized building companies throughout America. Most of the sales made for small contracting entities are broker originated and usually from off-site locations. Builders account for the rest of the sales made in those companies where the principals take an active role in selling their own homes.

The small builder is well advised to contract with real estate professionals who understand new home sales and marketing when the volume of the operation does not justify developing in-house talent. Even larger companies have found it advantageous to engage real estate brokers rather than attempt to build their own sales and marketing teams. A primary motivation for using contract marketing agencies is to free the builder to concentrate on what he does best: buying land and building homes. The danger in completely trusting a subcontractor relationship is losing control over vital marketing decisions. We believe that, while it is often in the builder's best interest to assign the broader marketing responsibilities to outside real estate professionals and to concentrate on the financial and production aspects of the business, it is equally vital to the health of the enterprise to maintain an active marketing forum that involves all of the needed disciplines. A marketing committee is one of the best ways to achieve the free flow of information that can correctly influence the decision makers.

Again we ask the question: Should builders or land developers be their own marketing managers? The answer must be partly yes if we view marketing as the comprehensive assignment of creating and positioning new residential housing. Those who have the most to gain or lose should never release total control of the economic future of the business to others. On the other hand, there is no need for any builder/developer to try to make decisions and manage marketing operations without the assistance of those who have more expertise in sales and marketing. Real estate brokers, full-time marketing directors, sales managers, consultants and other members of the builder's team should be involved in developing marketing strategies based on their knowledge and skills. It is a matter of structuring the marketing functions so that they meet the financial objectives of the enterprise. In this manual we provide specific guidelines for organizing marketing and sales operations for developers, builders and outside specialists who serve their needs.

## POSITION DESCRIPTION OF THE MARKETING DIRECTOR

As we have noted, the marketing director in a new home sales organization may be the builder, an outside broker, a specialist in marketing, or a sales manager with multiple responsibilities. The size and nature of the enterprise will usually dictate who should logically be in charge of marketing. Whoever plays that role should take the position seriously. The success of the company rests on the ability to sell new homes at a reasonable profit within logical time frames. Unless the director of marketing has clearly defined responsibilities, authority and accountability, sizable risk exists that many vital functions of sales and marketing will be neglected. We have assisted numerous clients in structuring their marketing operations to help them become more effective, including the preparation of position descriptions for directors of marketing and sales.

In this section of the manual, we summarize basic areas of responsibilities for those who are in charge of marketing functions in real estate development, home building and new home marketing companies. These guidelines should be tailored for the specific needs of individual enterprises.

## SHOULD MARKETING MANAGERS SUPERVISE SALES
## AND SALES MANAGERS?

Before we introduce the elements of a typical marketing manager's assignments, we must discuss sales management as it relates to marketing management. Historically, the evolution of specialists in marketing has been closely tied to the responsibility for sales performance. After all, marketing managers provide sales personnel with the tools and traffic they need to achieve their objectives. Thus, in most home building and real estate organizations where the volume of activities justifies a full-time marketing manager, the supervision of sales management is normally included in the position description. At the very least, the director of marketing should be in a close liaison role with those who are directly responsible for sales personnel.

The two roles are fundamentally different, even if performed by the same person. Marketing deals with *things* while sales management deals with *people*! The director of marketing must be primarily concerned with such things as research statistics, product design, model-home decorating, signs, brochures, advertising and promotion. The sales manager is concerned with recruiting, selecting, training and motivating salespeople. Effective sales managers will devote at least 50 percent of their time to the needs of the salespeople, helping them to resolve the issues that affect sales performance. Marketing managers are often so involved with the details of organizing the opening of a new community or the development of a major marketing campaign that they have little or no time to worry about training and motivating salespeople.

Often the qualities required to be a strong, results-oriented sales manager are not those characteristic of the creative people who supervise marketing and merchandising. True, we do have within the industry many individuals who can perform both functions reasonably well, but they are exceptions rather than the rule. Having a good feel for the preparation of brochures, ad copy, housing designs and decorating does not assure an understanding of the complexities of managing emotional salespeople or appreciating how to motivate them to higher levels of achievement. Even if marketing supervisors have a responsibility for sales functions, specialists often must assume the direct responsibility for sales management. The "people-motivating" profession demands a unique set of skills normally gained only by being directly involved in front-line sales. Most new home sales managers evolved from the ranks of front-line sales people. On the other hand, many marketing and merchandising people come from other fields where they developed creative skills in advertising, graphics, design and public relations without in-depth exposure to the sales processes.

So we ask again: Should the marketing manager also be the sales manager or supervise the sales manager? The answer to that question depends upon the skills and background of the individuals—not just on the logical corporate structure. We do not always attract people who have multidisciplined skills in marketing and sales. Ideally, the director of marketing should be responsible for everything that affects the attainment of the company's sales objectives, and this certainly includes sales management. That does not mean the marketing manager has to personally perform the sales management functions. Those with the time and talent to work in the field with sales people should have the direct line of authority in sales production. Sales managers normally report to marketing managers. However, if the nature of the organization dictates that a marketing manager be employed who has little or no sales management experience, it may be wise to place the two functions on the same corporate level in a cooperative role and have them, in turn, report to a president or general manager who has the ability to extract the best out of both disciplines.

## DIRECTOR OF MERCHANDISING SERVICES—A COORDINATING ROLE

In some companies, the marketing disciplines are divided into three broad functional areas:

1. strategic marketing management
2. sales management
3. merchandising services

Under this organizational plan, a general manager usually has the overall responsibility for developing marketing strategies and supervising the other disciplines on which the execution of those plans depends. Sales management and merchandising services are separated so that neither is burdened with details of the other disciplines. The sales manager supervises sales personnel, while the coordinator of merchandising services is concerned with model decor, brochures and the development of sales aids. The strategist at the top of this corporate structure maintains full responsibility for creating the products, managing the research, developing marketing campaigns and supervising the marketing department.

A number of home-building companies have essentially this format, and often the builder serves the role of the general strategist or director of marketing. He or she is supported by the two individuals (or departments) responsible for these separate areas.

In a few companies, a merchandising coordinator reports to the sales manager who, in turn, reports to the marketing manager. This is rare, although it is not without merit since the sales manager has the greatest concern for providing sales personnel with the merchandising support needed to make them effective. Providing sales managers with one or more assistants to expedite the details of on-site marketing and merchandising can be effective in tying responsibilities to those who have the most to lose or gain by proper implementation of merchandising details.

## THE MARKETING DIRECTOR AS STRATEGIST AND GENERAL MANAGER

The most common way to supervise marketing disciplines is to have one person (even if he or she wears other hats) in the primary role as director of marketing and chief strategist for designing and implementing basic marketing programs. On this premise, we include for your reference a typical position description for this key function. Following this broad definition of the major position in the marketing department, we will provide you with separate position descriptions for the sales manager and for the merchandising coordinator. Where one individual is doing all three functions you can digest and combine these position descriptions. It is important to remember that, no matter who has these assignments, they collectively represent the opportunities and challenges of efficiently managing the marketing functions on which the success of the enterprise is critically dependent.

## OBJECTIVES OF THE MARKETING MANAGER'S POSITION

The director of marketing in a real estate development entity has the basic responsibility for creating and managing all the strategies necessary to assure successful marketing of the properties offered by the company.

In that capacity, the following broad objectives are included:

- Develop marketing and general sales plans for each community, project or building phase as the company releases them to the marketing department for review and recommendations. These plans should be submitted in writing within the time assigned by executive management. This includes the preparation of marketing budgets as requested.

- Establish the criteria for all research needed to effectively determine the potential absorption and penetration rates for each of the projects and products offered by the company. Select and supervise the people and agencies necessary to maintain a comprehensive research capacity.
- Maintain control over all marketing elements with a dedicated concern for the image and reputation of the company as projected in the various mediums of marketing.
- Establish standards of performance for personnel in the marketing department and assist them to set and attain results-oriented objectives.
- Select and supervise the agencies and suppliers needed for implementation of marketing programs. These include advertising agencies, graphic display companies, printers, interior decorators and suppliers of marketing materials.
- Anticipate potential marketing and sales obstacles that might adversely affect attainment of company goals and recommend actions to minimize or avoid negative challenges.
- Chair the marketing committee, which will be composed of representatives from disciplines within the company and experts from consulting agencies important to the formulation and execution of marketing programs. This committee is a decision-influencing group, but the responsibilities for approval of marketing programs as well as their implementation rest with the director of marketing.
- Review and approve the sales strategies for each project and marketing program of the company as submitted by sales management. Supervise all functions of the sales department through personnel selected for sales management.
- Participate in local and national associations important to the company in education, public relations and research.
- Periodically attend conventions, seminars and conferences that can assist company objectives. Visit other communities and real estate operations for research objectives and prepare competitive reports.

## OBJECTIVES OF THE SALES MANAGER'S POSITION

The general sales manager may have one or more projects or communities to supervise. In some companies, the sales-management role is divided by assigning different people to each project. Thus, general management becomes the responsibility of either the director of marketing or the general manager of the enterprise. We will address the objectives and responsibilities of this position from the posture of one sales manager not directly involved with marketing management but devoted to meeting the company's sales goals in the role of managing sales and salespeople.

- Develop a general sales plan for each community, project and building program released to the sales department by executive management. These strategies should be summarized in writing as requested by general management. Budgets will be prepared and submitted when appropriate.

- Recruit and select sales personnel needed to staff the communities and sales offices of the company. This includes setting and maintaining standards for the quality of personnel and performance desired by the company.
- Educate and train all new-home sales personnel to assure adequate product knowledge and sales skills required to meet presentation and closing objectives.
- Supervise and motivate personnel to keep them at the highest possible performance levels. This includes monitoring and regularly evaluating the performance of each salesperson in the department.
- Establish and maintain relationships with all REALTORS® and the real estate professionals who cooperate in representing the company's housing to the general public.
- Supervise processing of all sales transactions and those involved in servicing sales from beginning to end.
- Lead the salespeople by example and administer duties in a fair, ethical and knowledgeable manner. This includes occasionally assisting sales representatives in handling prospects and closing sales.
- Serve as sales coordinator with other departments and personnel of the company. This includes resolving issues with construction, finance and development operations.
- Supervise the sales facilities and sales materials necessary for the operation of each assigned company project. This includes coordination with those responsible for model homes, landscaping, inventory homes and homesites.
- Submit reports as requested by executive management for the evaluation of personnel, sales in process, sales traffic, customer surveys and competitive research conducted by the sales department.
- Maintain challenging and stimulating environments for all the sales personnel within the department.

## OBJECTIVES OF THE MERCHANDISING COORDINATOR'S POSITION

In most new home sales organizations, the role of managing merchandising elements of marketing programs is handled either by the director of marketing, the sales director or one person responsible for both functions. However, some larger companies use a third party or separate department to manage these responsibilities. The following position assignments are covered in this category:

- Develop recommendations for the presentation of the homes, models, communities and services of the company. Submit these recommendations in writing as requested to the director of marketing for review and approval.
- Supervise the decorating of all model homes including coordinating with interior decorators, production personnel and designers. Maintain inventory controls for all furnishings and equipment involved in merchandising operations.

- Coordinate with sales management the installation of all graphics and displays required in the sales areas for professional presentation of the company's homes and communities.
- Supervise production and installation of all signs, billboards, flags and other elements needed to promote the housing communities offered by the company.
- Coordinate advertising and promotion. (There may be some in-house capacity to produce ads, brochures and promotional elements.)
- Supervise development and production of brochures, sales literature and collateral materials for marketing company housing.
- Assist, as requested, in customer-service programs, including move-ins and welcoming owners to their new homes, customer surveys and public-relations campaigns.
- Organize and supervise special events to help promote company communities. This includes preview parties, open houses, grand openings and special parties for owners and guests.
- Produce and distribute company newsletter(s) for both communication to employees and associates and for owners of homes built by the company.
- Perform other assignments for the marketing department as requested by executive management.

## THE MARKETING COMMITTEE—A USEFUL MANAGEMENT FORUM

Marketing encompasses all the other disciplines in a real estate enterprise. From land acquisition to final delivery of the last home in the community, marketing is responsible for pulling together all ingredients of the presentations and formulating programs and strategies for sell-out in the predicted time period. That is why a forum for communicating marketing objectives and resolving marketing issues within the company is essential. Any director of marketing, regardless of knowledge and skills, will be less effective trying to operate independently than when supported by a cooperative team from the other disciplines in the enterprise.

The formation of a marketing committee that can oversee all marketing operations of the company is a practical way to open communication lines and generate creative ideas to assist in the attainment of marketing objectives. Those who are normally members of this decision influencing group include:

1. the director of marketing (normally the chairperson)
2. the construction manager (optional)
3. the sales manager(s)
4. the merchandising coordinator
5. account executive from the advertising agency
6. consultants as required
7. sales personnel as required

In small companies, this committee is often an informal group that meets frequently for a variety of up-dating and planning functions. In larger, more disciplined enterprises the committee usually has regularly scheduled meetings (sometimes once a week in fast-moving operations) where agendas and minutes are formally organized. Whether formal or informal, a genuine need exists to provide those in charge of marketing and sales with a sense of direction. Proposals that will change the design of the land plan, the homes or condominiums, amenities, options and inclusions in the product line, financing packages, and myriad similar items that tend to be modified as you develop land and build residential structures are vital factors in effective marketing programs. Without an opportunity for the affected disciplines to exchange ideas and critique the proposed designs and campaigns, the risk is great that decisions detrimental to sales and marketing objectives and, ultimately, to company profits will be made.

We do not believe any unnecessary meeting should be held. Meetings that are poorly organized and attended by people whose input is not vital to the operation are a waste of time and money. Some companies seem to spend all of their management time in meetings. One wonders when the key people have time to follow through on what they decided in those meetings! Marketing meetings are no exception. If there are no topics that need to be discussed and everything is running smoothly, scheduled meetings can be cancelled. However, when new communities are being planned, new housing designs and models proposed, and adjusted marketing campaigns under consideration, group sharing is necessary before conclusions are reached. Actions should not be started that do not have the advantage of collective wisdom to prevent serious errors in judgment. The resulting synergy of bringing together those who can contribute to marketing strategies in an open and free-wheeling exchange of ideas often produces the difference that sets one company's marketing effectiveness apart from another's.

## GUIDELINES FOR ORGANIZING EFFECTIVE MARKETING MEETINGS

Management time is valuable and nonrecoverable. It needs to be jealousy guarded by all who are in charge of organizing meetings. When you multiply the dollar value of each hour by every individual present at a meeting, you become aware of the partial cost for assembling human resources in a decision-influencing session. The major reason so much time is wasted at meetings is little or no advance planning.

Every meeting held should have an agenda and a clearly defined set of objectives that are communicated to all participants prior to the meeting. Every member of the marketing committee should know what will be covered at the planning session and what each is required to bring to participate effectively. Statistics, exhibits, floor plans, merchandising proposals, etc., should be organized and distributed to the committee members before or during the meeting.

Any productive conference normally has a time limit—one as brief as possible as long as it permits accomplishment of the stated objectives. Most marketing meetings can be kept to one hour or less if well planned and efficiently conducted. Before the meeting begins, the chair should state the objectives, review the agenda, set time guidelines and ask participants to keep comments brief and to the point. When someone gets out of line or the meeting starts to wander, the chairperson has the responsibility of bringing objectives back into focus. At the end of the meeting, the chairperson should give a quick summary of decisions or recommendations and assignments made for following through on the actions taken.

Always appoint someone to keep notes of topics discussed and major points covered so that they can be digested and distributed to the attendees following the meeting. These notes should also be placed in a control binder in chronological sequence so they are available for review by management when needed.

## TYPICAL AGENDA FOR A MARKETING COMMITTEE MEETING

Here is a sample agenda of a well-planned marketing committee session for a home-building company.

---

**FIGURE 1.1   Marketing agenda.**

### Marketing Committee Agenda 10/16

1.  Review of Sales and Traffic By Project . . . . . . . . . . . . . . . . . . . . . . . . . . . . . . . . . . . . .R. Selly
2.  Critique of New Townhome Floor Plans . . . . . . . . . . . . . . . . . . . . . . . . . . . . . . . . . .B. Harris
3.  Value Index Research Evaluation . . . . . . . . . . . . . . . . . . . . . . . . . . . . . . . . . . . . . . .D. Sullivan
4.  Review Changes for Evening Sales Hours . . . . . . . . . . . . . . . . . . . . . . . . . . . . . . . .G. Maryleen
5.  Preview Marketing Campaign for Wood Lake . . . . . . . . . . . . . . . . . . . . . . . . . . . . . .R. Selly
6.  Interior Decorator Presentation . . . . . . . . . . . . . . . . . . . . . . . . . . . . . . . . . . . . . . . .M.Garcia
7.  Direct Mail Campaign Review—Chelsea . . . . . . . . . . . . . . . . . . . . . . . . . . . . . . . . .B. Harris
8.  New Business and Assignments

Note: Meeting will begin promptly at 8:00 A.M. in the main conference room and is scheduled to conclude no later than 10:00 A.M. Any amendments or additions to the agenda must be cleared with Susan Davidson before 5:00 P.M. Tuesday night. Come prepared with your exhibits and comments so we can make this another productive meeting.

---

A well-run meeting, like the one outlined above, can provide the stimulus of ideas and momentum to marketing programs that keeps your company out in front of your competition!

## WARNING: NEVER SACRIFICE SALES MANAGEMENT FOR OTHER MARKETING ACTIVITIES

Sales management is not a desk jockey's job! It is not possible to be an effective sales manager and devote most of your time to budgetary matters and paperwork! And yet hundreds of people claim to be managers of sales but spend very little time with the salespeople in the sales arenas they supposedly supervise. They have the titles but do not play the roles.

Effective sales managers devote most of their time to face-to-face, on-line sales management activities. The best way to monitor sales performance and help sales representatives improve their selling skills is to be with them in the sales environments they experience each day. If you are buried in paperwork, meetings with builders and developers, sessions with advertising agencies and a hundred other events, little or no time is left for direct involvement with the people on whom the success of the enterprise depends: *those who sell the homes you build!*

It is easy to fall into the paper trap. The position description for many sales managers is almost the same as for the director of marketing: supervising research, preparing market plans, working with designers and decorators, meeting with the agencies who handle publicity and promotion and serving as merchandising advisor to those in the company who have to interface with sales and marketing people. In small companies, one person must play all of these roles as a matter of economic necessity. Even outside brokerage companies can fall into this same administrative problem.

If you are the sales manager and not devoting at least half of your time to the direct supervision of salespeople, you should consider changing your title and letting someone else manage them. It is not sufficient to hold a once-a-week sales meeting in the central office and consider that brief encounter as fulfilling the requirements of sales leadership.

## PRIORITIES AND TIME MANAGEMENT

Motivating and stimulating sales personnel to meet the sales goals necessary to achieve corporate profit objectives is a primary responsibility of a sales manager. Anything that detracts from that results-oriented priority has to be carefully evaluated. Sometimes the problem is comfort-zone management. We tend to do things we like rather than focus on things we need to do. Not everyone is comfortable supervising the direct-line sales functions. If you do not fully relate to selling roles and find it stimulating to be with salespeople in the selling environment, chances are that you have the wrong position in the company. On the other hand, if you have gradually allowed less important matters to encroach on the sales management time necessary for one-on-one involvement with your representatives, then the rules should be changed.

The better-organized sales managers in this industry normally plan their days so that they can do all of their administrative housekeeping functions in the office (or elsewhere) in the morning hours and they reserve each afternoon to be out in the field with the sales associates of the company. They schedule their daily activities to leave plenty of time for "hands-on" sales programming with their agents.

## ROLES OF ON-LINE SALES MANAGERS

Daily involvement with salespeople should include the following roles:

- Reviewing the prospects that are not yet closed.
- Evaluating follow-up procedures used by the agents to assure continuity of contact and higher closing rates.

- Checking the inventory sites with sales personnel and determining what needs to be done to sell the remaining locations.
- Studying the sales methodology used by each associate to validate its effectiveness and determine which skills need improvement.
- Checking sales in process to be sure all necessary steps are being taken to assure successful and timely closings.
- Evaluating the physical sales environment to be sure it is in optimum condition to receive and motivate customers to buy.
- Reviewing the self-prospecting activities of each agent including building owner referrals, contacting cooperative brokers and working centers of influence.
- Rehearsing the salespeople on each function of the sales process including participating in role-playing sessions:

> Greeting
> Qualifying
> Building values with planned presentations
> Handling objections
> Creating urgency for specific sites
> Closing
> Handling financing and paperwork
> Following up the sales that have been made

- And most important, providing personal counseling and motivation for all salespersons in ways that lift their self esteem and cause them to rise to their full capacities.

The sales manager should be capable of taking over on a busy day and assisting the salespeople in handling traffic and closing sales. The turn-over role is also an essential part of this process. When a salesperson has a prospect who is difficult to close, the introduction of the manager can often be valuable in providing the reinforcement that results in a sale.

Many sales managers are also front-line salespeople serving dual functions. They sell as part of the team and manage part of the time. While this is a challenging position that demands an ability to keep the separate roles in perspective, it is a logical use of talent in a growing sales organization. A selling sales manager may be far more effective than a full time one who spends all of his or her time in the office rather than in the field. To influence the salespeople and help them achieve maximum results, you have to know their abilities and be alongside to motivate them to reach their full potential. There is no substitute for hands-on sales management. And if you or your company is suffering from marketing congestion blocking the sales channels, you should re-evaluate the use of human resources and put the emphasis where it belongs: on the front-line performers.

Marketing management must encompass all disciplines that affect the attainment of sales objectives—but none is more important than sales management!

The next section of this chapter is specifically designed for builders and developers who elect to engage outside brokerage companies (or individuals) to represent their properties. It will also be of interest to brokers seeking ways to more effectively attract clientele from the housing industry. If this does not apply to you or your company, you may want to skip to chapter two.


## CRITERIA FOR SELECTING A DESIGNATED BROKERAGE COMPANY

The choice of a brokerage firm to represent a builder or developer in the primary marketing functions is vitally important to successful fulfillment of marketing objectives. Not all brokerage firms are capable of representing builders' homes. If it is your responsibility to make the choice, select your target markets carefully so that your broker(s) can professionally fulfill the responsibilities and produce profitable results.


### Location of the Brokerage Company's Office

The brokerage company's office location can be a key criterion if you are expecting buyers to be produced by their off-site agents. Is it easy for prospects to visit the offices, to sit down and view audio-visual presentations, to learn about your housing and be qualified prior to showing your homes? You want prestige locations in neighborhoods that are representative of the profiled clientele who purchase your homes. You want offices ideally located in relation to traffic patterns; that is, easily accessible by major freeways or thoroughfares so as to attract people and to facilitate clear directions through the company's local advertising.

Companies with more than one office location may be preferable because of the advantage they offer in increased exposure. However, there is another side to that issue. Many small offices do not compare with the advantages of one well-located, prestigious office that has the facilities as well as the professional image to represent your homes. You normally should be more concerned about the coverage of one office than the scope of the total organization. In a major region, you may want more than one brokerage company involved. This matter must be researched carefully and a decision made as to the anticipated impact of one brokerage company based on the influence of its location as compared to other factors.


### Reputation of the Brokerage Company

Certainly, a company's adherence to a high standard of ethics must be a major consideration in selecting brokers. To some degree, that will be based upon their years in business and their credibility in the real estate markets they serve. A large referral volume together with professional recognition will increase public acceptance of their recommendations and, hopefully, your new homes. You will, in many cases, need the broker's support and reputation to compensate for the inherent fears of buyers who hesitate to become directly involved with builders and the construction process. A brokerage organization with a quality image can add measurably to the images of the builders and developers it represents.

### The Capacity of Brokerage Firms to Attract and Sell Your Buyers

Before selecting any brokerage company, evaluate the nature of the properties and clientele they presently service. Do not make exclusive listing arrangements with brokers who do not have access to your buyers.

You will want the marketing platform that reputable brokers can give to introduce your housing to the right people with whom they have established relationships. Capitalize on the broker's centers of influence within the community. These will probably lead you to more buyers through the broker's networks. These centers of influence can be very important marketing considerations. The broker who has a solid reputation for being involved with the right political and social circles will help you to introduce your homes to the right people. You can accelerate your marketing program by using the designed broker's advance groundwork.

Thus, as part of your criteria, identify the neighborhoods within each market area that represent the price range and caliber of buyers you seek. Then determine which brokerage firms in that market are most effective and have the finest reputations with the majority of local residents.

### Quality of the Broker's Personnel

The nature and quality of the broker's personnel should also be a prime factor in making your selection. You need salespeople who are respected by the prospects you are trying to attract and who have the knowledge and skills to work comfortably with your clientele. You also want salespeople involved mostly with new residential sales, preferably within a separate new-home sales or builder marketing-services department. Some companies specialize in new-home sales and marketing. There is a direct relationship between the number of contracts each agent has and the effectiveness of presenting new home opportunities. We know there is only a limited percentage of any specific market available to us, so the increased number of salespeople exposed to the area gives you a better chance to tap that share of the market.

Dedicated account managers are a necessity. One individual from the designated firm should coordinate with you and your staff. That person should have the prime responsibility for being the liaison between his or her organization and yours. From an administrative viewpoint, this is a requirement for effective communication. Look for brokerage companies with experience and a solid reputation in their market areas—and especially in the effective representation of new housing developments.

### Quality of Brokerage Administration

You can certainly appreciate the truth that not all brokers are effective administrators. In fact, poor administration is more the rule than the exception. A large number of real estate firms have little or no management control because those who operate them are basically sales individuals who operate in a world of independent contractors doing independent things. You want to associate with a well-managed real estate firm—one with an experienced broker or brokers capable of supervising their people and working effectively with you in all facets of your operation. You need brokers who are capable of representing you and who understand the special needs of the home-building industry. The account manager at the cooperative brokerage firm who will be working with your company should be mutually approved. You want an administrative commitment from the brokers that assures their willingness to extend sufficient time and attention to your marketing needs.

## CRITERIA FOR SUCCESSFUL OPERATION OF A DESIGNATED-BROKER PROGRAM

### The Commitments Made to the Brokers

It is essential that management realize that the commitments it makes to designated brokers must be fulfilled. Carefully evaluate promises that will be made to the designated broker and set up realistic goals. Your management must not abdicate its responsibilities to brokers any more than you should expect brokers to neglect their commitments to you.

### The Communication and Verification of the Broker Relationship

It is important for your company's objectives that a schedule be established to assure regular communication with designated brokers, preferably on a weekly basis. Ask the broker for opinions on presentations, designs, floor plans and other matters pertinent to marketing management. There is great validity in evidencing the executive team's concern about its relationship with its broker(s) and about reactions to your housing operations. Management should follow through with brokers to see how their salespeople have reacted after inspecting your properties. Standardized sales and marketing reports should be submitted to your company by the broker for your review. The reports should be thorough, detailing the number of people to whom your housing programs were presented, those who expressed interest in purchasing, sales in progress and recommendations for future marketing needs.

### Sales Training and Orientations

Sales and management training of a designated broker's staff is fundamental to your success. It is a matter of working closely with the designated brokers to help them understand the benefits of your housing programs. It is more effective for one individual, your account representative appointed by the designated broker, to coordinate efforts with your staff than to expect every agent to try to communicate with you. Some brokers need to control their own staffs and want to play that role; others are willing to assign someone else to be the specialized representative for your homes. Our experience suggests that, if strong internal control is exercised by the broker, there is more likely to be a better qualified group of prospects resulting from that designated broker's efforts.

### Responsibilities for Marketing and Merchandising

Brokers who serve the specialized needs of developers and builders have gradually concluded that it is not always in their best interests or their clients' to be totally responsible for all marketing functions such as advertising, merchandising and promotion. In some cases, brokers elect to pay for all of these costs out of their gross commissions. In others, they prefer to accept net contracts that make them financially responsible only for salespeople and sales management. The burden for advertising the homes, decorating models, installing billboards and preparing brochures or sales aids is left to the clients. The procedures for creating and administering marketing programs that efficiently generate qualified prospects, covered in more detail in chapter eight, always should be mutually conceived and managed. Agreements should specify responsibilities and provide for close coordination of these business development efforts. Regularly scheduled marketing meetings plus accurate monitoring systems are needed to avoid misuse of the budget or lost opportunities.

### Cooperation Between Designated Brokers and Other Brokers in the Area

It is normally desirable to be represented by a principle broker who totally cooperates with all the other real estate sales organizations in the region and actively promotes the builders' homes to sales agents in the multiple listing system and the real estate board. Exceptions exist in those few markets in America where outside brokers seldom show new housing communities because of local custom or the effectiveness of on-site criteria. Whatever the arrangements, be sure they are defined and not left to the broker's sole discretion. If the designated company will be staffing the site primarily with its own new home specialists and not seeking outside cooperation, that should be specified in the marketing plan. When the new home sales company is on a net contract, it is usually necessary to budget an additional fee to pay cooperating agents who produce prospects from off-site activities. Properly treated, this should be classified as a marketing expense and not a sales commission. The fee is paid for attracting buyers that might not otherwise be drawn to the community. We provide complete guidelines for developing cooperative broker programs in chapter eight.

## BUILDER-BROKER EXCLUSIVE AGENCY AGREEMENTS

The criteria for selling new housing developments dictate that special contracts be drawn covering the specific needs of the client and the mutual responsibilities of builders and agents. A checklist detailing what each organization supervises and who is responsible for the costs of marketing and management should either be incorporated in such a contract or added as an addendum.

---

**FIGURE 1.2   Position Descriptions for Builder Services Department New Home Sales**

---

POSITION DESCRIPTION: DIRECTOR OF SALES AND MARKETING
General Description of Position

The Director of Sales and Marketing has the primary responsibility of overseeing all of the projects and sales personnel within the Company. This position is less concerned with the development of new business opportunities than with the necessity of successfully marketing and selling all of the properties that are accepted by the Company for representation. Once a developer or builder entrusts us with a new project, this department assumes the full responsibility to see that it is professionally staffed and all necessary steps taken to ensure that a marketing plan is developed and implemented that will attract the number of qualified prospects to assure a reasonable conversion ratio and the attainment of pre-established sales goals.

This position has the full responsibility for recruiting, training, motivating and supervising new-home on-site sales specialists within the Company. This applies only to those sites that are under the direct on-site management of the Company.

The Director of Sales and Marketing is responsible for the attainment of the sales goals of the Company and this objective must take precedence over all other activities and assignments. The development of action-oriented sales plans and the direct management of Site Managers and the on-site sales specialists is the essence of this position. All other functions such as supervising closings, providing product recommendations, participating in group planning sessions are secondary to the prime objective: produce the number of sales per project that will satisfy the profit objectives of our clients and the Company.

Line of Authority

The Director of Sales and Marketing is a key member of the New Homes Sales Division team. The position is directly responsible to the Director of the New Homes Division and all authority for fulfilling the assigned responsibilities is derived from the Division Manager. The Division Manager is directly responsible to the Executive Vice President of the Company.

The Director of Sales and Marketing supervises the following departments and personnel:

a. The Site Managers and all sales consultants in this department.
b. The Marketing Services Department and the coordinators who provide marketing and merchandising services to the clients of the Company.
c. The Director of Training and Personnel Development encompassing all educational services provided to the sales consultants and others within the Company.

The Director of Sales and Marketing is a permanent member of the Marketing Committee and the chairperson of the Project Review Committee which evaluates performance effectiveness of all projects at least once each month.

The Director of Sales and Marketing must abide by the policies and procedures for the Company as established by the Executive Committee and the Executive Manager.

Responsibilities

The primary responsibilities of the Director of Sales and Marketing include the following:

1. Develop and implement a marketing plan for each assigned community or client. This requires the preparation of a written sales-oriented business plan prepared in cooperation with the Account Manager(s) and the Research Division of the Company. This plan must cover the following topics:

FIGURE 1.2    Position Descriptions for Builder Services Department New Home
Sales (continued)

Evaluation of anticipated market absorption and sales penetration rates.

Time frames for initiating sales and completing each released sales phase.

Demographic analysis of the profiles of prospective buyers including identification of primary buying motivations that will be incorporated in the sales and marketing strategies.

On-site staffing plans including number of personnel, compensation arrangements, and incentives.

On-site sales facilities: type, location, furnishings and related cost considerations.

Proposed advertising and promotion programs and budgets for implementing them.

Sales management procedures including specific responsibilities for site management.

General list of objectives and issues that need to be evaluated, resolved and monitored.

2. Supervise the Marketing Services Department and the activities of the Coordinators of Marketing Services. This includes a weekly status review of all assigned projects. The Coordinators in this department will receive their assignments from the Sales and Marketing Director.

3. Prepare the standard Company New Home Community Control Procedures Manual for each newly assigned project. This requires the development of information from a variety of sources together with a scheduled time frame for the performance of each item on the check list.

4. Recruit and select on-site sales specialists as required to meet all project staffing assignments. This function will involve the cooperation of Site Managers, the Director of Educational Services and the Account Managers. While the Director of Sales and Marketing may delegate the recruiting functions, the necessity to maintain the number and quality of sales personnel needed to fulfill the Company's objectives remains as his principle responsibility. Unless the Company continually attracts and retains the superior sales specialists for our on-site staffing assignments, the other goals and objectives cannot be realized. Thus, this is one of the most important of all positions within the organization, and it is expected that every effort will be made to maintain the highest standards of performance and the most effective on-going recruiting programs.

5. Supervise all orientation and training programs to assure that all sales personnel are provided with the knowledge and skill-improvement plans that will optimize their effectiveness in representing our clients' homes and communities. In this capacity, The Director of Sales and Marketing is responsible for the activities of the Director of Educational Services as defined in that position description.

6. Recruit, appoint and supervise the Site Managers who in turn have the direct front-line responsibilities for sales management of on-site sales specialists. These operating sales managers take their direction from the Director of Sales and Marketing and the fulfillment of specific site management objectives rests with this position.

**FIGURE 1.2   Position Descriptions for Builder Services Department New Home Sales (continued)**

7.  Provide the information that is needed by on-site sales specialists and their Site Managers to effectively meet the market opportunities and competitive challenges of the marketplace. This includes holding regularly scheduled sales meetings, conferences and workshops that are targeted to current sales needs.

8.  Motivate all of the personnel in this department to achieve optimum results by consistent reinforcement of the goals and objectives of the Company and its clients. This includes developing incentives that will inspire sales specialists and their managers to attain our goals.

9.  Personally inspect and monitor all on-site sales operations and verify that they meet Company defined objectives. Newly assigned communities that have not yet initiated sales will follow the checklisted Community Control Manual procedures as identified in #2 above. It is desirable that the Director of Sales and Marketing personally inspect each new community during its planning stages. It is required that he or she physically inspect the project at least two weeks before staffing commences except for on-going projects which we have accepted from other sales operations. In such situations, immediate inspection is required. Each inspection should be made with the use of the community evaluation checklist which identifies current site conditions and notations regarding progress in implementing company programs. Copies of community evaluation checklists' are to be promptly forwarded to the Division Manager, the assigned Marketing Services Coordinator, the Account Manager, the Site Manager, and the Vice President of the Company.

10. Supervise the research functions of checking all competitive projects directly impacting the assigned communities. This includes cooperation with the Director of Research in completing the competitive analysis program forms from the on-site sales specialists and Site Managers. It is essential that the Director of Sales and Marketing is personally aware of all competitive marketing conditions that affect our ability to develop and implement effective sales and marketing strategies.

11. Cooperate with the Sales Processing Manager in validating all purchase agreements and expediting the reporting process. The Director of Sales and Marketing has the responsibility of resolving those issues that arise in the processing of individual sales that cannot be efficiently handled by the Sales Processing Manager.

12. Prepare an annual forecast and budget for the department including all on-site projects with the assistance of the Controller. Necessary information must be gathered prior to September 1st and the budget in place by October 31st of each year. Monthly monitoring of the P&L is required.

13. Supervise the activities of the Assistant Director of Sales and Marketing. This position description encompasses all of the responsibilities of the Director of Sales and Marketing as assigned. The objective of the Assistant Director's role is to expedite those areas of the operation that currently need attention and to efficiently utilize the time and talents of all concerned. The primary emphasis of this position will be on personnel development, including recruiting, education and community management follow-up.

---

**FIGURE 1.2    Position Descriptions for Builder Services Department New Home Sales (continued)**

---

Communication Systems and Working Relationships

The Director of Sales and Marketing is truly at the very heart of our business. Everything revolves around our sales effectiveness. Thus, the communication lines between on-site sales specialists, Site Managers, Account Managers, our builder/developer clientele and central management must be clearly defined and openly maintained at all times. The role of the Director and the Assistant Director of Sales and Marketing in this process includes the following:

1. Completely document all activity for each on-site sales facility. This involves the weekly submission of the Sales and Traffic Report Form, the monthly Sales Efficiency Report, and the up-dating of the Community Control Manual. The most urgent report is the Sales and Traffic Summary, which must be received from the Site Managers by Monday of each week and promptly forwarded to the Coordinator of Marketing Services, The Account Manager, the Director of Research, the Director of the New Homes Division and the Vice President of the Company.

2. Conduct a weekly meeting with all Site Managers for a complete up-date of the status of all staffed projects from a sales management perspective. The development and implementation of sales strategies to meet established sales objectives is the primary purpose of this meeting. A review of sales personnel performance is an important aspect of this evaluation.

3. Chair the Project Review Committee which meets once each month with the heads of the departments involved in managing staffed communities.

4. Meet once each week with the Director of the New Homes Division to report on the status of all projects. This includes a review of high-priority objectives and issues that demand primary attention.

5. Participate in the regularly scheduled Marketing Committee which reviews all potential projects before their acceptance.

6. Meet with builder/developer clients only as requested by Account Managers and preferably in their presence.

7. Verify that Site Managers hold sales meetings once each week with their personnel and report topics and results.

8. Conduct a major sales meeting at least once each month. The agenda should be organized with the assistance of Site Managers and a portion of each meeting devoted to motivational and educational objectives.

9. Attend the monthly on-site sales P&L review and closing report evaluation as prepared by the Director of The New Homes Division.

10. Verify that each new community is provided with the complete start-up package that includes the following:

---

**FIGURE 1.2    Position Descriptions for Builder Services Department New Home Sales (concluded)**

Policies and Procedures Manual
Community Control Manual
Site Specifications Manual
Start-up files and forms.

The Director of Educational Services will, in most cases, perform these orientation and start-up functions under the supervision of the Director of Sales and Marketing.

Summary

The Director of Sales and Marketing carries the front-line responsibility to see that what we accept to sell is, in fact, sold and closed on time. This involves a wide range of responsibilities, most of which center on the selection and administration of new home sales specialists who work under our company banner. We are known by the people we keep—and that is never more true than in the sales role. Training, motivating and monitoring the performance of the sales specialists and their managers should be the dominant and overriding concern of this key position in the Company. We believe that is far better to be physically present and involved with the personnel than to administer from a protected corporate environment. The motto might well be: INSPECT RATHER THAN EXPECT!

---

**FIGURE 1.3    Position Descriptions for the Marketing Services Department**

---

POSITION DESCRIPTION: MARKETING SERVICES COORDINATOR
General Description of the Position

The Marketing Services Department provides a wide range of marketing and merchandising services for the clients of our company. The scope of those services depends upon the needs of our clients and the nature of the contractual relationships. The Marketing Services Coordinator is responsible for the implementation of all marketing and merchandising programs that have been authorized as a result of service agreements executed with our company.

Line of Authority

This department and its personnel are part of the New Homes Division of the Company. Its functions are under the immediate supervision of the Director of Sales and Marketing who in turn reports to the New Homes Division manager. Since the services are critical to the sales functions, the department coordinators are expected to work closely with those involved in the sales department and to take their direction from the Director of Sales and Marketing.

The Marketing Committee is the forum in which all of the basic strategies for representing new home communities are resolved. The Marketing Services Coordinators are permanent members of this vital committee. The committee establishes guidelines for meeting the marketing needs for each of the builders and new home projects we represent. It also serves as the body which determines which assignments will be accepted or rejected.

Responsibilities

1. Review all available research data for every new residential project assigned to the department and to make recommendations for marketing concepts and strategies to the Director of Sales and Marketing and to the Marketing Committee.

2. Prepare a pro forma for each proposed assignment with detailed budgets to be submitted to the Director of Sales and Marketing, the Division Manager and the Company Vice President for review and approval before incurring any costs.

3. Upon approval of a specific assignment, one of the Marketing Services Coordinators will be appointed by The Director of Sales and Marketing to be the primary 'coordinator' for that account. In that role, the coordinator is then responsible for selecting the other members of the support team. This includes all subcontractors and outside agencies who are drawn from a pre-approved list of qualified specialists. The recommended participants on the team must be submitted to the department head for approval before proceeding with appointments.

4. It is the responsibility of the assigned coordinator to personally inspect each project within the initial planning stage, hopefully within the first two weeks of its acceptance by the company. There is no substitute for the direct involvement and evaluation by the marketing coordinator who will be responsible for the execution of the marketing support services. It is preferable that this inspection be held in cooperation with the Account Manager who will be directly supervising the client relationships and the project. If other members of the planning team are available for a group inspection tour, it can be a valuable means of sharing reactions and providing mutually developed marketing ideas.

**FIGURE 1.3    Position Descriptions for the Marketing Services Department (continued)**

5. Help develop a community theme and related identity elements for each project where image positioning is not yet in place or to make recommendations when it is believed that a new image is needed to fulfill sales and marketing objectives. This can be accomplished by a team planning session or by assigning the creative roles to an approved member of the team.

6. Develop all collateral material such as theme brochures, sales aids and advertising elements. This is accomplished with the following steps:

   Review and approve the themes including colors, schematics and graphics representations of the housing community.

   Approve the artistic elements of the marketing plan including submission to clients for their written approval.

   Develop a proposed budget for these specific items after obtaining bid proposals from the selected agencies and suppliers.

   Execute an expense authorization and submit to management for approval and processing.

   Submit approved assignment to the designated agency or agencies for completion and/or placement.

   Monitor the progress of all assignments to be sure that pre-established deadlines are met and the quality of performance meets our established standards.

7. Develop and supervise the signage plan for each community where one does not already exist. This includes the following steps:

   Clearly define the responsibilities of the Company versus those of the developer or builder before incurring any costs for signage. As a matter of policy, permanent identity elements are always the responsibility of the developers and builders unless specific arrangements to provide such identity elements are approved by the Company Vice President.

   Prepare signage designs for on-site and off-site locations as covered by the agreement or the approved marketing budget.

   Submit design criteria to a minimum of two suppliers for bidding purposes and, when returned with sketches and figures, review with Department Manager for approval of the company to be used in producing and installing the signage.

   Supervise the installation of the signage by either personal inspection or appointment of a representative of the department.

   Photograph the results for the permanent records.

When billboard advertising is proposed or necessary, the coordinator will work with an approved agency to prepare bids, sketches and approval processes. Due to the limited availability of billboards and the relatively high cost for this medium of exposure, this form of marketing must have the review and approval of the Director of Sales and Marketing, the Division Manager and the Company Vice President before authorization to incur costs of development or installation.

**FIGURE 1.3   Position Descriptions for the Marketing Services Department (continued)**

8. Prepare recommendations for the physical on-site sales facilities within the scope of the client agreement and the approved budgets. This normally involves the following steps:

   Provide an office layout based on the criteria for space or type of facilities as provided by the Account Manager or the client.

   Identify all of the furnishings and equipment needed for the facility and submit a recommendation for the specific items to be acquired, leased or relocated from other facilities. This must include estimates of costs for meeting these recommendations.

   Order the equipment (once approvals are received) and supervise installation.

   Prepare an inventory control form for all items acquired (or relocated) and keep with master project file for permanent reference. Also enter the inventory data on the master equipment register maintained in the controller's offices.

   Arrange for insurance coverage (fire/theft) with our Insurance Department. Place copy of the binder in the project file.

9. When requested, assist in providing criteria for the decorating of model homes. In rare cases, the Company may be responsible for the acquisition and management of the furnished models. Normally, our role is purely advisory. The selection of a decorator or designer may be determined by the builder/developer or by our Company. Since this is a very delicate and expensive area of marketing, the concensus of the management team is required before recommendations are made to the client. The procedures for controlling the acquired furnishings are the same as those identified in #8 above.

10. Design direct-mail pieces and campaigns as required for specific projects. Some campaigns will be best directed from the central offices of the Company under the supervision of the coordinator, while others will be handled by the on-site sales representatives. This decision will be made by the Director of Sales and Marketing in conformance with the master plan and approved budgets.

11. Prepare recommended publicity and public relations programs for each assigned community. This responsibility is normally delegated to an outside public relations specialist selected from the pre-approved subcontractor list. To assure that each project receives the publicity and attention that it deserves the coordinator is expected to carefully monitor this function.

    The coordinator is responsible to see that photos are taken of all special events, grand openings, parties, and ground breakings. Free-lance photographers can be used for this purpose with budget approval.

    Community newsletters will be justified in some of the larger subdivisions. These will be supervised by the assigned coordinators even though the specific responsibility for preparation and distribution may be at the on-site sales level.

12. Maintain a complete record of all activities and exhibits associated with each assigned project. To accomplish this, a master portfolio will be kept at the department offices for each community and it will include copies of brochures, models and copies of all advertising and publicity properly identified and dated. This will serve as a permanent reference resource for the department and for our Account Managers. The marketing value of this library justifies the time required to assemble and maintain it.

---

**FIGURE 1.3   Position Descriptions for the Marketing Services Department (concluded)**

---

Communication Systems and Working Relationships

This department is at the very center of our marketing activities and will always be under the spotlight in terms of client expectations and on-site sales needs. Therefore it is vital to the success of our client relationships to be certain that we maintain optimum communication and reporting systems between the Marketing Services Coordinators and all those who are dependent upon its fulfillment of assignments. The communication systems and expected performance includes the following:

1. Receive and review weekly submitted sales and traffic analysis forms. (See attached exhibits) It is the responsibility of the Director of Sales and Marketing to see that this information is supplied on a timely basis by each site manager.

2. Evaluate the results of all marketing services and written summaries provided each week to the Director of Sales and Marketing with copies to the Division Manager, the Account Managers, the Site Managers, the Director of Research, and the Vice President of the Company.

3. Review all projects within each region with the appointed Account Manager. This review should occur at least once each week by pre-established appointments.

4. Attend the regular Marketing Committee Meeting and the Project Review Meeting with submission of summaries of current advertising and marketing programs together with recommendations for the future.

5. Communicate with each supplier and subcontractor on a regular basis to assure their constant attention to outstanding assignments and deadlines. Meet at least once each week with the major advertising agencies who represent the majority of our clients.

6. Meet once each week with the Controller to review budgets and pro formas with up-dated information for the computer models.

7. Meet directly with clients only when requested to do so by Regional Account Managers—and preferably always in their presence. This is to prevent any misunderstandings or create communication channels that by-pass the RAMS who have primary responsibility for client relationships.

Summary

The Coordinators in the Marketing Services Department provide the physical elements of marketing essential to the success of our sales representation of our client's merchandise. We have advised our clients and proposed clients that we are the best organized and most efficient new home sales organization in the markets we serve. This department visibly represents one of the key functions of marketing ... and unless all coordinators and the managers of the department accept their assigned responsibilities with the dedication to excellence that we have professed, our entire organization and its future potential can be adversely affected. This detailed position description has been created to help us stay on course and to assure that we will live up to our full potential.

---

**FIGURE 1.4    Position Descriptions for New Home Sales Division**

---

POSITION DESCRIPTION: NEW HOMESITE MANAGERS
General Description of Position

The Site Managers are the front-line sales supervisors who assist the Director of Sales and Marketing to provide the guidance and daily monitoring for the site specialists and their on-site staffed facilities. They are normally selected from the sales staff based on their experience in selling new housing communities and their management potential. They are assigned to regions based on the number of projects requiring sales monitoring and the relative distances to be traveled from one project to another.

Site managers are a vital link in the sales management functions. Because of the limited number of communities they must supervise daily and their ready availability to the on-site sales specialists, they can provide the one-on-one supervision needed to keep each project on target with Company goals and objectives. The people selected for this role are in an ideal position for further growth as the Company expands its operations. This is a management training arena for which many of our future managers at other levels of the Company will be drawn.

Line of Authority

The Director of Sales and Marketing in the New Homes Sales Division is fully responsible for selecting and supervising the Site Managers. They serve in an extended capacity of that all-encompassing sales management role. Their authority is limited to the specific assignments and responsibilities given them by the Director of Sales and Marketing. This position description provides broad guidelines for this sales management support function, but each Site Manager will be given very specific instructions based on the nature of the projects and personnel within the assigned region.

As assistants to the Director of Sales and Marketing, they are expected to secure all needed support materials directly from the central office and follow the supply request procedures as detailed in the policies and procedures manual. Site Managers are not authorized to incur expenses other than by written authorization of the Director of Sales and Marketing.

Responsibilities

The basic responsibilities of the Site Managers include the following:

1. To provide sales counseling assistance to each of the on-site sales specialists within the assigned region. This requires daily telephone conversations for monitoring and psychological support and a minimum of once a week in face-to-face counseling environments. The areas requiring concentrated support are:

    Follow up of existing business, sales in progress and all prospects not yet sold.

    Monitor sales in progress and not yet closed to provide guidance for expediting all items that affect potential closings including financing and contingencies.

    Review the sales skills of the specialists with emphasis on qualifying, value-building, demonstrating and closing.

    Review all sales obstacles that need special attention. This includes production and delivery issues to value perception challenges. Suggest courses of action and make written recommendations to the Director of Sales and Marketing.

---

**FIGURE 1.4    Position Descriptions for New Home Sales Division (continued)**

---

2. Inspect all sales facilities using the appropraite checklist. The checklist is to be forwarded upon completion to the Director of Sales and Marketing and a copy to the appropriate Account Manager. This should include recommendations for improving the on-site marketing systems. The status of all supplies for the sales office including brochures, sales literature, and sales aids, are reported on a Marketing Services checklist and forwarded to the Marketing Services Department. Office supplies must be ordered sufficiently in advance to allow for a 30-day delivery and are requested on the property form and forwarded to the Director of Operations.

3. Review inventory control records to verify all sold, for sale and not-yet-released properties. This should be matched against the master inventory control record which is maintained by the central office. Also verify that all prices conform with the listing inventory. Evaluate the remaining product mix in terms of salability and marketing emphasis. Make recommendations where an obvious need exists to concentrate our sales and marketing strategies on specific products.

4. Role play and rehearse sales presentations on those areas that need the most emphasis.

5. When appropriate, assist in servicing traffic and writing sales. Any sales made are to be credited to the assigned site specialist. This is one of the better methods of educating newer sales personnel in proven sales procedures.

6. Organize and conduct sales meetings where the Director of Sales and Marketing, the Assistant Director of Sales and Marketing and the Director of Educational Services are present. Such meetings should be held at least once each month.

7. Participate in the competitive project evaluation program and verify that site specialists are making competitive evaluations for their specific assignments.

8. Conduct quarterly goal-setting and evaluation reviews with assigned sales specialists. Submit the personnel review forms to the Director of Sales and Marketing along with specific recommendations.

Communication Systems and Working Relationships

We expect all Site Managers to be excellent salespeople as well as good managers. As such, they should observe their communication skills to maintain the positive sales-oriented environment most conducive to keeping salespeople as well as others enthusiastic, confident and productive. We consider these front-line sales managers most representative of our professional sales staff. The most effective leadership is by example. It is essential that Regional Site Managers provide solutions, not create problems! Relationships with the sales personnel should always be professional, business-oriented and above reproach.

When in the field working with our sales representatives, the Site Managers are the eyes and ears of the Sales and Marketing Department. They are also the essence of the Weichert image and should always conduct themselves with that fact in mind.

---

**FIGURE 1.4   Position Descriptions for New Home Sales Division (concluded)**

---

The primary communication systems to be used by these front-line sales managers are:

a. Standard reports as identified above
b. Attendance at weekly Regional Site Manager meetings with the Director of Sales and Marketing.
c. Establishment of effective working relationships with their Account Managers, with some form of weekly contact and regularly scheduled monthly meeting.
d. Attendance of the quarterly company management meeting and be prepared to present all of their assigned projects as to status, marketing programs and future plans.
e. To keep a consistent and united posture with our builder/developer clientele, the Site Managers should review with their Account Managers the communication procedures for specific clients. While it is desirable to establish direct communication lines between Site Managers and the assigned builders to expedite sales and marketing issues that need prompt attention, it is also essential to preserve the relationships that have been carefully cultivated by the Account Managers. When in doubt as to the reactions of the client to specific recommendations or issues, the matter should be referred to the appropriate Account Manager for his or her advice.

Summary

Site Managers are the first line of defense and of administrative support for the sales functions in this Company. They are almost always experienced salespeople who have proven their skills in new-home sales and understand what is required to be successful in the sales trenches. With that background and their personal commitment to help others grow with the new-home team, they provide the daily counseling and motivation that all the sales people need to continue to perfect their trade.

Dedication to the standards of excellence we have set for our Company begins with the way we serve the public and fulfill the sales goals of our valued clients. The Site Managers bring the Company to the sales people where it counts most: the on-site model sales environments.

**FIGURE 1.5　Departments of the Contemporary Homes Company (Organizational Chart)**

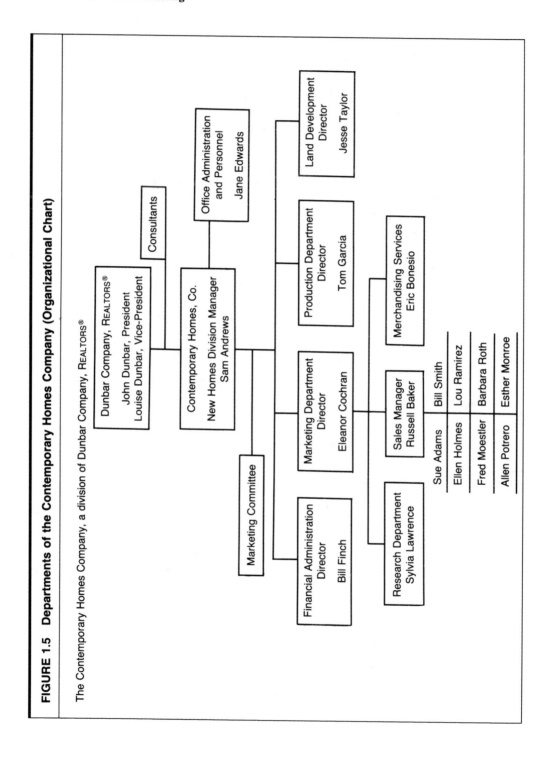

The Contemporary Homes Company, a division of Dunbar Company, REALTORS®

Dunbar Company, REALTORS®
John Dunbar, President
Louise Dunbar, Vice-President

Consultants

Office Administration
and Personnel
Jane Edwards

Contemporary Homes, Co.
New Homes Division Manager
Sam Andrews

Marketing Committee

Financial Administration
Director
Bill Finch

Marketing Department
Director
Eleanor Cochran

Production Department
Director
Tom Garcia

Land Development
Director
Jesse Taylor

Research Department
Sylvia Lawrence

Sales Manager
Russell Baker

Merchandising Services
Eric Bonesio

Sue Adams　　Bill Smith

Ellen Holmes　　Lou Ramirez

Fred Moestler　　Barbara Roth

Allen Potrero　　Esther Monroe

**FIGURE 1.6** **Research Checklist**

## RESEARCH CHECKLIST FOR COMMUNITY SERVICES GUIDE

| Classification | Community Service Facts | Sources of Information |
|---|---|---|
| Climate | —Average Temperatures<br>—Seasonal Variations<br>—Average Rainfall<br>—Number of Sunny Days<br>—Other Facts | —Weather Bureau<br>—Chamber of Commerce<br>—Tourist Bureau<br>—City or Regional<br>  Government Offices |
| Cultural Activities | —Theaters<br>—Museums<br>—Art Galleries<br>—Libraries<br>—Music Studios<br>—Special Events<br>—Other | —Chamber of Commerce<br>—Service Clubs<br>—Tourist Bureau<br>—Newspaper—Social Section<br>—Telephone Directory |
| Demographics (Population Characteristics) | —Total Population<br>—Population Mix<br>—Average Family Size<br>—Average Income<br>—Professions<br>—Growth Rates<br>—Projections | —U.S. (or Foreign) Census Bureau<br>—Commerce Department<br>—Banking Institutions<br>—Chamber of Commerce<br>—Tourist Bureau<br>—Government Offices |
| Educational Facilities | —Elementary Schools<br>—Junior/Senior High<br>—Junior Colleges<br>—Vocational Schools<br>—State Universities/Colleges<br>—Special (Pre-School, Gifted, Handicapped, Alternative)<br>—Quality of Education<br>—Teacher/Student Ratio<br>—Noted Achievements | —Department of Education<br>—Chamber of Commerce<br>—Government Offices<br>—School District<br>—Each Individual Institution |
| Financial Institutions | —Bank Locations and Services<br>—Savings & Loan Companies<br>—Trust Companies<br>—Assets and Financial Growth<br>—Future Projections<br>—Other Facts | —Chamber of Commerce<br>—Yellow Pages<br>—City Directory<br>—Bankers Association<br>—Commerce Department |

Community Services Guide 2

**FIGURE 1.6   Research Checklist (continued)**

| Classification | Community Service Facts | Sources of Information |
|---|---|---|
| Fire Protection | —Nature of Services<br>—Fire Rating Facts<br>—Fire Station Locations<br>—Equipment<br>—Other Facts | —Local Fire Department<br>—Insurance Underwriters<br>—Chamber of Commerce<br>—City Directory |
| Government | —Type of Local Government<br>—State and Regional<br>—People and Positions<br>—% Resident Participation<br>—Elections<br>—Social Services<br>—Achievements and Other Facts | —Mayor's Office<br>—Chamber of Commerce<br>—Media Sources<br>—Banks<br>—Service Organizations |
| Industry | —Number and Types<br>—Employment Figures<br>—Personnel Management<br>—Community Involvement<br>—Growth Rates and Projections<br>—Other Facts | —Chamber of Commerce<br>—Yellow Pages<br>—City/Regional Directories<br>—Government Offices<br>—Tax Assessor's Office |
| Land Planning | —Local and Regional Plan<br>—Zoning Ordinances<br>—Future Planning<br>—Local Attitudes<br>—Surrounding Influences<br>—Other Facts | —Planning Department<br>—Government Offices<br>—Land Developers<br>—Zoning Commission<br>—Architects/Engineers<br>—Chamber of Commerce |
| Medical/Dental Services | —List of Practitioners<br>—List of Clinics<br>—Special Health Services<br>—Specialists<br>—Assistance Programs | —Hospitals<br>—Yellow Pages<br>—Medical/Dental Society<br>—Health Department |
| Local Ordinances | —Dog, Bike, Car Licensing<br>—Street Parking<br>—Residential Property<br>Maintenance<br>—Fire Hazards<br>—Other Ordinances | —Government Offices<br>—Chamber of Commerce<br>—Local Bar Association<br>—Fire Station<br>—Police Station<br>—Building Permits Dept. |
| Places of Worship | —Denominations<br>—People and Positions<br>—Hours of Worship<br>—Accommodations (Transportation,<br>Child Care)<br>—Other Facts | —Chamber of Commerce<br>—Council of Churches<br>—Local Newspapers<br>—All Faiths Roster<br>—Yellow Pages |

## FIGURE 1.6   Research Checklist (continued)

| Classification | Community Service Facts | Sources of Information |
|---|---|---|
| Police Protection | —Size and Quality of Police Force<br>—Station Location<br>—Crime Rate Statistics<br>—Special Services | —Police Station<br>—Mayor's Office<br>—Media Source<br>—Civic Organizations |
| Real Estate Values | —Appreciation Factors<br>—Percentages of Ownership<br>  Versus Renters<br>—Vacancy/Turnover Rates<br>—Land Costs/Values<br>—Mortgage Availability<br>—Investor "Climate"<br>—Growth Rates<br>—Commercial Properties<br>—Other Facts | —Tax Assessor<br>—County Recorder<br>—Title Companies<br>—Chamber of Commerce<br>—Board of Realtors<br>—Banking Institutions<br>—Builder's Association<br>—Utility Companies<br>—Bankers' Association<br>—Local Appraisers |
| Recreation Facilities | —Location of Facilities<br>  Golf Courses<br>  Tennis Courts<br>  Swimming Pools<br>  Parks & Reservoirs<br>  Hiking/Bike Trails<br>  Special Clubs<br>—Special Events<br>—Special Regional Highlights | —Tourist Bureau<br>—Chamber of Commerce<br>—Parks & Recreation<br>—Civic Organizations<br>—Government Offices<br>—Dept. of Interior<br>—Direct Investigation |
| Service Clubs | —List of Service Clubs<br>—Scheduled Meetings<br>—Noted Achievements<br>—Community Charities<br>—Special Projects/People<br>—Other Facts | —Chamber of Commerce<br>—City Directory<br>—Tourist Bureau<br>—Direct Contact with<br>  Organizations |
| Shopping Facilities | —Major Shopping Centers<br>—Consumer Services and Products<br>—Transportation<br>—Hours (weekly, on weekends)<br>—Pricing Comparisons<br>—Plans for Expansion<br>—Access Routes<br>—Other Facts | —City Directory<br>—Chamber of Commerce<br>—Better Business Bureau<br>—Shopping Mall Promotional Flyers<br>—Banking Institutions<br>—Mass Transit Offices<br>—Local Newspapers<br>—Tax Assessor |

**FIGURE 1.6    Research Checklist (concluded)**

| Classification | Community Service Facts | Sources of Information |
|---|---|---|
| Taxation | —Tax Rate<br>—Services Included<br>—Comparisons of Neighborhood<br>  Areas<br>—Anticipated Tax Rates<br>—Distribution of Taxes by Service<br>—Other Facts | —Tax Assessor's Office<br>—Chamber of Commerce<br>—Planning Department<br>—Women's League of Voters<br>—Other Civic Groups<br>—City/County Offices<br>—Tax Records |
| Telephone Service | —Company and Offices<br>—Quality of Services<br>—Costs for Installation<br>—Other Facts | —Direct Contact with<br>  Branch Offices<br>—Utility Commission<br>—Personal Investigation |
| Transportation | —Access and Freeways<br>—Mass Transit<br>—Airlines, Bus and Train<br>—Moving and Storage<br>—Truck and Trailer Rental<br>—Other Facts | —City Directory<br>—Chamber of Commerce<br>—Bus, Train and Airline Terminals<br>—Yellow Pages |
| Utility (Fuel) | —Availability, Cost<br>—Installation<br>—Alternative Sources, i.e.,<br>  Wood, Coal, Solar, Nuclear Energy<br>—Other Facts<br>—Nuclear Energy Commis. | —Utility Companies<br>—Government Offices<br>—Media Sources<br>—Environment Groups<br>—Water Resources Dept. |
| Waste Disposal | —Types of Systems and Capacity<br>—Cost<br>—Locations<br>—Garbage Pickup and Disposal<br>—Tree Trimming | —Health/Welfare Dept.<br>—Sanitation Department<br>—Public Works Department<br>—Zoning Commission<br>—Planning Department<br>—Chamber of Commerce |

# 2: Research is Your Security Blanket

Developing, building and marketing real estate is a risk-taking venture that is complex and capital-intensive. Unpredictable factors exist in political arenas, vacillating mortgage markets, changing economies (both local and national) and increasing costs of land, building materials and labor. Add to those variables the uncertainty of what the buying public can afford or will accept, and you can quickly realize how vital research should be to our decision-making processes.

A large percentage of entrepreneurs in our home-building enterprise make only a cursory investigation of the marketplace before launching housing projects. Many of them operate on "gut" instinct alone! Their decisions to buy vacant or completed homesites, build their favorite floor plans, include or exclude specific amenities, price and finance the homes they build are often made without benefit of validated research. It has always amazed me that so many leveraged dollars can depend on so little documented information!

The failure rate in this industry is also relatively high. A substantial number of builders lose control of their properties to investors and lenders after months of construction and frustrating attempts at crisis management or patchwork marketing programs. Many buy land and start the development process without business plans founded on well-organized market research.

One of the prime objectives of the marketing director (whoever has that responsibility) is to prevent failure by documenting and interpreting the various factors that ultimately should influence the decision makers. Too many people in marketing are guilty of wearing rose-colored glasses! They believe in the positive sales attitude that you can sell anything if you have the right marketing plan. This can create a fool's paradise when it permeates executive boardrooms. Marketing specialists should always begin their assignments by identifying what might go wrong. Anyone can tell you what might go right! No genius is required when you are looking at all the positive influences and predicting success.

Decisions in a high-risk business should at least be shaped in a pragmatic environment that questions the validity of all conclusions against the background of documented research and reasonably well-defined options. By recommending conservative actions that begin to limit risks, the prudent manager/marketer protects invested capital and the energies of valuable human resources. Many benefits can be derived from doing your homework when launching a new community or new housing designs. If nothing else, research becomes your security blanket by reinforcing the tentative gut reactions you may have felt before the facts were assembled. Very often, the analysis of the marketplace when compared to economic variables leads to conclusions very different than those originally anticipated.

In this chapter we will review practical systems for evaluating market opportunities. We will then relate these to the decision-making process that business managers should pursue to avoid failures and ensure successes. We include a variety of proven checklists and forms developed by professionals who specialize in real estate research. Most important, we will demonstrate how to gather and use information to establish guidelines and strategies for real estate development.

## OBJECTIVES OF RESEARCH

When you approach the subject of research, you open doors to a variety of potential objectives. In our profession, the nature of the research assignment is frequently influenced by the motives of the one requesting the evaluation. For example, the seller of real estate often wants the evaluation to slant the market facts in favor of the price and development possibilities he or she believes will strengthen predetermined values. On the other hand, lenders in this business want research that will minimize the risks they are taking in lending money to developers. Builders who have already purchased property sometimes instruct those doing market research to present the most favorable cases for the planned absorption rates and designs they have already created. When research is done solely to determine whether or not a property should be acquired along with the criteria by which it should be developed, it tends to be more objective than when used to justify preconceived judgments.

All research studies are not the same. Few of them encompass all parameters that might be evaluated if you wanted to document every variable. For the purpose of this manual, we divide the types of research into five categories. While a comprehensive feasibility study might include all five, it is more common to find studies that use only one or two of the overviews. All approaches need not be included in a specific assignment. The developer/builder may have answered some of the normal concerns through extensive knowledge of the market and from personal experience gained from building other projects in the same market area.

## MARKET FEASIBILITY

The foundation for most real estate research is known as market feasibility. In its simplest form, this addresses the questions:

- Does a market exist for what was conceived or proposed?
- What are the criteria for housing types, sizes, prices, amenities and general architectural designs?

- What are the predicted total absorption rates for these classifications within the geographical area served by this location?
- What are the predicted penetration rates for this site and for each product type based on gaining a realistic market share?

Compiling the information needed for a comprehensive market study requires review of many sources of information. Some of these are in the public domain and easy to extract. Others require personal inspection and interpretation. Later in this chapter we will provide checklists and forms typically used by those who prepare market feasibility reports. At this juncture our emphasis is on appreciating the specific objectives of feasibility as contrasted with other approaches to data gathering assignments.

Marketing studies that are professionally organized and validated by well-documented data are invaluable decision influencers. Obviously, no profit-oriented manager wants to buy land or build housing that will not generate a profit. The first line of defense against making a serious mistake in this business is to know with reasonable certainty that a market exists for what you plan to build and sell. Equally as important, you need to know how many units can be sold within specific time frames. If you have no preconceived notions about what should be constructed, the entire process of structuring a business plan will depend upon the market directions indicated from your research.

If your job is marketing director, you role in organizing this type of research analysis is a fundamental aspect of the position description. If it is not, someone has made a classic error in defining the functions of your job. It is possible that you will not be involved in any other aspect of the research assignment but this one. It is the foundation on which all others depend for their ultimate conclusions. Thus, if the data are not adequately supported by known facts and backed up with realistic projections, the conclusions reached in all other disciplines and the future success of the venture may be in jeopardy.

## ECONOMIC FEASIBILITY

Economic feasibility is not market feasibility. It is a distinctly different approach to the total assignment of reviewing the potential for a new real estate development. Market feasibility attempts to define the nature, breadth and depth of demand for housing products by type and price range. Economic feasibility enters the picture after market research indicates a certain course of opportunity with the prime objective of determining whether or not it is economically feasible to develop and build what has been defined.

I have investigated many pieces of property for which there was clearly a solid demand for specific housing products, only to discover (when the economic feasibility study was completed) that there was no way the anticipated markets could be met. The costs of development forced the prices completely out of the ranges that market indicators had specified.

Economic feasibility checklists include such critical items as land development costs, political demands in zoning and planning, sources and costs of capital, time frames for construction and completion, availability of qualified labor, demands of lenders versus the efficiencies the builder team wants to employ and the impact on other projects and programs to which the company may already be committed.

It is not uncommon for the heads of the company to reserve this aspect of the decision-making process as their exclusive priority. Input from estimators, engineers, construction managers, the purchasing department and accountants is compiled. While this may be concurrent with the pursuit of marketing data, it is more frequently done after market factors have been first assembled and a logical land-use plan is prepared based on those findings.

Marketing directors are not always parties to this aspect of the analysis process. It is mutually beneficial when they are included, since a comprehensive understanding of why certain business decisions are made strengthens marketers' ability to look at future projects more objectively.

## ENVIRONMENTAL IMPACT STUDIES AND POLITICAL FEASIBILITY

This is a special type of research, usually done when demands are made by governmental agencies and local politicians requiring information that influences approvals of proposed land-use plans. In recent years the trend has been for political bodies to require developers to submit consumer-oriented documentation with their requests for land-use permits. This documentation will answer a wide variety of concerns of citizens who may be affected by the anticipated construction.

Environmental impact studies cover such subjects as the effect on local taxation from services to be delivered versus compensative benefits derived by the municipality. The projected additional load on schools, highways, public service agencies, police, fire, recreation facilities and parking areas are typical concerns that must be answered to the satisfaction of the supervising agencies before approvals to proceed are granted. Sometimes special interest groups must be satisfied as part of this process. Adjacent neighbors and the impact of proposed new development on their real estate values and lifestyles may be an underlying issue. The preservation of open space has precipitated many of these research requests.

It is very rare for a developer to include this kind of data in an initial feasibility study, although some more astute developers have learned it is wise to anticipate issues that concern community leaders and objectively respond to them before political obstacles are raised.

## CONSUMER ATTITUDES AND FOCUS-GROUP RESEARCH

When creating new housing designs that are uniquely different than traditional housing in your market area, it is wise to invest time and money in consumer attitude research. This type of research is much more difficult to conduct and interpret than the basic demographic and statistical approaches we have just identified. However, an increasing number of pragmatic developers invest in consumer-oriented studies prior to initiating new product lines or opening new residential communities.

One approach is known as focus-group research. A target group of prospective buyers is selected by a professional researcher and assembled for an intensive group-reaction session. At that meeting the discussion leader introduces a series of questions about housing, lifestyles, attitudes, and motivations that have been carefully identified before the session. Floor plans, elevations, options and checklists of priorities are normally used to stimulate reactions. These free-flowing discussions are usually taped so that others can listen to the comments later. When completed, the research team digests the results and makes recommendations.

This type of opinion gathering can be misleading unless it is well organized, conducted by experienced researchers and screened for subjective versus objective responses.

One of the more valuable approaches to behavioral interpretation has come from studies done by universities and private organizations that have compiled thousands of structured interviews and questionnaire responses to provide guidelines for identifying behavioral groups. The VAL* system is one of the best known of these study models.

It is not necessary to have such a formally organized group study to test consumer attitudes and reactions. A marketing director can establish periodic surveys of both people who have purchased housing and those who investigated new homes but did not purchase. Questionnaires, phone interviews and private one-on-one sessions can be very helpful when evaluating public reaction to what you are currently building and suggested improvements you might consider in future designs. We include in this chapter some practical questionnaires used by marketing people in this industry to measure reaction to existing and proposed housing.

## INTERPRETIVE MARKETING STRATEGIES

The ultimate objective of all research should be to develop profit-oriented and practical housing programs that will meet the needs of the marketplace and of the sponsoring entities. This means interpreting the research so that all facts and opinions result in definitive recommendations.

In this final, and most crucial, research area so many generalists in the field of fact-gathering are remiss. Too often the decision makers are presented with a compendium of facts assembled by the pound without clear-cut, meaningful and practical courses of action. I have reviewed hundreds of studies in my years in this profession and am disappointed in the majority of them. In the final analysis, the principals who paid for these studies reached their own conclusions after wading through the mass of pages and figures provided by the researchers. The recommendations made are often very general and not supported with specific guidelines that can be readily justified or implemented. Worse yet are feasibility studies that conclude with the wrong recommendations!

Interpretative research is probably the most important of the five approaches discussed. It goes far beyond just defining how many can be sold, what to build or

---

*Values and Lifestyles. Stanford Research Institute, Palo Alto, CA.

where to build it. This discipline digests all data and brings it into focus with specific strategies on pricing, financing, timing, phasing, model selection, methods of entering the market, where and how to reach the target prospects, and what conditions must be satisfied to create and sell the number of homes that general research indicates might be possible within designated time periods.

Since few researchers do this job well enough to justify unqualified acceptance of their conclusions, the marketing director and a committee of people within the company who are concerned with marketing usually must prepare this final summary in feasibility analysis. Marketing directors must know how to evaluate all data presented and then produce (perhaps with the help of trusted associates) the game plan for any proposed project assigned. They must be able to sort out fact from fiction, important from unimportant statistics and to crystallize all of the information into a workable formula for success.

This is best achieved by writing a business plan for the specific project. The marketing director may be responsible for writing all or part of the proposal. Marketing strategies play an integral part in this presentation and should be supported by critical-path checklists and planning forms.

| FIGURE 2.1   Residential Development Feasibility Checklist | | |
|---|---|---|
| *Item Number* | *Checklist Information/Assignments* | *Verification Dates/Notes* |
| 1.0 | PARCEL IDENTIFICATION DATA | |
| 1.1 | Reference title of parcel: | |
| 1.2 | Location (general): | |
| 1.3 | Owners/sellers/optionees: | |
| 1.4 | Submitting party: (contacts for data) | |
| 1.5 | Assignment(s) for internal review and evaluation: | |

| FIGURE 2.1 Residential Development Feasibility Checklist (continued) | | |
|---|---|---|
| Item Number | Checklist Information/Assignments | Verification Dates/Notes |
| 1.6 | General site description data | |
| 1.7 | Legal description (attach exhibits) | |
| 1.8 | Boundaries (survey if available) | |
| 1.9 | Access routes | |
| 1.10 | Topography (attach photos—general) | |
| 1.11 | Size of parcel (acreage & dimensions) | |
| 1.12 | Neighborhood influence (describe and relate to boundaries or size) | |
| 1.13 | List of people involved in parcel submission and processing<br>1.<br>2.<br>3.<br>4.<br>5.<br>6. | |

| Item Number | Checklist Information/Assignments | Verification Dates/Notes |
|---|---|---|
| | **FIGURE 2.1   Residential Development Feasibility Checklist (continued)** | |
| 2.0 | MARKET ANALYSIS AND FEASIBILITY | |
| 2.1 | Population statistics (U.S. Census or other resources)<br><br>Neighborhood<br>City<br>County<br>Regional | |
| 2.2 | Projected population growth rates<br><br>Neighborhood<br>City<br>County<br>Regional | |
| 2.3 | Population characteristics (persons per household, etc.) | |
| 2.4 | Income levels | |
| 2.5 | Estimated cost and fill grading requirements | |
| 2.6 | Existing buildings (Describe—photos) | |
| 2.7 | Demolition/removal requirements | |
| 2.8 | Amenities and potential preservation elements | |
| 2.9 | Sanitary sewers (availability and capacity) | |

| Item Number | Checklist Information/Assignments | Verification Dates/Notes |
|---|---|---|
| | **FIGURE 2.1 Residential Development Feasibility Checklist (continued)** | |
| 2.10 | Gas lines (availability) | |
| 2.11 | Soils—types/tests made | |
| 2.12 | Electricity (availability) | |
| 2.13 | Potable water (availability) | |
| 2.14 | Fire hydrants (location/capacity) | |
| 2.15 | Telephone service | |
| 2.16 | Cable T.V. service | |
| 2.17 | Street improvements required | |
| 2.18 | Existing easements (Describe—attach maps) | |
| 2.19 | Deed restrictions and protective covenants | |
| 2.20 | Potential dedications to municipal authorities or others | |

| Item Number | Checklist Information/Assignments | Verification Dates/Notes |
|---|---|---|
| | **FIGURE 2.1   Residential Development Feasibility Checklist (continued)** | |
| 3.0 | GOVERNMENTAL CRITERIA | |
| 3.1 | Municipalities involved | |
| 3.2 | Current zoning status | |
| 3.3 | Master plan and potential rezoning criteria | |
| 3.4 | Permit procedures and estimated time-tables for processing zoning and use permits | |
| 3.5 | Estimates of maximum yields of dwelling units per acre | |
| 3.6 | Attitudes of municipality and governmental agencies to development of this parcel | |
| 3.7 | Environment impact considerations<br>Traffic circulation<br>Parking<br>School load<br>Fire protection<br>Other issues | |

**FIGURE 2.1**    **Residential Development Feasibility Checklist (continued)**

| Item Number | Checklist Information/Assignments | Verification Dates/Notes |
|---|---|---|
| 3.8 | Tax information (assessor's map parcel #_____)<br>Rates_____<br>Bonds_____<br>Current tax status_____ | |
| 3.9 | Post office address and mail delivery<br>_____ | |
| 3.10 | Security services: police, sheriff, etc.<br>_____<br>_____<br>_____<br>_____ | |
| 4.0 | LAND PLAN AND PRODUCT DEVELOPMENT | |
| 4.1 | Establish land plan criteria and meet with planners for initial concepts | |
| 4.2 | Establish housing design criteria and meet with architect/designers for initial concepts | |
| 4.3 | Review initial land plan and housing designs with executive planning committee<br><br>Concepts related to profiled markets<br><br>Designs<br><br>Floor plans<br><br>Elevations<br><br>Price ranges<br><br>Product mix<br><br>Exterior materials<br><br>Exterior colors | |

| | FIGURE 2.1   Residential Development Feasibility Checklist (continued) | |
|---|---|---|
| *Item Number* | *Checklist Information/Assignments* | *Verification Dates/Notes* |
| 4.4 | Finalize working drawings for each floor plan and elevation | |
| 4.5 | Prepare preliminary cost estimates | |
| 4.6 | Plan first-phase mix, and streetscape elevation controls based on sites and anticipated sales patterns | |
| 4.7 | Coordinate exterior treatments such as patios, terraces, fencing and landscaping. Note key sites that need special landscaping attention | |
| 4.8 | Finalize sequence of construction on the sites that need to have early completions to protect community values | |
| 4.9 | Design all amenities and supervise their installation | |
| 4.10 | Prepare final master site plan showing all phasing, amenities, and neighboring values for use by sales personnel | |
| 5.0 | GENERAL MARKET ANALYSIS | |
| 5.1 | Population statistics (U.S. Census or other resources)<br>Neighborhood_____<br>City_____<br>County_____<br>Regional_____ | |
| 5.2 | Projected population growth rates<br>Neighborhood_____<br>City_____<br>County_____<br>Regional_____ | |

| FIGURE 2.1 | Residential Development Feasibility Checklist (continued) | |
|---|---|---|
| Item Number | Checklist Information/Assignments | Verification Dates/Notes |
| 5.3 | Demographics | |
| 5.4 | Population characteristics (persons per household, etc.) | |
| 5.3 | Income levels | |
| 5.3 | Employment patterns (labor availability & unemployment) | |
| 5.3 | Major industries (listed by size and volume)—(Add list to exhibit) | |
| 5.4 | Retail commerce per capita expenditures | |
| 5.4 | Retail sales analysis by category (Attach exhibits) | |
| 5.5 | Building permits/starts (provide time periods covered) (single-family vs multi-family) | |

| Item Number | Checklist Information/Assignments | Verification Dates/Notes |
|---|---|---|
| | **FIGURE 2.1   Residential Development Feasibility Checklist (continued)** | |
| 5.6 | Estimated building permits next 12 months (or longer)— (category) _____ _____ | |
| 5.7 | Percentage owner-occupied units _____ | |
| 5.8 | Percentage tenant-occupied units_____ | |
| 5.9 | Projected assumption rates or housing types by location and price range (attach work sheets) _____ _____ | |
| 5.10 | Summary of competitive projects currently in operation (Add detail competitive analysis forms for each project listed below) 1. _____ 2. _____ 3. _____ 4. _____ 5. _____ | |
| 5.11 | Summary of anticipated competitive projects 1. _____ 2. _____ 3. _____ 4. _____ 5. _____ | |
| 5.12 | Summary of existing housing near or adjacent to parcel (Attach photos) Tract ____ ____ ____ ____ Age ____ ____ ____ ____ Sizes ____ ____ ____ ____ Types ____ ____ ____ ____ Values ____ ____ ____ ____ Condition ____ ____ ____ ____ For sale ____ ____ ____ ____ Vacant ____ ____ ____ ____ Turn/rate ____ ____ ____ ____ | |

| FIGURE 2.1 Residential Development Feasibility Checklist (continued) | | |
|---|---|---|
| Item Number | Checklist Information/Assignments | Verification Dates/Notes |
| 5.13 | Profile(s) or anticipated buyers (Furnish back-up data) | |
| 6.0 | PRELIMINARY TITLE INFORMATION | |
| 6.1 | Title company or abstract attorney | |
| 6.2 | Title office or attorney | |
| 6.3 | Title vested in | |
| 6.4 | Taxes Current_____ Installments_____ | |
| 6.5 | Liens (other than taxes) | |
| 6.6 | Easement(s) (Attach exhibits) | |
| 6.6.1 | Limitations on building or development due to easement | |
| 6.6.2 | Easements that must be negotiated or acquired prior to development | |
| 6.7 | Encumbrances (Attach exhibits) (amount, beneficiaries, rates) 1. _____ 2. _____ 3. _____ 4. _____ | |

**FIGURE 2.1   Residential Development Feasibility Checklist (continued)**

| Item Number | Checklist Information/Assignments | Verification Dates/Notes |
|---|---|---|
| 6.8 | Status of mortgage encumbrances (due on sale/release clauses) | |
| 6.9 | Lis pendens | |
| 6.10 | Mineral rights (Attach exhibits) | |
| 6.11 | Existing leases or tenant farming contracts, etc. | |
| 6.12 | Ownership of improvements to the property | |
| 6.13 | Bonded indebtedness | |
| 6.13a | Amount_____ | |
| 6.13b | Interest rate_____ | |
| 6.13c | Term_____ | |
| 6.13d | Annual payment_____ | |
| 6.13e | Total outstanding principal_____ | |
| 6.14 | Other considerations involved in clearing title | |
| 7.0 | MARKETING FACTORS TO BE EVALUATED | |
| 7.1 | Accessibility of parcel (ingress/egress factors) | |
| 7.2 | Visual impact of parcel and approaches to site | |

| FIGURE 2.1 | Residential Development Feasibility Checklist (continued) | |
|---|---|---|
| *Item Number* | *Checklist Information/Assignments* | *Verification Dates/Notes* |
| 7.3 | Traffic generators—and traffic counts in area | |
| 7.4 | Availability of signage sites and directional billboards | |
| 7.5 | Negative influences that may require compensation in marketing strategies | |
| 7.6 | Amenities in area that add to value (List)<br>1.<br>2.<br>3.<br>4. | |
| 7.7 | Impact of major competitors in the area | |
| 7.8 | Target neighborhoods for potential purchasers | |
| 7.9 | Primary advertising media and comparative costs | |
| 7.10 | Impact of local real estate brokers on new homes sales (anticipated cooperation) | |
| 7.11 | Impact of "trade-up" market reference current resale market conditions | |

| | FIGURE 2.1　Residential Development Feasibility Checklist (continued) | |
|---|---|---|
| *Item Number* | *Checklist Information/Assignments* | *Verification Dates/Notes* |
| 7.12 | Impact of "transferees" and relocation buyers | |
| 7.13 | Impact of apartment renters and new family formations | |
| 8.0 | DESIGN CRITERIA | |
| 8.1 | Housing types to consider | |
| 8.2 | Square footages and approximate price ranges | |
| 8.3 | Bedroom mix | |
| 8.4 | Baths (number per plan and features) | |
| 8.5 | Architecture—(elevations) | |
| 8.6 | Garages—parking criteria | |
| 8.7 | Features to consider incorporating in the interior designs<br>1. _____<br>2. _____<br>3. _____ | |

**FIGURE 2.1   Residential Development Feasibility Checklist (continued)**

| Item Number | Checklist Information/Assignments | Verification Dates/Notes |
|---|---|---|
| 8.8 | Recommended exterior amenities and design features<br>1. _____<br>2. _____<br>3. _____<br>4. _____ | |
| 9.0 | ECONOMIC EVALUATION FACTORS | |
| 9.1 | Asking price for parcel_____ | |
| 9.2 | Proposed terms of purchase | |
| 9.3 | Potential subordination agreements—ventureships or other leverage considerations | |
| 9.4 | Anticipated capital required for acquisition | |
| 9.5 | Anticipated costs of development<br>(Prepare detailed checklists) | |
| 9.6 | Projected costs per unit for land acquisition and development (checklists—exhibits) | |
| 9.7 | Projected costs per unit for construction financing, marketing and profit (checklists & exhibits) | |

| FIGURE 2.1 | Residential Development Feasibility Checklist (continued) | |
|---|---|---|
| *Item Number* | *Checklist Information/Assignments* | *Verification Dates/Notes* |
| 9.8 | Evaluation of the anticipated gross prices in terms of perceived values and competition _____ _____ _____ | |
| 9.9 | Potential resources for capitalization and financing (List) _____ _____ | |
| 9.10 | Estimated normal appreciation if parcel purchased and held for investment (one to five years) _____ _____ | |
| 9.11 | Identify alternatives or development that could increase flexibility and resale financial runs _____ _____ | |
| 9.12 | Rate this parcel on a scale of 1–10 in terms of comparable sites available for acquisition and similar use _____ _____ | |
| 10.0 | ANTICIPATED TIME SCHEDULES | |
| 10.1 | Acquisition period<br>Preparation of agreement_____<br>Presentation_____<br>Acceptance_____<br>Funding_____<br>Close of escrow_____ | |
| 10.2 | Planning and approvals<br>Land plan_____<br>Zoning_____<br>Development permits_____<br>Housing designs_____<br>Lender approval_____ | |

| Item Number | Checklist Information/Assignments | Verification Dates/Notes |
|---|---|---|
| | **FIGURE 2.1   Residential Development Feasibility Checklist (concluded)** | |
| 10.3 | Anticipated phasing of construction<br><br>Phase 1_____<br>Phase 2_____<br>Phase 3_____<br>Phase 4_____ | |
| 10.4 | Pre-construction marketing phase<br><br>_____<br><br>_____ | |
| 10.5 | Construction phase<br><br>_____ | |
| 10.6 | Completion and post-construction period<br><br>_____ | |
| 10.7 | Anticipated total development and sell-out period<br><br>_____<br><br>_____ | |
| | | |

## SOURCES OF RESEARCH INFORMATION

Numerous resources are available to you or anyone else conducting market research in the housing industry. A large percentage of these are easily accessed and cost very little (except the time and effort to gather them). In metropolitan markets you will normally find an abundance of research statistics at your disposal, since many agencies and individuals need them. Common interest demands have generated numerous data-gathering programs. A list of these resources is provided at the end of this chapter.

## ORGANIZING RESEARCH SYSTEMS

When you operate in one general market area for a sustained period of time, it is in your best interests to have in place an on-going research capacity that is regularly up-dated. Basic indicators of market activity need to be monitored consistently for you to be well-informed and able to respond to changing conditions. Unless you identify your resources and have your methods of accessing them established for periodic measurement, you will most likely conduct research only when there is pressure to do so. You can avoid crisis-management reactions to the market by maintaining fingertip control over primary data sources that indicate the direction and depth of current housing activity.

The key elements in an organized research program include the following:

1.  Aerial photography and regional maps of market areas in which your company develops property.
2.  Identified list of all competitive housing communities and building operations, preferably shown on a control map.
3.  Copies of census tract data for the specific areas your housing serves.
4.  Copies of published reports on housing starts, building permits, construction activity, closings, etc.
5.  Multiple listing reports that show residential resale activity by geographic subneighborhoods.
6.  Current information on financing and available loans, interest rates, etc.
7.  Clipping file of articles containing information on the growth of the general communities in which you operate.
8.  Copy of the master plan and zoning regulations for each of the municipalities in which you are involved.
9.  General economic indicators and business development in the region. Banks and chambers of commerce are among your best sources for this data.
10. Maps and other exhibits that depict planned highway construction.
11. Maps and other exhibits that show the location of existing underground service utility lines plus planned extensions.
12. School district boundary lines shown on maps or other exhibits.
13. Political information file relating to the attitudes and actions of those who approve or reject new development plans.

## THE VALUE OF HAVING A WAR ROOM

There is real value in having one room or location within the corporate offices where all research information is available to those who need it. I have often referred to this concept as having a *war room*, where everything is visually available to those in command. Like generals in the military, you can grasp the significance of multiple pieces of information if they can be graphically displayed on maps and strategic-planning boards.

Aerial photographs are one of the most helpful visual aids in this environment. They permit you to see all of the land within the region and to spot developed and undeveloped areas. Topographical features that affect land development will be clearly evident. By using overlays, you can show existing and future highways, the location of underground utilities, school district boundaries and many other items that are significant when planning the acquisition and development of real estate.

By maintaining one map that shows all competitive developments, you can visually orient yourself to the housing environments that are a factor in your own planning. Anticipated future projects should also be denoted as they are discovered. Copies of competitive market studies of each project should be filed and up-dated regularly. Normally this should be done once a month with the help of your real estate agents or assistants.

This room is an excellent place to keep copies of plat maps for the new areas that are under various stages of development. Your own communities can be maintained on separate control boards showing the status of construction, sales, closings, occupancies and other relevant factors. Floor plans can be kept on racks or in cabinets so they are readily accessible to those who need them. Project control manuals that contain the original research studies, development history, sales records, prices, specifications, options, etc., are also valuable management resources for a research library.

The objective is to have one central location where every piece of research is readily accessible to those who need it for review in managing the business. If you cannot afford or do not require a separate room, at least have your research centrally organized so that you can locate facts you require without the frustration of searching through scattered, uncatalogued files!

## EMPLOYING RESEARCH SPECIALISTS

If you do not have the people or the time to devote to market research, you may elect to employ the services of an individual or a company that specializes in such studies. Every major metropolitan area has one or more consultants who will provide housing research studies for specific sites and for general analysis of the needs of the region. In smaller communities, you may have to employ someone from another city who is willing to take on assignments outside their home base. You can obtain the names of reputable researchers by checking with lending institutions, your local chapter of the Home Builders Association, your compatriots in the business, or by writing to the National Association of Home Builders in Washington, D.C. The authors also maintain a list of researchers around the nation who have gained a solid reputation for professional feasibility analysis, and you can write to us if your other resources do not answer your needs.

Our experience has certainly demonstrated that all researchers are not equal! Many who profess to know how to do competent analysis of housing markets have produced reports that were misleading and incomplete. Before you engage any researcher not personally known to you, check their references. Ask to see samples of recent studies they have done for others and compare the content and interpretative elements against your expectations. If your report is going to be used to help influence your banking sources, be certain that the researchers meet the qualifications required by these institutions.

Costs of research studies vary greatly. In many instances you will be quoted a flat fee that includes all time and expenses. Others quote hourly rates plus expenses.

Before you employ a researcher, obtain the quotation for services and ask for a detailed explanation of what this will encompass.

You can often save money if you provide some of the research data with the help of your own staff or of people less expensive than the outside consultants. Discuss this with the research company and identify what you can provide versus that which you expect from them.

## MARKET RESEARCH IS A CONTINUOUS ACTIVITY

Market research should not be viewed as a one-time activity that occurs only at the inception of a project. To gain maximum effectiveness from market research efforts, market data should be kept up-to-date and maintained by monitoring key elements that affect markets. Such elements include what the competition is currently doing, what is happening in the general economy and the local economy, prevailing conditions in financial markets and new trends in consumer preferences in products and product features.

The value of sound market research cannot be determined by measuring the direct costs of research. What really counts is the validity of the research information and the ability to interpret it as it applies to your particular needs. Definitive research helps everyone to know not only what is happening, but where you might be able to do successfully something not already being done.

The most productive type of foundation market research—the initial research from which the project's general directions are first taken—is that which discloses holes or voids that you can fill. Finding a niche in the market allows you to put your product on the market without much competition, thus giving you the distinct advantage of being a monopolistic competitor. A monopolistic competitor is one who has successfully introduced a product into a marketplace already active with similar but not identical products and features and who, through effective marketing techniques and strategies, is able to persuade the product-buying public that there is only one place to find that product. In an ideal world, you would have a market so accurately profiled and strategies so finely developed that your prospects face no decision between competing products—only whether or not they should buy your product now. While the ideal may rarely be achievable, comprehensive market research brings you closer to it.

Because of increasing dominance of markets by housing "giants" working on a national basis with top staffs and advisors who, in turn, are working with more comprehensive and sophisticated market research programs than has been typical of smaller operators, small- and medium-sized builder/developers are at an increasing disadvantage.

As the giants continue to increase their market share, they inevitably do it at the expense of the smaller builder. And where the giants are not gobbling up market share, the large, well-heeled regionals are. The medium- and small-sized builder/developer's chances for survival and continued growth must begin with major improvements in market research. Of great importance, improved market research programs include designing and implementing a sound system for continuing research as well as foundation research.

Continuing research begins with structuring an information-management system built around your sales activities. For a nominal investment you can buy a computer, necessary peripherals and a data-base management program sufficient for the information needs of a good, on-going market research program designed around your own marketing and sales activities. It takes just a few days of applied study for a total novice to become operational in a data-base management program operating with a microcomputer. With a proper data-input format designed for your needs, it takes no more than an hour or so to train a clerk with no experience in computers to input all the information you will ever want to retrieve and analyze.

The information you will want to store and regularly analyze is socio-economic profile data on prospects and buyers, sources of traffic, addresses at time of first visit, number of visits, length of time before purchase, record of sales by salesperson, popularity of product types and features along with other information that enables you to measure the effectiveness of project activities and expenditures.

Many by-products of such a program exist, not the least of which is the better follow-up of prospects. With names and addresses along with profile information and coded data such as financial strength, marital status, indices of product interest and other factors, you can generate follow-up letters of pin-point accuracy through the information management system when combined with a mail-merge system that enables personalized letters on a volume-run basis.

When you spend substantial dollars to produce buyers, it makes no sense to view those expenditures simply as a week-to-week marketing expense. In reality, with a good data-base management system that serves as the core resource for your continuing market research, you can convert your promotional expenses to capital expenses. The dollars you spend for a week of advertising can give you value not just for that week but for many months and even years, as you "trap" information from each prospect who visits after seeing an ad. That information enables you to better understand your market and often allows you to sell the slower-to-decide prospect as much as a year or more later. We have found, for example, that more conservative consumers often won't buy when a project is new because they won't put their money into something others have not previously accepted. Those persons may still be viable prospects many months later and, if you are properly working your data-base program, a systematic follow-up will keep your project's name in the prospects' consciousnesses. Because your continuing market research tells you who is buying and why, you will be better able to convey the success of the project and why it is successful to the shy prospect who needs only to be infected with what we call, "buyer contagion." Your research systems should provide a continuous reference base against which you can interpret marketing opportunities and develop cost-effective strategies that produce optimum results.

## THE VALUE OF MONITORING PROSPECTS AND OWNERS

The most effective research we can conduct in this home-selling industry is usually right at "home"! The people we have sold and those we have met as a result of our marketing efforts are the first resources we should tap when attempting to evaluate what we are doing right—and what we might improve. Our owners should always be one of our most important sources of additional business. Referrals are based on goodwill and the willing pursuit of these potential leads by your sales staff. Most important is the ability to use owners as a valuable source of information to help you locate and sell other prospects. Some of the clients of The Stone Institute do a very creditable job in following up their owners after they move in; others seem to find it hard to work this monitoring activity into the schedule.

The results that we have seen from an effective consumer research program are so dramatic that we have become convinced that any builder or marketing team not taking advantage of this resource is missing an essential part of the total marketing plan. Although it requires someone to administer the custom survey system, and a few dollars must be invested in survey forms, direct mail, and personnel to obtain and digest the information, the results always outweigh the costs. There are companies that specialize in providing independent monitoring systems by direct contact with new owners.

A well-organized program will contain the following elements:

1. prospect profile cards
2. buyer profile records
3. scheduled time periods to contact owners
4. owner survey questionnaires mailed/delivered after the sale is consummated
5. periodic sampling of prospects who have not yet purchased from your company
6. data compilation system for recording all responses
7. periodic summaries of findings for use by every level of management from designers to front-line sales people

Often the owner survey and monitoring system is incorporated in the total customer-service program. It is logical that it be included in this customer-relations package. While measuring the degree of satisfaction owners have with their new homes, you are also able to discover information that will help direct your marketing efforts. What do they like most about their homes? Why did they purchase this particular model? What would they improve if they had the opportunity? How do they feel about the service they have received? The company? Your sales personnel? Would they recommend your company and its homes to others? What do they consider the most outstanding feature of the home they selected? Of the community?

A wealth of valuable information can be derived from those who have purchased and are living with your housing environments. Not to ask their opinions and to use the information to improve the effectiveness of your operations is to overlook the most fundamental of all research objectives!

## NONPURCHASERS CAN OFTEN TELL YOU MORE THAN PURCHASERS

Prospects who visit your communities or sales offices but do not buy from you are even more important in evaluating your effectiveness than information gained from those who bought! After all, those you sold are going to be inclined to reinforce their own decisions. People do not like to fault their own judgments. We tend to justify our actions—or inactions—in life. On the other hand, the people who investigated your housing opportunities and did not decide to purchase are a valuable resource for discovering what is not working—and why.

Prospects are impossible to monitor if your salespeople do not keep accurate customer profile cards. Amazingly, the majority of sales operations in this industry do not have tight control on this critical area of marketing. Many companies do not even require that sales personnel use the prospect card at an early point in the greeting and qualifying process! How can you follow up or sell people whom you can't contact? Sales agents will excuse themselves from trying to secure names and addresses by saying, "People resent being asked to give that information." This is just an excuse. It is not rational. We know from experience that a skilled sales representative can secure the prospect's name, address and pertinent qualifying information in 90 percent of the cases when motivated and trained to do so. The first step in establishing a strong marketing research program and assuring your company of a chance to get a fair return from its promotional efforts is to have control over the prospect profiles. The second is to insist that every prospect be contacted on a regular basis until sold or deleted from the active list by qualified criteria.

Some of the companies we represent use the following system for monitoring the prospects that are in the open file.

1. Every prospect must be "carded" by the sales representative or hostess. Minimum information includes the following:

   name/address/phone
   reason they visited your community
   time-frame considerations in buying and moving
   present status: own, rent, local resident, transferee, etc.
   size and type of home sought

2. The sales representative adds as much additional information as possible obtained during the interview (or immediately thereafter). Essential areas of sales qualifications noted are:

   financial qualifying (income, price range and type of financing)
   motivations and interests
   contingent factors
   competitive shopping data

3. The sales representative adds personal observations on the card (usually the back side) and gives the prospect a rating classification. A typical rating system is:

   A  =  qualified buyer with no contingencies and a relatively short time span in which to make a decision
   B  =  qualified buyer but has either a contingency or a longer time frame for decision making
   C  =  prospect not presently qualified but does show interest in the homes you offer

D  =  all the others; essentially nonqualified and little or no interest in the homes you feature

4. The salesperson is responsible for following-up all A's immediately and at least three contacts are required within ten days after first visit. Five contacts are preferred.

B's should be contacted as A's if time permits. The minimum is two contacts within ten days.

C's are sent a thank-you note for coming to the community and contacted as time allows after A's and B's have been adequately serviced.

D's are held in the research files for future mailings and potential contact when business is slow and other resources are exhausted. A minimum objective should be sending a thank-you note for visiting in the hope it stimulates someone else's potential interest.

5. The A's and B's are not disturbed by management or researchers until:

The salesperson releases them after a reasonable follow up period.
The follow-up contact confirms they purchased competitive homes.
The prescribed follow-up time period has expired and management elects to investigate with a third-party contact.

6. Sales management or the marketing department reviews all prospect cards on a regular basis (at least once a month). Decisions are made with the sales representative's concurrence regarding each unclosed prospect.

7. Periodic monitoring of the unclosed prospects is then conducted at management's discretion. This may be done with the use of in-house personnel or an outside and independent monitoring team.

8. Results of all monitoring activities are shared with the salespeople as well as other members of the marketing and management system.

This type of controlled monitoring of prospects produces outstanding results. The first objective is to keep active prospects in the buying curve so that a high percentage is successfully closed. The other objective is to use the reservoir of unsold customers as a research fund that can provide valuable information about the effectiveness of promotions and presentations.


## THE TELEPHONE SURVEY IS MOST EFFECTIVE WITH UNCLOSED PROSPECTS

The return on direct-mail questionnaires for prospects who have visited models and not purchased is very low. People are not inclined to respond to this type of mailing. They consider it a promotional effort and, since they have not yet purchased, will avoid going on record as to their present motivations and interests. However, telephone interviews conducted by friendly and well-trained interviewers can produce excellent results. It is usually best to employ someone not related to the sales function to hold these interviews. The prospects are not as likely to tell another salesperson

**FIGURE 2.2    Sample Prospect Card**

### (Front Copy)

THANK YOU for visiting us.                                    DATE:_____
Please help us better meet your housing
   needs by completing this card.              COMMUNITY:_____

NAMES: _____

ADDRESS: _____ ZIP _____

TELEPHONE: (Home) _____ (Work) _____ (Work) _____

ARE YOU IN THE MARKET FOR A NEW HOME: Yes _____ No _____ Maybe _____

DO YOU PRESENTLY OWN OR RENT? Own _____ Rent _____ Lease (Term) _____

WHY ARE YOU CONSIDERING A MOVE? _____

WHAT SOURCE OF INFORMATION DID YOU USE TO HELP DECIDE WHERE TO SHOP FOR
A NEW HOME? CHECK ALL THAT APPLY.

        [ ]  Newspaper 1      [ ]  New Homes Guide
        [ ]  Newspaper 2      [ ]  New Homes Magazine
        [ ]  Radio Commercial   [ ]  Television Commercial
        [ ]  Homeowner Referral [ ]  Billboards and Signs
        [ ]  Referral or Friend  [ ]  Mail Advertisements
        [ ]  Driving Around    [ ]  Off-Site Sales Center
        [ ]  Realtor         [ ]  Other

Notes: _____
_____
_____

### (Back Copy)

NAME: _____ CHILDREN: Boys _____ Girls _____ Ages _____

EMPLOYER: _____ Job Title _____ Income _____

EMPLOYER: _____ Job Title _____ Income _____

SOURCE OF DOWN PAYMENT _____ FINANCING PROPOSED _____

MODEL BEING CONSIDERED _____ Homesite _____

OTHER BUILDERS BEING CONSIDERED _____

FOLLOW-UP RECORD

| Date of Contact | Type of Contact | Discussion Notes | Plan of Action |
|---|---|---|---|
|  |  |  |  |
|  |  |  |  |
|  |  |  |  |
|  |  |  |  |
|  |  |  |  |

what they felt about a particular housing program as they will an independent researcher. Here are some of the questions that are commonly asked in these telephone interviews:

> *"Mrs. Williams? . . . ("Yes?") Good evening, my name is. . . . I am a researcher with "Consumer Profiles, Inc." and your name was given to me to call as someone recently investigating new homes in this area. We are conducting an independent housing-interest survey to assist those planning new communities and new housing designs for our city. If you have a moment, I would like to ask you a few questions that are valuable to our research efforts. We will send you a gift in appreciation of your participation in this research assignment. Have you been seriously looking for a new home within the past six months?"*

*If no, ask: "Are you considering a move in the future?"*

*If yes, ask the following series:*

> *"How long have you been looking for a new home?*
> *"Have you been shopping on your own or working with a real estate broker?*
> *"How many homes have you inspected thus far?*
> *"Which new home communities or individual sellers have favorably impressed you? Why?"*

*If our community is not mentioned, ask specifically: "Have you seen _____?"*

*If yes, ask:*

> *"What were your impressions of _____?*
>
> *"May I ask your current status in trying to reach a decision about what and when to purchase a new home?*
> *"What features do you consider most important in the design of a new home?*
> *"How large is your present home?*
> *"How long have you lived there?*
> *"What features not in your present residence would you like in the new home?*
> *"When do you think you will be making a decision."*

Follow up with a thank-you note for time and interest. Advise that you will send a gift for their participation in the survey. Hang up. Record all notes not taken during the interview and make your next call.

The typical thank-you gift is a copy of a housing magazine or a booklet on decorating, etc. It is not essential to use a gift, but it does help to improve the quality of the responses and increases the number of people who will answer the questions.

Some researchers tape the conversations (with the respondent's permission) so that they do not have to write out all the answers during the interview. The principle objective is to discover the consumer's attitudes about your homes in comparison to others they have seen and to determine the status of their potential housing decisions. Secondary objectives include gaining some understanding of what are the "discontent factors" that motivate your prospects to move from present residences and discovering why they have delayed making those decisions. This can be valuable to your designers and marketing strategists.

## OWNERS RESPOND TO SURVEY QUESTIONNAIRES, BUT PERSONAL INTERVIEWS PRODUCE THE BEST RESULTS!

Your owners have a deeper interest in sharing information with you than do the people who have not yet purchased. They are far more likely to respond to your requests for their opinions, especially if they have something to bring to your attention! You will hear the negative concerns owners have accumulated since moving into the new homes, but you will also learn the positives that caused them to purchase. Not to survey and monitor your buyers is to miss information that can help you improve many aspects of your system. More important, it is your best way of saying to them "WE CARE!" When you ask their opinion in a sincere and friendly manner, you are indicating a genuine interest in their opinions and welfare. That alone justifies the time and money you invest in customer-satisfaction surveys.

The printed questionnaire is most commonly used by "the marketing-aware" in our industry. If someone is assigned to personally interview each owner within 60 to 90 days after move-in you may improve both your customer-service procedures and your consumer relations. That is one of the reasons that some companies combine these functions with the total customer-service plan.

The typical questionnaire contains some of the following questions along with special requests that are needed for a specific housing environment.

1. Are you enjoying the new home?
2. What are the features of the home that you consider most appealing as compared to your previous home?
3. Are there design adjustments you would recommend for future versions of this plan? Why?
4. Has our sales staff kept you informed throughout the process of purchasing and moving into your new home?
5. Were there any surprises or areas of concern that you felt could have been better handled?
6. Please rate the following on a scale of 1 to 10 (1 being the lowest value and 10 the highest) in terms of your satisfaction with our services:

   your sales representative        _____
   the mortgage processor        _____
   the walk-through inspection        _____
   customer service department        _____
   pre-move-in services        _____
   the owner's manual        _____
   the general attitude of our personnel        _____
   other comments        _____

7. How would you rate the value of the home and neighborhood compared to other choices you had? (Scale of 1 to 10)
8. Will you recommend our company and homes to others?
   Yes_____ No _____
9. As an owner in our new community, what would you most like to see accomplished in the forthcoming months to make this a better place to live?

---

**FIGURE 2.3  Home Buyers Survey**

---

# HOME BUYERS SURVEY

Survey #: _____ (1-4)

Card #: _____1_____ (5)

Market Area: _____ (6-7)

We would appreciate a few minutes of your time so we can determine how various features appeal to you and also how important they would be in your decision to move to a new home.

An annual survey conducted by BUILDER magazine and Fulton Research, Inc.

**1.** Check all of the items that would *strongly* influence you to move to a new community.

**A.** Recreation features:
- (8) _____ 18-hole golf course
- (9) _____ 9-hole executive golf course
- (10) _____ Country club
- (11) _____ Tennis courts
- (12) _____ Racquetball courts
- (13) _____ Walking/jogging trails
- (14) _____ Lake
- (15) _____ Boating
- (16) _____ Fishing
- (17) _____ Swimming pool
- (18) _____ Spa
- (19) _____ Sauna
- (20) _____ Horse stables/riding ring
- (21) _____ Exercise room
- (22) _____ Other

**B.** Activity areas:
- (23) _____ Card rooms
- (24) _____ Hobby rooms
- (25) _____ Social lounge
- (26) _____ Children's care center
- (27) _____ Playgrounds
- (28) _____ Woodworking shop
- (29) _____ Clubhouse
- (30) _____ Park area

**2.** (31) Which one of these floor plan types do you most prefer:
- 1 _____ Single-story
- 2 _____ Split-level
- 3 _____ Two-story
- 4 _____ Three-story

**3.** **A.** What is the maximum price you would be willing to pay for a new home? $ _____,000 (32-34)

**B.** What is the maximum down payment you would be willing to make? $ _____,000 (35-37)

**C.** What is the maximum monthly payment you would be willing to make? (Including property taxes and homeowner's insurance) $ _____ (38-41)

**D.** What is the square footage you would expect in a new home? _____ (42-45)

**4.** (46) Do you own or rent the home you are living in now?
- 1 _____ Own  2 _____ Rent

(What is your monthly rent? _____) (47-50)

(51) If own, type of home:
- 1 _____ Mid-rise condo
- 2 _____ Townhouse
- 3 _____ Single-family detached home

---

**FIGURE 2.3    Home Buyers Survey (continued)**

---

**5.** If you own your current residence:

    **A.** What is its approximate market value? $ _____ ,000
                                      (52-54)

    **B.** What is its approximate size? _____ sq. ft.
                                    (55-58)

    **C.** Approximately how much equity do you have in your
    home? $ _____ ,000
              (59-61)

**6.** Check the number of bedrooms desired in a new home.
(62)

| 1 | 2 | 3 | 4 | 5 or more |
|---|---|---|---|---|
| 1( ) | 2( ) | 3( ) | 4( ) | 5( ) |

**7.** Check the number of baths desired in a new home.
(63)

| 1 | 1½ | 2 | 2½ | 3 | 3½ | 4 or more |
|---|---|---|---|---|---|---|
| 1( ) | 2( ) | 3( ) | 4( ) | 5( ) | 6( ) | 7( ) |

(80)-9
(1-4) DUP
(5)-2

**8.** Rate the appeal of the following kitchen features or products with which you are familiar. (Rate each item on a scale of 1 to 5 with 1 being least appealing and 5 most appealing.)

| | | Least appealing | | | | Most appealing |
|---|---|---|---|---|---|---|
| | | 1 | 2 | 3 | 4 | 5 |
| Double-bowl sink | (6) | ( ) | ( ) | ( ) | ( ) | ( ) |
| Single-bowl sink | (7) | ( ) | ( ) | ( ) | ( ) | ( ) |
| Porcelain sink | (8) | ( ) | ( ) | ( ) | ( ) | ( ) |
| Stainless steel sink | (9) | ( ) | ( ) | ( ) | ( ) | ( ) |
| Wood-finish cabinetry | (10) | ( ) | ( ) | ( ) | ( ) | ( ) |
| European-style laminate-finish cabinetry | (11) | ( ) | ( ) | ( ) | ( ) | ( ) |
| Intercom | (12) | ( ) | ( ) | ( ) | ( ) | ( ) |
| Walk-in pantry | (13) | ( ) | ( ) | ( ) | ( ) | ( ) |
| Eating area | (14) | ( ) | ( ) | ( ) | ( ) | ( ) |
| Snack bar | (15) | ( ) | ( ) | ( ) | ( ) | ( ) |
| Greenhouse window | (16) | ( ) | ( ) | ( ) | ( ) | ( ) |
| Laminate counter top | (17) | ( ) | ( ) | ( ) | ( ) | ( ) |
| Ceramic tile counter top | (18) | ( ) | ( ) | ( ) | ( ) | ( ) |
| Corian counter top | (19) | ( ) | ( ) | ( ) | ( ) | ( ) |
| Resilient vinyl flooring | (20) | ( ) | ( ) | ( ) | ( ) | ( ) |
| Wood flooring | (21) | ( ) | ( ) | ( ) | ( ) | ( ) |
| Ceramic tile flooring | (22) | ( ) | ( ) | ( ) | ( ) | ( ) |
| Island work area | (23) | ( ) | ( ) | ( ) | ( ) | ( ) |
| Microwave oven | (24) | ( ) | ( ) | ( ) | ( ) | ( ) |
| Single oven | (25) | ( ) | ( ) | ( ) | ( ) | ( ) |
| Double oven | (26) | ( ) | ( ) | ( ) | ( ) | ( ) |
| Barbeque cook top | (27) | ( ) | ( ) | ( ) | ( ) | ( ) |
| Trash compactor | (28) | ( ) | ( ) | ( ) | ( ) | ( ) |
| Built-in food processor | (29) | ( ) | ( ) | ( ) | ( ) | ( ) |

**9.** Assuming you were buying a home, rate the appeal of the following *exterior* features or products. (Rate each item on a scale of 1 to 5 with 1 being least appealing and 5 most appealing.)

**A.** Siding that is primarily:

| | | Least appealing | | | | Most appealing |
|---|---|---|---|---|---|---|
| | | 1 | 2 | 3 | 4 | 5 |
| Plywood | (30) | ( ) | ( ) | ( ) | ( ) | ( ) |
| Stone | (31) | ( ) | ( ) | ( ) | ( ) | ( ) |
| Stucco | (32) | ( ) | ( ) | ( ) | ( ) | ( ) |
| Wood | (33) | ( ) | ( ) | ( ) | ( ) | ( ) |
| Brick | (34) | ( ) | ( ) | ( ) | ( ) | ( ) |
| Wood shingles | (35) | ( ) | ( ) | ( ) | ( ) | ( ) |
| Hardboard | (36) | ( ) | ( ) | ( ) | ( ) | ( ) |
| Aluminum | (37) | ( ) | ( ) | ( ) | ( ) | ( ) |
| Cement block | (38) | ( ) | ( ) | ( ) | ( ) | ( ) |
| Vinyl | (39) | ( ) | ( ) | ( ) | ( ) | ( ) |
| Other | (40) | ( ) | ( ) | ( ) | ( ) | ( ) |

**B.** Roofs that are:

| | | 1 | 2 | 3 | 4 | 5 |
|---|---|---|---|---|---|---|
| Wood shake | (41) | ( ) | ( ) | ( ) | ( ) | ( ) |
| Asphalt composition | (42) | ( ) | ( ) | ( ) | ( ) | ( ) |
| Clay or concrete roof tile | (43) | ( ) | ( ) | ( ) | ( ) | ( ) |
| Other (e.g., slate or metal) | (44) | ( ) | ( ) | ( ) | ( ) | ( ) |

**C.** Entry doors that are:

| | | 1 | 2 | 3 | 4 | 5 |
|---|---|---|---|---|---|---|
| Plain wood | (45) | ( ) | ( ) | ( ) | ( ) | ( ) |
| Decorative wood | (46) | ( ) | ( ) | ( ) | ( ) | ( ) |
| Plain steel | (47) | ( ) | ( ) | ( ) | ( ) | ( ) |
| Decorative steel | (48) | ( ) | ( ) | ( ) | ( ) | ( ) |

**D.** Windows (double-glazed) that are:

| | | 1 | 2 | 3 | 4 | 5 |
|---|---|---|---|---|---|---|
| Aluminum | (49) | ( ) | ( ) | ( ) | ( ) | ( ) |
| Wood | (50) | ( ) | ( ) | ( ) | ( ) | ( ) |
| Vinyl-clad wood | (51) | ( ) | ( ) | ( ) | ( ) | ( ) |

**10.** In terms of age groups, which type of community would you prefer?
(52)

  (1) _____ All adults 35 years or older, no children.
  (2) _____ All adults 50 years or older, no children.
  (3) _____ Adults of all ages, no children.
  (4) _____ No restriction on age of adults or children.

**11.** Are you currently retired or planning to retire within five years?
(53)

  (1) _____ Currently retired
  (2) _____ Planning to retire within five years
  (3) _____ Neither

## FIGURE 2.3  Home Buyers Survey (continued)

**12.** What would you consider the maximum distance you would move from your current home (other than a job transfer)?

(54)

- (1) _____ 0-5 miles
- (2) _____ 6-10 miles
- (3) _____ 11-15 miles
- (4) _____ 16-20 miles
- (5) _____ 21-30 miles
- (6) _____ 31-50 miles
- (7) _____ 51-100 miles
- (8) _____ More than 100 miles

**13.** Assuming you were going to buy a new home, which of these home types would you seriously consider purchasing? (Check all applicable housing types.)

- (55) _____ Single-family detached
- (56) _____ Garden (patio) home
- (57) _____ Townhouse
- (58) _____ Mid-rise condominium (2 or 3 floors)
- (59) _____ High-rise condominium (4 or more floors)

**14.** What is your favorite house design? (Check only one.)

- (1) _____ Tudor
- (2) _____ Colonial
- (3) _____ Traditional
- (4) _____ Ranch
- (5) _____ Modern
- (6) _____ Spanish
- (7) _____ Victorian
- (8) _____ Other

**15.** In a two-story home would you prefer to have the master bedroom on the first or second floor? (All other bedrooms would be on the second floor.)

- (1) _____ Master bedroom on the first floor
- (2) _____ Master bedroom on the second floor

(80)-9
(1-4) DUP
(5)-3

**16.** Rate the appeal of the following *interior* features or products. (Rate each item on a scale of 1 to 5 with 1 being least appealing and 5 most appealing.)

| | | Least appealing | | | | Most appealing |
|---|---|---|---|---|---|---|
| | | 1 | 2 | 3 | 4 | 5 |
| Tile flooring | (6) | ( ) | ( ) | ( ) | ( ) | ( ) |
| Hardwood flooring | (7) | ( ) | ( ) | ( ) | ( ) | ( ) |
| Upgraded carpeting | (8) | ( ) | ( ) | ( ) | ( ) | ( ) |
| Skylight | (9) | ( ) | ( ) | ( ) | ( ) | ( ) |
| Ceiling fan | (10) | ( ) | ( ) | ( ) | ( ) | ( ) |
| Greenhouse window | (11) | ( ) | ( ) | ( ) | ( ) | ( ) |
| Greenhouse section (sunroom) | (12) | ( ) | ( ) | ( ) | ( ) | ( ) |
| Fireplace | (13) | ( ) | ( ) | ( ) | ( ) | ( ) |
| Vaulted ceiling | (14) | ( ) | ( ) | ( ) | ( ) | ( ) |
| Wet bar | (15) | ( ) | ( ) | ( ) | ( ) | ( ) |
| Window seat | (16) | ( ) | ( ) | ( ) | ( ) | ( ) |
| Recessed or track lighting | (17) | ( ) | ( ) | ( ) | ( ) | ( ) |
| Built-in shelving | (18) | ( ) | ( ) | ( ) | ( ) | ( ) |
| Mirrored walls | (19) | ( ) | ( ) | ( ) | ( ) | ( ) |
| Sliding doors | (20) | ( ) | ( ) | ( ) | ( ) | ( ) |
| French doors | (21) | ( ) | ( ) | ( ) | ( ) | ( ) |
| Step-up or step-down rooms | (22) | ( ) | ( ) | ( ) | ( ) | ( ) |
| Wood paneling | (23) | ( ) | ( ) | ( ) | ( ) | ( ) |
| Decorative moldings | (24) | ( ) | ( ) | ( ) | ( ) | ( ) |
| Security system | (25) | ( ) | ( ) | ( ) | ( ) | ( ) |
| Deadbolt locks | (26) | ( ) | ( ) | ( ) | ( ) | ( ) |
| Central vacuum | (27) | ( ) | ( ) | ( ) | ( ) | ( ) |

**17.** Rate the appeal of the following *exterior* features. (Rate each item on a scale of 1 to 5 with 1 being least appealing and 5 most appealing.)

| | | Least appealing | | | | Most appealing |
|---|---|---|---|---|---|---|
| | | 1 | 2 | 3 | 4 | 5 |
| Covered porch | (28) | ( ) | ( ) | ( ) | ( ) | ( ) |
| Wood deck | (29) | ( ) | ( ) | ( ) | ( ) | ( ) |
| Patio slab | (30) | ( ) | ( ) | ( ) | ( ) | ( ) |
| Hot tub or spa | (31) | ( ) | ( ) | ( ) | ( ) | ( ) |
| Carport | (32) | ( ) | ( ) | ( ) | ( ) | ( ) |
| One-car garage | (33) | ( ) | ( ) | ( ) | ( ) | ( ) |
| Two-car garage | (34) | ( ) | ( ) | ( ) | ( ) | ( ) |
| Three-car garage | (35) | ( ) | ( ) | ( ) | ( ) | ( ) |
| Automatic garage door | (36) | ( ) | ( ) | ( ) | ( ) | ( ) |
| Security lighting | (37) | ( ) | ( ) | ( ) | ( ) | ( ) |

## FIGURE 2.3   Home Buyers Survey (concluded)

**18.** Check the items that would *most* encourage you to purchase a new home. (Check all applicable.)

(38) _____ Larger home
(39) _____ Larger yard
(40) _____ Smaller home
(41) _____ Less yard maintenance
(42) _____ New product features
(43) _____ New design features
(44) _____ An energy-efficient home
(45) _____ Investment potential
(46) _____ Tax advantages
(47) _____ Growing family
(48) _____ Job transfer
(49) _____ Closer to work
(50) _____ Better neighborhood
(51) _____ Better schools
(52) _____ Change of scene
(53) _____ Tired of renting
(54) _____ Children have left or are leaving home
(55) _____ Community with recreation facilities
(56) _____ Change in marital status
(57) _____ Warranty on construction

**19.** Rate the appeal of the following features or products for the *master bedroom* and *master bath*. (Rate each item on a scale of 1 to 5 with 1 being least appealing and 5 most appealing.)

| | | Least appealing | | | | Most appealing |
|---|---|---|---|---|---|---|
| | | 1 | 2 | 3 | 4 | 5 |
| Private balcony or patio | (58) | ( ) | ( ) | ( ) | ( ) | ( ) |
| Sitting area | (59) | ( ) | ( ) | ( ) | ( ) | ( ) |
| Fireplace | (60) | ( ) | ( ) | ( ) | ( ) | ( ) |
| Walk-in closet | (61) | ( ) | ( ) | ( ) | ( ) | ( ) |
| Bay window (bedroom) | (62) | ( ) | ( ) | ( ) | ( ) | ( ) |
| Whirlpool tub | (63) | ( ) | ( ) | ( ) | ( ) | ( ) |
| Separate shower enclosure | (64) | ( ) | ( ) | ( ) | ( ) | ( ) |
| Two sinks (instead of one) | (65) | ( ) | ( ) | ( ) | ( ) | ( ) |
| Colored fixtures | (66) | ( ) | ( ) | ( ) | ( ) | ( ) |
| Upgraded fittings (i.e., faucets) | (67) | ( ) | ( ) | ( ) | ( ) | ( ) |
| Linen closet | (68) | ( ) | ( ) | ( ) | ( ) | ( ) |
| Ceramic tile flooring in bath | (69) | ( ) | ( ) | ( ) | ( ) | ( ) |
| Ceramic tile walls in tub and shower | (70) | ( ) | ( ) | ( ) | ( ) | ( ) |
| Mirrors in bath | (71) | ( ) | ( ) | ( ) | ( ) | ( ) |
| Vanity storage | (72) | ( ) | ( ) | ( ) | ( ) | ( ) |
| Water-saving fixtures | (73) | ( ) | ( ) | ( ) | ( ) | ( ) |

**20.** How would you describe your buying intentions? (Check one.)
(74)
(1) _____ Plan to buy now
(2) _____ Plan to buy within one year
(3) _____ No plans, just looking

**21.** Please check which category represents the age of your head of household:
(75)
(1) _____ 25 or under
(2) _____ 26-35
(3) _____ 36-45
(4) _____ 46-55
(5) _____ 56-65
(6) _____ over 65

**22.** Which of these categories best describes your household?
(76)
(1) _____ Single male adult
(2) _____ Single female adult
(3) _____ Couple without children (or none at home)
(4) _____ Couple with children
(5) _____ Single parent with children at home
(6) _____ Unrelated individuals

**23.** How many people, including yourself, are there living in your household? _____
(77)

**24.** Please check which range indicates your total annual household income, before taxes. (Including wages of all family members.)
(78-79)
(1) _____ $15,000 or less
(2) _____ $15,001-$20,000
(3) _____ $20,001-$25,000
(4) _____ $25,001-$30,000
(5) _____ $30,001-$35,000
(6) _____ $35,001-$40,000
(7) _____ $40,001-$45,000
(8) _____ $45,001-$50,000
(9) _____ $50,001-$65,000
(10) _____ $65,001-$75,000
(11) _____ $75,001-$100,000
(12) _____ More than $100,000

**25.** Does more than one person contribute to the above household income figure? Yes _____(1)    No _____(2)
(80)

*Thank you for your help.*

---

**FIGURE 2.4   Buyer Information Sheet**

---

# *Signature*
# H O M E S
## Buyer Information Sheet

Name: _____

**Old Residence**

Address: _____        Phone: _____ (hm)

_____                  _____ (wk-male)

Years lived there?: _____        _____ (wk-female)

Type of Residence: _____ Home                **Features:**

_____ Condominium              No. of bedrooms    1   2   3   4   5   6

_____ Townhouse                No. & type of baths _____ Full _____ 3/4 _____ 1/2

_____ Apartment                Other (circle/list):

_____ Mobile Home              Den      Family Room    Sauna    Jacuzzi

Do you: _____ Own _____ Rent      _____

What are your monthly payments/rent? $_____     **Financing:**

Reasons for moving:                 Type: ___ VA ___ FHA ___ Bond ___ Conventional

_____ Tired of renting             Other _____

_____ Closer to work               Loan Amount: $ _____

_____ Larger home                  Interest Rate: _____ %

_____ Smaller home                 Balance: $ _____

_____ Better schools               Current marketing value: $ _____

_____ Better community             Status of home:

_____ Job transfer                          _____ Sold

_____ Change in marital status              _____ Not listed/must sell

_____ Less maintenance                      _____ Listed/must sell

_____ Change in family size                 _____ Listed/no need to sell

_____ Other (specify)                       _____ Not selling

_____               _____ Other

---

**New Residence**

Development Name _____        Sales Agent: _____

Block No. _____ Lot No. _____     Sales Price: $ _____

Address: _____        Square footage: _____

Plan Name/No. _____        **Features:**

_____ One story _____ Two story    No. of bedrooms   1   2   3   4   5   6   7

_____ Detached _____ Attached      No. & type of baths ___ Full ___ 3/4 ___ 1/2

Other (circle/list):

Den     Family Room    Sauna    Jacuzzi

_____

## FIGURE 2.4   Buyer Information Sheet (continued)

How did you hear about us?

_____ Signs        _____ Friends/relatives
_____ Newspaper  _____ Previous buyer
_____ Radio        _____ Realtor
_____ TV           _____ Builder
_____ Magazine    _____ Other (specify)
_____

Financing:

Type: ___ VA ___ FHA ___ Bond ___ Conventional

Other _____

Loan Amount: $ _____

Down payment: $ _____

Name of Financial Institution:_____

**Family**

Names:

Heads(s) of household: _____
_____

Status: _____ Married _____ Single _____ Divorced

Ages of household heads:  (circle one)

20-24   25-29   30-34   35-39   40-44   45-49   50-54   55+

Education of household heads:  (circle one)

High School          Some College          College Graduate          Post Graduate Work

Children: Name(s)        Age          Gender          School

_____   _____   _____   _____
_____   _____   _____   _____
_____   _____   _____   _____
_____   _____   _____   _____

Total No. of Children   _____

**Employment**

|  | Male | Female |
|---|---|---|
| Employer | | |
| City Located In | | |
| Occupation | | |
| Field | | |
| No. of Years there | | |
| Miles to Work | | |

**FIGURE 2.4   Buyer Information Sheet (concluded)**

Annual Family Income:  (circle one)

| | | |
|---|---|---|
| $20,000-25,000 | $25,000-30,000 | $30,000-35,000 |
| $35,000-40,000 | $40,000-45,000 | $45,000-50,000 |
| $50,000-55,000 | $55,000-60,000 | $60,000-65,000 |
| $65,000-75,000 | $75,000-85,000 | $85,000-up |

**Lifestyle**

Hobbies/Interests: _____

Achievements: _____

Social Clubs/Memberships: _____

Recreation: _____

Centers of Influence: _____

Religion: _____

Where do you shop? _____

**Control Record**

| Date | Method | Notes |
|---|---|---|
| _____ | _____ | _____ |
| _____ | _____ | _____ |
| _____ | _____ | _____ |
| _____ | _____ | _____ |

CUSTOM ONE Survey

_____

_____

_____

_____

**Referrals**

| Date | Method | Notes |
|---|---|---|
| _____ | _____ | _____ |
| _____ | _____ | _____ |
| _____ | _____ | _____ |

10. To help us improve the quality of our services and to reward those who have been helpful to you, please share with us the names of people you believe have rendered superior service?

These are brief samples of home buyers survey forms. Each company should design its own and personalize it to topics that are of special interest to that organization. It is appropriate to provide a small token of appreciation for those who return their questionnaires within prescribed time limits. Certificates for nursery plants, dinners-for-two, books on decorating or gardening, etc. are inexpensive and in good taste.

If a one-on-one interview can be scheduled by an experienced member of your team to personally sit with each owner within a few months of move-in, the amount of information you obtain will be even greater and more reliable.

## THE MARKETING IMPACT OF CONSUMER-RESEARCH PROGRAMS

Perhaps the greatest value of this type of research is its impact on prospective buyers. Documented profiles of your owners become a reinforcing tool when the sales representatives are talking to potential purchasers about the benefits of living in your homes and neighborhoods. The social/economic profiles can help to instill confidence in the decision-making process for hesitant buyers. The credibility of owners who say things like: *"We love it here!" "Best decision we ever made!" "Your people are wonderful!"* is a hundred times more effective than the great things you might say about yourself!

When using third-party sources to research prospects, you also provide sales-people and decision makers with the unbiased opinions of those who are outside of the company's political scene. This can help sell the changes necessary to improve the effectiveness of the team.

If you are not currently collecting and using information from those you sell—and those you want to sell—perhaps it is time to organize and initiate a program so that your future operations will benefit from this valuable research resource!

### Responsibilities of the Director of Research

The responsibilities of the Director of Research include the following:

1. Total control over all research activities of the Company regardless of which division or department seeks to initiate or pursue them. Requests for research must be processed through this position to receive approval before they are initiated.
2. Supervision and control of all research files, libraries, computer software programs, microfiche records, master maps, feasibility reports and related exhibits. This includes the responsibility to:

   Maintain a complete index of all files and research resources for reference by authorized personnel.

   Provide security for all such records and verify that only those with access clearance are given permission to inspect the data files.

Establish research networks to secure all data and see that it is properly indexed and entered into the system. Some of the external sources to be used include:
multiple listing systems
building department reports
lending institution reports
chamber of commerce reports
United States Census Bureau
others
Internal sources include:
competitive project reports from all sources
buyer profiles on all projects
company activity reports
company-prepared feasibility studies
others

3.  Manage the competitive project program as one of the major research services of the company. This includes the following steps:
Maintain a list of all regular contributors to this competitive market analysis system and monitor their response to project inspections to assure continuous input. Regular participants include:
project managers
land managers
site managers
on-site sales specialists
all company managers who visit sites as part of their normal duties
others who are voluntarily enlisted

Keep all participants supplied with necessary forms and regular reminders plus thank-you notes to assure that this data-gathering effort is given priority attention.

Receive, verify, log and file each project comparison form along with supporting documents.

Summarize the data once each month or more often as requested and forward to all division heads.

4.  Respond to all requests by division directors for research data for individual projects. Requests for research support must be approved by the division heads prior to initiating assistance.

5.  Anticipate research data needs as related to all proposed projects on the agenda of the Marketing Committee. The Director of Research should be sensitive to all new project proposals that are known to be circulating through the system and recognize in advance the need to have as much data as possible to help the managers and the Marketing Committee reach informed decisions as to the feasibility and criteria for representation.

6.  Explore ways to improve the research systems and make recommendations to the Executive Committee for expanding the capacity of the Research Division.

---

**FIGURE 2.5  Competitive Project Evaluation Form**

A. *GENERAL:*                                                                      DATE: _____
  1. Development name: _____
  2. Location: _____
  3. Total acres in development: _____
  4. Total master plan calls for: _____ single family residences.
                                  _____ multiple family units.

  5. Building company: _____
  6. Sales started _____ Approximate sales to date_____
  7. Number of homes completed _____; homes under construction _____
  8. Approximate number of homes available for sale: completed_____
                                                     uncompleted_____

| B. *FINANCING:* | *INTEREST:* | *BUYER'S CLOSING COSTS* |
|---|---|---|
| 9. Conventional 5% | _____ | _____ |
| " " 10% | _____ | _____ |
| " " 20% | _____ | _____ |
| F.H.A. | _____ + ___ MMI. | _____ |
| V.A. | _____ | _____ |

C. HOUSE PROFILES:

| | | PLAN | | | | |
|---|---|---|---|---|---|---|
| 10. | Number of stories | | | | | |
| 11. | Number of bedrooms | | | | | |
| 12. | Number of baths | | | | | |
| 13. | Sales price | | | | | |
| 14. | Lot size (sq. ft.) | | | | | |
| 15. | Sales price ÷ home sq. ft. | | | | | |
| 16. | Architectural style | | | | | |
| 17. | Family room? | | | | | |
| 18. | Dining room? | | | | | |
| 19. | Garage (2 car or 3) | | | | | |
| 20. | Special rooms | | | | | |
| 21. | Bonus room (unfinished sq. ft.) | | | | | |
| 22. | Kitchen counter:☐ tile ☐ laminate | | | | | |
| 23. | Bath: wainscot ☐ tile ☐ laminate ☐ fiberglass ☐ none | | | | | |
| 24. | Bathtub ☐ Pressed steel ☐ iron ☐ fiberglass | | | | | |
| 25. | Appliances ☐ gas ☐ electric | | | | | |
| 26. | F.A.U. Heating (b.t.u. output) | | | | | |
| 27. | Heating ducts ☐ galvanized ☐ alum bestos | | | | | |
| 28. | Insulation ☐ ceilings ☐ walls | | | | | |
| 29. | Other features: a _____ b _____ c _____ | | | | | |

| D. *BASIC ITEMS* | *INCLUDED* | *OPTIONAL* | *PRICE* | *DESCRIPTION* |
|---|---|---|---|---|
| 1. Carpets | | | | |
| 2. Fireplace | | | | |
| 3. Dishwasher | | | | |
| 4. Fencing | | | | |
| 5. Landscaping (front) | | | | |
| 6. Landscaping (rear) | | | | |
| 7. | | | | |
| 8. | | | | |

---

**FIGURE 2.6   Housing Project Analysis**

Date: _____

BY: _____

*1.0   DESCRIPTION OF THE PROJECT AND BACKGROUND DATA*

Project name: _____

Developer(s): _____

Builder(s): _____

Office address: _____

_____

Phone(s): _____

Project location and directions: _____

_____

_____

_____

_____

Sales office or project phone: _____

Personnel on duty: _____

_____

Project size: _____

Housing units: _____

_____

_____

_____

*2.0   PROJECT DEVELOPMENT AND SALES HISTORY*

Acquisition & development history: _____

_____

_____

_____

Sales history:

Date sales commenced/anticipated: _____

Presales activity/scheduled: _____

Grand opening(s): _____

Total net sales to date: _____

Total net closings: _____

Pending unclosed sales: _____

Cancellation history: _____

---

**FIGURE 2.6   Housing Project Analysis (continued)**

---

Present sales status:

  Past 3 months activity summary:

  Net sales: _____ Number per plan type: _____

  _____

  _____

  Number sales closed: _____ Occupied: _____

  Cancellations: _____

Inventory status:

  Total units released for sale to date: _____

  Number per plan unsold: _____

  _____

  _____


*3.0   EVALUATION OF LOCATION AND ACCESSIBILITY*

  Observations about the general region: _____

  _____

  _____

  Observations about the adjacent neighborhoods: _____

  _____

  _____

  Major access routes: _____

  _____

Observations about accessibility:

  Billboards and directional signage: _____

  _____

  _____

  Flags or other visual elements: _____

  _____

  Possible improvements: _____

  _____

  _____

  General advantages of location: _____

  _____

  _____

  Issues to evaluate: _____

  _____

  _____

**FIGURE 2.6   Housing Project Analysis (continued)**

4.0   *EVALUATION OF IDENTITY AND IMAGE FACTORS*

General approach: _____

_____

_____

Entry area: _____

_____

_____

Theme name and use: _____

_____

_____

Landscaping: _____

_____

_____

Parking: _____

_____

Fencing or natural barriers: _____

_____

Construction and construction traffic: _____

_____

Neighborhood identifications: _____

_____

Theme signing—paths—amenities—etc.: _____

_____

_____

Other image/identity observations: _____

_____

_____

5.0   *EVALUATION OF SALES FACILITIES & GENERAL SALES ENVIRONMENT*

Description of facilities: _____

_____

_____

Access and approach: _____

_____

_____

Visual control of arriving traffic: _____

_____

**FIGURE 2.6   Housing Project Analysis (continued)**

Total size of sales office facilities:_____

Evaluation of design and layout:_____

Theme coordination:_____

Observations re: decor & color scheme:_____

Sales personnel counselling areas:_____

Rate impact for following objectives: (Scale 1–10)

Credibility:_____     Urgency-tempo:_____
Quality/performance:_____     Prospect control:_____
Freshness:_____       Presentation:_____

*6.0   EVALUATION OF PRESENTATION ELEMENTS, GRAPHICS, & DISPLAYS*

General observations re: quality & value of exhibits:

_____

Location display(s):_____

Builder(s)/developer(s) displays:_____

Site map—table display(s):_____

Floor plans:_____

Elevations:_____

Amenities:_____

Lifestyle photos, etc:_____

Product features—construction benefits:_____

**FIGURE 2.6  Housing Project Analysis (continued)**

Options, selections, choices:_____

_____

Community activities—people—events:_____

_____

Property managements—association management:_____

_____

*7.0  EVALUATION OF SALES LITERATURE, BROCHURES, HANDOUTS*
General observations re: brochure(s):_____

_____

_____

_____

Floor plans:_____

_____

Prices—price sheets:_____

_____

Site plan:_____

_____

Competitive feature list(s):_____

_____

Environment—history—lifestyles:_____

_____

Options and alternate choices:_____

_____

*DIRECT MAIL PIECES*
Thank-you notes:_____
Informational items:_____

_____

_____

_____

Newsletters:_____

_____

*RATE LITERATURE FOR FOLLOWING* (Scale: 1–10)
Flexibility _____ Quality _____ Value _____
*8.0  EVALUATION OF MODELS, SHOW HOMES, & INVENTORY OR SITES*
*MODEL HOMES*
Number: _____ Plan types: _____
Sequence:_____

---

**FIGURE 2.6   Housing Project Analysis (continued)**

Relationships to available inventory:_____
_____
_____

Landscaping:_____
Decorating:_____
General conditions:_____
Decorator items:_____
Observations about decor & furnishings re:
    Profile of potential buyers:_____

*INVENTORY HOMES AND SITES*
Number of completed unsold homes:_____
Total unsold (completed plus incomplete):_____
Mix of inventory for sale:_____
_____

General condition of inventory homes:_____
_____
_____

Target properties for current emphasis:_____
_____

Phasing observations & inventory control:_____
_____
_____


*9.0   EVALUATION OF AMENITIES, RECREATION FACILITIES, COMMON AREAS*
*List of all amenities and recreational facilities:*
_____
_____
_____
_____
_____
_____

Observations re: use, condition, & value:
_____
_____
_____
_____
_____
_____
_____

---

**FIGURE 2.6   Housing Project Analysis (continued)**

Marketing impact of presentation of amenities:

_____

_____

_____

_____

*10.0   PERSONNEL EVALUATION (one sheet per sales person)*

Name:_____ Sex: _____

Status:_____

Days & hours assigned:_____

Home address: _____

_____ Phone: _____

Experience in real estate:_____

_____

Experience in new-home sales:_____

_____

Date associated with this company:_____

*GENERAL OBSERVATIONS*

Appearance:_____

Attitude:_____

Product knowledge:_____

Assertiveness:_____

Sociability:_____

Resourcefulness:_____

Desire to learn:_____

Time management:_____

Ability to communicate:_____

Emotional stability:_____

Other:_____

_____

_____

*11.0   EVALUATION OF MARKETING STRATEGIES*

Identification of profiled markets:

_____

_____

_____

_____

---

**FIGURE 2.6   Housing Project Analysis (continued)**

On-site marketing programs:

_____

_____

_____

Off-site marketing programs:

_____

_____

_____

Newspaper advertising (Identify publications used):

_____

_____

_____

Electronic media (Identify stations/channels):

_____

_____

_____

Publicity & public relations:

_____

_____

_____

Direct mail campaigns:

_____

_____

_____

Competitive positioning (List major competition):

_____

_____

_____

_____

_____

Cooperative broker programs:

_____

_____

_____

Resident referral programs:

_____

_____

_____

---

**FIGURE 2.6   Housing Project Analysis (continued)**

Industry contact programs:

_____

_____

_____

Literature placement programs:

_____

_____

_____

Equity assistance plans:

_____

_____

_____

Financing plans featured (Attach detailed sheets):

_____

_____

_____

Transferee and relocation programs:

_____

_____

_____

Speaker's bureau—audio/visual presentations off-site:

_____

_____

_____

Other marketing programs:
   Testimonials:_____
   Photo albums:_____
   Special events:_____

12.0   *OWNER'S ASSOCIATION MANAGEMENT (When Applicable)*
   Status of owner's association:

_____

_____

_____

Indoctrination programs:

_____

_____

_____

**FIGURE 2.6   Housing Project Analysis (continued)**

Current directors of the association:

_____
_____
_____

Operating committees:

_____
_____
_____

Property management team:

_____
_____
_____

Evaluation of resident involvement:

_____
_____
_____

13.0   *EVALUATION OF AFTER-SALE SERVICE & CUSTOMER MOVE-IN PROGRAMS*
Warranty programs & materials given to buyers:

_____
_____
_____

Pre-move-in procedures & involvement programs:

_____
_____
_____

Walk-through & move-in procedures:

_____
_____
_____

Sales follow-up & welcoming programs:

_____
_____
_____

Special events & activities for owners:

_____
_____
_____

**FIGURE 2.6  Housing Project Analysis (concluded)**

Surveys & measurements of resident satisfaction:

_____

_____

_____

_____

*14.0  EVALUATION OF MAJOR QUESTIONS, OBJECTIONS & SALES OBSTACLES*

Location:_____

_____

_____

Development team:_____

_____

Site plan:_____

_____

_____

Floor plans:_____

_____

_____

Construction:_____

_____

_____

Amenities:_____

_____

_____

Available inventory:_____

_____

_____

Options, choices:_____

_____

Financing:_____

_____

NOTE: If there are other categories, list on separate page.

*15.0  SUMMARY OF OBSERVATIONS AND RECOMMENDATIONS*

_____

_____

_____

_____

(Use as much space and add pages as necessary)

**FIGURE 2.7  Housing Market Checklist**

## HOUSING MARKET EVALUATION CHECKLIST

| Item | 1970 | 1980 | 1986 | 1987 | Projected 1988 | 1989 | 1990 | Percent Change 1970–1980 | 1980–1986 |
|---|---|---|---|---|---|---|---|---|---|
| Population | | | | | | | | | |
| Employment | | | | | | | | | |
| Civilian Labor Force | | | | | | | | | |
| Total Employed | | | | | | | | | |
| Unemployed | | | | | | | | | |
| Unemployment Rate (%) | | | | | | | | | |
| Total Wage in Salary | | | | | | | | | |
| Manufacturing | | | | | | | | | |
| Construction/Transportation/Utilities | | | | | | | | | |
| Trade/Services/Professions | | | | | | | | | |
| Government | | | | | | | | | |
| Household Formation Rate | | | | | | | | | |
| Households | | | | | | | | | |
| Household Size | | | | | | | | | |
| Household Average Income | | | | | | | | | |
| Housing Stock | | | | | | | | | |
| Housing Stock-Owned/Rent % | | | | | | | | | |
| Platted Lots | | | | | | | | | |
| Building Permits | | | | | | | | | |
| S.F.D. | | | | | | | | | |
| Two Family | | | | | | | | | |
| Three-Four | | | | | | | | | |
| Four + | | | | | | | | | |
| MLS Listings | | | | | | | | | |
| MLS Sales | | | | | | | | | |
| Turnover Rate | | | | | | | | | |
| Anticipated Housing Demand | | | | | | | | | |
| Anticipated Project Area Demand | | | | | | | | | |
| Anticipated "Captureable" Demand | | | | | | | | | |

**FIGURE 2.8   Development Profile**

GRAPH SYMBOL:

PROJECT NAME _____DATE:

DEVELOPER _____PHONE:

LOCATION _____

PRODUCT TYPE _____Lot Size/Density:

**PLAN DESCRIPTION**

PLAN NO. _____
PLAN PRICE _____
SOLD-OUT _____
SQ. FT. _____
PRICE SQ. FT. _____

NO. OF LEVELS _____
BEDROOMS _____
BATHS _____
GARAGE _____

FORMAL DINING _____
FAMILY ROOM _____
BASEMENT _____

**PLAN MIX**

NO. PLOTTED _____
NO. UNSOLD _____

**PRICE INCREASES**

PAST _____ MONTHS _____

**FEATURES**

- ☐ Driveway
- ☐ Roof
- ☐ Fencing
- ☐ Landscaping
- ☐ Sprinklers
- ☐ Balcony
- ☐ Patio
- ☐ Carpets
- ☐ Fireplace

- ☐ Drapes
- ☐ Dishwasher
- ☐ Double Oven
- ☐ Self-Cleaning Oven
- ☐ Microwave
- ☐ Trash Compactor
- ☐ Wet Bar
- ☐ Air Conditioning
- ☐ Other

**FINANCING**

- ☐ FHA
- ☐ VA
- ☐ CONVENTIONAL

DOWN      INT. RATE

**SALES PROFILE**

| | Total | Current Phase |
|---|---|---|
| A. Sales Started | A. | A. |
| B. Total No. Lots in Project | B. | B. |
| C. Total No. Lots Offered for Sale | C. | C. |
| D. Total Completed & Unsold | D. | D. |
| E. Total Under Construction & Unsold | E. | E. |
| F. Total Pre-Construction & Unsold | F. | F. |
| G. Total Sold To Date | G. | G. |
| H. Weekly Sales Average | H. | H. |
| I. Total Remaining for Development | I. | I. |

PAST            Months

Number of Sales

Weekly Sales Rate

---

**FIGURE 2.8   Development Profile (concluded)**

---

PROJECT NAME                                              GRAPH SYMBOL:

RECREATIONAL AMENITIES                                    ASSOCIATION FEE:

☐ SWIMMING POOL          ☐ CLUBHOUSE/REC. ROOM      ☐ TENNIS COURTS
☐ SAUNA                  ☐ JACUZZI                  ☐ OTHER

**DESIGN ELEMENTS**

| KITCHEN | MASTER BEDROOM | SECONDARY BATHS |
|---|---|---|
| ☐ Defined Nook | ☐ Double Doors | ☐ Double Vanities |
| ☐ Breakfast Bar | ☐ Retreat | ☐ Compartmented |
| ☐ Table Space | ☐ Walk-in Closet | ☐ Other |
| ☐ Greenhouse Windows | **MASTER BATH** | **OTHER FEATURES** |
| ☐ Tile Countertops | ☐ Compartmented | ☐ Volume Ceilings |
| ☐ Luminous Ceiling | ☐ Dressing Alcove | ☐ Beamed Ceilings |
| **ENTRY** | ☐ Double Basin Vanities | ☐ Sunken/Raised Rooms |
| ☐ Double Doors | ☐ Separate Shower & Tub | ☐ Conversation Pit |
| ☐ Raised Area | ☐ Deluxe Tub | ☐ Atrium |
| ☐ Tile or Parquet | ☐ Ceramic Tile Surround | ☐ Interior Utility Area |
| **STAIRCASES** | ☐ Planter Area | ☐ Direct Garage Access |
|  | ☐ Luminous Ceiling | ☐ Den |
|  | ☐ Window | ☐ Other |

ELEVATIONS _____

BEST-SELLING FLOORPLAN _____

PRIME COMPETITION _____

LOT PREMIUMS _____

BUYER PROFILE _____

**MARKETING/MERCHANDISING**

☐ Sales Office
☐ Model Complex
☐ Model Decoration
☐ Advertising

COMMENTS:




Source: Courtesy of Fulton Research Group

---

**FIGURE 2.9  Basic Sources for Real Estate Research**

---

General Demographic Data

- U.S. Census Bureau
  (Census tract studies)
- Local Chamber of Commerce
- City/County Planning Commissions
- Commercial banks (research depts.)
- Savings and Loans (research depts.)
- School Boards
- City/County Directories
- Local research organizations
- Tourist bureaus

General Economic Data

- State/Federal Departments of Human Resources (employment statistics)
- Economic Development Commissions
- State Department of Commerce
- Local Chamber of Commerce
- Commercial banks (research depts.)
- Highway development authorities
- Local industries (research depts.)
- Research companies operating in the area

National Housing Trends

- Professional magazines (i.e., *Professional Builder, Builder Magazine, Multi-Housing News*, Regional builder publications)
- National Association of Home Builders
- National Association of REALTORS®
- Urban Land Institute
- Private newsletters
- National real estate networks
- National relocation companies

Real Estate Values and Activity

- Appraiser(s)
- Building permits (Recorders office)
- Real estate broker(s)
- Assessor's office
- Deed transfers (courthouse—hall of records)
- Sales and Marketing Council (local home builders)
- Title companies
- Escrow companies
- Home Builders Association or Building Industry Association
- General Contractors Association
- Local board of realtors
- Multiple Listing Services

FIGURE 2.9   Basic Sources for Real Estate Research (concluded)

- Mortgage Bankers Association
- Federal Housing Administration
- Utility services (connections)
- Apartment Owners Association
- Property management and rental service companies
- Real estate research companies operating in the area

Miscellaneous Sources

- Historical societies
- Universities and colleges (research projects)
- Charitable organizations
- Political organizations
- Civic and social clubs
- Retail merchants associations
- Sales and marketing executive clubs

# 3: Game Plans and Marketing Strategies

Successful development of effective marketing strategies begins with the research preceding or following land or lot acquisition. As emphasized in the previous chapter, research is the security blanket of this business. It minimizes risk and increases opportunities for profits if correctly interpreted and applied. Failure to thoroughly investigate the nature of the housing market prior to designing and building housing products is a sure way to court financial disaster. Taking research as just one of the critical knowledge areas that must play an integral role in the decision-making process, we ask the question: Who is best qualified to gather, review and interpret data sources? Is it the builder? The developer? The real estate broker? The architect? An outside specialist? Or the salesperson who will sell the homes?

Who should design the homes and decide what to include in the basic package? Is it an outside architect, the builder, the land engineer, the research specialist or the sales organization?

It is obvious that few of us are capable of playing all roles involved in the development and marketing of new homes, condominiums, resort sites or other real estate ventures. The orchestrating of these disciplines with effective management skills determines whether or not the entrepreneur will successfully meet anticipated sales and profit objectives.

Creation of practical marketing strategies is not a simple process when you are operating in a real estate environment that offers a choice of diverse communities and housing concepts. That is why marketing administrators must have access to people and systems that will help them meet the specific challenges and opportunities of each assigned project.

## EVOLUTION OF AN EFFECTIVE MARKETING PLAN

Organized marketers follow a practical decision track when asked to create a business plan for marketing a new housing community. This process begins, rather logically, with definitive research. Since we have covered this subject in detail in the preceding chapter, we will concentrate now on how that research is used in the actual decision-influencing process. The essence of all research is knowing what questions to ask and where to obtain information that will answer these queries. Strategists in this business begin the analysis of the research assignment by asking the following questions and satisfying themselves that they have reasonably quantified and validated the answers before proceeding with the rest of the marketing road map:

- Is there a market potential for the proposed land use and anticipated housing designs?
- How deep is that market opportunity?
- What will be the profiles of prospective buyers?
- What reasonable penetration rates can be projected for this site during the coming months or years?
- What design parameters will help assure housing products that meet demand criteria?
- What are the dominant motivations of the target profile groups?
- What key value indicators must be met to be certain the housing designs are competitive?
- How do you efficiently reach targeted audiences?
- What key marketing messages must be communicated to stimulate customer response?
- Who should be employed to represent the housing community to the buying public?
- How do anticipated timing factors for acquisition, development, construction and sales promotion affect local marketing criteria?

These and other issues require careful analysis by those responsible for overall marketing decisions—and they should be answered before impulsive *management* decides to move ahead with construction of untested concepts.

Knowledge is power! Research is risk insurance! And preparation of comprehensive marketing plans before housing is launched is the only way to provide the enterprise with a reasonable chance to achieve envisioned profits. Decisions should not be made in a vacuum. Smart marketers always ask themselves what might go wrong. The marketing plan should evolve with that overriding concern as a guiding light for those doing the planning.

## CHECKLISTS AND THE CRITICAL-PATH PLANNING PROCESS

Complete checklists are invaluable when trying to pursue a complex process with many variables and possibilities for errors. Checklists and critical-path planning charts are essential tools for managing the sequence of inter-related events and decision points in the home building profession. At the outset of a newly proposed project, the individual ultimately responsible for developing the marketing plan should open a file or a project-control manual and systematically check off the various steps that must be completed satisfactorily along the decision track. We include on the next few pages an organized decision chart, which acts both as a guide to the successful completion of a marketing plan and a red flag for key determinants along the way.

**FIGURE 3.1   Marketing Checklist**

| | DATE REQUIRED | COST ESTIMATE | COST ACTUAL | COMPLETED | INITIAL |
|---|---|---|---|---|---|
| **General** Marketing Input | | | | | |
| Survey Competition | | | | | |
| Review Design Criteria | | | | | |
| Select Architect | | | | | |
| Establish Criteria | | | | | |
| Monitor Preliminary and Working Drawings | | | | | |
| Select Decorator and Landscaper | | | | | |
| Review Preliminary Plans | | | | | |
| Marketing | | | | | |
| Architect | | | | | |
| Landscaper | | | | | |
| Prepare Working Drawings & Schedules | | | | | |
| Review Working Drawings | | | | | |
| Preliminary Cost | | | | | |
| Estimate | | | | | |
| Marketing | | | | | |
| Architect | | | | | |
| Decorator | | | | | |
| Landscaper | | | | | |
| Sales Schedule & Preliminary Sales (12 per month) | | | | | |
| Plotting | | | | | |
| After Receiving Data, Establish Percentage Breakdown for Each Plan and Elevation, Physically Plot Houses and Send Out to Preselected Land Engineer for Input Regarding Drainage, Etc. | | | | | |

**FIGURE 3.1   Marketing Checklist (continued)**

| | DATE REQUIRED | COST ESTIMATE | COST ACTUAL | COMPLETED | INITIAL |
|---|---|---|---|---|---|
| Finalize Plot Plan with Sales Department | | | | | |
| Exterior/Interior Colors | | | | | |
| Color Coordinator | | | | | |
| Exterior Landscaping | | | | | |
| Interior Decorator | | | | | |
| Submit to FHA, VA, etc. | | | | | |
| Supervise Model Construction from Foundation Grade Pad to Finish | | | | | |
| Walk Framing with Architect/Decorator | | | | | |
| Walk Drywall with Architect/Decorator Landscaper | | | | | |
| Inspect Finish with Architect/Decorator/ Landscaper | | | | | |
| Landscaping | | | | | |
| Coordinate with Decorator on Patios | | | | | |
| Model Site Location with Landscaper | | | | | |
| Final | | | | | |
| Walk with Decorator Landscaper and Area Manager | | | | | |
| As-Built Changes in Plans | | | | | |
| Product Set for Final Construction | | | | | |
| See Representatives with New Products | | | | | |
| Bid on and Start, or Modify, Product | | | | | |
| Preliminary Review of Land Plan | | | | | |

## FIGURE 3.1   Marketing Checklist (continued)

|  | DATE REQUIRED | COST ESTIMATE | COST ACTUAL | COMPLETED | INITIAL |
|---|---|---|---|---|---|
| Preliminary Review of Budget—Establish: |  |  |  |  |  |
| Architect |  |  |  |  |  |
| Landscaper |  |  |  |  |  |
| Decorator |  |  |  |  |  |
| Models |  |  |  |  |  |
| Review Renderings for Correctness/Presentation |  |  |  |  |  |
| Review Decor Drawings for Design Acceptability |  |  |  |  |  |
| Review Exterior Colors for Design Acceptability |  |  |  |  |  |
| "On-Call" Problem Solve |  |  |  |  |  |
| Monitor Sales Office Design |  |  |  |  |  |
| Inspect Construction Conformance with Plans |  |  |  |  |  |
| Design Marketability |  |  |  |  |  |
| Inspect Landscape Conformance with Plans |  |  |  |  |  |
| Design Marketability |  |  |  |  |  |
| Select Light Fixtures |  |  |  |  |  |
| Inspect Exterior Colors Conformance with Plans |  |  |  |  |  |
| Review Landscape Drawings for Design Acceptability |  |  |  |  |  |
| Review and Evaluate Market Impact |  |  |  |  |  |
| Production |  |  |  |  |  |
| Monitor As-Built Drawings |  |  |  |  |  |
| Design Entry Gate |  |  |  |  |  |

**FIGURE 3.1   Marketing Checklist (continued)**

| | DATE REQUIRED | COST ESTIMATE | COST ACTUAL | COMPLETED | INITIAL |
|---|---|---|---|---|---|
| Monitor Progress of Engineers and Sub-contractors | | | | | |
| Special Situation Houses—Design | | | | | |
| Special Situation— Monitor Drafting | | | | | |
| "On-Call" Problem Solve | | | | | |
| **Checklist for Setting Up Sales Office, Model Homes and Signing Program** *Office Supplies* Calendar | | | | | |
| Files | | | | | |
| Ash Trays | | | | | |
| Stapler, Staples | | | | | |
| Stapler Remover | | | | | |
| Typewriters | | | | | |
| Desks | | | | | |
| Desk Chairs | | | | | |
| Pens | | | | | |
| Pads | | | | | |
| Phone Lists | | | | | |
| Business Cards | | | | | |
| Stationery | | | | | |
| Real Estate License | | | | | |
| Counseling Center Furnishings (i.e., Chairs, Tables, etc.) | | | | | |
| Plants/Flowers | | | | | |
| Music System | | | | | |
| Name Tags | | | | | |
| Desk Nameplates | | | | | |
| Coffee Equipment | | | | | |

FIGURE 3.1   Marketing Checklist (continued)

| | DATE REQUIRED | COST ESTIMATE | COST ACTUAL | COMPLETED | INITIAL |
|---|---|---|---|---|---|
| Supplies for Food Center | | | | | |
| *Marketing Tools* Office Entrance Sign | | | | | |
| Model Directional Sign | | | | | |
| "Hours Open" Sign | | | | | |
| Plot Maps Printed | | | | | |
| Plot Map Scale Model | | | | | |
| Topographic Plot Map | | | | | |
| Plot Map Table | | | | | |
| Aerial Photo | | | | | |
| Sales Booklet | | | | | |
| Slide Show Program(s) | | | | | |
| Slide Projector | | | | | |
| Color Selections (Interior) | | | | | |
| Color Selections (Exterior) | | | | | |
| Sample Materials: Carpets, Drapes | | | | | |
| Sample Optional Materials | | | | | |
| Construction Details | | | | | |
| Construction Materials | | | | | |
| Custom Changes and Bonus Area Details | | | | | |
| Special Options | | | | | |
| *Brochures* Quantity | | | | | |
| Date Needed | | | | | |
| Plans Finalized | | | | | |
| Feature Details Made Available by | | | | | |
| Area Details Made Available by | | | | | |

**FIGURE 3.1   Marketing Checklist (continued)**

| | DATE REQUIRED | COST ESTIMATE | COST ACTUAL | COMPLETED | INITIAL |
|---|---|---|---|---|---|
| Price Information Available by | | | | | |
| Square Footage List | | | | | |
| Special Photography | | | | | |
| Artwork | | | | | |
| Special Maps | | | | | |
| *Miscellaneous* Model Doormats | | | | | |
| Model "Turnkey" Signs | | | | | |
| "Disclaimers" Signs | | | | | |
| Model Merchandising Area Signs | | | | | |
| Tot Lot Equipment | | | | | |
| Flag/Poles | | | | | |
| Lead-In Signs | | | | | |
| Billboard Program | | | | | |
| Monument Design | | | | | |
| **Media Advertising Program** Sneak Preview | | | | | |
| Grand Opening | | | | | |
| "Theme" Ad Series, ie. Area, Special Buyer, Age, etc. | | | | | |
| "Product" Ad Series | | | | | |
| "Price" Ad Series | | | | | |
| Radio | | | | | |
| Classified | | | | | |
| Direct mailing | | | | | |
| Magazine Ads | | | | | |
| Ground Breaking Ceremony Photos | | | | | |
| "Sneak Preview" P.R. | | | | | |
| Special Promotion Events Planning | | | | | |

**FIGURE 3.1   Marketing Checklist (concluded)**

|  | DATE REQUIRED | COST ESTIMATE | COST ACTUAL | COMPLETED | INITIAL |
|---|---|---|---|---|---|
| Model Home Photos | | | | | |
| Press Kits | | | | | |
| Trade Press Kit Mailing | | | | | |
| Tour Models with Local Real Estate Editors, VIP's | | | | | |
| On-going Publicity in Local Media | | | | | |

**FIGURE 3.2   Community Marketing Management Checklist**

MARKETING PLAN FOR: _____

Community Name:_____ Date: _____

| Item Number | Category-Marketing Element | Action | Due Date | Final Date |
|---|---|---|---|---|
| THEME—IDENTITY—IMAGE | | | | |
| 1. | Theme name-image | | | |
| 2. | Graphic interpretation | | | |
| 3. | Logo type-image | | | |
| 4. | Neighborhood identities | | | |
| 5. | Street names | | | |
| 6. | Model names | | | |
| 7. | Colors—impact/appeal | | | |
| 8. | Stationery/business cards | | | |
| 9. | Brochure sales aide | | | |
| 10. | Corporate identity | | | |
| ENTRY AND SUB-ENTRIES | | | | |
| 11. | Identification dominance | | | |
| 12. | Visibility to arriving traffic | | | |
| 13. | Hardscaping design | | | |
| 14. | Landscaping design | | | |
| 15. | Lighting | | | |
| 16. | Flag(s) | | | |
| 17. | Focal elements | | | |
| 18. | > Fountain | | | |
| 19. | > Gatehouse | | | |
| 20. | > Gates/fencing | | | |
| 21. | > Water amenity | | | |
| 22. | > Trees | | | |
| 23. | > Flowers/shrubs | | | |
| 24. | > Lawns | | | |
| 25. | Maintenance/conditions | | | |
| 26. | Security | | | |
| 27. | Directional signage | | | |
| MODEL SALES AREA | | | | |
| 28. | Accessibility/visibility | | | |

| FIGURE 3.2 | Community Marketing Management Checklist (continued) | | | |
|---|---|---|---|---|
| Item Number | Category-Marketing Element | Action | Due Date | Final Date |
| 29. | Parking spaces—signage | | | |
| 30. | Model park entry identification | | | |
| 31. | Flags/accent elements | | | |
| 32. | Model landscaping design | | | |
| 33. | Traffic—customer control | | | |
| 34. | Driveways—rails—sidewalks | | | |
| 35. | Night lighting (exterior) | | | |
| 36. | Sales office identification | | | |
| 37. | Model identification/signs | | | |
| 38. | Exterior approach to each model | | | |
| 39. | Landscaping conditions | | | |
| 40. | Adjacent property conditions | | | |
| SALES OFFICE | | | | |
| 41. | General office design | | | |
| 42. | Approach/entry—visual control | | | |
| 43. | Colors—emotional appeal | | | |
| 44. | Lighting—cheerfulness | | | |
| 45. | Greeting area | | | |
| 46. | Display station graphics | | | |
| 47. | > General location map | | | |
| 48. | > Aerial photography | | | |
| 49. | > Photos—schools, shopping, etc. | | | |
| 50. | > Developer/builder credibility panel | | | |
| 51. | > Welcome identity graphic | | | |
| 52. | > Master site plan (table) | | | |
| 53. | > Community benefits panel | | | |
| 54. | > Amenities displays | | | |
| 55. | > Life style photographs | | | |
| 56. | > Product feature—benefit panel | | | |
| 57. | > Floor plans | | | |
| 58. | > Exterior elevations | | | |
| 59. | > Streetscape rendering(s) | | | |
| 60. | > Community activity board | | | |

**FIGURE 3.2   Community Marketing Management Checklist (continued)**

| Item Number | Category-Marketing Element | Action | Due Date | Final Date |
|---|---|---|---|---|
| 61. | > Customer service warranty | | | |
| 62. | Closing-counseling area | | | |
| 63. | Internal traffic flow | | | |
| 64. | Decorator selection area | | | |
| 65. | Option selection displays | | | |
| 66. | Audio-visual area/equipment | | | |
| 67. | Sitting/holding area(s) | | | |
| 68. | Flowers—plants—color | | | |
| 69. | General appearance—maintenance | | | |
| 70. | Background music | | | |
| 71. | Refreshments area—water dispenser | | | |
| 72. | Filing-storage space | | | |
| 73. | Brochure control | | | |
| 74. | Registration area/pedestal | | | |
| 75. | Manufacturer displays | | | |
| 76. | Secondary phase maps for sales control | | | |
| 77. | Customer impact rating | | | |
| 78. | > At-home feeling | | | |
| 79. | > Credibility | | | |
| 80. | > Sense of urgency—success | | | |
| 81. | Perception of values | | | |
| MODEL HOMES (FURNISHED) | | | | |
| 83. | Models furnished to buyer profiles | | | |
| 84. | Space relationship enhanced by decor | | | |
| 85. | Value range of furnishings appropriate | | | |
| 86. | Decorator items identified | | | |
| 87. | Number of options per model | | | |
| 88. | Rate each model: | | | |
| 89. | > Emotional appeal—identity | | | |
| 90. | > Use of colors—textures | | | |
| 91. | > Accessories | | | |
| 92. | > Interior lighting | | | |

**FIGURE 3.2  Community Marketing Management Checklist (continued)**

| Item Number | Category-Marketing Element | Action | Due Date | Final Date |
|---|---|---|---|---|
| 93. | > Livable space merchandising | | | |
| 94. | > Quality of furnishings | | | |
| 95. | > Ease of value interpretation | | | |
| 96. | Doors removed in crowded areas | | | |
| 97. | Silent sales tools appropriate | | | |
| 98. | Patios/decks/merchandised | | | |
| 99. | Rear yards landscaped | | | |
| 100. | Background music (profiled to buyer groups) | | | |
| 101. | Air-fresheners and fragrances | | | |
| 102. | Plants and flowers | | | |
| 103. | Appliances—tags removed | | | |
| 104. | Garage clean and merchandised | | | |
| 105. | Closets/storage merchandised | | | |
| 106. | Lighting fixtures on master switch | | | |
| 107. | Features and Benefits accented | | | |
| 108. | Front door cigarette urn | | | |
| 109. | Model welcome sign at entry | | | |
| 110. | General maintenance conditions | | | |
| AMENITIES-RECREATIONAL FACILITIES | | | | |
| 111. | General maint./conditions | | | |
| 112. | Signage depicting future amenities | | | |
| 113. | Directional signs | | | |
| 114. | Theme signage for each amenity | | | |
| 115. | Pedestrian paths—trails | | | |
| 116. | Vista points—sitting areas | | | |
| 117. | Social gathering points | | | |
| 118. | Security and supervision | | | |
| 119. | Merchandising exhibits in place | | | |
| 120. | Resident participation/membership | | | |
| 121. | Calendar of events—posted | | | |
| 122. | Community publicity and photography | | | |
| 123. | Management/service personnel | | | |

**FIGURE 3.2   Community Marketing Management Checklist (continued)**

| Item Number | Category-Marketing Element | Action | Due Date | Final Date |
|---|---|---|---|---|
| 124. | Association fees—perceived values | | | |
| COLLATERAL MATERIALS | | | | |
| 125. | Institutional brochure(s) | | | |
| 126. | Floor plan—product inserts | | | |
| 127. | Feature–benefit value lists | | | |
| 128. | Model tour guide | | | |
| 129. | Mailers and leaflets | | | |
| 130. | Publicity story reprints | | | |
| 131. | Picture postcards | | | |
| 132. | Business cards | | | |
| 133. | Regular stationery | | | |
| 134. | Follow-up cards stationery | | | |
| 135. | Registration—survey cards | | | |
| 136. | Traffic report forms | | | |
| 137. | Sales processing forms | | | |
| 138. | Customer service forms | | | |
| 139. | Current phase plat maps | | | |
| 140. | For lot sales—individual lot folders | | | |
| 141. | Contract packages assembled | | | |
| 142. | Model/office hours sign | | | |
| 143. | "Out showing property" sign | | | |
| 144. | Emergency security notice on door | | | |
| 145. | Warranties assembled | | | |
| 146. | Homeowners' manual | | | |
| 147. | Financing pkgs. assembled | | | |
| 148. | Homesites staked/marked | | | |
| 149. | "Sold" signs for lots/homes | | | |
| 150. | Sold buttons/decals for plat maps | | | |
| 151. | "Available" signs for selected sites | | | |
| 152. | Questions and answers booklet | | | |
| PUBLICITY-NEWSLETTERS | | | | |
| 153. | Pre-opening/history articles prepared | | | |
| 154. | Local real estate editor cooperation | | | |

**FIGURE 3.2   Community Marketing Management Checklist (continued)**

| Item Number | Category-Marketing Element | Action | Due Date | Final Date |
|---|---|---|---|---|
| 155. | Scheduled releases–assigned | | | |
| 156. | Photographic history of community | | | |
| 157. | Aerial photos depicting progress | | | |
| 158. | Charter-founders club formed | | | |
| 159. | Advisory H.O.A. board selected | | | |
| 160. | Articles/photos about residents | | | |
| 161. | Grand opening publicity | | | |
| 162. | Special events featured | | | |
| 163. | Builder/developer interest stories | | | |
| 164. | Design/award/recognition stories | | | |
| 165. | Manufacturer tie-ins—publicity | | | |
| 166. | Sponsor community activities | | | |
| 167. | Specialty items: T-shirts, etc. | | | |
| 168. | Owner identity items: car stickers, etc. | | | |
| 169. | Establish community newsletter | | | |
| 170. | > Assign responsibilities | | | |
| 171. | > Secure resident support | | | |
| 172. | > Maintain news of resident interest | | | |
| 173. | > Use extra copies for public | | | |
| 174. | Establish broker relations (see separate checklist) | | | |
| 175. | "Thank-you-for-buying" letters | | | |
| 176. | Customer survey questionnaires | | | |
| 177. | Involve subcontractors/suppliers | | | |
| 178. | Photos and publicity posted (banks, suppliers offices, etc.) | | | |
| 179. | Feature "industry of the month" | | | |
| 180. | Feature home or yard of the month | | | |
| 181. | Invite professionals to critique the community | | | |
| 182. | Pursue stories—magazines/periodicals | | | |
| 183. | Maintain publicity and photo albums | | | |

**FIGURE 3.2   Community Marketing Management Checklist (continued)**

| Item Number | Category-Marketing Element | Action | Due Date | Final Date |
|---|---|---|---|---|
| ADVERTISING AND PROMOTION | | | | |
| 184. | Selection of advertising specialists | | | |
| 185. | Research target markets | | | |
| 186. | Research media effectiveness | | | |
| 187. | Evaluate competitors' advertising | | | |
| 188. | Establish point-of-difference marketing | | | |
| 189. | Monitor/evaluate traffic sources | | | |
| 190. | Monitor/evaluate cost of sale by media source | | | |
| 191. | Evaluate off-site signage | | | |
| 192. | Evaluate broker co-op support | | | |
| 193. | Evaluate owner referrals | | | |
| 194. | Evaluate quality of street traffic | | | |
| 195. | Review adequacy of advertising budget | | | |
| 196. | Pinpoint market demographics | | | |
| 197. | Establish campaigns with repetitive image values | | | |
| 198. | Invest dollars in proposition to returns | | | |
| 199. | Maintain ad scrapbook with traffic notes | | | |
| PHASING-PRICING STRATEGIES | | | | |
| 200. | Inventory release not to exceed 90–120 days of sales | | | |
| 201. | "Perceived-value" pricing of individual sites | | | |
| 202. | Price models based on value perceptions | | | |
| 203. | Planned price increases with time frames or release dates | | | |
| 204. | Maintain pricing—move inventory in right product mix | | | |
| 205. | Price options and extras based on sales objectives and value perceptions | | | |

## FIGURE 3.2  Community Marketing Management Checklist (concluded)

| Item Number | Category-Marketing Element | Action | Due Date | Final Date |
|---|---|---|---|---|
| 206. | Competitive value index comparisons | | | |
| 207. | Create/maintain sense of urgency | | | |
| 208. | Target sales to high-visibility sites | | | |
| 209. | Complete streetscapes/avoid scattered sales | | | |
| 210. | Evaluate financing incentives for competitive positioning | | | |
| 211. | Evaluate buyer costs builder might include in pricing | | | |
| 212. | Nonconfusing pricing | | | |
| 213. | Inclusion/exclusion of optional features | | | |
| 214. | Contingency procedures for resales | | | |
| 215. | Incentives for preconstruction sales | | | |
| 216. | Building Specifications—difficult sites | | | |
| 217. | Realistic underwriting or guarantee of first year's homeowner assn. costs | | | |
| 218. | Each new phase released with tempo strategies/precnstrct. to grand opening pricing | | | |
| 219. | Construction activity used to stimulate sales | | | |
| 220. | Construction environment separated from models and sales center | | | |
| 221. | Development maintained with concern for visual appearance to arriving traffic | | | |
| 222. | Sales and management personnel pull together—team commitment to community goals | | | |

## IMAGE AND IDENTITY POSITIONING FOR THE HOUSING COMMUNITY

Once the initial research has been completed and the market opportunity validated, an early step in the planning process is the development of identity-positioning criteria for the proposed housing designs and the neighborhoods in which they are to be constructed. If the project is a large, master-planned community with a variety of housing types and clustered neighborhoods, a major concentration of creative talent is required to position the entire development program. On the other hand, if it concerns merely the selection of a few homesites in an existing community, the process is limited to the immediate neighborhood and the design criteria for homes to be constructed in that controlled area.

For the purpose of this book, we will approach the basic strategy of theme-positioning from its broadest objectives and then apply these concepts to the smaller elements involved in designing and building housing products.

## IDENTITY IS A PRIMARY MARKETING MOTIVATOR

At the heart of strategy planning for any housing community is the matter of establishing an identity for the homes and housing environment that will provide the right nesting envelope for future residents. Behavioral scientists tell us that all humans seek to reinforce their identities as part of the drive for individuality and social participation. Many factors come into play when you evaluate self-identity concepts. Each of us has a unique way of measuring and reacting to identity statements about ourselves. For example, if you ask individuals to tell you a few pertinent facts about themselves that might help us to understand better who they are, they will normally include one or more of the following:

- their given name
- their professional achievements
- marital status (including progeny)
- where they live
- their educational achievements
- their age
- friends and associates with whom they identify
- social groups to which they belong
- description of the home they own
- automobiles or other possessions they own

These elements help establish individual identity. All of us seek, in our own way, to reinforce our self-images through identification with what we do, where we live, what we own, whom we know, etc. Psychologists verify that a primary motivation in most major buying decisions is the matter of self-image—personal identity factors—that most of us tend not to violate unless we have no choice.

High on the list of self-image motivators for most of us is the decision about where we live, and the homes in which we choose to live. Although its relative importance in identity reinforcement varies greatly from one person to another, it is usually a major motivator even if it has not yet been tapped. For example, when we start out in adult life and try to gain some independence from our parents and protectors, one of the first steps is locating a residence separate from our previous guardians. Maybe we can only afford a small apartment that is substantially less spacious than the home in which we were raised, but the fact that it gives us a sense of independence helps us to find a stronger self-image in everything else we do. Back in the recesses of our mind, we still have our dreams of the home and other possessions we picture owning someday. Those dreams are the fuel for our daily fulfillment of tasks we must accomplish to reach them. I have often said to real estate salespeople that one of their primary functions is to harness the dreams of their prospects and breed discontent with what they now own that does not satisfy those visions of self-fulfillment. The homes we own as we progress through the pathways of life are distinctive symbols of our identities and our dreams, fulfilled or unfulfilled.

That is why one basic concern in creating marketing strategies for any new development must be the determination of criteria for establishing a strong, positive sense of identity that relates to the motivations and self-images of your profiled prospects. Everything that affects the image of the community, neighborhoods, and the design of the homes plays a role in consumer acceptance or rejection. Often the small elements are most influential in establishing the identity values perceived by the customers. Without a positive and value-reinforcing image that relates to the interests of your target audience, your marketing campaign can fail or fall short of its mark.

## IDENTITY AREAS THAT DESERVE MARKETING ATTENTION

Location is obviously the first identity consideration for prospective home buyers. They most often make that choice before they even begin looking and thus confine their housing search to areas where they perceive the values and services justify investigations. Since general location often has preconceived value factors, we must objectively evaluate all aspects of the location as they affect the value images we need to convey to profiled consumers. Negatives, if present, need to be minimized, offset, or justified as part of our basic marketing program. Some major considerations of image identity for home buyers are:

- adjacent real estate development
- value ranges of homes in that area
- schools and the quality of education
- social acceptance of area by peer groups
- demographics of the general location
- community activities and political compatibility
- lifestyle benefits related to personal interests
- address value contrasted to alternative areas

When you have an opportunity to develop housing in an accepted and well-established neighborhood where values have been protected and enhanced, it is fairly easy to capitalize on the images already in place. However, if you acquire a site on "the wrong side of the tracks," as perceived by the local populace, and surrounding housing environments are substandard compared to your anticipated product lines, you have a real marketing challenge. In the first situation you should seek to become identified with the existing community, while in the latter case you might want to try to isolate your project from its surroundings. This is part of the basic strategy that needs resolution before you create the visual and psychological elements of your marketing plan.

Theme-positioning the housing neighborhoods and establishing positive, visual graphics and architectural structures that set the stage for your housing designs are vital aspects of the strategic planning process. What messages are you trying to convey to prospects as they approach the community and visually experience your housing? How can you help them to picture the psychological benefits of living in one of your new residential structures? What image-enhancers can you employ to set your community and housing apart from the competition or surrounding properties of lesser value?

We have helped clients meet some very difficult challenges in theme-positioning a new community. On many occasions our best approach to the image issues of adjacent environments was to isolate ourselves completely from the surroundings by creating a "walled city" or an oasis of landscaping with a dominant entry that gave residents a sense of independence and security. On occasions, when we were truly on the wrong side of town as perceived by the local squatters, we had to launch major marketing campaigns to counter the established attitudes of the entrenched population. Often the transferees and relocated families change attitudes about local markets, where the natives have grown up with biased judgments regarding what is acceptable and what is not. Targeting for the trendsetters is another strategy in helping to launch an unproven location.

## WHAT IS IN A NAME—AND DOES THE PUBLIC CARE?

As one traverses the country and studies thousands of housing communities, it is easy to question the judgment of builders who have selected names for their neighborhoods and homes seemingly by pulling them out of a hat. It reminds me of the story I heard about a boy who was named seven-and-one-eighth because his name was pulled from a hat! In too many cases, community identities have little or nothing to do with the housing, the people or the self-image of the residents.

We have seen communities with names like Pine Acres where not a pine tree was on the landscape. Willow Creek where there were no willows and no creek! Rolling Hills in a prairie neighborhood of flat lands and few trees. There is nothing detrimental about these names in their own right. It is the disparity between the themes and the actual characteristics of the areas they are supposed to represent.

When you theme-name a community of homes, a unique opportunity exists to reflect the natural environment or the imaged dreams of potential residents. Wherever you have the freedom to name subdivisions, streets, amenities, trail systems, and model homes, carefully think through the thematics and image-positioning from the vantage point of the potential pride of ownership future owners will enjoy. Memorable identity statements will help you establish the community and your housing much more readily than those that are not. Names that capture the positive imagination of your profiled customers' interests will strengthen your advertising capacity to attract prospects to your sales facilities.

There is real marketing power in choosing for your housing environments theme names that reinforce the values of the homes you build and the communities you create. However, far more is involved in establishing marketable identities than just selecting appropriate theme images. The process really should begin with land planning. The objective is to create neighborhoods and housing clusters that fulfill basic human needs and motivations. The most effective land plans are those that take into consideration the lifestyle needs of the anticipated residents. Large neighborhoods are not as desirable as small ones. When you can provide streetscapes and controlled access areas of less than fifty homes or condominiums, you offer owners a comfortable sense of identity with their immediate neighbors. If you can bring those groupings to even smaller clusters such as 15 to 35, you will significantly add to the friendliness and privacy of the environments. Large, massive, undefined housing patterns tend to lessen the sense of community and to decrease personal identification with streets, neighborhoods and housing types. A little forethought by land planners and those who influence master plans can often convert a boring, undefined subdivision into a series of charming little nesting areas, where each grouping of homes gains its identity from the streetscapes and approaches to the separate villages.

## PROVIDE OWNERS WITH A SENSE OF COMMUNITY

Developers who really understand the underlying motivations of homeowners concentrate on creating communities, not just building homes. They realize that the home is only part of a larger environment and that the effectiveness of the community will depend upon the degree of involvement and commitment that residents give to improving and supporting group interests. Even large neighborhoods can have a strong sense of community if those who designed them gave special consideration to preserving human values. Most owners want to care for their possessions. The neighborhoods in which they live can be perceived as including those interests if builders and marketers work at making it happen.

What gives people a true sense of community and, thus, a strong identity? Many elements, both physical and psychological, combine to either nurture or destroy planning, execution, marketing and servicing the created environments. Physical elements come first, because they are the ones prospects see and react to before moving into the community. That is why it is so important to design and install graphic representations of neighborhood images at the beginning of each new section of housing and especially to provide for a sense of arrival into the community from its various access points. Entry monuments, landscaped approaches, architecturally pleasing fencing, and theme name markers are part of that sense of arrival that can quickly establish values before the prospect even arrives at the new housing sites. These entry areas help to offset the seeming loss of identity that clustered multi-family housing in particular tends to produce.

As we must use land more efficiently to obtain ever increasing densities due to costs and availability of services, we force people to live closer together in housing that is often fairly uniform in design and architectural characteristics. The single-family home has the greatest physical identity for most of us because it sits alone on a defined homesite with the owner free to personalize the property in a variety of ways that reinforce identity factors. High-rise condominiums and stacked housing units tend to take away the separate identities we enjoy in single-family neighborhoods. That is why it is even more important in these types of housing environments to find substitute ways to give occupants pride of ownership. If they must arrive at the third floor of a condominium building where all residents have the same type of doors facing a common hallway, we should compensate by providing an alternate sense of arrival. Entry gates to the general area, neighborhood identities, building names, separate lobbies, and elevator arrival points on each floor are all potential areas where you can restore the personal identity of the owners.

When trail systems and recreational amenities are shared by the residents, there is an additional opportunity to provide romantic reinforcing image-enhancers. Naming trails, treating gardens and sitting places with special attention to landscaping and providing vista points and community gathering places are valid and very positive ways to add to the perceived values of ownership.

Beyond these visual elements is the much greater objective of helping owners to feel they are a part of a meaningful and life-rewarding community. That is achieved by more sound land planning and well-designed neighborhoods. It depends equally upon the spirit of friendliness and community service promulgated by the community founders. Marketing has a vested interest in fostering positive interrelationships within the community and in seeing that charter residents are made to feel like important contributors to the success of the area as it matures.

## BUILDING VALUE PERCEPTIONS ON COMFORT MOTIVATORS

Another basic marketing strategy centers on creating perceived value advantages for your homes and communities in terms of comfort and convenience comparisons. When you demonstrate that your housing environments add to the personal comfort of your owners as contrasted with previous experiences, you have tapped a motivational force that can trigger interest. People do not necessarily want a different lifestyle, but they do respond to improved lifestyles! Anything that makes life more pleasant and enjoyable can potentially be a stimulant to positive action.

When evaluating your housing designs, amenities, construction features and locational advantages, focus your attention on elements that will add to the potential comfort-conditioning of targeted clients. People make comparisons first to what they have experienced, owned or used. They seek improvements in creature comforts. Anything that makes life easier, less complex and more enjoyable will gain favorable attention.

If your profiled customers are first-time buyers who have been living in small apartments with limited facilities, the mere opportunity to own a modest condominium or home that has two bathrooms instead of one and a serviceable kitchen with modern appliances can be a real motivator to purchase rather than rent. On the other hand, an elderly couple currently enjoying the spaciousness of an older home with fine furnishings and appointments will not be satisfied with a smaller one unless it contains equivalent or more comfortable design elements. They will seldom sacrifice luxury just for less space. The manageable space relationships in a more efficient condominium that others maintain is a primary design consideration, but it must at least have the quality and prestige that the customers have previously known.

Perceived values are those that prospects understand and accept as being important to them, not those that the production department independently decides they should have. Just because a builder includes a particular feature in a home does not assure that prospects will appreciate or pay for it!

Carefully research your competition to discover what your profiled buyers are purchasing. Look for areas in design and features that you can add to increase the value perceptions of comfort and quality. Often the small things we do make the big difference. You may not be able to increase footage, but you can add special design elements that make the home far more attractive and comfortable. Research the housing environments from which you will be drawing prospective buyers and determine what they do not now enjoy in terms of creature comforts that you might include in your housing.

## THE VALUE-INDEX SYSTEM INCREASES SALES POWER

New home sales specialists are discovering the power of using value index systems to help convince buyers of the benefits of their builder's home versus those offered by the competition. The general idea is not new, but the techniques for applying these rating concepts are generating new approaches and improved visual aids.

## WHAT IS A VALUE-INDEX SYSTEM?

A value-index system is a checklisted rating chart that identifies your housing product's features and thus guides prospective buyers to compare your product's best features with features your competition has (or does not have). The simplest form of this concept is merely a list of features printed for inclusion in a brochure, used as a separate handout, a guide for salespersons in sales sessions or in an enlarged form in sales center graphic displays as a feature board.

Such simple special feature checklists are not as effective as a more complete list that has columns for the prospect to use in adding to or subtracting from feature points of the competition's products.

Prioritize the checklist for greater effectiveness. This means identifying all features in the order of how you believe the average prospect would rate them, as well as how valuable you believe them to be. Since you are designing the value index, you can be creative in how you influence the prospective purchaser to compare your product with the competition's. The key to effective use of such a rating system is grading or starring the items so that the prospect feels he or she is following the natural order of importance in rating a good home buy.

**FIGURE 3.3  Comparative Value Index Checklist (Compare Beacon Hill with the others)**

| Y/N | BEACON HILL | OTHERS | | |
|---|---|---|---|---|
| Y | From $64,000 | | | |
| Y | 1 to 3 bedrooms | | | |
| Y | As little as 5% down | | | |
| Y | 30-year loans—fully assumable | | | |
| Y | Tennis courts | | | |
| Y | Pool and spa | | | |
| Y | Men's and women's saunas | | | |
| Y | Clubhouse with full kitchen | | | |
| Y | Billiard room and gas B.B.Q. | | | |
| Y | Lovely landscaped grounds w/waterfall | | | |
| Y | Central heating and refrigerated A/C | | | |
| Y | Brass ceiling fans | | | |
| Y | Large country-style kitchens | | | |
| Y | Deluxe birch kitchen cabinets | | | |
| Y | Ceramic tile kitchen counters | | | |
| Y | Large pantries with spice racks | | | |
| Y | Gas range and self-cleaning ovens | | | |
| Y | Microwave and refrigerator | | | |
| Y | Stainless-steel double kitchen sinks | | | |
| Y | Energy saving automatic dish washers | | | |
| Y | Patios or balconies | | | |
| Y | Wall-to-wall carpeting | | | |
| Y | Draperies throughout | | | |
| Y | Woodburning, heat recirculated f/places | | | |
| Y | Country community on the lake | | | |
| Y | Home trade-in program | | | |
| Y | Historic home town | | | |
| Y | Location—shortest drive to town | | | |
| Y | Plenty of storage and closet space | | | |
| Y | Open, flowing space | | | |
| Y | 5-year warranty on A/C compressor | | | |
| Y | 25-year roof warranty | | | |

FIGURE 3.3  Comparative Value Index Checklist (Compare Beacon Hill with the others) (concluded)

| Y/N | BEACON HILL | OTHERS | | |
|---|---|---|---|---|
| Y | Thick fiberglass insulation | | | |
| Y | Washer and dryer | | | |
| Y | Beautiful garden baths | | | |
| Y | Large marble Jacuzzi tub in master bath | | | |
| Y | Ceramic tile stall shower in mstr bath | | | |
| Y | Vanities in each bath | | | |
| Y | Custom double vanity in master suite | | | |
| Y | Acoustical ceilings | | | |
| Y | Cable TV pre-wiring | | | |
| Y | Smoke detectors | | | |
| Y | Fully sodded front and rear yards | | | |
| Y | Automatic garage door opener | | | |
| Y | Hand-finished stair rails | | | |
| Y | Custom door knobs | | | |
| Y | Embossed doors throughout | | | |
| Y | Ventilated attics | | | |
| Y | Tinted glass windows | | | |
| Y | High-quality brick exteriors | | | |
| Y | Decorator base molding and door molding | | | |
| Y | Lots of square footage | | | |
| Y | Custom fitted construction | | | |
| Y | Computerized security system | | | |

The value index subtly helps prospects see how much more you offer than the competition. Of course, almost every builder offers special items or exceptional product advantages, but by emphasizing in your collateral materials those items that your homes feature in a manner that contrasts them with those of your competition, you are using the well-established principle of human perception of value marketing that psychologists call the contrast principle.

Many salespeople in other fields use the contrast principle between various products they are selling (as you, no doubt, have experienced on an automobile showroom floor). But in new home sales, the most effective use of the contrast principle is when comparisons between your homes and those of your competition are artfully promoted to the prospect. It shows confidence in your own product when you invite prospective purchasers to compare. Prospects who really become interested in buying someone's product generally expect (and desire) guidance. Remember Lee Iaccoca's exhortation: "If you can find a better car, buy it!" He had set up a conceptual, if not detailed, value index before he issued that gutsy invitation to the car buyers of America.

Do not use standard items when you can emphasize exclusive features with the community or builder's name reinforced. Alert marketers today have recognized the value of eliminating the word *standard* from brochures, model signs and sales displays. The words *standard* and *basic* are not positive words. To be standard is ordinary; it is representative of an expectation not worthy of special notice. For example, you would hardly say in a brochure that the "bathroom is standard." Instead of using such undistinguishing words, substitute such phrases as *exclusive feature*, or *builder feature* to dress up the ordinary. For example, you can use the name of the builder and tie it to the word feature: This is a *Sullivan feature*.

Items included in the quoted price should be spotlighted by accent phrases such as *this is an included feature*. Silent sales aids in models should also use terms like, *quality feature, home craft feature*, etc. We also have generally dropped the words, *extras* and *options* from promotional materials and sale conversations. Instead, we are using such terms as *custom features, decorator features* and *designer selection features*.

*Remember:* A feature is going to be perceived by the prospect as far more valuable than a standard item. Salespeople, of course, need to translate features into benefits in the buyer's mind. Buyers are not as concerned with what it is as what it will do for them. Give your prospects feature-benefit rating lists; then under the guidance of an able salesperson, let them reinforce the reasons why your homes deserve their confidence. As handouts and visual aid charts, these value index systems stimulate buyer interest and increase your sales power. It is a proven approach.

## ROMANTIC ENVIRONMENTS STIMULATE POSITIVE RESPONSE

We are all influenced by our physical surroundings. Our natural instincts draw us to environments that stimulate our visual sense and give us a sense of well-being and purpose. Open, green, park-like spaces that extend the living areas of our homes are always welcome visual relief from urban streetscapes that dominate most cities in America. There is little beauty or human identification with asphalt, cement, parking lots, cluttered yards, and confused architecture. Conversely, we have affinity for natural environments with trees, flowers, waterscapes, mountains and native terrain.

One of the strategic objectives of marketing should be to create amidst construction turmoil sample environments that help the prospects picture the living benefits of the community once the homes are built and the area is landscaped. Model sales areas should try to capture a bit of that dream and romantically portray what the future will bring. One of the best investments you can make in most model settings is in mature, professionally planned landscaping. Trees, shrubs, flowers, berms and interesting water amenities can do much to take pressure off of exterior architecture and surroundings that may be less than exciting influences.

We communicate values and concepts to most individuals through the nonverbal sensory system much more effectively than through the spoken word. People tend to react to, believe and remember more of what they see than what they hear. That is why you should place a great deal of emphasis on the visual elements of your on-site merchandising program. Today's marketing leaders are going far beyond just normal landscaping and decorating of model homes. They try to appeal to all of the senses in very positive ways. Fragrances that convey homey messages are being used in appropriate rooms in each model. Music identified with the profile of prospective customers is played softly on background stereo equipment in models and sales areas. Outdoor sitting areas are created around homes to help prospects picture their potential enjoyment of the landscaped settings. This is a holistic approach to marketing. It encompasses the romantic aspects of living and appeals to emotions that can be powerful when unleashed.

As professional salespeople know, you sell to emotions first! People buy on emotion and justify with facts. They seldom reverse that process where primary housing decisions are concerned. The thrust of the strategy is to help your profiled prospects become emotionally involved with your homes and housing environments so that they sell themselves on wanting to live there.

In chapter five, we will discuss in depth various aspects of on-site marketing proven effective for builders and marketers. Romantic positioning and emotionally positive communication are basic objectives of residential marketing strategies.

## SECURITY AND PRIVACY ARE PRIMARY MOTIVATORS

When designing neighborhoods and housing, planners and marketing people should pay special attention to the twin motivators of security and privacy. In urban centers of the country, these are far more important than in rural market areas. The very congestion of high-density housing dictates that we compensate for the increased exposure with genuine concern for the safeguards we can use to avoid human conflict and loss of privacy.

Security in many communities is even more important than privacy. Where external risks of intrusion and pressures of urban society might encroach on the sanctity of personal life patterns, planners must provide for barriers and safety valves. Security (privacy) walls, security gates, sentry guards, lighting systems, electronic monitoring devices and roving patrols are frequently part of a major community security program. Designers must study ways to make a home environment feel secure physically as well as psychologically. A delicate balance exists between perceived security that is still friendly and that which translates into prison mentality. No one wants to live in a fort where you feel like you have to report just to leave or enter your home.

Privacy extends to other considerations beyond physical security. Essentially, three aspects of privacy deserve attention in design and marketing:

- social privacy
- sound (audio) privacy
- visual privacy

Social privacy is a subtle and critical interpretation of people/space relationships. Crowded areas will always produce some negative emotions for most of us. We do not want to be packed into our environments without enough personal space to feel we can be ourselves and breathe without jostling someone else. When you have high-density, large communities, you have a special marketing need to decrease the potential perception of lost privacy. A buyer does not need to know that there are 20 condos to the acre! In fact, if it feels that dense, there will be resistance to the housing. Architects who have studied ways to carefully balance the needs of man, land and housing create relationships that make the blend seem far less dense that it really is. The movement of streetscapes, changing setbacks and positioning buildings so that visual interest is maintained as you move from one place to another is part of the superior orchestrating of interesting land plans. It is how it feels that counts!

The strategy in promoting any community, large or small, is to make the neighborhoods and housing seem private while strengthening the cohesive aspects of community design so that it feels compatible and friendly. You always want to avoid threatening numbers and massive housing concepts. If prospects feel that they are going to be forced to meet a lot of people they do not know and become lost in multitudes of unfriendly residents, they will instinctively retreat to less threatening environments. For example, suppose your site plan called for a community of 500 homes of different types to be built over the next few years. If you emphasize in the introductory information given to new customers that 500 homes and 2000 people will be in that community, you risk losing the average buyer. Most of us do not want to meet that many people! We certainly do not want to get lost in that crowd!

Social privacy needs dictate that we approach the presentation of any large or densely populated housing project by first conveying the small, friendly, private aspects of the land plan.

> *"Note that we have several private residential neighborhoods. For example our first little village is Quail Court with only 35 homesites of which 21 have already been sold. Then we have Walden Place with another 55 that have just been released. The other neighborhoods will be just as private and protected as these and, when they are completed, we will have 11 living areas that combine to make the Lake of the Woods a marvelous place to be!"*

The point we are underscoring with this scenario is simply that socially comfortable and private neighborhoods must be conveyed incrementally to establish the larger picture offered by major housing environments. Your marketing strategies should protect the human need to relate to just a few people and places as well as provide prospects a place to retreat from the group. They have to understand through marketing messages that not everyone swims in the pool at the same time. There are other places to be in the community. The homes are nestled and protected from each other by the way they are designed. Admittedly, this is difficult to do with some land plans. However, when given the challenge of communicating social privacy, effective marketers find a way through presentations and promotional copy to minimize the potential issues.

Sound privacy is another dominant motivation of home buyers. Intrusive sounds lessen the quality of life and invade our personal sense of privacy. If you have ever lived in an apartment building with paper-thin walls, you know the problems this creates psychologically for residents. Whenever you are marketing attached housing of any type, you want to work closely with those in charge of design and construction to see that appropriate steps are taken to lessen the chances of sound transmission.

Visual privacy is attained by designing homes and apartments to allow residents to use their interior space and part of their exterior space without exposure to neighboring occupants. Staggering building setbacks, providing wing walls for rear yard privacy, protecting deck and patio spaces, and placing the sleeping zones of homes where they are isolated from more active waking areas are primary design elements that deserve special consideration.

Although the director of marketing may not be able to directly affect product development decisions, he or she should certainly be aware of the detrimental effect that lack of visual privacy will have on public acceptance. When well-designed housing has resolved the typical problems we face in trying to maintain privacy in a densely populated area, it needs to be given marketing emphasis in all aspects of promotion, both on-site and in the media.

## CONTROLLING INVENTORY AND CREATING URGENCY ARE MAJOR STRATEGIES

Few marketing strategies are more important to your objectives than those that focus on creating momentum for the housing programs you represent. Numerous factors influence the tempo of success, but controlling the amount of inventory offered to the marketplace is the key to all the others. By inventory we are referring to homesites for sale, homes under construction—unsold, and speculative housing completed— unsold. Excess inventory in any commodity, including housing, lessens values and reduces the sense of urgency to act now.

All disciplines in the operation need to appreciate this truth. If administration releases more lots, homes, condos or apartments than the market can reasonably absorb in a short period of time, the result will be decreased urgency, reduced values and potential customer confusion. If production starts too many homes at one time, and they fail to be absorbed as they are completed, the vacant inventory will not only reduce profits because of increased holding costs, it will also adversely affect the confidence and interest of the prospects. Before the decision is made to release homes or lots to the sales staff, the marketing team should evaluate inventory needs and propose what should be offered based on projected sales rates.

A classic rule in this business is if the known, available inventory of homesites or housing units exceeds the capacity of the market to absorb them within three to six months, the result will automatically be:

- decreased confidence to purchase
- lessened urgency
- increased confusion because of selection alternatives
- potential reduced values

It is best to keep inventory within 60 to 90 days' supply rather than 90 to 120. This is especially true of housing under construction. You can afford to be slightly more lenient on the inventory control formula for lots not yet sold than for spec housing. However, in either case, the published availability of new opportunities can play havoc with sales strategies once buyers feel they can afford to wait. The motivating factors are desire and fear. When you want something and you fear you may lose it by waiting, you are prompted to take action now. Excessive choice and slow sales activity communicates to prospects that they can wait without risk because there is plenty from which to choose and few are buying.

The opposite is true when you manage released properties efficiently. The limited number of choices, coupled with the sales made that are evident on your sales control board, help to stimulate the hesitant buyer to act now. When everything works well, the housing area generates a momentum of its own that feeds on the apparent rapid pace of sales made from a limited inventory base. As new homes and homesites are released (following the same absorption guidelines), prospects react favorably to the opportunity to buy at today's prices before these are also gone.

If you truly appreciate the marketing power of this fundamental strategy, you will fight to control inventory and make certain that you keep the sales staff concentrating on what needs to be sold to maintain the confidence of prospects and residents. We feel this is so crucial to the planning process that we are covering this subject more extensively by now analyzing some specific areas of opportunity and concern you need to constantly monitor.

## PLAN THE PHASING STRATEGY AT THE INCEPTION OF THE PROJECT

The time to get a firm grasp on strategic phasing is at the beginning. Planning sessions held before construction begins or sites are released are the right forums for addressing this vital concept. Marketing is responsible for research and, thus, for making projections as to what percentages of the total market can be penetrated by type and price range within specified time periods. When you make those predictions, it is always best to be conservative than overly optimistic. Releasing too much inventory is a much greater marketing risk than releasing too little. In most cases you can add to inventory on regular dates if sales justify, but it is more difficult to withdraw properties from the market once they have been posted for sale.

Builders do not always understand why we need to control inventory so carefully. Economics rather than marketing psychology, often guides their decisions. If it is cheaper to build a number of homes at one time or open an entire area of lots because underground utilities and streets are less expensive when installed on larger scale, production managers will frequently opt for the larger undertaking. As marketers, we need to educate and influence those who make these decisions.

Remember that a big difference exists between developing lots, starting construction and releasing housing sites to the market for public consumption. The development company may find it economically desirable to install improvements or begin early construction of housing without concurrently releasing those properties to the sales staff. This truth needs emphasis with construction management as well as sales personnel in a building enterprise. We control inventory decisions based on many factors: sequencing development so that we have completed neighborhoods and also reserving sites for price increases and later occupancy.

As we will emphasize in chapter four, the site plan display in a sales office should only reflect those properties that marketing desires to feature at a specific time. The rest of the property needs to be identified as future construction or future releases. The phasing of a community has many advantages for both buyers and developers:

- Neighborhoods are completed without scattered lots of unoccupied housing.
- Values of housing environments are protected because of finished streetscapes and occupancy.
- Builders save money in time and material management by sequential construction operations.
- Owners need not contend with noise of construction activities because the homes surrounding theirs are finished.
- Developers and marketers can maintain control over the amount of property offered and avoid depreciation of assets and lessening of tempo.
- Residents have a greater sense of community as they take possession. People take pride in their homes and share in community activities more readily.

## DETERMINE WHICH HOMES SHOULD BE SOLD AND BUILT FIRST

Beyond the strategy of controlling the logical flow of housing and lot inventory to the market based on projected sales volume for 90-day time frames is the matter of choosing sites that should be built, sold and occupied early in each phase of the project. Marketing management should evaluate the entire community-development plan in terms of potential marketing advantages and disadvantages of selling key locations at the beginning of each phase. The visual impact of having construction start early on some sites versus others can benefit the sales objectives as well as the credibility of the project. For example, when the land plan is exposed to unattractive vacant land or abuts property that tends to depreciate values, it is logical to start housing on locations that close off those adverse views. There is also the distinct advantage of having a group of homes brought into a sense of community by having arriving prospects view completed streetscapes instead of unfinished land areas.

The strategic sale of one key site can have many times the sales value of another not as visible or important to the overall momentum of the neighborhood. Earmark key sites and locations that need early attention and set in motion plans that will assure their sale and occupancy.

## CONCENTRATE MARKETING EFFORTS ON THE RIGHT PRODUCTS

Another basic objective is to place your marketing emphasis on homes and categories of sites that represent the majority of your inventory. For example, if most of your single-family lots are 7200 square feet and only a minority at 10,000 or more, you will not want to sell all the large sites first nor have the agents promoting or featuring these choice locations. Advertising and presentation needs to focus on the inventory in balance to the total mix. If there are more C condo models than A's, do not focus attention on the A's.

Selection of models, spec inventory and lots needs to be guided by appropriate concentration on inventory availability. There is little need to put models on the best lots when the majority of sites for sales are of lesser value. Models belong on average lots and should represent the majority of your inventory. If marketing management does not think about these things in advance, construction may be dictated by other interests less sensitive to marketing objectives.

## PRICING STRATEGIES AND THE MARKETING PROCESS

Pricing your homes and determining how to gain the most momentum and profit from the home building game is not simply a matter of working percentage formulas that lead to arbitrary values. Although there should be a reasonable relationship of hard costs, soft costs and profit objectives, the pricing of individual models and homesites should consider the variables that affect value perceptions and the total tempo of the community throughout its building phases. Gaining an exact percentage of profit from each home or condominium you construct is not as important as being certain that the complete inventory is sold and delivered at reasonable profits within workable time frames.

Builders who do not fully appreciate the significance of developing market-oriented pricing strategies at the beginning of a new venture often discover they have lost money in the long run. Profit is seldom in the sale of one home, unless you are only building one at a time and have no lot inventory or overhead to worry about. Most of us must complete a minimum number of sales and closings each year to meet basic overhead costs before we realize any profit. In land development, all of the gain is normally in the last 20 percent to 30 percent of each development phase. Prior to that it is mostly overhead and underground!

What is a reasonable profit margin? Some might answer: "What the market will bear." That is not unreasonable, because the market often dictates that a product is worth less than it costs to produce. Within the industry the accepted target range for builder profit margins is normally between 10 percent and 15 percent of gross sales price. However, only a small percentage of builders realize that much profit. Volume or merchant builders will accept lower percentages to stay competitive and produce a greater number of sales.

If you can do so, it is wise to separate land development profits from building profits. A developer creates values by plotting and land planning. When sites are ready for construction, they have a value-added base that deserves an adequate return on risk capital expended to that point. Land profits can often be much greater than those from comparable dollar volume in home building. When the same company develops the land and also builds the homes in a major project, the profits may be separated into a number of accounts or merged into one total sum for the entire development.

I am of the opinion that any developer or home builder willing to take the sizable risks of this capital-intensive business deserves all the profits that can reasonably be generated by creating legitimate values. From a marketing viewpoint, profits are far easier to gain and preserve if pricing and perceived values are strategized to build increased consumer acceptance by the way they are introduced in various stages of construction.

Although marketers seldom have the final decision on pricing strategies in the home building business, they should certainly have a major vote in influencing the decision makers. Failure to take into account certain fundamental pricing principles can be very costly and sometimes disastrous to the entire venture. In the best-managed home building and development companies, pricing strategies are the mutual determination of a marketing team, with each discipline playing a role in helping management to reach decisions that will insure a profitable operation. Estimators, accountants, production supervisors, financial managers, and entrepreneurial owners need the advantage of having a marketing viewpoint before reaching pricing conclusions. The objective is a results-oriented strategy that takes into account the following key factors:

1.  The reasonable penetration rate this site or program can achieve within a specific time frame based on market feasibility analysis.
2.  The maximum or desired product rate that the builder/developer can achieve in that location or market environment, regardless of the sales potential. It is important to recognize that the opportunities of the market place may exceed the capacity of a specific production company's ability to fulfill them.
3.  The competitive positioning for the homes and the sites as viewed by prospective buyers who will make their value comparisons. Perceived-value indexes must be used to insure that the public will respond favorably to the pricing and terms of purchase.
4.  The dollar amount of closed sales that must occur within predetermined time frames to meet overhead and land release objectives.
5.  The gross and net profit objectives of the developers and builders for this particular venture. This must include the expectations of joint-venture investors whose involvement is often less flexible than many projects require for optimum performance schedules.

To create a pricing plan without seriously evaluating these five critical determinants is to court disaster. Over-expectations frequently lead to disappointments. The unexpected is a more common result than the expected in this industry, as our last few tumultuous years of fluctuating interest rates and rapidly changing economic conditions have dramatically proven.

One of the more frequent scenarios we encounter as consultants to this industry is the ACT IV ending, where the builder, developer or investors sit with the last 10 percent of the project unsold and unwanted! Of course, these are the sites and the homes that should supply most of the profits of the entire community. Yet, the sales staff has sold the best sites, the cream puffs and the desirable locations up front—for less money than they would have been worth if they had sold last.

Pricing strategies should always take into account the need to protect and enhance values as you move from one released series of lots to the next. They must assure that the developer/builder profit margins are preserved, even if that means reducing some sites below cost to sell others at sizable premiums. Always be cognizant of the truth that the basic values in this business are in *land*—not in housing! It is what happens to land that makes or lessens the ultimate perception of value for the consumer—the final judge of how valuable anything is!

## HOW MUCH PRICING SPREAD IS DESIRABLE OR MARKETABLE?

One of the early decisions that must be reached when planning a new community is the matter of practical and marketable pricing ranges. How much difference between bottom and the top should there be in a given neighborhood? What happens to upper-range values if substantially lower-priced properties exist in the immediate area? How will the public rate the community if a particular pricing strategy is pursued?

These are not idle questions. The conclusions you reach on fundamental value ranges and product pricing will have a major impact on consumers' perceptions of value for the entire project. We are addressing the subject of image and identity values. In America, we are socially programmed to believe that the value of the homes we live in reflects our status in life. There is a direct correlation between one's self-image and success rating and the price of the home one owns.

Every experienced real estate agent and appraiser knows the challenges of *over-improvement* and *economic obsolescence*. It is far easier to sell the less expensive home in a high-priced neighborhood than the most expensive in a low-priced neighborhood A $150,000 home next door to one priced at $300,000 may be perceived as worth more because of the adjacent value. The reverse may be true for the upper-end property. When you lay out a business plan for a new community you need to first profile the people whom you hope to attract and validate the available numbers to assure the attainment of your penetration goals before you decide on either the price range or the products to be featured.

What is a reasonable and marketable range? The answer must be: It depends upon local market attitudes and the historic value ranges acceptable to the profiled buyers. However, experience suggests some practical general guidelines.

The social economics of profiled buyers will dictate their comfort zone in accepting adjacent values. For example, first-time buyers barely able to afford the starter home are far less concerned with value ranges than luxury buyers who have discretionary dollars and a prior equity base. When affordability is the primary issue, the matter of surrounding values is relative only to comparative shopping experiences. However, the same buyers several years later will consciously seek better neighborhoods and improved values to prove to themselves that they are coming up in the world.

Define your neighborhoods (or building groups) and keep your value ranges within the social expectations and identity perceptions of your profiled prospects. A well-defined grouping of homes should sustain the values of all the homes within that neighborhood, with none being a deterrent to the upper price levels. For example, a range of $50,000 to $100,000 in direct competition with each other on the same street is not reasonable unless clustering and landscaping separations create the sense of independent neighborhoods. That is very hard to achieve, although some master-planned communities have done it reasonably well. (The Woodlands near Houston, Texas, is a good example). Fundamentally, the $50,000 buyer is not in the same social economic class as the $100,000+ buyer. While you may be able to readily sell all of your $50's in this area, you will probably have difficulty marketing the $100,000 range for optimum profits.

Protect the value range by controlling the architecture and streetscapes. Regardless of the range, the appearance of the community and the exterior design statements will greatly affect the perceptions of the public. Well-designed elevations that are not duplicated like monopoly pieces can preserve a much greater difference in values than those that are look-alike boxes.

When your target market is the more affluent buyer in the upper price ranges, always maintain tight control of price variances. For example, in a neighborhood that averages $500,000, you might have a $350,000 home and a $750,000 home (architecturally controlled), but you probably would not allow one at $150,000. There is a reasonable range that buyers of these prestige homes would consider acceptable to their own socioeconomic measurements, and there is a point below which they would be seriously concerned with the impact on their investment.

Behavioralists in recent years have concluded that Americans make their buying decisions (and their choices in most things) in terms of their values and lifestyles. The *belonger* is seeking a different environment and identity statement than an *achiever*. We are socially programmed in life as a result of our experiences and attitudes. Expectations and cultural acceptance of our environments dictate our choices.

Some people who have money and can afford to live in the most exclusive (snobbish) neighborhoods elect not to do so. Some individuals with little economic security consciously strive to be in the right neighborhoods and belong to the most prestigious groups, even if they cannot afford to do so comfortably. Money alone does not dictate where we live or how we relate to others. It is important to realize that pricing strategies and product positioning affects much more than obvious land-use patterns. Lifestyles and social images are every bit as important as dollars invested in housing communities!

## PRICING IS A MARKETING TOOL THAT AFFECTS SALES TEMPO

When you first introduce a new community, neighborhood or housing line, you have an opportunity to employ pricing strategies to accelerate sales and create a desired tempo of activity. The launching pad is the right time to think through the entire development scenario and project the desired results. What you do (or do not do) at the outset will affect the results you realize for the total community.

Phasing strategies should always be employed in any community where the number of sites to be offered exceeds a 90-day inventory. Likewise, it is almost always in your best interest to structure a preconstruction, preopening marketing plan designed to capture a number of sales before you have completed models or a major event to launch the project. Pioneer and preview pricing should allow prospects to feel they are realizing a price advantage by making the housing decision before everything is completed. Prices three to five percent less than grand-opening levels will usually give adequate momentum to the project. If you limit the number of homes or sites you plan to sell at each price level, you can easily raise prices even before grand opening. One proven formula is to offer inventory in a manner that permits you to sell no more than 20–25 of every released group of homes or sites at the lower prices so that you can incrementally increase them until you have attained the desired total dollars from the entire release. This increases the sense of urgency to act and reinforces the values of homes sold to early purchasers, who must wait the longest for delivery dates. This strategy provides maximum incentives of charter members of your owners' club!

A fast start is a valid marketing objective. However, the counter point is the risk of selling all of your first-phase homes or condominiums so fast that you fail to recover the extra profit dollars possible had pricing and releasing strategies been carefully planned and executed from the beginning. We are all familiar with projects that sold out on opening day, but the builders lost money or could not deliver for the prices they asked, because sales were too far in advance of deliveries and production costs increased beyond expectations. Unless you have rigid controls over costs, production schedules, financing and closing procedures, it is not wise to let consumers dictate your profits by selling all homes in one brief period at a fixed price with no opportunity to increase or adjust values.

Strive for a reasonable balance between sales pace, profit margins and pricing formulas. By setting limits on the number or percentage of properties to be sold at specific preconstruction prices, decision makers can monitor results and make appropriate adjustments to maintain the desired momentum and bottom-line numbers. On a fast-moving community, you can increase inventory and adjust prices on an hourly basis if necessary. In contrasting situations where sales are not occurring rapidly enough, rebalancing and allowances for initial sales can produce the necessary nucleus of owners to provide the credibility that motivates others to buy. The pricing-strategy game is a sensitive pivoting point around which other marketing plans must revolve.

An additional pricing strategy should be noted at this point. It is the *loss leader theory*. The principle is based on pricing a small percentage of total inventory below your actual costs to stimulate total sales volume in the community. This is a relatively common practice in major developments where there is a need to accelerate sales and gain a market position quickly. One plan might be selected as a leader and discounted to an entry-level figure that will attract heavy consumer interest. It is not unlike the fundamental strategy of many retail stores that purposely lose money on one product to attract customers so they can sell the rest of their merchandise. If adopted, this strategy should be used with discretion and limited in numbers of units offered. It should also be closely controlled in terms of percentage of profit sacrificed.

## PRICE INDIVIDUAL HOMES OR CONDOMINIUM SITES TO PROVIDE VALID COMPARISONS

One major variable in most new home communities that affect both the sales rate and profits is the pricing of individual sites. While there are plats where few, if any, distinctions can be found to support premiums or allowances for differences in values, the majority of subdivisions have the opportunity to create pricing comparisons for one location over another. In many years of researching this industry, I have discovered that one sure way of determining the values developers and builders missed is to study the resale market in those same communities three or four years later! The public marketplace quickly reveals the differences people were willing to pay for larger home sites, cul-de-sac lots, extra trees, superior views and other subtle value considerations. As a good marketer, I believe it is our duty to ask in advance: Where are the potential perceptions of value that the future marketplace will reveal? Then take advantage of those perceptions today to help builder clients increase their margins and improve their sales rates.

By carefully studying each site and using a checklist of value comparisons for everything from views to privacy, you can establish premiums and base lot values that will translate into higher returns and more balanced absorption rates. Whenever you end a subdivision with the most difficult sites to sell, it is almost always because no one took the time in the beginning to anticipate or study the value comparisons necessary to be sure these properties were favorably marketed. Ideally, you do not offer your best sites first or start the subdivision on the most expensive ground. If you are forced to do so, anticipate how the balances must be made to allow for the ultimate cleanup of the entire development. If you start with the best sites and the highest prices, you have nowhere to go in providing for increases or created appreciation on the balance of the project. When builders fall into that trap, they usually have a difficult time selling the portions of the land acquisitions that represent the majority of the profits.

Dollar averaging for the entire community is sound business management. Marketers need to know in advance the profit objectives of the developers and builders and contingent factors of land releases, cash flow requirements and development concerns that will affect the bottom line. To reach pricing decisions in the first phase of a subdivision without knowing the consequences of those actions on the final phase and the projects' total profitability is like trying to chart a course without knowing the desired destination!

In a long-term community (three years or longer to complete), there is another subtle, but potent, consideration. What will the resale market do to marketing strategies and profit margins? I have seen many developments that suffered from their own resale competition. It was not the builder down the street that was the obstacle to new sales. It was the homes that the company built two or three years earlier that were now on the market at prices lower (or substantially the same) as the new merchandise. It is difficult to convince new buyers to pay higher prices for the same floor plans and models that are reselling for less in the same neighborhood. Even though the new units have the protection of new warranties and a few special features, the lack of appreciation in the neighborhood makes it difficult for the builder to justify values.

---

**FIGURE 3.4   Lot Rating Chart**

| Lot number | Size | Views | Build-ability | Privacy | Amenities | Security | Prestige | Trees | Total points |
|---|---|---|---|---|---|---|---|---|---|
| | | | | | | | | | |
| | | | | | | | | | |
| | | | | | | | | | |
| | | | | | | | | | |
| | | | | | | | | | |
| | | | | | | | | | |
| | | | | | | | | | |
| | | | | | | | | | |
| | | | | | | | | | |
| | | | | | | | | | |
| | | | | | | | | | |
| | | | | | | | | | |
| | | | | | | | | | |
| | | | | | | | | | |
| | | | | | | | | | |
| | | | | | | | | | |
| | | | | | | | | | |
| | | | | | | | | | |
| | | | | | | | | | |

NOTE: 0 = Average or base site for each amenity. The scale is then 1 to 10 above or below a zero. A dollar value to the adjusted levels or percentage value to dollars should then be established for the 1 to 10 rating. For example, if each one point above or below represented one percent of the lot value and the lot was priced at $6,000, then every point would be worth $60. Points should be rated according to the importance of that particular item to the salability of the site. The total on the far right represents the balance between pluses and minuses above and below the base lot. The first lot selected for that group should be as near as possible to being the average lot with no pluses or minuses in reference to the eight rated elements.

---

One of the basic marketing objectives (especially in a community that must compete with itself because of the length of the marketing time) is to see that values are created and enhanced in every phase and as consistently as the marketplace will allow. This is one reason why you should avoid starting a project at the top of the market range or without room to increase prices as additional sales are made. Having preplanned and built-in strategies for raising prices during each phase of development is one of the best ways to preserve public confidence and insure consistent sales. Individual site pricing is one of the ways you can achieve this goal. Without having sustained periods of inflation, it is hard to justify major increases in construction costs. By taking into consideration lot values, pre-opening opportunities, phasing allowances and planned appreciation, you can build internal values that are isolated from general market conditions. It is sometimes necessary to be an island in the middle of economic confusion. You seldom win by joining the losing majority!

One of the better ways to preserve values and profit margins is to plan for the introduction of new floor plans, more exciting models and added amenities. If you stay with the same merchandise too long, you create some of your own competition. The automobile industry has learned the value of planned obsolescence. New designs make the older ones less desirable. It is the fundamental marketing concept of breeding discontent with the past so you can sell the future. Plan to add or change models at least every 18–24 months. Add a new model or two, even if you keep some of the proven winners. Do not get into the position of forcing comparisons with your older homes where values are directly visible. It is hard for the public to measure difference when the homes they are viewing are unlike anything else they have seen!

## THE APPRAISAL AND LOAN-TO-VALUE ISSUE

Appraisers and lending institutions play a role in our pricing policies, whether we want them to or not. They determine what is an acceptable market price based on the usual formulas of cost reproduction, comparative data and income streams. In a new community where we are trying to establish values through the use of planned pricing systems, we need to take appraisers and lenders into our confidence. Often, it is necessary to do all the documentation of competition, costs and projected values from completed programs to influence the institutional forces. Just because an appraiser may not perceive the differences in one site over another or the justification for preopening prices does not mean you should abandon this valid strategy. I know from experience that you can influence the opinion makers if you do your homework and are prepared to spend some time educating them. In the final analysis, you may have to make some adjustments to meet appraisal standards, but do not start by believing that uniformity is a desirable marketing standard.

## HOW OFTEN AND FOR WHAT REASONS SHOULD YOU CHANGE PRICES?

Answers to these questions are not found in a pat formula. There are too many variables in this business to be able to establish exact answers to the broad marketing issues of pricing and timing. There are reasonable guidelines. One of them is to try to set into motion a value-building program that will at least allow for nominal (if not major) price increases every three months. This should be an outside objective. If prices can justifiably be raised more often than once per quarter (and not destroy sales momentum or customer acceptance), the faster pace should be pursued. A new home community or condominium project that lasts longer than 90 days and has no price increases within its entire marketing time was incorrectly strategized at the outset. Stagnation and sales resistance occur when the public does not perceive that values are improving. It is a known fact that only 16 percent of new home buyers purchase on the first visit. Although better salesmanship and improved closing skills can alter this percentage, it is unlikely that we will change the shopping habits of well-educated consumers. If a buyer visits a community on one weekend and comes back another and no additional sales are evident, the confidence to purchase is logically lessened. Equally important, the public that inspects housing neighborhoods over a sustained period of time and sees no evidence of increasing values has little motive to purchase.

Anticipated or actual increases in the costs of developing lots or building homes will dictate price increases at some point. However, a builder frequently has the chance to use a forthcoming increase to create more sales. It is one of the better techniques for creating a sense of urgency and motivating hesitant home buyers to act before prices are raised. Buyers are often suspicious of this ploy when it is not based on reality. It is better to document the forthcoming increases and to have a valid reason for them than just to say: "Our prices are going up soon."

There are also times when the builder is well advised not to increase prices, even if costs have narrowed profit margins. Competitive and economic conditions may not be right for trying to keep pace with actual costs. This is one reason why builders are justified in making profit margins whatever the market will bear, when they can do so! There are always times in this industry when the cycle turns, and those former profits become the means of sustaining present operations.

It is essential to create a feeling of value-added benefits as the project progresses, even if you have to do it by some structured marketing techniques. No change says to to the consumer that there is no urgency to purchase and may be a valid reason to avoid the decision. Any project that goes an entire year without some perception of increasing prices is in difficulty. There is only one logical time to tackle that issue effectively: at the starting point. If you miss it then, it may be impossible to recover from the consequences.

If sales are not moving quickly enough, you should look at the values of rebalancing prices. Lower some; raise others—whether by site, model or limited quantity incentives.

How do you justify to the public your pricing policies? Here are a few very good reasons that can be included in sales presentations in ways acceptable and convincing:

> *"In this pre-opening period, we are saving marketing expenses that will be incurred when we finish our models and hold our grand opening. We are reflecting those savings in these special prices and giving you the benefit of both selection and extra value if you act now."*

> *"We build communities that hold their value, and that includes establishing a pricing policy that permits early purchasers to share with us in the values we create as the dream becomes a reality."*

> *"The developers know that charter owners deserve to profit from improved values as we progress from one stage and neighborhood to another. After all, those who come early are willing to wait for the community to come together, while those who come later deserve to pay for the established benefits."*

> *"Each location in this community has been value indexed against established value points, and the prices you see reflect those differences. Some sites are*

*larger, others have variations in views, trees and similar distinguishing characteristics. That is why we can offer you this same floor plan or model priced from _____ and to _____.''*

*''We have experienced increases in construction costs that have not yet been reflected in our current pricing. However, as of __(date)__, the builder has scheduled a necessary increase to offset these additional expenditures.'' (Best to show proof of the date and amount of increase on builder stationery.)*

*''Each neighborhood (phase) of this community has been master planned for the protection of its own values. The developers believe in preserving and enhancing the values of the homes by seeing that all homes in one area are built in one sequenced schedule. Thus, your home has been priced as part of that phase, and you benefit from the economies of scale we achieve through our efficient construction systems.''*

## HOW TO DETERMINE THE BASE PRICE VERSUS THE PRICE WITH OPTIONS

One of the more important aspects of pricing is the matter of base-pricing strategies versus adding optional or up-grade selection items. Many factors should be taken into consideration before the final package is presented to the sales staff or the public. Value perceptions can be heavily influenced by the customer's expectations of what should normally be included in the basic price contrasted with the variables. Prior to making any of these decisions, the building enterprise should define its primary objectives and then be guided by those fundamental guidelines when approaching this assignment.

If the construction company is essentially a production-oriented merchant building enterprise, options and extras may be viewed as obstacles to the construction flow and, thus, not something to be encouraged. Conversely, if this is a custom building operation in which the total design process is an elective process (the ultimate option package), these areas of choice will be viewed as both necessary and desirable. Some companies look at options as ways to make additional profit (often substantial margins above normal building percentages), while others see them as roadblocks to the administration system that delay construction and increase overhead.

It is not a question of which philosophy is right. You can justify either approach depending on the nature of the company, the volume of building that must be managed at one time and the procedures proven most effective in preserving margins. However, it is a mistake to confuse objectives by trying to administer a large option package and still retain a fast-moving volume construction program where pricing has been based on competitive positioning. Marketing faces the challenge of trying to present the properties in a manner acceptable in terms of value perceptions and consumer understanding. Anything that confuses the prospects or forces them to make line-item comparisons with competing properties has a tendency to reduce sales effectiveness.

From the viewpoint of sales and ease of administration, the easiest way to sell any home is to be able to say to the prospective buyer:

*"The home is priced at $_____, and that includes all of the features you see. . . ."*

This is a positive approach to the presentation of the total values included in a model home or production spec. In economy housing, this is the normal pricing approach. Choices are usually limited to carpet colors and interior decor. The more expensive housing will usually feature a fairly wide selection of custom options, simply because buyers expect to be able to tailor the home to their individual specifications.

The following factors should be evaluated when determining what to include in a featured home or model and what should be treated as consumer options:

1. The competition's inclusions and options for comparable price ranges and housing types.
2. The ability of typically profiled buyers to qualify for the home with all proposed inclusions.
3. The potential for creating the perception of more value by including something the competition does not offer.
4. The expectations of potential buyers as related to their existing residences and the discontent motivators that may stimulate extra sales.
5. The relative ease of administering the options without adversely affecting construction operations.
6. The added profit margins that can be legitimately produced by featuring options rather than including these items in the total price.
7. The relative ease of selling the base-price home without including all options versus building them into the price and marketing the total package.

From a marketing viewpoint, we must always be concerned with anything that potentially creates confusion in the selling process. We must also avoid the credibility challenge of causing buyers to wonder what else we are hiding from them. If one expected item is not included the customers may start looking for other exceptions and become defensive about our marketing tactics.

The pricing strategies for inclusions versus options is not an area of decision making that should be casually approached. The consequences of the decisions will have a major impact on the consumer's perceptions of your housing values.

## THE ROLE OF BUYER FINANCING IN THE PRICING GAME

In recent years it has become standard practice for many builders to include take-out (permanent) financing costs in the original pricing quotes. This practice was rampant in the hectic markets of 1980 to early 1983 when interest rates were then at their all time high. Buy-downs, discounts for cash, prepaid closing and financing costs became popular tools to lessen the qualifying challenges and the resistance to such high rates. Many builders, especially those appealing to first-time buyers and the modest-priced housing markets, still use this procedure to soften the monthly investment costs and remain competitive with others who use financing as a primary buyer-attraction device. Changes in the guidelines used by underwriting agencies like

Fannie Mae and Ginnie Mae have limited the amount that a builder can agree to absorb into the price of a home to be financed through the secondary markets. Five or six percentage points is usually the maximum allowable amount.

When you are designing pricing strategies for your product line, the issue of financing should be evaluated and addressed. If the builder down the street with whom you are directly competing is paying five points for the mortgage buy-down to give his homes an interest-rate advantage, you have two primary alternatives:

1. Meet him head-on with a similar buy-down program and raise your prices to cover this added marketing cost or . . .
2. Do not include any costs of financing in your pricing and keep your prices five percent lower, which will reflect a lower per-square-foot cost comparison.

Which course of action you choose can have a dramatic effect (plus or minus) on your sales volume and your profit. In some situations the interest rate buy-down may be the wisest choice, because your buyers may have difficulty qualifying for the higher rate, when the monthly investments are the key factor in their decision-making process. In other cases, especially with more affluent buyers, the lower costs for comparable footage will be a significant advantage. Only an objective analysis and understanding of your market area should guide your ultimate pricing decisions.

One of the adverse by-products of increasing prices to offset heavy buy-downs is the inflated values this tends to create. Some markets in America (like Houston, Texas) suffered from a decrease of housing values as much as 15 to 20 percent or more in 1985 to 1986 because of the impact of local economics and the artificially high mortgage levels on homes sold in 1980 to 1983 when rates were 13 to 15 percent. When the market dropped to rates at ten percent or less, these older homes were almost impossible to sell or refinance without substantial losses. If you are building homes in an area where you will continue to complete in the marketplace for several years because of the size of the project or scope of your operations, there should be some concern for protecting resale values. If the homes you sold two or three years ago are either difficult to resell or have lost their value base, you will have created a marketing challenge for your new homes. That is why we believe that pricing strategies and product positioning is not a short-term game, unless you are in a parcel where you will be sold out and building elsewhere in the future.

## STRATEGIES FOR DISCLOSING PRICING INFORMATION TO PROSPECTS

Once you have decided on how you will price your homes, options and homesites, you need to evaluate how best to present your total pricing package to your customers. You have a wide variety of approaches to consider, and the way you handle the information will be important to your sales representatives' objectives.

One of your choices is to leave most of the control for communicating pricing information in the hands of the sales personnel. Instead of publishing a complete price list with all of the listed options, etc., you can elect to give the agents the advantage of disbursing these vital facts on a one-on-one basis as each prospect is introduced to the community and individual homes. Merely publishing a price range or ''priced from . . .'' can achieve this control objective. In custom housing operations that is a fairly normal marketing approach. After all, the exact price will depend upon what the prospect wants included in the home that will be custom tailored to personal motivations, abilities and needs.

On the other hand, your marketing strategy may be very straightforward and uncomplicated. If you have five models all prepriced with few, if any, variables, the prices might be boldly featured in your advertising, in the sales office and in hand-out price sheets given to prospects when they arrive. High-traffic projects often require this kind of marketing to simplify the sales process. There are times when this is the appropriate marketing scenario.

There is also the possible advantage of blending these two pricing systems into a plan that promotes basic prices and ranges but leaves the presentation of all variables to the sales representatives. Rather than provide a price list that contains all the information about the options and other selection areas, the information sheet merely covers the base prices and contains a disclaimer identifying a list of options available from the sales personnel.

A product line with a number of variables and difficult to understand without the guidance of sales representatives forces buyers to try to figure out all the details for themselves. Confusion and lack of appreciation for values are two major reasons sales that could have been made are lost. The most effective sales strategy is usually to leave as much control as possible with the sales counselor, so that the art of qualifying and value building can be combined to meet the specific interests of individual customers. Too much advance information can deny salespeople the opportunity even to get themselves into a position where they can counsel and close buyers.

Marketing strategies, to be effective, must complement sales strategies if they are to be successfully executed. The on-site presentations should be taken into consideration when designing collateral aids that will be used to communicate product and pricing information to prospective home buyers. For example, if salespeople are forced to give customers all housing facts and pricing details in a complete brochure at the front door of the sales office, they lose control of the presentation elements. The customers now have in hand the answers (they believe) to what they came to learn, and they do not need to talk to the agents or ask questions. They can look at the models, read the price lists and study the literature. If they discover anything they do not like or believe fits their needs, they will leave without a face-to-face selling involvement with the builder's representative.

Let's take the example of a prepriced merchant builder's model home that has a base price of $98,500. But the home is shown with 16 options the way it has been constructed in the sales environment. How should the salespeople handle this pricing challenge? Do they try to explain every item that does not come with the base-priced home—all 16? Do they give buyers a price list and show all the options with prices beside each of them, which the customers can try to inspect and add up as they tour the model? Should they go with every customer and point out all the nonincluded items in a demonstration process? Or perhaps they should quote the model with everything in it and not try to explain the options that can be deleted from that price until after the inspection has been completed.

These are fundamental considerations in trying to develop sales strategies that work. If the salesperson says to the buyer:

*"The Barony model has a base price of $98,500, but the model shows many designer items that are optional additions. . . ."*

Has that agent added to the potential confusion of the prospect? Will the customer spend valuable time trying to figure out what comes with the home at the expense of the time that should be used to obtain emotional involvement with the living benefits of the floor plan and designs? Sales presentations make or break sales opportunities. Information alone does not sell property. We can never afford to lose sight of the fact that most people buy on emotion and justify with facts, not the reverse! Providing credible pricing data that is easy to understand is an essential part of the presentation process, but the question is when and how? The point we want to emphasize here is simply: Do not confuse production-pricing needs with the presentation-control needs of your front-line sales personnel!

## HOW TO HANDLE THE PRESENTATION OF OPTIONS AND EXTRAS

Every new home salesperson who has ever presented a product line that contained a wide variety of options, upgrades and extras knows the challenges of correctly handling the smorgasbord menu of variables without losing control of the customer. There is always the possibility of confusing customers by too many choices. There is the risk that individual items on the list may become issues and divert attention from the major objective of completing the sale. In this section, we will share some observations about various strategies for handling the presentation of options and selection choices in new home marketing.

### Physical Location of the Choices

It has been our experience that options, selection boards and other variables in the decision-making process are best located in an area of the office or model environment that does not conflict with the major presentation objectives of the sales representatives. If such items are visible in the greeting area where salespeople need to welcome and initially qualify prospective buyers, they are likely to become obstacles rather than sales tools. If they are prematurely discovered or discussed, they can divert attention from the early objective of providing an overview to the community and the housing environment. The sales presentation process has a logical sequence. A logical qualifying procedure should also precede involvement with specific floor plans, designs and optional selection items. Prospects tends to gravitate to displays that interest them, and if the color boards, carpet samples and tile choices are visible and accessible at the entry to the sales arena, they frequently divert the presentation sequence.

Most salespeople, if given their choice, elect to place these color-selection boards, up-grades, decorator items and optional features in controlled locations, where they can, at their election and timing, introduce them to prospects. An independent design-counseling room can be an effective sales tool. If isolated from the principle selling environment, it permits purchasers to spend time at their own convenience making their choices without taking the valuable time of sales representatives or bothering other buyers. If a specialist in the field of interior design is available to meet with buyers by appointment following confirmation of sales, this is one of the very best ways to control the selection process.

A basic rule that should not be violated is to be sure that nothing is displayed in the primary sales arena that might adversely affect sales. For example, if you show fireplace options, cabinetry, tiles, etc., that are not available on all models or only applicable if specified early in the construction sequence, these visual displays may encourage prospects to ask for things they cannot have. It is also possible to price the buyers out of the market. If they want more than they can afford, it becomes psychologically difficult to delete the up-grades they have seen and picture owning.

We believe that it is always in the best interests of the building enterprise to organize the sales office in a way that permits the sales representatives to completely control the presentation. Anything that detracts from the qualifying and value-building decision track should be repositioned or eliminated. This includes options and extras that are variables for specific homes and price ranges. Isolating them so that they are only introduced when appropriate to the sales process is often the very best approach.

## IDENTIFYING THE NONINCLUDED EXTRAS IN MODELS

Although we must unquestionably alert our customers to the up-grades and options displayed in model homes so that we will avoid misunderstandings, it is also important not to confuse them during the inspection process. A number of accepted ways exist to handle this marketing issue. Conflicting objectives must also be weighed when making marketing decisions on how, where and when to introduce optional features and discretionary choices. Let's review some of your options in presenting these selection variables.

### Identifying Each Item in the Display Model

Some builders prefer to have every optional feature clearly marked in their models at a spot directly related to each item. The term *optional feature* is often used as the means of marking these additions to the published price. That term is certainly preferable to *not included*! In high-traffic sales operations where prospects visit the models without salespeople to point out the features and benefits, there is some merit to this means of identifying items not included in the published base price list. However, the disadvantage exists of drawing undue attention to these items that do not come with the home, rather than focusing on the positives of those that are included.

Marketers agree that, if you are going to identify each nonincluded option at the exact spot where it is featured in the model, you should make the display message as unobtrusive as possible. Attractive plastic markers no more than an inch or so wide and two or three inches long are preferable to show cards that shout at the visiting prospects. Always prevent the model from feeling like a museum. If your customers spend their time reading show cards and information about the home rather than picturing the living benefits that might emotionally induce them to purchase, you have lost the primary objective for which models are created.

## Providing One Summary Display that Identifies All Options

The most practical method of handling options and up-grades in models where salespeople are not in attendance at inspection is the use of an attractive summary display element that identifies all items that are shown but not included in the base price. The preferred method of providing this identification is having a graphics specialist imprint the message on acrylic (usually transparent) display stands. These are fairly attractive and do not detract from the decor and presentation values of the model. Normally, it is necessary to have only one of these in prominent position in each model to cover the liability factors of posting consumers about pricing variations.

## Price-Sheet Hand-Outs That Identify Optional Choices for Model

Many marketers in this industry elect to handle the matter of options, extras, up-grades and other variables by use of a printed hand-out sheet given to each prospect before visiting the models. If the information is complete and easy to interpret, this procedure will probably meet the requirements of consumer-protection policies. This approach resolves the problems of trying to mark every item in each home. It permits the decorator to create the physical and psychological moods so important to portraying the living benefits of each design without having to be concerned for the labeling of non-included items. The disclaimer for decorator items that are not part of the home or options may have to be covered by a special display piece, but even that can be handled on the introductory sheet given to customers prior to model inspection.

## Showing Models with a Sales Representative Always Present

The remaining choice is to control all model home presentations by having prospects escorted by well-trained sales counselors who provide information about what is and is not included in the pricing program. Where there is limited traffic and you can obtain this kind of control, it is obviously the best procedure for meeting sales objectives. Demonstrating the benefits of a model to a prospective buyer is the best way to validate value statements. It is also the most effective way of qualifying and counseling prospects. Luxury housing communities often use this VIP approach. Condominium buildings, which have a need to protect the security of the environment, will frequently employ this mandatory showing procedure. Experience has shown that this is the most effective way to obtain a high closing ratio to exposed traffic and is well worth considering whenever the presentation criteria permits.

## HOW MUCH INFORMATION SHOULD BE GIVEN TO THE PROSPECT— AND WHEN?

We know that home buyers can easily become confused when they have too many things to think about at one time. If the list of choices is long and complex, it adds to the decision-making time. More important, it can delay or prevent a decision, because it forces the prospective buyer to weigh so many items that the sheer volume of information to be processed through the human computer (the mind) throws it into a no-decision mode. While there is merit in some product lines, especially custom-housing communities, for providing a wide selection of optional choices, the attendant risk of confusion should never be underestimated.

Salespeople know that the easiest way to sell any home is to show it to a qualified buyer and be able to say:

*"Everything you see is included in the price . . . !"* Or; *"With the exception of the decorator furnishings, the home will include all of the features you see. . . ."*

The most difficult position is usually the one where the agent has to explain away what does not come with the home! Worse yet, are questions where the salesperson must say no.

*"Does that come with the home?"* *"No."*

*"Does this come with the home?"* *"No."*

. . . and after three or more of these negative responses the customer is in a negative mood and the sales representative in a defensive posture.

The objective should be to provide the prospect with a very positive, value-building presentation that emphasizes what is included, thus minimizing the add-ons.

*"Your new home comes with all of these fine features. . . ."*

Executives who decide what they will ask for each model and what items will or will not be included in the asking price should give careful consideration to the sales psychology involved in the prospect's decision-making process. Too many choices can be detrimental to the sales track. Too few can be noncompetitive and perceived as arbitrary. The balancing act should take into consideration the expectations of profiled prospects, the competition, the value of each proposed option as related to total demand and the economics of administering the production system. Having no options may be as big an obstacle to sales as having too many.

## THE DIFFERENCE BETWEEN STANDARD AND NONSTANDARD OPTIONS

It is often wise to separate your options into two categories:

1. Items promoted and presented to all prospects
2. Items only introduced when specifically requested or needed

Options and customer-selection items that are in high demand for the type and price range of the housing you offer certainly merit promotion. Others that are only occasionally needed to meet a limited market profile might best be handled by not publishing them in the hand-out literature or displaying them in the models. The determination of what is logical to feature and what should be kept in a separate pricing binder for use on special occasions should be dictated by demand and competitive positioning. One guideline used by many builder/marketers is to feature only those options that will have at least a 50 percent use factor. All others that may be necessary for smaller percentages of the marketplace will be kept in a sales-controlled option binder for selective use. This is sound strategy. It helps to keep the number of options and up-grades within controllable ranges and eliminates much of the confusion that can otherwise be generated when there is a complete catalogue of choices given to every prospect.

## HOW TO MARKET AND PRESENT A MODEL THAT INCLUDES NUMEROUS OPTIONS

Most new home sales specialists will agree that one of the more difficult challenges of working with builder models is trying to present one that seems to have almost everything in it as an optional item. If the list of displayed variables exceeds five to seven, the sales representative has the dilemma of trying to index everything not included or generalizing, both of which can lead to misunderstandings. If the prospect cannot look at the home and quickly understand what is included with the quoted or published price, the resulting confusion is often so counterproductive to the sales process that everyone loses!

Ideally, the model can be shown and quoted with the majority of all displayed physical real estate elements included in the stated price. Exceptions can then be easily addressed with a covering statement like:

> *"The Cypress model includes all of the luxury features you will see with the minor exception of the wall coverings, mirrors, and up-graded carpets."*

If, on the other hand, the model contains a long shopping list of displayed extras, it is far better to quote the home from the top down than from the bottom up. For example, the agent might say:

> *"The price of this model is $149,000, but that does not include many of the displayed features such as. . . ."*

The sales representative is now forced to either explain each item that does not come with the home or answer the questions of the prospect as he or she views the property. The silent cards do not help when you have an extensive selection list. We have found that it is best in these cases to quote from the higher figure and work to the lower one:

> *"This is a designer model with a number of selection features that you can include or eliminate at your option. As you see it, the home is priced at $161,000, with the exception of only the furnishings and wall coverings. The home can also be purchased for as little as $149,000. The differences are personal choices that you can tailor to your own desires."*

At that point, the sales representative can either identify the electives or wait until the home has been inspected and then use them as involvement and potential closing tools.

There is a large risk in showing a model that has a major structural difference from the homes produced in the field! Few things are more irritating or challenging to salespeople than trying to explain a model that is not built in the production system the way it is shown in the model area! Minor adjustments can be handled, but major ones are real sales obstacles! An example would be showing a home with a vaulted ceiling when only a conventional ceiling is offered in production. Another would be changing the shape of a room so that the actual inventory is totally different than the model. We recommend closing models that do not meet the inventory pattern and having the salespeople work with production housing if that is the only alternative.

## MAKE IT EASY FOR YOUR CUSTOMERS TO MAKE A DECISION!

The bottom line from a sales perspective is to be aware that, in all marketing decisions concerning the handling of options and decorator items, you should make it easy for people to understand what you are selling. Present it in a manner that makes it relatively easy for them to make positive decisions. If it is confusing to your prospects, it will cost you sales volume! If it is confusing to your sales representatives, it will certainly be confusing to your buyers!

The primary objective is to sell the home and the homesite, not to focus on minor variables that people may want to consider once they have made the larger decision. If you get them off the track when they enter the sales arena by the way you quote and present your selection package, the result will be lost sales!

The basic game plan in this business is to create and communicate housing values that will stimulate your profiled prospects to action!

## HOW TO PREPARE A WRITTEN MARKETING PLAN AND BUDGET

The preparation of a written marketing plan and a supporting budget is either the responsibility of the director of marketing or of the administrative team. When an outside contract brokerage company has total responsibility for marketing, this function should be performed by the builder's account representative or the marketing committee, which includes the brokerage advisors. Trying to operate a multimillion-dollar sales program without a well-defined and documented game plan is like trying to fly a plane without filing a flight plan or having a charted course.

In its simplest form, a marketing plan is a digest of seven key decision-influencing topics, including a preliminary marketing budget. In its most refined form, it is a detailed road map that covers every aspect of anticipated marketing strategies from land acquisition through final clean-up phases. Brokers who specialize in new home sales can separate themselves from the average residential resale agencies by providing thoughtfully prepared marketing plans for each of their builder/developer clients. The in-house marketing manager certainly needs the knowledge and skills to generate and communicate the pro forma on which the sales success and profitability of the building venture is dependent.

The seven major topics typically addressed in a new home marketing plan are:

1. *The property and development objectives.* This identifies the subject property (proposed or already acquired) as related to its geographical location and the market areas it may serve. It also states the objectives of the principals and marketing team. When specific products and development programs have already been formulated, the written plan will acknowledge these conclusions and list all issues and opportunities that will affect marketing objectives. If one purpose of the document is to establish product criteria, the broader spectrum of opportunities will be pursued with the objective of providing specific recommendations for management's consideration. Site maps and orientation exhibits are normally included in this section of the report.

2. *The economy and basic housing demand factors.* This portion of the business plan provides an analysis of the current and projected demand for housing within the market region, usually segmented by housing type, price range and buyer profiles. If a researcher has been employed to prepare a separate feasibility study, that document is appropriately referenced and/or summarized. Topics included usually begin with a review of the economic stability, growth and future of the area. The general demographics (population characteristics) are identified. This leads to an analysis of housing demand factors, market segmentation, household income, housing supply and overall housing absorption rates by categories.

3. *The competition and recommended product positioning.* The analysis of projects and properties now that are (or will soon be) competing for the same targeted prospects is a key segment of the total marketing plan. Detailed summaries with comparative value-index forms should be included for those products directly competitive in price, type and buyer profiles. Matching this information with the general market analysis in section two provides the basis for specific product-development guidelines positioned to attract well-identified buyer types. Recommendations on floor plans, inclusions, options, pricing and presentation should be covered in this section.

4. *Absorption rates and projected sales pro forma.* Having defined the general market, the competition and the specific opportunities for product development and presentation, the marketing plan should next provide projections for penetrating the available housing demand at this particular site. The factors that affect development and delivery of the housing units must be addressed before the numbers can be realistically interpreted. This is where the marketing experts put themselves on record as being able to achieve a certain sales pace, annual absorption rate and net number of closed transactions within the time frames set forth in the first section.

5. *Proposed marketing strategies.* The projections in section four should now be supported by a definitive plan for reaching the profiled buyers in sufficient quantity to assure a conversion rate that will fulfill anticipated closings. Whether or not to have models, employ a preconstruction sales plan, establish a broker network, develop major media campaigns, etc., are detailed in this portion of the marketing game plan. These are topics that we will extensively explore in the remaining chapters of this book. This is the heart of the marketing scenario, and it is in the success of these strategies

that marketing management will be judged. The subjects of phasing, creating urgency through inventory control, targeting to the motivations of identified customers, as well as the selection, staffing assignments and training of the sales personnel are vital ingredients in the success of these marketing strategies.

6. *Preliminary marketing budget.* The pro forma ultimately must be translated into a budget: the projected costs for accomplishing marketing objectives as identified in the first five sections of the report. Those in charge of marketing should be willing to commit themselves to a plan that includes projected sales, closings and marketing costs. A wide variety of forms and formats are employed by professional new home marketers for documenting these figures. We are including two examples in this chapter. Figure 3.6 begins with a special analysis for model construction, decorating, landscaping and administrative costs amortized over the life of the project. Figure 3.7 was provided courtesy of Development Directions, Inc. of Rochester, Minnesota. It is an actual preliminary plan prepared for Calia Development Corporation of Barrington, Illinois for a proposed project known as "Fox Trails." It was used as an estimate in the early stages of finalizing a comprehensive marketing program.

7. *Summary and conclusions.* The marketing document normally begins or ends with a summary of the recommendations and conclusions contained in the report. This section is also used to establish broad criteria and disclaimers for changes in the economy and the general marketplace. It is the appropriate place to identify the people who will be involved in executing the marketing plan, along with time-frame estimates and assignments. The inclusions of a CPM chart (Critical Path Management graphic) is a helpful visual tool for illustrating the time-line relationships of various activities and expenditures.

The final exhibit in this chapter was provided courtesy of the Grupe Development Company of Stockton, California (a major residential developer in the western states) and Herbert L. Aist and Associates, of Calabasas, California (a professional real estate research organization). This is an example of a total financial analysis developed from a recommended housing program for a specific project. This type of detailed pro forma is the ultimate objective of a complete marketing plan.

## PLANNING AND BUDGETING ARE HALLMARKS OF MARKETING PROFESSIONALS

The ability to analyze the marketplace and interpret the reactions of prospects to competitive housing programs is a valuable skill. It is gained from experience more than intuition. Marketing directors who have attained national recognition among their peers have all cultivated their interpretive talents. Even more important is their ability to plan and execute cost-effective marketing strategies. As participants in the decision-influencing processes, they learn from other pros and try new approaches, when needed, to attain sales projections. Planning is the best insurance for avoiding failures. The long list of ingredients that can affect your sales and profits is not something you can readily commit to memory, no matter how good your recall may be! It is the consistent use of proven checklists, continual research and monitoring that ultimately win the game! With so much at stake, attention to the smallest marketing details is well justified! If you are responsible for organizing marketing strategies for your company or clients, you need to consistently attend to the details that make the difference!

---

**FIGURE 3.5   Contents of Marketing Plan**

| ITEM | DESCRIPTION |
|---|---|
| 1. Table of Contents | Subjects covered in plan and where to find them. |
| 2. Introduction | Purpose and uses of plan. |
| 3. Executive Digest | Summary of major provisions of plan. |
| 4. Company Mission, Scope and Goals | Nature of business (markets) and product lines; contribution to corporate purpose; company profile; capabilities; where company wants to go. |
| 5. Situation Analysis | Facts and assumptions on which plan is based. |
| Assumptions | Report on economy, environment, politics, social, technological and competitive factors. |
| Company Resources | Key personnel, talents, resources, capabilities and techniques. |
| Market Potentials/ Forecasts/Facts | Quantitative and qualitative information on size (dollars & units) of each market, growth rates, customer profiles, customer wants, needs and attitudes. |
| Market Share | Company share of total industry sales. |
| Sales History | Sales over past 3–5 years in each market; current position vs. previous years' objectives. |
| Sales, Expense and Profit Forecasts | Product line—volume—profit-investment forecasts. |
| Current & New Opportunities | High potential markets and products. |
| 6. Current Marketing Organization | Structure and purpose; lines of authority; responsibilities. |
| 7. Marketing Objectives | Results to be produced and where you want to be next year (and future years). |
| 8. Marketing Strategies, Policies, Procedures | General courses of action to reach objectives. |
| 9. Marketing Programs | Specific courses of action (tactics) with respect to sales, service, promotion, advertising, pricing, distribution, marketing research, and product planning and development. |
| 10. Schedules/Assignments | Who does what, where, how and when (milestones). |
| 11. Personnel Plan | Availability and needs. |
| 12. Budgets | Required resources, costs and risks. |
| 13. Pro forma P&L Balance Sheet | Accounting statements from controller. |
| 14. Controls | Procedure for measuring and controlling progress of planned actions. |
| 15. Continuity | Procedures for keeping plan updated. |

## FIGURE 3.6 Marketing-Budget Forms

Divisions: _____
Building Partnership: _____
Prepared by: _____ Date: _____

**MARKETING BUDGET**

Tract: _____
Opening Date: _____
Projected Sellout Time: _____

Total Dollar Sales: _____
Average Sales Price: _____
No. of Houses: _____

| Account Number | Month | Month | Month | Month | Month | Month | Month | Month | Month | Month | Month | Month |
|---|---|---|---|---|---|---|---|---|---|---|---|---|
| Model Homes Expense—Total | | | | | | | | | | | | |
| Model Homes—Utilities | | | | | | | | | | | | |
| Insurance on Models and Contents | | | | | | | | | | | | |
| Model Home Gardening Expense | | | | | | | | | | | | |
| Model Home Cleaning Expense | | | | | | | | | | | | |
| Music in Models | | | | | | | | | | | | |
| Model Furnishings Replacement Expense | | | | | | | | | | | | |
| Model Home Expense—Other | | | | | | | | | | | | |
| Closing Costs—Total (From 4A of 5) | | | | | | | | | | | | |
| Transportation, Entertainment and Subsistence—Total | | | | | | | | | | | | |
| Travel | | | | | | | | | | | | |
| Entertainment | | | | | | | | | | | | |
| Subsistence | | | | | | | | | | | | |
| Automobile Expense | | | | | | | | | | | | |
| Professional Fees—Total | | | | | | | | | | | | |
| Consultant | | | | | | | | | | | | |
| Market Research | | | | | | | | | | | | |

## FIGURE 3.6   Marketing-Budget Forms (continued)

Divisions: _____
Building Partnership: _____
Prepared by: _____   Date: ____

MARKETING BUDGET

Tract: _____
Opening Date: _____
Projected Sellout Time: _____

Total Dollar Sales: _____
Average Sales Price: _____
No. of Houses: _____

| Account Number | | Month | Month | Month | Month | Month | Month | Month | Month | Month | Month | Month | Month |
|---|---|---|---|---|---|---|---|---|---|---|---|---|---|
| | Miscellaneous Selling Expense—Total | | | | | | | | | | | | |
| | Sales Training and Seminars | | | | | | | | | | | | |
| | Dues and Subscriptions | | | | | | | | | | | | |
| | Miscellaneous Selling Expense | | | | | | | | | | | | |
| | | | | | | | | | | | | | |
| | Total Expenses | | | | | | | | | | | | |
| | Grand Total Model Home and Marketing Expense | | | | | | | | | | | | |
| | | | | | | | | | | | | | |
| | Promotion—Total | | | | | | | | | | | | |
| | Sales Displays | | | | | | | | | | | | |
| | Giveaways | | | | | | | | | | | | |
| | Buyer—Motel Bills | | | | | | | | | | | | |
| | Home Shows | | | | | | | | | | | | |
| | Referrals | | | | | | | | | | | | |
| | Sales Promotion Contest | | | | | | | | | | | | |
| | Promotion—Other | | | | | | | | | | | | |

**FIGURE 3.6  Marketing-Budget Forms (continued)**

Divisions: _____

Building Partnership: _____

Prepared by: _____  Date: _____

MARKETING BUDGET

Tract: _____

Opening Date: _____

Projected Sellout Time: _____

Total Dollar Sales: _____

Average Sales Price: _____

No. of Houses: _____

| Account Number | | Month | Month | Month | Month | Month | Month | Month | Month | Month | Month | Month | Month |
|---|---|---|---|---|---|---|---|---|---|---|---|---|---|
| | Sales Office Expense—Total | | | | | | | | | | | | |
| | Sales Trailer | | | | | | | | | | | | |
| | Sales Office Supplies | | | | | | | | | | | | |
| | Credit Reports | | | | | | | | | | | | |
| | Photostats, Picture & Blueprint | | | | | | | | | | | | |
| | Utilities (if separate from models) | | | | | | | | | | | | |
| | Telephone | | | | | | | | | | | | |
| | Sales Office Expense—Other | | | | | | | | | | | | |
| | | | | | | | | | | | | | |
| | | | | | | | | | | | | | |
| | | | | | | | | | | | | | |
| | | | | | | | | | | | | | |
| | | | | | | | | | | | | | |
| | | | | | | | | | | | | | |
| | EXPENSES | | | | | | | | | | | | |
| | Salaries, Commissions, and Related | | | | | | | | | | | | |
| | Payroll Costs—Total | | | | | | | | | | | | |
| | Salaries—Sales | | | | | | | | | | | | |
| | Commissions—Sales | | | | | | | | | | | | |

**FIGURE 3.6    Marketing-Budget Forms (continued)**

Divisions: _____
Building Partnership: _____
Prepared by: _____ Date: _____

MARKETING BUDGET

Tract: _____
Opening Date: _____
Projected Sellout Time: _____

Total Dollar Sales: _____
Average Sales Price: _____
No. of Houses: _____

| Account Number | | Month | Month | Month | Month | Month | Month | Month | Month | Month | Month | Month | Month |
|---|---|---|---|---|---|---|---|---|---|---|---|---|---|
| | Salaries—Model Clean and Landscaped | | | | | | | | | | | | |
| | Salaries—Bonuses | | | | | | | | | | | | |
| | Salaries—Other | | | | | | | | | | | | |
| | Commissions—Outside Brokers | | | | | | | | | | | | |
| | Payroll Taxes | | | | | | | | | | | | |
| | Compensation Insurance | | | | | | | | | | | | |
| | Health Insurance | | | | | | | | | | | | |
| | | | | | | | | | | | | | |
| | | | | | | | | | | | | | |
| | | | | | | | | | | | | | |
| | | | | | | | | | | | | | |
| | Advertising—Total | | | | | | | | | | | | |
| | Advertising—Newspapers | | | | | | | | | | | | |
| | Advertising—Radio & Television | | | | | | | | | | | | |
| | Advertising Agency Fee | | | | | | | | | | | | |
| | Advertising—Direct Mail | | | | | | | | | | | | |
| | Advertising—Other | | | | | | | | | | | | |
| | Brochures | | | | | | | | | | | | |
| | Sign Rental and Leasing Fees | | | | | | | | | | | | |
| | Signs Expense—Erection & Maintenance | | | | | | | | | | | | |
| | Public Relations | | | | | | | | | | | | |

## FIGURE 3.6 Marketing-Budget Forms (continued)

PROJECT REPORT—MARKETING

Divisions: _____
Building Partnership: _____
Prepared by: _____

Tract: _____
No. of Houses: _____
Date: _____

| | Month Ended: | | | Tract to Date | | | Projected for Tract | | | |
|---|---|---|---|---|---|---|---|---|---|---|
| | Actual | Variance | % Var. | Actual | Variance | % Var. | Total | Variance | % Var. | |
| Model Home Complex Costs: | | | | | | | | | | |
| Model Home Land Acquisition, Carrying and Improvement | | | | | | | | | | |
| Model Home Hard Construction Costs | | | | | | | | | | |
| Model Home Job Overhead | | | | | | | | | | |
| Model Home Landscaping | | | | | | | | | | |
| Model Home Decorating Fee | | | | | | | | | | |
| Alterations Before Selling Models | | | | | | | | | | |
| Total Model Homes | | | | | | | | | | |
| Less: Sales Price—Gross | | | | | | | | | | |
| Add: Sales Commission | | | | | | | | | | |
| Closing Costs | | | | | | | | | | |
| Discount and Loan Expense | | | | | | | | | | |
| Subtotal | | | | | | | | | | |
| Furniture for Models | | | | | | | | | | |
| Less Resale | | | | | | | | | | |
| Subtotal | | | | | | | | | | |
| Sales Office Hard Construction Costs | | | | | | | | | | |
| Less Resale | | | | | | | | | | |
| Subtotal | | | | | | | | | | |

# FIGURE 3.6  Marketing-Budget Forms (concluded)

PROJECT REPORT—MARKETING

Divisions: _____
Building Partnership: _____
Prepared by: _____

Tract: _____
No. of Houses: _____
Date: _____

| | Month Ended: | | Tract to Date | | | Projected for Tract | | | |
|---|---|---|---|---|---|---|---|---|---|
| | Actual | Variance | % Var. | Actual | Variance | % Var. | Total | Variance | % Var. |
| Construction and Land Improvement Loan Expense | | | | | | | | | |
| Loan Interest on Model Furnishings | | | | | | | | | |
| Marketing Allocation—Models | | | | | | | | | |
| Administrative Allocation—Models | | | | | | | | | |
| Customer Service Allocation—Models | | | | | | | | | |
| Total Model Home Complex Costs | | | | | | | | | |

---

**FIGURE 3.7   Preliminary Plan**

## GENERAL MARKETING RECOMMENDATIONS AND BUDGETS

The following chart diagrams our recommended approach to creating a sound and successful development team and new residential community.

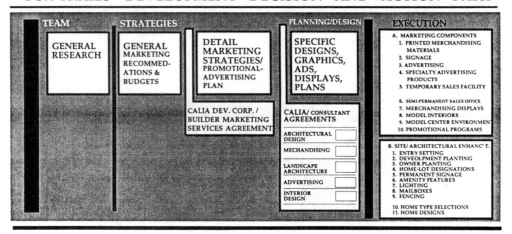

"FOX TRAILS" DEVELOPMENT DECISION AND ACTION PATH

| TEAM | STRATEGIES | | PLANNING/DESIGN | EXECUTION |
|------|-----------|---|-----------------|-----------|
| GENERAL RESEARCH | GENERAL MARKETING RECOMMEDATIONS & BUDGETS | DETAIL MARKETING STRATEGIES/ PROMOTIONAL- ADVERTISING PLAN | SPECIFIC DESIGNS, GRAPHICS, ADS, DISPLAYS, PLANS | A. MARKETING COMPONENTS<br>1. PRINTED MERCHANDISING MATERIALS<br>2. SIGNAGE<br>3. ADVERTISING<br>4. SPECIALTY ADVERTISING PRODUCTS<br>5. TEMPORARY SALES FACILITY |
| | | CALIA DEV. CORP. / BUILDER MARKETING SERVICES AGREEMENT | CALIA/ CONSULTANT AGREEMENTS | 6. SEMI-PERMANENT SALES OFFICE<br>7. MERCHANDISING DISPLAYS<br>8. MODEL INTERIORS<br>9. MODEL CENTER ENVIRONMEN<br>10. PROMOTIONAL PROGRAMS |
| | | | ARCHITECTURAL DESIGN | |
| | | | MECHANDISING | B. SITE/ ARCHITECTURAL ENHANC T.<br>1. ENTRY SETTING<br>2. DEVELOPMENT PLANTING<br>3. OWNER PLANTING<br>4. HOME-LOT DESIGNATIONS<br>5. PERMANENT SIGNAGE<br>6. AMENITY FEATURES<br>7. LIGHTING<br>8. MAILBOXES<br>9. FENCING |
| | | | LANDSCAPE ARCHITECTURE | |
| | | | ADVERTISING | |
| | | | INTERIOR DESIGN | 10. HOME TYPE SELECTIONS<br>11. HOME DESIGNS |

## I. GENERAL COMMENTARY & STRATEGIES.

For the purposes of this series of guidelines, the word "marketing" is used as an umbrella term, under which are placed all tasks and categories such as marketing management, collateral advertising materials, merchandising, displays, promotion and print, signage and media advertising.

MARKETING BUDGET:  Budgets for these items (exclusive of marketing management, sales management and sales commissions) typically range from $1\frac{1}{8}$ to $2\frac{1}{8}$ of sales price.

**FIGURE 3.7   Preliminary Plan (continued)**

DEVELOPMENT DIRECTIONS, INC.   UNIFIED COMMUNITY MARKETING TASKS & TOOLS...a ☑ checklist & budget worksheet

Disciplines / Category / Specific Tools

LAND
- ☐ DEVELOPMENT
  - ☐ LAND PLANNING
  - ☐ LANDSCAPE ARCHITECTURE
  - ☐ CIVIL ENGINEERING
- ☐ RESEARCH
- ☐ MARKETING PLAN

MARKETING
- ☐ SALES
- ☐ BUILDING
  - ☐ GRAPHIC DESIGN
  - ☐ ADVERTISING
  - ☐ MERCHANDISING
  - ☐ PROMOTIONS

BUILDING
- ☐ ARCHITECTURAL DESIGN
- ☐ BUILDING PLANS, DETAILS & SPECS
- ☐ INTERIOR DESIGN/MERCHANDISING

Development Component/Permanent Site Amenities; Permanent Signage & Features; Temporary Signage; Collateral Advertising Material; Merchandising Displays; Advertising & Promotion; Sales Facilities; Home & Building Design

Notes & Calculations

budget total →

© 1988 Development Directions, Inc./ Putman & Co., Rochester, MN

# FIGURE 3.7 Preliminary Plan (continued)

| III. MARKETING TOOLS INVENTORY AND BUDGETS | ESTIMATED CONSULTATION FEES AND EXPENSES | PRODUCTION/PRINTING/CONSTRUCTION/INSTALLATION COST ESTIMATE | | | SELECTED AMOUNT |
|---|---|---|---|---|---|
| | | GOOD | BETTER | BEST | |
| A. MARKETING COMPONENTS | | | | | |
| 1. MARKETING STRATEGIES | | | | | |
| a. DEVELOPMENT/MARKETING PLAN | | | | — | |
| b. PROJECT MARKETING THEME | | | | — | INCLUDED WITHIN B.M.S. 3% CAMMN. |
| c. DETAIL ADVERTISING/PROMOTIONAL PLAN & SPREAD SHEET BUDGET | | | | — | |
| 2. PRINTED MERCHANDISING MATERIALS | | | | | |
| a. THEME ADAPTATION - GRAPHIC IDENTITY | $650-1250 | $650. | $750 | 1250 | |
| b. ILLUSTRATION ART WORK | $700/PLAN 245/BROCH. (220/KIT.EXT.) 360, 375, 245 | | | | |
| 1) HOME FLOOR PLAN | | | | | |
| 2) HOME EXTERIOR PERSPECTIVES | | | | | |
| 3) INTERIOR PERSPECTIVES | | | | | |
| 4) SITE PLAN ART | | $3800 | $5200 | 640 | |
| 5) SITE ENTRY/AMENITY ILLUSTRATIONS | | | | | |
| c. PHOTOGRAPHY | | | | | |
| 1) MODEL HOMES PURCHASE | | $1,000 | $7200 | $5400 | |
| 2) SITE PURCHASE | | | | | |
| 3) LIFESTYLE | | | | | |
| d. BROCHURES | | $4600. | $12,000. | $8,750 | |
| e. BROCHURE INSERTS | | $2000 | $4,700. | $2,500 | |
| f. FOLDER/HANDOUTS | | $2,500 | $5,100 | $3,500 | |
| g. DIRECT MAIL | | $3000 | $11,000 | $20,000 | |
| h. NEWSLETTER | | $6700 | $5,820 | $9,000 | |
| TOTAL PRINTED MERCHANDISING MATERIALS ESTIMATES | | 25,000 | 50,000 | 75,000 | |
| 3. SIGNAGE | $2650.00 | | | | |
| a. DESIGNS, PLANS, SPECS | | | | | |
| b. BILLBOARDS | | | | | |
| c. DIRECTIONAL SIGNS | | | | | |
| d. LEADER OR "BANDIT" SIGNS | | | | | |
| e. TELEPHONE POLE DIRECTIONAL SIGNS | | | | | |
| f. SALES SIGN(S) AT PROJECT ENTRY(IES) SIGNS | | | | | |
| g. LOT CORNER SIGNS | | | | | |
| h. AMENITY LOCATION SIGNS | | | | | |
| i. INFORMATION CENTER DIRECTIONAL SIGNS | | | | | |
| j. INFORMATION CENTER SIGN | | | | | |
| k. PHASE/LOT AND ORIENTATION SIGNS | | | | | |
| l. MODEL HOME NAME IDENTIFICATION SIGNS | | | | | |
| m. MODEL HOME DIRECTIONAL SIGNS | | | | | |
| TOTAL SIGNS COST ESTIMATES | | 13,900 | 24,300 | $3,600 | |

## FIGURE 3.7 Preliminary Plan (continued)

| III. MARKETING TOOLS INVENTORY AND BUDGETS. | CONSULTATION FEES AND EXPENSES | PRODUCTION/PRINTING/CONSTRUCTION/INSTALLATION COST ESTIMATE NOTES/QUANTITIES | AVG. | BETTER | BEST | SELECTED AMOUNT |
|---|---|---|---|---|---|---|
| 4. ADVERTISING | | | | | | |
| a. NEWSPAPER | | | | | | |
| b. MAGAZINES | | | | | | |
| c. AIRPORT | | | | | | |
| d. OTHER | | | | | | |
| e. AGENCY - CREATIVE PRODUCTION | | | | | | |
| TOTAL ADVERTISING ESTIMATES | | | $11,000 Yr. | $24,000 | $36,000/yr | |
| 5. SPECIALTY ADVERTISING PRODUCTS | | | | | | |
| a. MUGS | | | | | | |
| b. RULERS | | | | | | |
| c. TOTE BAGS | | | | | | |
| d. PAPER PADS | | | | | | |
| e. BALLOONS | | | | | | |
| TOTAL SPECIALTY ADVERTISING PRODUCTS ESTIMATES | | | | $11,000. | | |
| 6. TEMPORARY SALES FACILITY (TRAILER) | | | | | | |
| a. PLANNING, LAYOUT DISPLAY DESIGN | $1,625. | | | 1,625 | | |
| b. INTERIOR DECORATOR | $500-1000 | | | 500-1000 | | |
| c. PERMITS | | ? | ? | | | |
| d. TRAILER | | | | $7,000 | | |
| e. SITE PREPARATION HOOK UP | | | | $1,500 | | |
| f. PARKING | | | 500 | $400 | 2,500 | |
| g. LANDSCAPE/WALKWAYS | | | | $200 | | |
| h. LIGHTING | | | | $1,500 | | |
| i. EXTERIOR FACADE/TREATMENTS | | | 0 | 3,000 | 6,000 | |
| j. PARTITIONS | | | 1 | — | 500 | |
| k. FLOOR COVERINGS | | | | | | |
| l. WALL COVERINGS | | | | | | |
| m. PHONES | | | | 700 | | |
| n. PAGING/MUSIC | | | | 300 | | |
| o. FURNITURE | | | | 2,000 | | |
| p. PLAT TABLE | | | | 500 | | |
| TOTAL TEMPORARY SALES FACILITY ESTIMATES | | | | 16,005 | | |

# FIGURE 3.7  Preliminary Plan (continued)

| III. MARKETING TOOLS INVENTORY AND BUDGETS | ESTIMATED CONSULTATION FEES AND EXPENSES | PRODUCTION/PRINTING/CONSTRUCTION/INSTALLATION COST ESTIMATE | | | | SELECTED AMOUNT |
|---|---|---|---|---|---|---|
| | | NOTES/QUANTITIES | GOOD | BETTER | BEST | |
| 7. SEMI-PERMANENT SALES OFFICE | | | | | | |
| a.  PLANNING, LAYOUT DISPLAY DESIGN | | | | $1,000. | | |
| b.  INTERIOR DECORATOR | | | | $500.+ | | |
| c.  PERMITS | | | | ?, — | | |
| d.  SITE PREPARATION HOOK UP | | | | $ — PRESENT | | |
| e.  PARKING | | | 500 | $1,500. | 2500 | |
| f.  LANDSCAPE/WALKWAYS | | | | $2,500. | | |
| g.  LIGHTING | | | | $ — | | |
| h.  EXTERIOR FACADE/TREATMENTS | | | | $1,000. | | |
| i.  PARTITIONS | | | | $1500. | | |
| j.  FLOOR COVERINGS | | | | $1500. | | |
| k.  WALL COVERINGS | | | | $500/R | | |
| l.  PHONES | | | | $600 | | |
| m.  PAGING/MUSIC | | | | $600 | | |
| n.  FURNITURE | | | | $4500 | | |
| o.  PLAT TABLE | | | | FROM TRAILER | | |
| p.  DISPLAY BRACKETS/CABINETS | | | 3000 | 2500 | | |
| TOTAL SEMI-PERMANENT SALES OFFICE ESTIMATES | | | | 17,000 | 25,000 | |
| 8.  MERCHANDISING DISPLAYS | | | | | | |
| a.  SALES OFFICE & ELEMENTS DESIGN | 625. | | | | | |
| b.  SALES OFFICE DISPLAYS | | | | | | |
|     1)  PROJECT LOCATOR DISPLAY | | | | | | |
|     2)  BUILDER CREDENTIAL DISPLAY | | | | | | |
|     3)  AVAILABLE PHASE SITE PLAN DISPLAY | | | | | | |
|     4)  OVERALL/MASTER SITE PLAN DISPLAY | | | | | | |
|     5)  LIFESTYLE DISPLAY | | | | | | |
|     6)  QUALITY & UNIQUE FEATURES DISPLAY | | | | | | |
|     7)  HOME PERSPECTIVE/ELEVATIONS DISPLAY(S) | | | | | | |
|     8)  HOME FLOOR PLAN DISPLAY(S) | | | | | | |
|     9)  MERCHANDISING SCALE MODELS | | | — | $7,000. | $8,000. | |
| TOTAL MERCHANDISING DISPLAYS ESTIMATES | | | $3,500. | $10,500 | $7,000 | |
| 9.  MODEL FURNISHINGS | | | | | | |
| a.  COST OF FURNISHINGS | | | $15/sf. | $20/sf | $20/sf. | |
| b.  OTHER | | | | | | |
| TOTAL MODEL FURNISHINGS ESTIMATES | | | | $4,80+ 22,400. | | |

## FIGURE 3.7  Preliminary Plan (continued)

| III. MARKETING TOOLS INVENTORY AND BUDGETS | ESTIMATED CONSULTATION FEES AND EXPENSES | PRODUCTION/PRINTING/CONSTRUCTION/INSTALLATION COST ESTIMATE | | | | SELECTED AMOUNT |
|---|---|---|---|---|---|---|
| | | NOTES/QUANTITIES | GOOD | BETTER | BEST | |
| 10. MODEL LANDSCAPING | | | | | | |
| a. SPRINKLERS | | | | $500/h + | | |
| b. PLANTING | | | | $300/h + | | |
| c. SEEDED LAWN (SOD) | | | | IN LUMP PRICE | | |
| d. FENCES OR WALLS | | | | | | |
| 1) TYPE | | | | | | |
| 2) ESTIMATED FOOTAGE | | $1,000/h. | | | | |
| 3) COST PER FOOT | | 2000/2h. | | | | |
| e. PATIO | | | | $2,000 + | | |
| f. PATIO COVER | | | | $400 | | |
| g. PARKING LOT | | | | $400 | | |
| h. OTHER | | | | | | |
| i. ESTIMATED RECOVERY (100%) | | | | | | |
| TOTAL LANDSCAPING (MODEL AREA) | | | | | | |
| 11. MODEL EXTERIOR LIGHTING | | | | | | |
| a. FULL FLOOD/LANDSCAPE HIGHLIGHTING | | | | | | |
| TOTAL MODEL LIGHTING ESTIMATES | | | 2,000 | $500 | | |
| 12. MODEL MAINTENANCE | | | | | | |
| a. LANDSCAPING/MODEL INTERIORS | | | | $10,000/h | | |
| TOTAL MODEL MAINTENANCE ESTIMATES | | | | | | |
| 13. PROMOTIONAL PROGRAMS | | | | | | |
| a. PROSPECTS | | | | | | |
| b. BROKER/REALTORS/BROKERS | | | | | | |
| c. REPEATERS | | | | $200. | | |
| TOTAL PROMOTIONAL PROGRAMS ESTIMATES | | | | | | |
| 14. MARKETING MANAGEMENT, SALES MANAGEMENT & SALES COMMISSIONS | | | | | | INCLUDED WITHIN B.M.S. 3% COMM'N. |
| a. AVERAGE SALES PRICE | | | | | | |
| 1) SALESMAN COMMISSION | | | | | | |
| 2) MANAGER OVERRIDE | | | | | | |
| 3) SALESMAN INCENTIVE | | | | | | |
| 4) TRADE PROGRAM | | | | | | |
| 5) SALES TRAINING | | | | | | |
| 15. ESCROW COSTS | | | | | | USE JUDGMENT LOAN CHARGES |
| a. TITLE CHANGES | | | | | | |
| b. ESCROW FEES | | | | | | |
| c. CITY TRANSFER TAX | | | | | | |
| d. STATE TRANSFER TAX | | | | | | |
| TOTAL ESCROW COST ESTIMATES | | | | | | |

# FIGURE 3.7  Preliminary Plan (concluded)

| III. MARKETING TOOLS INVENTORY AND BUDGETS | ESTIMATED CONSULTATION FEES AND EXPENSES | PRODUCTION/PRINTING/CONSTRUCTION/INSTALLATION COST ESTIMATE NOTES/QUANTITIES | GOOD | BETTER | BEST | SELECTED AMOUNT |
|---|---|---|---|---|---|---|
| B. SITE/ARCHITECTURAL VALUE ENHANCEMENT | | | | | | |
| 1. 1" = 50' HOMESITE SITE/HOME TYPE RECOMMENDATIONS | $2,000. | | – | – | – | |
| 2. 1" = 20' DEVELOPER/RESIDENT PLANTING RECOMMENDATIONS PLAN | $2,000. | | 50/LOT | 1000/LOT | 4,000'.LOT+ | |
| 3. 1" = 20' INDIVIDUAL HOMESITE ANALYSIS & RECOMMENDATION FORM | $35/LOT. $12,500 | | – | – | – | |
| 4. ENTRY SETTING DESIGN | $2,500 | | $5,000. | $12,000. | $19,000. | |
| 5. PERMANENT SIGNAGE DESIGN | $1,500. | | 1,000. | 4,000. | 8,000. | |
| 6. AMENITY FEATURES DESIGN | $1,500-3,000. | | ? | | | |
| 7. LIGHTING DESIGN | $2,500, ? CITY REQ'S? | | ? | | | |
| 8. FENCING/MAILBOX RECOMMENDATIONS (POTENTIAL SUN/LIGHT INTEGRATION) | $2,000. | | | $30 LOT+ | | |
| 9. FACING/LOT PRICING | $1,500. | | – | – | – | |
| 10. RESIDENTIAL PRODUCT DESIGN/STYLE SUGGESTION | $1,000-3,000/PLAN (SQL BLDG) | | | | | |

## FIGURE 3.8    Recommended Housing Program

|  | PLAN 1 | PLAN 2 | PLAN 3 | PLAN 4 | Weighted Avg. |
|---|---|---|---|---|---|
| Base Price | $250,000 | $270,000 | $290,000 | $310,000 | $283,945 |
| Square Footage | 2,060 | 2,430 | 2,800 | 3,150 | 2,682 |
| P/S Ratio of Base Price | $121.36 | $111.11 | $103.57 | $98.41 | $105.87 |
| Number of Stories/Floors | 1 | 2 | Tri-level | 2 | |
| Total Number of Bedrooms | 3 | 4 | 4 | 4 | |
| Includes Regular Bedrooms | 2 | 3 | 3 | 3 | |
| Includes Convert. Bedroom/Den | 1 | 1 | 1 | 1 | |
| Includes Maid's Room | 0 | 0 | 0 | 0 | |
| Includes Guest Suite or Wing | 0 | 0 | 0 | 0 | |
| Master Bedroom Retreat | Yes | Yes | Yes | Yes | |
| Number of Bathrooms | 2.5 | 3.0 | 3.0 | 3.0 | |
| Family Room | Yes | Yes | Yes | Yes | |
| Den/Library | No | No | No | Yes | |
| Separate Dining Room | Yes | Yes | Yes | Yes | |
| Informal Breakfast Nook | Yes | Yes | Yes | Yes | |
| Fireplace Location | LR-FR | LR-FR | LR-FR | LR-FR-MBDR | |
| Wet Bar | Yes | Yes | Yes | Yes | TOTAL |
| Mix (Percent) | 20.2% | 20.2% | 29.4% | 30.3% | 100.0% |
| Mix (Units) | 22 | 22 | 32 | 33 | 109 |
| Total Revenues | $5,500,000 | $5,940,000 | $9,280,000 | >$10,229,99 | $30,950,000 |
| Weighted Average Price | $250,000 | $270,000 | $290,000 | $310,000 | $283,945 |
| Total Profits | $661,298 | $713,614 | $1,114,080 | $1,252,845 | $3,741,837 |

|  | PLAN 1 | PLAN 2 | PLAN 3 | PLAN 4 | Weighted Avg. | |
|---|---|---|---|---|---|---|
| Lot Cost (Incl. Landscaping) | $98,675 | $98,675 | $98,675 | $98,675 | $98,675 | 34.8% |
| Const. Cost per Square Foot | $38.60 | $38.60 | $38.60 | $38.60 | $38.60 | |
| Direct Construction Cost | $79,516 | $93,798 | $108,080 | $121,590 | $103,522 | 36.5% |
| (Lot and Construction) | $178,191 | $192,473 | $206,755 | $220,265 | $202,197 | 74.7% |
| Financing Cost (% Sales Price) | $13,000 | $14,040 | $15,080 | $16,120 | $14,765 | 5.2% |
| Marketing Cost (% Sales Price) | $15,000 | $16,200 | $17,400 | $18,600 | $17,037 | 6.0% |
| Indirect Costs (% Sales Price) | $5,000 | $5,400 | $5,800 | $6,200 | $5,679 | 2.0% |
| Overhead (% of Sales Price) | $7,500 | $8,100 | $8,700 | $9,300 | $8,518 | 3.0% |
| R. E. Taxes (% of Sales Price) | $1,250 | $1,350 | $1,450 | $1,550 | $1,420 | 0.5% |
| Profit (% of Sales Price) | $30,059 | $32,437 | $34,815 | $37,965 | $34,329 | 12.1% |
| % Profit by Plan | 12.0% | 12.0% | 12.0% | 12.2% | | 12.1% |

|  | PLAN 1 | PLAN 2 | PLAN 3 | PLAN 4 | TOTAL | |
|---|---|---|---|---|---|---|
| Total Lot Cost Incl. Landscaping | $2,170,850 | $2,170,850 | $3,157,600 | $3,256,275 | $10,755,575 | 34.8% |
| Total Construction Cost | $1,749,352 | $2,063,556 | $3,458,560 | $4,012,470 | $11,283,938 | 36.5% |
| Total Financing Cost | $286,000 | $308,880 | $482,560 | $531,960 | $1,609,400 | 5.2% |
| Total Marketing Cost | $330,000 | $356,400 | $556,800 | $613,800 | $1,857,000 | 6.0% |
| Total Indirect Cost | $110,000 | $118,800 | $185,600 | $204,600 | $619,000 | 2.0% |
| Total Overhead Cost | $165,000 | $178,200 | $278,400 | $306,900 | $928,500 | 3.0% |
| R.E. Taxes | $27,500 | $29,700 | $46,400 | $51,150 | $154,750 | 0.5% |
| Total Profit | $661,298 | $713,614 | $1,114,080 | $1,252,845 | $3,741,837 | 12.1% |
| Total Costs | $4,646,202 | $5,018,486 | $7,841,120 | $8,619,105 | $27,208,163 | 87.9% |
| Total Square Footage | 45,320 | 53,460 | 89,600 | 103,950 | 292,330 | |

SOURCE: Herbert L. Aist & Associates

# 4: On-Site Merchandising

The physical environment in which prospective homebuyers are expected to make decisions plays a dominant role in the psychological aspects of the sales process. Whether it is just one speculative home under construction on an individual site, or a central sales facility complete with furnished and well-landscaped models, the impact of the visual presentation on the senses and emotions of customers is a crucial factor in the way they respond to the featured housing values. Judgments are made based on a variety of sensory messages to the brain. As prospects inspect a housing environment, they relate what they see to prior information and personal experiences. The general appearance of the sales and construction areas are compared to other properties they have inspected. Each prospect has a certain level of expectation as a new housing environment is reviewed. It is rated against one's present residence as well as other housing opportunities previously investigated. We also judge property by the criteria that our advisors have given us. When the home or its surroundings fail to meet standards implanted in the memory, there is little chance for emotional interest to take root.

The primary objective of all on-site marketing is to provide an emotionally stimulating environment that excites customers and prepares them for well-organized sales presentations. A builder who cannot afford a furnished model because production is limited to five homes a year has a totally different on-site marketing requirement than a merchant builder who is creating a major community and selling several hundred homes each year. There is an economy of scale that financially influences the development of the marketing pro forma. However, fundamental marketing objectives do not change just because the homes are fewer. The values of the homes and neighborhood must be communicated to prospective homebuyers, whether by well-trained sales professionals or by the silent visual messages contained in the models, sales aids and supporting graphics.

## SET THE STAGE FOR POSITIVE PERCEPTIONS

Many prospects arrive on their own, while others are escorted by cooperating real estate professionals. What are their first impressions? Unless blind, we receive most messages to the brain through the eyes. Visual experiences are usually more important to our mental impressions than the things we hear. A salesperson has to work very hard to overcome visual negatives already planted in the brain. Those immediate reactions to the general area, the adjacent neighborhoods and the new housing sites often predetermine whether or not the customers even get out of their automobiles to inspect our housing.

It is not always possible to mask adverse neighboring influences. If you are adjacent to depreciating real estate conditions, the objective is to isolate your environment so that it has its own independence and self-contained values. On the other hand, if everything along the approaches to the community is equal to or better than what you are offering, the objective is to become part of those reinforcing values.

**FIGURE 4.1    First Impressions**

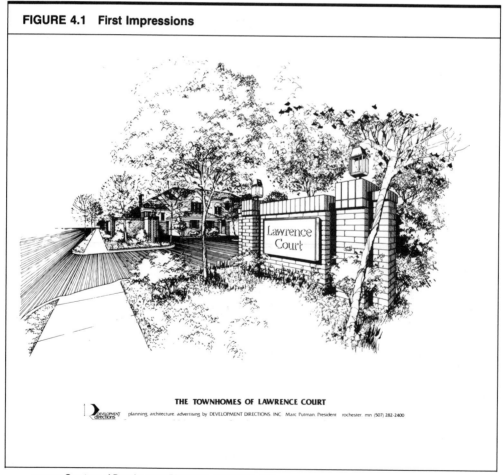

THE TOWNHOMES OF LAWRENCE COURT

planning. architecture. advertising by DEVELOPMENT DIRECTIONS. INC   Marc Putman. President   rochester. mn (507) 282-2400

SOURCE: Courtesy of Development Directions, Rochester, MN

**FIGURE 4.2   Site Identification Signage**

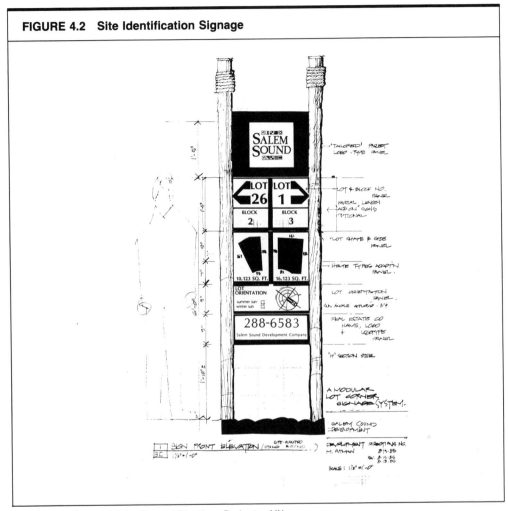

SOURCE: Courtesy of Development Directions, Rochester, MN

You should look at your properties through the eyes of prospective buyers. What will they see as they approach your housing community? Are the influences potentially negative to the value levels you are trying to project? What fears and concerns about the area might be generated as a result of what they are visually inspecting? How can you protect your new homes and homesites from potentially depreciating factors?

This analysis of the site includes a careful review of the best way to direct or bring prospects to the sales area. If you have your choice of routing them through established neighborhoods of higher values or through those that are not well-maintained, you will obviously choose the more prestigious approach. Likewise, you need to think about competitive housing projects visible along a primary access to the

**FIGURE 4.3   Directional Sign**

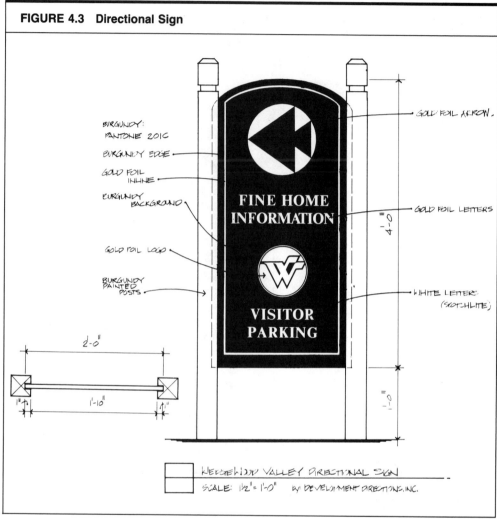

SOURCE: Courtesy of Development Directions, Rochester, MN

property. Sometimes it is wise to capitalize directly on the other builder's operations, particularly if you are less expensive and have more value footage to feature. Conversely, there are situations where you want to discourage exposure to the other housing choices, because the risk of losing control to competition will be much greater if their properties are seen first.

## TRY TO CREATE A POSITIVE SENSE OF ARRIVAL

The objective is to set the stage for your homes by either controlling the approach or compensating for it by the way you treat the *sense of arrival*. The impressions prospects experience before arrival must be compensated for by what they see when they approach the construction area. If you can justify the expense of special entry treatments and landscaped settings that accent your housing environments, the investment is often more than justified in the increased values that buyers sense when they arrive at the models. At the very least, the construction site should be reasonably clean, free of excess debris and effectively identified.

The sense of arrival at a residential housing neighborhood is a value-influencing factor that reinforces identity. Frequently a substantial number of dollars is invested in creation and installation of entry monuments, gates, landscaped meridians, theme-fencing and accent features that provide instant recognition for new communities. The land developer is usually responsible for this aspect of marketing, and the scale of investment is related to the size of the project. However, even if you cannot influence or control the merchandising at the main entry, you should do all that is economically feasible to set the stage for your homes in the immediate neighborhood where you are engaged in sales activities. This includes the following:

1. Attractive theme-signage that identifies neighborhoods and the homes you are featuring.
2. Landscaping appropriate for the housing environment. Berms and accent areas can be very effective in setting the approach area apart from the general surroundings.
3. Flags can be helpful in identifying the location of your building area, sales facility and model homes. The United States flag does not require any special approvals before installation. The right to display the American flag is a constitutional privilege.
4. Planter boxes are very useful in identifying key points of access and in controlling traffic areas. They can be placed to block construction areas from general access and used to define parking, sales office paths and model areas.
5. Fencing serves as an identity element that can also mask some negative influences. While masonry fences are the most elaborate and expensive, even a well-constructed wooden fence can achieve the effect often needed to set the neighborhood or model-cluster apart from the surroundings.
6. Lighting can play a very important role in marketing the community at night. Spotlights on entry elements, landscape lighting and accent spots on models will set them apart from their nighttime surroundings.
7. Signage that provides information about the community, sales facilities, models and current availability of homesites or housing is important for capturing the interest of local traffic.

Theme names that evoke a strong sense of personal identity help to strengthen the prospect's association with the community. Whenever possible, you should include the romance elements of the theme in the on-site merchandising programs. Graphic

## FIGURE 4.4   On-Site Phasing Sign

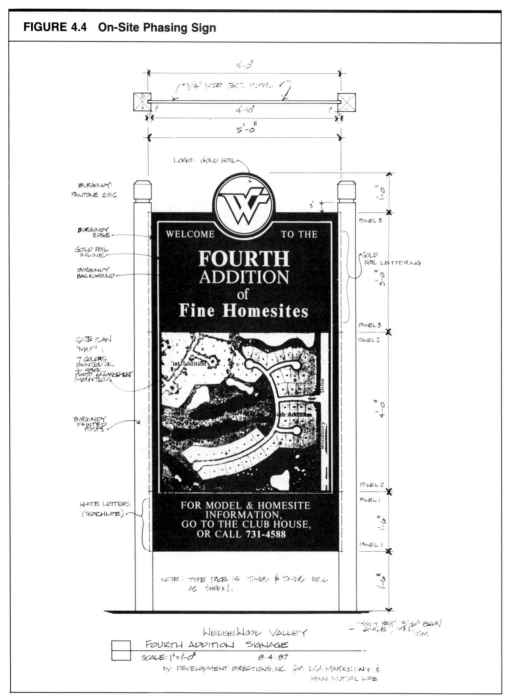

representations of theme names in street signage, amenity markers, neighborhood monuments and sales displays adds to the cohesiveness of the total marketing plan while increasing the sense of community for prospects and residents.

## LOCATING AND DESIGNING ON-SITE SALES FACILITIES

The best place to sell a new home or condominium is in its natural environment. While we may use real estate brokerage offices to attract and counsel customers who need guidance in selecting new homes, we invariably sell real estate by going to its location and exploiting its advantages. Modern methods of marketing new homes and new home communities encompass a wide variety of on-site merchandising programs. In the past two or three decades, the merchant developers and builders of North America have become increasingly aggressive in providing stimulating sales environments that motivate consumers to act. The on-site sales and information center should be a focal point of these marketing concepts.

Each environment has its own demands, and it is impossible to anticipate every situation that might be encountered. However, there are guidelines for successful on-site marketing that have proven to be very effective in stimulating more new home sales. As we share these concepts with you, we ask that you interpret them according to local market conditions and to opportunities presented by a particular housing assignment.

## GENERAL GUIDELINES FOR LOCATING THE SALES OFFICE

When trying to determine where to locate the on-site sales office or models, the following factors should be carefully evaluated:

1. Exposure to passing or arriving traffic and the ability for salespeople to see who is arriving.
2. Adjacent housing influences.
3. Available parking for prospective customers.
4. The potential adverse influences of construction traffic, noise and development activities.
5. The location of the sites and housing inventory in relation to models or sales office.
6. The longevity of the facility in terms of future development plans.
7. The proximity of amenities that deserve to be viewed and promoted.

In addition to these considerations, there is always the matter of the marketing budget. How much is available, or can be justified, for creating a sales center? The normal approach is to use all or part of a speculative model home as the least expensive and most practical place from which to conduct sales activities. In large communities, where the number of homes to be sold can readily justify a major commitment to on-site marketing, the independent sales center is frequently constructed with the objective of converting it to other uses in the future. Planned-unit developments with major recreational facilities will often use a portion of the clubhouse or amenity package to accommodate sales needs until the community is well-established.

## THE GARAGE OF A MODEL HOME AS A CONVERTIBLE SALES OFFICE

The most popular arrangement for new home sales is the conversion of a garage area into a temporary sales center until that model has been sold or a new phase opened to replace the model location. This is certainly one of the most economical approaches to accommodating the presentation and counseling needs of on-site sales representatives. A two-car garage provides about 400 square feet of open space that is easily organized to accommodate the various exhibits and closing spaces essential to the sales process. Sometimes the only choice is to use a single-car garage. This space tends to be too small to do justice to the value-building programs. We recommend that you try to avoid the single-car facility if there is any other reasonable alternative. When you must locate in a small garage, try to open the space by extending it to the outdoors or into the home. An example of a creative approach to a single-car garage is included in the exhibit section.

The two-car garage has many variations in design and use. The three-car garage is even better. There is also the possibility of linking two garages with a covered breezeway or enclosure that allows the functions of greeting to closing to flow from one area to the other.

If you elect to use a garage as a convertible sales arena, here are some suggestions in positioning the particular home and site:

1.  Position the garage so that your salespeople have sight of arriving traffic as well as the model homes.
2.  A corner lot is often the most practical location, since it has a commanding view and is easy for arriving customers to spot from a distance.
3.  Preserving the corner lot for parking can provide a side garage entry more convenient and impressive than a driveway approach. This requires the use of two sites for the sales area: the corner for parking and the adjacent site for the model with its garage entry. The plan may have to be reversed to accommodate a side entry off the temporary parking area.
4.  It is often wise to leave a vacant lot between the sales office and the models or speculative homes to allow breathing room for the sales center and provide landscaped areas that set the stage for the display homes. This same lot can serve as a place for an additional model if it is needed at some future date.
5.  To provide a more dramatic direct entry from the street, you can leave out the driveway(s) until the model is sold as a home. This is commonly done where a group of models is anchored by one garage sales office in a controlled sales environment. The visual impact of the green lawns and landscaping does much to set the models and office apart from the inventory homes and construction area.

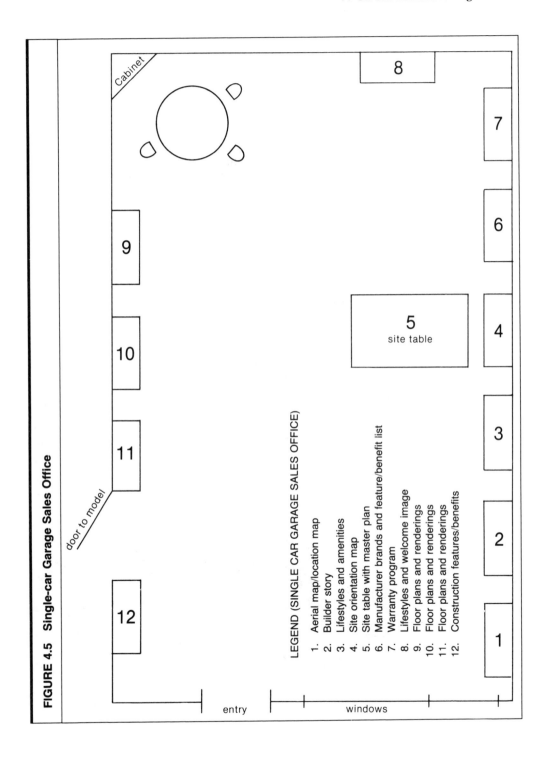

**FIGURE 4.5   Single-car Garage Sales Office**

LEGEND (SINGLE CAR GARAGE SALES OFFICE)

1. Aerial map/location map
2. Builder story
3. Lifestyles and amenities
4. Site orientation map
5. Site table with master plan
6. Manufacturer brands and feature/benefit list
7. Warranty program
8. Lifestyles and welcome image
9. Floor plans and renderings
10. Floor plans and renderings
11. Floor plans and renderings
12. Construction features/benefits

Cabinet

5
site table

door to model

entry          windows

6. If the garage does not have windows where needed to observe arriving traffic and control the model homes, it is wise to make an exception in the one garage you choose for a sales office. Insert the windows where they give the sales representatives the ability to monitor exterior conditions at all times.

7. Employ planter boxes and other landscaping elements to direct customers to the main entry of the sales office. When appropriate, use a canopy, trellis or patio entry design to create visual interest and focus attention on the access point to sales information.

## USING A MOBILE TRAILER FOR PRECONSTRUCTION SALES

Sometimes it is both expedient and practical to set up a sales facility long before you have the opportunity to construct a model home or permanent office. The preconstruction sales period provides many advantages to both the builders and the

---

**FIGURE 4.6    Exterior Sales-Office Features**

SOURCE: Photos courtesy of Habitat, Tempe, AZ.

sales organization. The more contracts you secure before you start construction, the less risk for all concerned. In multi-family housing projects such as high-rise condominiums, planned unit developments and townhome clusters, there is often the necessity of demonstrating to a lending institution an adequate sales pattern before construction financing can be obtained. It is not uncommon to have a goal of 50–60 percent presales level before the go signal will be given by a venture partner or financial institution. In such cases, the use of a temporary sales office becomes even more important.

The most widely adopted procedure is to lease a mobile unit from a service company and position it on site to accommodate interim marketing requirements. Some companies that build in volume in a number of locations will maintain their own mobile sales office and arrange to pull it from one location to another as needed. If you lease a mobile home or trailer, you must normally agree to a minimum lease period, even if you do not need it for the entire time. Six or 12 months is the usual for a lease of this kind.

Here are some guidelines for securing and positioning a trailer or mobile building as a temporary on-site sales office:

1. The minimum size to seek is 12′ wide by 40′ long. Width is important. If you can lease a 14′-wide, so much the better. That extra two feet makes a big difference in the space that can be allocated for exhibits and sales furnishings.

2. If you are going to be in the location for an extended period of time, or you represent a major housing community that deserves a complete presale presentation, arrange for a double-wide mobile facility. The extra space gives you the opportunity to arrange site tables and set up displays, counseling areas, etc., in a more dramatic and effective way.

3. Create a facade that will soften the harsh and somewhat sterile appearance of the trailer. A wide deck across the entire front of the trailer is one of the more effective ways of accomplishing this. Planter boxes, canopies, landscaping and deck furniture do much to convert the mobile building into an attractive facility.

4. Locate the trailer where it can easily function as the sales office until the models and/or permanent facility are completed. This means putting it on a site out of the way of construction so it will not have to be moved until desired. However, you still want to follow the guidelines for positioning the building, so that you have control of arriving traffic and adequate parking for guests.

5. Do not use the trailer as a combination construction and sales center unless you absolutely have no other choice. Construction activities are seldom compatible with sales objectives. Subs and suppliers are not sales-oriented. The conversations, noise, confusion and general reactions of those in construction should be isolated from the sales environment.

6. Use signage at the sales trailer that clearly indicates this is a temporary facility. Do not leave the impression that the building will be there for any great length of time or that the construction company cannot afford a permanent facility. The entire strategy is based on offering opportunities to

**FIGURE 4.7   Mobile Sales Offices**

SOURCE: Photos courtesy of Centex, Cary, Illinois and Wood Brothers, Denver, CO.

the public that would not be possible if this advance sales plan were not in place.

7.   Flag the trailer so it can be seen from every arriving direction. Since the building is not large, it should be highlighted visually with eye-catching tools such as flags and directional signage.

We have provided you with examples of sales trailers that you can adapt to your specific needs. Many of the interior displays will have to be compromised in size or neglected until you move to larger quarters. However, if you carefully plan portable displays and size them to meet the flexible space requirements of trailers and garage offices, you will be able to accomplish both objectives without incurring additional graphic expenses.

## CRITERIA FOR INTERIOR SPACE ARRANGEMENTS

As a marketing director, you have the responsibility of organizing the physical environments for your representatives' sales presentations. You cannot depend upon the real estate agents to design or produce the exhibits and sales tools that will adequately communicate the values your builder or developer has created. Regardless of the size or nature of the on-site physical facilities, a fundamental need exists for graphic displays and visual marketing aids that will supplement the verbal messages given by salespeople. For most prospects, the visual impact of the things they see will overshadow the messages they hear. Therefore, it is essential that marketers provide reinforcing visual experiences that dramatically and effectively provide the value-building elements that compose the total picture and create the composite values.

Merely creating displays and installing them in some loose format in a sales environment does not assure they will achieve all sales objectives.

The sales process is not simply the showing of a home or homesite. The decision track of the prospective homebuyer follows a series of influencing factors that must be measured and weighed before a purchase commitment will be made. The prospects arrive at the property with some preconceived notions and value judgments. If they have been guided to the home by a professional real estate agent, they will have gained additional information that will play a role in setting the stage for the inspection and presentation. However, they will be heavily influenced by personal experiences and advice from those they respect. Prior to being introduced to your housing environment, your customers have at least two-thirds of the input that will determine their value judgments when viewing your homes and neighborhoods. What you do in the sales center and the models or display homes determines the balance.

**FIGURE 4.8    Shepherd's Vineyard Sales Center**

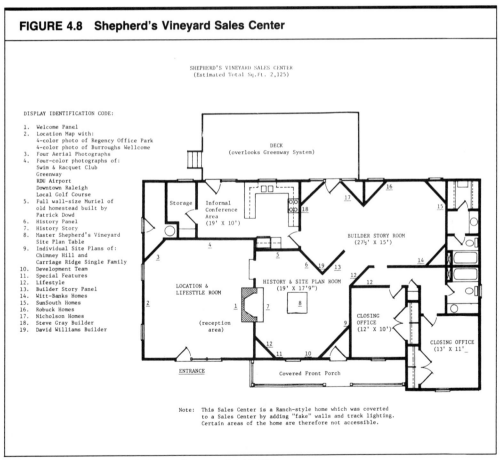

SHEPHERD'S VINEYARD SALES CENTER
(Estimated Total Sq.Ft. 2,125)

DISPLAY IDENTIFICATION CODE:

1. Welcome Panel
2. Location Map with:
   4-color photo of Regency Office Park
   4-color photo of Burroughs Wellcome
3. Four Aerial Photographs
4. Four-color photographs of:
   Swim & Racquet Club
   Greenway
   RDU Airport
   Downtown Raleigh
   Local Golf Course
5. Full wall-size Muriel of
   old homestead built by
   Patrick Dowd
6. History Panel
7. History Story
8. Master Shepherd's Vineyard
   Site Plan Table
9. Individual Site Plans of:
   Chimney Hill and
   Carriage Ridge Single Family
10. Development Team
11. Special Features
12. Lifestyle
13. Builder Story Panel
14. Witt-Banks Homes
15. SunSouth Homes
16. Robuck Homes
17. Nicholson Homes
18. Steve Gray Builder
19. David Williams Builder

DECK
(overlooks Greenway System)

Storage

Informal
Conference
Area
(19' X 10')

BUILDER STORY ROOM
(27½' X 15')

LOCATION &
LIFESTYLE ROOM

(reception
area)

HISTORY & SITE PLAN ROOM
(19' X 17'9")

CLOSING
OFFICE
(12' X 10')

CLOSING OFFICE
(13' X 11'

ENTRANCE

Covered Front Porch

Note: This Sales Center is a Ranch-style home which was coverted
to a Sales Center by adding "fake" walls and track lighting.
Certain areas of the home are therefore not accessible.

SOURCE: Courtesy of Fonville-Morisry Company, Raleigh, NC.

**FIGURE 4.9   Canal Pointe Sales Center**

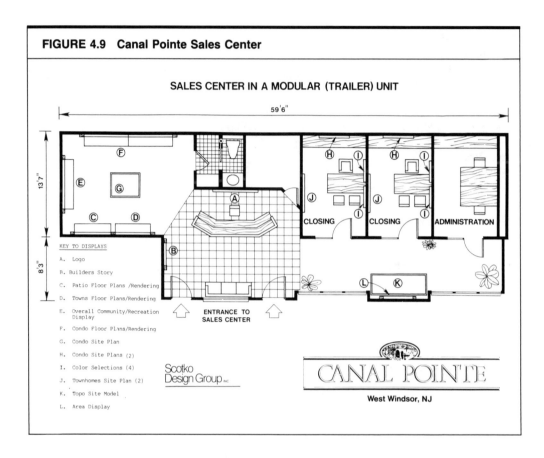

SALES CENTER IN A MODULAR (TRAILER) UNIT

59'6"

13'7"

8'3"

KEY TO DISPLAYS

A.  Logo

B.  Builders Story

C.  Patio Floor Plans /Rendering

D.  Towns Floor Plans/Rendering

E.  Overall Community/Recreation
    Display

F.  Condo Floor Plans/Rendering

G.  Condo Site Plan

H.  Condo Site Plans (2)

I.  Color Selections (4)

J.  Townhomes Site Plan (2)

K.  Topo Site Model

L.  Area Display

CLOSING    CLOSING    ADMINISTRATION

ENTRANCE TO
SALES CENTER

Scotko
Design Group inc

CANAL POINTE

West Windsor, NJ

That is the critical point of sale where everything has to come into focus to help a hesitant prospect reach a positive buying decision.

When designing the interior space arrangements for an on-site sales facility, keep these objectives in mind:

1.   The control needed by sales representatives to provide the time to involve and qualify customers.
2.   The friendliness and warmth of the environment. It should feel more like a home than an office.
3.   The stations of involvement must be organized to permit sales representatives to build values in a logical sequence while pursuing their qualifying objectives.
4.   Evidence of success and a sense of credible urgency to act must be conveyed by the displays and general appearance of the environment.
5.   Colors and furnishings should put people into positive moods and stimulate emotions that prepare them to think seriously about homebuying.
6.   There must be room for private counseling and closing without sacrificing the need for adequate presentation of decision-influencing messages.

**FIGURE 4.10  Carrefour Sales Center**

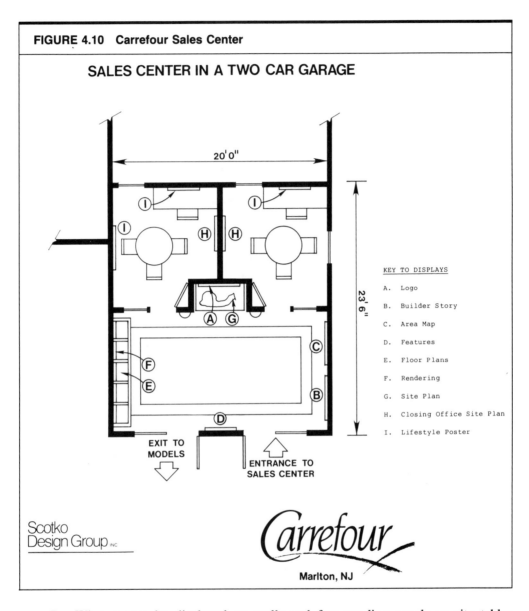

SALES CENTER IN A TWO CAR GARAGE

KEY TO DISPLAYS

A.  Logo

B.  Builder Story

C.  Area Map

D.  Features

E.  Floor Plans

F.  Rendering

G.  Site Plan

H.  Closing Office Site Plan

I.  Lifestyle Poster

Scotko Design Group INC

*Carrefour*

Marlton, NJ

7. What cannot be displayed on walls and free-standing panels or site tables should be available in some other visual form, such as mobile cards, binders and retrievable files.

A wide variety of conditions will influence the design of a new home sales office. We are frequently forced to live with less than the amount of space needed to fulfill all of our objectives. The compromises we make must be very carefully weighed to avoid losing the impact of the big messages.

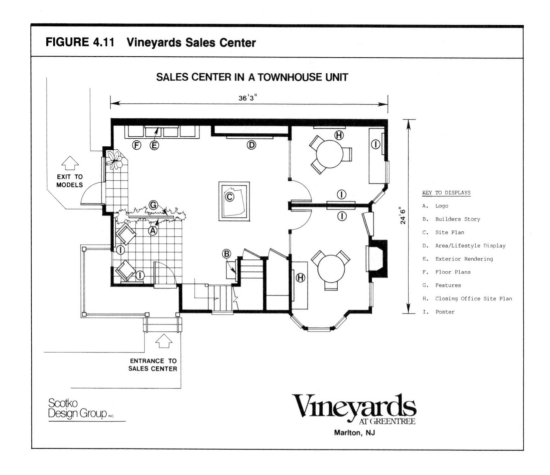

**FIGURE 4.11    Vineyards Sales Center**

SALES CENTER IN A TOWNHOUSE UNIT

KEY TO DISPLAYS

A.  Logo

B.  Builders Story

C.  Site Plan

D.  Area/Lifestyle Display

E.  Exterior Rendering

F.  Floor Plans

G.  Features

H.  Closing Office Site Plan

I.  Poster

EXIT TO MODELS

ENTRANCE TO SALES CENTER

Scotko Design Group inc.

**Vineyards**
AT GREENTREE
Marlton, NJ

## PRINCIPAL ZONES OF A SALES CENTER

Five major zones or functional areas need to be accommodated within the sales arena:

1.  Welcoming and greeting area
2.  Overview and concept-presentation area
3.  Counseling and closing area
4.  Designs, floor plans and/or models
5.  Decorator and option-selection functions

The first three functions are essential in every on-site office. The other two can be handled outside the primary arena and treated by individually controlled presentations with salespeople and design counselors. The majority of sales centers will include items one through four. Selection of colors, up-grades, options and extras is often handled in either a separate design-counseling room or by appointment with a professional decorating service. When this function must be included within a sales

## FIGURE 4.12    Hunter's Creek Sales Office

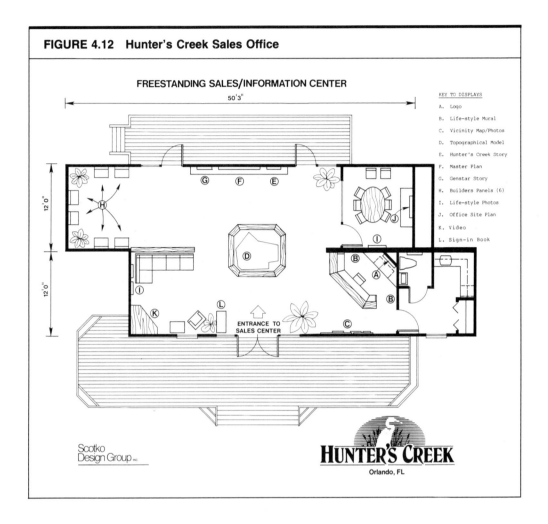

FREESTANDING SALES/INFORMATION CENTER

KEY TO DISPLAYS

A.  Logo
B.  Life-style Mural
C.  Vicinity Map/Photos
D.  Topographical Model
E.  Hunter's Creek Story
F.  Master Plan
G.  Genstar Story
H.  Builders Panels (6)
I.  Life-style Photos
J.  Office Site Plan
K.  Video
L.  Sign-in Book

ENTRANCE TO
SALES CENTER

Scotko
Design Group inc.

HUNTER'S CREEK
Orlando, FL

facility, locate it where it does not confuse the prospect or lessen control by forcing premature involvement with these minor choices versus concentration on major home-buying decisions.

Before identifying specific elements that might be included in each of the functional areas of the presentation arena, you should look at some broad guidelines that might influence the location and space relationships of each of these primary areas.

## GREETING AND WELCOMING LOBBY

Every sales office needs a sense of arrival and a comfortable place to greet and quickly qualify prospective buyers prior to introduction to the community and the housing product lines. The first three to four minutes of exposure to a prospect is the most critical time in the entire sales process! If the environment is not conducive to a relaxed and nonthreatening introduction, all other objectives may never be attained. Homebuyers who arrive on their own are usually not ready to become involved with sales agents prior to discovering what is for sale. They want to investigate the property and pick up any information, which they can then leisurely review back at their present residence. Everything the salespeople must accomplish can only occur if they are able to gain attention and win the respect of the customers. You always need to set the stage for a positive involvement with prospective buyers. If the space is cramped, has too many confusing messages or seems threatening in any way, you will find it difficult to put people into the necessary comfort zone that is the prelude to meaningful dialogue and effective presentation of your housing opportunities.

During the introductory phase of the sales process, the salesperson needs to be able to qualify the prospect quickly and build rapport without having to discuss in detail the site plan, housing floor plans or construction features. Thus, it is best to keep primary exhibits and displays that deal with such topics out of the entry area. Appropriate visual aids for the greeting zone are those that establish the identity of the community and the builders, the location advantages and the lifestyle of the profiled residents. Ideally, there should be enough space in this portion of the office to permit the salesperson to talk comfortably with two or three people in a family group. The space range should be a minimum of 50 square feet to about 100. That's an area of about seven-by-seven to ten-by-ten feet. When you have the luxury of working with a large sales pavilion or multi-room structure, the greeting and warm-up section can be even larger. It is often appropriate to include a small sitting arrangement in the lobby, but it should be positioned so it will not interfere with the greeting needs of the sales staff. The use of planter boxes, half-wall dividers and specially designed display panels can help to separate this warm-up space from the primary presentation zones.

## OVERVIEW AND CONCEPT PRESENTATION AREA

The transition zone between the entry lobby and the product displays should be devoted to selling the master plan of the neighborhood and the concepts that represent the basis for the housing values. This includes renderings and pictures of amenities as well as feature benefit boards that emphasize the advantages of life in that particular environment. If you are selling a variety of housing types in a number of neighborhoods or are representing a major community, the focal display will usually be a concept site plan. Whenever possible, this should be designed to fit on a site table that is easily viewed in a standing position and oriented to the points of the compass exactly as the parcel of land relates to the prospect's visual orientation. It is not necessary for this master plan to show specific lot lines or available inventory, although that is occasionally appropriate. As we will review in greater detail, all site maps must avoid confusing the customer and offering so much inventory that the sense of urgency to purchase is reduced.

The primary objective of this centerpiece in the sales office is to establish larger values that will carry the smaller ones. The land plan, streetscapes, amenities and

**FIGURE 4.13  Site Map**

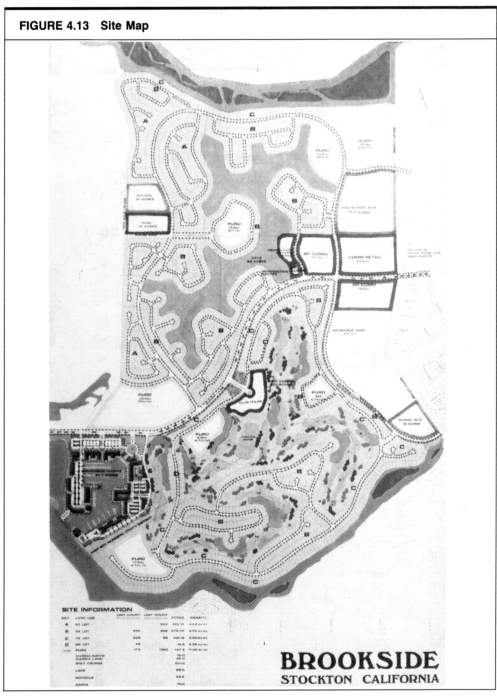

## FIGURE 4.14 Sales-Office Interiors

SOURCE: A. Courtesy of Exhibits, Inc., Denver, CO. B, C, and D. Courtesy of Habitat, Tempe, AZ.

neighborhood characteristics should first be reinforced in the value-building process before individual plans and available homes are discussed. It is often wise to have two separate site plans, whether on one site table or in two different locations. The first one features the overview of the entire community land plan. The second is an enlargement of just the streets or buildings currently available for sale. By divorcing the two presentations, you can help prospects understand the bigger picture and then direct their full attention to the one area of construction where you need to begin building a sense of urgency for specific housing choices.

## CRITERIA FOR DESIGN AND USE OF THE MASTER SITE PLAN

Because the neighborhood master plan is the focal point of the overview sales presentation module, it should be designed with the objective of communicating the values that may not yet be evident in the emerging community. The visual impact of this site plan influences prospect perceptions. That is why it should always be designed to romance the environment with the proper use of colors, textures and eye-appealing layouts. The minimum requirement is the use of an engineer's site plan (typically blueprint-sized) appropriately colored to depict open spaces, landscaping, streetscapes, housing pads and amenities. Colors like green for trees, lawns and parks or blue for ponds, streams and lakes are logical ways to help prospects picture the completed community. Avoid colors that are not natural. Green and blue are enriching colors associated with positive experiences. Always attempt to give customers the benefit of emotionally satisfying messages both visually and verbally. In its ultimate form, the master plan will be a topographical relief map depicting all three dimensions and showing all of the natural characteristics of the physical environment. These are relatively expensive and normally only justified when you have a major community where the number of homes or homesites to be sold will justify the amortized cost of a professionally created diorama.

Here is a checklist for those who are designing this key sales-presentation element.

1. Display the land plan in a horizontal position at a standing height level for easy viewing (three-and-a-half feet is normal).

2. Position the map so that it is correctly oriented to the compass points the way it will be viewed in the sales office. That way, salespeople do not need to re-orient prospects while standing at the display.

3. Provide a framed mat that allows the site plan to be accented and leaves room for legend or copy that emphasizes key feature/benefit messages.

4. Use only materials and colors that are true to nature. Make the site plan believable by depicting the future landscapes and surroundings that accent the buildings.

5. Include any adjacent parcels of land that will add to value perceptions. Open spaces, parks, natural woods, lakes, marinas and more expensive neighborhoods are examples of buffers worth featuring.

6. If there are more homesites or housing units than can be predictably absorbed within three to six months, it is far better to phase the releases and depict the master plan with overlays for the sections or buildings not yet on the market. Excess inventory will defeat the urgency objectives of the sales process and lessen values through confusion and decreased activity. A variety of ways exist to accomplish this inventory control objective:

    a. Complete the entire map with all sites properly portrayed, and then add colored poster board templates that can be removed as individual sites are released. Only the current phases are shown, the balance are covered. Street patterns, amenities, etc., and the future areas are shown. The templates are designed only to cover the building sites. These are labeled "future residential" or left unmarked—at the discretion of sales management.

        b. Prepare the master map without showing individual homesites or buildings. The plan shows only neighborhoods, villages and street patterns. This orientation vehicle is then used to explain the total concept, and a secondary site map is created (preferably located away from the master plan) that shows an enlarged section or phase where current housing is available. This is the one used to post the solds and accent remaining inventory. This technique helps to create more urgency and better control than is possible with a single master plan that attempts to accomplish both objectives at once.

        c. When you create a topographical relief map, it is best to design it with removable sections that can be pulled out and modified as neighborhoods are released and new product offerings are added. This is slightly more expensive than doing a one-piece topo, but the control benefits are usually worth the extra investment.

7. All homesites should be depicted as large as feasible for the allotted space. It is always a mistake to show homesites in small dimensions that decrease the feelings of spaciousness, privacy and identity—fundamental motivators of prospective homebuyers. If there are too many sites to display individually at a reasonable scale, use the primary master plan to show neighborhoods instead of individual sites. Use secondary displays to depict separate neighborhoods with enlarged sections that are urgency controlled.

8. Whenever possible, use photographs in conjunction with the site map to portray the living benefits of the neighborhood. Photos of owners using parks, trails and other amenities will add to the emotional impact of the display. Simple snapshots of owners enjoying their homes and yards will enhance the value statements ten-fold. Cameos and cut-outs in a matting frame can provide a professional look to these informal shots.

9. Allow room for a summary of environmental benefits that can be read by people who are looking at the site plan without a salesperson in attendance. These silent sales messages help to reinforce the verbal presentations and also serve as cue cards to real estate agents.

10. Always provide adequate lighting that focuses on the table top. Be careful to avoid reflections that distort or diminish the value of this tool. Exercise caution in using glass, since it will have to be lifted for up-dating the map. It can be hazardous if not properly handled.

11. When possible, design the site table so that it can be used as a writing surface—or add a ledge for registration and note taking. Also, use the space under the site table for brochure storage. This is the logical location for extra brochures and the easiest control point for salespeople to procure and assemble information needed by prospective buyers.

12. When the site table is positioned against a wall (leaving three sides for the salespeople to involve customers), use the wall space immediately above the table to display one or more of the following:

        a. An aerial or location orientation map that helps customers relate the master plan to the larger geographical area.

b. A phasing map that shows sections currently being offered and relates them to the master plan on the primary site table.
c. A feature/benefit summary (including photographs) with examples of the great advantages of living in that neighborhood and general location.

When a master site map is not well designed, it limits the capacity of sales representatives to build the neighborhood values that are the foundation of individual housing values. Properly done, this can be the most important single sales exhibit in the office. Its design, construction and use should be controlled by sales management—not advertising agencies!

## MAJOR AMENITIES DESERVE SPECIAL EXHIBITS

In the general concept and overview area, you should display the exhibits that depict major amenities, either existing or proposed. They should be easily visible when salespeople are standing at the site table with their customers. The objective is to have salespeople relate the benefits of neighborhood living as they present the bigger message about the history, protected values, design concepts and current availability of product in the phasing of the community plan. If you have a number of amenities such as a swimming pool, tennis courts, golf courses, marina, etc., each deserves separate graphic representation. If you have a limited package, such as a small park, pond or open space area, the message can be accomplished in one display. The most effective way to communicate these amenities is to use photographs. Pictures of people enjoying the area, playing in the park, or walking beside the pond communicate the real values you offer better than the spoken word ever can.

History of the area is often an overlooked amenity. People enjoy knowing more about the past, especially if you can capture any romance about the people who lived in the area, special events that occurred there or roles this region played in the history of the country. Even the chain of title to the land is a potential resource for creating interest in the property. Who owned the land in the past and what were their lives like? Old photographs of the early days that show life in this area before it was developed can be conversation points to stimulate consumer interest.

This same section of the sales office needs to summarize the major benefits your company offers to the people who purchase from you. It is a good place to reinforce customer service programs, warranties, testimonials about your past performance and what sets you apart from your competition. Brand names and manufacturer displays can provide a transition to the product-orientation areas or the models. The objective is to add to value before the specific housing designs, models and homesites are inspected.

## CLOSING AND COUNSELING AREAS

One or more places within the sales environment should be available to conduct private counseling sessions where salespeople can help prospects reach positive buying decisions as well as qualify for confidential information essential in structuring a real estate contract. These can be formal and completely private, or open and semiprivate, depending upon the nature of the office and the needs of the particular salespeople assigned to that facility.

It is most common to construct at least one sales office area that is acoustically semi-insulated from the general sales arena and public traffic patterns. Specific configuration options for these closing rooms or zones will vary greatly from one project to another. However, we believe that some basic guidelines are worthy of the designer's consideration in structuring this counseling space. Among these is the matter of giving the prospects a nonthreatening environment in which to communicate with the sales representatives. If the space is cramped or too confined, either physically or visually, it can be an inhibiting factor for both the sales counselors and their customers. Whatever space is selected for an office or closing area, it should be designed to make it relatively easy to encourage clients to enter and comfortably share their thoughts with the sales agents. This is best achieved by defining the space with plenty of light in pleasant surroundings.

Opinions differ on the merits of formal versus informal closing areas. In the more formal setting, there is usually a desk, office furniture, regular straight-back chairs, filing cabinets and the accessories that characterize a business office. In the informal arena, the desks are eliminated in favor of either round conference tables or credenzas with comfortable sitting areas. The latter is more representative of the way families decorate a den or flex room in a home. The family-room look is being adopted by an increasing number of marketing directors because they believe it is less restrictive to the communication needs of salespeople.

We favor the informal counseling areas, particularly when dealing with more expensive price ranges. When dealing with first-time buyers and the lower price ranges the area can be more structured, since you are working with people who need to be given a stronger sense of direction. More affluent customers and those who have bought and sold homes before are generally more comfortable in informal settings. The round conference table is far less authoritative than a big oak desk. This psychological difference needs to be evaluated when deciding on furnishings for the closing rooms. There are valid reasons for electing to have a desk rather than a round table. These include the following:

1.  The salesperson may need the desk as an authority element to augment personal strength in communicating with the prospects. Diminutive salespeople, those whose personalities are not very assertive and those who have developed a personal preference for the desk may be best served by providing the more formal setting.
2.  The profile of the prospective customers may indicate that the salesperson must be able to exert authority to effectively qualify and close. The demographics of the market as related to the product line may be a determinant in how the sales office should function.
3.  The character or feel of the housing designs may exert a subtle influence in this matter. The projects that are marketed with no frills or that feature maximum space for the dollar (without extensive amenities) may be more

effectively promoted in the same direct way. The business office setting is a no-nonsense environment. When the product communicates that direct approach, there may be a valid case for a simple sales office.

There are many valid reasons for creating the more comfortable and informal sales office setting. In fact, in our opinion, that should be the basic objective for most situations, unless one of the above identified factors dictates that it should be altered. It is far easier to encourage people to sit down in an informal area than to invite them into what appears to be a closing room. Serious buyers will communicate in either environment. But hesitant prospects who are not sure they want to become involved with a salesperson (one who may try to sell them a home), will very often avoid the opportunity to sit down in perceived closing areas.

A classic rule for this intense communication setting is to avoid having any displays or items on the walls that may distract the attention of potential buyers. For example, you do not want to be in the middle of a closing session and discover that your buyers are studying a list of optional items displayed on the wall or reading materials that raise questions that will then have to be answered. Any element that might cause the salesperson to lose control of the closing presentation is detrimental to the decision-making process. Items shown on the walls and the surrounding areas in the closing arena should support the sales decision—and lessen any chance for confusion or distraction.

Colors, wall covering, pictures and visual elements need to be carefully selected to provide a positive and nonconfusing backdrop for the confidential closing sessions.

## DESIGNS, FLOOR PLANS AND/OR MODELS

The product-presentation zone of the sales office must be structured to meet the specific criteria of each community. When the builder is featuring a limited number of prepriced models that will be replicated throughout the community in a variety of elevations, the need is different than when the builder is designing and constructing custom homes and a diverse housing line.

In the first case, there is validity in having floor plans and elevations displayed in the sales center in complete form. In the custom situation, the need is different. Representative homes may be shown as examples, but the objective is to counsel qualified prospects and help them to reach a personal decision through a skillfully conducted interview and portfolio-review process.

There are times when the best approach is to show no specific floor plans or models in the primary area. Streetscapes and sketches of typical housing may adorn the walls, but the detailed floor plans are often best handled by individual selection and presentation under the control of professional sales representatives. This is especially true when you are in preconstruction marketing phases in a new community where the use of floor plans in the primary arena denies salespeople the opportunity to involve consumers privately in one-on-one counseling sessions.

A major rule to remember about positioning floor-plan and product displays is to avoid having them at the entry lobby and greeting zone. As we have noted, this area should be reserved for qualifying the prospects' experience, urgency and general knowledge of the area. It is always unwise to deal with the benefits of the housing plans until the stage has been set and the qualifying started on the larger issues of location, neighborhood benefits and developer credibility.

It is sometimes effective to have the product line displayed in an area not visible upon entry. This can be achieved by the way panels and dividers define the space. By keeping the main area focused on larger concepts, the salespeople can qualify and control customers more efficiently. When it is appropriate to lead prospects to examples of housing designs, the salespeople can do so with a discovery process that helps to heighten interest levels.

When you have model homes that should be seen before people become involved with floor plans, any floor-plan display is best positioned where it can be used when clients return from the inspection tour. Better yet, in a low-volume traffic community, the salesperson should escort prospects through the models and use these occasions to further qualify and build trusting relationships that may lead to more sales. Remember that floor plans do not make sales—salespeople do!

Floor plans do not make interesting wall displays when seen from a distance. That is why experienced marketers position them so that they can be studied only by standing over or near them. Angled wall mounts that permit floor plans to be viewed from above are preferable to those that hang on wall panels. Once you are more than three or four feet from a floor plan, it appears as just a series of lines and markings. It is visually more effective to have pictures or artist's renderings of exteriors of homes displayed on the walls so that they add an element of interest even from a distance. Only when you are close to the displays will the blueprints or keyline drawings be of value.

When you have an extensive portfolio of floor plans, limit the ones shown in the display area to a representative group arranged by classification. For example, if you have several traditional two-story homes, a variety of ranch styles and split-levels, select representative plans for each type for your public viewing areas and maintain the rest in accessible locations for use in personal counseling sessions. The objective is to permit the salesperson to qualify for interest and financial ability before narrowing the choices to a particular size, style and price range. The primary issue is the risk of confusing prospective buyers with too many choices and complicating the selling process.

If you have a number of different product lines within one community (such as townhomes, single-family detached, condominiums and custom homes), each product display area should be separated from the other categories of housing to permit the sales representatives to concentrate on one classification at a time. This can be achieved either by scattering the the product presentations within the sales arena or by using vertical display panels that visually control what the buyer can see at any one position in the office. For example, a six-foot-high display panel might feature one product line on one side and another on the opposite. A triangular display or a kiosk could accommodate at least three housing categories while visually separating them from each other. In a custom housing environment, emphasize exterior design treatments, rather than floor plans. Let salespeople work from well-organized plan portfolios to paint the dream of ownership with the personal touch that brings the homes to life.

The basic rule is to limit the number of floor plans or choices to seven or less as viewed from a single location within the office. We know from extensive research that confusion and indecision are major deterrents to the selling process. Once you introduce more than seven choices at one time, you risk losing the prospect's attention as well as his or her ability to reach a preliminary sense of direction. The range of five to seven plans is followed by most knowledgeable sales managers and merchandisers in this profession. Once this range is exceeded, it is time to provide an alternative method of addressing the selection process. Plan portfolios from which designs can be introduced to the prospects one at a time are far more effective than a wall of confusing floor plans.

## SIZE AND PERSPECTIVES AFFECT VALUE PERCEPTIONS

The relative size of the floor plans used in the sales presentation affects value perceptions. We know that the smaller the floor-plan examples, the more likely the buyers will judge that the space relationships are less than desired. First impressions are a factor in our value judgments. It is a mistake to compromise on floor-plan sizes in your sales office. The ideal display arrangement is to use full-sized blueprint dimensions for every floor plan, whether mounted on a display panel or shown individually from a controlled portfolio. The smaller the home, the more important it is to visually depict liveable spaces.

Equally important is the use of color and dimensional shading to highlight rooms, exterior landscaping, decks, patios and traffic patterns. Too many builders use plain vanilla presentations of their floor plans! Why not put some color into the picture? You can make an average floor plan far more exciting and understandable with the addition of colors like yellow, green, and light tan. Dramatize the living benefits of each offering by accenting space relationships and incorporating future surroundings. Show landscaping concepts and help the two-dimensional graphics to come to life in ways that help overcome the difficulty of interpreting floor plans.

When displaying floor plans that have been previously modeled or built for individual owners, consider using interior photography to communicate unseen values. Why not incorporate a few color photos as part of each floor plan display panel? Mount around a floor plan cameo shots that colorfully depict the interior design features you need to illustrate. This will do much to overcome the limitations of two-dimensional plans. Studies indicate that 70 percent of the population cannot read a two-dimensional floor plan and picture the third dimension. Anything that helps translate these spatial relationships in positive ways will assist the value-building process.

The preconstruction phase is the most demanding of all new home sales environments. When you do not have models available, no completed homes can be shown as production examples and everything must be portrayed through words and graphics, so sales personnel need effective visual tools to paint the future dream. This is when show-and-tell becomes a well-rehearsed game. We believe in limiting floor-plan exhibits in preconstruction sales offices so that the sales personnel can use every moment with the prospective buyers to maximum advantage. By selecting individually mounted floor plans from an enclosed cabinet or plan container, sales representatives can increase the amount of time they have with each prospect, while verbally and visually portraying future benefits to those who buy during the pioneer period. In the best-designed sales trailers, the information shown in the main lobby is limited to the overview and lifestyle exhibits that set the stage for private counseling in an adjacent room.

While it is desirable to depict on the walls exterior elevations and streetscapes of the new neighborhoods, the discovery of any particular design should rest with the salespeople for one-on-one counseling. In these dream environments, the ideal method of handling floor plans is to use blueprint-sized reproductions that are keylined to show only the primary walls and mount them on a firm material (like white foam core) for easy handling. The surface of each plan should be covered with an acetate transparency so the sales representatives can use dry-erase markers to personalize the living benefits for each customer. These markings can be erased after each use to ready the floor plan for the next prospects.

## MULTIPLE-BUILDER DEVELOPMENT WITH A CENTRAL SALES FACILITY

The multiple-builder community with a central sales facility needs special designing to accommodate all of the participants in the venture. One of the functions is to emphasize the developer's credibility story in the greeting and overview portion of the sales office and reserve the builders' stories where they can be related to product differentiation. While it may be appropriate to list the preferred builders along with the developer at an early entry station, the marketing of each organization, its principle and programs justifies separate displays. When space permits, it is most effective to provide an individual alcove or visually controlled location for each company. A representative selection of the homes offered can be shown, while the rest are handled by the sales representatives after qualifying for motivations, abilities and interests. Sometimes the best way to handle individual builder programs is to place them in their own models or sales areas. As sales counselors take prospects to the demonstration products, they can use the builder-credibility messages with their merchandise. They can also use plan portfolios and sample displays of products and features in these same locations. If you have a model row that features one home by each builder in a controlled presentation sequence, easels promoting the builders can be prominently displayed inside each model and supported by appropriate product-benefit information panels.

## SPECIAL PRODUCT FEATURE DISPLAYS

The unique merits of one builder's construction systems versus another's can make a difference when homebuyers are weighing their purchase decisions. That is why it is important to visually promote your features and their related benefits in ways that effectively dramatize these special values. The feature/benefit display should be positioned in the sales office, where it can be used by sales representatives prior to the showing of models or inventory housing as well as afterwards for reinforcement of the quality delivery message. The contents of this area in order of importance include the following:

1.   a summary of major features and benefits listed in order of priority (the item that creates the greatest value difference for comparative shoppers should be first, followed by the next most important benefit and so on)
2.   the builder's commitment to service and the related warranties provided to each purchaser
3.   awards, testimonials and publicity articles
4.   brand names and product photos or endorsements
5.   energy-efficiency display and related endorsements
6.   wall cutaway or equivalent graphic identifying construction techniques and benefits
7.   photos of construction systems showing the building process in the field

Video tape or slide presentations are occasionally used to explain construction techniques or emphasize the builder's quality delivery story.

## COMMUNITY ACTIVITY BOARDS, HISTORY AND NATURE

The human side of the development story can best be depicted with photography mixed with memorabilia about community activities, historical articles and the natural environment. Whenever you capture the romance of the past and blend it with the creation of new neighborhoods, you add a special dimension to the sales presentation that can win hearts as well as pocketbooks! Where the history of the site has romantic value, it should be incorporated in the storyboards. Sometimes it deserves major emphasis as part of the overview or information in the entry or lobby.

It always pays to have a community activity board with candid photos, publicity stories and general community news. We suggest locating this tool near the sales representatives' counseling desks, so they can reference people and events as part of their informal conversation with prospects.

Nature is always worth promoting. If the environment is interesting, it merits visual representation in the sales arena. Stories about recreational parks, lakes and trails, as well as the flora and fauna of the region, can stimulate conversations and emotions. Always try to think beyond the housing you are building to the larger environments of which they are a part. When you combine lifestyles and natural amenities with your construction messages, you tap the underlying motivations that cause people to select one location over another. Your purchasers buy neighborhoods and surrounding values before they buy your homes!

## DECORATOR AND OPTION SELECTION AREA

The very nature of various options and design choices often available in the selection process creates a potential conflict of interest in the decision-influencing environment. While these choices frequently help reinforce values and assist salespeople in getting minor decisions to verify major commitments, they can be real deterrents to the logical sequence of topics and decisions that must be reviewed before the sale is consummated. Most sales professionals in this business prefer to have the decorator-selection items kept out of the major sales arena and located where they can be referred to as needed. If at all possible, a separate design center or a design counselor should be used to keep these potentially confusing decisions from muddying the sales track and causing salespeople to lose control.

Cabinets can be constructed to store these items so they are retrieved by sales representatives only when appropriate to their presentations. An independent room, which is accessed under sales control, is among the better ways to handle options, extras and decorator choices.

## PUT PEOPLE IN THE PICTURE!

Selling residential real estate is an emotional business! It takes more than facts and figures to convince prospects they should own specific homes in neighborhoods with uncertain social and psychological prospects. We may be able to buy investment property we do not plan to occupy (or even see) without needing to know the social elements related to that decision, but it is unlikely that any potential home buyer is going to decide to live in a neighborhood without some knowledge of the social benefits and the people who will live there and an appreciation of the lifestyles that characterize that housing environment. In your profession, you sell people to people as much as you sell property to people!

The better marketers in this profession understand that truth. They take time to gather all of the demographic information they can before they develop marketing campaigns. They interpret housing designs and environments in terms of human needs and emotional security factors. Sales presentations, sales offices, advertising campaigns and all collateral literature should be designed and used in terms of the human emotions that must be fulfilled before sales are consummated.

Knowing the importance of this social message, I am always amazed at the number of real estate offices and on-site community sales facilities I investigate that are almost devoid of *people*! It is not the exception that bothers me—it is the frequency of this experience! The typical subdivision office or builder's model home will have absolutely no evidence that real people have purchased homes there, will ever live there or will enjoy the benefits of living there. Walls are covered with displays of housing exteriors, floor plans, maps, information about the builder, the products and the community. But few, if any, human faces reflect the living concepts the marketers are trying to portray.

One of the most effective sales tools you can have in a sales office is a display of pictures showing the owners of your homes. Better yet, have photos that were taken in front of their new residences or in the interiors of their newly decorated homes. Add some testimonials and personal endorsements and you have the most effective reinforcer for any sales presentation. If there is not room to show a number of photos on the walls, you can always have a family photo album with pictures of people, events and testimonial elements, which your prospects can review at an appropriate time during sales presentations.

The typical sales office will display artists' renditions of the exterior elevations of various housing designs, but without any people or evidence of livability. The homes are almost always shown in a sterile environment, which does not paint the dream of what it would be like to put yourself in the picture. Why not show these same elevations and perspectives with people? Why not select profiled individuals or buyer types and place them in the photos or artists' scenes? Doesn't it make sense to try to communicate the emotional and psychological benefits of ownership with the use of characters representative of that specific housing area?

I am reminded of a time when I was helping a client design a new sales office for a medium-priced, single-family housing project in the midwest. We were looking at the renderings, aerial photos, master site plan and related exhibits that he planned to use in the visual support system. We both noted that not a single graphic showed any evidence of human activity—or future living benefits. As we talked about his prior success in a similar subdivision not far from this location, I asked him if he had ever taken pictures of those homes with the owners included in the photography? He had not, but he immediately grasped the significance of the idea. That afternoon, we laid out a sales office that was purposely designed to bring his profiled prospects and prior successes into the visual sales arena. We elected to do away with artists' renderings in favor of enlarged photos of those same elevations taken with real people who own them in the other location. We eliminated the typical floor-plan displays and substituted full-size blueprints on a rack, which sales representatives individually select to place on a drafting table to review with customers. On the walls above the drafting table and blueprint rack, we mounted photos (professionally taken) that showed the interiors of each of these homes with actual owners, not models. The result is a gallery of interesting photos that translate the benefits of each design while reinforcing the personal aspects of the people who have purchased, currently enjoy and live in them.

In addition, we took the site map (the usual horizontal site table-display) and incorporated cameos (cropped photos) and living scenes taken from the lifestyle portfolio that our photographer had gathered. As people look at the site plan, they see scenes of real people who live in the community artistically inserted in the surrounding border. It provides the salesperson with a marvelous opportunity to talk about the types of families, community activities and social advantages of living in this protected neighborhood.

The builder's credibility story was executed with the same consideration. We showed scenes of the builder, architect and production people working on site, not in a formal environment. There were photos showing the sequential history of the development and statements that reinforced the commitment to preserve trees and maintain the natural beauty of the environment. The result was an interesting and believable visual presentation that substantially strengthen the role of the sale representatives.

In this particular community, we carried the personalization further by using blueprint-type floor plans that had artist's notes (the architect's comments handwritten on them instead of formal, commercial printing.) The salespeople used them to add their own notes and put their customer's names on the plans with which they most identify!

**FIGURE 4.15 Marketing Tools**

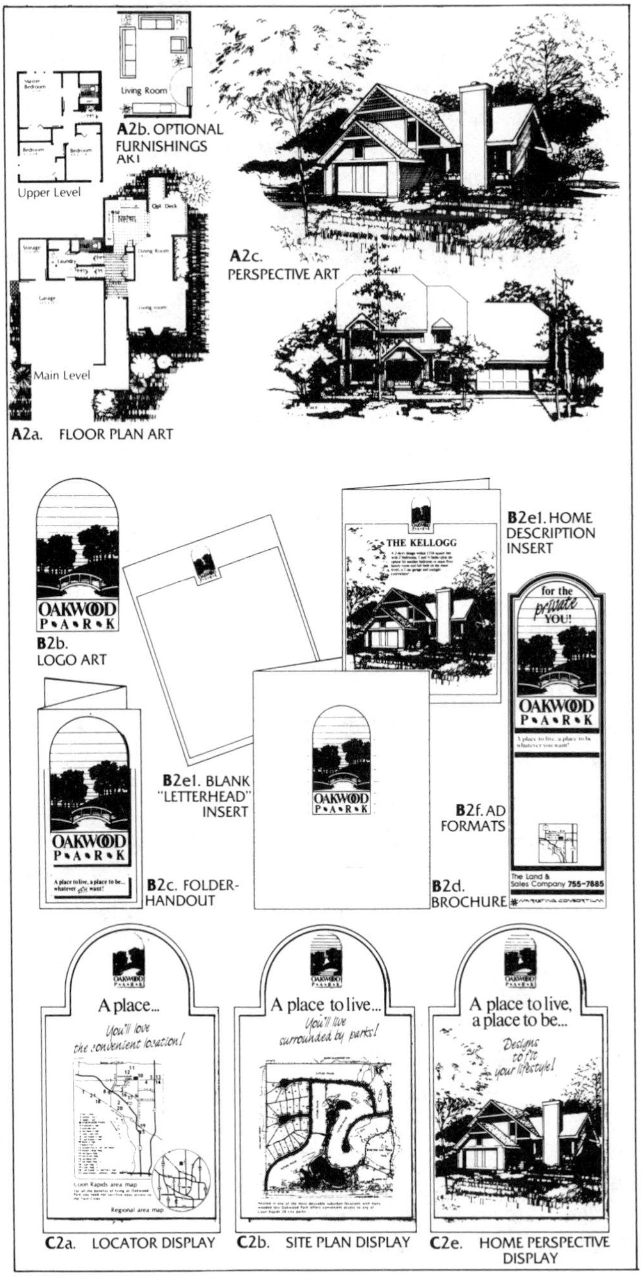
Upper Level
Living Room
A2b. OPTIONAL FURNISHINGS ART
Main Level
A2a. FLOOR PLAN ART
A2c. PERSPECTIVE ART
OAKWOOD PARK
B2b. LOGO ART
THE KELLOGG
B2e1. HOME DESCRIPTION INSERT
for the private YOU!
B2e1. BLANK "LETTERHEAD" INSERT
B2f. AD FORMATS
B2c. FOLDER-HANDOUT
B2d. BROCHURE
The Land & Sales Company 755-7885
A place...
You'll love the convenient location!
A place to live...
You'll live surrounded by parks!
A place to live, a place to be...
Designs to fit your lifestyle!
C2a. LOCATOR DISPLAY
C2b. SITE PLAN DISPLAY
C2e. HOME PERSPECTIVE DISPLAY

SOURCE: Courtesy of Development Directions, Inc., Rochester, NY

The entire office now serves as a testimonial support system for the sales messages. You can easily picture yourself in that environment and you can relate to the people who live there or will live there soon.

Take a look at the sales environments in which you conduct your marketing activities. Do they communicate the personal, emotional and romantic aspects of living in your homes and neighborhoods? Do they visually say: "We have happy people living here (like you) who believe in our homes and are convinced they made the right decision!" If not, maybe you should put more *people in the picture*!!!

## POSITION THE STATIONS OF INVOLVEMENT TO MAXIMIZE SALES CONTROL

Closing is not a point in time—it is a complete process! For salespeople to efficiently produce sales from the opportunities they are presented, they must qualify, involve, build values and reduce resistance. The processes are interlinked, but they move forward along a decision track that must be strong enough to withstand the pressures of uncertainty, confusion, lack of urgency and normal resistance to change.

When organizing a sales center of any kind, think through the objectives that must be kept in focus if a high yield is to be realized from the efforts of the sales representatives. Maintaining a positive psychological climate while quickly qualifying and building perceived values requires a number of professional skills. It is far easier for the salesperson to perform these assignments if the office and displays are logically organized.

A minimum of seven major decision points always apply in each new home sale. Five of these usually justify special visual displays in the sales environment. These five are:

1.  selling the general location as the right place to live
2.  reinforcing the credibility of the development team
3.  selling the values of the land plan and neighborhoods
4.  selling the special features and benefits of the homes and amenities that characterize the specific offering
5.  selecting and presenting of the floor plans, models and designs available in that community

The other two decision points of homesite selection and financing are normally handled through personal counseling, although occasionally it is helpful to have exhibits dealing with these two subjects.

If you are dealing with a builder who builds on scattered sites or on lots owned by the prospects, the above sequence will begin with the builder story and move to the quality features and design choices. Location and neighborhood sales have already occurred.

## CRITERIA FOR MODELS AND SHOW HOMES

The decisions made for on-site marketing scenarios in new residential subdivisions are influenced by numerous factors, and frequently the judgment calls prove inadequate and at times disastrous. Developers and home builders look at their opportunities and then their pocketbooks when faced with choices for presenting their merchandise to the buying public. Many successful builders never feature speculative models. While these are typically small-volume operations, they are often very profitable for the entrepreneurs who run them. They keep overhead low and risks to a minimum. Thus, they are flexible and tend to survive market downturns and the gyrations of the economy. Most of these builders depend upon either referrals from prior customers or the support of real estate brokers capable of selling from blueprints using previously delivered homes as examples. On the other end of the marketing spectrum are merchant builders who attempt to capture a high percentage of target markets by investing substantial sums in beautifully furnished model homes, well landscaped sales environments and graphically effective sales facilities.

We are often asked by our clients whether they need furnished models or elaborate merchandising programs to meet their sales objectives. There is no simple answer to that question. Like so many choices we make in new home marketing, we must review alternatives against a checklist of proven guidelines. It is appropriate at this point to address those criteria in some detail.


## THE CASE FOR MODEL HOMES

Do you need model homes to meet your sales pro formas and, if so, how many? That is not a question that can be answered quickly. Among marketers, you will find almost unanimous agreement that models measurably add to the potential for achieving sales quotas. With rare exception, they are a plus in the marketing equation. The reason is simple: The average prospective home buyer has difficulty picturing a finished home from a set of blueprints. The imagination level of most individuals is insufficient to understand a three-dimensional home from two-dimensional plans. Equally important is their inability to picture an unfurnished home in a decorated mode. When given the choice, prospects will gravitate to furnished, well-decorated models in preference to blueprint shopping, even if the homes they ultimately purchase were finally selected from a plan portfolio or were custom-drawn just for them. Those builders who offer well-decorated show homes tend to attract more customers and generate more sales, because they have provided sample dream environments that compensate for the lack of visual translation.

Whether or not a specific project requires models depends upon a number of variables, not the least of which is the competitive nature of the marketplace and the amount of pent-up demand for the type of housing products you are offering. If you have a choice location and a proven product with a demonstrated need, you might be able to sell all of your production from a preconstruction sales trailer or an off-site office without ever incurring the costs of models. It is often done in high-demand markets when interest rates and public acceptance of housing are favorable factors. However, there is always a risk that what you perceive to be a slam-dunk will turn out to be a hard-fought battle.

Markets change. You may begin your planning when everything is rosy, only to discover that the rules are altered before you are halfway through! Experience with wild gyrations in the mortgage markets have conditioned most of us to realize we do not control our own destinies. It is a wise marketer who plans for the worst-case scenarios and then conserves marketing dollars to move efficiently everything that can be sold without making big expenditures unless necessary. Thus, presale campaigns that capitalize upon consumer demand are a means of reducing risk while testing the strength of the marketplace. Planning for one or more models, even if they are never used, is good business insurance! Not to have them in your marketing budget is to risk reduction of profits if models become necessary.

The small-volume builder will not be able to afford the models or the sales environment that a merchant builder can justify. That does not mean he or she does not need a representative home or two from which to demonstrate design and quality. The term *model* is understood in our industry. What is a model? It can be a speculative home that is for sale and, until sold, serves as a display home or show home for public viewing. It can also be a production home that has been sold to an individual buyer but is used in the interim to produce other sales.

Models need not be furnished to illustrate values. In fact, an unfurnished home is sometimes a much better marketing tool. It permits the sales representative to demonstrate quality of construction and to show the home the way it will be delivered. If the craftsmanship is evident, the sales agent can make the point that this builder is putting the dollars into homes rather than into expensive merchandising like other builders. The buyer benefits by not having to pay for the frills of model marketing. Partially furnished (vignetted) models can be a solution where limited budgets are a factor. The use of plants, effective lighting and a few silent sales tools can make an unfurnished model a showplace for demonstrating unique benefits of design and construction.

The number of models and whether or not to furnish them involve discretionary decisions that should be weighed against the following criteria:

### Absorption Rates and the Total Number to Be Sold

Economy of scale must be taken into consideration when planning model merchandising. A fully furnished model that is to be kept off the market for a year or more is an expensive investment. The interest carry and management costs alone can be substantial. Decorating will range from $15 to $30 per square foot in most markets. A 2,000-square-foot home can easily represent $30,000–$60,000 in furnishings if done by a professional interior designer, and this is exclusive of landscaping and model maintenance. If you are planning to sell only five to ten homes in a year, it would be very difficult to justify a fully furnished model, unless that was almost your only form of marketing and you had adequate pricing margins to absorb these costs. Normally, merchant builders attempt to stay within the range of 20 to 40 sales per furnished model home per year. Thus, a location that will generate 100 sales a year could probably justify a minimum of two to a maximum of five fully decorated model homes. This does not mean that each model must produce a proportionate share of the total volume; the point is to have enough homes to amortize the costs of model merchandising within a reasonable budget range. If the absorption rate for one builder is less than 20 per year, the judgment call must now involve other factors.

## The Competitive Market and the Prospect's Expectations

When operating in a market area where every builder is doing a superb job of merchandising models, and prospective buyers are conditioned to seeing well-furnished display homes, you can suffer by comparison if your homes are not equally well presented. The expectations of your customers are a primary factor in the marketing equation. Model homes serve as traffic generators. Without them, you tend to draw fewer customers. They are marketing tools that keep you in business. If everyone around you is using show homes to advantage and you are operating without a place from which to do business, you can lose your market share to the competition. One solution to this dilemma is to build in communities where you will gain exposure simply because a number of builders are producing homes, and then to feature one home that shows well—even if unfurnished. If staffed and partially merchandised, you can live off some of the sales traffic generated by the other entrepreneurs.

## The Uniqueness of Housing Plans or Design Concepts

The more difficult it is to understand a floor plan or design concept, the more important it is to furnish and dramatize its benefits. When you are building traditional Williamsburg two-story colonials that everyone in the area understands (including most buyers who have been in a number of them before seeing yours), it is not as important to furnish or even maintain a model as when you have a contemporary design not seen before in that market place. It is the lack of imagination and the inability to picture the finished home that are the challenges. When unable to visualize and appreciate a new, unfamiliar design, buyers may gravitate to finished products rather than purchase in the pre-construction phase. Likewise, even if the homes are completed, buyers may not be able to appreciate how to furnish them unless someone illustrates it for them. Most condominiums and attached housing designs require some furnishing to make them appear livable; the smaller the spaces, the more important it is to show what can be done with them. If you are dealing with some of the newer cluster housing concepts of zero lot lines, "Z" lots, and patio homes, the need for models to illustrate livability is greater than when dealing with single-family detached homes.

## Available Dollars and the Total Marketing Plan

Model homes are usually the centerpiece in the marketing pro forma. Without them, advertising and other promotional efforts can be wasted. Therefore, as you study alternatives, you need to put into perspective the number of marketing dollars you can justify for your total business plan and weigh the relative value of on-site merchandising to the off-site promotional budget. A safe rule to follow is: Always have at least one well-merchandised example to show to the public to reinforce confidence in your delivery system and stimulate discontent with other housing comparisons.

## Competitive Positioning to Increase Market Penetration

A building company that has made a commitment to substantially increase its market share by aggressive merchandising can sometimes justify a major investment in

**FIGURE 4.16    Atlanta Model**

SOURCE: Courtesy of Carol Clark & Co.

models, model home parks and extensive advertising on the basis of buying the market for future growth objectives. By simply leading the pack with superior on-site presentations, it is possible to make the buying public more aware of your company and its housing programs. If the selection and execution of model homes is dramatically better than the competition's, an increase in sales at the expense of the other builders is a probable result. However, at some point the costs for those adventures will have to be met. If profits do not increase along with sales, the decision to invest a few hundred thousand dollars in the merchandising budget may jeopardize the survival of the enterprise!

## Creating an Image of Excellence that Improves Perceived Values and Profits

The saying "a picture is equal to a thousand words" has a corollary in new home marketing. "A professionally decorated model is better than a thousand brochures!" Perceptions of value are subtle. How do you show quality to a home buyer? Every builder proclaims to have a quality product, and most are convinced they do a better job than their competitors. A well-designed and decorated model home finished with an eye to craftsmanship can communicate in a few moments what a salesperson or a thousand brochures may never accomplish. Conviction is achieved when people can see, touch and feel a quality home.

## The Need for a Place to Do Business

A small-volume home builder will sometimes elect to build and maintain a furnished model home as the primary place of business. A portion of the home, such as a den, bedroom or lower level, is used as the builder's office, while the rest of the home is shown as one example from the available portfolio of plans. This same home might have a garage sales office plus one room assigned to the builder's management needs. Although this is less desirable than having a model that does not conflict with construction and management activities, it is a reasonable compromise when budgets do not justify both. We know many builders who started operations with just such humble beginnings and grew to be major forces in their marketplaces.

## Establishing Values for a Neighborhood

Sometimes a developer needs to create values for the remaining homesites in a particular community or neighborhood, and the course chosen is to build one or more luxury models that will raise the values of surrounding properties. A subdivider dependent upon other builders to unlock the real estate values he or she has attempted to create may need to take the lead in salting the community with one or two models that set the tone for the designs and price levels desired for the entire project. In such cases, the costs of the models may be borne by the increased values of the remaining lots and passed on to builders or individual site purchasers. This is sound strategy when the area being developed does not already have an established perception of value equal to the targeted price levels.

## LOCATING YOUR MODELS

When choosing the location for your models or housing showcase, your overriding objective should be establishment of a sample environment that will communicate the future values of your homes and the community to optimum advantage. At the same time, you want to avoid creating unfavorable comparisons between your model homes and the actual inventory sites for sale. The choice of model homesites deserves more than casual review. Short- and long-range objectives need to be taken into consideration. If the model setting is also going to serve as the sales center for the community, the criteria are different than if the homes are going to be shown by appointment and scattered throughout the development. Assuming that your models must be positioned where they will achieve multiple objectives for sales and presentation, here is a checklist we use in determining the best place(s) for positioning demonstration housing.

### Traffic Control and Accessibility to Prospective Buyers

Exposure to arriving traffic in the general area and within the community is a key factor. A principal reason you construct model homes is to have a magnet to attract your profiled customers. If you are hard to find, or at a competitive disadvantage because of your location, compensating promotional efforts are required to offset this factor, and in some cases, you may never be able to overcome the disadvantages. When operating in a multiple-builder community, the model-home game has a more complex set of rules than when you totally control your own destiny. In reference to this issue, it is desirable that you meet the following objectives:

1. Position models where they can be seen from the high-traffic streets and, preferably, where you can control the gate or access point into the specific neighborhoods you are marketing.
2. Locate on the right side of the access street so it is easy for prospects to stop or turn into our parking areas.
3. Anchor your sales facility or model home that serves as a sales office so that it has visual control of arriving and passing traffic.
4. Situate where parking will not be a challenge to your customers. If necessary, convert one homesite or two into a parking area from which you can provide attractive access to the model sales office.
5. Gain a competitive advantage when possible, so that prospects see or stop at your models before they visit any others in the immediate area.

### Model Sites Representative of Inventory

It is normally unwise to put models on your best sites or the prime locations in the community. The problem is one of over-expectation by prospects who see these lots and then are shown less-desirable inventory locations. It is tough for salespeople to overcome the psychological letdown that results when customers are exposed to superior model settings and then taken to production homes or vacant sites not nearly as attractive as those first encountered. Even worse is the situation where none of the homesites is comparable to the ones selected for the models! In most situations, it is sound merchandising strategy to place the model homes on homesites most representative of the ones you will be selling. The best sites are easy to sell and will probably go for premiums. In addition, you have the added value of landscaping and model-home streetscaping to demonstrate the advantages of the typical locations.

The exceptions to this rule are when the control factors would be violated or when proximity to major amenities is necessary to demonstrate properly community benefits such as a clubhouse, lake, golf course or marina. Even then, the choice should be carefully weighed so that potential negatives of existing inventory are not accentuated by contrasts with the model environments. Topography, sun orientation, views, trees and neighboring influences deserve evaluation. Demonstration homes need to dramatize the benefits and compensate for any possible negatives with superior merchandising that helps your prospects picture what they can do with similar homesites.

### Location Should Permit Demonstration of Basic Plans

If you have floor plans designed to fit a variety of sites because of differences in topography or land-planning, it is important to try to find a model setting that will permit you to demonstrate most of them in the same vicinity. Sometimes it is not possible to do this and still fulfill the higher priorities. Then elect to show some of them in the model area and the rest either as speculative production homes or from illustrations.

### Provide a Self-Contained Setting that Controls Model Exposure

Whenever possible, place your models in an area that will not be adversely affected by through traffic, congestion or neighboring influences. One of the least desirable situations is to have models on both sides of a street that is open to the public for through traffic. Merely crossing the street becomes a risk to you and your prospects. When you must use a busy street, choose one side for a model series partially protected by landscaping and fencing. A preferred arrangement is to devote a cul-de-sac totally to model presentations. Control is optimum because there is no through traffic. Models are given a superior setting with landscaped yards, and sometimes the street can be treated as a park with sitting areas and interesting walking paths between the models. An alternative is the use of a partial street blocked off on one end to serve as a model park while production housing is started elsewhere or barricaded and accessed from the opposite end of the street.

### Allow Space for Adding Future Models and
### Provide Breathing Room for Your Show Homes

Unless you have only a few sites and a short building cycle, you should plan for tomorrow's marketing needs. That is why smart marketers usually leave one or two adjacent homesites vacant when designing model sales areas. This accomplishes two objectives:

1.  Room exists to add models if the first ones do not fully meet sales goals.
2.  There is breathing space around show homes to set them apart from regular construction. These open spaces can also serve as transitional parks between models, tot lots, and additional parking.

### Avoid Construction Traffic and Noise If Possible

Model environments should be isolated from unsightly and noisy construction areas whenever practical. The confusion, dust, traffic and sounds of building operations present challenges for the maintenance of peaceful and productive sales arenas. Sometimes there are no alternatives. In those cases, learn to live with construction activity. However, planning frequently solves the problem. Establishing access points for construction traffic to bypass model areas (even if only temporary) is in everyone's best interests. Keeping construction trailers at locations that do not conflict with sales presentations is always desirable. Construction workers are seldom a positive influence when directly exposed to prospects and salespeople on a daily basis.

## HOW MANY MODELS DO YOU NEED AND WHICH DO YOU FEATURE?

Economics tend to drive the model-home decision. The number of models is a discretionary choice guided by both competitive positioning and merchandising budgets. If you have an extensive portfolio of designs (more than three or four) or are in the customizing business, your model choices must be limited to those that best fulfill the needs of your sales representatives in presenting your homes to advantage. Your selection should be guided by answering the following questions:

* Which plans will represent the majority of sales—or be necessary to fit the sites you have to sell?
* Which will generate the most interest in terms of competitive positioning?
* How many plans have similar design features, and which of these can best illustrate the variables?
* How many basic housing types are needed to meet anticipated buyer profiles?

When you have the answers to these questions, you can rate your priorities and then make logical choices. If you can justify only one model home from the list, it should be the one that will do the following:

1.  fit the needs of most of your buyers
2.  generate the greatest interest when compared to competitive housing
3.  demonstrate both the variables of the plan and the quality of construction
4.  be priced to attract the largest number of potential prospects

If you can afford more than one demonstration home, the designs chosen should appeal to different prospect profiles to broaden your market potential.

## MODEL SEQUENCE GUIDELINES

Schools of thought differ on model-sequencing. Some builders like to position their most expensive homes first; others prefer them to be last in the model area. The majority give little consideration to the psychology of customer-conditioning in model-home tours. Lot sizes and streetscapes tend to get more attention than the impact of sequencing housing designs to create maximum buyer interest. Our experiences seem to validate the following:

- The first home seen should not be the most expensive or the largest. If it is, all other homes by comparison will be at a disadvantage.
- It is preferable to select the first home in the sequence to be a qualifier property: that is, one that enables salespeople to determine whether a more or less expensive home is needed. This means selecting a plan in the middle price range that is able to set the stage for the other homes.
- The initial model should stimulate emotions and prepare prospects for the rest of the tour. This means selecting a plan that has some exciting features and is not just a Plain Jane!
- Smaller or less expensive homes should be anchored by mid-range or more expensive models.
- Models that fit similar buyer profiles and lifestyles should be separated, so that contrasts and interest levels will peak as comparisons are made.
- The relationships between models should accent the values of exterior designs, landscaping and spaces with a view to both visual values and privacy.

## THE MODEL-SALES TRAP: A PLUS OR MINUS?

Marketers debate the value of controlled model-sales areas designed to trap prospects within their borders. The majority favor them for obvious reasons:

1. They permit salespeople to greet, qualify and demonstrate the homes to every prospect.
2. They protect the investment in model-home furnishings and accessories since they are less vulnerable to theft.
3. Models will usually be seen in the order presented, and this assists the basic conditioning strategies.
4. Customers attracted to controlled model areas know they will be interviewed and tend to be more prepared for the sales representative's involvement.

Those who do *not* favor sales traps base their arguments on the following key points:

1. Some prospects are intimidated by these barriers and, thus, are discouraged from investigating housing they should see.
2. Competition that has a more relaxed approach to presenting properties may secure some sales simply because customers felt less pressured.

3.  Brokers are a major source of business in many markets, and they also tend to resist model traps because they prefer to control their own prospects and avoid new home sales specialists.
4.  Model areas are expensive and traps increase landscaping and fencing costs.

In our studies of hundreds of housing operations in North America, we find that local customs as much as anything else seem to influence this presentation issue. There are markets where sales traps have never been used and, in the opinion of local marketers, might be a disadvantage in the face of alternative housing environments. In others like the fiercely competitive southern California market, almost every builder of any consequence features both superior on-site model presentations and controlled trapping. Buyers expect them and salespeople prefer them. It is my opinion that a well-designed trap does not feel like one. It is a landscaped area that properly protects and enhances the exterior appearance of the homes and surroundings. Water barriers, berms, trees, varied fencing treatments and mature landscaping help to mute the sense of being controlled. Benefits outweigh possible negatives. The bottom-line factor should be the impact on sales, and it is easier to sell someone you qualify and talk to than someone you do not!

When designing model areas, always remember that a home should be approached from its best vantage point. This means that walkways should swing away from models and lead prospects from one to another so that each home is seen and addressed from the angle that gives maximum value to the architecture and a sense of arrival.

## IS THERE A CASE FOR SCATTERED MODELS?

The answer is yes—if you have salespeople who will escort their prospects to each location and maintain control over the showing process. Sometimes you have no choice but to locate production models on scattered homesites as you fill-in a subdivision that was not sequentially controlled. In these situations, you can use one strategic location to pick up sales traffic, qualify and provide the overview. Then you can take customers on a planned approach to the models or demonstration homes located in various parts of the community. This is frequently the concept employed when selling custom-home communities or major planned-unit developments, where a variety of housing types are positioned in separate subneighborhoods. Multiple-builder communities with a central sales staff typically function with widely separated models or speculative inventory. The key to success for individual builders is to be sure their homes are shown to qualified buyers by the community sales team. That requires personal attention to the interests of the sales agents and the promotion of your values and services to those who dictate what is shown.

A very effective way to provide equal exposure and assure every builder of a setting that will draw consumer interest is to create a multiple-builder showcase of model homes all located in one controlled environment. There are many fine examples of well-planned model parks that display the homes offered by a variety of builders. Customers can see them all in one location and have a chance to make comparisons as well as become enthused about the diversity of housing concepts they see. When developers understand the value of group-marketing programs, everyone can profit from a dream street or model parade that is open to the public seven days a week. In well-organized multiple-builder programs, developers establish guidelines to which all participants subscribe. This includes plan registration and protection, control of speculative inventory, model-home responsibilities, group promotional funds and lot-pooling or exchange privileges to assure continuity of the development. Readers interested in more details on these policies and procedures can write the author for access to additional resources.

## MODEL CRITERIA FOR CONDOMINIUMS AND MULTIFAMILY HOUSING

Marketing condominiums and other multifamily projects is more demanding than marketing single-family housing. There is far less flexibility, simply because buildings must be constructed in groups or all at one time. A high-rise condominium usually depends upon an extensive preconstruction sales program, because of the time it takes to build the structure and the financial requirements. A high percentage of presales is necessary before lenders are willing to release construction funds. Low-rise communities are a little more manageable, since some groupings can be started without waiting for one key building to be completed.

In the case of a high-rise condominium building, the solution to models is often the construction of a sample design located off-site, where it can be inspected while the structure is being erected. Mock-up three-dimensional replicas of each plan are usually justified—along with a scaled version of the building complex. The graphics used in this type of marketing environment are much more critical than in typical single-family developments. They have to portray future concepts that are hard to visualize unless shown in detailed perspectives—inside and out.

Once access to the condominium building is available, locate models where they will be most representative of the inventory and the views. For example, it is a mistake, in my opinion, to have the models on the ground floor of a high rise. When you do, buyers do not have the perspective of the views, which can only be captured on the upper floors. It is also unwise to be in penthouse locations or in the upper one-third of the building. These are normally premium locations. Also, some prospects are afraid of heights and nervous about elevators. Logic dictates placement of models on one of the middle floors, unless you can justify the cost of a number of models on different levels. General sales information can be provided on the ground floor, but all prospects should be escorted up the elevators with informative sales counselors who can make the elevator rides interesting and short. Arrival at the mid-level gives them a chance to qualify for location and price without being in the most or least expensive models. Our pricing studies on high-rise condominiums reveal that the first five to seven levels are frequently more valuable than the middle floors. Those afraid of fires, elevators and heights will choose them over the upper floors. The prestige locations are almost always on the top floors, where views are the key to value.

Low-rise clusters should follow the basic guidelines we have provided for single-family models, with the additional caution that control is usually achieved either by placing models adjacent to the sales unit or by keeping them closed to be shown only to prospects escorted by salespeople. In buildings that feature security services, it is easy to justify why you must be present when buyers tour models. You are emphasizing one of the major benefits of this type of housing environment as you show the various models. When you are concerned about the effect of noise and confusion from those already occupying the building on the viewing public, it is best to close off the floor, building or street selected for sales and models for the exclusive use of the sales staff until most of your sales are achieved.

## MAKING YOUR HOMES MEMORABLE

In most major metropolitan markets in America, competition for the attention of today's home buyer is complex and intense. Housing candidates investigate numerous opportunities before deciding upon those they ultimately select. National research indicates that the average new home buyer sees a minimum of 12 to 15 different housing environments and/or model areas during a shopping period in excess of three months. This includes the few buyers who purchase the first homes they inspect and the preretirees who seem to take forever to reach decisions.

The size of the housing-investment decision justifies this in-depth investigation. It is not a choice lightly made. New home buyers live with their decisions for many years. Real estate brokers who work with transferees recognize the challenge of trying to orient new arrivals to the community.

Typically, such brokers must review a wide selection of homes before their customers are ready to narrow the decision to one or two. The risk of house indigestion is very high! Consider, then, the unescorted potential buyers who wander from one housing neighborhood to another without benefit of someone to help them eliminate the homes they do not need to see. A weekend of inspecting a variety of new homes can leave consumers totally confused and mentally exhausted.

Is it any wonder that only 16 percent of our new homes are sold to buyers who purchase the first day they see them? After looking at so many, how do they relate to one or two and decide to return to make a purchase decision? The propensity for such high return percentages is built into the shopping system. Even with closing masters on the front line, seldom will the closing ratio be over 10 percent of all traffic, and the majority of those closed return more than once before finalizing the sale. Master closers do a better job of bringing customers to the closing table and have greater conversion ratios than the amateurs in this business, but most of them will readily admit that trying to win the favorable attention of their prospects is a fiercely competitive game.

## CREATING MEMORABLE MODELS IS SOUND MARKETING STRATEGY

If your homes are not memorable, you may lose the game before it starts! The average homebuyer has a very low imagination level and, if the homes inspected do not translate the dream into an emotionally exciting experience, the tendency is to continue looking. People forget the things that do not make a favorable impression on our senses. That is why most marketers prefer one well-furnished model rather than two or three poorly done show homes. If the choices of colors, decorating themes and furnishings do not stimulate the prospects' emotions in positive ways, the design benefits may be lost in the maze of competing images. If the homes are not decorated to the tastes and dreams of the profiled prospects, the people you want to impress most will not relate to them. You are competing for the attention of the senses! Memorable models reach out and grab the emotions in such positive ways that the prospects instantly begin to picture themselves living in the new environments! Such homes tap the inner dreams of the targeted homebuyers. A marketer in this industry can be paid no better compliment than to be told that almost everyone who sees the model home falls in love with it! Such homes will capture a high percentage of their profiled prospects, because they capture imaginations and dreams!

Today's new home marketers attempt to appeal to all of the senses when they merchandise their models. They employ background music for each model, specially programmed for the lifestyles and ages of their profiled customers. Carefully selected fragrances are emitted in each room to stimulate the nostrils and induce memories of pleasant experiences associated with their dream homes. Color, light, textures and materials make every room in a model a memorable experience. We tend to recall favorably those homes that made us feel alive, confident and comfortable at the same time. If we can picture ourselves living in those environments, we will instinctively be drawn back to them!

Your first marketing dollars should always be invested on-site with the models and model setting. If the sales message is not visually conveyed by the way it is organized, the dollars you spend to bring prospects to the site will be lost. Conversely, an exciting presentation will stimulate word-of-mouth promotion that can be worth far more than expensive media advertising. Careful planning of presentation objectives can pay big dividends. Failure to do so can be very costly! Always study the competitive environment, and then develop your presentation with the primary objective of being the most exciting and memorable experience for targeted prospects as they review and compare housing alternatives. This does not mean the most expensive presentation—it means the most memorable one!

## HOW TO SELECT AN INTERIOR DESIGNER WHO UNDERSTANDS MERCHANDISING

The specialized knowledge and skills required to become an effective model merchandiser versus a custom-home decorator are as different as those of the professional land planner versus the civil engineer who occasionally does land plans. Interior designers who have risen to national prominence in the housing industry during the last few decades have earned their professional standing, just as leading architects, land planners and marketers have gained theirs. The interior merchandisers who win awards and create exciting models that increase sales results for their clients understand the difference between just decorating a new home and making it a place that profiled customers instinctively picture having for themselves. They have mastered the art of balancing light, space, colors, textures and materials to stimulate emotional appeal. While it is not necessary to employ nationally recognized model merchandisers, they set the standards by which all others in the interior design business should be measured. Builders are tempted by economics or friendship to employ people close to them who will decorate their model homes for nominal fees. Builders frequently ask their wives to undertake this responsibility. Admittedly, some of them do creditable work. I have seen a few cases where the close relative has applied the basic concepts employed by the professionals with acceptable results. However, they are exceptions rather than the rule! The majority of cases have been less than satisfactory when viewed from a merchandiser's perspective.

Even less desirable is asking the local furniture store to decorate the models with the help of their staff decor specialist. Most of these cases result in model homes looking like showplaces for furniture rather than models intimately in tune with the moods and interests of prospective home buyers. This is not to imply that you should never consider using an interior designer affiliated with a furniture store or that working with those who sell furniture is not practical. There are economies and sometimes cooperative marketing objectives that can serve the interests of builders and retail furnishers. The danger is in allowing those who do not fully appreciate your merchandising objectives or the profiles of your buyers to impose their ideas without challenging their selection procedures.

If the budget permits, the benefits of employing a proven professional who has learned how to interpret builders' models and can provide guidance in both design and decor tailored to the specific needs of the marketplace outweigh the slight additional costs that may be involved. Your search for a competent interior merchandiser should begin in your immediate market area. Most metropolitan markets have more than one skilled interior designer who has gained local recognition from the building industry. Knowledge of local attitudes, competition, cooperating marketers and supply sources can both decrease costs and increase the quality of services. Merely having daily access to your interior design specialist can prove very beneficial as you review plans, make proposed changes and react to emergencies incurred in the marketing game.

One problem experience by local design experts is overexposure to the same marketplace. I have been in cities where eight out of ten models in the area were decorated by the same person. No matter how good they are, model merchandisers are like artists, and after a while you can see their mark on a model as soon as you enter. Staying ahead of competition and providing fresh concepts that give you a marketing edge may dictate that you search farther afield.

Wherever you choose your talent, your criteria for selecting a merchandiser should include the following:

1. Having basic knowledge of the difference between furnishing a home, and merchandising it to accent all of its features to prospective buyers
2. Having experience in decorating builder models or training that has prepared them for the opportunity. Inspect his or her work, if possible, or ask to see photos and letters of recommendation.
3. Having the willingness to be guided by marketers and researchers regarding buyer profiles, attitudes and interests. Preferably, the candidate knows the market and has a feel for the likes and dislikes of targeted consumers.

4. Making an agreement to attend planning sessions, meet with the builder, marketing director, architect, land planners and sales personnel in preparation for the initial proposal.

5. Showing willingness to prepare detailed layouts and color boards prior to ordering any furnishings or materials.

6. Making an agreement to live within the authorized merchandising budget and to obtain approval for any changes or extras deemed desirable prior to installation.

7. Making the commitment to personally supervise installation of all approved selections and to be responsible for repairing or replacing anything that does not meet original specifications.

Good merchandisers are also good communicators. I would worry about employing any designer that does not adequately communicate in advance the concepts he or she plans to execute. If you do not know what is going to be achieved and there is not a full understanding of the objectives for each model and the total merchandising effort, your risks far outweigh the investment.

## Agreement for Designer Services

Designers should provide the following in an interior designer's working agreement with a builder[1]:

- Interior design presentation boards for _(number)_ models with color and theme specifications.
- Furniture layouts and selections.
- Design drawings and specifications for mirror treatments and special custom treatments and moldings with detailed wall preparation and paint specifications.
- Supervision of the installation of all interior decor and furnishings.
- A final inventory of all furniture and accessories by model and room location, including one set of 35mm color prints showing each room as finished.

The designer shall specify, procure, deliver and install:

- interior furnishings
- lamps
- artwork and graphics
- decorative accessories

The designer shall specify by model:

- wallcoverings
- paint colors and wall preparation
- mirror treatments
- custom treatments and moldings
- affixed lighting

---

[1]Criteria for the designer-services agreement was furnished courtesy of Karen Butera, Inc., Palo Alto, CA.

- standard interior finishes by model as requested by client
- live plants and containers

## Client's Responsibilities

Prior to commencement of installation of materials by designer, client shall have procured and installed the following:

- wallcoverings (installation only)
- paint colors and wall preparation
- custom mirror treatments
- custom design detailing and moldings
- affixed lighting
- standard interior finishes
- live plants and containers

Client shall provide for the following prior to installation by the designer:

- adequate roads and walkways for the delivery of materials
- running water, electricity, heat and/or air conditioning at the time of installation of the furniture
- cleaning services for windows and all areas relating to the services of the designer
- secured locks to protect the furnishings

Client shall provide at commencement of installation of materials by the designer:

- casual on-site labor
- continuing interior clean-up services for models
- final cleanup including removal of debris and packing materials

Finally, there is the matter of fees. Some designers work on a fixed fee per model plus the costs of all furnishings and materials. Others set a gross price for their services including all furnishings and materials. They work on whatever margins they can salvage. A few price their services by the square footage of each model home, such as $25 a foot, etc. Occasionally, a designer will propose a contract based on a percentage of the gross expenses for the job such as 10 or 15 percent above actual costs. Retainers are normal, and where furnishings are to be ordered by the designer, they are either paid in advance or directly billed to the client. To avoid unpleasant surprises, be sure to put all financial arrangements in writing!

## VARIABLES OF FURNISHING AND DECORATING MODELS

The rest of this book could be devoted to decorating model homes if all of the ideas and opinions offered by interior designers were presented. Since numerous resources such as monthly trade publications treat this subject extensively, the focus of attention will be on the merchandising issues that affect sales strategies and the effectiveness of sales personnel in working with model homes. It is also appropriate to provide a digest of guidelines for selecting interior designers and establishing the budgets.

A model need not be furnished to serve its basic objective of providing customers with a home they can visualize and understand. In fact, some homes are best seen without furnishings! Furniture may detract from significant aspects of design and finish that would be less obvious if the home were fully decorated. A finished home with floor coverings, window treatments and a limited number of accessories like plants and lighting fixtures can be very effective if the plan is easy to interpret.

Even in a model setting where several homes are completely decorated, there is value to having one home unfurnished so that prospects can focus attention on workmanship and design features and can use their imaginations to personalize the environment. An unfurnished model can serve as a sales tool for salespeople who need to show prospects how a home is delivered after they have toured homes with options, upgrades and extensive decorating. A variation of this theme is to vignette one or more rooms in a model rather than having it entirely decorated. A single room with a sitting area, plants and a few amenities can set the tone for the rest of the home without comprehensive decorating schemes.

Given our alternatives and priorities, most of us will recommend decorating and furnishing at least one model if the budget permits. It is better to do one model well than three poorly. If you can justify decorating all the models, be sure to meet the expectation levels of your targeted buyers.

## MATCH MODEL DECOR TO PROFILED PROSPECTS

Today's housing markets are segmented into a variety of buyer types, price ranges, lifestyles and design concepts. When you are establishing criteria for furnishing and decorating model homes, the first step should be to clearly define the potential prospects you seek to attract to each design. Interior designers should be given specific guidelines for furnishing and decorating the homes in keeping with the profiled buyers' tastes and budgets. Too often we see model decor totally miss the target markets. A well-designed home that is a good value can become a poor seller if the people who should identify with it do not see themselves in the picture.

A common mistake is to furnish the homes to the tastes of the builder, the decorator or others who are not the ultimate buyers. Every interior design specialist will have personal opinions about how a home should be shown. Like other creative artists, each tends to express his or her skills in a personal manner. That is why it is important to reach agreement on the objectives for each model and to review the schematics and budgets carefully before authorizing installation. Following are some general guidelines gleaned from a number of recognized leaders in the interior design profession for model-matching for three predominant buyer groups.

### First-Time Buyers

Young singles and couples starting the path to home ownership are mostly working with very limited budgets. The key factor in decorating a model for these beginners is to keep it within the reality of their economic perceptions. *Do not over-decorate*! You can turn them off if your models are elaborately done with furnishings and accessories they cannot duplicate. These start-up buyers are most responsive to decor they can picture achieving themselves with modest budgets. If they are young, they will normally be turned on to bright primary colors, inexpensive but colorful accents like pillows, bedspreads, plants and pottery. It is often wiser to paint the walls than to use wallpaper, since the costs of the latter can be too high for those on tight budgets. Also, since starter homes or condominiums tend to be small, care must be taken not to crowd rooms with too much furniture. Scale the furniture to fit the dimensions of the rooms, and remember: It is better to be underfurnished than overfurnished!

### The Move-up Mid-life Family Buyers

As your starters leave their first or second homes and move up to better living environments, they seek things they did not have in their first homes. They have acquired a few pieces of furniture that will probably stay with them for a number of years. They must be able to mix these early marriage pieces into the new setting. Eclectic furnishings in good taste may be appropriate for the main living areas of the home, while matched bedroom sets—somewhat better than they now have—are appropriate for that increasingly important master suite. As the young mature, they tend to become more traditional. The move-up home will often feature the formal dining room they did not have in their earlier residences. This can be a focal point of attention with classy furnishings and accessories. Children are now a key factor, and appealing to their ages and interests in decorating secondary bedrooms and recreation rooms deserves special attention.

### Active Adults Who Become Empty Nesters

This is often the move-down market. The children have either flown the nest or are about to do so, and the parents are looking forward to pursuing their personal interests. When children dominate the scene, homes are usually less formal and center more on family rooms, country kitchens and media rooms. Mature adults approaching the golden years look for some of the personal things they may not have been able to justify while the kids were at home. Elegance in the detailing and finish of cabinetwork, hardware, lighting fixtures and trim becomes important to them. The master bedroom suite and especially the bath are luxury elements in design and decor they probably did not have before. Although they may be moving down to less space, they want and demand better quality. In design, it is wise to pay special attention to hard-finish surface materials, such as hardwoods, ceramic tiles and brick. The majority of the empty nesters are very traditional in lifestyles, and they value treasures of the past. They have collectibles, usually including some pieces of fine art and other mementos they will want to display. Furniture should reflect traditional values and a touch of elegance.

## THE FORMULA FOR MERCHANDISING A MODEL HOME[2]

Basically four things must occur to have a good model:

1. Identification of the market
2. Fine-tuning of the space
3. Creation of the statement
4. Execution of the process

I. Identification of the Market

    A. *What* you must learn:
        1. marital status
        2. age
        3. income (white- or blue-collar)
        4. lifestyle
        5. values
        6. hobbies
        7. heroes—movies, books, music
        8. color preference—(studies by psychologists)
        9. furniture preference

    B. *How*:
        1. national studies
        2. local studies
        3. focus groups
        4. interview individuals inside their homes
        5. consultants
        6. real estate agents

II. Fine-tuning of the plan (Sometimes only a few minor changes really make the room sing.)

    A. Points of consideration:
        1. foyer (overall impact)
            a. mirrors
            b. lighting
            c. finishes
            d. leading the eye with color and furnishings

        2. furniture placement
            a. sufficient wall space for furniture

        3. windows
            a. symmetry and size
            b. adequate amounts of natural light
            c. upper-end situations with leaded glass or stained glass—statements of luxury and quality

---

[2]Some of the following suggestions are courtesy of Carol Clark & Co., Atlanta, GA.

4. door swings
   a. traffic flow
   b. space planning

5. kitchens
   a. access
   b. work areas
   c. triangle
   d. lighting
   e. special markets—move-up, vacation, elderly

6. room sizes
   a. adequate size for furniture

7. baths
   a. access
   b. sufficient number for bedrooms
   c. master bath
      i. separate wet and dry areas
      ii. no open water closets
      iii. sufficient vanity space
      iv. use of mirrors—are you lost in the maze?
      v. consider the market
      vi. lighting—vanities, make-up
      vii. sex appeal created with tub and finishes

8. lighting
   a. adequate
   b. drama
   c. special effects
   d. low-voltage spots to show art collections or architectural interest

9. special features
   a. bars in master bedroom
   b. garden rooms and atriums
   c. morning rooms
   d. keeping rooms
   e. geared to a specific activity
   f. built-ins

III. Creation of the statement: Three items must be considered when deciding the overall scheme of things; budget, appeal, and relationship to the whole. Do the elements work together in leading the potential owner from space to space?

A. furniture
   1. believable?
   2. scale—no dark or heavy pieces
   3. tall pieces blocking the eye's view?
   4. varied and unusual character pieces from flea markets, etc.

     5.  softness—plump round sofas and chairs with comfortable, inviting, sink-in feeling and pillows where room allows

     6.  glass and brass used sparingly, but softened with flowering plants and candlelight

     7.  50 percent of your budget for furniture

     8.  layout—leads the eye to the best features of the home—remains functional and creative

B.  finishes—wall space visualized in its relationship to all the elements of creation

     1.  paints
         a.  psychology
         b.  lower spectrum
         c.  warm colors
         d.  entry-level preferences
         e.  move-up market
         f.  crystal-clear colors make people happy
         g.  treating small spaces
         h.  larger-volume spaces

     2.  wallpaper—points of consideration
         a.  the statement
         b.  budget
         c.  overpowering patterns—too masculine or too feminine

C.  flooring
     1.  defines the space
     2.  warms the space

D.  lighting
     1.  enhances the space to the maximum?
     2.  special art pieces accented?
     3.  hot spots in the home lighted to create moods?

E.  drapery treatments
     1.  budget—ready-mades fine in some areas
     2.  fullness
     3.  no more than 20 percent of the window covered
     4.  considers the view
     5.  complement the architecture and general theme of the home?—small spaces: band of color—large spaces: splashes of color
     6.  25 percent of your budget

F.  artwork and accessories
     1.  highly personal—the statement for the home
     2.  realistic or achievable
     3.  complement and enhancement to the overall scheme
     4.  frames and matting—consider the overall scheme

5.   20 percent to 25 percent of budget to be spent here
6.   emphasize the color scheme—contrast
7.   theme
8.   personalize
9.   accessorize
10.   scale and condition of plants
11.   punch-out list for items still needed—makes your shopping easier

## Creativity

Most people want the latest and best that modern life affords—but all the flashiest gadgets in the world will not make a house a home. A home must be created. Home touches a human chord. The challenge of home builders and designers is to touch that human chord. High-Touch Design is the name assigned to the process which includes: process, nostalgia, warmth, softness, fun.

The following tips might prove useful in completing your plans:

1.   Allow 8–12 weeks—all kinds of delays and work orders can occur.
2.   Select main accessories in the beginning; find pieces with character.
3.   Work with a drapery expert and supervise work.
4.   Find a custom frame shop with a good knowledge of art.
5.   Make a list of all items that must be included (i.e.: towels, china) then make a folder with all fabrics—it makes shopping easier.
6.   Schedule the furniture to arrive all on the same day. Be there to place and check for any pieces that do not work.
7.   Draperies should not be installed on the same day as the furniture.
8.   Artwork should come in after the furniture and draperies.

The five elements, when properly considered in the overall scheme of design, are certain to bring you the results you want.

Ask your interior merchandisers to provide complete color selection boards that depict the colors, fabrics, textures and themes proposed for each room and each model. This gives marketing advisors an opportunity to critique and challenge, when necessary, any approach that does not seem appropriate. There should be no surprises at model-opening day! If you carefully monitor the decorating functions and have open communication lines with the designer, you can prevent expensive mistakes.

## STRETCH SPACE AND INCREASE PERCEIVED VALUES

Experts have learned how to achieve maximum livability and emotional impact in limited spaces. As costs of land and construction increase, builders must try to keep prices affordable, and that means reducing the size of housing and homesites. Thus, the challenge grows for model merchandisers to visually demonstrate livability with less space. The best of them have made an art out of taking small rooms and making them appear larger. They avoid doing anything that would reduce visual space. Here are a few of the tips from the pros:

- Use monochromatic color schemes in light and bright tones, and avoid color breaks that visually fragment sight lines. White walls, for example, make a room appear larger than do darker colors. When the same color flows from one space or room to the next, the sense of space is visually extended.
- Try to provide a focal point of interest at the farthest point in the room. Draw the eyes to a distant point first to stretch the visual impact and stretch the surrounding areas. This is often done with lamps, plants, spotlights and art pieces.
- Be cautious in the use of patterns and paneling that can bring the walls of a room closer together. Bold patterns and dominant prints shrink a room, while subdued designs that harmonize with light colors preserve or expand space.
- Employ light in a variety of interesting ways. Do not skimp on lighting when trying to compensate for smaller spaces. Accent walls with light from floor spots, indirect lighting, skylights and appropriately placed ceiling lights. In models, use full-wattage light bulbs in most lamps, especially in winter months and in gray climates.
- Mirrors are an effective way of stretching space. Floor-to-ceiling mirroring on a single-accent wall can do wonders for a small room. Mirrors should be used in good taste and not overdone, as they can detract from other elements if they appear garish.
- Potted plants on the inside can help to carry the space to the outdoors. By placing them near sliders or windows that extend to gardens or patios, you can visually carry the eye to the landscaped exteriors and make the interior space appear larger as a result.
- Small baths and powder rooms can be made visually larger with the use of reflective wall covering or with murals that achieve a vanishing point so that there is an illusion of infinity.
- Blend wall coverings into the environment by matching them with bedspreads, pillows and other accent pieces of the same fabric or pattern.
- Select carpeting with an eye to its impact on all spatial relationships. Floor coverings tend to be the most dominant element in interior designs. Dark colors reduce the size of the rooms. It is best to stay with light or neutral floor coverings and let your accessories provide the accent colors when you have limited space.
- Built-in cabinets (such as media centers) that are part of the walls rather than piece-meal additions can make a room more spacious and livable. Wall treatments around fireplaces, in dens and secondary bedrooms can provide usable space that lessens the need for additional furniture.
- Leave one section of a wall completely undecorated and the rest of the room will appear larger.
- Most important, select furniture in scale with room dimensions. Oversized and bulky furniture in a small room destroy space more than any other factor. Avoid using dark-grained woods and massive-appearing pieces when trying to expand room sizes.

## PUT PEOPLE INTO THE MODEL-HOME PICTURE

As I tour model homes across the nation, I seldom find pictures of people in the decorating schemes. This is one area too frequently overlooked by designers. One objective of model merchandising is to make houses look and feel like real homes. Your home or mine will have framed photographs of the ones we love, pictures of memorable experiences and other mementos that represent our values and lifestyles. Our model homes should give the same sense of belonging. Instruct your decorators to find photographs—pictures in sync with the profiles of your targeted prospects—and frame them for use in models. Children's rooms need the kinds of toys and other items representative of the way the children live. Posters, school books and pictures of rock stars or sports heroes are part of that setting.

Another overlooked area is the books people read and collect. Bookshelves loaded with old books (they can be acquired inexpensively at second hand book stores) add a special touch of livability that cannot be achieved by other furnishings. The same is true for magazines and periodicals. A normal home has them in abundance. Make your models believable by including the kinds of collectibles real people keep in their homes.

## HOW TO HANDLE THE COSTS OF BUILDING AND MAINTAINING MODELS

It is appropriate that we address model-home expenses and touch on ways to handle the capital investment for those who find it difficult to commit the funds needed to do a first-class model-home presentation. Many builders have discovered the value of selling their models to investors at the beginning of each new development, so they do not freeze valuable capital in model equities. The normal way to achieve this goal is to line up a number of individuals looking for appreciation, some tax write-offs and assured income for the period of time the models are leased by the building company. If the models are sold at cost, plus a small mark-up for administration, the value differences between what you sell them for at the beginning of the community and what they will be worth when the neighborhood is completed is usually enough to insure investor support. The sale/leaseback instrument achieves the financial objectives of the builder and the investor. Usually, we provide a minimum of one year for the leaseback privilege with the right to extend it if needed. In some cases, you can sell the model home and furnishings as a complete package, thus substantially reducing your capital requirements.

Some builders sell their model homes to pre-established syndication groups, and, occasionally, these are part of family trusts or personal investment programs. Bankers can provide special arrangements for model construction and holding costs if properly structured as part of the land development package. If necessary, some builders guarantee a minimum return to the investors after acquisition and resale.

Furniture can also be leased instead of purchased. Some furniture outlets provide financing packages for builders. These tend to be relatively expensive when you compare with the costs of the interest you would pay if you purchased and then carried under a normal line of credit with your banking institution.

For budgeting purposes, most builders write off all interest and carrying costs on models as a marketing expense and capitalize the furnishings and property. When sold, the net differences (if a loss is incurred) are charged to the marketing budget.

## WHAT'S IN A MODEL NAME?

Picture typical housing consumers touring projects and models in your market area on a busy weekend. How many will they inspect? How many brochures will they pick up and take home? How many models or floor plans will be depicted or represented in those brochures? Which ones will they remember? Most important, which ones will sufficiently capture their attention to cause them to seriously consider owning them? When they walk through your models (hopefully escorted by knowledgeable sales representatives) will they identify with them? When they get back to the starting point, will they think of your homes first? Will they be so impressed that they will want to return immediately to yours rather than to your competitors'? How positive will be their first impressions?

It has always amazed me that builders will design and construct expensive model homes and then give them such demeaning identifications as Plan A, Plan B, Plan I, Plan II, in a nondescript, alpha/numerical scheme. If you pick up several brochures on a weekend of shopping for a new home, probably 50 percent of them will use this trite method of identifying the plans. Others will use plan numbers that are equal to square footages: PLAN 1560, PLAN 2245, ad nauseam! Even those who use model names tend to pick them on some basis that has no relationship to architecture, design or consumer interests. The theme approach is certainly superior to the unimaginative alphabet or number game. People identify more with human-sounding names than with letters or numbers. Auto manufacturers long ago discovered that truth! Only the sports-car enthusiasts elect sexy-sounding terms—like XZ–500! A comparable factor may exist with the singles and swingles market in housing. Most of us relate to names that conjure up romantic images and permit us to put ourselves in the picture.

American manufacturers of big-ticket items have learned through research that the labeling of products plays a major role in their acceptance by their consumers. It certainly plays a role in helping people to remember them! Home builders represent the most expensive product that 95 percent of the population will ever acquire. Is it not logical to give housing designs identity labels that maximize marketing potential by being memorable to profiled prospects? Instead of just tossing out a few names in the pressure of trying to get ready for an opening event, would it not be wise to give as much thought to the naming process as the buyers will give to the purchasing decision? And haven't we progressed beyond the alliteration need to select names that represent letters like: ASPEN (A); BIRCH (B); CEDAR (C)? Surely sales agents and production personnel can remember names that are not alphabetized.

Names should evoke images that strengthen the customer's identification with the design and the living benefits of ownership. If it is appropriate to give them the traditional flavors of Williamsburg, Victorian, Colonial, etc., then remain true to the images you are projecting. Often, a big difference is apparent between the floor plans and the variety of elevations that complement them. How can you use a traditional name on a floor plan that has both a tudor and contemporary elevation? Why not consider naming each home by the architecture and not just the floor plans? Better yet, why not give the design a unique identity that truly sets it apart from all the others your shoppers inspect in that market region?

Those who use theme-oriented model names frequently pursue one of these broad categories:

- historical places or cities in that region: common on the east coast of America
- famous people from that region: the Jefferson, the Daniel Boone, the Pearson, etc.
- famous events connected with the history of the area: the Landing, the Pilgrim, the Pathfinder, etc.
- old country cities (particularly English, French and Spanish)
- flora/fauna themes (trees, animals, sea shells, etc.)
- famous landmarks related to the setting (names of golf courses, ski resorts, islands, lakes, mountains and ships)
- natural elements associated with the environment: Lakeview, Greens, Parkside, Woodland, etc.
- recreational events and lifestyle activities: The Mariner, The Surfer, The Islander, etc.
- modern events and technology (associated with hi-tech housing or the starter markets): Voyager, Explorer, Enterprise, Traveler, etc.

While all of these themes tend to create general interest and certainly help to strengthen the identity of the homes with the new community (if appropriately named), few give any serious thought in regard to competitive positioning or mental recall. In fact, in some market areas of the country (like southern California), you can go from one project to another in the course of a day and find similar (sometimes identical) names on models within a short distance of each other! Those who decided on the model labels were in too much of a hurry to study the competition and find a way to be unique in positioning their designs.

If you want to win the battle of mental images that will move your homes to the forefront of the competitive housing game, keep the following key factors in mind:

1.  Your prospects are normally going to see at least a dozen or more housing opportunities in that region. They will be easily confused unless you come up with something memorable.
2.  The sea of models and floor plans they inspect will run together and lose definition unless you create a memorable experience on-site that forces your homes to the surface.
3.  Until the prospects' decisions have been narrowed to three or fewer, confusion will reign! Make sure that one of your homes is mentally and emotionally imprinted on the buyer's mind on the first visit—and tie that involvement to a specific homesite they can envision owning now!

4.  Label and communicate the uniqueness of each plan so that it will not be lost when the customers leave to inspect other homes or return to their nests!

5.  Use creative and imaginative approaches to dramatize the benefits of owning a particular plan. This is an essential part of the sales representative's assignment. The sale is not made at the end. It is made in the presentation. If you do not win that game, you will not win the big one!

## SALESPEOPLE SHOULD USE THEIR OWN DESCRIPTIVE LABELS

When showing and demonstrating a model home, it is important to help customers identify with the floor plan and architectural elements so that they will easily recall them later. The more you do to set each of your homes apart from the smorgasbord of housing, the greater the chances are that you will sell yours when the others are languishing on the sales vine! This means having sales agents use descriptive terms and phrases to accent the benefits of each home.

A superior technique for creating a memorable impression for each model home is to give it a descriptive *sales label*, regardless of what it is called in the brochure or on the model identity sign. The objective is to dramatize each home in such a way that it can readily be recalled when the prospect is sitting back in his or her front room trying to remember what was seen. It is a battle for mental images, and you win when you do things that leave positive and distinctive impressions in the brain. The word choices for creating those images are as varied as the salespeople selling the housing. The key is doing something different and unique that will set them apart from competition . . . and help bring them back if they do not purchase today!

For example, you can describe a home by its architectural features:

> *"This is the* Classical Williamsburg *that is authentic in every detail . . ."*

> *"This model is a* Cape Cod Original. *It feels like it belongs to the era in which it was first created!"*

> *"Here is the essence of the* Spanish Hacienda. *It captures the romance of the conquistadors and early settlers."*

You can use the decor of the models as the key memory point. Look at the decorating in terms of distinctive appearances and translate them for the buyers:

> *"The first model is our* Country French *decor theme. It has the colors and romantic elegance of the French country."*

> *"This is our* Cheerful Yellow *home! The decorator has shown how bright and cheerful the home can be by using various shades of sunlight yellows."*

> *"Here is our* Pirate's Den! *The designer has used a nautical theme to bring out the romantic tones and room settings."*

One of the best ways to label the home is to refer to an emotional experience or feeling one gets from seeing it. After all, emotions dictate our housing decisions, and the more that you can play to them, the easier it is to be memorable—and to sell!

*"This is our* Sunshine Home. *Notice how light and bright it is and how it opens to the outdoors to give you the cheerful feeling that you are part of the sunshine environment that is Florida!"*

*"The next model has been called the* Elegant Entertainer *by several of the homeowners who have purchased it. Note the distinctive and elegant room arrangements that will make entertaining your guests such a memorable event for everyone!"*

*"This is our* Country Kitchen *home! The kitchen is literally the conversation center of the home. It is designed for families like yours who like the casual lifestyle that is part of this recreational community."*

When your salespeople take the time to think through ways to make their homes something other than Plan A, The Barony, or Number 1726, they will increase the potential for setting them apart from the multitude of housing options their buyers will entertain. This is *show biz*—and success is to win the audience's attention by the way you present your acts!

When selling custom homes, a superior technique is to name each plan for the buyer for whom it was designed. The one-of-a-kind is the ultimate in customer appeal. The *signature home* has exceptional merit when you are able to modify and create plans for individual owners!

## MAKE PERSONAL NOTES AND MARKINGS ON SALES LITERATURE

Some salespeople and their marketing directors feel that brochures and hand-out literature are sacred and should not be defaced! To the contrary, if you do not personalize the pieces that you send home with prospects, they may never remember or identify with your homes sufficiently to return—or live there. As most pros know from experience, it is not wise to give the complete brochure to arriving visitors. If you do, you lose the opportunity to control the information they see, and the chance to become involved with them after they tour the models or sites. Handing them a price list, or a model tour and feature/benefit guide is appropriate. When you accompany them to see the first model, you have the chance to reinforce and label the identity images so they will remember them. You can make notes (or have them do so) on the price sheets and other exhibits. When they return to the sales office, you should try to lead them to a place where you can counsel, involve and, hopefully, close. If nothing else, you need to make some personal notes on the items they take back to their present residences so that you will deepen the impression of your community—a favorite floor plan—and a remaining site or two that are available now and may be sold by tomorrow!

The entire process centers on *involvement*. We must be skilled at involving prospects with their *dream homes* and helping them to picture the future benefits of ownership. Labeling the models, talking about specific sites, making notes on estimate sheets or brochures is all part of that larger game plan. You win when your homes are so memorable that they block out everything else the prospect has seen or will see. To be remembered, you must be different, and that means creating positive and value-building images that will outlast the confusing housing selection process!

## ON-SITE MERCHANDISING INCLUDES ACTION—ORIENTED SIGNAGE

Communication of marketing messages to prospective buyers often begins with on-site signage long before advertising and construction commence. Preconstruction billboards announce the early opportunities that attract pioneers and help to get the sales program into high gear. Display signage of smaller dimensions direct customers to sales facilities, models and available properties. Future amenities and construction phases can be promoted with strategically placed information boards. Most important, the success of the community can be dramatically emphasized with *sold* signs and personalized identification of homes being constructed for specific buyers.

Maximum effectiveness is realized when all signage objectives are identified at the outset of the project and rules for maintaining high-quality exposure are enforced. Salespeople typically bear the responsibility for ordering, installing and monitoring *available* and *sold* signs for individual sites. Sales management will be concerned with supervising the execution of these duties as well as reviewing other signage needs each week. Marketing directors have ultimate authority to see that signage is designed and installed to previously established standards.

One objective should be minimizing confusing messages and cluttered conditions. A poorly managed subdivision has no signage rules, allows every builder and sales agent to install signs of any size, shape, color or message and has no program for keeping the sites clean and attractive. Multiple-builder developments need a master sign-control program instituted and enforced by the developer. Unless guidelines are inaugurated with the initial marketing plan, it is almost impossible to correct cluttered and uncoordinated signage conditions that automatically seem to evolve.

Here are some signage principles followed by marketing professionals for their well-managed communities:

- Graphic standards are established as part of the original marketing plan, and they detail the use of the community name, logo design, colors and signage formats.
- A consistent theme is employed throughout the community so that all signage and internal graphics communicate images in a professional manner.
- Property signs (*available* and *sold*) are limited to one style with predetermined riders or attachments to promote builders, availability and sales status.
- Suppliers and subcontractors are not allowed to advertise on the site with personal signage, except as prescribed by management.
- Outside brokers who list and sell within the community are required by covenants, conditions and restrictions to abide by the developer's signage policies.
- Salespeople must promptly install *sold* signs on all sold or reserved properties and check daily to see that they are up, clean and correct.
- All subcontractors and company employees are notified about the importance of the sign program as it relates to sales success and are given incentives to protect the signs as they conduct their construction activities.

Superior marketers realize the importance of controlling all merchandising elements that influence consumers' value perceptions. By creating professionally managed and protected environments, they generate more confidence in their products and enhance the sense of urgency to purchase.

---

**FIGURE 4.17   Sales Office Set-Up Checklist**

---

SUBJECT: POLICY: SALES OFFICE SET-UP CHECKLIST

The following checklist is provided for each salesperson and/or sales manager for convenience in setting up a new or temporary or permanent sales office.

In the case of the temporary sales office, sufficient space is provided for you so you may establish a date when something promised to you will, in fact, be delivered to your sales office and as far as the "now have" column, you may check those off as the items come in to you.

|  | DUE BY | NOW HAVE |
|---|---|---|
| Business cards | _____ | _____ |
| Prospect "registration-drawing" cards | _____ | _____ |
| Registration table and box | _____ | _____ |
| Follow-up cards | _____ | _____ |
| Tradesman referral cards (gifts to tradesmen who obtain referrals) | | |
| Sales and deposit agreement: | | |
| a. Conventional | _____ | _____ |
| b. FHA & VA | _____ | _____ |
| c. Conditional sales contract | _____ | _____ |
| Authorization to HOLD a deposit (hold form) | _____ | _____ |
| Loan applications | _____ | _____ |
| Credit applications | _____ | _____ |
| Statement of information | _____ | _____ |
| Buyer's selection approval forms | _____ | _____ |
| Change requests | _____ | _____ |
| Cancellation request forms (Notice of Intention to Cancel) | _____ | _____ |
| Declaration of acceptance | _____ | _____ |
| Agreement for possession prior to recordation (Rental Agreement) | _____ | _____ |
| Plans | _____ | _____ |
| Specification sheet | _____ | _____ |
| Plot plan | _____ | _____ |
| Renderings of elevations | _____ | _____ |
| Price sheets showing: | | |
| a. Development name | _____ | _____ |
| b. Plan number and footage | _____ | _____ |
| c. Plan description and price | _____ | _____ |
| d. Outstanding items included | _____ | _____ |
| Files | _____ | _____ |
| File folders with escrow control printed on folder | _____ | _____ |
| Master-control journal | _____ | _____ |
| Salesperson's sales manual | _____ | _____ |
| Salesperson's pro forma book (showing complete forms and description) | _____ | _____ |

**FIGURE 4.17   Sales Office Set-Up Checklist (continued)**

| | DUE BY | NOW HAVE |
|---|---|---|
| Small *sold* tags for plot map | ———— | ———— |
| Cardboard *sold* signs for production homes (after framing) | ———— | ———— |
| Giveaways: | | |
| a. Chamber of Commerce pamphlets | ———— | ———— |
| b. Retail giveaways | ———— | ———— |
| c. Other | ———— | ———— |
| Utility cards with telephone numbers | ———— | ———— |
| Receipt books | ———— | ———— |
| Counter-check books | ———— | ———— |
| Promissory notes | ———— | ———— |
| Miniature tract maps showing: | | |
| a. lots & dimensions | ———— | ———— |
| b. streets & house plotting | ———— | ———— |
| c. plan number and elevation | ———— | ———— |
| d. distance from house plottings to lot lines | ———— | ———— |
| Flags: | | |
| a. permanent in place on high poles | ———— | ———— |
| b. moveable type | ———— | ———— |
| Portable open sign (the larger the better—use wheels if necessary) | ———— | ———— |
| Postage stamps | ———— | ———— |
| Brochures: | | |
| a. temporary | ———— | ———— |
| b. inexpensive | ———— | ———— |
| c. expensive | ———— | ———— |
| Phone | ———— | ———— |
| Phone numbers of sales manager, escrow and construction companies | ———— | ———— |
| Rubber bands | ———— | ———— |
| Paper clips | ———— | ———— |
| Memo pads (don't say it—write it) | ———— | ———— |
| Rubber stamps with salesperson's name and phone number | ———— | ———— |
| Envelopes: | | |
| a. regular | ———— | ———— |
| b. 9″ × 12″ | ———— | ———— |
| Cleaning materials (soap, window cleaner) | ———— | ———— |
| Brooms, mops, rags, towels and toilet paper | ———— | ———— |
| Light bulbs | ———— | ———— |
| Scotch tape | ———— | ———— |
| Polaroid camera and color film | ———— | ———— |
| Desk (or conference table) and chairs | ———— | ———— |
| Storage facilities | ———— | ———— |

---

**FIGURE 4.17    Sales Office Set-Up Checklist (concluded)**

|  | DUE BY | NOW HAVE |
|---|---|---|
| Vacuum | _____ | _____ |
| Water cooler | _____ | _____ |
| *"No deposit reservation control"* book | _____ | _____ |
| Sales trailer or garage sales office with air conditioning | _____ | _____ |
| Cleaning people | _____ | _____ |
| Billboards | _____ | _____ |
| Traffic-count forms | _____ | _____ |
| Weekly sales summary report form | _____ | _____ |
| Completed financing sheets for VA, FHA, VA-FHA, Conventional (5, 10 20%, etc.) | _____ | _____ |
| Form 1880—Request for certificate of eligibility | _____ | _____ |
| Garage release | _____ | _____ |
| Option books and forms | _____ | _____ |
| Reverse telephone directory | _____ | _____ |
| Company follow-up card | _____ | _____ |
| Color cut-off dates | _____ | _____ |
| Color boards and/or color books: a. interior | _____ | _____ |
| b. exterior | _____ | _____ |
| Rendering or photos of same | _____ | _____ |
| Tract, lot, sequence, address, price forms | _____ | _____ |
| Delivery dates by lot with option cut-off dates | _____ | _____ |
| Garage release forms | _____ | _____ |
| Presale information checklist | _____ | _____ |
| Rental agreements | _____ | _____ |
| Material releases | _____ | _____ |
| Manning schedules | _____ | _____ |
| Irrevocable order to assign funds from sale of present home | _____ | _____ |
| Escrow activity report card | _____ | _____ |
| Occupancy and clearance notice | _____ | _____ |

_____

Submitted by

_____

Date

# 5: Recruiting Sales Counselors

Many critical decision points arise in the development of a new housing community. If you pay too much for the land, the original seller may have made all the profit before you even start your building operation. If you design and build the wrong product for the market, you may suffer rejection of your homes by those to whom you had hoped to sell them. If your financing package is not tailored to both your development needs and the ultimate consumer's qualification criteria, you may have to let the money lenders try to market the properties after you have bailed out! These are a few vital decision-making areas in which wrong choices can adversely affect the potential success of any building enterprise.

The most effective sales teams cannot completely compensate for serious errors in management judgment regarding product design, pricing or research. However, even if you purchase the land at a reasonable price, design and build your homes efficiently and arrange for adequate financing, you will not automatically sell what you build at the desired prices or absorption rates that must be maintained to realize a satisfactory profit margin. Equally critical to sales success in this business is recruitment and selection of sales personnel who can effectively sell what is offered to the market place! Without the right people representing the merchandise to the right prospective home buyers, the desired sales will seldom occur!

The real estate industry is basically very fragmented and unorganized when it comes to marketing new homes and new housing environments. Within the general brokerage community, you have thousands of independent agents who make their own decisions on what they will list, show and sell. The quality and selling skills of this diverse group vary dramatically. As in most sales fields, the minority of the salespeople do the majority of the business. The most effective sales representatives have learned how to build a solid personal referral business and to use their time wisely by concentrating on what will yield the best possible return for their efforts. The masses struggle to make a living, and only about 20 percent survive five years in the profession.

During the past 25 years, a substantial improvement occurred in the emphasis on education and general training of real estate agents by the larger companies, franchises and well-run independent brokerage offices in America. However, only a small percentage of brokers offer any type of special training for new home sales. Even fewer have specialists who devote all of their time to this aspect of the business. Recruiting people best suited for new home sales and then offering them a well-managed orientation and personal development plan is still a rarity among those who manage general brokerage companies.

This is a primary reason why many builders elect to recruit their own controlled sales personnel. The in-house captive sales team is the choice of many merchant builders whose volume and economics permit them to employ the managers and systems needed to sustain their own sales staffs. Smaller builders usually elect to work with outside brokers and are subject to the whims of listing agents and independent contractors, whose dedicated commitment to selling specific new home inventory is often difficult to obtain.

Many professional and effective real estate companies do an excellent job of representing their builders. A growing number of companies have developed specialized departments and separate sales organizations devoted solely to the representation of builders' and developers' housing opportunities. The Builders' Marketing Society is a recently created association of new home marketing specialists who recognize the need to provide programs for those who concentrate on new home sales. The industry is paying more attention today to the development of new home sales personnel than it ever has in the past. There is still a long way to go, however, before any real sense of pride can be displayed in the way America's builders and their products are represented to the home buying public!

## THE QUALITY OF THE PLAYERS DETERMINES SCORING RESULTS

Andrew Carnegie, one of America's great industrial leaders, once said: "My competitors can match me in many ways, but if my people are better, I have a priceless advantage!" Most companies have only three resources that matter: their financial assets, their reputations and their people!

In our industry, human resources tend to be more important than financial assets. Without the right people who know how to convert property into sales, whatever financial position we have today may dwindle or disappear tomorrow. If we attract and recruit agents who do not have the capacity, education and motivation to communicate effectively the benefits of our new housing environments to today's discriminating buyers, we will not attain the levels of success that are possible when we have the best players in the game!

## CRITERIA FOR THE STAFFING AND SELECTION PROCESS

Before you begin any recruiting campaign, the building group must decide how it is going to handle sales management. If an outside brokerage company or subcontracting sales organization is to be chosen, then the critera for selection begin with identifying those companies and individual agents best qualified for sales management. The recruiting baton then passes to the selected subcontracted marketing company.

However, profit-oriented developer/builders are going to evaluate the performance of those assigned to their projects. For the purposes of this chapter, presume that recruiting objectives for a specific assignment are the same whether managed by a contracting brokerage company or the builder's own controlled in-house sales staff.

A basic checklist identifies the factors that should influence the recruiting of new home sales personnel for a particular staffing opportunity:

1. How many homes, homesites or condominiums will the marketplace reasonably absorb in this location within the next 12 months? (Shorter or longer time frames can be used if appropriate).

2. What gross dollar volume will that absorption rate produce?

3. Can the builder (developer) produce and deliver all units within that time frame? If not, what realistic figures should be used to determine potential gross sales dollars from closings in that sales period?

4. How many salespeople or support personnel will be required to service effectively the anticipated traffic at the site?

5. What is a reasonable annual earnings level in your market area for the quality of sales professionals you hope to attract? (Compute annual earnings level, bring to a monthly figure and match to the number of months identified in #1, 2, and 3 above.)

6. What percentage of sales will originate from on-site specialists? From off-site cooperating real estate agents?

7. How much effort do you expect the sales staff to devote to prospecting or generating leads compared to the marketing efforts of the company to bring qualified prospects to them?

8. What are the profiles of the anticipated prospective buyers? What characteristics must your sales personnel have to match these profiles?

9. How are your competitors staffing their housing sites, and how are they compensating their sales personnel? Are qualified new home specialists in the general area, or must new people not currently in the profession be attracted and trained?

10. How much supervision from sales management will these candidates need? Will managers be available to help resolve issues and close sales, or must the salespeople be sufficiently skilled to operate with little or no day-to-day management?

11. Are you recruiting just for this one project or for ongoing opportunities that the company will provide in other locations and departments?

12. How much are you prepared to invest in sales commissions as a percentage of sales price to meet the criteria and maintain desired profit objectives?

When you have answered these questions to your satisfaction, you are ready to establish specific criteria for your selection and recruiting efforts. Obviously, no magic answers exist. Multiple factors always affect these decisions. The ultimate choice is usually a compromise. The primary objective should always be to select and recruit salespeople who can effectively close buyers, not just those who show property and sit open houses! Closers are the ones who produce the results that keep the enterprise in business. Numerous agents will gladly staff model homes and sit in sales offices for builders. They may occasionally show and sell new homes, but they cannot be classified as professional closers. If you are to win the sales game, you must have players who know the score!

## EVALUATE YOUR STAFFING NEEDS AND ALTERNATIVES

Chapter 8 will review effective ways to generate prospects to assure attainment of sales objectives. One of the most obvious means of creating sales opportunities is to be certain that the homes are shown to as many customers as possible. In turn, that implies that the homes (or on-site office) should be staffed to receive prospective buyers at all reasonable hours. At least one-third of new home sales result from street traffic, visitors drawn to the site as the result of signage, model exposure and media promotion. In many markets, this percentage is 50 percent or more. When homes are not available to be readily inspected by the public, opportunities for closing sales are substantially reduced. Thus, one major factor in establishing recruiting needs is determination of the staffing program and the number of on-site personnel necessary to achieve sales goals.

As a general guideline, commissions for on-site sales personnel range from one to three percent of gross sales prices. Arithmetic will quickly reveal the optimum number of full-time sales counselors and support personnel once these questions have been answered. The variables in the formula center on the use of part-time personnel, off-site brokerage agents and support people who are not necessarily sales professionals.

Any site that can predictably absorb 25 or more housing units a year will normally justify one full-time sales professional. When sales traffic exceeds 15 to 25 per week per agent, it is time to consider adding additional sales power, unless there are no additional homes to be sold as a result of the extra coverage. When one salesperson is closing 50 or more units a year, there is validity in adding more salespeople or support roles if production capacity permits.

Understaffing is expensive. The efficiency of salespeople in handling traffic diminishes as the numbers increase—and so do conversion ratios! It is often better to adjust the commissions to accommodate more salespeople than to try to develop all of your sales from one individual's efforts. High-traffic periods also must be accommodated. Grand openings, busy weekends and special events typically generate large numbers of customers compared to relatively low-traffic periods during the average week. We must also allow for time off (one or two days a week) and, if coverage is needed during these relief periods, we may want to use floaters or sales assistants who take up the slack.

## HIERARCHY OF ON-SITE STAFFING ARRANGEMENTS

Any community or project that can justify at least one full-time sales specialist based on the 5 point criteria just identified has the potential for expanding coverage and sales power with the addition of other personnel. Here is the normal hierarchy of staffing variables for your review:

- Level one: one full-time sales counselor
  eight-hour days
  five- to six-day week
  minimum 20–25 closings annually
- Level two: one counselor plus receptionist/hostess
  covers days off
  greets and holds excess traffic
  assists on paperwork
- Level three: one senior counselor plus sales assistant
  senior carries primary staffing responsibilities
  assistant is full-time
  senior normally paid override
  days off rotated
- Level four: two or more senior counselors
  seven-days-a-week coverage
  counselors equal in authority
  days off rotated
  minimum 50–75 closings
- Level five: community manager plus two or more seniors
  manager supervises, trains, motivates
  manager takes overage traffic
  manager avoids direct competition unless economically necessary
- Level six: community manager plus two or more seniors plus full compliment
  of support personnel
  manager supervises, trains, motivates
  manager does not compete with the sales counselors
  receptionists and hostesses supervised by manager
  processing and administrative assistance provided as needed

Other variables apply, particularly when general-brokerage offices are responsible for staffing. The least desirable situation is the use of inexperienced resale agents who rotate open-house hours and are available only on Sunday afternoons. Rotating salespeople is one of the most costly of all staffing errors. Since more than 85 percent of new home sales are the result of return visitors, lack of continuity by the same agents working their prospects will automatically reduce conversion ratios. Hostesses untrained on what to say and how to conduct themselves will also lessen the efficiency of staffing programs.

Where sales volume does not justify full-time staffing, the alternatives must at least provide for the ready availability of salespeople to show the builder's homes when called. Prompt response of the salesperson when a prospect asks to see a model or inventory home is essential to the retention of impulse business.

On-site signage needs to communicate clearly how customers can contact sales representatives as well as provide sufficient information to precondition the sales role. The rule is: provide on-site staffing whenever it can be economically justified! More important, assure yourself that you have closers and not losers working with your customers when they arrive to see your homes!

## LOOK FOR THOSE WHO HAVE THE CLOSING ATTITUDE

People who usually attain the highest levels of closing success in the sales game are those with very positive attitudes about themselves and about winning the game. Closers like people, and they like winning the people-property game even more! They are achievers and they take risks along the way. That means they have experienced failure. Salespeople who maintain high closing ratios are normally tenacious. They do not give up easily. They perceive that "no," or "I want to think it over," is often a sign that prospects need more information, counseling and reinforcement. They are assertive in pleasant, persistent ways. Money, and what it can do for them, is one of their dominant motivations. They also play the game for recognition and a sense of personal accomplishment. Closers accept challenges in the sales process in the same way an athlete approaches hurdles in a race: They are there to be jumped. They see them as stepping stones instead of stumbling blocks.

The quality you need most in your new home sales candidates is the winning attitude. This must be highest on the list! That behavioral characteristic is often referred to as the degree of ego drive or self-assertiveness. We talk about finding individuals who are self-motivated. That is not always easy to detect. Many can talk a good job and sound as though they are motivated, until you put them in front of a customer who raises objections and is difficult to close!

## RECRUITING IS PREDICTION AND ALL PREDICTION IS A GAMBLE

When you search for people to fill specific positions within any enterprise, always look for those who can best meet the specifications of the assignment. When you ultimately choose one person over another, you have made a prediction as to which one you felt had the best chance of meeting those requirements and your performance standards. You are making a judgment call. A measure of risk is always involved and therefore a chance of failure.

The primary objective of the recruiting process is to minimize risks and increase opportunities for successful choices. Many of us in sales management are guilty of making impulsive decisions about sales candidates. We short-circuit the process because we are busy or convinced our intuitions will outweigh any prescribed systematic screening procedures. The consequences are very often far more expensive to the enterprise than the brief amount of time we think we saved.

What is the true cost of having the wrong sales personnel staffing and representing your housing communities? What is the real cost of not closing a prospect who would have purchased had a professional been involved? What happens to the bottom line of the building company that does not achieve and maintain the sales pace required to meet the pro forma given to the lending institutions, investors and managers? What does it cost to carry completed, unsold inventory month after month? How expensive is it to try to regenerate interest in a new home community, after the grand opening and initial promotion were wasted because sales were not made?

The intangibles in recruiting are difficult to pinpoint or project. All of us who have hired and trained real estate agents know that there is a big difference between

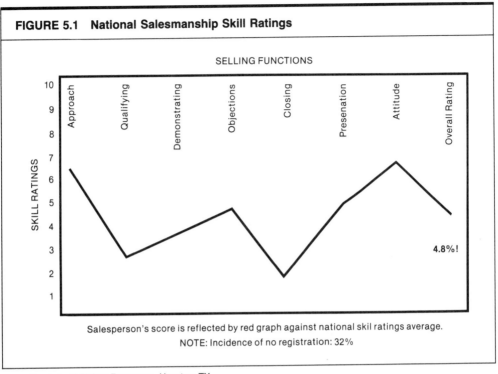

FIGURE 5.1   National Salesmanship Skill Ratings

SELLING FUNCTIONS

Salesperson's score is reflected by red graph against national skil ratings average.
NOTE: Incidence of no registration: 32%

Courtesy of Righey Resources, Houston, TX.

the winners and the losers. They have discovered guidelines that reduce the risk of hiring the wrong people while adding to the chances of attracting solid performers.

## WHERE DO YOU FIND THOSE NEW HOME SALES STARS?

Recruiting sources for salespeople are as extensive as the list of human enterprises in which they may be presently engaged. Sometimes they come to us from businesses where we least expect to find them, such as engineering and accounting. More often, they originate from fields that have already given them an opportunity to develop their skills in communication and persuasion, such as selling other products or services, teaching, managing and even parenting. You cannot judge the potential of sales candidates by their previous occupations, but you can test their propensity for selling by employing proven screening interview procedures.

Where should you search first? Unless you have a proven new home sales training program and time for managers to administer it, look for experienced real estate agents who have successfully sold new homes before. That means salespeople in general real estate and those currently working for other builders. Respect the recruiting ethics of the profession, but let people know you are in business and looking for qualified, experienced sales representatives.

Before you pursue residential resale agents, be sure to establish standards and guidelines for those you are seeking. Most general brokerage salespeople do not understand the differences between selling new homes and preowned ones. Distinctions exist in the way property is presented: how we market dreams for homes not yet constructed, avoiding negotiation traps that are a regular part of resale philosophy and servicing purchasers after sales are made. Not everyone who sells real estate is suited for the demands of new home marketing.

If you are looking for on-site personnel, you must be sure you attract salespeople who can work within a controlled environment and not experience emotional stress from the restrictions these sales areas impose. Most brokerage sales agents are uncomfortable selling just one product line or working in a single controlled model sales area every day.

Some of the best new home sales specialists have come directly from the general resale market. More have come from other sales fields and outside professions, where their previous careers prepared them, in part, for the challenges of this profession. Here is a checklist of practical recruiting sources:

1.  Recommendations and referrals from your present sales associates.
2.  Salespeople currently working for other builders.
3.  Leading real estate agents in brokerage offices who have a proclivity for new home sales.
4.  Homeowners who have purchased from you or live in your homes or in the same general neighborhood.
5.  Hostesses employed to serve peak traffic periods who show promise as future sales agents.
6.  Salespeople in other industries whom you deal with by mail, phone or in person.
7.  Suppliers, subcontractors and those businesses that have an interest in your success. They can be solicited to recommend candidates.
8.  Advertising for people who are not in the business now but might be interested in a career change.
9.  Career-opportunity nights are practical for larger recruiting efforts, such as those sponsored by major real estate companies.
10. Prelicensing real estate schools are sometimes effective, but more so for general brokerage companies than for new home sales.
11. Talking to everyone you meet about your recruiting needs. You never know who might be the key to opening the door to your next star player!

Recruiting is an ongoing process in a growing real estate enterprise. There is always a normal amount of turnover, sometimes more than we want.

Openings always exist for better producers. Maintaining a list of prospective candidates, even when you have no immediate needs, will come in very handy when that unexpected change occurs. Shopping your competition can serve multiple purposes. If you encounter a few outstanding sales representatives in the process, you can set the stage for future moves when conditions are ripe!

# HOW TO REDUCE THE RISKS IN THE RECRUITING PROCESS

Management decision making always involves a degree of risk. When you purchase a particular parcel of land with the intent to develop a residential community, your risk factors begin. Making sales forecasts, predicting public acceptance for your proposed product line, and anticipating income and expenses are all based on estimates of probability. Whether or not you have made the best possible decisions is heavily influenced by the quality of the information you gathered and evaluated before confirming your courses of action. This is certainly true when it comes to recruiting salespeople! The human ingredient is much more complicated and difficult to quantify than the values of a specific piece of land. To reduce your risks in choosing players who are going to be on the front line of your sales operation demands that you implement an information feedback system that will help you knock out the losers and choose the winners in the new home sales game!

# DO NOT WASTE TIME ON THOSE WHO DO NOT MEET YOUR STANDARDS

The recruiter in a real estate operation is usually involved in many other projects and wears several management hats. If he or she is the director of marketing, there will be a continuing demand to concentrate on those issues and opportunities that affect the marketing of a new residential community or housing enterprise. Avoid wasting time in any aspect of daily operations—including the recruiting process. It pays to have systems in place that will reduce the time it takes to prescreen candidates for sales positions. To preserve valuable business hours, we need procedures that knock out the people to whom we should devote little or no time.

Efficient recruiters use the following guidelines to assure that they are interviewing only those who meet at least the minimum standards established by the enterprise:

1. Establish written standards of association for your company and make these available to applicants prior to meeting with them.
2. Ask applicants for résumés to be submitted and screened before time is devoted to face-to-face interviews.
3. Employ the services of a secretary to perform prescreening functions.
4. Ask knock-out questions and evaluate the answers before asking candidates to fill out application forms or talk to recruiters.
5. Have candidates complete comprehensive position application forms prior to the first interview, unless the submitted résumés contain all necessary background information.
6. Employ some form of testing during the interview process to validate basic psychological profiles and behavior characteristics if candidates pass initial screening.
7. Ensure that the screening and selection process is always a minimum of two interviews if not more. Between the first and second sessions, information is checked, and others may be involved to give the recruiter a more accurate profile of the individual. Preferably, more than one manager is involved in the review session.

When you are seeking information on which to base a selection decision, you need to use a variety of sources and a number of proven techniques. Guard against wasting your time on the wrong candidates and, at the same time, secure sufficient facts on which to base your judgment calls. At this point in our marketing manual, it is appropriate to explore in greater detail the steps just identified.

## DETERMINE THE CHARACTERISTICS YOU CONSIDER ESSENTIAL

It is unfair to ask people to work for you without giving them an accurate picture of what will be expected of them. We have often been asked how to comfortably terminate nonperforming real estate agents. My first question to the manager is usually:

*"Did the employees or associates know what you expected of them when they accepted the position? Were there written standards of performance or association agreements that specified responsibilities?"*

Terminating salespeople is always painful. It admits failure. Somewhere along the line you either recruited the wrong person for the position or they did not fully understand what was expected of them. Although you know that you will have some failures simply because you are taking risks, you have an obligation to yourself, the people you employ and the enterprises you run at least to be very specific about your expectations of performance.

Unless you have a clear picture of the behavioral characteristics you believe are essential to the sales position, you may be tempted to recruit individuals who fail to rise to your expectations. It is very expensive to hire people and try to mold them into your own image. It is far more rewarding to recruit people who already possess the more important qualities inherent in successful sales personalities. Although salespeople come in all sizes, shapes, colors and backgrounds, they typically possess certain fundamental traits shared by those who achieve superior results. When you are searching for candidates, you should be concentrating on those who have dynamic, success-oriented qualities.

### Ability to Communicate and Be Persuasive

The entire selling process from qualifying to closing is based on the communication skills of the salesperson. People do not readily share their fears and concerns with sales agents unless they feel comfortable with the relationships. The ability to probe for motivations, financial capacity and personal interests requires an understanding and trusting personality. Helping indecisive prospects to make housing decisions means overcoming resistance to the risk-taking steps of moving forward rather than retreating to the nests in which they currently reside. Along the way to the sale, numerous opportunities to win or lose the sense of direction while trying to keep prospective buyers on target will arise. Closing the sale is a matter of obtaining minor agreements on the component parts of the major decision. Persuading people to take action when they should rather than yielding to instinctive delaying emotions requires confident counseling attitudes and persistent pursuit of sales objectives.

Ability to communicate effectively with people is high on the list of necessary skills in any field of selling. It is crucial in the real estate sales profession! We are dealing with one of the largest purchases most of us ever make, and it is emotionally more complex than other acquisition decisions. Buying a home means moving from one place to another. It entails leaving environments in which we have usually established some relationships and emotional ties. It involves sizable financial commitments. Frequently, it requires that we sell one property before we can purchase the new one. All of these factors intrude into the sales arena and must be proficiently handled by sales representatives if the final results are to be positive for all concerned.

When you are looking for sales candidates, keep in mind this vital communication ingredient. One reason we concentrate our recruiting efforts on those in related sales profession is that we reduce our risks of hiring the wrong individuals when we attract those who already know how to sell. If the applicant has a proven record in selling, especially with big-ticket merchandise or professional services, you can be reasonably assured that that person knows how to persuade. Truly skilled closers know the value of asking more questions than they are asked. They realize that everything they want is attained by getting other people to share their inner thoughts and emotions with them. They are good listeners and know how to help people clarify their thoughts through two-way reflective feedback processes.

When you are interviewing applicants, be very observant of their communication techniques. We will discuss this in greater detail later in this chapter.

## Ability to Learn, Think and Respond to the Unexpected

Very few selling occupations require practitioners to respond to as many variables and complexities as does real estate sales. Real estate agents must have a working knowledge of financing, construction, property values, real estate law, community regulations and the selling processes. Conditions in the real estate environment are constantly changing, and salespeople must be prepared to adjust quickly to new financing plans, housing designs, local economic conditions and fluctuating public attitudes. The ability to think on your feet and creatively adjust to social and economic factors that suddenly change is essential in becoming a top producer in real estate sales.

Although an above-average intellect is not essential to success, it certainly helps. Most outstanding producers in this profession have the capacity to learn quickly and respond to new conditions. If the profile of the people you sell includes many who are employed in high-paying professions and who hold college degrees, it is best to recruit sales personnel who can communicate on their level. Even if your demographics represent a broad range of people in all walks of life, the salesperson who thinks quickly and readily responds to the many variables in this business has a better opportunity to help people make decisions than someone who is slower in reaching the right conclusions.

## Ambition and the Desire to Achieve

Individuals who have no strong sense of direction in their lives never accomplish much. We are not born with a desire to achieve. It is a learned response to life.

Whatever the motivating forces, those with a deep personal need to get ahead in life usually find a way to do so. Those without that drive are normally content to accept mediocrity in their career paths. Selling is a profession in which the size of the paycheck is directly related to the degree of personal effort expended by the salesperson. The ambitious salesperson will strive to improve selling skills and personal knowledge of all disciplines needed in this industry. The thirst to learn and earn leads successful agents to ever greater levels of achievement.

Exploring what your candidates have done in the past to improve themselves is one way of qualifying them for degrees of personal drive. What a person has done is a fairly strong indication of what he or she will do. Few people make radical changes in life after the age of 30. Most life patterns have been set long before graduation from educational institutions.

Those who have no apparent idea about what they want to do or how to get there are obviously not ambitious. Even if our goals change from time to time throughout life, achievers always have both short-term and long-term goals with realistic objectives toward which they are striving. Some clues that indicate degrees of ambition can be gained from a review of previous career activities and interests. Others are gained from in-depth conversations. Psychological tests can provide additional evidence.

## Assertiveness

Assertiveness (or aggressiveness) is an important ingredient in the sales profile. People who are submissive, withdrawn, introverted and unwilling to assert themselves cannot make it in this profession unless they totally change. Since it is unlikely that we can motivate people to make drastic personality adjustments, it is unwise to employ anyone for a sales position who is not reasonably assertive.

Assertiveness is a measurable human behavior characteristic that should always be evaluated during the recruiting and selection process. It is directly related to ego drive, that subtle force in life that causes some to advance while others retreat. The willingness to take risks, meet new people, be the first to speak up and challenge an idea or jump into the middle of a social scene rather than hang along the fringes of the group is a strong indicator of an assertive personality.

It requires a fair measure of self-confidence to prospect for buyers, overcome objections, handle rejection, and live with the uncertainties new home buyers experience. A strong ego-drive is like the Rock of Gibraltar. Nothing shakes it from its foundation. The assertive salesperson seeks ways to solve problems rather than duck them. When a prospect says ''no,'' the assertive agent will explore what that means and continue to move toward the desired objective until it is proven that there is no possibility of making the sale. This willingness to be strong and assertive helps people reach positive decisions and results in closed transactions. It takes leadership to overcome normal resistance to change.

## Social Sensitivity and Empathy

The ability to communicate does not necessarily mean that one has empathy for others. It is true that the most effective communicators normally have a high empathy rating. However, many people in the sales profession survive on a self-interest form of communication related primarily to their own needs and objectives. Empathetic persons feel the emotional responses of those with whom they communicate. They move beyond the surface reactions of human dialogue to become aware of what is occurring at the feeling level.

Empathy and sensitivity to the feelings of people around you is a tremendous asset in selling. A feeling individual can reach people whom those without empathy cannot touch. Empathy may occasionally take the form of sympathy when that is the nature of the relationship, but, most of the time, this superior ability to relate to the inner feelings and motivational needs of others is a powerful source of strength that helps negotiate emotional hurdles.

Certain psychological tests can reasonably measure the degree of empathy you possess. Empathy is one of two characteristics that expert recruiters rate as essential in the basic profile of successful salespeople. (The other is ego-drive). As you communicate with prospective sales candidates, you can sometimes detect empathetic qualities by the way they react to you and to situations you describe about others. Personal interest in helping others and concern with the challenges people must overcome in life are indications of an empathetic personality.

The ability to feel for and understand your prospects and correctly interpret emotional reactions is a very valuable skill. When you are sensitive to the vibrations you receive from your prospects, you can adjust your approach to fit their needs. Combined with a reasonable amount of assertiveness, empathy helps to hold the communication on course and maintain a high level of trust and confidence in the process.

### Sense of Values and Ethics

When recruiting sales personnel, one of the more important personality factors that needs to be evaluated is the area of ethics: personal value systems. Some individuals do not view their relationships with honest concern for socially acceptable conduct. Some people lie, manipulate others to achieve their objectives, take things that do not belong to them and violate social standards. You certainly do not need people in your employ who have little or no sense of ethics.

It is possible to be fooled by some of these people because they have learned to con their way in and out of situations throughout life. That is one reason why it is vital to check references and talk to others who can vouch for the character of sales applicants. You must be reasonably sure that individuals you place in positions of trust and confidence with your properties and prospects are worthy of that trust. The consumer is normally suspicious of salespeople simply because they are in sales. A platform of trust and confidence is essential for creating sales and a solid referral business. When the motives of the salesperson are not in harmony with the motives of the consumer, the vital communication linkage is never adequately established. When in doubt about the integrity of a candidate for a sales position with your company, check and double-check before you accept that person on your sales team. A company is known by the people it keeps, and the reputation of the enterprise will be adversely affected if its salespeople perform their functions without concern for the ethical merits of their actions.

## Enthusiasm

Selling is a psychological profession. Success is directly related to the attitudes of those who are trying to influence the decisions of the consumer. That is why enthusiasm is always listed among any sales manager's criteria as a vital characteristic for hiring sales personnel.

You cannot give salespeople a magic pill that will make them enthusiastic in the presence of a customer. The attitudes you display in your daily encounters with others are the result of years of programming. You have learned to think and act in ways that seem appropriate to you because they are the responses you have chosen to the situations you experience in life. You are the sum total of everything that has happened to you, and your attitudes are like habits: They stay with you because they are an integral part of our normal response mechanisms. It is very difficult to break bad habits! Likewise, it is difficult to take negatively programmed people and convert them into enthusiastic personalities. Mentors and behavioral experts can influence others to help them change their lives, but that is not the role of a marketing director or sales manager for a real estate company! You need to start with people who already possess the characteristics you know are critical to success in this challenging business.

Unlike some of the personality traits already identified, attitude is fairly easy to detect with direct evaluation and a little probing. Enthusiastic people show that quality of life in everything they do and say. They radiate confidence and an upbeat approach to life. Their eyes sparkle, and they do and say things that show they have zest for life. They see opportunities instead of problems. Enthusiasm is one ingredient in human nature that is very difficult to hide! Conversely, those not fortunate enough to have accumulated the power of this mental lubricant will evince their lack of enthusiasm by their actions and comments. Some people can act enthusiastic for brief intervals. But stay around them for any sustained period of time, and the veneer of artificial confidence gives way to the underlying insecurities of negative thinking.

Avoid like a plague anyone whose basic attitudes in life are more negative than positive. There is no time to try to save them. Leave that to someone else who is paid to convert minds. Start with individuals who display sincere interest in life, in their careers and in the positive aspects of the exciting world of real estate!

## Self-Discipline and Sense of Responsibility

Finally, there is the matter of time management and personal discipline. Most salespeople are good at selling but poor at managing their time. This is not so much a matter of not caring about time as it is a matter of undisciplined habits. You will discover that some of your most effective communicators are people who find it distasteful to fill out forms, keep records, manage the processing details after the sales are made and keep appointment calendars with meticulous concern for being on time. An agent who has the characteristics desired but is lacking in the self-discipline department is seldom turned down. They can be educated in the importance of planning their time more effectively and shown the rewards for improving areas of personal discipline. This area is often compromised in order to attract enthusiastic and creative persuaders who can consistently close sales.

However, if you are fortunate to find candidates who have the dominant traits plus the bonus of being well-organized, you have potential superstars. It is a subject that deserves rating and careful interpretation. It is worth the time to help a potentially strong salesperson learn how to better use time management systems that will improve performance. If necessary, provide back-up support in the form of secretaries, managers, mortgage processors and others to make up for the deficiencies in this category.

## DEVELOP YOUR OWN PERFORMANCE SPECIFICATIONS FOR THE SALES ROLE

A written position description for the sales assignment is a very practical management tool that helps you clarify your expectations prior to interviewing or finalizing agreements of association. With these performance specifications as the standard for comparison in screening and selection, you can be more objective about the qualifications of a specific candidate. When you describe the requirements of the position and set standards by which the salesperson will be measured, you should be realistic rather than idealistic. Only a few superstars are in this selling profession. The basis of recruiting should be flexible enough to attract top producers and not so restrictive that you discourage reasonably good people who may be able to blossom into even better performers in a well-managed sales environment.

The position description and performance specification should describe in detail the duties, responsibilities and opportunities of the potential sales associate. This includes the following topics:

1. Specific assignments that you expect the salesperson to perform with proficiency.
2. General conditions and environments in which the sales associate will carry out the sales functions.
3. Minimum performance requirements expected of the sales representative to maintain the association with your company.
4. Knowledge, training, personal characteristics and skills that you believe are essential for success.
5. The communication responsibilities of the salesperson as related to the managment of the enterprise and a definition of the lines of authority and accountability.
6. Compensation incentives and methods of payment along with an explanation of merit systems.
7. Monitoring systems employed by the company to measure levels of performance.

Often the position description and the details of management's programs for evaluating and retaining salespeople are contained in the policies and procedures manual. If you have one that adequately covers these topics, it is wise to permit the candidate to read the policy manual before completing any agreement of association. The existence of such a management manual has the additional value of giving the applicant a feeling of confidence about your company. Well-organized enterprises tend to survive and grow, unlike those that operate without any sense of direction. Salespeople live in a world of uncertainty, and the more aspects of their environment that can be buffered from unexpected events, the more secure they feel in performing their emotionally charged roles.

We have included in this manual a number of examples of well-written position descriptions for your evaluation. However, we strongly recommend that you use them only as guidelines for one you develop exclusively for your own organization.

## THE VALUE OF A WELL-DESIGNED APPLICATION FORM

The application form is the first step in obtaining information that can be used to validate the candidate's background and qualifications. It should always be part of your information feedback process. This form, along with other supporting documents, is the beginning of the personnel file in which you can keep the association agreement, commission memorandums, performance reviews and other pertinent data. Information derived from the application for employment (or independent contractor association) serves as the format for the interview. It gives you a biographical condensation of events and circumstances that have brought the applicant to this career decision point. When completed, it should reveal the basic details about the individual's past performance. What has happened before is usually an excellent indicator of what may happen in the future.

A well-designed application form explores those areas of the candidate's background and experience directly related to the requirements of the assignment. It should be easy for the applicant to read, understand and complete. Include a disclaimer statement that permits the applicant to cover any omissions or mistakes without recrimination. Typical wording is:

"This information is factual and accurate to the best of the applicant's knowledge, and the employer is authorized to verify the details as desired."

The application form is normally composed of five basic areas of personal information. The first four categories usually contain data that can be verified if you choose to do so. The fifth area deals with the applicant's opinions and attitudes about the sales opportunity you are offering. If completed objectively, it may be of value in understanding the applicant's mental and emotional make-up. The sections covered are:

1. personal data (name, address, age, marital status, etc.)
2. education and training
3. employment history
4. special skills and qualifications for the position
5. reasons why the applicant is seeking the position

It is a good idea to leave the last section of the application blank and with no lines so that applicants, can express in writing their reasons for seeking the sales position. This permits you to make some observations about the degree of organization, orderliness and creativity of the candidate.

---

**FIGURE 5.2   Sample Application Form**

---

**Application
For Employment**

---

> Applicants are considered for all positions without regard to race, color, religion, sex, national origin, age, marital or veteran status, or the presence of a non-job-related medical condition or handicap.

*(PLEASE PRINT)*

Date of Application _____

Position(s) Applied For _____

Referral Source:   ☐ Advertisement   ☐ Friend   ☐ Relative   ☐ Walk-In

☐ Employment Agency   ☐ Other _____

---

Name _____
                LAST                          FIRST                         MIDDLE

Address _____
               NUMBER            STREET              CITY            STATE       ZIP CODE

Telephone (____) _____ Social Security Number __|__|_____
          Area Code

Are you employed now? ☐ Yes   ☐ No    May we contact your present employer? ☐ Yes   ☐ No

Are you prevented from lawfully becoming employed
in this country because of Visa or Immigration Status?   ☐ Yes   ☐ No
(Proof of citizenship or immigration status
may be required upon employment.)

On what date would you be available for work? _____

Are you available to work   ☐ Full Time   ☐ Part-Time

Are you on a lay-off and subject to recall?   ☐ Yes   ☐ No

---

Give name, address and telephone number of three references who are not related to you and are not previous employers.

_____

_____

_____

**FIGURE 5.2   Sample Application Form (continued)**

**Employment Experience**

Start with your present or last job. Include military service assignments and volunteer activities. Exclude organization names which indicate race, color, religion, sex or national origin.

| | Employer          Telephone ( ) | Dates Employed | | Work Performed |
|---|---|---|---|---|
| **1** | | From | To | |
| | Address | | | |
| | Job Title | Hourly Rate/Salary | | |
| | | Starting | Final | |
| | Supervisor | | | |
| | Reason for Leaving | | | |
| **2** | Employer          Telephone ( ) | Dates Employed | | Work Performed |
| | | From | To | |
| | Address | | | |
| | Job Title | Hourly Rate/Salary | | |
| | | Starting | Final | |
| | Supervisor | | | |
| | Reason for Leaving | | | |
| **3** | Employer          Telephone ( ) | Dates Employed | | Work Performed |
| | | From | To | |
| | Address | | | |
| | Job Title | Hourly Rate/Salary | | |
| | | Starting | Final | |
| | Supervisor | | | |
| | Reason for Leaving | | | |
| **4** | Employer          Telephone ( ) | Dates Employed | | Work Performed |
| | | From | To | |
| | Address | | | |
| | Job Title | Hourly Rate/Salary | | |
| | | Starting | Final | |
| | Supervisor | | | |
| | Reason for Leaving | | | |

If you need additional space, please continue on a separate sheet of paper.

*Special Skills and Qualifications*
Summarize special skills and qualifications acquired from employment or other experience_____
_____
_____
_____

**FIGURE 5.2   Sample Application Form (continued)**

**Education**

|  | Elementary | High | College/University | Graduate/ Professional |
|---|---|---|---|---|
| School Name |  |  |  |  |
| Years Completed: (Circle) | 4  5  6  7  8 | 9  10  11  12 | 1  2  3  4 | 1  2  3  4 |
| Diploma/Degree |  |  |  |  |
| Describe Course Of Study: |  |  |  |  |
| Desribe Specialized Training, Apprenticeship, Skills, and Extra-Curricular Activities |  |  |  |  |

Honors Received: _____

State any additional information you feel may be helpful to us in considering your application.



Indicate languages you speak, read, and/or write.

|  | FLUENT | GOOD | FAIR |
|---|---|---|---|
| SPEAK |  |  |  |
| READ |  |  |  |
| WRITE |  |  |  |

List professional, trade, business or civic activities and offices held.
(You may exclude those which indicate race, color, religion, sex or national origin): _____

_____
_____
_____

---

**FIGURE 5.2   Sample Application Form (concluded)**

---

**Applicant's Statement**

I certify that answers given herein are true and complete to the best of my knowledge.

I authorize investigation of all statements contained in this application for employment as may be necessary in arriving at an employment decision. I understand that this application is not and is not intended to be a contract of employment.

In the event of employment. I understand that false or misleading information given in my application or interview(s) may result in discharge. I understand, also, that I am required to abide by all rules and regulations of the Company.

| | |
|---|---|
| Signature of Applicant | Date |

## MERITS OF USING ONE OR MORE TESTING SYSTEMS

While it is not accepted by all sales managers in our industry that career testing systems are necessary or practical, an increasing number of the more organized real estate sales and home-building companies have adopted one or more testing programs as part of their recruiting procedures. Our experience validates that such tests have genuine merit. If nothing else, they give the applicant an increased sense of confidence in the company and in themselves when they qualify for association. When you have a professional screening system for the selection of sales associates, it shows that your company is well-run, concerned about its image and most likely profitable. An element of reverse psychology is involved when you use testing and behavioral review programs to help qualify personnel before their formal employment. Even the candidates sense that those who are selected probably are above-average individuals. Thus, they may aspire to be part of that team. Winners like to be with winners!

The real value of a good personnel evaluation plan, one that includes some testing, is its ability to reduce risks inherent in the recruiting process. Tests can provide you with information about a sales candidate that may not be clearly evident to the applicant. They can reveal specific traits and characteristics that may be masked in personal conversations. By identifying individual strengths and weaknesses, you are better prepared to train and supervise those you hire as a result of the screening program. The better tests will knock out the real losers and detect the marginal performers. If they served no other function, they would merit use for those reasons alone.

The study of human behavior and the development of psychological profile programs have become a major science. Thousands of specialists have been trained in the evaluation of human traits and can reasonably predict future behavior patterns of those they interview and test. This is not to imply that all such tests are of equal value. A wide choice is available to any manager, as you will shortly explore in this section of the manual.

The first decision to be made is whether or not to use any test at all. Our recommendation is to seriously consider doing so, if you have continuing recruiting needs and do not have a nucleus of proven performers who will stay with you for a sustained period of time.


## HOW TO SELECT A TESTING PROGRAM

When selecting a testing plan for screening sales applicants, you first need to define your objectives and determine the budget you are prepared to invest in testing your personnel. The quality and value of personnel evaluation systems vary substantially from one program to another. Costs also cover a wide range. Least expensive are self-administered systems that you grade using a master matrix score grid card. You plot the results. Choices range from simple vocational-interest tests that do not attempt to evaluate behavioral patterns to very sophisticated systems that require interviews with outside industrial psychologists and a battery of tests. Costs vary in direct proportion to the degree of involvement with administrative expertise.

Any meaningful test for evaluating human behavior and potential performance capacity must meet two technical standards. First, it must be reliable. The results that it produces must be consistent and measurable. The reliability of a test is determined by the statistical rating value measured by the number of controlled cases in which it has been used and monitored. Those tests that have had the widest use, and for which documented results are available, tend to give us more confidence than newly devised programs that may not meet the test of time. The other standard that should be carefully investigated is the degree of validity in measuring the specific behavior patterns important to the sales profile. The test should effectively measure what it is supposed to measure. There should be an easy-to-interpret relationship between the testing questions and the results of individual respondents.

An effective employment screening test provides two types of information. First, it gives a range of test scores. This is extremely important because you must have a score in order to compare the applicant's results with predetermined models. Score value ranges should permit the manager to predict the level of performance of the applicants. The other type of information is interpretive in nature. The explanations given by the authors of the testing system should be objective and understandable. Self-administered tests usually come with a manual or handbook that gives the manager a complete explanation of how to administer the tests and interpret the results.

## LIMITATIONS OF TESTING SYSTEMS

Testing, like other steps in the screening and selection process, has definite limitations. A test is intended to plug a certain information gap in the feedback process. It is not a crystal ball. It should not be the only determining factor in making the decision to recruit one person over another. It is safe to say that tests do not work every time, just as interview techniques do not always uncover the real motivations of a sales candidate. Application form data can often be inaccurate and misleading. That is why the best management system for recruiting is one that employs a number of information feedback methods and provides for investigative work to validate the findings. When you add a proven test to the system, you increase the potential for making a more informed decision while reducing the risk of hiring someone totally outside the desired profile.

## ENVIRONMENT FOR CONDUCTING THE INITIAL INTERVIEW

If you have personally ever had to apply for a position of employment, you know how awkward and uncomfortable you can feel about the whole process. Seeking a career change can be traumatic in itself. Someone not currently in real estate sales and knowing little of what to expect about the roles involved in selling homes may feel somewhat intimidated during the interview session. Your objectives of discovering your candidate and learning enough about him or her to make a judgment call dictate that you do everything possible to put your applicant at ease, especially in the first session.

While you are evaluating the prospective sales candidate, he or she is evaluating you. Remember you do not get a second chance to make a first impression! It is best to hold the interview in a location where you will not be interrupted unless it is an emergency. If numerous breaks occur in the interview process because of intrusions by others (including telephone calls), the candidate will be unable to maintain a flow of information in a manner that permits you to make an objective evaluation. If your management style indicates to the applicant that you are more concerned with other business details than the needs of your salespeople, the result may well be a decision not to work for your company.

You need to demonstrate sincere and dedicated interest in those who seek employment with your organization. The quality of time spent at the beginning sets the stage for the quality of the relationship. That is why you should set aside at least 30 to 45 minutes (or more) of uninterrupted time for that initial investigative interview with a prescreened sales candidate. Have your phone calls intercepted by a secretary or someone else during this time. Some sales managers prefer to hold these interviews after the normal business day or early in the morning before the telephones start to ring and typical crisis management activities begin. It may be that your own office is an effective environment for this first interview. But if it is not totally private with doors that close and where you have control over phones and other external forces, consider using some other location. A model home an on-site sales office, a conference room, or a private area at a club or restaurant is sometimes better for this initial encounter.

Privacy and an environment conducive to free interchange of information are the primary criteria. You are going to ask some very incisive questions, and the applicant will, you hope, reveal very personal thoughts about aspirations and past experiences that need a climate of confidential integrity. Since at least 55 percent of our communication with others is nonverbal, it is important to structure an environment conducive to a relaxed, normal response mode. You want to be able to read the body language and kinetics of human expression.

## CONTROL THE SEQUENCE AND OBJECTIVES OF THE INTERVIEW

Although probably as many different interview techniques are used as there are people doing interviews, professional recruiters follow basic guidelines during this discovery process. Seven phases make up a well-structured interview, and they follow a logical sequence.

### Greet the Candidate in a Warm, Friendly Manner

Your approach to the prospective sales representative should be one that makes the personal feel as comfortable and emotionally secure as possible in this potentially insecure scene. Your objective is to help the candidate feel important and relaxed. When you make people feel secure and important, you help them to reveal themselves in unguarded ways. You do not get to know someone who is uncomfortable about sharing personal thoughts and emotions. Sincere compliments are appropriate, as is natural humor and relaxed small talk. This is a good time to put the candidate into a conversational setting and offer soft drinks, coffee, or tea. The more informal the process, the more likely you will really uncover the person who is behind the mask.

## Provide An Overview of the Position and Your Objectives for the Interview

Do not assume that the candidate understands your objectives. Just as a good talk needs an introduction, so does an effective employment interview. This does not mean you should start telling the applicant about your company or how great you are! That is the wrong topic to discuss at the beginning. Instead, merely summarize why you are holding this interview, the position to be filled and the results to be expected from the process. For example, you might begin by saying:

> *"As you know, we are currently interviewing a number of people in our search for two additional members for our new home sales team. We have recently opened a new residential community known as 'Wildwood,' and we feel the anticipated sales volume justifies five full-time associates. Three of those five have already been chosen from our seasoned staff. We are interviewing only candidates who have proven experience in real estate sales, and your application has been reviewed with interest because of your extensive background in sales.*

> *"What I would like to gain from this interview is a general sense of your experience, your sales background and of the skills you might bring to our company."*

It is not appropriate to answer a lot of questions about the position, compensation or project at this juncture. However, observe how much interest is shown by the candidate. If he or she asks good questions, that is a very positive sign. Salespeople are trained to ask more questions than they hear, and you should always treat an inquisitive personality as a positive. If such queries are made, just politely indicate that you will discuss the various aspects of the assignment and the company after you have had the opportunity to become better acquainted. If you start talking about your company and the job before you have gained information from the candidate, you are working in reverse. Let the applicant sell his or her attitudes and skills first, and then you can decide how much you want to share about your company's goals. If this is someone which you decide does not fit your profile, why waste the time trying to sell the company at all? Besides, all the time you devote to telling your story limits the amount of time you have for the applicant's story.

## Ask Good Questions, Listen and Observe

As in all selling, you win by letting the customer do most of the talking. Let your sales applicant reveal the things you must hear and see to make some value judgments. Everything you say should be targeted toward the objective of getting your candidate to openly share information about his or her motivations, abilities and needs.

With the completed application form in front of you, there is a natural outline of topics to explore. Most of us like to begin by asking the prospect to give us a brief biography as it amplifies what is contained in the resume or application form. It can be a very informal opening like:

*"Tell me a little bit about yourself,"*

or more structured like:

*"I see from your application that you have been in various selling positions for nine years. Tell me what you did for each of those companies and why you elected to leave them?"*

Explore the five basic areas identified in the application form:

- personal data (age, marital, residency, etc.)
- educational background and training
- employment history
- financial status and current needs
- motivations for seeking the position

Ask nonthreatening questions. Especially at the beginning of the interview, avoid getting the applicant on the defensive or into a retreat syndrome. Remember that how the questions are asked is just as important as the questions themselves. Open questions are the most effective: those that cannot be answered yes or no and do not imply a specific answer.

*"How long have you been in the sales profession?"*

*"When did you decide that selling was a career you would like to explore?"*

*"What educational programs or courses have you taken to help you improve your knowledge of selling skills?"*

*"Why are you considering leaving your present position to seek this opportunity with our company?"*

*"Where have you lived during the past ten years?"*

*"Of all the positions you have held in the past, which one did you enjoy the most?"*

*"Why?"*

To interview effectively, you must be a good listener. Do not just listen to the verbal responses of the applicant. Listen *and* observe the emotions, hidden meanings, body language, and other visual impressions that are often more important than the spoken word. Focus not just on what is being said, but how it is said!

Do not be quick to react or respond to the candidate's comments. Silence is an effective tool of communication. Pauses will tell you whether or not the applicant can remain poised under pressure and how quick he or she thinks when there is a break in the conversation. Nodding your head silently and maintaining strong eye contact is a good way to help the candidate to clarify what he or she has already said. Try to keep your reactions to yourself. Do not prejudge. Give the individual the courtesy of a complete hearing. Do not give body signals that indicate you have already made up your mind one way or the other. If you are interviewing a really strong sales personality, that individual is trained to read people and will spot your own insecurities and emotional reactions.

If the flow of information begins to lag, use some subtle prodding, ask some specific and useful questions and help redirect the course of the interview.

## Describe the Position and Performance Standards

After the prospective salesperson has fully answered your basic questions, you are in a position to go into greater detail about the specific opportunity you are offering. However, if you have discovered that this is not an individual you want associated with your enterprise, you can politely terminate the interview at this point. Why waste time going into business matters that will not be productive? Normally, this is the half-way point in the interview process. You decide if it is valuable to continue with the phase that deals with the financial and procedural aspects of the position.

If you elect to proceed, this is the appropriate point to elaborate on the responsibilities, authority, accountability and opportunities of the salesperson you seek. Provide a brief description of what you expect from your sales associates. Use examples of employees currently with your company who are successful. Define the communities and properties your company is marketing. The forms and methods of compensating sales associates is now an appropriate topic. Realistic earnings projections can be given.

If you have a policies and procedures manual and other support materials, you might briefly introduce them at this point. Some managers like to give these documents to applicants that pass the first interview to enable them to learn more about how the company operates prior to the second interview session.

## Entertain Questions and Encourage Involvement in the Process

This is a logical place in the interview sequence to ask the candidate to react to the position opportunity. Encourage questions and try to achieve an open, honest dialogue. If the candidate has no questions, be very skeptical about his or her interest in the position. Sincere candidates concerned about their futures want to know as much as possible about the companies they choose for possible employment. Normal questions will deal with the success of other sales associates in your company, the management systems and people in the country, the nature of the properties and the marketing systems that will be used to bring them qualified traffic.

## Sell Your Company and its Opportunities

As you approach the end of the interview, you have the prime opportunity to sell the prospective salesperson on the merits of your organization and the immediate benefits available for the right person. You can also choose to delay this aspect of the interview until the second session. However, if you are convinced you have strong candidates for the job, don't let them get away without creating a desire to work for you rather than someone else. During earlier phases of the interview, you have been able to listen and observe. Now you can decide how this person compares to the candidates you have met and what degree of interest you have in trying to win his or her support. Where real estate agents are concerned, it is wise to remember that they employ us as much as we employ them. Real performers have no difficulty finding a place to use their talents.

Sometimes it is helpful to use an audio-visual presentation about your company if one is available. You might give the candidate a tour of your offices and a review of the homes and communities your company has developed. This is your presentation time to win another convert—if you want one!

### Conclude the Interview and Set an Appointment for the Next One

As you come to the conclusion of the first interview, you must decide what to do next. Is this a candidate you want to pursue? Is there value in proceeding with the interview process? If not, be honest with the applicant. It is better to say no now, than to waste both persons' time tomorrow. If the candidate does not meet the minimum standards of experience, education or other criteria, politely share that conclusion and thank the party for taking the time to consider your company. When an applicant looks promising but is only one of many whom you must continue to interview and evaluate, you can express some interest, but be careful about overcommitting yourself. Set a time for contacting the applicant. Give a deadline for reaching a decision so there will be no uncertainty about the time frame.

If this is a top contender for the sales position, you will want to expedite the process and keep the candidate fully involved in the momentum of the decision. One of the better techniques at this point is to set up appointments for the candidate to visit your communities and meet with sales associates who are proven performers. By involving your senior agents, you can avoid some of the challenges we often face in trying to introduce a new salesperson to the team.

Now is also the appropriate time to tell the candidate that you will be checking on various aspects of the application information form. Permission to contact personal references and past employers and other matters should be clarified and obtained. It can be very expensive not to verify the information given to you by potential associates.

### HOW TO EVALUATE OBJECTIVELY THE INTERVIEW RESULTS

During the course of your first interview you will be making mental notes about the applicant. Unless your memory is superb you should also have written notes on some type of patterned interview form. We have included examples of typical evaluation forms used by some recruiters during and following their interview sessions. Your interpretations of the prospective sales agent's attitude, poise, confidence, enthusiasm, and related characteristics will play a major role in determining your opinion. Obviously, you need to recruit people who have most of the necessary social skills to communicate effectively with others. Many of these qualities are

**FIGURE 5.3   Interview Forms**

SCREENING INTERVIEW FORM

| | 1 | 2 | 3 | 4 | 5 | 6 | 7 | 8 | 9 | 10 |
|---|---|---|---|---|---|---|---|---|---|---|
| PERSONAL APPEARANCE | Poor appearance, careless, unkempt | | Lack of attention to dress and personal grooming | | Generally neat and of good appearance | | Very careful of appearance | | Immaculate in dress and person | |
| VOICE | Unpleasant, not positive | | Indistinct, hard to hear, not forceful | | Pleasant, clear, well-modulated tone | | Very clear, easy to understand | | Unusually pleasing in quality, strength and clarity | |
| POISE | Shows some lack of self-control | | Ill at ease—embarrassed | | Normal amount of poise | | Entirely at ease | | Unusually self-possessed | |
| ABILITY TO COMMUNICATE | Confused, illogical | | Somewhat vague, or foggy | | Gets ideas across well | | Logical, clear and convincing | | Superior ability to communicate | |
| ALERTNESS | Slow, does not respond quickly | | Somewhat slow, asks poor questions | | Grasps things easily, a good listener | | Alert, asks intelligent questions | | Exceptionally keen, alert, and understanding | |
| PERSONALITY | Not positive | | Personality questionable for our job | | Pleasant personality, satisfactory for our job | | Very desirable personality | | Outstanding personality for our job | |
| TOTAL RATING | UNACCEPTABLE | | DISMISSED | | GAVE APPLICATION | | MADE APPOINTMENT FOR _____ | | TIME: _____   PLACE: _____ | |

**FIGURE 5.3 Interview Forms (continued)**

FIRST INTERVIEW FORM

| | 1 | 2 | 3 | 4 | 5 | 6 | 7 | 8 | 9 | 10 |
|---|---|---|---|---|---|---|---|---|---|---|
| DOMESTIC SITUATION | Questionable, stressful | | Definite weakness is evident | | Normal home life, no negatives | | All indications are positive | | Should be helpful to him or her | |
| EDUCATION | High school with no evidence of self-education | | High school plus some self-education | | Two years of college | | Three years of college | | Four years of college, earned degree | |
| PART-TIME WORK RECORD | No part-time work experience | | Spasmodic record of work | | Average amount of work | | Good record, helpful to him or her | | Consistent, mainly in sales | |
| WORK RECORD INTEREST IN SALES WORK | No experience in sales | | Small amount of sales experience | | Average amount of experience in sales | | Better-than-average experience in sales | | All past experience in sales | |
| STABILITY | Too many jobs, long periods of unemployment | | Changed jobs frequently, periods of unemployment too long | | Reasonably average time on each job | | Average of 2 years on each job, short periods of unemployment | | Long time on each job. No time of unemployment | |
| PROGRESS | No apparent progress | | Slight evidence of some progress | | Average progress made to date | | Above average progress | | An outstanding progress record for a man or woman of this age | |

**FIGURE 5.3    Interview Forms (continued)**

FIRST INTERVIEW FORM (CONTINUED)

| | No increase in rank, no explanation | | No increase in rank, Good explanation | | Small increase in rank | | Increase in non-commissioned officer rank | | Increase in commissioned officer rank | |
|---|---|---|---|---|---|---|---|---|---|---|
| SERVICE RECORD, INCLUDING INCREASE IN RANK | 1 | 2 | 3 | 4 | 5 | 6 | 7 | 8 | 9 | 10 |
| FUTURE GROWTH AND DEVELOPMENT | No chance that s/he will grow or develop | | Very slight indication that s/he will develop | | Average possibility for growth and development | | Better than average growth possibilities | | Can picture developing into management position | |
| | 1 | 2 | 3 | 4 | 5 | 6 | 7 | 8 | 9 | 10 |

REMARKS: _____

_____

_____

_____

_____

Note:  After the distribution of a formal job application and review of same, the interviewer should fill out the evaluation of this form, scaling it on a basis of 1–10 for each group.

**FIGURE 5.3  Interview Forms (continued)**

### SECOND INTERVIEW FORM

| NATURAL ENTHUSIASM | Listless, tired, bored | | Calm, possibly indifferent | | Normal interest, some enthusiasm | | Lively expression both facial and oral | | Sparkling and effervescent, full of life | |
|---|---|---|---|---|---|---|---|---|---|---|
| | 1 | 2 | 3 | 4 | 5 | 6 | 7 | 8 | 9 | 10 |

What clubs or organizations did you belong to during school? _____

Do you like to play cards? _____

Do you enjoy parties with lots of people? _____

Do you ever introduce yourself to strangers? _____

| ABILITY TO MAKE PEOPLE LIKE AND RESPECT HIM/ HER | Cold, aloof, Tendency to alienate people | | Slow to warm up, somewhat lacking in friendliness | | Friendly and adaptable, normal sociability | | Warm and friendly, easy to like | | Outstanding sociability, makes friends quickly | |
|---|---|---|---|---|---|---|---|---|---|---|
| | 1 | 2 | 3 | 4 | 5 | 6 | 7 | 8 | 9 | 10 |

What was your ambition when you graduated from high school? _____

When did this ambition change? Why? _____

What position would you like to hold 10 years from now? _____

What do you plan to do to obtain such a position at that time? _____

| AMBITION | No apparent idea of desires and future | | Uncertain ideas about future | | Normal desire to succeed | | Clear ideas as to future desires | | Strong, healthy ambition | |
|---|---|---|---|---|---|---|---|---|---|---|
| | 1 | 2 | 3 | 4 | 5 | 6 | 7 | 8 | 9 | 10 |

How did you get to this (or that) job? _____

How do you handle objections when selling? _____

**FIGURE 5.3   Interview Forms (continued)**

SECOND INTERVIEW FORM (CONTINUED)

Why do you want to work for our company? _____

Why do you feel that we should hire you? _____

| SALES DRIVE | Submissive, easily influenced | Lacking in drive and desire to persuade | Normal desire to persuade | Strong drive, tendency to dominate | Vigorous drive to persuade people |
|---|---|---|---|---|---|
| | 1    2 | 3    4 | 5    6 | 7    8 | 9    10 |

Did you ever hold positions of leadership during school? _____

Do you ever feel that you must hold against being overly aggressive? _____

Have you ever felt that you should try to develop your forcefulness? _____

| AGGRESSIVE-NESS | Weak, submissive, withdrawing | Lacks force and purpose | Normal forcefulness and self-confidence | Above-average force and aggressiveness | Very aggressive, forceful, tenacious |
|---|---|---|---|---|---|
| | 1    2 | 3    4 | 5    6 | 7    8 | 9    10 |

How did your previous employers treat you? Explain? _____

Have you ever worked on a committee? Explain? _____

What do you do when you need someone's cooperation? _____

**FIGURE 5.3  Interview Forms (concluded)**

SECOND INTERVIEW FORM (CONCLUDED)

| COOPERATION | Lacks the ability to cooperate | Below average in cooperativeness, possibly a problem | Normal cooperativeness | Easy to get along with | Highly cooperative, a pleasure to work with |
|---|---|---|---|---|---|
| | 1    2 | 3    4 | 5    6 | 7    8 | 9    10 |

What is the one greatest requirement of any man or woman for a successful career in selling?

_____

_____

_____

_____

evident during the give and take of the interview process. Try to objectively observe the candidate's behavior, and look for signs that indicate strength or weakness in sales situations. Be especially aware of how the applicant uses physical expressions that are part of the communication process. The eyes are a vital part of nonverbal communication. Did the candidate look at you most of the time and were the eyes sparkling with interest and vitality? Salespeople who can use their eyes effectively are normally much more successful in holding attention and building rapport than those who do not. Did the applicant smile and act friendly from the point of greeting right through the entire interchange? Was the body language positive? Did the applicant lean in or remain erect and confident during most of the session, or was there a very casual laid-back attitude evident from posture and bearing?

How about the voice? Was it modulated, resonantly pleasing to the ear and easy to understand? Did the prospective agent show enthusiasm in the inflections of the words and phrases chosen? Did he or she use appropriate language and indicate the educational background needed to fit comfortably the profile of the prospective buyers your company will attract to your housing communities. Was the pace of the spoken word assuring and positive? How about enunciation, pronunciation and projection?

During the conversation, did the applicant ask any questions? How many? Were they appropriate? As noted, you should be leery of salespeople who do not ask questions during a position interview. It is natural for any trained salesperson to want to control a conversation and lead it to positive conclusions. It is vital to sales success that the agent ask questions that will permit the prospective buyer to reveal inner feelings. Even more important, did the applicant listen actively and attentively? Was the body language indicative of someone who listens with interest to others and knows how to use the listening art to get people to share more of themselves?

What about the answers given to the questions you asked? Were they forthright and sincere? Or was there a tendency to embellish information with the puff often evident in salespeople who try to inflate their own importance to impress others? Were there any hesitancies in responding to your queries? Were there gaps in the information you requested that might indicate the party was hiding or evading something? When you asked inclusive questions about motivations and reasons for wanting to sell homes, did the agent become defensive in any way?

Admittedly, any job interview is going to be somewhat uncomfortable for most people. After all, it is not something you do everyday—and it does require that you try to be at your very best. This is not the natural environment in which you normally express your feelings to others. However, sales scenarios are filled with difficult and challenging interplays with customers who have emotional hurdles to jump before finalizing a decision. The agent who is uncomfortable in seeking employment may be also uncomfortable in trying to overcome the buyer's objections. You should use this setting to probe for real responses and reactions representative of encounters with prospective homebuyers. How a person handles the position interview can indicate how he or she would probably act in a challenging sales situation.

Be observant about physical aspects that indicate pride in personal appearance and a fair degree of self-esteem. If one comes to the interview for a new sales position with a careless attitude about attire and grooming, you would be justified in reaching the conclusion that this person would most likely do the same thing on site. More important, how a person takes care of little things such as personal grooming tends to reflect the way they handle other matters. When people evince concern about the way they look and dress, they are very likely to be conscientious about the way they follow through on other responsibilities in life. There is a direct relationship between one's self-image and how one dresses and acts.

Be cautious about stereotyping potential candidates. You may have some personal prejudices that cloud your judgment about people. If, for example, you believe that certain physical characteristics like weak chins, mustaches, or bald heads are an indication of a certain behavioral pattern, you will rule out individuals who otherwise might have valuable talents. Very few rules about physical characteristics can be used as indicators of mental and emotional strengths.

Likewise, avoid being influenced by the halo effect. This is the tendency to overlook other aspects of a personality because one or two characteristics seem so positive. For example, a person with a winning smile and a strong handshake might make you feel good about that individual's ability to relate to people. However, these are trained responses and may be masking deeper personality traits that are adverse to the sales profile. Try to be objective about the complete person that sits in front of you. Ask yourself: Would I buy a new home from this person? Does this applicant give me the impression that he or she could win and maintain confident relationships with our prospects? Does self-discipline and mental acuity reveal itself in the way the candidate organizes responses to the questions? In final analysis, it is often our training and intuitions that give us the best clues about how well applicants for sales positions will respond to the real-world environment of selling.

One other tendency needs a caution signal. Most of us tend to want to hire salespeople who are like ourselves. Hiring in your own image can be both self-limiting and impractical. We need a variety of personalities and skills in any successful real estate company. If you use the two-interview process and enlist another person to conduct the other review session, you will reduce the potential for seeking specific profiles with which you personally identify to the exclusion of other individuals who may add variety and strength to your group.

## ARRANGE FOR A SECOND INTERVIEW, PREFERABLY WITH ANOTHER INTERVIEWER

Hiring on the first interview is not a wise procedure unless you have been absolutely convinced that waiting may cost you someone you cannot afford to lose! It is far better to stage the process into two phases. The first is an initial screening session that determines whether or not the person will be selected for the second phase. Those who do not meet your specifications are eliminated during the first phase. Those who show promise are given encouragement and placed into phase two follow-up activities. This usually includes the following:

1. Provide an opportunity for the candidate to inspect your operations, visit on-site sales offices, review models, read policy and procedure manuals, view films, etc.

2.  Make an intensive check of references by the sales manager or recruiting assistants. Previous employers, personal references and financial institutions are contacted for background information.
3.  Have scheduled meetings with other sales personnel if appropriate.
4.  Hold an intensive second interview is held, preferably with another interviewer skilled in management of personnel.
5.  Hold a conference with the other people who have been exposed to the candidate and a general summary of observations compiled.
6.  Make the decision to finalize the association or decline the opportunity.
7.  Notify the applicant.

In a sales organization, it is very common to have the first interview held by the sales manager or individual who will be directly responsible for supervising the new associate. If that party does not want to take the applicant to phase two, it is his or her decision. Often the second interview is held by the general manager, broker or builder who in turn supervises the sales manager. In a major building company, more than two people might be involved in the screening process including the on-site sales manager, the director of marketing and the builder.

Two heads are usually better than one, as the old saying goes. When two people interview the applicant independently, they will see aspects of the applicant from different perspectives. What one manager may have overlooked another will uncover. The additional value to this process is its strengthening of the company image and reputation. Salespeople like to work for companies that are well-managed. The very fact that more than one person took time to interview the applicant gives the newcomer the feeling that this enterprise is run by individuals who care about people as well as about business. Another benefit is being able to reject someone without having that responsibility on one person's shoulders. The committee approach alleviates some of the hard feelings that develop when it is a personality issue. If you have ever had to reject someone who was a relative or close friend of the builder or some other influential party in the company, you know how complicated those nepotistic situations can be!

## ALWAYS CHECK REFERENCES

When you neglect to check the references given to you by the applicant, you miss an opportunity to validate information that can be critical in determining the veracity and capacity of the candidate. Written letters of recommendation are not a guarantee that the information they contain is believable. It has been said that some people receive great letters of recommendation when they depart from the employ of a company because management is still in a statement of euphoria about their departure! If you have ever had to terminate or dismiss someone, you know that there is always a lingering guilt you would like to alleviate. That is especially true if you were the one who employed that person in the first place. You would like to salve your conscience by helping the dismissed parties to find new employment. Thus, you are tempted to say nice things about them, even though you would not hire them again ourselves.

It is also a fact of business life today that one must be extremely careful about what is said about a person you did not hire or that you terminated. Employees are quick to sue if they feel they were unjustly treated and their incomes threatened by management's actions. Some companies refuse to make any comments at all about the individuals they release simply to protect themselves from lawsuits and poor publicity.

Despite these concerns, it is still worthwhile to do some checking. A phone call is an inexpensive and quick way to do some investigative work. With the applicants' knowledge and permission, you can easily check prior employers (not necessarily the current position). You can also check with people you mutually know. During the interviews it is wise to ask whom they know in the industry. If they are people you also know, they may be a good reference source.

When calling former employers, four major questions are worth asking:

- Did the applicants work for those companies in the positions represented and for the periods of time shown on the application form?
- Why did the applicants leave these companies?
- How did the applicant perform, including getting along with other people?
- Would you hire this person again under the same circumstances if the opportunity presented itself?

This last question is one that many employers will evade when they have reservations about the qualifications of the former employee. A little probing may encourage the respondent to share more information that will shed light on the personality and performance of the individual in question. Few of us ever want purposely to blackball or malign a former employee. In fact, we will bend over backwards to try to help those for whom we feel some moral responsibility. It requires a gentle but persistent investigative attitude to uncover some of the negative aspects of prior relationships.

Integrity, loyalty, sincerity and a personal value system that is evident in all relationships are traits you need to see exhibited by your potential sales personnel. This is not a hit-and-run business. If your salesperson is willing to say or do anything to make a sale, you will have the constant need to clean up the complications and try to solve the consumer problems that automatically ensue. A relationship exists between how one conducts one's private affairs, and the degree of responsibility and integrity displayed in public business affairs. The reputation and future of your enterprise depends upon the goodwill of satisfied owners of your homes. Watch for danger signs in flighty sales personalities often attracted to big-ticket selling. Those who believe they can make a fast dollar without regard to ethics will leave trails of unhappiness and management challenges behind!

## MAINTAIN COMPLETE PERSONNEL FILES FOR ALL APPLICANTS

Each candidate you have screened beyond the knock-out phase deserves to have a file folder created to hold all documents and notes resulting from the interview screening process. It is good business procedure to keep those records in the event they are needed for future reference, even if you did not hire the candidates involved.

---

**FIGURE 5.4   Sales Associate's Employment Agreement**

---

THIS AGREEMENT by and between _____, hereinafter referred to as "Company", and _____, hereinafter referred to as "sales associate", for and in consideration of their mutual promises and for their mutual benefits WITNESSETH:

THAT, WHEREAS the Company is duly registered as a licensed Colorado Real Estate Broker and is duly qualified to and does sell residential housing to qualified purchasers and has and enjoys the goodwill of and a reputation for dealing with the public and also has and maintains an office properly equipped and staffed suitable to serving the public and clients, and

WHEREAS the sales associate is now engaged in business as a real estate sales associate and has enjoyed and does enjoy a good reputation for fair and honest dealing with the public as such, and

WHEREAS it is deemed to be to the mutual advantage of said Company and said sales associate to form the association hereinafter agreed to, THEREFORE

(1) The Company agrees that sales associate may sell homes for Company on a commission basis as agreed to by a separate agreement known as "Compensation Addendum to Employment Agreement" and sales associate hereby agrees to sell homes for Company on a commission basis as agreed to by this separate agreement.

(2) The Company agrees to make available to the sales associate all current information regarding the homes offered for sale and agrees to assist the sales associate by giving that person advice, instruction and full cooperation in every way possible.

(3) The Company agrees that the sales associate may share with other Company sales associates all the facilities of the offices now operated by the Company in connection with the subject matter of this contract.

(4) The sales associate agrees to conduct business and regulate habits so as to maintain and increase the goodwill and reputation of the Company and the parties hereto agree to conform to and abide by all rules and regulations and the code of ethics binding upon or applicable to real estate brokers and all the Company's policies for sales associates.

(5) The sales associate agrees to work diligently and with best efforts to sell homes represented by the Company and to promote the business of serving our clients in the transaction of real estate to the end that each party hereto may serve the greatest profit possible.

(6) The sales associate agrees to observe and concur with the present policy and procedure manual, a copy of which is made available to the sales associate. Said policy and procedure manual is hereby made part of this agreement.

(7) The sales associate agrees to carry liability insurance to cover the use of an automobile in showing clients houses. Minimum coverage required will be One Hundred Thousand ($100,000) Dollars for any one person, and Three Hundred Thousand ($300,000) Dollars for any one accident and Fifty Thousand ($50,000) Dollars for property damage.

(8) The Company shall not be liable to the sales associate for any expenses incurred or for any acts, nor shall the sales associate be liable to the Company for office help or expenses. Sales associate shall have no authority to bind the Company by a promise or representation made, unless specifically authorized in writing.

---

**FIGURE 5.4   Sales Associate's Employment Agreement (continued)**

---

(9) From time to time, the Company will furnish files and miscellaneous information to sales associates concerning properties, sales in process and buyer data which shall be and always remain the property of the Company. Upon termination of this contract this information shall be accounted for and kept in the Company's possession.

(10) This agreement and the association hereby created may be terminated by either party hereto at any time upon notice given to the other, but the rights of the parties to any commission accrued prior to said notice, except as otherwise provided for in the policies and procedures manual, shall not be diverted by the termination of this contract. However, all rights, interests, commissions or claims of sales associates upon any pending sales not formalized on a written contrast shall cease at the time of said termination.

(11) The sales associates shall not, after termination of this contract, use to personal advantage or the advantage of any other person or corporation, any material or information gained for or from the files or business of the Company. Upon termination all leads, prospect cards and/or potential clients remain the property of the Company.

IN WITNESS WHEREOF the parties hereto signed or caused to be signed, these presents this _____ day of _____ 19 _____.

<br>

_____
Company

_____    _____
Sales Associate                      Authorized Signature              Title

_____    _____
Date                                 Date

(12) The Company reserves the right to retain up to Fifty (50%) percent of all commissions or sales in process that will not close within thirty (30) days and Twenty-Five (25%) percent of all commissions on sales in process that will close within thirty (30) days of the termination of sales associate. This retention is a servicing fee to insure the satisfactory closing of all open sales of terminated sales associates.

---

**COMPENSATION ADDENDUM TO EMPLOYMENT AGREEMENT**

---

TO: _____
                        Sales Associate
RE: _____
                        Project Name
DATE: _____

---

The commission to be paid per sale is as follows:

Commissions are considered earned after the closing and transfer of title to the purchasers and will be paid once each month within seven (7) days from the last day of the previous month. Any advances against open sales, whether it be a draw or partial payment upon loan approval, will be subject to recapture if that sale does not close.

---

**FIGURE 5.4   Sales Associate's Employment Agreement (concluded)**

The Company reserves the right to retain up to Fifty (50%) Percent of all commissions on sales in process that will not close within thirty (30) days and Twenty-Five (25%) percent of all commissions on sales in process that will close within thirty (30) days of the termination of sales associate. This retention is a servicing fee to insure the satisfactory closing of all open sales of terminated sales associates.

ON-SITE STAFFING HOURS WILL BE _____

OTHER COMPENSATION NOTES _____

_____

_____

| | |
|---|---|
| Sales Associate | Company |
| Date | Authorized Signature          Title |
| | Date |

---

You never know when you will need replacement personnel, and you may want to go back to the files to review people previously passed over. Also, there is value in researching the people you rejected to see how good your evaluation system really is! If you have turned down some real winners who went on to work for other real estate companies, it would be nice to know what you overlooked and why. None of us makes 100 percent on the decision scorecard! Something can be learned from our failures as well as our successes.

The people you bring aboard will need a comprehensive personnel file for your mutual protection and control. From the initial application form to the employment (or independent contractor's) agreement, you should have complete documentation of the initiation into the company. As you have evaluation reviews and related events with your salespeople, the notes resulting from those sessions should also be placed in their files. Should there be a change in management, the new supervisors should have the benefit of complete personnel records to assist them in making the transition in administration.

## SIGN AGREEMENT OF UNDERSTANDING AND WELCOME THE NEW ASSOCIATE

When you have made your final selection, it is good business procedure to enter into formal agreements that specify your mutual understandings about the nature of the relationships. If you are functioning as an employer, you need an employment agreement. If you do not want the responsibilities of an employer or for other business reasons must maintain some independence from the sales administration, use an independent contractor's agreement.

Completing the formal working arrangements is important, but so is being certain that the new associate is welcomed into the organization. We have known companies that employ salespeople, put them into their positions and fail to introduce them to the other people in the company for some time after their engagement. This is demoralizing to a salesperson. The function of selling has enough negatives; we should avoid adding others. People in salaried positions will believe they are more valuable than a salesperson if you allow that attitude to be reinforced by the way new people are brought into the sales team.

News bulletins, welcoming sessions at meetings, personal introductions to each of the key people and departments, and a general announcement that gives the new people a feeling of belonging, rather than being outsiders, can do much to put them into the right attitude about themselves and the company. Send a welcoming letter to the mate of the salesperson (if married). Let the people in the family support-system know the company appreciates the talents and services of their loved one. The more things you do to smooth the path into the new sales position, the more productive will be the relationship.

## HOW TO SELECT A DESIGNATED BROKERAGE COMPANY THAT ALREADY HAS THE TEAM IN PLACE

For those readers who are associated with builders and developers who use outside contract sales agencies to represent their homes, we are including this section of the marketing manual to identify the procedures for selecting and working with independent brokerage companies. If this does not apply to your organization, you may desire to skip the balance of this chapter and proceed to the next one. However, if you are by chance a brokerage company or a new home sales company that markets its services to client accounts, you will probably find this material of value in recognizing how best to structure your services on behalf of your clientele. Those who elect to choose subcontracting brokerage agencies to fulfill their sales objectives normally have a wide variety of choices in any market area of the country. Who wins the assignments usually depends upon who has the track record and the complete package of support systems that assure the builder of receiving professional attention.

## CRITERIA FOR BROKER SELECTION

### General Observations

Obviously, the choice of brokerage firms to represent your company is extremely important to your success and to the fulfillment of your marketing objectives. Not all brokerage firms are capable of representing new homes. In fact, many would not qualify. A very high percentage of real estate brokers do not want to become involved in any activity outside of their immediate interests. This means that you should carefully select your target markets to be certain that your designated brokers can do the job and that they will readily experience rewards from their efforts.

## Location of the Brokerage Company's Office

The brokerage company's office location is a vital selection criterion. Is it easy for prospects to visit the offices, to sit down and view audio-visual presentations, to learn about your housing and be qualified prior to showing homes? You want prestige locations in neighborhoods that are representative of the type of clientele who purchases your homes. You want offices that are ideally located in relation to traffic patterns; that is, easily accessible by major freeways or thoroughfares.

Companies with more than one office location may be preferable because of the advantage they offer in increased exposure. However, another side to that issue is that many small offices do not compare with the advantages of one well-located, prestigious office with the facilities and the image to represent your homes. We are normally more concerned about the coverage of one office than the scope of the total organization. This matter must be researched carefully and a decision made about the impact of one brokerage company based on its location and sphere of influence compared to other factors.

## Reputation of the Brokerage Company

Certainly, a company's adherence to a high standard of ethics must be a major consideration in selecting designated brokers. To some degree, that will be based upon their years in business and the credibility they have established in the markets they serve. The size of their referral volume, together with their professional recognition, will increase public acceptance of your homes. You will, in many cases, need the broker's support and reputation to compensate for the inherent fears of buyers who hesitate becoming involved with builders and the construction process.

## Financial Capacity of the Designated Brokerage Firms

It is also important that designated brokers are adequately capitalized with solid financial reputations. You cannot afford to link your name with an undercapitalized, poorly financed real estate enterprise. A company's lack of capital and its inability to meet obligations can seriously jeopardize your relationships with them and with your buyers. This means you should investigate the companies' reputations and their standings with lending institutions in the areas they serve. This can be done without too much difficulty and should be done quietly while making your initial investigation.

## Clientele of the Designated Brokerage Firm

Before selecting any brokerage company, evaluate the nature of the properties and clientele they presently service. You do not want to make arrangements with brokers who do not have access to your profiled buyers. You want the marketing platform that reputable brokers can give to introduce your housing to the right people with whom they have established relationships. You also want to capitalize on the broker's centers of influence developed within the community. These should lead you to more buyers through the broker's contacts. The broker who has a good personal reputation for being involved with the right political and social circles will help you to set the stage for introducing your homes to the right people. You can accelerate your marketing program by using the designated broker's advance groundwork.

Thus, as part of your criteria, you must first identify the neighborhoods within each market area that represent the price range and caliber of buyers you are seeking. Then determine which brokerage firms in that market are the most effective and have the finest reputations with the majority of local residents.

## Quality of the Broker's Personnel

The nature and quality of the broker's personnel are also prime factors in your decision making. You will need salespeople who are respected by those whom you are trying to attract and those who have the selling skills and knowledge to work comfortably with your clientele. You also want salespeople who are specialists in new residential sales rather than just resale housing.

Work with a brokerage company that has at least 10 to 15 residential sales agents per office (and preferably more). A direct relationship exists between the number of contacts each agent has and the effectiveness of presenting new home opportunities. We know that only a limited percentage of any specific market is available to us, so the increased number of salespeople exposed to the area gives you a better chance to tap that share of the market.

You need to have an account manager—one or more individuals from a brokerage firm who can coordinate with your staff and who will take the responsibility of being the liaison between their organization and yours. This is essential for effective communication.

## Marketing Capacity of the Brokerage Company

A major consideration is the brokerage firm's capacity to market your homes effectively in competition with other housing. You need to know the extent of the marketing systems they will provide your company. Will they be able to communicate by direct-mail to the owners they have served in the past and set up appointments after qualifying prospects in person or by phone? Will they be able effectively to incorporate your marketing program with their existing marketing systems? And, more important, in their organization do they have some individual who will assume responsibility for promoting your housing and establishing communication with other agents and prospects? Who is available for on-site staffing and what commitments will they make to provide adequate coverage?

Ultimately, it comes down to marketing!! You want to know how efficient the companies are and how cooperative they will be. An organization may be effective in doing things but not everything. Likewise, because of present responsibilities, additional commitments may take them to the breaking point. This is one of the more

**FIGURE 5.5    Project and Planning Control Forms**

| PROJECT AND PLANNING CONTROL FORM 1.0 | PAGE 1 |
|---|---|
| MAJOR CLASSIFICATION NOTATIONS: DESIGNATED BROKER PROGRAM | General Notes: |
| THE SELECTION AND SCREENING PROCESS | |

| PROJECT CONTROL NUMBERS | PROJECT OR PLANNING ASSIGNMENT / DESCRIPTION OF ASSIGNMENT AND RELATED NOTATIONS | PROJECT DIRECTOR | BEGIN | REVIEW | DUE | FINAL |
|---|---|---|---|---|---|---|
| 1.1 Define market areas | Using a map of the general region, identify the specific neighborhoods, communities and real estate districts where you need sales coverage. | | | | | |
| 1.2 Identify real estate offices | Using the same map and either colored pens or pins, mark the specific locations of residential brokers' offices. Where one company has multiple offices, use the same color to identify all locations. | | | | | |
| 1.3 Analyze your needs | Complete Analysis Form 1.3A to identify your needs as related to potential brokerage representation. | | | | | |
| 1.4 Preselect candidate companies | Based on the conclusions of Form 1.3A, pre-select potential candidate companies and prepare Profile Forms with known information prior to interviews. Use Form 1.4A. | | | | | |
| | COORDINATION NOTES | | | | | |
| | | | | | | |
| | | | | | | |
| | | | | | | |

## FIGURE 5.5  Project and Planning Control Forms (continued)

| | PROJECT AND PLANNING CONTROL FORM 1.0 | PAGE 2 | | | | |
|---|---|---|---|---|---|---|
| | MAJOR CLASSIFICATION NOTATIONS: DESIGNATED BROKER PROGRAM | General Notes: | | | | |
| | THE SELECTION AND SCREENING PROCESS | | | | | |
| | | | | | | |
| PROJECT CONTROL NUMBERS | PROJECT OR PLANNING ASSIGNMENT / DESCRIPTION OF ASSIGNMENT AND RELATED NOTATIONS | PROJECT DIRECTOR | BEGIN | REVIEW | DUE | FINAL |
| 1.5 Conduct broker interviews | Set up interview appointments with candidate brokerage firms (always with a key member of the management team). Answer the balance of questions on the Profile Form (1.4A). | | | | | |
| 1.6 Make tentative selections | Evaluate initial results of the interviews and the Profile Forms. Eliminate those who do not meet basic qualifications. Conduct second interviews with remainder. | | | | | |
| 1.7 Obtain broker marketing plans | Ask each of the remaining candidate brokerage firms to prepare a proposed marketing plan (in writing). Give these candidates the Marketing Plan Checklist to follow (Form 1.7A). | | | | | |
| 1.8 Finalize your decisions | Review the marketing proposals. Hold final interviews with the brokers and your potential Account Managers. Make your decision for one or more designated brokers. | | | | | |
| | COORDINATION NOTES | | | | | |
| | | | | | | |
| | | | | | | |
| | | | | | | |

**FIGURE 5.5   Project and Planning Control Forms (continued)**

**DESIGNATED BROKER CANDIDATE**
**BUILDER SALES ANALYSIS FORM**

BUILDER_____     DATE _____

*SALES PROJECTIONS*                                       Time frame _____
  Total new homes to be sold _____
  Projections by plan, type, price:
  _____
  _____
  _____

*INVENTORY STATUS*
  Presales from floor plans                               _____
  Inventory homes (specs)                                 _____
  Build-to-order on homebuyer's own sites                 _____
  Availability of display homes or models for sales agents _____

*STAFFING NEEDS*
  Staffing hours expected for on-site personnel           _____
  Number of salespeople needed for open houses on on-site sales facilities  _____
  Size of preferred real estate company                   _____
  Other notes:
  _____
  _____
  _____
  _____

*BUYER PROFILE*

*Instructions*: Profile the typical buyers anticipated for builder's homes or digest prior sales made
to document actual profiles.
  _____
  _____
  _____
  _____

*ESTIMATE OF BUYER SOURCES*
  Local buyers (number or percentage)                     _____
  Locations of origin within the region:
  _____
  _____
  _____
  _____
  Transferees (number or percentage)                      _____
  Builder-originated referrals                            _____
  Importance of cooperative broker sales:
  _____

---

## FIGURE 5.5    Project and Planning Control Forms (continued)

Trades or contingencies (number or percentage)    _____
Other factors:

_____
_____
_____
_____

*MARKETING SERVICES DESIRED FROM DESIGNATED BROKER*

*Instructions*: Rate the importance of each item.
   Market research    _____
   Transferee services    _____
   Equity assistance plans    _____
   Sales personnel willing to staff open homes    _____
   Special real estate office displays    _____
   Newspaper advertising    _____
     Classified    _____
     Display    _____
   Direct-mail campaigns    _____
   Radio    _____
   Television    _____
   Cooperative broker networks    _____
     Local    _____
     Regional    _____
     National    _____
   Multiple-listing service    _____
   Brochure production    _____
   Photography    _____
   Display graphics    _____
   Newsletters    _____
   Satellite displays    _____
   Model home furnishings    _____
   On-site sales offices    _____
   Brochure distribution services    _____
   Billboards    _____
   Special signs    _____
   Public relations    _____
   Other marketing services:

_____
_____
_____
_____

*MANAGEMENT SYSTEMS AND PROCEDURES*

*Instructions*: Rate relative importance of each item.
   Policies and procedures manual    _____
   Recruiting capacity    _____
   Training and education    _____

**FIGURE 5.5    Project and Planning Control Forms (continued)**

Compensation incentives            _____
Recognition and motivation         _____
Sales-processing services          _____
Mortgage-processing services      _____
Telephone and message-forwarding services   _____
Land/lot acquisition services         _____
Property management                   _____
Other management services:

_____
_____
_____

### DESIGNATED BROKER CANDIDATE
### PROFILE ANALYSIS FORM

*GENERAL*

Firm name_____
Address (main office)_____
City _____ State _____ Zip _____
Phones:  (    ) _____ - _____
        (    ) _____ - _____

Principal                          Office
brokers:        Number: _____     locations:     Number: _____

General history of the company

_____
_____
_____
_____
_____
_____

Years in business _____    Total sales personnel _____
No. of managers _____      Resale specialists _____
No. of office staff _____     New home specialists _____
Annual gross sales $ _____   Commercial/investment _____
Annual no. of housing units             Resort sales _____
    sold _____                   Land sales _____
                                     Other _____

*EVALUATION OF NEW HOME SALES CAPACITY*

Separate new home sales department?       Yes _____   No _____
Years of experience in new home sales _____
Gross sales volume in past 12 months        $ _____ Units _____
Price ranges sold _____ Av. price $ _____

**FIGURE 5.5   Project and Planning Control Forms (continued)**

Experience in selling from floor plans?                     Yes _____  No _____
Experience in staffing open houses?                         Yes _____  No _____
Experience in project management?                           Yes _____  No _____
Builders currently served by company:

_____
_____
_____
_____
_____


*MARKET RESEARCH SERVICES*

Does brokerage firm have a research dept.?                  Yes _____  No _____
Computerized data base?                                     Yes _____  No _____
MLS?                                                        Yes _____  No _____
Preparation of market feasibility studies?                 Yes _____  No _____
Published reports?                                          Yes _____  No _____
Competitive market studies?                                Yes _____  No _____
Inventory of homesites and land?                           Yes _____  No _____
Examples of previous research studies?                     Yes _____  No _____

Obtain a summary of sources of buyers and the percentages in each category.


*RELOCATION AND TRANSFEREE SERVICES*

Estimate of current percentage of sales volume attributable to transferees       _____
Does brokerage firm have a specialized relocation dept. with an
organized program?                                         Yes _____  No _____
List the national referral networks to which this company belongs:

_____
_____
_____
_____
_____


List any direct equity (third party) companies represented:

_____
_____
_____
_____
_____


Which of the following relocation services does the broker offer?
Transferee kits                      _____
Welcome-to-community services        _____
Orientation programs                 _____
Office displays, maps, visual aids   _____

---

**FIGURE 5.5    Project and Planning Control Forms (continued)**

---

*EQUITY ASSISTANCE PLANS*

Does the brokerage company offer a guaranteed-equity or trade plan?    Yes _____    No _____

Do they offer equity advances and bridge loans?    Yes _____    No _____

Total number of completed trades or contingent transactions during past 12 months    Yes _____    No _____

Does the company have a special marketing plan for handling contingencies?    Yes _____    No _____

If yes, describe:

_____

_____

_____

_____

_____


*NEW HOME MARKETING SERVICES*

Sales personnel willing to staff open homes as needed?    Yes _____    No _____

Special real estate office display for builder(s)?    Yes _____    No _____

Newspaper advertising?    Yes _____    No _____

   Classified?    Yes _____    No _____

   Display?    Yes _____    No _____

Direct-mail campaigns?    Yes _____    No _____

Radio?    Yes _____    No _____

Television?    Yes _____    No _____

Cooperative broker networks:

   Local    Yes _____    No _____

   Regional    Yes _____    No _____

   National    Yes _____    No _____

Multiple-listing service?    Yes _____    No _____

Brochure production?    Yes _____    No _____

Photography?    Yes _____    No _____

Display graphics?    Yes _____    No _____

Newsletters?    Yes _____    No _____

Satellite displays?    Yes _____    No _____

Model home furnishings?    Yes _____    No _____

On-site sales offices?    Yes _____    No _____

Brochure distribution services?    Yes _____    No _____

Billboards?    Yes _____    No _____

Special signs?    Yes _____    No _____

Public relations?    Yes _____    No _____

Other marketing services:

_____

_____

_____

_____

---

**FIGURE 5.5   Project and Planning Control Forms (continued)**

---

*MANAGEMENT SYSTEMS AND PROCEDURES*

| | |
|---|---|
| Policies and procedures manual? | Yes _____   No _____ |
| Recruiting systems? | Yes _____   No _____ |
|   If yes, describe:_____ | |

_____

_____

| | |
|---|---|
| Training and education? | Yes _____   No _____ |
|   If yes, describe:_____ | |

_____

_____

| | |
|---|---|
| Compensation system for new home personnel? | Yes _____   No _____ |
|   If yes, describe:_____ | |

_____

_____

| | |
|---|---|
| Recognition/motivational programs? | Yes _____   No _____ |
|   If yes, describe:_____ | |

_____

_____

| | |
|---|---|
| Sales-processing services | Yes _____   No _____ |
|   If yes, describe:_____ | |

_____

_____

| | |
|---|---|
| Mortgage-processing services? | Yes _____   No _____ |
|   If yes, describe:_____ | |

_____

_____

| | |
|---|---|
| Telephone and message-forwarding services? | Yes _____   No _____ |
| Land/lot acquisition services? | Yes _____   No _____ |
|   If yes, describe:_____ | |

_____

_____

| | |
|---|---|
| Property management? | Yes _____   No _____ |
|   If yes, describe:_____ | |

_____

_____

*KEY QUESTIONS TO EVALUATE*

1.  Who would be the account manager if you choose this company?

    _____

2.  How much time will the account manager be able to devote to your needs?

    _____

3.  What kind of support will the rest of the staff give to the account manager?

    _____

4.  Are the internal commission incentives of the company appropriate for new home sales management?

    _____

---

### FIGURE 5.5    Project and Planning Control Forms (continued)

---

5. Is the attitude of the principal brokers positive toward new home sales and builder representation?
   _____

6. What staffing commitments will they make for on-site coverage?_____
   _____

7. How extensive and effective are their marketing activities for new housing projects?_____
   _____
   _____

### DESIGNATED BROKER PROGRAM
### MARKETING PLAN CHECKLIST

COMPANY _____ DATE _____
BROKER _____

*INSTRUCTIONS*: Prepare a written marketing plan for the builder covering the major points listed below. Be sure to provide specifics rather than generalities where possible. Also, attach any exhibits which will illustrate or validate *your* recommendations.

- Proposed procedures for account management, including who, time available for management and team members involved.
- Summary of brokerage company's history and success.
- Description of services available to the builder.
- General observations regarding builder's plans, location(s) and prices.
- Profile of anticipated buyers.
- Identification of target markets in terms of origin of buyers.
- Proposal for on-site marketing, including staffing.
- Recommendations for advertising and promotion, including how costs will be handled.
- Proposal for obtaining maximum support from cooperating brokers.
- Proposal for obtaining preconstruction sales.
- Proposal for building referral leads.
- Proposal for reaching various target groups: (Define yours)
     First-time buyers
        Singles-mingles
        Young married
     Trade-up buyers
     Transferees
     Empty-nesters
     Others
- Commissions and budgets
     Identify the commission schedule to be applied to this builder program.

     Develop a proposed marketing budget and indicate the costs to be borne by broker versus those by the builder.

     Estimate the number of sales to be made and the time periods in which they will occur (use a monthly projection chart).

     Identify your own qualifications (or those of your associates) to represent the builder.

| FIGURE 5.5 | Project and Planning Control Forms (continued) |
| --- | --- |

| | PROJECT AND PLANNING CONTROL FORM 2.0 | | General Notes: |
| | MAJOR CLASSIFICATION NOTATIONS: DESIGNATED BROKER PROGRAM | |
| | BUILDER-REALTOR® AGREEMENTS | |
| | | |

| PROJECT CONTROL NUMBERS | PROJECT OR PLANNING ASSIGNMENT | PROJECT DIRECTOR | BEGIN | REVIEW | DUE | FINAL |
| --- | --- | --- | --- | --- | --- | --- |
| | DESCRIPTION OF ASSIGNMENT AND RELATED NOTATIONS | | | | | |
| 2.1 Services Checklist | Review all checklisted items on Form 2.1A and obtain agreement from the designated broker as to the responsibilities and obligations of both entities. | | | | | |
| 2.2 Execute Agreement | Execute a written agreement with the designated broker. Prepare your own form checklist (Form 2.2A) or use agreement prepared by broker. Be sure to cover all major points in checklist. | | | | | |
| | | | | | | |
| | | | | | | |
| | COORDINATION NOTES | | | | | |
| | | | | | | |
| | | | | | | |
| | | | | | | |

---

**FIGURE 5.5   Project and Planning Control Forms (continued)**

---

### CHECKLIST OF TOPICS TO REVIEW
### WITH DESIGNATED BROKERS
### PRIOR TO CONFIRMATION OF RELATIONSHIPS

*COMPENSATION AGREEMENTS*

- Commissions
- Consultation fees
- Reimbursement of expenses
- Draws and advances to agents
- Accounting procedures

*STAFFING ASSIGNMENTS AND RESPONSIBILITIES*

- Identity of the account manager(s)
- Personnel assigned to the account
- Right of builder review
- On-site staffing hours
- Responsibilities for costs of on-site sales facilities
  - Office furnishings
  - Displays
  - Office supplies
  - Telephone/answering service
  - Maintenance
  - Landscape
  - Janitorial
  - Utilities
  - Insurance
- Model homes and show homes
  - Furnishings/decorating
  - Maintenance
  - Landscaping
  - Janitorial
  - Utilities
  - Insurance

*ORIGINATING AND PROCESSING PURCHASE AGREEMENTS*

- Prospect registration and prospect profile data
- Prospect follow-up procedures
- Product presentations
- Purchase agreements to be used
- Disposition of deposit monies
- Presentation and acceptance of purchase agreements
- Mortgage-processing procedures
- Buyer profile form
- Color choices and design advice
- Change orders, options, custom extras
- Production-scheduling procedures

---

**FIGURE 5.5    Project and Planning Control Forms (continued)**

---

- Homeowner's insurance policies
- Cancellations and noncompletions
- Contingent transactions and trades


*CONSTRUCTION COORDINATION AND MOVE-IN PROCEDURES*

- Coordination between builder's staff and designated broker's staff
- Premove-in inspection procedures
- Key release procedures
- Move-in and utility connection procedures
- Builder's warranty package
- Customer service policies
- Welcome-to-new-home programs


*MARKET RESEARCH AND CONSULTATION*

- Broker's submission of current market data on regular basis
- Competitive market analysis
- Available lots inventoried and evaluated
- Design consultation
- Consumer surveys and customer satisfaction studies
- Financing sources reviewed and recommendations made to builder on regular basis


*ADVERTISING AND PROMOTION*

- Establishing budgets and payment of costs
  - Broker's responsibilities
  - Builder's responsibilities
- Production of ads
- Placement of ads
- Brochures
- Sales literature
- Direct-mail pieces
- Direct-mail campaigns
- Radio
- Television
- Signs/billboards
- Satellite displays
- Displays in broker's office(s)
- Public relations
- Special events
- Sales presentation exhibits
- Sales presentation binders for use by agents
- Cooperation and promotion with other brokers
  - Local
  - Regional
  - National

---

**FIGURE 5.5   Project and Planning Control Forms (continued)**

---

*BROKER'S ADMINISTRATION OF MARKETING, SALES AND SALES PERSONNEL*

- Orientation sessions
- Sales training on builder's products and programs
- Commission incentives to sales staff
- Completion and submission of sales and marketing reports
  - Identify forms to be used
  - Identify responsibilities for submission
- Policies and procedures manual
- Personnel policies
  - Attitude and conduct of staff
  - Dress code(s)
  - Referrals between agents and other brokers
  - Motivational programs

**DESIGNATED-BROKER PROGRAM**
**SELECTIVE CLAUSES FOR BUILDER-REALTOR® AGREEMENTS**

*EXCLUSIVE RIGHT TO SELL AND TERM OF AGREEMENTS*

Builder hereby grants to Agent the exclusive right to sell homes constructed by the Builder on the following areas:

(list by address, lot number, tract number, or other legal descriptions)

For a period commencing ___(date)___ and terminating ___(date)___ on the following terms and conditions.

*COMPENSATION*

Builder shall pay the Agent _____ per transaction as the total consideration for professional services rendered. This commission shall be payable at the close of escrow and recordation of title transfer.

*PRICES AND TERMS OF SALE*

Builder agrees to furnish Agent current price lists of all floor plans, homesites, models, and options and to keep Agent informed in writing of any changes prior to their effective dates. The Builder reserves the right to adjust prices in accordance with changing costs of construction and related factors.

*SALES PERSONNEL*

The Agent shall be fully responsible for selecting and supervising all sales personnel to staff the Builder's properties as agreed in this contract. The Agent will serve as the responsible representative for communicating and negotiating with cooperative brokerage companies.

---

**FIGURE 5.5    Project and Planning Control Forms (continued)**

---

*SALES FACILITIES*

The Agent will use all the sales facilities available in present brokerage offices to adequately represent the Builder's properties. The Agent will arrange a display of Builder's homes in the Agent's primary office located at _____. At the Builder's option, an on-site sales office and design center may be constructed and assigned to the Agent for staffing and use. In that event, the Agent will be responsible for the following costs:

(list of costs)

The Builder will be responsible for the following costs:

(list of costs)

The Agent will use due diligence in caring for the sales office and all model homes or displays.

*STAFFING RESPONSIBILITIES*

The Agent agrees to staff and represent the homes covered by this agreement and to service the traffic in a manner that will assure satisfactory sales coverage. The minimum staffing hours for the on-site sales center or display homes will be _____(specify hours and days)_____.

*ADVERTISING AND MERCHANDISING*

*Clause A*

The Builder assigns to the Agent the responsibility for coordinating all advertising and merchandising of the Builder's properties. Costs for said advertising and merchandising will be paid for as follows:

(define method of payment)

*ALTERNATE*

*Clause B*

The Builder shall from time to time at his sole cost and expense promote the sale of his housing programs by advertising through various media, such as newspapers, magazines, direct-mail, billboards, signs, radio and in such other ways as the Builder in his sole discretion deems appropriate.

*ALTERNATE*

*Clause C*

The Builder and Agent shall mutually agree upon all advertising and merchandising to be employed in promoting the Builder's housing programs. Regularly scheduled meetings will be attended by the Builder (or his representative) and the Agent to plan future marketing activities. The cost for all advertising and merchandising will be paid for as follows:

(defined method of payment)

**FIGURE 5.5   Project and Planning Control Forms (continued)**

*PURCHASE AGREEMENTS AND DEPOSITS*

Upon execution of an agreement to purchase for one of the Builder's homes, the Agent shall obtain from such Purchaser a deposit in cash or check which shall be delivered to the Builder (or the Builder's authorized representative) to be applied toward the purchase price of the real property. The Agent shall instruct its personnel to make all checks payable to _____.
The only authorized contract to purchase acceptable to the Builder will be the one attached to and made a part of this agreement and noted as "Exhibit A."

*DELIVERY OF DOCUMENTS*

The Agent shall deliver the receipt for the deposit and the purchase agreement to the local offices of the Builder (or such designated locations as he elects to use) within two (2) business days following receipt from the Purchaser.

*ACCEPTANCE OF PURCHASE AGREEMENTS*

Within forty-eight (48) hours of receipt of the purchase agreement, the Builder shall accept (or reject) such contract and release it for delivery to the Agent's office, title company, or escrow agent for expeditious processing. Acceptance shall not unreasonably be withheld. Contracts presented to the Builder by the Agent that do not conform to the written, authorized prices and terms may be rejected. If the Builder elects to present a counteroffer to the Purchaser, the Agent shall use due diligence in presenting the alternative proposal for the prospective Purchaser's acceptance.

*CONTRACT PROCESSING AND MORTGAGE FINANCING*

Agent agrees to maintain individual sales records of all transactions on the Builder's homes available for the Builder's inspection at any time.

Agent agrees to expedite all processing details necessary to complete the Purchaser's qualifying and obtaining mortgage financing (when needed). The Agent will abide by the Builder's instructions regarding placement of mortgages. The status of all sales in progress will be submitted once each week to the Builder on a transaction-processing flowchart for the mutual review of all concerned parties.

The Builder will similarly keep the Agent informed as to the status of construction for each contracted housing unit.

*PRODUCT KNOWLEDGE AND SALES REPRESENTATIONS*

The Agent agrees to attend the indoctrination sessions scheduled by the Builder and to see that all Agents involved in representing the Builder's homes are given a complete orientation. In addition, all new information furnished to the Agent will be promptly relayed to all sales personnel as well as cooperating brokers.

The Agent and the cooperating Subagents are only authorized to quote and use the information in writing by the Builder. The Agent will be fully responsible for the representation made by the Agent or Subagents regarding the Builder's properties.

---

**FIGURE 5.5    Project and Planning Control Forms (continued)**

---

*CONDITION OF PROPERTIES*

Builder agrees to maintain all of the properties covered by this listing agreement in presentable condition and to promptly respond to and handle Purchaser's complaints as prescribed by the Builder's service warranty.

*NONCOMPETITION CLAUSES*

*Clause A*

The Agent agrees not to represent another Builder or Developer whose homes or projects might be deemed to be directly competitive to the Builder's properties without the express written consent of the Builder.

*Clause B*

The Builder shall not during the term of this agreement and for a period of six months thereafter employ or offer to employ or contract for services with any employees or associates of the Agent without the written consent of the Agent.

*COMMISSION(S) AFTER TERMINATION*

The Builder shall pay to the Agent the commission prescribed in this contract in the event a sale is made within 30 days after the termination or expiration of this agreement to a third-party Purchaser with whom the Agent shall have negotiated during the term of the agreement.

*TERMINATION OF AGREEMENT*

This agreement shall be terminated upon the closing of escrow of the last home sold during the life of this agreement. However, the agreement is terminable by either party hereto, without the necessity of giving reasons, by a written notice from the party electing to terminate delivered to the other party at least thirty (30) days in advance. Termination of the agreement shall not alter the mutual responsibilities of the participants for acts made during its active term.

*NO ASSIGNMENT*

This agreement or any interest therein may not be assigned by the Agent or the Builder without the written consent of both parties.

*INDEMNITY*

The Builder shall indemnify the Agent against and hold the Agent harmless from any and all claims, demands, losses, causes of action, arbitrations, attorneys' fees, costs, liabilities and judgments, including fees and costs of defense arising out of or in any way related to actions, inactions, representations, concealments or nondisclosures of the Builder or his employees or Agents that materially affect the real estate offering of the Builder's properties and programs.

The Agent shall hold the Builder harmless for representations of its employees or Agents beyond the scope of this agreement that result in litigated claims.

| FIGURE 5.5 | Project and Planning Control Forms (concluded) | | | | | | |
|---|---|---|---|---|---|---|---|
| | PROJECT AND PLANNING CONTROL FORM 3.0 | | General Notes: | | | | |
| | MAJOR CLASSIFICATION NOTATIONS: DESIGNATED BROKER PROGRAM | | | | | | |
| | REALTOR® ORIENTATION AND COMMUNICATION PROCEDURES | | | | | | |
| | | | | | | | |
| PROJECT CONTROL NUMBERS | PROJECT OR PLANNING ASSIGNMENT | PROJECT DIRECTOR | BEGIN | REVIEW | DUE | FINAL |
| | DESCRIPTION OF ASSIGNMENT AND RELATED NOTATIONS | | | | | | |
| 3.1 Furnish indoctrination materials | Supply the broker and the associated salespeople all of the necessary indoctrination materials on your housing programs. Set date(s) for group orientation session(s). | | | | | | |
| 3.2 Conduct orientation session | Conduct one or more product orientation sessions with the agents and their associates. Involve suppliers, designers, planners and others as deemed advisable. | | | | | | |
| 3.3 Review position descriptions | Review position descriptions for the Account Manager and Sales Manager. Verify the procedures for managing your projects and properties. | | | | | | |
| 3.4 Establish a marketing committee | Organize a Marketing Committee, consisting of the agency, key members of your staff, and others as needed. Set regular schedule for meetings to review all marketing. | | | | | | |
| | COORDINATION NOTES | | | | | | |
| | | | | | | | |
| | | | | | | | |
| | | | | | | | |

subtle aspects of your criteria, and you should explore further the motives of your candidates in interviews held with potential brokers.

### Capacity for Administration

You can well imagine that not all brokers are good administrators. In fact, poor administration is more the rule than the exception. A large number of real estate firms have little or no management control because those who operate them are basically sales individuals who operate loosely. You want a well-managed real estate firm, one with an experienced broker or brokers capable of supervising their people and effectively working with you in all facets of the operation. You want brokers capable of representing you well, and who maintain control of their sales staff to avoid misrepresenting you. This will depend upon how effective they are in day-to-day supervision of their sales organization. You should be concerned if they do not have in place training programs that emphasize new home selling techniques. Obtain a commitment from the brokers that they are willing to expend the proper amount of time and attention to help you fulfill your marketing needs.

## MARKETING YOUR COMPANY TO THE PEOPLE YOU WANT

I have always been of the opinion that brokers and marketers do not select high-achieving salespeople. They select us! Experienced people who know that they have something to offer and can prove their worth do not have to worry about finding sales positions. They are in such high demand and so few of them are around that they can take their pick of opportunities within their market areas. The inexperienced recruit may be tempted to take a position anywhere that he or she feels will provide a logical starting point for a new career path. The pro will study the alternatives and determine where he or she wants to work. The preselection is usually done before they ever come to your attention. If they never knock on your door, you should worry about the reputation of your organization as a place that top producers want to be.

In interviewing the peak performers, we have asked them to identify the things that attracted them to the companies with whom they are currently associated and what would cause them to ever change employers. Below (in order of priority) are the determinants they have shared with us.

### Location and Size of the Operations

The locale and the size of the venture were selected by most of the pros as one of the most important considerations. The majority of them are established within specific marketing regions, have family ties and do not want to move or travel long distances from home base. There are exceptions. The relative size of the organization is also a key factor. Some want to be with large, growing enterprises that have a number of projects and programs in place, while others are looking for smaller, more personal companies where they can be big frogs in small ponds rather than small frogs in big ponds. This choice is very personal and will vary from one agent to another.

## Type of Real Estate Projects

It is interesting to note that most top producers have identified the type of communities and environments they enjoy selling. While some can handle anything from mobile homes to castles, their own self-images are usually involved in what they like to represent. For example, some new home sales specialists prefer dealing with luxury housing in the upper price ranges, and others are more comfortable selling first-time buyers and the entry-level properties. Some prefer condominiums; others are good at lot sales or custom homes. It is usually a matter of what they have found comfortable and easy to do from past experience. A small percentage are always seeking new challenges and broadening their skills by selling entirely new concepts with which they have had no previous experience. Salespeople become typecast just like actors and actresses. Time-share agents who do very well in fast-track resort markets frequently feel like fish out of water when working the slower-paced, single-family, custom home (hand-holding type) buyers. This is why recruiters need to look for professionals in comparable sales environments before they seek those unfamiliar with that type of selling criteria. The complete salesperson with maturity can handle anything, regardless of type or price. That capacity usually comes after years of well-rounded experience and is not acquired early in one's sales career.

## Amount and Scope of Company Marketing

Ahead of commissions or other forms of compensation, knowledgeable professional will evaluate how easy it will be to make a good living working with one company compared to another. If the company has a very effective marketing program that attracts hundreds of prospects each month, the achiever will usually carefully weigh that factor against other employers who are less effective or who do not spend as much to produce potential home buyers. After all, it is easier to reach your financial goals if you have a good number of prospects coming to you rather than having to find them yourself.

## Reputation of the Company

The reputation of the company with its customers is a major concern with professionals who have a high self-image. They do not want to work for companies that do not maintain high standards of performance. Those in the business of new home sales will normally measure the prospective employers' reputation with their owners. Service-after-sale is an area that can produce tremendous frustrations for front-line salespeople who must live with those buyers after they move into their new homes. If the warranties, call-backs, and promised services are not met, the agents on duty will bear the brunt of the consumers' dissatisfaction.

The pros also know that referrals should account for at least 20 to 35 percent of their annual sales volume. It is almost impossible to achieve that level of referred sales volume when the production department does not meet its obligations. There is the added risk of the potential lessening of one's self-image when associated with enterprises not respected by the public.

## Continuity and Capacity of Operations

After you have been in the housing business for a while, you quickly learn that a big difference exists between the capacity to sell homes and that of delivering and closing them! Many an agent has run into the situation where he or she has sold far more than the production department can build in a reasonable period of time. Then their sales skills mean nothing, because they are effectively out of business until production catches up. Land development roadblocks often prevent future phases from coming on line. What does the peak performer do while waiting? A company with continuity of production and/or alternative housing projects that assure the winners of having a place to use their skills will attract and keep better than those who are in and out of the market without economic security for the front-line sales staff.

## Compensation Incentives

Contrary to what managers tend to believe, commissions and other forms of financial incentives are not the first item on the lists of most high achievers. They want the big dollars, but they want them in the context of other things that are important to them.

What good is a high commission rate if the company cannot assure delivery of what the salesperson sells, or cannot meet the numbers on which the commission is predicted? Six percent of nothing is nothing!

There is also the matter of short-range versus long-range incentives. Bonuses for achieving reasonable goals are a valid consideration in attracting and retaining producers, especially if they truly reward the stars in proportion to achievements. Most top producers would rather work on commission than on any form of guarantee that lessens their opportunity to earn at the highest level. They like to be paid according to performance: the more they sell the more they earn. No incentive system is better than that one! Those who pay self-limiting salaries and do not acknowledge the achievements of outstanding master closers are not likely to recruit or keep these highly motivated individuals. Your total compensation package is what's important, and it should include ways for those who do more than the average to earn far more than the average!

## Quality of Management and Other Personnel

The pros of the world like to be with other pros! The way you get better is to associate with people who are at least as good as you are—and perhaps better. We learn more from our peers than from amateurs. Salespeople want to be with managers and others in the sales team who can add to their own dimensions in life. They also want to work with and for people they respect. Given a choice of working for a manager whom they do not respect and one they do, they will select the latter even at a lesser commission base! That is why the best coaches have the best teams!

Marketing the strengths and caring attitudes of your managers and associates is an important part of your recruiting message.

### Education and Personal Learning Opportunities

Among the better attraction elements in a recruiting program are the quality and scope of the training and educational systems offered by the company. With all of the other prioritized items having been satisfied, the amount and quality of continuing education will play a role in drawing the attention of achievers.

More than most, the best want to get better. They have a desire to grow and learn more about how to improve their skills. Organizations that have well-structured training programs will be more effective in recruiting producers than those who do not. While it is true that self-starters will go to seminars on their own, purchase their own books and tapes, and continue to improve by personal experience, they prefer to be associated with enterprises that make that process more available to them.

### Recognition Incentives and Fringe Benefit Programs

Outstanding sales performers do not select a company because it hands out plaques and status awards, but such items are a subtle factor in their evaluation criteria. They want to work where they are appreciated and they enjoy receiving the plaudits of success. If everything else is equal, the reason to go with one company over another is the added recognition and fringe benefits you will realize. Fringe benefits for these stars range from belonging to special in-house clubs to getting free vacations at company-owned condominiums. They can range from simple plaque-of-the-month status symbols to major things, like having a chance to purchase shares in the company. Fringes in the package must be weighed against other economic objectives, but when there are none, commissions usually have to be at the peak of the market place.

These are the nine leading factors listed by the stars in real estate sales. While any one individual might prioritize them differently, our sample has listed them as they are perceived by the majority we interviewed. It should be evident in reviewing these factors that those who know what they want in life and have the talents to achieve it are very discriminating about the companies with whom they associate. If you want to recruit master marketers, counselors and closers, you need to hold a hand that includes the right draw-cards!

## YOU TEND NOT TO RECRUIT BETTER PEOPLE THAN THOSE YOU HAVE NOW

Once you have a nucleus of salespeople, your future recruiting will normally continue to attract the same caliber of people as you already have. Until you have a few star performers, it is difficult to bring more. Pros attract pros. That is why it is so vital to build upon strengths and to set high standards for the selection and recruiting process. Once you have the reputation of being the place where the peak performers are and where they can earn most in both financial and social rewards, you will discover that the candidates you want will seek you out instead of vice versa. Getting to that point is not easy, and most companies never achieve that level of recruiting security. Time spent searching for the better material is well worth it in the long run. Do not short-circuit this decision process just because you have too many other demands on your time and talents. If you lose the battle for the winners in the sales field, you may lose the war in the competitive marketplace—where the difference between success and failure is in the quality of the sales representation of your merchandise!

# 6: Training and Motivating New Home Sales Representatives

Sales professionals are a dominant factor in the success of any enterprise that depends upon consumers for the ultimate capital that drives the economic machine. Real estate salespeople who are skilled at their trade are among the highest earners in the sales world because they represent big-ticket products and must counsel with more empathy and understanding than is typically required with other purchases. However, as in all sales fields, a minority accounts for the majority of total transactions. The 80/20 principle is evident in the closing records. Eighty percent of sales are made by 20 percent of licensed real estate agents. Recruiting and selecting the right talent are essential to reduce the risks of failure. Once the right talent is aboard, the psychological environment conducive to above-average performance needs to be nurtured by all concerned about sales results. This includes the stimulants of training and motivation.

New home sales requires special knowledge and skills not automatically part of the general brokerage agent's understanding and practiced disciplines. Ability to communicate and empathetically relate to the needs of people leaving one nest to move physically to another is vital, whether selling existing housing or new construction. Those proficient in helping prospects to make positive decisions will always be more effective than average representatives, who have difficulty in the closing arena. However, it takes more than enthusiam and the willingness to ask for the order to achieve a consistently high ratio of sales of new housing products. The training of new home sales professionals has received more attention in the past few years than was true in the 1960s and 1970s. Awareness has increased among builders, Realtors® and marketers of the value of specialized educational programs for those who represent new homes, condominiums and custom-building programs.

General real estate agents are taught to negotiate, to sell what already exists and to take prospects from one location to another until they discover homes that fit their customers' interests. New home sales representatives are often married to a physical location with the necessity of selling what they have to sell with no freedom to handle resales and without a wide variety of alternatives. Even if they have the privilege of showing both new and used housing, new home salespeople must learn how to sell dreams rather than reality, since most new housing is not finished at the time it is sold. Frequently, they must sell from blueprints and site maps that depict what may ultimately be a reality but is now only a vision.

Along with that factor is the subtle difference in servicing new home buyers. Due to the myriad details involved in selecting, building, decorating and delivering a new home, the professional salespeople master the art of follow-up and customer service, which extends for many months following the initial sale. Builders' sales representatives must know how to demonstrate effectively new construction systems and to accent value differences that set one builder's homes apart from others. In addition, they must be able to interpret and promote the warranties, customer-service systems and protective covenants important for creating customer confidence in the decision to buy a new rather than a used home and to choose a particular contractor. On-site representatives who work with model homes or a controlled sales environment have to master the ability to involve and qualify customers quickly during periods of high traffic and to use to maximum effectiveness the limited time they may have with any particular customer.

New home buyers historically do more shopping on their own than do resale customers, and they take longer to make their housing decisions. The majority return more than once to the new homes they ultimately select before making the final decision. The is one of the reasons that the new home sales specialists must be trained in methods of increasing the initial involvement experience and consistently following-up prospects who have not yet purchased. Also important are handling site releases, learning how to sell one homesite versus another and using valid urgency factors to gain decisions from prospects who want to think it over.

Pricing strategies in new housing are entirely different than in resale. Builders' models are used as examples, and reproductions are normally priced higher if decisions are not made within specific time frames. Knowing how to handle options, up-grades, change orders and decorating choices for each builder are unique aspects of new home presentations. Finally, there is construction coordination. Unless sales representatives know specific details about construction procedures applicable to a particular builder's operation, they risk misrepresentations, confusion and lost sales.

Because of these valid differences, builders, developers and brokers who want to achieve outstanding results from their sales personnel recognize the importance of investing time and money in educational programs that improve sales performance.

## WHO SHOULD DO THE TRAINING?

Real estate brokers who elect to represent developers and builders bear a primary responsibility for educating themselves and their sales associates about professional techniques for effectively selling new construction. Their clients have the right to expect the very best from them. Progressive brokers in markets where demand justifies special attention to new housing projects often establish separate new home sales departments and develop training programs for members of their organizations who concentrate on builders' merchandise. One primary reason that builders decide to list with brokers rather than represent their own homes is that they believe there are efficiencies in working with outside professionals who practice proven sales skills. As we shall identify in this chapter, numerous training aids and systems are available to brokers and individuals who want to become proficient in selling new housing.

When a developer or builder has an in-house sales organization, the responsibilities for educating the sales staff fall on the principals of the enterprise, unless they have hired sales managers or marketing directors who can perform that role. It takes knowledge to be an effective teacher. If the key people in the development company do not have the expertise to train new home representatives, they should seek assistance from consultants or employ the talents of individuals within the sales organization who can teach. Often, the training needs are a low priority because so many other activities seem more urgent. This is a costly mistake. Everyone in the system depends upon sales to meet financial goals. Nothing really happens until someone sells something! Training methods can be adopted that will work for small builders as well as larger companies.

Regardless of who does the job, builders cannot abdicate their responsibilities of communicating their knowledge about design, construction, values and procedures critical to the professional representation of their housing environments.

## BUDGETING FOR TRAINING AND SALES DEVELOPMENT

It takes talent, time and money to support a results-oriented training system. In most cases, the major cost is the time of managers that is allocated to training (distinct from other activities that always tend to come first). For example, many full-time sales managers find themselves psychologically trapped in positions that force them to spend most of their time doing paperwork, participating in management meetings, working with advertising people and supervising case processing. Time available for one-on-one or group-training events is very limited and sometimes nonexistent! The cost for the time adjustment to put training on the priority list is weighed against perceptions of other urgencies. Solutions to this management trap include reapportioning activities, enlisting others on the team to assume training responsibilities or hiring outside training consultants who assume part of the training role.

Every sales and marketing budget should include enough dollars for educating salespeople and managers to be sure that the reinforcements are there when needed. Outside experts are available to assist in this endeavor, but less expensive ways exist to achieve the educational objectives. Paying for salespeople to attend special conferences as well as providing them with learning aids is a practical way to give them the encouragement they need to improve their knowledge and skills. In addition to the time of in-house trainers and managers, a minimum budget per salesperson of at least $500 to $1000 per year is a bare-bones level of commitment in the opinion of experts. Some new home sales companies invest more than $2500 per year per agent for educational programs, and these organizations have the sales results to justify that size budget.

## SET STANDARDS OF PERFORMANCE AND TRAIN TO THESE LEVELS

How much can you expect from your sales representatives? What is a reasonable performance level in your market with the opportunities presented? How can you be sure they are making a professional presentation each time they review your housing programs with potential buyers? Unless you or your sales management team have clearly established minimum standards of performance it will be very difficult to judge results. All sales training should be aimed at development of specific skills based on an understanding of the principles on which those skills are founded. Without a clear definition of training objectives as measured by actual results, little chance exists that the investment in education will produce desired returns.

The initial steps in creating a results-oriented training program are to identify the primary disciplines that must be mastered and then to set the criteria by which each of those skills is to be measured. For example, a new home educational system that covers the simple fundamentals of this profession would have at least nine modules of knowledge and a related minimum level of acceptable performance applicable to each:

1. preparation (including product knowledge)
2. prospecting for the profiled buyers
3. greeting (including attitudes and actions)
4. qualifying for motivations, abilities, needs
5. demonstration and presentation
6. reducing resistance and overcoming objections
7. closing (including urgency for one of a kind)
8. follow-up of unclosed prospects
9. service after sale and construction coordination

Depending upon the objectives of the sales organization, each of these disciplines justifies a set of standards by which sales representatives can be measured.

## MULTIPLE WAYS TO TRAIN

Like most fine things in life, education is most effective and valued when it is received on the installment plan: a little at a time! No single method of training works so well that it does not need the support of other systems. In fact, unless a balance of techniques is used and a commitment to continuous education made by all concerned, results from what is transmitted will normally be short-lived. Primary methods of training include the following:

1. one-on-one management counseling with a schedule of learning objectives
2. buddy-system field-oriented training
3. classroom sessions scheduled by topic
4. sales meetings that include training modules
5. self-learning programs supervised by management
6. seminars, conferences and special events

**FIGURE 6.1   Performance Standards for Salespeople**

The Ryland Group, Inc.
RYLAND HOMES
RYLAND HOMES PERFORMANCE STANDARDS
SALES REPRESENTATIVES

Month of _____

1._____NET SALES IN 1988 (SALES TO DATE:_____)

2._____MINIMUM CUSTOMER RELATIONS RATING OF 4.0
CUSTOMER RATING TO DATE: _____

Achieved by:  100%  Registration of Traffic
              20%   Self-Generation of Traffic
              100%  24-36 Hour Follow-up with A & B Prospects
              100%  Monthly Review of C Prospects

              1st Visit Closing: Goal: 25%
                                 MPS: 15%

              Appointments:   Goal: 100% of A & B Prospects
                              MPS: _____ per week

              "Closing Table": Goal: 100% of A & B Prospects
                               MPS: _____ per week

              Sales per Week: _____
              Conditioning:   100% of Sales

              Referrals:      Goal: 1 per Sale
                              MPS: 20%

**FIGURE 6.1 Performance Standards for Salespeople (continued)**

NAME: _____

REGION/LOCATION _____

JOB TITLE: _____

TIME IN POSITION: _____

I. APPRAISAL SCALE & DEFINITIONS: Appraise the individual's performance on the performance objectives below and assign point values to year-to-date results in the PTS. ☐ by the scale and definitions below:

MARGINAL..1–2 Points Generally failed to meet minimum acceptable standards of quality, quantity, capability and human relations skills.

FAIR..3–4 Points Met or somewhat above acceptable level of quality, quantity, capability and human relations skills.

FULLY SATISFACTORY..5–6 Points Regulary demonstrated fully satisfactory quality, quantity, capability and human relations skills.

COMMENDABLE..7–8 Points Performance regularly exceed the full requirement of quality, quantity, capability and human relations skills

DISTINGUISHED..9–10 Points Demonstrated exceptional quality, quantity capability and human relations skills.

(STANDARD = 5 POINTS)

| PERFORMANCE OBJECTIVES | MEASUREMENT AND STANDARD | YEAR-TO-DATE RESULTS | PTS | PERFORMANCE GOALS NEXT RATING PERIOD. MUTUALLY SET TO IMPROVE YEAR-TO-DATE RESULTS. SET PRIORITIES, STANDARDS & TARGET COMPLETION DATE |
|---|---|---|---|---|
| 1. NET SALES | % of pro-rata shares of forecast Std: 100% of pro-rata share (1 pt. for each 10% over) | | | |
| 2. ASSIGNED NEIGHBORHOOD DUTIES—MODELS, SIGNS DISPLAY, AREA, YARD, ETC. | Number of duties communicated as "need attention" STD: Maximum of 3 duties indicated as need attention/ rating period. | | | |
| 3. PROSPECT FOLLOW-UP | Prospect recorded and contact attempted within 24 hours of job site contact and records of continuous follow-up activity. Std: Maximum of 2 not up-to-date on follow-up/rating period. | | | |

**FIGURE 6.1  Performance Standards for Salespeople (continued)**

| PERFORMANCE OBJECTIVES | MEASUREMENT AND STANDARD | YEAR-TO-DATE RESULTS | PTS | PERFORMANCE GOALS NEXT RATING PERIOD. MUTUALLY SET TO IMPROVE YEAR-TO-DATE RESULTS. SET PRIORITIES, STANDARDS & TARGET COMPLETION DATE |
|---|---|---|---|---|
| 4. BUYER FOLLOW-UP COMMUNICATING PERTINENT INFORMATION | Buyer recorded within 24 hours of sales agreement and re-cords of continuous schedule contacts to move-in. Std: Maximum of 2 not up-to-date on follow-up/rating period. | | | |
| 5. SALES WARRANTY SERVICE | Number times listed on 30-day inspection recap. STD: Maxi-mum of 5 on every 2-week list/ rating period. | | | |
| 6. RECORDS, REPORTS SELECTION SCHEDULES AND REVISIONS | Number of errors and/or late-ness of records, reports, se-lection schedules & revisions. STD: Maximum of 3/rating periods. | | | |
| 7. PROMPTNESS IN OPENING MODELS AND ATTENDING COMPANY BUSINESS MEETINGS | Number of times late or absent. STD: Maximum of 1 unexcused/ rating period. | | | |
| 8. PROSPECT BROCHURES IN CENTERS OF INFLUENCE | Number of times brochures are not serviced. STD: Maximum of 2/rating period. | | | |

**FIGURE 6.1   Performance Standards for Salespeople (continued)**

II. *APPRAISAL SCALE & DEFINITION*

Appraise the individual's performance on the abilities listed to the right by the scale and definitions (See page 1, Item-1) below:

Indetermined: Insufficient knowledge due to time in position

+1 Marginal
+2 Fair
+3 Fully Satisfactory
+4 Commendable
+5 Distinguished

DETAILS OF PERFORMANCE

1. SALES PRESENTATION & DEMONSTRATION: Adapts presentation to the situation, able to handle most objections.
2. TIME MANAGEMENT: Manages time to meet or exceed time schedules, deadlines for maximum results.
3. RELATIONSHIPS: Works harmoniously and consistent with all customers and others, securing cooperation minimizing peaks and valleys.
4. SELF-MOTIVATED and FLEXIBILITY: Takes actions without suggestions, adjusts to changes with a continued high rate of results.
5. REACTION TO INSTRUCTIONS and REQUEST: A positive reaction and acceptance of suggestions, instructions, critique and/or requests.
6. PROFESSIONAL COMPETENCE: Knowledgeable about F and J, its products, competition, assigned area and maintains appearance and conduct.
7. RESPONSIVENESS: Is responsive to the needs of all prospects/customers, not just their own.
8. PERFORMANCE UNDER STRESS: Coping with tough customers, accepting disappointments and reality of business life; making unpopular decisions and maintaining a positive attitude.
9. INFORMING MANAGEMENT: Timely keeps management informed about customers likes, dislikes, trends, competitive activity and changes needed.
10. PROMOTES COMPANY IMAGE: A positive effort to maintain & improve company image with others inside or outside the company.

TOTAL

III. What self-development is planned to better him/her for present position? (Reading; Special Projects; Training Programs; Outside Development Activities, Etc.)—(Bonus Points: Up to 2 Points/Planned activity—maximum of 10 points.)

*PLANNED ACTIVITY*          *TIMING*          *OBJECTIVE*
A.
B.
C.
D.

IV.  OVERALL EVALUATION OF PERFORMANCE:_____
TOTAL POINTS I + II + BONUS = ☐

---

**FIGURE 6.1   Performance Standards for Salespeople (concluded)**

V. Discussion of review
  a. Salesperson's Acknowledgement: The contents of this form have been reviewed with me.
    SALESPERSON'S SIGNATURE_____ DATE_____
  b. Salesperson's comments to this performance review_____
  _____
  _____
  c. Appraiser's signature_____ DATE_____
VI. Reviewer's Comments:_____
  _____
  _____
  Reviewer's Signature_____ DATE_____
VII. General Sales Manager's Signature_____DATE_____

---

Courtesy of Fox and Jacobs, Dallas, TX

Each of these can become an effective part of a total training plan. The key to the success of any educational program that achieves results is commitment by all participants to maintain a schedule and to validate what has been learned.

## PREPARE AN ORIENTATION SCHEDULE

Over years of helping our clients develop meaningful training programs, we have proven the value of having an orientation checklist or schedule that identifies all knowledge areas that a new sales representative needs to assimilate and practice to achieve a satisfactory performance level. The responsibility for preparing this list usually falls to the individual who is supervising sales functions, although input from all disciplines is recommended. This is a much more detailed reference guide than the broad-based list of primary knowledge categories. It breaks each subject into logical sub-modules and then references where and how that information can be secured.

The most efficient orientation schedules provide a verification column for each topic so that the supervising party can validate the learning curve. This method of supervising the educational process prevents omissions that can be very costly to sales goals. It provides both managers and salespeople the security of a definite road map that will help them to cover all checkpoints that lead to becoming a complete professional. This should be a framework that supports all other training systems. The learning matrix and attendant verification notes become the foundation for measuring the progress of each salesperson whether experienced or inexperienced at the time of association.

---

## FIGURE 6.2    New Home Sales Orientation Schedule

Salesperson:_____Date:_____
Manager:_____Office:_____
Project assignment:_____
Training director:_____

| Item Number | Assignment-notes category and topic | Source | Date | Verified |
|---|---|---|---|---|
| **OFFICE ORIENTATION** | | | | |
| 1 | Association agreement executed | | | |
| 2 | License transfer procedure | | | |
| 3 | Personnel file opened | | | |
| 4 | Business cards and supplies ordered | | | |
| 5 | Position description reviewed | | | |
| 6 | Policy manual assigned/reviewed | | | |
| 7 | Auto and liability insurance | | | |
| 8 | Office key(s) assigned | | | |
| 9 | Internal announcement of affiliation | | | |
| 10 | Personal introductions to staff | | | |
| 11 | Compensation memorandum signed | | | |
| 12 | Accounting records completed | | | |
| 13 | Assigned sales training manual | | | |
| 14 | Tour of all company facilities | | | |
| 15 | Inspection of all current projects | | | |
| 16 | Application (transfer) NAHB membership | | | |
| 17 | Application (transfer) NAR membership | | | |
| 18 | Meet with president/CEO | | | |
| 19 | Photo session for publicity | | | |
| 20 | Publicity article scheduled | | | |
| **GENERAL ORIENTATION** | | | | |
| 21 | History, structure of company | | | |
| 22 | Office communication procedures | | | |
| 23 | Legal and professional guidelines | | | |
| 24 | Attitude and image guidelines | | | |
| 25 | Verification of all written policies | | | |
| 26 | Forms assembled/reviewed | | | |
| 27 | General community facts reviewed | | | |
| 28 | General construction orientation | | | |
| 29 | Mortgage processing (general) | | | |

**FIGURE 6.2   New Home Sales Orientation Schedule (continued)**

| Item Number | Assignment-notes category and topic | Source | Date | Verified |
|---|---|---|---|---|
| 30 | Purchase contracts (general) | | | |
| SALES SKILLS | | | | |
| 31 | The challenges and opportunities (new home sales) | | | |
| 32 | The value of well-planned presentations | | | |
| 33 | Qualifying and involving prospects | | | |
| 34 | How to demonstrate a new home | | | |
| 35 | Model demonstration (role-play) | | | |
| 36 | Production housing demonstration | | | |
| 37 | Selecting and demonstrating sites | | | |
| 38 | Handling difficult questions and objections | | | |
| 39 | Creating a sense of urgency to act | | | |
| 40 | Counseling and follow-up techniques | | | |
| 41 | Closing skills: obtaining agreements | | | |
| 42 | Service after sale and follow-up | | | |
| 43 | Prospecting for new buyers | | | |
| 44 | Telephone techniques | | | |
| 45 | Maintaining confidence and control | | | |
| PROJECT ORIENTATION (SPECIFIC) | | | | |
| 46 | Builder and project facts reviewed | | | |
| 47 | Location benefits listed/rehearsed | | | |
| 48 | Community benefits listed/rehearsed | | | |
| 49 | Builder/developer credibility message | | | |
| 50 | Orientation to models, sales office, area | | | |
| 51 | Review all displays and sales tools | | | |
| 52 | Traffic control and greeting | | | |
| 53 | Specific qualifying objectives | | | |
| 54 | Anticipating and handling specific objections | | | |
| 55 | Review of construction features | | | |
| 56 | Analysis of all competitive projects | | | |
| 57 | Value-indexed presentation prepared | | | |
| 58 | Demonstration of each floor plan | | | |
| 59 | Demonstration of construction models | | | |
| 60 | Demonstration of available homesites | | | |
| 61 | Closing on estimate sheet/selections | | | |

## FIGURE 6.2   New Home Sales Orientation Schedule (concluded)

| Item Number | Assignment-notes category and topic | Source | Date | Verified |
|---|---|---|---|---|
| 62 | Closing on sites and inventory | | | |
| 63 | Closing on urgency factors | | | |
| 64 | Construction coordination procedures | | | |
| 65 | Sales-processing procedures | | | |
| 66 | Checklist or specific responsibilities | | | |
| 67 | Contract preparation (specific to project) | | | |
| FINANCING ORIENTATION | | | | |
| 68 | Review all basic programs offered | | | |
| 69 | Review qualifying criteria each plan | | | |
| 70 | Review processing procedures each plan | | | |
| 71 | Review of by-laws | | | |
| 72 | Review of protective covenants | | | |
| 73 | Assessments and budgets | | | |
| 74 | Community management procedures | | | |
| 75 | Privileges and responsibilities of owners | | | |
| 76 | Review potential H.O.A. objections | | | |
| SALES SKILLS (ADVANCED) | | | | |
| 77 | Time management systems | | | |
| 78 | Cultivating owner referrals | | | |
| 79 | Working effectively with cooperative brokers | | | |
| 80 | Qualifying for buyer types | | | |
| 81 | Qualifying for dominant motivations | | | |
| 82 | Advanced closing skills | | | |
| 83 | Handling third-party advisors | | | |
| 84 | Improving listening/counseling skills | | | |
| 85 | Handling difficult customers/owners | | | |
| 86 | Handling interruptions effectively | | | |
| 87 | Preventing cancellations and remorse | | | |
| 88 | Creative prospecting techniques | | | |
| 89 | The sales role in quality delivery system | | | |
| 90 | How to move the less desirable sites | | | |
| 91 | Winning emotional involvement | | | |
| 92 | How to remember and use names | | | |
| 93 | Self-actualization and visualization | | | |
| 94 | Become a "peak performer" and "master closer" | | | |

## VALUE OF EXPERIENTIAL LEARNING SYSTEMS

Most of us learn more by doing than by listening to others or reading about the subject. Sales training is a skill-oriented learning process. The most efficient method for assuring that salespeople have retained and understood the concepts taught is to have them practice these concepts in the presence of their facilitators. The more you bring educational objectives into a participatory teaching mode, the more likely it is that students will absorb the information and be able to apply it in their daily activities. It is also true that we tend to retain more when we are actively involved in the communication process. Salespeople who listen to lectures normally absorb only a small percentage of what has been transmitted by the lecturer. Conversely, when they are involved in answering questions—practicing what they have learned—the retention curve is dramatically accelerated.

It is also a matter of holding attention. A high percentage of those we bring into this profession have been out of school for some time and have lost some of their ability to retain what they see and hear. Holding their attention by actively involving them in case studies, give-and-take sessions and role-playing is the best means of keeping mental receivers open and in tune with the objectives of the training sessions.

Role-playing has become a favorite teaching method for sales trainers. It embodies all of the objectives of reinforcing learning curves and measuring what has been assimilated. While it is true that some salespeople resist this form of training because they are fearful of being judged by their peers in artificially structured learning environments, most sales agents accept the opportunity to improve themselves through role-modeling as long as the sessions are positive rather than negative experiences.

One of the easiest ways of initiating these make-believe exchanges is to identify a specific case study or situation and ask the sales representatives to share ideas on how they might handle it without asking them to stand up and act out the parts. Once you have them involved, it is easy to move to more formal role-playing. For example, the meeting leader might set the stage by saying:

> *"Your prospects have seen your model home on the first visit and are about to leave without sharing their observations. They make the comment: 'We are just looking and haven't seen enough homes yet, so we will come back later.' Question: What would you try to do at that point to draw the prospects out so you could determine whether you had the opportunity of a sale at some point?"*

This will probably lead to a variety of ideas expressed from the informal location of each representative in the room. When several ideas have been briefly discussed, the leader might suggest that two of the sales representatives role play the scene while the rest observe.

Once the scene is finished, each participant should be asked to express his or her thoughts about what transpired and to explore alternative approaches. The other sales agents can then be polled to share first what they thought was handled well and then what might be improved. If each representative knows that he or she will have to appear in a role play at some point, the tendency to critique harshly will be softened by the realistic awareness of the learning opportunity.

---

**FIGURE 6.3    Role-Playing Scenarios**

---

THE VOCAL HOUSING EXPERT IN THE MOB

It is Sunday afternoon on a busy traffic day. People are arriving at your model sales center in bunches and it is hard to stay in control of the scene. Just as you are finishing up with one group and sending people on their way to inspect your models so you can return to address the others in the office, six people arrive in a group and quickly make their presence known by the one loud voice in their midst. A burly gentleman with an obvious need for attention says in a voice all of your guests can hear:

"We do not have much time. I understand that you do not have as much to offer as BRAND X, but we thought we would see them before we finalize our decision. Just give us brochures and we will take a quick look. What are your prices and do they include everything you show in the models?"

At this point, you do not know if the six people are really together or just happened to come through the door at the same time, since you did not see whether or not they got out of the same car when they arrived. You suspect that only one couple may be involved in the looking process, but you are not certain. The intimidating personality of the male who asked the question dominates the psychological environment at the moment. You still have four other parties in the office who have heard his comments and questions.

Identify the issues and possible objectives. How would you respond to his inquiry? Would you ignore or address his comment about your homes not having as much to offer as your competition? Is he speaking for the group, himself or merely as an advisor to someone else? If he visits the model unescorted with all the other prospects viewing them, could he create an adverse scene by loudly discussing his perceptions of your deficiencies compared to what is offered by the competition? How could you control this situation and potentially turn it into a positive rather than negative one?

Let's role-play this scenario!


THE RELUCTANT RETURN

Jack and Cynthia Borgman visited your sales office yesterday and you spent nearly an hour with them reviewing their housing interests and presenting the opportunities your company features. You found that they liked your most popular model and could financially qualify for it. During the presentation you were able to get them to one homesite that had the exposure and setting that appealed to them. You attempted to close by asking several closing questions but were unable to get a commitment from them. When you tried for a specific appointment for the next day, they evaded making one by indicating they were going to look at several other properties that day and did not know what their time schedule would be until they had completed their investigation. You gave them a comparative checklist of value-added features which your company includes that most others either do not have or charge extra to add and suggested that they evaluate these benefits when looking at other homes. After they left you made the following notes on the back of your prospect registration card:

"Liked Hampton model: Four bedrooms essential; large family room key factor. Present home too small. Three children: Joe: 14, Mary: 10, Benjamin: 7. School district plus. Site 47 shown, liked. Commented on large backyard for kids to enjoy. Sold home: 90 days to move. Shopped five projects, want to see more. Concerned about resale values since subject to transfer within three to five years."

Based on this information what would you do to follow up this prospect? How soon would you contact? What would you use as a reason for a phone call? What incentives might be provided to induce them to return?

SOURCE: Berne, *Buddy-System Training.*

---

**FIGURE 6.3   Role-Playing Scenarios (continued)**

---

Role-play one or more phone-call approaches. List the steps you would normally take in pursuing the Borgmans. How long would you keep them in your prospect control system?

*Note to sales managers: This is a good subject for group discussion and several role-plays by different salespeople.*

### THE TRANSFEREE SHOPPER

Mr. Herb Harrison and his wife, Alma, have just toured your models and returned to your sales office. You discover that they are visiting for the first time and, while interested in your largest home because of its size and room arrangements, they plan to do some more looking before deciding on which neighborhood and builder to concentrate.

Further questioning reveals that they are being transferred to your city by one of the high-tech firms that is expanding its local operations. They have been looking at housing for three days and have not covered everything they want to see and know. They indicate they are working with a local real estate broker and are also considering one or two resale properties.

You also uncover the fact that they have made arrangements for the home they own in the city of origin to be acquired by the company under its direct-equity plan. They have two teenage daughters who are still in school, so the possession dates will be scheduled to coincide with the summer vacation period. The schooling system in your neighborhood, while reasonably good, is not rated as highly as the other district in town where they have been conducting most of their housing search.

When you attempt to get them to inspect a homesite or two, Mr. Harrison says:

"We are going to check some other locations first—but we do like the model home, so we will probably be back in the next day or so. Besides, we make it a point never to buy anything the first time we see it."

Mrs. Harrison has not been very responsive during this interchange. You are not certain whether or not she likes the home and what her attitudes on this home-shopping process really are.

You do have some choice sites you would like to show them . . . and you sense that if you do not do something soon, they will leave and may never return. What would you do to deepen this involvement and how could you avoid losing this opportunity?

Try this role play and convert the eternal shoppers into buyers!

### THE BROKER WITH MIXED EMOTIONS

Mr. and Mrs. Jackson arrive at your new home community escorted by a real estate broker, Jane Sorge. This is their first visit and you are not acquainted with this particular real estate sales agent. During the introductions you discover that it was the Jackson's request that they stop and look at your new homes while the broker was escorting them to see resale homes in the area.

You discover that the Jacksons have two children, a boy, seven, and a girl, ten. Your community has the types of amenities that appeal to the wife and she expresses that thought in the interview. She wants her children to be in the right area where they will enjoy the recreational and educational benefits this location affords. However, in looking at your models, the wife raises objections about the size of the bedrooms and the small lots. The husband seems to be more amenable to the lot sizes, but is noncommital about the interior-design issues.

During the discussions, you learn that the real estate broker is trying to interest the Jacksons in one of her resale listings that has a larger yard and a bigger four-bedroom home. Upon questioning, you discover, however, that this property is 30 minutes farther from the husband's employment center and in an undeveloped area without nearby shopping or recreational facilities. The school district is also less desirable based on your documented information.

---

**FIGURE 6.3   Role-Playing Scenarios (continued)**

---

As you are trying to qualify and build values for your homes and location, the broker makes numerous comments to encourage the Jacksons to see the other home again before making a decision of any kind. You strongly suspect that the larger commission in the sale of the pre-owned property is influencing her actions.

Role-play objectives: How to overcome the objections that are raised and how to neutralize the broker's position so that the Jacksons can seriously consider the merits of your housing environment.

A CASE OF AFTER-BUYING BLUES

Mr. and Mrs. Henry Brown have given you a deposit on your most popular model home and for a choice site that is the only one left on the cul-de-sac where current construction has begun. The Browns have been nervous buyers from the very beginning. They returned three times over a ten-day period before you were finally able to get their signatures and a deposit check.

It is now three days later, and Henry has called you to tell you he and Martha (his wife), have decided to cancel the contract. The phone conversation indicated he had just learned that he may be transferred this year and he does not want to be obligated to a new home under the circumstances. You suspect that this is only an excuse to avoid completing the sale. You have advised him that you cannot cancel the contract by phone and that he and Martha must come to the office to review the matter. They are now in your office and visibly uncomfortable with the entire process. Henry is doing all the talking—and indicating he is really not prepared to complete the purchase due to his potential career move.

When you first sold them the home, you noted that Mrs. Brown seemed very interested in the design, and she was particularly impressed with the quality of the neighborhood and the schools. They have two children (Johnny and Marie) who are in the seventh and ninth grades. She has made comments in your presence that indicate she is tired of moving around the country and changing schools. But she also seems to yield to her husband's desires, since he is the breadwinner in the family, and there is a strong family commitment.

As they sit in your presence asking for the return of their check, you have another opportunity to try to salvage the sale. How would you approach this potential cancellation. What might you do to avoid losing it?

Let's role-play this scenario!

THE BUYER WHO WANTS EVERY CHANGE IN THE BOOK!

You represent a home builder who does not allow structural changes to his pre-priced model homes and has only a limited number of options for upgrades and additions to the basic package. Your price range of $150,000 to $175,000 for single-family detached homes in your area is in the upper-mid-range for the move-up buyers who are your primary customers. There is extensive competition in this price range, including some custom builders who will design and build to the specific interests of their customers. You have one major competitor in a nearby community who is promoting customized changes and offering a long list of options. His price values per square foot are about $7 to $10 more than yours for comparable basic construction, but his success has been generated with buyers who want personalized changes.

You have been working with Larry and Jean Upwards for the past two weeks. They originally placed a deposit on your three-bedroom two-story that features an elegant master suite and luxurious bath as well as an outstanding garden kitchen which has been the focal point of attention for Jean. Since the first deposit of $1,000, the Upwards have been visiting your major competitor and negotiating for a home that has about the same footage. They have returned for the fourth time to advise you that unless your builder will permit them to extend the family room

---

**FIGURE 6.3    Role-Playing Scenarios (concluded)**

with a patio enclosure, allow them to upgrade hardware throughout, and install extra wiring for his computer room, they plan to cancel and purchase from the other company. You have checked with your supervisor and been informed that the company will not make the changes they request as they have no way to supervise these adjustments without complicating their entire construction process.

   You are now in session with the Upwards and faced with the necessity of relaying this information. What can you do or say to salvage this sale? Let's role-play this scenario and overcome this change-order challenge!

THE CASE OF THE SITE-CHOICE DILEMMA

   You are currently marketing the last few sites in the first phase of your new Highland Oaks community, all of which back up to the local expressway. The initial release of 27 homesites included a variety of locational differences, and seven abutted the freeway boundaries. Two of these have been sold at a price difference of $5000 less than the premium sites on cul-de-sacs at the entry of the neighborhood, and five remain to be sold. The other homesites have been sold and you are awaiting phase two, which will not be on the market for another 60 days due to development delays. Meanwhile, your builder/developer is pushing to get action on these final lots before launching the new area. Your homes have been well-accepted and the real issue now centers on available locations.

   John and Cecilia Hawthorne have expressed interest in the community and the four-bedroom colonial two-story that has proven your most popular design. This is their third visit to your sales office in the last two weeks. You have shown them sites 23 and 26, which are along the freeway buffer zone. They indicate to you that they are concerned about freeway noise and future resale values. Your next phase is where they prefer to be but you cannot sell these for at least two months and you do not have prices.

   There is an indication that new phase lot prices will increase by at least 10 percent over the present base values. The Hawthornes need to be in a completed home within 120 days, as they have been transferred to this city and they want to be settled before school starts in the fall since they have two pre-teens whose education is very important to them. If your construction department could start a new home within 30 days, it could meet that deadline. John tells you he likes the neighborhood, the schools and the design but really is uncomfortable with the freeway locations available. There is another subdivision in a less-desirable general location that has homesites with trees and privacy, which he and Cecilia are debating. You recognize that if you cannot help them over this hurdle and sell them on the merits of the home they like on one of these remaining sites, you will lose them. What would you think of doing to try to salvage this opportunity? What benefits or information can you use to help them accept the sites backing up to the busy highway? Let's role-play this scenario and close the Hawthornes in Highland Oaks!

---

Role-reversals are one of the better methods of getting salespeople to learn from each other. One salesperson plays the agent's role while the other takes the buyer's position. When through, roles are switched so that each gets the benefit of experiencing the dynamics of the process. We have provided a few sample role-play scenarios used in typical new home training formats as a guide for those who may be using this book to help them create training modules.

## BUDDY-SYSTEM TRAINING

One preferred method of training new sales associates in the real estate industry is the buddy system. This involves assigning a newer person to a senior sales associate who accepts part of the responsibility for indoctrinating the neophyte. Where you have a well-seasoned staff of sales professionals and a team spirit of cooperation in helping everyone to mature, this is a very practical way of achieving educational objectives at little or no cost. Sometimes it is appropriate to compensate the seniors for the time they devote to assisting beginners. The form of compensation most often employed is tied to a percentage of commissions earned by the new recruit. Another approach is to place the trainees on a salary or draw during the training period and allow all of the commissions to accrue to the seniors who assist them until the indoctrination period is completed. Where there is a selling sales manager who earns a fair portion of his or her income from personal sales efforts, the buddy system is merely an extension of the sales management function. Rotating beginners from one buddy to another in different locations is also valuable to provide them broader exposure to the sales staff and to avoid having just one role model, who may be deficient in some aspects of ideal sales performance. By observing other salespeople in action, newly affiliated representatives can absorb practical sales techniques from real-world experiences and decide how best to apply concepts for personal use.

## CLASSROOM TRAINING SESSIONS

The classroom provides a structured environment in which to accomplish training objectives. Teaching several people at one time is more economical than trying to impart information on a time-consuming, one-on-one basis. Where the number of recruits and associates justifies group education, the organized classroom setting is a practical means of communicating information. Some subjects are best taught in group sessions rather than one-on-one. Examples are:

- company policies and procedures
- financing
- contract preparation
- attitudes, ethics and personal conduct

All of the items listed on the master orientation schedule could be included in a comprehensive classroom series, but it is seldom practical to spend that much time in group sessions relative to the time needed for on-site field training experiences.

A few companies offer a fast-start program for beginners that includes a digested series of classroom topics such as greeting, qualifying, demonstration, closing and servicing. This might range from as little as three days to as much as two weeks of closed-environment training. Classroom training can also be a means of continuing education for both novices and experienced agents covering a planned calendar of topics over an extended period of time.

The most appropriate time for training sessions is in the mornings or evenings to avoid conflicting with prime selling time. Afternoons should be reserved for face-to-face selling.

## SELF-LEARNING SYSTEMS

Regardless of other training methods used by the builder, broker or marketing group, there should always be a planned approach for providing sales associates with resources for educating themselves on their own time and in the manner with which they are most comfortable. We do not all learn the same way with equal effectiveness. Some people do well absorbing information from books and written articles. Others learn by listening to audiotapes. Almost all can profit from audio-visual programs that incorporate both communication advantages.

Videotape training systems are growing in popularity. The more progressive companies in this industry produce their own videos taken from live recordings of their sales training events. The minimum level of self-learning assistance that you should provide to potential new home sales specialists is a list of available resources with the recommendation that they invest in their own growth. Where a number of salespeople are involved, it is beneficial to establish a central learning library from which each can draw based on personal educational needs. Establishing a learning center is not complicated, and the investment in dollars is nominal compared to costs of other forms of training. A wealth of learning aids is already in existence and can be purchased from the National Association of Home Builders, the National Association of REALTORS® and many private educational companies. We provide a list of resources in the appendix of this book.

To protect the investment in a circulating library, access should be controlled with some type of monitored check-out and check-in system. One method of being certain that items are returned after being used is to assign a value to them that is recovered from the salespeople who fail to bring them back.

When you use a comprehensive orientation schedule as part of your indoctrination procedures, its value can be enhanced if it also cross-references the books, audiotapes, videos and other resources available to the sales associates by specific topics on the checklist. By encouraging salespeople to improve their knowledge and skills by drawing upon the learning resources available from professionals in the industry, you assist your training objectives and stimulate the desire to attain optimum performance levels.

## SALES MEETINGS PROVIDE A BASIC FORUM FOR EDUCATION

The weekly sales meeting is one of the better vehicles for on-going training. Most real estate companies and in-house builder sales organizations hold some type of regular meetings for the collective review of business activities. A substantial number of enterprises like to hold these meetings on Monday mornings so they can use them to summarize the results of the previous weekend and administer the details of processing new transactions. Unfortunately, too many of these meetings become purely administrative sessions and do little to provide education or motivation for the sales staff. While it is necessary to administrate, it is equally important to educate and motivate! Every sales meeting should be used to impart information that will add to the knowledge and skills of sales personnel. A well-balanced meeting devotes not more than 20 to 30 percent of the time to administrative details. The balance is reserved for training and motivating. Those most active in sales training and sales management recommend that sales meetings be held on Friday rather than Monday since it prepares the sales associates to be ready for a positive and productive weekend—the most important selling time in the new home sales profession! Figure 6–4 contains examples of well-planned sales meetings.

## SALES MANAGEMENT SHOULD ALWAYS BE PREPARED TO EDUCATE

A primary responsibility of sales management is to provide the psychological environment that helps to stimulate sales personnel to perform at optimum levels. Since every salesperson has individual attitudes and behavior patterns, it is impossible to create a system that will automatically assure that everyone exposed to it will respond with equal results.

Understanding and influencing human behavior to accomplish desired performance objectives is a relatively young science. Those who have devoted lifetimes to the study of the way humans learn, react, and modify attitudes and actions have given us new clues to the most effective ways to evoke desired responses and results. When dealing with emotionally charged sales personalities and the unpredictable nature of the business environments in which we perform, it takes a special appreciation for the needs of new home salespeople to be an effective sales manager.

Most of us have accepted certain basic principles as valuable guidelines for creating and maintaining positive relationships with our sales associates. Education can be a primary motivator. When people believe they are learning valuable lessons from their associates, they are inclined to seek ways to satisfy the expectations of these mentors. The desire to learn and improve is a basic characteristic of top performers in any profession. By providing a stimulating learning environment and giving people recognition for what they have accomplished as a result of applying new-found knowledge, you can build bonds of loyalty and commitment that surpass typical employer–employee relationships. Assisting new home sales representatives to become more proficient in converting prospects into satisfied homeowners has both financial and psychological rewards. That is why every sales manager should have the educator ethic as he or she pursues day-to-day administrative functions. For example, when visiting a sales office and encountering a salesperson who expresses frustration over some aspect of the selling process as it relates to a specific case, the administrator might be inclined to tell the agent how to handle it, while the educator will use the occasion to full advantage in trying to establish an improvement in the learning curve.

---

**FIGURE 6.4   Sales-Meeting Plans**

---

YOUR NEXT SALES MEETING

:00–:05   OPENING COMMENTS

:05–:15   THE IMPORTANCE OF DISCOVERING DISCONTENT FACTORS IN HOME BUYERS' MOTIVATIONS FOR SHOPPING

A discussion or talk that focuses on the benefits of exploring each prospect's reasons for considering a move. In-depth questioning about the things each is trying to improve as compared to his or her present housing provides the clues: the 'hot buttons!'

:15–:30   HOW TO QUALIFY FOR DOMINANT MOTIVATIONS

A group discussion and/or role-play on ways to uncover the key motivators in the housing decision. During the discussion, try to have the group explore each of the following qualifying techniques:

• Visual observations.
• Prospect's questions.
• Salesperson's open-questioning skills.
• Use of reflective questioning: repeating and clarifying what prospects have said or seem to want to say.
• Reactions to property.

:30–:45   CREATING A SENSE OF URGENCY IN CURRENT HOUSING MARKETS

A summary of the status of current inventories, market conditions, etc., with open questions to the sales associates about ways to generate more urgency in the buying process.

:45–:55   REVIEW THE TRENDS OF THE MORTGAGE MARKET AND WAYS FOR STIMULAT-ING SALES BY USING THESE TRENDS TO ADVANTAGE

:55–:60   CLOSING COMMENTS AND GOALS FOR THE WEEK

YOUR NEXT SALES MEETING

:00–:05   WELCOME AND ADMINISTRATIVE COMMENTS

:05–:15   THE IMPORTANCE OF CUSTOMER FOLLOW-UP AS A KEY TO CLOSING MORE SALES

A presentation by the sales manager on the impact of prospect follow-up to net sales results. If records are available from which you can extract the facts that show how many times the typical buyer returns before consummating a sale and the number of follow-up calls that are indicated as a result, these should be shared as the basis for a group discussion.

:15–:30   WAYS TO FOLLOW UP THE PROSPECTS YOU HAVE GENERATED

A group discussion that elicits ideas from each salesperson ways he or she contacts customers after initial visits. List ideas on the board and then ask salespeople to rate the ones that seem to produce the best results.

---

**FIGURE 6.4   Sales-Meeting Plans (continued)**

:30–:45   HOW TO USE THE TELEPHONE TO ADVANTAGE

A discussion about the best ways to use the telephone for contacting prospective customers as well as servicing those who have purchased. Telephone courtesy, reasons for initiating calls, ways of maintaining interest and attention, and controlling the conversation are appropriate topics to explore.

:45–:55   MOST CREATIVE SALES OF THE WEEK

A review of the sales made this week (or month) that required creative applications of sales skills. Have each salesperson share information about the prospects he or she has recently closed.

:55–:60   SUMMARY AND GOALS FOR THE WEEK

YOUR NEXT SALES MEETING

:00–:05   WELCOME AND OPENING REMARKS

:05–:15   HOW TO SELL INDIVIDUAL SITES AND HOMES THAT NEED SPECIAL EFFORT

A general review of the inventory currently represented by the sales organization and identification of the properties that need attention. The sales manager can use this segment to discuss the importance of selling all of the properties in the right mix in order to assure the success of each phase of the projects.

:15–:35   CHECKLIST REVIEW OF WAYS TO CREATE PERCEIVED VALUES FOR INDIVIDUAL SITES

Group discussion with the use of a blackboard or flip-chart to summarize ways to create values and sell the benefits of various sites and homes. To assist in providing a value index list, refer to the article on 'Value Indexing Individual Homesites' in the June, 1987 issue of *Trends and Strategies.*

:35–:50   THE USE OF THE T-BAR OR BALANCE SHEET CLOSE TO OVERCOME RESISTANCE TO A SPECIFIC SITE.

The sales manager or some other member of the sales force should illustrate the use of the T-bar close (also known as the Ben Franklin close) to provide an effective tool in selling property that has both pluses and minuses in terms of consumer interests. This is best done by selecting a specific home or lot that is not yet sold and which has been rated as somewhat difficult to sell, and using it as the example. Get the sales staff to volunteer ideas on the items they feel belong on the plus side and to review how they would overcome the negatives on the minus column.

:50–:55   RECOGNITION OF THIS WEEKS' ACHIEVERS

:55–:60   SUMMARY OF WEEK'S OBJECTIVES AND CLOSING COMMENTS

YOUR NEXT SALES MEETING

:00–:05   OPENING COMMENTS

:05–:15   THE IMPACT OF CUSTOMER SERVICE ON SALES AND PROFITS

A ten-minute talk or discussion by the sales manager on the reasons that it is so important to service customers before, during and after the sale. Company records of customer satisfaction might be introduced to demonstrate effectiveness of your programs.

---

**FIGURE 6.4    Sales-Meeting Plans (continued)**

---

:15–:30    SERVICE CHECKPOINTS THAT ARE CRITICAL TO CUSTOMER SERVICE OBJECTIVES

Open group discussion of the things salespeople, coordinators and managers should do to assist the service objectives.

1. At the "point of sale."
2. Immediately after the sale.
3. Post-sale processing.
4. Pre-move-in period.
5. Walk-through orientation to new home.
6. On move-in day and immediately afterward.
7. Post-move-in period.

:30–:45    HOW TO CULTIVATE MORE REFERRAL BUSINESS

Discussion about the ways to get the support of buyers and others to refer new prospective home buyers to you.

:45–:55    CREATIVE WAYS TO GENERATE MORE BE-BACKS FROM YOUR CUSTOMER FOLLOW UP PROCEDURES

Have each salesperson give at least one creative idea for ways to get people to return after an initial visit at which a close was not achieved.

:55–:60    GOALS FOR THE WEEK—AND CLOSE

YOUR NEXT SALES MEETING

:00–:05    WELCOME, INTRODUCTORY REMARKS AND ADMINISTRATIVE ITEMS

:05–:15    THE VALUE OF COMPETITIVE SHOPPING

(A group discussion led by the sales manager on the merits of regularly shopping and evaluating the competition in the marketplace. The emphasis should be on how such periodic studies help the sales representatives to better present their own product values and overcome resistance when the differences seem to favor other builders.)

:15–:30    REPORTS ON SELECTED COMPETITIVE PROJECTS

(Assigned sales personnel report on specific housing communities or builders' models and identify the perceived value differences from the consumers' point of view. Strategies for selling against each competitor are discussed and summarized.)

:30–:40    HOW TO SELL THE ETERNAL SHOPPER (GROUP ROLE PLAY)

The sales manager sets the stage for a group role-play discussion by describing a particular prospect who is looking at specific projects and who uses the common escape statement: "We want to see more homes before we make a decision . . ." The group is asked to individually share ideas on how they would handle that type of prospect.

---

**FIGURE 6.4   Sales-Meeting Plans (continued)**

---

:40–:55   AWARD FOR THIS WEEK'S MOST CREATIVE SALE

Management has either previously determined which sale should be recounted and recognized, or asks for volunteers to describe the sale made which most challenged their selling skills. An appropriate gift or form of recognition is presented by the sales manage to the winner.

:55–:60   IDENTIFY THIS WEEK'S GOALS AND CLOSE

YOUR NEXT SALES MEETING

:00–:05   WELCOME AND OPENING COMMENTS

:05–:15   HOW TO CREATE A SENSE OF URGENCY WITH TODAY'S INTEREST RATES AND MORTGAGE MARKET

This can be either a brief summary of the market by a member of management together with a checklist of alternatives for stimulating a sense of urgency or a group discussion inviting the ideas of all the sales associates.

:15–:30   PLANNING YOUR FOLLOW-UP AT THE FIRST VISIT

Review with the sales staff the various steps that can be taken to assure a higher percentage of 'be-backs' from those who cannot be closed on the first visit. Some of the subjects to discuss might include:

- Selling specific appointments.
- Watching for verbal clues to trigger follow-up opportunities.
- Watching non-verbal cues.
- Using controlled information.
- Using research.
- Using partial information that permits piggy-backing with a phone call.
- Targeting specific family interests.
- Being a good 'counselor' who wants to assist people in the buying process.

:30–:45   ROLE PLAY FOLLOW-UP PROCEDURES

Possibly use the case history in this *Trends* issue as a group role-play session. Call on your best salespeople who use follow-up procedures to explain their approaches to the others. List follow up opportunities:

- site availability
- financing information
- availability of specific products
- school enrollment information
- pending price increases
- possession dates
- neighborhood information
- living benefits of making a decision now

---

**FIGURE 6.4    Sales-Meeting Plans (concluded)**

---

:45–:55    HOW TO MAINTAIN YOUR ENTHUSIASM EACH DAY

In this section you might have an open discussion about the various ways each sales-person approaches the need to keep himself or herself in positive mental states every day. An inspirational tape or film would also be appropriate. If comfortable with a pep talk . . . this is an excellent subject for a ten-minute cheerleading event.

:55–:60    SUMMARY OF GOALS FOR THE WEEK—CLOSE

---

*"What have you thought about doing to solve that situation?"*

*"What are the motivations of the customer and how can you use those to solve your dilemma?"*

*"Have you had this experience before?"*

*"What did you do in the other cases?"*

*"Have you thought about this possibility . . . ?"*

The sales manager who thinks *education* first will approach each situation from the vantage point of the salesperson with the objective of stimulating the learning process. This is also sound time management, since the primary goal is to develop people to skill levels that minimize management supervision time.

## THE MOST PROFICIENT TEACHERS ARE THE BEST STUDENTS

A sales manager or marketing director who has the responsibility of educating others needs to continue his or her own education in a consistent way. The best instructors are historically the best students. A shortage of competent sales trainers and sales managers afflicts the new housing industry. Those who have attained recognition as superior educators are in constant demand and have no difficulty finding clients who value their services.

On a national level, organizations provide forums for aspiring professionals in the sales and marketing disciplines. The National Sales and Marketing Council of the National Association of Home Builders is the premier educational and social organization for residential construction specialists. Every sales manager in this industry should be active in this network of experienced marketers. In addition, the special designation of MIRM (Member of the Institute of Residential Marketing) is awarded to those within this association who take specified courses and prepare written case studies for the approval of its board of trustees. The MIRM certificate and designation is the equivalent to the GRI (Graduate REALTORS® Institute) of the National Association of REALTORS® for general brokerage professionals.

The Urban Land Institute is an elite association of experts from all disciplines of the development world. Its educational programs are among the finest offered in areas of land management, planning, research, and community development and marketing. Membership in this organization provides a wealth of documented information about real estate development activities. While it may be tailored more to the needs of planners and developers of major projects, it is a resource for valuable research that residential marketers and sales managers can apply to local real estate opportunities.

The National Association of REALTORS® is a broad-based resource for information on general brokerage sales and marketing. Only a small portion of its educational programs are devoted to the interests of builders and new home merchandising. That is only logical, since the majority of its membership concentrates primarily on existing housing or commercial industrial sales. At its national headquarters in Chicago, NAR maintains an extensive research library that is available to all members. Many books, tapes and articles of interest to new home sales managers are available through this circulating library.

The Builders' Marketing Society, founded in 1985, is a private institution that limits membership to companies and individuals who specialize in representing the sales and marketing operations of developers and builders as outside subcontracting agencies. The group was formed to provide a high-level forum for experienced professionals who are not part of in-house developer/builder enterprises. Captive sales managers or marketers are not eligible for membership in this society. The growing number of REALTORS® and marketing experts who have established separate operations for managing the sales and marketing needs of developers and builders has increased awareness for the need to share information between practitioners in this somewhat exclusive field.

In addition to formal institutions and societies available for professionals in new residential marketing, private networks have spontaneously evolved as one expert meets another and discovers common interests in learning more about the refinements of this business. Attending conferences and major conventions like the annual convention of the National Association of Home Builders provides an opportunity to meet people from all parts of the nation with similar interests and needs. One of the best ways to improve your knowledge is to travel to other cities and see how they do it there! One of my valued clients defined the theory as "caring enough to steal from the very best!" When you get out of your own backyard and investigate what others are doing, you invariably discover concepts that can be applied to your own operations.

The sales manager/teacher has an obligation to those he or she supervises to always be out on the front of the knowledge curve so as to be effective in helping others to grow. If your competition is tapping outside resources and you are not, it is only a question of time before they surpass you in capturing a greater share of the market. The manager who does not read, study new information, listen to cassette tapes or attend learning events is of little value to those who depend upon this person to guide them in a rapidly changing and highly competitive world.

## HOW TO MOTIVATE SALESPEOPLE TO PEAK PERFORMANCE LEVELS

Motivating salespeople to attain optimum levels of personal achievement is one of the three principal responsibilities of any sales manager. The position description could be summarized by these simple imperatives: administrate, educate, motivate. The how-to's of the first one are much easier to define than the third one. Administration invariably has a specific list of things to do that can be readily measured if not performed. The challenge of motivating salespeople tends to be a subject role that is difficult to quantify. How do you know whether or not Mary or Bill is really motivated to succeed? What can you measure to determine if you are getting 100 percent from a particular sales representative? Perhaps Mary has been face-to-face with 25 visitors at your open house this month and only written one sale. Did she lose people she could have closed if she had been more motivated to involve them with specific properties when they were there, or to follow-up more often after they left? Bill is always cheerful and in good humor. He seems to have an answer for everything and seldom shows any sign of depression or serious mood swings. Yet his sales performance is below the standards you have established for that project. Is he motivated? What is hidden behind that cheerful facade that is not surfacing in your personal communications?

The more we learn about human motivation, the more we realize how much we have yet to learn! Each individual has a personal agenda of interests that dominates his or her attitudes and energies. A sales agent who is well-motivated one month can be the most depressing person to be around the next month! How can you attain consistency in performance with personalities that tend to peak and dip? Harry writes a sale and is on top of the world one day. The sale cancels the next day and he goes into a tailspin for three days before he gets back on course again! Why? How do you modify his peak-to-valley moods so he operates efficiently every day? Or is it possible to change his behavior at all?

As all so-called experts in sales management will assure you, no simple way exists to motivate a complex human being. What is required is a desire to understand people and to seek the motivational factors that will work with each individual. We are distinctly different creatures! We do not all respond the same to the same stimuli. In my early career as a manager, one of my mentors gave me a clue to motivating salespeople that has helped me better to understand the role than almost anything else I ever learned. His point was simply to always remember that *the customers of the sales manager are not the buyers of the homes we sell—they are the salespeople!* If we work as hard to understand and motivate individual salespeople as we would if we were trying to sell to prospective buyers, we will be more likely to achieve our objectives than if we treat them as employees or people we have the right to manage!

The psychological environment you create in which to conduct sales-management functions is the catalyst that determines your potential effectiveness. The best sales managers are leaders who understand that it's easier to get others to perform if you first take into consideration their motivations, abilities and needs. The role of an effective sales manager is to be a coach, not an autocratic administrator. Coaches win ballgames when they challenge and reinforce the inner motivations of the players.

Coaching implies practicing with the players. The best sales managers are usually those with sales backgrounds and front-line experience. They motivate by being able to sell right alongside their pros when the need arises. They treat salespersons as special and spend time getting to know their individual aspirations, fears, dreams and goals. Sales management is, and always will be, a hands-on occupation!

Four primary motivators need to be interpreted for each salesperson and consistently monitored to be certain you have the optimum climate in which to inspire peak performance:

1.  Money and all related compensation benefits.
2.  Opportunity to grow and be involved in meaningful activities now and in the future.
3.  Recognition in every form to reinforce self-images.
4.  Ego-drive and personal desire to be a pro.

When you evaluate and apply these four major motivators to the framework of your management systems, you have the necessary structure to maintain a positive self-sustaining environment in which individual needs can be addressed and fulfilled.


## MONEY IS A PRIMARY MOTIVATOR

Nothing can substitute for money as a dominant motivator for real estate sales representatives! People are drawn to this profession because of the financial opportunities it provides compared to many other occupations, including other sales fields. Because it is a commission industry, returns for personal achievement are relatively high, and so are risks for those who never master the arts of communication and persuasion. Top sales performers expect to be paid based on what they accomplish—not by salaries that limit them to the average of others in the same profession. The ability to write your own paycheck based on your personal sales performance is an ego-satisfying stimulus to the true sales personality. The ultimate financial incentive system is to compensate individuals based on what they personally achieve and not on what is accepted as an industry average. The master closers in this field know that they have automatic job security! They can go anywhere and secure positions that allow them to demonstrate their sales proficiency. Only a few top performers are in any market area in America, and almost everyone in the business knows who they are. They consistently out-sell the general group of real estate agents who have not honed their skills to the same degree and who are not as highly motivated to be in the multi-million dollar clubs!

The best security developers or home builders can have to assure economic success is to have the finest sales representatives staffing and showing their new residential environments to qualified prospects. Only a small percentage of the population is profiled to be in high-performing sales circles. Attracting the right ones to your organization and keeping them motivated to remain with you is solid business insurance! Financial incentives are a major part of the package needed to recruit these winners.

## WHAT IS REASONABLE COMPENSATION FOR SALES REPRESENTATIVES?

That is a question that our clients frequently ask us. Builders occasionally express their frustration with the amount of money they pay sales representatives in relation to their perception of the amount of work salespeople do to earn these fees. Brokers operate within a competitive market that somewhat dictates what they must pay to attract and retain producers. Each market area in America has its own customs and expectations. No universal agreement exists as to what is fair compensation for salespeople, especially when it relates to in-house controlled sales staffs. In chapter five we reviewed general criteria for recruiting and staffing on-site builder-marketing operations. A review of these 12 points would be appropriate if they are not freshly in mind.

Key factors for on-site personnel as contrasted with general brokerage agents who have the freedom to sell a variety of products are:

1. Annual anticipated volume in units and dollars.
2. Number of salespeople required to service traffic.
3. Competitive value of top performers in comparable staffing opportunities.
4. Amount of self-prospecting expected versus ease of selling traffic produced from builder's marketing efforts.
5. Security of continuity of employment and housing production of one company versus another.

Percentages of gross sales price allocated for sales commissions range from as low as .05 percent to as high as 5.0 percent. Industry averages tend to fall between 1.0 and 1.5 percent. These figures do not include any allocation for sales management or marketing. Real estate brokers who most often work on gross commissions that cover both sales and marketing expenses must split the dollars between the functions with the net result that the selling agent is very often paid at about the same level as the on-site representative for his or her portion of the gross fee. Small-volume builders depend upon brokers and their roving sales force, since they do not produce enough volume in any one location to justify full-time specialists who devote all their selling skills to one product line. The gross fees paid are somewhat higher than experienced by larger-volume operations, but that is reasonable when you consider the reduced risks, the absorption of all marketing expenses by the broker and the management time that is only compensated if and when the homes are sold and closed. Most brokers negotiate fees with volume builders based on what costs and services they are asked to perform versus those born by the client.

## COMPENSATION PACKAGES TYPICAL OF
## IN-HOUSE OR SPECIALIZED STAFFS

While the basic method of remunerating new home sales personnel is commissions paid from closed transactions, a variety of plans are employed by developers, builders and marketing groups involved in residential marketing. The plans range from straight salary to straight commission. Here is a list of the combinations our research has uncovered:

1. Straight salary (employee status with some fringe benefits).
2. Salary plus overrides on each unit sold.
3. Salary plus overrides plus bonuses for achieving predetermined unit or dollar-volume levels.
4. Guaranteed draw against commissions.
5. Draw with minimum sales performance standard and higher commissions when draw is in the positive column.
6. Draw plus bonus incentives for achieving predetermined unit or dollar-volume levels.
7. Base commission, no draw. Occasional advances against commissions managed by exception.
8. Base commission plus bonus incentives for individual achievement of predetermined unit or dollar volume.
9. Base commission plus bonus incentives for individual achievement, plus additional bonus if group meets goal.
10. Straight commissions paid only at closing.

Within this broad framework are numerous variations designed by individual companies to increase the financial incentivies for salespeople who perform at above-average levels. Fringe benefits can include free trips, vacations, use of company-owned recreation facilities, attendance at national conventions, etc. Obviously, the bottom line is determined by the sales representative who must weigh the financial rewards in terms of perceived values and personal motivations.

The subject of pooling commissions for on-site sales representatives deserves a few comments. Our research indicates that the majority of builders and sales managers favor paying each salesperson based on individual performance rather than encouraging them to pool and divide their earnings when more than one person is assigned to the same sales office. However, a number of organizations have adopted the pooling concept, and they can make a strong case for its use. Their principal argument is that pooling avoids claim-jumping, unhealthy competition and dog-eat-dog attitudes about customer-protection policies. They also maintain that customers receive more attention from the team when everyone is involved in the ultimate financial reward for maintaining each sale. We have several clients who have tried both methods and who prefer the pooling approach.

A much larger constituency of managers believes that salespeople perform best when they have the maximum incentive: total commission for total effort. A middle ground also exists between these two compensation philosophies. The functions of the commission are identified and the compensation is paid to the individual who performs them.

Technically, the selling side of any real estate commission can be separated into three categories:

1. Procuring cause or origination of the potential sale.
2. Writing the purchase agreement or contract.
3. Servicing the customer after purchase through settlement.

If you assign a percentage of the sales commission to each function and monitor who provides which services, some of the inequities of group staffing can be effectively resolved. For example, if you allocate one-third of the commission to each, here are some possibilities for disbursement:

1.  Salesperson A registers a prospect on Sunday and makes the initial presentation. Prospect leaves without purchasing.
2.  Prospect returns on Wednesday, which is the day off for A. Salesperson B continues the presentation and writes the purchase agreement.
3.  By agreement, salesperson A services the buyer through final closing.

In this case, salesperson A would receive two-thirds of the commission and B one-third. The percentages could have been reversed based on the policies of the company or the agreement of the agents. Sometimes, the servicing function is split on all sales while the other two-thirds remain with those who performed them. This helps to resolve the concern that customers might not receive maximum attention from everyone if the selling agent is entitled to the total commission. We have seen a number of variations of this theme that have creatively met the needs of specific staffing situations. The above formula works very well when you have roving salespeople or floaters taking days off and providing supplemental staffing needs. The travelling agent is always entitled to at least the registration and procuring portion of the commission regardless of who sells the prospect at a later date.

One weakness of this plan is the assignment of follow-up responsibilities. There must always be a strong incentive to pursue the people who did not purchase on their first visit. Follow-up accounts for the majority of new housing sales! If you employ some form of this functional separation of commission roles, be sure to have a firm policy in place that makes either the procuring agent or the seniors on the staff responsible for on-going contact after initial exposure to the project.

## CAN YOU OVERPAY SALESPEOPLE?

The obvious answer to that question is yes. A salesperson capable of effortlessly converting 100 buyers a year from street traffic does not provide a comparable selling situation to another who is staffing a difficult-to-sell product in a remote location with little or no street traffic to draw upon. Our clients with diverse operations and unequal selling opportunities are recommended to adopt a policy of setting commissions or compensation programs on a project-by-project basis. Each community and staffing situation has its own demands. By working with individual compensation agreements or memorandums for specific assignments, the marketing organization can balance the needs of the sales representatives against the economic pro formas of each project.

Some national companies and volume operators have found this variable-commission policy difficult to administrate. Instead of changing commissions to satisfy inequities, they prefer to move salespeople to sites where opportunities can be balanced on the merit system.

Suppose that you need one of your best full-time sales professionals to staff Hidden Valley, which is hard to find and has a projected absorption rate of only one to two sales a month at an average price of $100,000. If the annual expected income levels of new home pros in your area is between $40,000 and $60,000 and your normal percentage paid in other locations is only 1 percent of gross sales price, this representative would have an income potential of only $12,000 to $24,000. If the commission were raised to two percent, the chance of hitting $48,000 for optimum performance becomes attainable. It might even pay to provide an additional incentive if the goal of 24 homes sold is attained! If your other community is producing substantial traffic and generating four sales a month, there is no need to change the base level of one percent, unless you elect to add more sales representatives or want to increase the absorption rate.

Another approach to this same concept is to have annual contracts with the sales representatives and to establish annual compensation or bonus incentive goals based on the business plan for the coming year. No fixed rule says commissions must always remain the same. It is in the best interests of the builder/sellers and the sales representatives to agree upon realistic goals and financial rewards based on the requirements for attaining those objectives.

## COMPENSATION PLANS MUST BE WEIGHED AGAINST STAFFING NEEDS

Sales managers differ in their opinions about how many salespeople are needed to staff on-site facilities effectively. Some believe in loading the office to capacity and working on the theory that the best will survive and the others will leave. This may work well when you are covering a scattered market with numerous builders and the agents are free to find their own prospects and sell anything that suits their needs. It is not a wise approach when you have limited production capacity and predictable absorption rates. The formulas for staffing and the balancing of commission incentives that have evolved among the top sales management expert in this industry include the following:

- Most new home professionals reach a peak of effectiveness when they handle approximately 50 closed sales a year. This presumes that they have to do all of the processing work following the sale—including securing financing, coordinating construction details, and handling final settlements. At 75 a year with these total responsibilities, the sales professionals are running at full-speed.
- The amount of traffic a salesperson can effectively service per week also enters the picture. Somewhere between 25 and 35 new customers a week seems to be the maximum that can be handled efficiently before lack of attention results in lost opportunities.
- When long time delays occur in delivering housing that has been sold, the need for hand-holding and constant follow-up increases. This puts a strain on the sales representative's time available for new business. Thus, some adjustments in staffing or compensation are needed when these situations develop.

- The acceptable conversion rate of traffic to sales in on-site environments varies from as low as two percent to as high as ten percent, based on the quality of the traffic and the skills of the sales representatives. Compensation formulas should be related to reasonable conversion ratios. Many sales managers set that ratio at a minimum of five percent. Thus, every 100 prospects should produce a minimum of five sales. Master closers will consistently hit higher ratios—sometimes as much as 20 percent or better. The difference in sales skills is really evident when you can realistically measure conversion ratios against qualified prospect totals.
- Support personnel should be used to assist salespeople during high-volume periods or with communities where the paperwork and follow-up activities tend to keep your pros from their selling time.

As you can see, a number of variables must be taken into consideration when establishing a compensation plan that will attract the winners and still remain within the economic models established by developer/builder clients. One word of advice to summarize this subject: If you want to recruit and retain the cream of the crop in the sales profession, be willing to pay a little more than your competition! A few extra dollars in the commission column can be translated into thousands of extra dollars in gross sales and bottom-line profit figures!

## OPPORTUNITY TO GROW AND TO PARTICIPATE IN COMPANY ACTIVITIES

Although monetary compensation has historically been the leading motivating factor for salespeople entering our industry, other considerations play a role in holding the interest of the proven performers. Continuity of employment opportunities is certainly one of them. Our industry has a record of being very volatile. Developers and builders are in and out of the market for a variety of reasons. Availability of the essential raw ingredient of land suitable for development is always a controlling influence. Market conditions change, including rapid fluctuations in mortgage rates and the availability of capital with which to finance and operate a capital-intensive business. Delays in construction precipitated by outside forces such as planning and zoning processes, labor and material shortages, and the time frames required to install underground utilities for new development phases can play havoc with sales projections and the earnings' potential of new home sales representatives. A developer or home builder who has a consistent record of producing homesites and housing has a distinct advantage in attracting salespeople over those whose futures are more uncertain. Small builders who do not have the capacity to maintain enough production volume to keep full-time sales professionals in business are forced to take a back seat to competition that has control over sustained construction schedules. Most often, these smaller entrepreneurs seek the services of real estate brokers who include their merchandise in a multiple-listing pool for exposure to all the agents in the area. What personal attention they may obtain is usually limited to a few hours of open-house marketing on Sunday afternoons. For the same reasons, some new home sales specialists prefer to work for an independent builder marketing services company that represents a large number of clients rather than affiliate with one builder whose volume is unpredictable. Organizations that have proven track records and reasonably secure futures have a recruiting advantage over those who do not.

An equally strong motivator is the subtle factor of how salespeople feel about the companies for which they work. Pride of association with a company that cares for all of its employees and pays particular attention to the needs of sales representatives will sustain relationships even when others are paying larger commissions. The desire to belong to an enterprise that appreciates you and values your services is fundamental to your instinctive need to participate with others in meaningful activities. We all have a desire to belong. We need to feel important. Our self-image is influenced by the feedback we receive from others and our sense of purpose in life.

Companies that understand this truth invariably realize superior performance from their employees. Tom Peters's well-documented books, *In Search of Excellence* and *Passion for Excellence*, clearly illustrate the differences between achievers and average players. Where business managers have made a special effort to involve employees in the objectives of their companies and have consistently reinforced the value of individual participation toward those goals, the results have been felt at the front line where it really counts: with the customers who are the ultimate *boss*! Not enough developers and builders appreciate the knowledge and values that salespeople can bring to the decision table!

Salespeople become more motivated to improve themselves and serve their employers when they are made to feel part of the total enterprise—not just a necessary evil. Smart sales managers and principals of building companies spend time seeking the advice of their front-line personnel. They invite salespeople to critique new floor plans, review strategies for lot releases and phasing, share the observations of prospects and home buyers and suggest ways to improve sales and marketing operations. Such involvement in company planning gives each sales representative the special feeling of being part of the family and not just an appendage. Salespeople have much of value to contribute to decision makers. They certainly know what their prospects are saying about the products they represent. They have a personal relationship with each owner they have sold, and that leads to an opportunity to share information that can improve productivity and customer satisfaction. Not to involve them in the research phases of the business is to miss a dual opportunity to learn from them and to strengthen their commitment to the success of the ventures.

Some organizations have established marketing committees that include sales representatives who serve as advisors to the decision influencers. Others have sales councils or builders' councils, where key sales representatives participate with management teams to share ideas and to learn from others at these sessions. This is an excellent way to begin developing leadership qualities to discover which salespeople may be suitable for promotion as growth permits. A wise manager plans for his or her replacement as the company grows. Sales management and marketing talent is not suddenly discovered! It is cultivated in a climate of participatory activities that stimulate the desire to learn and improve.

Family spirit is one of the most valued attributes of a well-run sales organization. When there is a conscious effort by management to make everyone in the system feel important, less strain is placed on the emotional fabric of interdepartmental relations. Sales and construction are not known as compatible disciplines. In too many companies a running battle goes on between production and sales personnel. Production-driven companies have a tendency to ignore salespeople and to criticize every mistake they make. Sales-driven enterprises can be slanted too much the other way and ignore the pragmatic needs of construction coordinators. Accounting departments and finance managers are also targets for the frustrations of outsiders, particularly salespeople who are seldom detail oriented. When strong leadership at the top recognizes the value of having all members of the system pulling in the same direction, cohesive and positive relationships develop at all levels of the organization.

## TAKE A PERSONAL INTEREST IN THE CAREER PATHS OF SALESPEOPLE

One of the most decisive factors in maintaining the goodwill of salespeople is the time you devote to counseling and reviewing where they are going with their careers. That is why education is such a strong attraction to new people in particular. Any person with a sense of self-worth wants to know how he or she is doing in comparison to others, especially in the peer group. We want to be given assurance that we are progressing, not standing still. A well-motivated sales agent is constantly seeking opportunities to learn and to increase earnings potential. When sales management takes time to review the career path of each salesperson and provides guidance as well as commendation for achievements, bonds of loyalty and commitment develop. That is why it is wise to have periodic performance evaluation sessions. Mystery shoppers can play a role in providing independent critiques that are helpful if used as self-improvement motivators rather than as job threats. The time spent helping salespeople to define their career objectives and improve levels of performance can produce returns that far exceed the value of the investment.

## CHECKLIST OF IDEAS FOR PROMOTING TEAM SPIRIT AND PERSONAL PROGRESS

1. Use a company newsletter or in-house bulletin to circulate information that makes everyone feel part of the team. Company activities, newsworthy events, recognition of performers and interesting stories about the people in the company are typical subjects for general distribution.
2. Organize company events that bring together all of the personnel and their families so they can get to know each other outside the context of daily business activities. Company picnics, sports events such as softball or bowling teams and annual awards banquets are examples.
3. Always welcome new sales associates and introduce them to all members of the company team. This includes construction departments, secretaries, processing and accounting divisions.

4. Publish business plans that define the goals and objectives of the company and share them with all employees including sales representatives.

5. Invest in educational courses for salespeople and others based either on time with the company or performance goals.

6. Provide opportunity for physical exercise through either company-owned equipment and facilities or club memberships.

7. Organize a sales council or a marketing committee and appoint salespeople to represent the sales disciplines at the regularly scheduled sessions.

8. Employ professional mystery shoppers to evaluate each salesperson's performance on the front line. The results of the shopping experience should be privately reviewed with each representative for its learning value and as a guide for self improvement.

9. Hold quarterly evaluation sessions with each salesperson to measure progress against the goals and objectives that were mutually agreed upon at the beginning of the year.

10. Invite professionals from other companies and industries to address your people at general meetings. Experts on land planning, industrial development, the school systems and other community interests are examples of topics that add to the sales representatives' knowledge base.

11. When salespeople are widely scattered and must drive long distances to attend meetings, use telephone conference calls as a substitute. Have telephone operators arrange for all of the staff to be on the phones at the same time and hold an up-date session from your office.

12. Keep complete personnel files that identify the personal items that deserve management attention, such as names and ages of children, hobbies, educational interests and financial goals. Review regularly and always personalize your one-on-one meetings with observations about the things that motivate a particular individual.

## THE THIRD MAJOR MOTIVATOR:
## RECOGNITION FOR PERSONAL ACHIEVEMENT

I have yet to meet a salesperson (or anyone else for that matter) who does not favorably respond to a sincere compliment. People seek reinforcement and group support to strengthen their sense of self-worth. Salespeople seem to require more reinforcement than people in other occupations. That is probably attributable to the emotional nature of the roles they play and the uncertainties of being measured each day by the sales they write or lose. When sales are going well, they can be on top of the world! When sales decline and problems in construction or the marketplace begin to dominate their thoughts, it is easy for a salesperson to lose perspective.

Sales slumps are often the result of self-induced psychological pressure. Empathetic sales managers realize how important recognition is as a sales stimulator. Self-confidence is an absolute essential in the selling profession. A confident salesperson will produce more sales than an insecure agent. The level of enthusiasm that is a direct by-product of a feeling of self-worth is measurable. When it drops, so does sales volume! Raise it, and sales performance improves. That is why the most productive coaches in the sales world are so valuable. They have developed to a fine art the ability to keep salespeople feeling good about themselves and in positive moods that translate into additional sales.

Nurturing salespeople does not come easily to people in other disciplines who often feel that agents are overpaid and pampered already! I have heard more than one builder and construction manager say things like: "Why should I tell them they are good? God knows I pay them enough for what little they do! Compared to my carpenters and superintendents, they earn more and still never seen to be on the team!" This attitude prevails in the industry. Only a few builders or developers take the time to thank the salespeople who write the contracts that keep their enterprises in business. Receiving a personal note of appreciation from the president of the company, from the builder whose name is on the model office or from the developer whose land is being unlocked by each lot sale made can be almost a bigger morale booster for a sales representative than a bonus check!

Recognition can take many forms. It does not require expenditure of large sums of money. In fact, the most effective forms of reinforcement are those that acknowledge performance achievements within the peer group of sales professionals. Certificates of recognition from the National Sales and Marketing Council as a multi-million dollar producer are inexpensive but very effective. Publicity articles about the salesperson of the year in the local newspaper that is read by associates and the general public can provide a shot of adrenaline that will carry a salesperson for several months! Being recognized at the weekly sales meeting among equals as the sales associate who accomplished something special last week will lift the confidence level another degree or two and may result in an extra sale the following week! When it comes to recognition motivators, the little things make the big difference! Here is a list of ideas we have gathered from clients and associates:

1. Enlist each salesperson in the local and/or National Sales and Marketing Council or the NAHB. Enter their sales records annually when they exceed the required million-dollar minimum. The awards are published and each qualifying sales representative receives a certificate to hang in the office.
2. Institute an in-office award system for your performers. Salesperson of the month, of the year, etc. Establish incentives for attaining this recognition, such as dinner for two at a fine restaurant, gift certificate for clothing at a quality store or credit toward trips and vacations.
3. Make it a point to send thank-you notes to individual sales associates whenever appropriate. Also, when special achievements have been accomplished, send notes of appreciation to the spouses of these sales personalities.
4. Prepare publicity articles (with photos) and feature them in local publications when a salesperson has attained special status.
5. Hold a private party at the home of the president of the company, the sales manager or any other VIP to recognize those who achieved their goals.
6. Place the photo of the salesperson of the month in the lobby or conference room of the main office. Some companies hang these photos in the office of the president or chief executive officer.

7.  Maintain a roster or plaque in the main office listing all award-winners by month and year.
8.  Use customer survey cards to measure your buyers' ratings of salespeople and read all positive comments before the entire group at sales meetings.
9.  Maintain records of the number of buyers secured as a result of personal referrals. Establish an award for salespeople who consistently do the best job in cultivating owner referrals.
10. If you have a cooperative-broker plan that encourages your salespeople to promote your homes to other real estate agents, give special recognition to those who extend themselves by visiting cooperating offices and who secure additional business as a direct result.
11. Make it a point at each sales meeting to have those who excell share with the others how they made recent sales or prospected for business, etc. When the achievers are telling the others how they did it, they gain peer-group recognition and help to motivate the rest to imitate their success.
12. For newer people, establish awards or recognition events to acknowledge their progress: rookie-of-the-year award, award to the individual who has made the most progress in one year; certificates of graduation for completing a prescribed company training program, etc.

## TAP THE COMPETITIVE SPIRIT AND THE INNER DRIVE TO BE THE BEST

All peak performers have an inner drive to be the very best at what they do, and they enjoy the competitive nature of the business that allows them to be measured against others whom they admire. Most people have role models in life who have given them inspiration to do more than they might have without their influence. Effective sales coaches can become role models. Top salespeople in the local SMC provide goals for others to shoot at. People tend to get better when they have to play against individuals who challenge them. This is as true in sports as in business. A golfer who always plays alone will never learn what can be gained by playing with other golfers who are better at some portions of the game. When you challenge salespeople to improve and pursue standards of excellent in all areas of business and life, you help them to fulfill themselves.

Most people accomplish only a small fraction of the things they are capable of. Friendly competition and ego-satisfaction for attaining goals are tremendous stimulants to most sales personalities. The best way to tap the inner drives of your salespeople is to spend private time getting to know them well. By showing genuine interest in the things that are important to them in their lives, you can assist them to reach for these dreams. Stimulating development programs will keep them on course. Setting realistic goals and giving them incentives to achieve them are major parts of this process. Goals must first be tied to company objectives and then expanded to incorporate new challenges and growth experiences for each individual. Being number one in sales is not necessarily a realistic expectation for every associate on the sales team. New people without experience may be shooting to move up the ladder with the help of management.

A salesperson assigned to a clean-up location or a more difficult product to market begins with a handicap in terms of volume. That is why all goal-setting should be personalized to individual opportunities and experience levels rather than to team averages or the target set by the master closer. The competitive spirit that needs to be kindled to put fun into the business and stretch sales associates to new heights should be stimulated through contests, point systems and percentages of goals attained rather than solely by the numbers game.

## CONTESTS AND TEAM ACHIEVEMENT ACTIVITES
## HELP TAP INNER DRIVES

Contests and other group or team events have multiple benefits in maintaining morale and stimulating superior sales records. One advantage is the fun that salespeople have in participating and competing with each other. Selling and closing new home transactions is not always fun. Challenges arise in mortgage processing, construction coordination, delayed move-ins and a fair share of customer complaints after the sales are consummated. Home buyers are frequently frustrated by the entire process, and they tend to vent their feelings at the salespeople! Keeping the motivators motivated is a never-ending task for sales managers. By using contests and special awards to focus attention on positive rather than negative aspectes of the business, a more relaxed and cheerful sales environment is maintained. Contests also have the benefit of bringing to the surface the competitive instincts of sales personalities. Playing to win is both fun and challenging. In addition, properly structured, these events can help management attain specific objectives, such as moving homes that need to be sold or meeting quotas that affect bottom-line profits.

A contest every week or sponsoring one just because it has been a long time since one was held is not recommended. If you use them, do so wisely. Plan them to fit into the timing of the marketplace or the objectives of marketing strategies. For example, little value results in having a major contest to sell more homes when production cannot keep pace with the sales already made. Contests are needed less when sales are naturally going well, but are valuable when markets turn downward or conditions change that adversely affect the sales pace. During slow seasons of the year (late fall, for example) a stimulating game with rewards for those who hit the targets can provide momentum instead of stagnation.

The goals and rewards should always be attainable. Any contest that has unrealistic targets will be a self-defeating exercise the moment it is launched. Salespeople need to have the experience of winning, and management should plan events that add to, not subtract from, that needed sense of accomplishment.

The best contests in the opinion of most experts are those that allow every participant to win something if individual goals are met, and also provide special awards for those who turn in truly superior records. Another guideline shared by leading sales managers is to avoid contests that cover several months before recognition levels are attained. If the program is going to last longer than thirty days, provide for interim awards based on monthly accomplishments toward the bigger goal.

Contests should be both challenging and exciting. Keeping participants involved in the progress of the scores provides some emotional fuel that stimulates more activity. Setting rewards worth attaining adds to the incentive to achieve. Events that involve teams as well as individuals can be very productive. For example, you might have three subdivisions staffed with different teams. The first level of the contest pits the teams against each other with possible handicaps for economic differences in products or locations. The next level includes individual competition for top performance regardless of the team to which you are assigned. This allows high achievers to maintain their strong ego-drives to be first while encouraging cooperation to help their assigned teams outshine the others.

The most effective rewards for contests or individual recognition are those that enhance the winners' self-image. If the award allows the recipients to experience or do something they might not have done on their own but had an inner longing to try, the company helps to strengthen the desire to continue earning at levels that allow such happenings to become more frequent.

Improving lifestyles is a reasonable objective of the rewards for reaching new goals. Sending the winner and his or her mate on a special vacation to a dream resort they might not have visited on their own is an example of a positive lifestyle reward. Providing salespeople with a wish-book from which they can select their own rewards if they hit target goals is another way of fulfilling this improved life-style objective. However, the reward is not the key to the success of a contest. It is the increased sales or other accomplishments that result from this synergized effort and the fun everyone has while participating in the game!

## TYPICAL CONTEST IDEAS

1.  Set point values on different functions of the sales process and keep score of total points earned by each representative. Reward those who reach highest point levels from a published list of awards. This type of contest is ideal for targeting activities to meet very specific objectives. The points can be weighted to favor items most important to the company or client. Examples of target items are:

    Moving standing completed spec inventory.

    Writing preconstruction contracts without the benefit of models.

    Attaining the most closed transactions or move-ins within the contest period.

    Selling options and upgrades where this is a profit objective of the company.

    Selling specific floor plans or models that have not previously been moving as well as the other designs.

    Securing more cooperative brokers and showings.

    Converting the most contingencies to firm contracts.

2.  Organize an auction with a list of items to be bid for at a specific date. In the interim, print play money with the company name and distribute it based on attainment of weekly goals and for special achievements whenever they occur. The amount of money awarded for each activity can be varied based on objectives. For example: each sale might be worth $1,000 in play money; a spec sold—$2,000; a self-generated prospect sold—an extra $500; etc. Since it is only paper money, you can be as liberal as you like. The money is distributed at each sales meeting. When the date comes for the auction, everyone with money can bid for the items on display but, obviously, those with the most money have the best chance of out-bidding the others for the awards they particularly want. Everyone has fun . . . and the company controls the cost of the contest because all items were budgeted and purchased in advance.

3.  Travel contests are popular events. For example, pick one or more destination resorts to which you are prepared to send those who meet the established sales goals. Set up a travel map and plot the distances toward the destinations as they are tallied each week. Provide the sales agents with literature and tantalizing messages about the resorts they have chosen to keep their interests peaked. Only those who have enough points to make the round trip are awarded the vacations. Award minor prizes to others who got only part-way on the chart.

4.  Team contests can be based on the same goals used for other types but with team rewards instead of individual items. The steak-and-bean idea has been around for years. Winning teams eat steak at a fine restaurant while the losers at the same setting must eat beans. Variations on this include having the winning teams catered to by the losing teams at company Christmas parties or award banquets.

## HOW TO EVALUATE SALES PERFORMANCE

We are frequently asked questions like these:

*"How do I know that my salespeople are doing their best?"*

*"How do you measure the effectiveness of a salesperson?"*

*"What are the standards for judging sales performance?"*

Obviously, there are no pat answers. Many factors must be taken into consideration when assessing the performance of sales personnel. The tendency is to conclude that it must be the sales agent's fault if sales are slow. These front-line representatives of America's housing opportunities are in the most vulnerable position—also the most important one! When sales are not meeting anticipated projections, the first visible target is the salesperson. Management frequently jumps to the conclusion that it is not getting the quality of personal skills necessary to do the job. While it is true that the representative plays a key role in the sales challenge, other factors outside the salesperson's control can play an equally important part. These should be evaluated before the agent becomes the focal point of the critique. Some of these contributing elements that determine sales success are:

1.  the public's acceptance of value, based on design and price comparisons with other available alternatives
2.  the quality and nature of prospects attracted to the product
3.  the financial ability of prospective buyers to purchase homes based on available terms
4.  the economic conditions of the marketplace and the general confidence of the buying public
5.  the condition of the homes and the sales environment

These vital influencing factors should be carefully evaluated when looking at possible reasons why sales have not been up to expectations. However, whether your sales are at a reasonable level or not, every sales professional deserves an opportunity to be monitored and evaluated periodically. If sales are critical and goals are not being met, it is essential to study the human resources and rate their performance.

## HOW TO MONITOR SALES PERFORMANCE EFFICIENTLY

Several ways are available to verify the quality of the sales representative's skills. No one approach is normally sufficient by itself. It takes a combination of techniques and reporting systems to provide sales management with the information needed to make valid judgments about the effectiveness of individual sales agents.

We can categorize the various sales monitoring systems into five broad classifications:

1.  personal (on-site) involvement and observations
2.  records and reports that are regularly reviewed
3.  surveys of buyers and prospects
4.  professional personnel shopping services
5.  professional testing and counseling

We will briefly explore the relative merits of each of these supervisory programs.

### Personal On-Site Involvement and Observations

One of the best methods of evaluating any salesperson's selling skills is to observe the agent in action. That is why the sales managers who can invest sufficient time on-site to participate in the sales process with their salespeople are usually much more effective than those isolated in management offices at corporate headquarters. No substitute will do for face-to-face opportunities to work with sales personnel in their selling environments. Through constructive conversations, in-depth debriefings and trained observation, you are able to discover how each sales representative thinks and functions.

A community large enough to justify full-time on-site sales management has a distinct advantage over those that can not. An experienced sales leader who knows what it takes to be truly effective in qualifying, involving and closing prospective buyers is in the ideal position to measure the performance of the agents he or she supervises. Day-to-day evaluation and guidance almost always produces far better results, because the synergy of group participation and personal leadership is not to be had merely by reading reports and conducting once a week sales meetings.

Realistically, however, only a minority of projects can economically sustain multiple sales agents and full-time on-site sales managers. The majority of our sales environments are staffed by one or two salespeople, and many only on weekends, because of their size and the anticipated sales volume they will generate. Thus, management must find other ways to validate the quality of the sales performance. Whatever support programs are added to provide the needed information, every sales manager or director of marketing should personally visit the sites and observe the agents in action as often as possible.

## Records and Reports

Sales performance records and reports are fundamental tools of sales management. Without them, it is impossible to maintain adequate control over the many factors that influence marketing decisions, from advertising efficiency to salespeople. The basic documents essential to these monitoring objectives are the following:

- prospect information cards
- traffic report forms (usually filed weekly)
- sales reports
- buyer-profile records
- sales-processing controls
- personnel files with performance records

Each of these reporting systems serves a valuable function in the overall interpretation of sales and marketing strategies. In our opinion, the first three are absolutely essential to sales management in the evaluation of the efficiency of each salesperson. Individual prospect cards are not only essential for the use of salespeople in following up the business they are developing, but they also provide management with a daily record of customers and an opportunity to debrief agents on the steps they are taking to pursue potential purchasers. The ideal system uses a three-part prospect-control card. The original is kept in the salesperson's tickler file for follow-up, one copy goes to sales management and the third is retained for marketing research.

The traffic report provides a summary of the total number of people who visit the housing center, the be-backs, the broker inspections, number of brochures distributed and other vital data. The responsibility for completing this form is usually that of the on-site sales agents, and, thus, the accuracy of the figures is subject to question. If a salesperson desires not to record everyone who visited on any particular day, it is easy to fudge the numbers. Sales managers must educate and motivate agents to help them appreciate the value of these statistics. Advertising and related marketing decisions are affected by the research information available to management. In some companies, these figures are recorded by an on-site hostess.

Ratios of total traffic to closed sales are guidelines to individual sales perfor- mance. For example, many of the professional sales managers in this industry expect a closing rate of anywhere from 10 to 20 percent of qualified traffic. The challenge is to determine what is qualified traffic! Periodic comparisons of prospect cards to traffic report figures can give you a general feel for the nature and quality of the people visiting your communities.

Sales-transaction records are obviously the most reliable determinant of sales performance. When the number of sales meets or exceeds expectations, we tend to relax our other monitoring systems. Conversely, when sales decline or are nonexistent, we usually begin looking for reasons and often are panicked into some course of action that may not be justified.

Other controls (buyer profiles, processing records and sales personnel files) are essential support programs for the efficient supervision of the entire sales operation. Collectively, all of these paper-tracking devices give managers a means of maintaining a daily understanding of the statistical realities of the sales process. However, they do not tell you how well the salespeople are really doing when they are one-to-one with prospective buyers. For example, they may be making sales simply because the product is easy to sell and they are creaming the traffic. On the other hand, they may be working very diligently, but the real issues lie with the product or the market conditions. That is why we cannot totally rely on written reports.

### Surveys and Interviews with Buyers and Prospects

Your buyers, as well as prospects who do not buy from you, are a valuable source of information. They can provide an independent rating of your salespeoples' performance. Although the consumers' opinion may be nonsales-oriented, it is certainly an important factor in public relations, and it directly affects the amount of referral business you enjoy.

Many home building companies and marketing organizations make it a policy to send survey letters to their purchasers after they have moved into their new homes. These questionnaires explore various areas of consumer satisfaction; one of them is the customers' rating of the salespeople with whom they dealt. Primary factors that are rated include:

- knowledge and proficiency of the salesperson
- reliability and honesty
- overall impressions including attitude and interest in the purchaser's needs

Some of the clients of the Stone Institute hold personal interviews with each owner after move-in. These sessions permit the company to build a solid relationship for the builders and the development team. They are usually held by individuals in the customer-service department or some adjunct of the public relations department of the marketing company. In these interviews, new owners are asked about their treatment by the sales force, along with many other areas of research interest. Telephone interviews are also effective when time does not permit personal visits.

Spot-checking prospects who have not purchased is also a very good way to discover their attitudes about both housing products and salespeople.

One of the major clients of the Stone Institute uses customer rating information as one of the three grading systems for recognizing superior performance; annual contests and awards are partly based on these consumer report cards.


## Professional Personnel Shopping Services

Because of increasing demand by builders, marketers and sales managers to know how well their sales representatives perform in a direct relationship with prospective buyers, a number of professional personnel shopping service companies have been formed during the last few years. While the availability of these companies is usually limited to major metropolitan areas of the country, some of them will travel to any community (for the agreed fees) to evaluate individual salespeople and projects. The quality of the shopping services does vary, and it is wise to verify the credentials of anyone you might consider employing for this evaluation function by checking with other clients they have served.


**Approaches and Techniques.**    The methods used by different sales shopping services vary, as does the type of reporting system you receive after the shop has been completed. Some of the mystery shoppers use hidden tape recorders (upon approval of the client), while others do not. Some record the personal observations of the shopper immediately following the session with the salesperson, so that their thoughts are fresh and responsive. Others use only the standard form check-off sheets to record their observations.

Another difference worth noting is the willingness of the shopping service to do a second interview (often with a different shopper), if the agent receives below-average marks on the first investigation. Any salesperson should be given the benefit of the doubt about a particular session, since even the best agents have bad days now and then.

Personally, we prefer to use shoppers who will follow specific guidelines given to them by sales management and who are willing to use tape recorders if requested. When you rely solely on the judgment of the mystery shopper about the quality of the responses they receive from the salespeople, you run the risk of having them evaluated unfairly for one or more reasons. When in doubt, the tape-recorded conversations give you special insight regarding the effectiveness of the interchange without any bias. If you plan to have your agents' conversations with the mystery shopper tape recorded, it is wisest to obtain written releases in advance of the shopping event. Some builders include in their employment agreements a standard clause that covers the right of the company to shop and tape-record at any time they desire.

The better shopping services train their mystery shoppers to perform like actors and actresses and to maintain a typical buying profile in selling encounters. This includes resisting the salesperson when closing techniques are tried and raising sufficient objections to force the agents to use fully their closing skills.

**Evaluation and Rating Categories.** The basic areas of evaluation may be classified differently by the various companies that provide these services, but most of them include a breakdown of major aspects of the sales functions including:

- the approach (greeting and warm-up)
- qualifying
- demonstration and value building presentation
- handling objections and serious questions
- closing

Special evaluations are often given to the following additional categories:

- attitude
- over-all presentation
- financing knowledge and skill in handling numbers

In rating the agent's efficiency, some methods use more of a yes/no approach to each question or item on the checklist, while others offer a much more detailed system based on a scale of one to ten or some variation of grading. Written or tape-recorded narratives are often submitted with the report to permit the managers to evaluate the findings with the mystery shoppers' personal perspectives in mind.

**Costs and Values of Mystery-Shopping Reports.** Costs for shopping personnel range from a low of about $100 per salesperson to as much as $750. The majority of reports in today's market average in the range of $125 to $175, plus the costs of travel if outside of primary market regions. Some efficiencies are obtained if you work with one company and do a quantity of evaluation sessions within a specified time.

Is it worth the investment? Opinions differ on this subject, but our research indicates that most companies who have used professional shopping services felt they got more than they invested and are convinced they need to shop their people at least once a year. The main value is often the objectivity and systematic summary of an independent review of the sales process. It gives management and the salespeople involved a chance to look at performance levels based on desired standards of achievement. It is an opportunity to help sales associates to improve as well as to commend those who obtain an above average rating. It also helps to justify decisions to replace agents when that is the pragmatic thing to do.

**Use Local Talent for Mystery Shops.** Although many advantages result from using the services of companies and individuals who professionally evaluate new home salespeople as an ongoing business, you can control your own shopping needs without going to this added expense. Many builders and marketing companies use people they know in the local marketplace to spot check specific housing environments and salespeople. Some even run advertisements that read:

### HOME BUYERS ATTENTION!

*If you qualify, we will pay you to look for your new home! Our company is interested in maintaining the high standards of excellence that have made us housing leaders in our city. As part of that continuing effort, we are interested in the unbiased opinions of prospective home buyers in the quality of our sales representatives' presentations. If interested, please call . . .*

This is a unique way to prospect for home buyers and find shoppers as well. What you pay them per investigation can be as much as you feel the task is worth, but the mere fact that you are dealing with real buyers gives both you and your salespeople a distinct advantage.

Others who are often effective in the shopping role are school teachers, actors and actresses, ministers, salespeople in other professions and people whose business activities involve dealing with the public. Avoid using close friends whose opinions may be biased or whose advice you will find difficult to reject. Match your shoppers to the profile of the typical buyers for the housing involved.

Whomever you use, be sure to have some type of orientation session that prepares the mystery shoppers for the way you expect them to profile themselves in the presentation and the things you want them to do to rate your agents objectively.

**FIGURE 6.5   Tom Richey's Planned Encounters Management Checklist**

Salesperson:———————————     Date:———————————
     Project:———————————

1. Salesperson role-plays typical presentation on arrival of manager. (optional)
2. Manager reviews overall project status and answers pressing questions.
3. Manager asks how many were taken to the closing table the last seven days; reviews sales.
4. Manager reviews self-prospecting efforts.
5. Manager tracks incidence of referral sales.
6. Manager monitors prospect card box on a card-by-card basis; asks specific suggestions for follow-up.
7. Manager spotlights the ten best prospects for follow-up on the follow-up.
8. Manager surveys sales office for efficiency and cleanliness.
9. Manager audits the salesperson's sales spreadsheet to insure efficient case-processing.
10. Manager audits salesperson's filing system, plat map (sold buttons) and selling visualizer.
11. Manager tours models and corrects deficiencies according to the merchandising checklist.
12. Manager quizzes salesperson for rule-of-five's knowledge, i.e., reviews management rule-of-five's worksheet.
13. Manager tracks urgency creation.
14. Manager addresses salesperson's knowledge of project ESP's and specific USP's to inventory *in the field*.
15. Manager administrates any new company policies and answers questions.
16. Manager asks for salesperson's biggest objections; helps neutralize them.
17. Manager inspects salesperson's car for cleanliness and tours subdivision for presence of *sold* signs, *available* signs, general cleanliness.
18. Manager role plays presentation in salesperson's opportunity house.
19. Salesperson recites his/her closing techniques utilized to write the last sale (or two).
20. Manager sets closing table (and sales goal) for salesperson in next seven-day time frame.
21. Manager departs on a high note with an appropriate motivation item.
     "My competitors can match me in a thousand ways, but if my people are better, I have a priceless advantage."

Corrective action:

1. ————————————————————————————

2. ————————————————————————————

3. ————————————————————————————

4. ————————————————————————————

5. ————————————————————————————

6. ————————————————————————————

Courtesy of Richey Resources, Houston, TX.

---

### FIGURE 6.6   Personnel Evaluations—Confidential Shopping Report

**Sales Effort Evaluation**

DEVELOPMENT:_____ SALES CONSULTANT:_____

DATE:_____ DAY OF WEEK:_____ TIME:_____

MODEL TRAFFIC:_____ WEATHER: _____

|  | YES | NO | SOMEWHAT | N/A |
|---|---|---|---|---|
| **1. PHONE CONTACT WITH COMMUNITY:** | | | | |
| a. Was number easily obtainable? | | | | |
| b. Was the office easy to reach via phone? | | | | |
| c. Did the representative identify himself/herself? | | | | |
| d. Did you know the representative's capacity? | | | | |
| e. Was your name requested? | | | | |
| f. Was the phone manner professional? | | | | |
| g. Was an appointment attempt made? | | | | |
| h. Were directions accurate and easy to understand? | | | | |
| i. Were you encouraged to visit this community? | | | | |
| **2. ADVERTISING:** | | | | |
| a. Did you locate an ad for this community? | | | | |
| b. Was the ad eye-catching? | | | | |
| c. Were directions in ad accurate? | | | | |
| d. Was the phone number in ad accurate? | | | | |
| **3. LOCATING THE COMMUNITY:** | | | | |
| a. Were signs noted en route? | | | | |
| b. Were they well placed? | | | | |
| c. Were they legible? | | | | |
| d. Was first visual impression of community favorable? | | | | |
| **4. SALES OFFICE:** | | | | |
| a. Was it well-identified? | | | | |
| b. Was office professional in appearance? | | | | |
| c. Were provisions made for prospect comfort? | | | | |
| d. Were there adequate visuals? | | | | |
| e. Did the visuals attract your attention? | | | | |
| f. Was a brochure offered? | | | | |

**FIGURE 6.6    Personnel Evaluations—Confidential Shopping Report (continued)**

| | YES | NO | SOMEWHAT | N/A |
|---|---|---|---|---|
| 5. **ENTERING THE SALES OFFICE:** | | | | |
| a. Were you greeted by a sales assistant? | | | | |
| b. Were you greeted by a sales consultant? | | | | |
| c. Did this representative introduce himself/herself to you at this point? | | | | |
| d. Were you immediately made aware of the capacity of this person? | | | | |
| e. Was there a verbal attempt to discover what prompted your visit? | | | | |
| f. Was a verbal attempt made to determine your housing needs or what you were looking for? | | | | |
| g. Were you asked to complete a guest card or register? | | | | |
| 6. **DIRECT CONTACT WITH THE SALES CONSULTANT:** | | | | |
| a. Was the sales consultant introduced to you? | | | | |
| b. Did the sales consultant learn your name? | | | | |
| c. Did the sales consultant determine if this was your first visit? | | | | |
| d. Was there an attempt made to determine your seriousness or time frame? | | | | |
| e. Did the sales consultant determine your current residential status? | | | | |
| f. Was there an initial attempt to determine your current residential status? | | | | |
| 7. **THE SALES CONSULTANT'S PRESENTATION:** | | | | |
| a. Did the sales consultant lead and control the presentation? | | | | |
| b. Was it organized? | | | | |
| c. Did the sales consultant avoid sounding mechanical? | | | | |
| d. Was the presentation personalized? | | | | |
| e. Was it tailored to your specific requirements and concerns? | | | | |
| f. Did the sales consultant know the product? | | | | |
| g. Did the sales consultant sell the product? | | | | |

---

### FIGURE 6.6    Personnel Evaluations—Confidential Shopping Report (continued)

| | YES | NO | SOMEWHAT | N/A |
|---|---|---|---|---|
| THE SALES CONSULTANT'S PRESENTATION: (continued) | | | | |
| h. Did the sales consultant offer you any community orientation? | | | | |
| i. Did the sales consultant offer any information about the builder/developer? | | | | |
| j. Did the sales consultant sell location? | | | | |
| k. Did the sales consultant build value in living here? | | | | |
| l. Did the sales consultant have the needed visuals and "tools" to present the product? | | | | |
| m. Were visuals utilized in the presentation? | | | | |
| n. Did the sales consultant translate features into benefits? | | | | |
| **8. THE MODEL AND MODEL DEMONSTRATION** | | | | |
| a. Were you escorted through a model by the sales consultant? | | | | |
| b. Were you escorted by the sales assistant? | | | | |
| c. Was there an actual model demonstration? | | | | |
| d. Were the features translated into benefits to you? | | | | |
| e. Was "emotional sell" employed during this demonstration? | | | | |
| f. Was the model well-maintained? | | | | |
| g. Was the model attractive and appealing? | | | | |
| h. Can the model be easily recalled? | | | | |
| **9. FINANCING** | | | | |
| a. Did you receive financing information? | | | | |
| b. Did the sales consultant offer these details? | | | | |
| c. Did this discussion take place in privacy? | | | | |
| d. Was the sales consultant selling the product as well as the financing? | | | | |
| e. Was the sales consultant well informed regarding financing? | | | | |
| f. Were financing alternatives narrowed down? | | | | |

**FIGURE 6.6   Personnel Evaluations—Confidential Shopping Report (continued)**

| | YES | NO | SOMEWHAT | N/A |
|---|---|---|---|---|
| **FINANCING** (continued) | | | | |
| g. Was there a definite attempt made to determine your financial qualifications? | | | | |
| h. Was financial information written down by the sales consultant? | | | | |
| • If so, were you kept involved during this work-up? | | | | |
| i. Was financial information provided on a preprinted form? | | | | |
| • If so, was it explained to you? | | | | |
| j. Were the figures clearly labeled? | | | | |
| k. Were the tax benefits of home ownership made clear? | | | | |
| l. Was there any attempt made to discern your acceptance of these figures? | | | | |
| m. Were you given a work-up to take with you? | | | | |
| **10. LOT AND MODEL SELECTION:** | | | | |
| a. Was there an attempt to narrow down your interests to one specific model? | | | | |
| b. Did the sales consultant point out, on a plat or such, available lots or units? | | | | |
| c. Was an offer made to show you some specific lots or vacant units? | | | | |
| d. Did you walk the lot or see an available unit with the sales consultant? | | | | |
| e. Did you walk the lot or see an available unit unescorted? | | | | |
| **11. CLOSING:** | | | | |
| a. Was a sense of urgency created for you to make a purchase decision? | | | | |
| b. Was deposit procedure information volunteered? | | | | |
| c. Were the steps involved in a purchase offered? | | | | |
| d. Did the sales consultant ask for the sale? | | | | |
| e. Did the sales consultant ask for a deposit? | | | | |
| f. Did the sales consultant attempt to establish a specific return appointment? | | | | |

---

**FIGURE 6.6   Personnel Evaluations—Confidential Shopping Report (concluded)**

| | YES | NO | SOMEWHAT | N/A |
|---|---|---|---|---|
| 12. THE SALES CONSULTANT: | | | | |
| a. Was the sales consultant's appearance professional? | | | | |
| b. Did the sales consultant seem interested in you? | | | | |
| c. Was the sales consultant enthusiastic? | | | | |
| d. Was the sales consultant energetic? | | | | |
| e. Was the sales consultant willing to spend time with you? | | | | |
| f. Was the sales consultant tactful? | | | | |
| g. Did the sales consultant seem sincere? | | | | |
| h. Was the sales consultant's body language and eye contact positive? | | | | |
| i. Did the sales consultant attempt to build rapport? | | | | |
| j. Was the sales consultant acting in an advisory capacity? | | | | |
| k. Was the sales consultant's attitude positive regarding: • The builder/developer? | | | | |
| • The product? | | | | |
| • The community? | | | | |
| • The price? | | | | |
| • The financing being offered? | | | | |
| l. Did the sales consultant employ "emotional sell?" | | | | |
| m. Was the sales consultant actively selling? | | | | |
| n. Was the sales consultant able to convert negatives to positives? | | | | |
| o. Was the sales consultant adept at handling traffic? | | | | |
| p. Did the sales consultant makes an effort market himself/herself? | | | | |
| AS OF THIS DATE, HAS THE SALES CONSULTANT FOLLOWED UP IN ANY WAY? | | | | |

Courtesy of Nicki Joy and Associates, Brookeville, MD

## Professional Testing and Counseling

Finally, the entire evaluation system can be placed under the guidance of organizations experienced in personnel evaluations for industry in general.

Behavioral research has become a specialized field that has attracted both academic and business experts. Companies throughout America offer personnel-testing systems and will include personal counseling sessions, if necessary.

Schools and courses are available to teach you to become more proficient in selecting and evaluating people for your business.

Many real estate enterprises use testing systems in recruiting as well as for periodic updates when contemplating promoting or relocating personnel. These tests and evaluation programs are no valid substitute for one-on-one involvement and personal counseling. Effective sales management recognizes that the primary concern is to supervise and evaluate salespeople to gain the highest and best performance levels possible for the benefit of all involved. The coaching role of sales management is a hands-on assignment!

## How to Spot a Potential Sales Slump

Alert sales managers know how to spot potential sales slumps before they become serious. The key is knowing each salesperson's personality and performance patterns through consistent monitoring. Planned and casual encounters are the best means of staying on top of the sales picture. Managers monitor effectiveness and measure attitudes as they do so. The outstanding sales coaches are in touch with their associates and can read them just as a sports coach learns to interpret each player on a team. (See Tom Richey's planned encounters checklist)

Seven primary indicators tell when a salesperson is either already in trouble or soon will be!

1. *Loss of Enthusiasm.* The first clue to decreased sales ability is when a salesperson shows less sparkle and interest in the business. Enthusiasm is a principal characteristic of top performers. When it starts to wane, a drop in sales performance is not far behind.
2. *Lessened empathy.* The partner to enthusiasm is empathy. When your salespeople show less concern for their clients' needs, become defensive with present residents, are less inclined to follow through with the prospects they are servicing, the second clue is in place. Only caring, empathetic salespeople achieve optimum sales goals.
3. *Decreased energy.* When a salesperson shows signs of decreased energy, including tiredness, burn-out and listlessness, he or she is either sick or showing one of the principal symptoms of stress. This is very often the by-product of other factors, such as loss of enthusiasm and decreased confidence.
4. *Declining participation in group events.* Declining sales are often accompanied by a desire to retreat from peer-pressure situations, such as attending sales meetings, participating in group discussions and sharing in educational

events. Insecurities begin to manifest themselves in either aggressive or defensive reactions when mixing with other professionals is demanded.

5. *Ethics and Value Systems Begin to Erode.* As psychological pressure builds insecurities, it also may lead to a lowering of professional standards. Salespeople who sense they must do anything to get results begin making promises or commitments they cannot keep. It is serious when they bend the truth to make sales on any terms.

6. *Negative thinking dominates the conversation.* A sure sign of lessened confidence and a sales slump is negative thinking that is openly expressed. Constant complaining, finding fault with everything and everybody are obvious indicators of a salesperson who is in deep psychological trouble!

7. *Depression and retreat.* The final stages of the sales-slump malady is deep depression, retreat from responsibility, and apathy. When it reaches this level, it is difficult to correct. It is the by-product of prolonged periods of self-doubt, increased stress, and perceptions of self-failure. Professional guidance is needed to help someone out of the valley of lost sales.

## Education and Motivation are Fuel
## for Attaining Maximum Performance

The human resources that fuel a residential marketing organization include many disciplines, but none is more important than front-line sales personnel charged with the responsibilities of finding and converting prospective buyers into satisfied home-owners. The quality of the people you recruit and retain determines your results. Two major pillars of the sales management system are *education* and *motivation*. They are not occasional activities engaged in when time permits. They are vital on-going functions that deserve priority roles on the time-management schedule. If the people within the company do not have the time or the skills necessary adequately to perform these personnel development systems, others from the outside should be recruited to accomplish the objectives. Motivation begins at the top of the company, not the bottom! The principals who have the most to gain from superior sales efforts need to communicate their convictions in motivating ways so they reach the individuals who most need to remain confident and fully dedicated to the pursuit of excellence in the sales arena!

# 7: Organizing the Sales Presentation

The quality of the sales presentation directly influences the decision-making process. Home buyers do not make decisions in a vacuum. They require information that helps them sort out the advantages and disadvantages of one home over another. In fact, the very nature of the typical shopping experience for most prospective home buyers is one of elimination rather than selection! Prospective buyers investigate a number of opportunities and make comparisons before they decide to buy or not to buy. In the process, the majority of properties they inspect are eliminated—ruled out for one reason or another. They start with some preconceived ideas about what they think they want. Normally, they have partially qualified themselves for what they are prepared to invest, either in total capital or monthly payments, and they have determined a general location in which they will concentrate their search. They also may have established basic criteria for the relative size of the home they prefer and made a mental list of features they expect it to contain. It is not uncommon for women, in particular, to purchase magazines that illustrate dream homes with all of the refinements that appeal to those who have been living in less satisfying environments. Armed with these mental pictures, they begin the house-hunting process with expectations often beyond their economic capacity. How do they reach a decision point and select one home at the expense of all the others they could continue to investigate? What causes them to purchase?

The truth is that most people who go shopping for a new home do not purchase one—at least for a long time after beginning the process. The biggest competitor for any salesperson in this business is not the builder with another model or location; it is the existing nest to which potential prospects can readily retreat! The average decision time for new home buyers is over three months of searching—and that is just for those who ultimately decide in favor of moving! A large percentage remain in their present residences. Uprooting people and putting them through the complicated process of buying a new home in a virgin neighborhood and waiting for it to be completed is not the easiest thing to accomplish.

Salespeople concentrate on things they believe they are selling and, more often than not, overlook issues being weighed by their prospects. As marketers we should be more concerned with the buying track than the selling track!

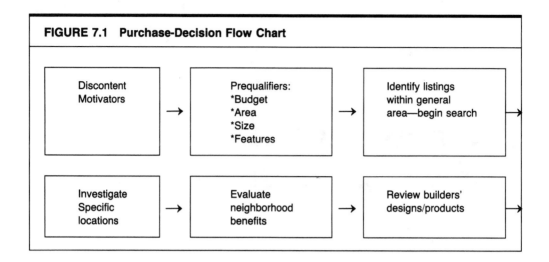

**FIGURE 7.1    Purchase-Decision Flow Chart**

- What are your potential buyers experiencing?
- What unresolved issues stand in the way of making the decisions to purchase new homes?
- What messages or reinforcement do they need before they will be emotionally assured to step forward and accept the benefits of our new housing environments?
- How can you best provide the information and emotional security that will facilitate the decision-making process?

Although the ultimate decision is influenced more by emotions than facts, it is essential that you design your sales presentation to provide justification for the desired emotional responses. All home purchasers make a series of decisions to finally reach the major one: which home to purchase. They begin the process by debating whether or not to leave the nest they currently occupy. Unless some form of natural or forced discontent exists, the instinct to avoid the complications of relocating will outweigh anticipated benefits.

Breeding discontent is an objective of all successful marketing and must be incorporated directly into the sales presentation and the sales environment. Until the targeted prospects have received an initial prompting to get out of their comfortable chairs and begin investigating alternatives, the new home sales agent has no way even to begin the sales process.

The critical path to the sale from the potential buyers' perspective is illustrated in Figure 7.1.

Organizing a well-planned sales presentation that facilitates the buying process and increases the opportunities of having your homes selected instead of your competitors' is not something you can afford to treat lightly. A primary objective is to avoid being eliminated by prospects who are qualified and profiled as targeted

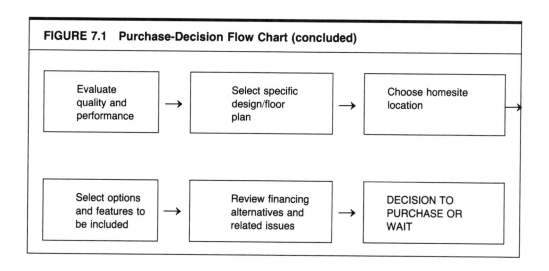

FIGURE 7.1   Purchase-Decision Flow Chart (concluded)

purchasers for your housing portfolio. If the comparative analysis puts your homes at a disadvantage, sales will be lost simply because customers gravitate to properties that they perceive as having the greater value relative to their motivations. A principal role of your professional new home sales representative is to communicate the values you offer in ways that will offset perception differences between your housing and the alternatives they have been presented. People who investigate homes without the benefit of a knowledgeable representative are seldom able to see and interpret all of the factors that justify their involvement and investment.

Every developer and builder deserves to be represented by a salesperson or a real estate company that has taken the time to prepare and practice value-building presentations that will be effective with qualified customers. This is not something that should be left to chance or extemporaneously delivered by sales agents who have not researched and rehearsed the presentation elements. The sale is made in the presentation, not at the end. Closing or confirming the decision is the result of all the decision-influencing steps that have been carefully reinforced prior to that time.

The critical path to the sale from the professional salesperson's perspective should include a mastery of the presentation and emotional involvement points in the sequence in which they normally occur before a sale is ratified. It is similar to increasing the temperature in a chemical mixture to the proper point before obtaining the reaction you want. A psychological buying state is produced along the critical path in the decision-making process. Each level along the way must produce evidence that you are ready to proceed to the next one. Measuring and maintaining control over the process is what master closers do best! In the book *New Home Sales*, this subject is reviewed in more detail than we will cover here. However, we provide a digest of the topic at this point because it is essential to the material that follows.

## THE VALUE-BUILDING PRESENTATION PROCESS

In the development of an effective new home sales presentation, the representative should tailor the modules of information that must be communicated to customers so they flow logically from one key decision point to another, while remaining flexible and able to adjust to the level of interest and involvement shown by any particular prospect. A minimum of seven basic knowledge modules should be mastered prior to making any presentation. Each requires advance research and requires careful attention to establish the information priorities for specific prospects. What may be important to one customer could be relatively unimportant to another. Fundamental value messages must be communicated and reinforced with every potential home buyer prior to attempting the close. You risk losing a sale if you try to close without having built a solid foundation on which the ultimate decision can securely rest.

The basic modules are:

1. general location and community values
2. yhe credibility story for both developer and builder
3. yhe master plan and amenities of the new neighborhood
4. features and benefits of the basic construction
5. features and benefits of each floor plan and model
6. values of available homesites and specific locations
7. financing terms and factors affecting ownership

When representing common interest communities or condominiums, at least two additional presentation modules are required:

8. structure of the homeowners or condominium association

9. protective convenants and privileges of the owners

Moving along the critical path to the sale, the salesperson should use the knowledge he or she has gained on each of these vital subjects to increase interest while qualifying and involving customers in ways that hold their attention. The bridge to agreement is laid one plank at a time. It is a mistake to try to leapfrog across the valley of indecision without having nailed the planks that sustain the values. The process can be illustrated as a series of steps or levels of increasing interest which hopefully will lead to a confirmed purchase agreement.

### Level One: Attention Gained

- greeting
- first impressions
- initial qualifying
- customer made to feel at home

**FIGURE 7.2   Stations of Involvement**

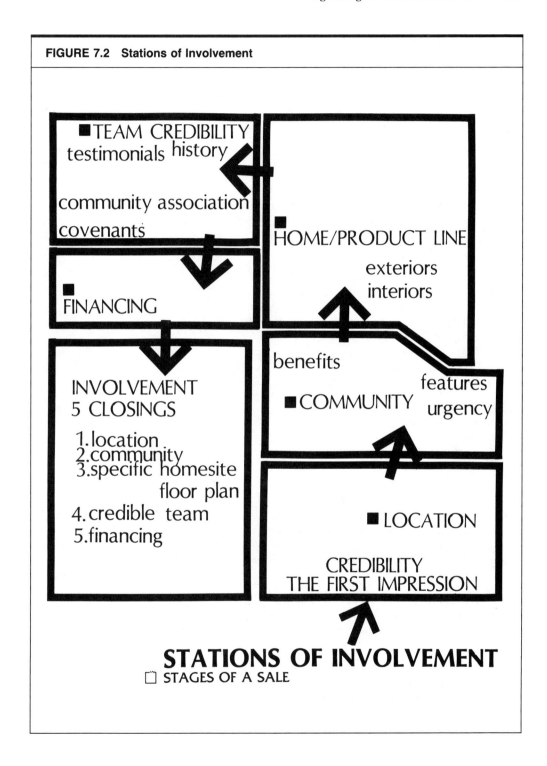

TEAM CREDIBILITY
testimonials history
community association
covenants

HOME/PRODUCT LINE
exteriors
interiors

FINANCING

benefits
COMMUNITY
features
urgency

INVOLVEMENT
5 CLOSINGS
1. location
2. community
3. specific homesite
        floor plan
4. credible team
5. financing

LOCATION

CREDIBILITY
THE FIRST IMPRESSION

**STATIONS OF INVOLVEMENT**
STAGES OF A SALE

### Level Two: Interest Generated

- Priority presentation points on:

  general location benefits
  builder/developer credibility
  master site plan and neighborhood
  amenities and features of the community

- qualify for experience, timing, financial capacity

### Level Three: Emotional Involvement

- models inspected or qualified designs presented
- demonstration of specific features and benefits
- qualify for needs, status of decision, motivations

### Level Four: Desire Evident and Ownership Pictured

- involvement narrowed to one plan and homesite
- financial factors reviewed—estimate sheets
- emotions begin to peak; ownership benefits portrayed
- emotional memory links reinforced
- trial closes attempted

### Level Five: Resistance Barriers Encountered

- objections raised
- empathetic counseling
- retreat—think-it-over syndrome
- reinforcements of key benefits
- create sense of urgency to act based on valid points
- counselor closes attempted
- minimum objective: partial decision and return appointment established

### Level Six: Conviction (Possibly a Return Visit)

- assumptive attitude must prevail
- summary closing
- deep counseling
- resolution of any blocking objections or issues
- emotional involvement must be at maximum
- comparative value-indexing if needed

### Level Seven: Commitment—Closing

- all resistance overcome
- anticipation of gain; future benefits emphasized
- urgency to act motivated by fear of loss
- decision committed to writing

## SALES MANAGEMENT'S ROLE IN ORGANIZING SALES PRESENTATIONS

It is the responsibility of those in charge of sales and marketing to assemble and organize information needed by sales representatives to assure reasonably effective sales presentations. While it is practical to ask your own full-time specialists to participate in gathering the information and preparing checklists that can be referenced as needed, outside brokers cannot be expected to have the same interest in performing these research functions. The use of checklists to identify value points and information of general interest to some customers is the best way to avoid overlooking important data. Everyone involved on the developers' or builders' team should be solicited to provide information and ideas helpful to salespeople.

Land planners, architects, interior designers, suppliers and subcontractors have a vested interest in the success of the project, and they will usually share ideas with the sales team if requested. Some facts can be gained only by physical inspection, such as studying competitive properties. Others are available by reviewing specifications and owner documents. Whatever may be needed in face-to-face selling situations to help convince potential prospects to purchase should be anticipated and documented in advance. On the following pages are the checklists we use with our clients in preparing background data for organizing effective sales presentations.

## VALUE INDEXING INDIVIDUAL HOMESITES

Every parcel of real estate has its unique characteristics. Appreciating that fact is essential in understanding how to create the one-of-a-kind difference that will motivate prospects to perceive the benefits of owning specific housing locations. Unless your customers become involved with individual sites they can picture owning, you have little or no urgency generated in the closing process. We all know that having too much inventory on the plat map from which prospects can select is a potential negative to decision making. Too much choice produces confusion and decreases incentives to act now. Professional marketers understand and capitalize on the unique values of each housing location within the master plan or neighborhood to achieve the greatest degree of prospect involvement.

Value indexing is a fundamental strategy that applies to every aspect of the presentation. Unless you have positioned your properties correctly and communicated the values that make them distinctive, better or more desirable than competitive opportunities, you will lose the sales contest. We all want to realize the most we can from the money we have to invest in property. We also have individual tastes and personal motivations. What one person perceives as a value, another may perceive as a detriment. That is why we must analyze our site inventories very carefully and identify the factors that separate them from one another. If we do not appreciate the differences, we certainly cannot communicate them to our customers!

To illustrate this concept, let's use a case history. Hidden Valley is a single-family housing community consisting of 137 homesites nestled in the rolling hills of Pennsylvania. Annual projected absorption rates for the mid-range housing is estimated at between 50 and 60, or about one sale per week. The homesites average

---

**FIGURE 7.3    Statement of Quality Features**

# QUALITY FEATURES

The homes at Carriage Hill feature quality materials throughout and careful attention has been paid to every construction detail to assure lasting value. As you tour our models, please notice the many extra features that have been included to enhance the style and comfort of these fine homes.

**As You Enter...**
- Beautiful solid core raised panel entry doors
- Stylish ceramic tile or wood parquet entry
- High vaulted ceilings
- Multi-paned window treatments
- Beautiful wood-capped handrails

**Throughout The Living Area...**
- Woodburning fireplaces
- Wall-to-wall carpeting
- Spacious living rooms
- Formal dining rooms
- Family rooms (Plan Three)
- Breakfast nook with patio access (Plan Three)
- One bedroom adaptable for use as a den (Plans Two & Three)

**In The Expansive Kitchen...**
- Gas range with continuous-cleaning oven
- Deluxe multi-cycle dishwasher

- European-style cabinets
- Pantry for extra storage
- Wood-trimmed luminous ceiling
- Plumbed for icemaker
- Porcelain-coated cast-iron sinks

**In The Luxurious Master Bedroom Suite...**
- Private bath/dressing area with double basin/Corian pullman and glass-enclosed shower stall
- Walk-in closet (Most Plans)
- Antique brushed brass plumbing fixtures

**Construction Features...**
- Enclosed two-car garages
- Brick exterior detailing
- Gas forced-air heating
- Tempered safety glass in sliding glass doors
- Interior laundry areas (Plans One & Three)
- Gas/220 electrical outlet in laundry area

- Decorator-selected lighting fixtures
- Concrete driveways
- Gas barbeque stub in rear yard patio area
- Trouble-free copper water lines
- Pre-wired for television and telephone outlets
- Underground utilities
- Raised-panel Colonist doors
- Fire-retardant treated shake roofs

**Energy-Saving Features...**
- Exterior wall and ceiling insulation
- Energy-efficient gas water heater
- Insulated air ducts
- Maximum 3 GPM flow control on all shower outlets and faucets
- Weatherstripping on exterior doors
- Pilotless ignition forced-air heating
- Automatic setback thermostat

---

8,000 square feet, but they range from approximately 7,000 to as much as 10,000 in some cases. There are cul-de-sacs as well as typical rectangular primary street sites. Since the land is rolling in nature, street patterns take advantage of the valley, hillsides and gentle slopes to create an interesting and private community.

Following sound marketing principles, release patterns will include no more than a ninety-day sales pace. To assure continuity of the development and avoid scattered-site situations that decrease both urgency and community values, the releases will be designed to provide contiguous housing that is constructed early enough to give

Hidden Valley a strong sense of community. Streetscapes are studied to assure that the sites that need to be sold first are given the attention they deserve. Since there is an open field on the south side of the entry area that is not part of this development, the models and first homes to be featured will be built along that perimeter. This will block out the open fields that might tend to reduce the sense of community.

With room for three models and two reserved sites on either side to allow for additions as well as to protect the model sales environment, the marketers decided to release 18 lots in phase one. The next phase will not be released until at least 12 of the first phase are sold, despite the fact that economics of physical improvements dictate development of 39 sites. The section not released will be blocked off both on site and on the plat table in the sales office to focus prospect attention on the 18 that are the target group.

Having made these decisions, the next step is to develop a detailed value index for each of these 18 homesites. The objective is to break them into categories and then into subcategories that will help salespeople and buyers understand the individual exclusivity of each property. No two are alike, and that must be communicated to customers or they will not feel the degree of desire and urgency necessary to precipitate action—today!

Begin by analyzing housing types and preselecting ideal locations for different floor plans. Some lots are best for certain plans while others may accomodate a wide variety. Attempt to isolate lots that work best for particular designs and, thus, broadly separate them into classifications that reduce confusion. A limited number will accomodate walk-outs, and these are considered premium locations, since the profiled family buyers tend to favorably respond to family rooms on the lower level that take advantage of direct access to protected yards. Only a few will justify the ranch-style home, and these are indexed. More mature buyers and empty nesters prefer one-level living, and you need to provide homes for this market segment. The two-story plans will fit almost every site, so you can be a little more liberal in working with the traditional two-level designs.

Having made this broad separation, prepare individual worksheets for each site and have sales associates, management and production personnel give their input to the value-index formulas. Here are the basic items rated in the order of priority:

1. *Lot sizes, configurations and square-footage factors.* Usually the first major determinant of value in a single-family development (this is not applicable to condominiums) is the relative size of each site. This is not just a matter of dimensions such as width and depth. It is best translated in terms of actual square-footage figures. A site that has 8,922 square feet is psychologically worth more than one that has 7,856 square feet. Ask an engineer or numbers expert to compute these figures prior to beginning the value-indexing process. Of course the following must also be taken into consideration:

   usable yard space based on types of floor plans proposed for the site
   topography as it relates to ideal siting of the home for views, streetscape appearance, ingress and egress and physical relationships to adjacent sites
   protection of natural assets such as trees and native landscaping

2. *The internalized views each owner will experience.* Home buyers pay for views. The orientation of a home in terms of its immediate environment and the vistas that it will enjoy is one of the most important value-perception items on this index. These views vary from one location to another. They will also be affected by the type of housing plan placed on a given site. If you are not certain which floor plan will be selected for a particular location, generalize the views as they will most likely relate to a typical plan. If you will be recommending or building a specific design, you will then index the views from each room of the home and accent the most valuable. Always be concerned with the primary views from living centers, kitchen and master suites. If a two-story plan is most likely to be constructed on a site, then the second-floor views will be given special attention, since they are frequently more valuable than first-level ones. Distant sites and long-range vistas not evident on the first floor can be seen from the second level.

3. *Sun orientation, energy and weather factors.* Also high on the rating system will be determination of the pluses and minuses of siting as it relates to the sun, weather and general energy concerns. Since you are in a four-season market, that will be a measurable rating factor. A few of the sites have the preferred southerly exposure that gives the home maximum sun in the winter, thus reducing heat loss and energy costs. They will also have some distinctive advantages in summer, where backyard exposure will be protected from much of the midday heat. These will command a premium from buyers who are energy conscious.

   Other weather considerations will be taken into account, such as prevailing winds, buffered sites that shelter the homes from winter storms, and treed versus open locations as they relate to more or less sunshine exposure. Those sites that are not the most desirable for sun and weather will be studied for compensating benefits.

4. *The number and quality of trees and natural growth.* Sites with specimen trees almost always command more value than sites without them. Most people express a desire to have trees on the horizon of their properties, even though they may not want them smothering the home from sunlight. This particular project has a virgin stand of beautiful hardwoods, some of which are more than 100 years old. There is also a good mix of birches, elms and evergreens. As part of the planning process those trees that need to be preserved were marked and logical footprint locations for various floor plans were identified to take advantage of natural landscaping values. While it may be obvious you will have to remove some trees as the normal cost of construction, you should protect the natural treescape and native landscaping to increase perceived values for the ultimate owners.

5. *Topography and Buildability factors.* The specific characteristics of this property provide interesting differences from one homesite to another simply because of the way the land is configured. These same factors influence construction sites. A few of them will require some form of retaining walls or earth berms to handle transitions between the residences.

Erosion considerations in landscaping will be a concern with a few sites which abut a natural drainage area. Rate the topography from two viewpoints:

What are the additional costs for providing special treatments to meet construction requirements and maintain an attractive relationship of buildings and surrounding environments?

What are the relative values in general appearance and interest as viewed by our profiled prospects? Streetside appearance as it impacts architectural appeal is a major consideration. Elevated sites that put the home above the surroundings will have an entirely different appeal than those which drop below street grade. Driveway approaches are part of this evaluation.

6. *Proximity to amenities and open-space areas.* Hidden Valley is an open-space community. About 25 percent of the land has been retained as common park land to be held for the mutual enjoyment of all the owners under a homeowners association. The land that has been placed in this protective reserve is essentially the ravines, creekbed, and hillside slopes not suitable for construction purposes. Like so many of these common-interest communities, the improved land planning has added measurable values to the individual sites and increased marketing values to the entire land plan. With that in mind, rate each of the homesites in terms of immediate exposure to the common park lands or proximity for use by individual owners. Those that directly extend into the open area will be worth more than those that have no abutting park space. Residents of some internal lots have to cross streets to get to the open space unlike those who are on the same side of the street. Such small factors influence perceived values and should be translated into both pricing and presentation differences.

Six tot lots or playground areas are built into this master plan. People with young children will perceive the proximity to these recreation areas as a major plus, while those without children may prefer to be farther away from potentially noisy children at play. It is that kind of value balancing that helps us determine who should be shown certain sites, their premium or discount relationship to base lots and what points to emphasize with individual prospects.

7. *Proximity to potentially adverse influences.* While rating sites for positive values derived from amenities as parks or play areas, we must also study those locations that have potentially adverse influences. In Hidden Valley, ten homesites will back up to a busy and often noisy highway. Even though these lots are somewhat deeper than others, we know that many prospective buyers will be concerned with the sound levels of passing traffic, particularly trucks that must negotiate the hills by changing gears.

For these locations, value index the negatives and reflect that in lot pricing. Also, include a masonry wall buffer that will help to reduce some of the sound and improve privacy. There will be some offsetting pluses that can be used in the presentations, providing the salespeople understand and use them correctly. The street traffic will be more of a concern to local buyers than those moving from metropolitan areas on the east coast where they have become accustomed to even greater noise pollution.

Five sites abut a drainage ditch that cannot legitimately be called a creek. This is a ditch . . . and it only has water after major rain storms. Some prospects will be concerned about flooding . . . and others with the general appearance of the area. Landscaping will help, but this negative influence was taken into consideration when establishing the lot balancing act. Either by pricing, landscaping allowances, or inclusions, these factors were kept in mind when those sites were introduced to the market place. market place.


## Social Value Factors

While most of these first seven key evaluators affect the social values of each site, they are quantifiable factors that can be presented to prospects without regard to personal needs. These are visual distinctions readily evident to a trained observer. We rate them first as they set the foundation for more subjective indexing. The next five ratings are interpretative considerations that sales representatives can use at their discretion when emphasizing the merits of one location versus another. By profiling prospects to match available homesites, agents can emphasize the social and emotional perceptions of value that will help to provide further uniqueness for each property.

8. *Privacy considerations: Social, auditory and visual.* Privacy is one of the basic motivations in housing environments. Most buyers want a reasonable amount of privacy. Some demand total privacy. Privacy is influenced by the following:

> proximity of other residents
> distance from streets and traffic
> amount of screening provided by natural or added landscaping, especially trees and shrubs
> protection from viewing by neighboring homes to the rear
> siting of adjacent homes in terms of potential noise transmission
>     Example: separation of family living areas from next-door bedrooms or buffering of sound by garages, privacy walls or low-use areas
> limited access for local residents
> separation from heavily used amenities such as public pools, play areas, tennis courts, etc
> architectural designs that provide privacy walls and limit views to screened areas and private yards

> Our research indicates that most people are concerned with social privacy, that is, the ability to remove themselves from the group and be

alone when they choose. They may like the idea of living in a community that has a social activity center where they can mix with their neighbors, but they want their homes to be as private as possible from the visual and auditory exposure to others. Many individuals will pay a premium to achieve a greater degree of privacy than may be afforded by the normal siting. The desire for privacy relates to age, lifestyles and physical needs. Those who want security will often choose to be closer to neighbors than others who are less concerned with this motivator.

9. *Security considerations and their social implications.* Security has long been recognized as a fundamental consideration in the design and marketing of residential communities. The public is justifiably concerned with the risks of living in neighborhoods where they are subject to outside forces that can disrupt their lives. Security factors are broadly classified into three considerations:

*Protection of health and life.* The key element in the security concerns of home buyers is the protection of personal health and life. Everyone is interested in living where their lives are not threatened by people or the environment. New communities often appeal to people who currently live in cities where declining values and increased security challenges have motivated them to move out. They seek assurances of a safer and more secure lifestyle. Neighborhood and site considerations that affect these issues include:

> street patterns and traffic flow
> accessibility of the sites by nonresidents
> proximity to any public area that attracts people who do not live there
> distance to other homes (closeness can be a plus, especially for older people who do not want to be isolated in case they have unexpected problems)
> built-in security systems such as guards, roving patrols, security gates, electronic security devices, etc.
> street and pathway lighting systems
> visual exposure to other homes so that monitoring by neighbors is easier to maintain
> proximity of nearest fire hydrant and in some cases fire stations
> proximity of nearest medical services (particularly for those with health problems or the elderly)

*Protection of property values and resale potential.* Financial security is the second important element in this package. The value of the entire project is affected by the quality of the housing designs, protective covenants and the way that owners maintain their homes. Individual homesites are immediately affected by the following:

> value of the adjacent homes
> condition of adjacent homes
> relative values of the homesites as measured by the other factors

When making site presentations, the sales representatives at Hidden Valley can emphasize the relative merits of specific locations in terms of their surroundings. Where a larger home has been constructed, there will be a residual value to the adjacent lots. Where there are protected areas such as open space and landscaped common areas that border particular homesites, the resale values will definitely be enhanced for these properties. Those homesites that are for sale in the first phase where sales and construction have removed the unknowns can be demonstrated as having the advantage of early existing values on which to build versus the more expensive and, as yet, unreleased sections.

*Social security: Neighbors and lifestyles.* A subtle but important facet of value indexing homesites is the matter of people matching and lifestyle compatibility. When you have totally contrasting lifestyles in immediate proximity, you can lessen desirability for one or more adjacent neighbors. People who have children often want to be next door to others with children so they will have playmates and can share common interests. Older people often want peace and quiet. They may be threatened if they live where children are active and noisy. Those who live alone, particularly single women, will feel more secure if they have other singles nearby with whom they can share interests and social needs.

Prior to commencing sales at Hidden Valley, identify those homesites that will appeal to specific social profiles. The quiet cul-de-sac removed from play areas may be a logical place to direct the couples over-50 who have raised their children and are seeking a more leisurely lifestyle. Homes next to the active areas are logical locations for families with children.

Once sales commence, the representatives index the profiles of the purchasers and add an element of knowledge that will help them to match social values for different groups. This never involves a discussion of race, creed, politics or personalities. It focuses on the demographics of family size, ages of children, social interests, professions and cultural activities.

10. *Identity factors: Prestige, self-image and position.* Research and personal experience have shown that self-image or personal identity is one of the strongest motivating factors in the home-buying decision. People tend to purchase those properties that enhance their personal images. With some profiles this is a major consideration. The prestige buyer wants a homesite and a home that makes a strong statement about the owner. There are those who will pay more to live on corners or in highly visible locations where everyone entering the community will see their homes.

Homesites should be rated for prestige and identity values. Prominent locations will appeal to the social needs of the prestige purchaser while the hidden sites will draw those who are more reclusive in nature. Even elevation types will influence this social factor. At Hidden Valley only a few locations will accommodate the colonial home with pillars. Too many on a street would adversely impact the streetscape. This type of exterior needs to be placed on those sites which can be seen from a distance and where they will not overdominate adjacent homes.

Identity valuing is more than just looking for the obvious ego badge purchaser. It is also recognizing how to match the identity needs of every potential prospect from the creative romantic to the people who are trying to keep up with the proverbial Jones family.

11. *The convenience factors: Comfort, use and proximity.* Most people want to live their lives with as little inconvenience as possible. As they can afford to move up the ladder of life, they will seek environments that are more comfortable, less trouble and more convenient to the support services they need to maintain their lifestyle. In the value indexing of homesites, that includes:

> distance to amenities
> ease of ingress to and egress from the site
> available parking for your cars and those of your guests
> proximity to convenience shopping (especially for elderly people)
> access to public transportation or internal shuttle services
> for families with children, distance to school bus stops
> proximity of mailboxes
> amount of property to be maintained
> availability of management services

12. *The romance elements: Individuality, beauty, self-expression, recreation and personal interests.* Finally, there are the personal-use factors that directly relate to individual lifestyles. These are referred to as the romance elements. These take into consideration the special and romantic ways that people like to personalize their homes and homesites. For example, some people love to garden and maintain beautifully landscaped yards. Others want to have swimming pools and private cabañas where they can relax and entertain friends. There are special needs for pets like dogs and in some communities, larger animals like horses. Every homesite can be studied and value indexed for potential personalization. Here are a few of the more obvious:

> sites that will accomodate swimming pools
> sites that have room for dog runs, fenced yards, etc.
> places to build play areas, tree houses, hobby rooms
> areas that permit the green thumbs to practice their gardening arts
> sites large enough to permit expansion of bonus rooms as the family
>   grows and needs change
> environments that appeal to artistic interests such as painting, writing
>   and collecting

By looking at each homesite with a creative viewpoint, you can often find unique points of value that will help your sales representatives match individual buyer needs to the special advantages of one site rather than another. The more skilled they are in validating the one-of-a-kind sales message with each prospect, the more sales will be made. Urgency is generated by creating desire for a property and establishing that it has unique benefits. Fear of losing a particular property at today's price is very often the precipitating force that produces the sale.

## Value Points Will Be Determined By the Environment

Hidden Valley, in the rolling hills and verdant landscape of Pennsylvania, has a much greater variety of choices and value points than would a flat, treeless setting in Phoenix, Arizona! You cannot create differences that do not exist. However, whether desert land in Arizona, wheat plains in Kansas or seashores in California, valid and important characteristics for each homesite in a given community merit value indexing and planned demonstrations. Failure to prepare a detailed checklist of these perceived value differences will lessen the opportunity to create optimum involvement and genuine urgency to act.

## Condominiums and Attached Housing Have Some Special Value Considerations

Condominiums, townhomes, and mixed-use communities have some special value considerations. The sizes of individual parcels of real estate are seldom important or valid differences. Instead, more accent is on such things as enjoyment of amenities, distances to parking, social relationships and views. Security and privacy surface as the two most important elements that deserve special attention. In high-rise buildings, concerns for being on levels that provide easy exit from the buildings may affect some buyers, while prestige penthouse vistas will appeal to others. There tends to be less individuality of design in such housing environments, which necessitates more emphasis on the other distinguishing features. There is also the disadvantage of having a large number of units on the market at one time in a major multifamily community. Separating inventory into areas that have locational differences is usually sound strategy to permit control of the selection process. Examples:

- poolside
- lobby levels
- parkside
- lakeside
- city view
- mid-building
- vista levels
- meadow view

The objective is to bring the inventory under control and begin to isolate individual properties that match lifestyle and economic needs as early in the process as is reasonably possible. Failure to accomplish that goal leads to delayed action—and lost sales.

## Summary

The best strategy for selling every homesite or condominium you offer is to be certain that the unique benefits and distinguishing features created by the physical properties of the locations are evaluated, rated and indexed for effective use in the one-on-one presentations to prospective buyers. The ideal way to achieve that objective is to physically inspect every location and study it from the perspective of the profiled prospects. The next step is to document the differences, and role-play with others to sharpen your skills in translating these one-of-a-kind values. When people are not taking the properties away from you or you have some sites that just do not seem to win the customer's favorable attention, it is time to reevaluate the differences and rehearse the presentation points!

## PREPARE FLOOR PLAN AND MODEL DEMONSTRATION GUIDELINES

Each floor plan or model featured in the builder's portfolio deserves to be presented in a professional manner that accents its features and benefits in ways that create maximum interest for prospective owners. If you are in a preconstruction mode and working from blueprints, salespeople will be most effective if they have full-sized (preferably key-lined and colored) floor plans that can be dramatized with creative presentations. Since only a small percentage of people can read a two-dimensional floor plan and picture the third dimension, it rests with salespeople to help them visualize the completed design. Our research proves that salespeople who follow well-organized demonstration procedures outperform those who let prospects inspect and judge housing merits on their own.

To assist sales agents, the following steps should be followed:

1. Profile the typical prospects for whom each plan has been designed. Describe lifestyles, motivations and areas of interest in the design concept that merit special attention.
2. Identify the living benefits of each plan. This means visualizing how future owners would live in the homes and the features of greatest value relative to zones, traffic patterns, privacy, romance, convenience and security.
3. Review all aspects of architectural styling, both exterior and interior. Relate to prospect self-image and lifestyles. Incorporate architect's or designer's comments as appropriate to reinforce value statements. Interpret streetscapes and neighborhood characteristics defined by the architectural treatments.
4. Provide each salesperson with a complete specifications sheet for each design. Identify features that are either exclusive or noteworthy in your price range when compared to competitive products.
5. List all options, upgrades and approved choices for each plan. Review their values and strategies for introducing them to prospects.
6. Once models are available for demonstration, establish a demonstration plan incorporating the above objectives in a physical presentation of each home. Establish body-positioning guidelines so that property is always shown to visual advantage.

**FIGURE 7.4   Lot Rating Chart**

| Lot number | Size | Views | Build-ability | Privacy | Amenities | Security | Prestige | Trees | Total points |
|------------|------|-------|---------------|---------|-----------|----------|----------|-------|--------------|
|            |      |       |               |         |           |          |          |       |              |
|            |      |       |               |         |           |          |          |       |              |
|            |      |       |               |         |           |          |          |       |              |
|            |      |       |               |         |           |          |          |       |              |
|            |      |       |               |         |           |          |          |       |              |
|            |      |       |               |         |           |          |          |       |              |
|            |      |       |               |         |           |          |          |       |              |
|            |      |       |               |         |           |          |          |       |              |
|            |      |       |               |         |           |          |          |       |              |
|            |      |       |               |         |           |          |          |       |              |
|            |      |       |               |         |           |          |          |       |              |
|            |      |       |               |         |           |          |          |       |              |
|            |      |       |               |         |           |          |          |       |              |
|            |      |       |               |         |           |          |          |       |              |
|            |      |       |               |         |           |          |          |       |              |

NOTE: 0 = Average or base site for each amenity. The scale is then 1 to 10 above or below a zero. A dollar value to the adjusted levels or percentage value to dollars should then be established for the 1 to 10 rating. For example, if each one point above or below represented one percent of the lot value and the lot was priced at $6,000, then every point would be worth $60. Points should be rated according to the importance of that particular item to the salability of the site. The total on the far right represents the balance between pluses and minuses above and below the base lot. The first lot selected for that group should be as near as possible to being the average lot with no pluses or minuses in reference to the eight rated elements.

---

**FIGURE 7.5   Special Features Literature**

## WHAT MAKES A SIGNATURE HOME SPECIAL?

### IS PRICE PER SQUARE FOOT A GOOD CRITERION FOR BUYING A NEW HOME?

Many people compare one builder to another by dividing the sales price by the estimated square footage of the house. We feel this would be like buying your next new car by the cost per pound. You may find that rather silly, but isn't that what most buyers do when comparing the value of homes to each other? If the lowest price per square foot is your sole criterion for determining which home you purchase, you may not purchase a Signature Home. Although we are very competitive with other builders on a cost per square foot basis, the quality of a new home can not be judged solely as a cost per square foot. A home and neighborhood must be judged by the features, design, materials and the quality of construction that are provided relative to the price per square foot. That is where we are set apart from out competition and where you should analyze the value to cost ratio. If you are still thinking of shopping on only cost per square foot basis you need to varify the dimensions as quoted from outside wall to outside wall, or inside wall to inside wall. This simple calculation can mean as much as a 30 to 50 square foot difference per some floor plans.

### WHAT DO YOU LOOK FOR ON THE OUTSIDE OF A SIGNATURE HOME?

As you approach a Signature Home you will first notice the neighborhood in which it is located. We provide a master planned community of separate neighborhoods designed to enhance value with compatible architectural home styles, sizes and prices. No matter what your investment may be, shouldn't your neighborhood rate a distinctive entry?

Over forty thousand dollars have been invested in the entry to your new Signature Home neighborhood. Professionally designed graphics, landscaping, sprinkler systems and lighting, as well as a custom designed bridge, sets the proper tone for your guests when they visit you in your new Signature Home. You've worked hard to buy a new home, shouldn't you get a quality neighborhood with your quality home?

Over 27 acres of Beacon Hill are being preserved with open spaces for parks, stocked lakes, walks and picnic areas. Over 7000 Tulip and Daffodil bulbs will spring to life each year in your neighborhood. One hundred and eighty seven trees have been planted in the open areas and along Beacon Hill road as it winds into each neighborhood. In addition, several hundred trees have and will be preserved on the property. When you choose to resell your home, don't you think your home will command a higher value or sell quicker than those homes located in neighborhoods where little or no investment was made by the builder?

Architectural styling in fashion with many old quality neighborhoods are featured on Signature Homes. Front porches with brick edges (2 story home), entry doors with sidelites, narrow New England lap siding, turned porch posts, cedar trim, dental molding, shutters and heavy dimensional shingle roofs. In addition, every effort is made to keep fresh pastel colors on all homes with no similar color or design next to, or across the street from each other. Finally, all Signature Homes come with baked enamel guttering and down spouts eliminating mud splashing and water shooting around our homes.

5318 Pembrook    -    Wichita, KS 67220    -    316-682-5002

---

**FIGURE 7.5   Special Features Literature (continued)**

---

**WILL THE COURTS AT BEACON HILL HAVE THE TYPICAL HODGE-PODGE OF MAIL BOXES, OR UGLY GANG BOXES IN SOMEONES YARD?**

No, it won't.  A New England style post office has been built in the entry to your neighborhood.  You can pick-up your mail and oversized parcels inside, out of the weather.  Your mail is protected by secure, locked boxes conveniently located on your way into or out of the neighborhood.  You can also keep up on the neighborhood news with the bulletin board located in the post office.

**A SIGNATURE HOME FOUNDATION IS BUILT FOR A LIFE TIME.**

We pay particular attention to the foundation a Signature Home is built on.  Unlike most builders, we use drain tiles, both inside and outside the foundation footings to assure water will be kept away from our homes.  Our foundations contain high strength 3500 PSI concrete and can have up to 2240 lineal feet of steel rebar.  The amount of rebar will depend upon the size of your foundation.  As an example, 2240 lineal feet of steel consists of 112 pieces of 20 foot rebar, 77 pieces of 8 foot rebar and 22 pieces of 4 foot rebar.

Also study the concrete patio areas around a Signature Home to those of other new homes.  Ours are large and usable but they are also built with rebar as are our walks and garage floors.  Our entry walks to our front doors are wide and curving.  They are not the usual narrow bowling alley style walks provided to front doors by other builders.

Signature Homes is one of the few, if not the only East side builders putting rebar in our walks, patios and garage floors.  We felt this was necessary due to the clay soil East Wichita has and the amount of cracking and breaking we found in the competitions patios, garage floors and walks.  The amount of rebar we put in our homes costs more and so does the labor to install it, but don't you want your foundation walls, patios and walks to last?

**WHAT ABOUT ENERGY CONSIDERATIONS?**

Every Signature Home built qualifies as a THERMAL CRAFTED HOME (TM) by Owens Corning.  Before you buy you will get a computer assisted state-of-the-art design study.  This study was developed by Owens Corning Fiberglas and will tell you the cost of heating and cooling your new home per year, taking into consideration factors such as home design, lot selection and family size.

Not only do we insulate the walls and ceiling with high quality Owens Corning Fiberglas, but we also fur-out and insulate your unfinished basement walls.  We can show you that insulating basement walls will save you in excess of $200 a year in heating and cooling bills.  It costs more to do initially, but the savings provided down the road will make it a plus to your monthly budget.

Signature Homes are sheathed with a 7/16th potlatch oxboard and reduces drafts and cold walls, which are common in less insulated homes.  Many other builders either use paper sheathing or styro-foam boxing.  The styro-foam provides an uneven wall to nail siding  and has less structural strength.  In addition the insulating values of the styro-foam is negated when a hole is punched in it, which always happens when siding is installed.  The oxboard sheathing provides an exrtremely tight exterior shell to the home, reducing drafts and heat loss while providing structural strength.  In addition, R-13 insulting batts are used in the wall cavity, thus giving your home an "R" value of at least 17.  The ceiling areas are well insulated with R -30 insulating batts.  All exterior penetrations into a Signature Homes' thermal envelope and the cracks between the framing sill plate, door and window openings are filled with a foam sealant, which further eliminates drafts and will save you dollars on heating and cooling bills.

---

**FIGURE 7.5   Special Features Literature (continued)**

---

Every Signature Home is built with a Coleman Company 70% furnace and a 9.0 SEER air conditioner. The highest efficient (91%) furnace and air conditioner built in the industry is also available to all Signature buyers at a slight additional cost. The Coleman Company is a leader in the heating and cooling industry and have the quality we expect and what we feel our buyers deserve in the heating and cooling area.

### COMPARE WINDOWS...WHAT PRODUCT AND DESIGN IS BEST FOR YOUR NEW HOME?

We found aluminum windows a definate design and maintenance plus for our buyers. The windows found in all Signature Homes were chosen to obtain the best architectural look, performance and long term maintenance freedom that is available in the market today. The space age "A-Them" thermal barrier system minimizes heat flow and condensation on the frame. This is the first aluminum window that provides the warmth of wood. A "cold test" made by the manufacturer placed a piece of dry ice at 110 degrees below zero piled on the outside section of our window and a conventional metal window. In five minutes the conventional window section is solidly frosted its entire length, inside and out. Our window frosted only as far as the thermal barrier. The inside stayed warm and frost free. This window, used by Signature Homes, can save up to 48% heating costs over standard double glazed products. A problem with wood windows is they will swell and shrink as temperatures change, causing cosmetic damage to the paint and air infiltration. Our aluminum windows won't swell or shrink due to their design. This creates a maintenance free window, no painting, no hassel and minimum heat loss.

We feel the amount of glass area compared to floor area is an important design feature in our homes. We provide an airy, bright and open feeling in our homes due to the generous amount of window space we include. Compare our window to floor area to any of our competition in a similar price range. We take pride in providing our home buyers with the high ratio of window area. Also the large amount of operable windows allows you to have greater ventilation possibilities than many other new homes in our market. During nice days you can air out your home plus, save on air conditioning costs. Fixed glass windows are cheaper, but are they the most practical and comfortable for you?

### EXTERIOR DOORS ARE ATTRACTIVE AND MAINTENANCE FREE.

The impressions and maintenance of exterior doors and garage doors after one or two years are going to be the same as when you first moved into your home, because we took the time to research and find the most attractive and maintenance free doors and garage doors for our buyers.

Our entry doors are metal, insulation filled, and sealed with magnetic weather stripping. The weather stripping is similar to that found around your refrigerator door. Most front entries of our homes are also covered, protecting you from the elements. We are the only builder that standardly offers you decorative glass sidelites around your door. We think they look better from the front as well as providing nice lighting to your entry.

The garage door is a metal, raised panel sectional. The advantage of metal over wood is that the metal door won't rot out and sag like a typical wood door will do after a few years. We find this to be a substantial savings to our buyer and one they will appreciate down the road.

---

**FIGURE 7.5   Special Features Literature (continued)**

---

### IN A SIGNATURE HOME, GET A FINISHED GARAGE.

Many other builders simply sheetrock the warm walls to the house (required by code) but do not finish anything else. Our garages are completely sheetrocked, taped and painted, plus, we prewire for your garage door opener. Why don't all builders finish the garage? Because it cost $400 to $500 more to do. Our finished garages are just another hidden value you'll find in a Signature Home.

### ARE ALL BUILDER ALLOWANCES CREATED EQUAL?

The answer is a resounding.....NO....Many builders include such small allowances in their homes that you will have to spend several hundred dollars more to get a decent quality of decorator items or at least the quality that you saw in the models. All floor covers, lighting, tile and counter tops shown in the model homes can be used in your new home without spending a dime more. We want to offer you a good grade of decorator materials that you will be proud to have in your new home.

### IT IS HARD TO FIND A BETTER APPLIANCE PACKAGE.

Compare the total cost of our Whirlpool appliances at any appliance store in town to the cost of the appliances other builders offer. We think you will find that this package is of top quality and represents a higher cost. All warranties on these appliance products are, of course, passed through to our home buyers.

### EVERY SIGNATURE HOME FEATURES TWO EATING AREAS.

The Signature Home design, features two separate eating areas, formal and informal. We believe we are the only builder in our price range that offers such a feature throughout our product line. Years from now, this single item will be a great plus when you decide to resell your home.

### SOME THINGS TO LOOK FOR IN OUR KITCHENS.

Please note the quality of the oak cabinets in our kitchens. Our cabinets can be stained in a variety of stain colors because they are custom built for your home in Wichita. All drawers are supported by double glides, which gives you more support and smoother operation.

Your kitchen sink is stainless steel with a spray attachment. The sink offers a smaller rinse off and disposal area along with a large bowl that is perfect for bigger pots and pans.

Note how the counter top extends into the window area. In most plans it will end behind the sink. We believe this feature gives a clean expensive look to the kitchen and makes cleanup easier when water spills into the area behind the sink. Your Signature Home comes with a ceramic tile back splash and a laminated counter top which is a superior performer in the kitchen area. This surface is not difficult to clean, and best of all, it comes in such a vast range of colors, that there isn't a future wallpaper, paint or drape that can't be matched or enhanced.

All Signature Homes come pre-plumbed with an ice maker rough-in, compared to our competition which charges $25 to $30, and considers this as an option. This rough-in is a recessed box for easy connection and prevents the valve from pushing the refrigerator into the kitchen traffic area.

---

**FIGURE 7.5   Special Features Literature (continued)**

---

Note the lighting in our kitchens. We believe that kitchen lighting is extremely critical and demands more than a single light over the sink, which most builders provide. Count the number and types of light fixtures. We want you to compare ours to anyone elses, even in much higher priced homes. For every extra fixture we have included, you can expect to pay at least $35 per fixture in other builders homes. Additionally, almost all of our kitchens offer either a full height cabinet or a traditional pantry with standard doors and shelving. We want to provide the most storage possible, because we know our home buyers need the storage space in their kitchens.

**THE BATHROOM SUITE IS OUR PRIDE AND JOY.**

All our master bathrooms feature a generous use of mirrors, large counter tops and double lavatories. The Signature Home exclusive is also our use of separate tubs and showers, which are featured in all our master baths with the exception of the Thomas model. We felt this was a crucial area for our buyers as so many of you both work and need the separate bath areas. Most bath areas offer conveniently located linen closets as well as large closets with both double and single rods and shelf spaces. Again, note the generous use of lights over the tubs and sinks. Plenty of natural light is also provided from oversized windows that brighten the bath area. We doubt that you can find master baths the size of a Signature Home in any of our competitors homes at our prices.

**COMPARE OUR FIREPLACES.**

Standard in every Signature Home you will find a fireplace with glass doors, gas log lighters and outside combustion air intakes. In most other new homes offered in this price range, you would pay more for the extras. In addition, we offer four different customized fireplace fronts and mantels. These fronts have been designed exclusively for your Signature Home. When you consider the variety of materials and combination of fronts offered with our fireplaces, your fireplace will become a special one of a kind focal point of each room. We think you'll agree, a Signature Home fireplace is elegant looking enough to be in a home that costs two or three times more than our homes.

**HOW DO I KNOW SIGNATURE HOMES WILL DELIVER THE HOME THEY PROMISE?**

This question represents the age old question every new home buyer asks. When you select a Signature Home, you will become a part of the CUSTOM ONE HOMEBUYER'S ASSURANCE PLAN, which is a national program with headquarters located in Minneapolis, Minnesota. Their CUSTOM ONE SEAL is awarded only to a selected few qualified builders nationally. This seal is to the homebuilding industry, what a five star rating is to a fine hotel or restaurant.

The Custom One system provides builders and their sales representatives a very credible demonstration of their commitment and achievements regarding customer service and satisfaction. We have put our system in writing for our buyers for each evaluation and comprehension of the home delivery process. We feel this unique, integrated delivery system is designed to assure maximum satisfaction to our home buyers. Our buyers will be in direct contact with a Custom One representative to monitor buyer satisfaction.

In addition to the Custom One program we will do a walk through inspection prior to the closing of the home, and will follow-up with you at intervals of one week, 5 months and 11 months after you have moved in. We want to monitor your warranty service work at those intervals plus provide service request forms when things come up between the intervals.

---

**FIGURE 7.5   Special Features Literature (concluded)**

---

Signature Homes has purchased the services of Quality Specialists to assure you fast, quality response to your service needs. Most builders try to get their subcontractors back to finish the "call back" service requests. This is normally not convenient for the home owner to schedule and it usually requires weeks of waiting for service. Our arrangement with Quality Specialists requires that we are in contact with you 48 hours after your written requests. We are proud of our homes and gladly stand behind them. In fact we've located our Corporate Office in the community so that we can be easily accessible to our home owners needs.

**YOUR SIGNATURE HOME CARRIES A 10 YR INSURED STRUCTURAL WARRANTY.**

Each new home built by Signature Homes carries not only a one year limited warranty, but also a 10 year insured structural warranty. Not all builders are approved for this type of Homebuyers Warranty Program. Each year we are screened in areas of technical competence, financial soundness and customer satisfaction to remain in this program. We want you to be sure to discuss the warranty of your home with the builder you choose, as every home should receive a written warranty. We also feel confident you will find our warranty program superior to our competitors.

**WEIGH THE ADVANTAGES OF LIVING IN A SIGNATURE HOME.**

We challenge you to put our homes against any of the competition in our price range. We are confident you will find a Signature Home not only of top quality, but also innovative in design, competitive in price and equipped with the plusses every buyer dreams of getting with their new home. With a Signature Home you will receive the quality and extras that will set our standards and market value ahead of the competition. We have built not only the dreams of our buyers, but also the neighborhood they thought would only come with a resale home in an established area. The Courts at Beacon Hill, built by Signature Homes. A Critchfield Incorporated neighborhood.

---

# EDUCATE AND MOTIVATE SALESPEOPLE TO DEMONSTRATE YOUR HOMES

Many sales agents resist the demonstration process. This is particularly true when builders provide a sales center that includes decorated models where prospects are encouraged to look on their own. While every customer does not need an escort through all of the models, salespeople should at least make an effort to control the initial introduction to the homes and set the stage for possible value-building demonstrations. The assumptive attitude should be the fundamental approach in all selling situations. By assuming that customers want your information, more of them will accept the opportunity to see the property with you. Phrases like: ''Permit me to

---

**FIGURE 7.6   Checklist for Demonstrating a New Home**

General features
- [ ] Designs/floor plans
- [ ] Architecture
- [ ] Energy-conservation construction elements
- [ ] Foundations
- [ ] Roofs
- [ ] Siding/masonry
- [ ] Exterior finish

Entry area
- [ ] Entry flooring (when applicable)
- [ ] Definition of space
- [ ] Guest closet/coat closet
- [ ] Lighting fixture

Living room
- [ ] Location advantages
- [ ] Dimensions (when appropriate)
- [ ] Furniture placement alternatives
- [ ] Paneling/wall treatments
- [ ] Sound engineering systems
- [ ] Functional use for entertaining
- [ ] Windows and window treatments
- [ ] Heating and air-conditioning system
- [ ] Special effects (such as vaulted ceilings, step-down areas, conversation pits, fireplaces)
- [ ] Indoor-outdoor relationships
- [ ] Decorating alternatives
- [ ] Other items

Dining room or dining areas
- [ ] Functional relationship to kitchen and entertaining areas
- [ ] Dimensions (when appropriate)
- [ ] Dining room table placement and alternatives
- [ ] Buffet serving area
- [ ] Lighting fixtures (when applicable)
- [ ] Wall treatments
- [ ] Indoor-outdoor relationships
- [ ] Windows/patio doors (when appropriate)
- [ ] Other items

Kitchen
- [ ] Locational advantages (accessibility for grocery delivery)
- [ ] Dimensions (when appropriate)
- [ ] Cabinet space and extra storage areas
- [ ] Countertop space/finish
- [ ] Appliances
  - [ ] Range

Kitchen (continued)
  - [ ] Oven
  - [ ] Dishwasher
  - [ ] Garbage disposal
  - [ ] Refrigerator
  - [ ] Other appliances
- [ ] Lighting fixtures (when appropriate)
- [ ] Electrical outlets
- [ ] Serving functions
- [ ] Food preparation functions
- [ ] Indoor-outdoor relationships
- [ ] Visual screening from formal areas
- [ ] Conversational opportunity with family in other areas of home
- [ ] Wall treatment(s) (application to care and maintenance)
- [ ] Floor covering(s)
- [ ] Windows, pass-throughs, doors (where applicable)
  Other items

Family room or area
- [ ] Location advantages
- [ ] Dimensions (when appropriate)
- [ ] Furniture orientation
- [ ] Functional use of room
- [ ] Fireplace (when applicable)
- [ ] Wall finishes
- [ ] Flooring or floor covering
- [ ] Patio doors (ingress, egress)
- [ ] Lighting fixtures (where appropriate)
- [ ] Sound controls (particularly entertaining and children's activities related to rest of the home)
- [ ] Special effects (beams, vaults, lofts, step-downs, conversation pits)

Bathrooms
- [ ] Locations (accessibility, privacy)
- [ ] Bathroom fixtures
- [ ] Lighting fixtures
- [ ] Cabinetry/storage areas
- [ ] Counter surfaces
- [ ] Wall treatments
- [ ] Safety devices
- [ ] Plumbing fixtures
- [ ] Mirrors
- [ ] Decorating alternatives
- [ ] Other items

---

**FIGURE 7.6   Checklist for Demonstrating a New Home (concluded)**

Master bedroom suite (other bedrooms as necessary)
- [ ] Location (privacy, accessibility to service)
- [ ] Dimensions (when appropriate)
- [ ] Bed placement alternatives
- [ ] Dressers
- [ ] Wall treatment(s)
- [ ] Flooring or floor covering
- [ ] Lighting fixtures (when appropriate)
- [ ] Indoor-outdoor relationships
- [ ] Mirrors
- [ ] Closets (demonstrate space when a positive)
- [ ] Accessibility to bath and dressing areas
- [ ] Windows
- [ ] Doors, patios, decks (as appropriate)
- [ ] Other items

Service area(s)
- [ ] Locational advantages

Service area(s) (continued)
- [ ] Washer-dryer (space)
- [ ] Plumbing outlets
- [ ] Floor treatment (safety, care, maintenance)
- [ ] Sound-conditioning factors
- [ ] Water heater
- [ ] Furnace
- [ ] Air conditioning
- [ ] Cabinets and storage
- [ ] Other items

Other areas of demonstration as applicable
- [ ] Basements (lower levels)
- [ ] Garages, carports
- [ ] Outdoor storage facilities
- [ ] Decks, patios, balconies, porches
- [ ] Attic storage (access)
- [ ] Expandable areas of the home
- [ ] Special-purpose or multipurpose rooms

---

point out some of the exclusive features that distinguish our homes and to explain the optional features that allow you to personalize them to your tastes, then you can browse on your own . . .'' help to control the demonstration process. Always remember that people who inspect new homes without escort seldom see everything important for creating maximum perceptions of values. The benefits of demonstration outweigh the risks of offending a few people who may not want to talk to salespeople. The additional time invested with the customers allows the representatives to strengthen relationships and discover the motivations that may trigger sales.

## PREPARE SALES PRESENTATION GUIDES

The best-organized marketing programs include written sales presentation guidelines with suggested topics to be covered at each station of involvement. Rather than trust individual sales representatives to develop their own, many sales coaches create road maps or detailed checklists to assist the staff in making the most effective use of the exhibits, amenities, models and homesites. These presentation guides are prepared with the following objectives in mind:

1. List the stations or exhibits to be used during the natural flow of the presentation with a recommended sequence for use with most prospects.

2. Identify primary topics to be discussed at each location or exhibit point.
3. Establish value points to be emphasized at each station and rate them in order of importance so that first things will always be covered first if possible.
4. List qualifying questions or topics to be discussed that will uncover the motivations, abilities and needs of prospective buyers.
5. Refine the guide for flexibility to meet the needs of individual buyers with variances based on profiles and interests.

### Professionally Prepared Videotape or Slide Presentations

Use of professionally prepared videotapes and audio-visual multimedia slide presentations has become increasingly popular over the last few years. Larger developments frequently incorporate them as part of the basic on-site sales office package. They have special value when the messages to be communicated are difficult for salespeople to present without dramatic visual aids. For example, at the beginning of a new master-planned community, when everyone is inspecting the site at a stage when literally nothing is there to see yet, dream-painting scenarios graphically pictured in a slide or video production help to compensate for lack of actual amenities to show your prospects. Carefully scripted and produced, these presentations also assure that every customer hears and sees the messages in the same professionally delivered manner. In a high-traffic community, they serve as excellent holding devices to keep people involved while preconditioning them for the sales representatives.

Another practical use of videotapess is the reinforcing value they have when you allow customers and buyers to take copies home to review on their own VCRs. Resort marketers have taken advantage of this superior marketing tool more than those operating in primary housing areas. Prospects frequently receive videotapes in the mail after visiting recreation centers, with messages attached asking them to enjoy the memory—with the hope they will soon return and become owners of one of the condos or homes. A few progressive marketers in primary housing environments have take a cue from the promoters of recreational real estate.

Since today's home buyers are fairly sophisticated and conditioned to video screens where millions are spent to influence their buying decisions, it is essential to invest in quality productions rather than risk looking like amateurs in a world of pros. If you decide not to invest in a first-class video with a professional voice, we recommend that you use a slide carousel, which will not be judged in the same league as video presentations. If you elect to remain with a low-budget production, make sure it is one that will be credible and not detract from the value statements your sales staff are attempting to reinforce. In most markets, there are companies that specialize in audio-visual productions, and it is recommended that you personally preview examples of their work before employing any particular agency.

**FIGURE 7.7  Sales Presentation Guide**

**Community:** Minnesota Valley Country Club Condominiums        **Date** 7-6-89

| Station | Major Topic | Key Value Points | Qualifiers |
|---|---|---|---|
| ENTRY LOBBY first level | GREETING AND INTRODUCTION | Welcome<br><br>This is our first building in the new Minnesota Valley C.C.<br><br>54 private residences with just six homes in each separate wing level<br><br>All of the condominiums have views of either the golf course or choice river bluffs and valley | "Is this your first visit?"<br><br>"Are you familiar with our country club?"<br><br>"What other condominium communities have you visited?" |
| ENTRY LOBBY aerial map | LOCATION STORY | Protected environment just minutes from the Edina—Bloomington area<br><br>Moments from Hwy. 494 with access to major employment centers, airport and shopping<br><br>Established area with secure real estate values . . . and isolated by the natural boundaries of the golf course and river bluffs | "Where do you presently live?"<br><br>"Do you play golf?"<br><br>"Where do you commute for employment?<br><br>"What other recreational interests do you enjoy?" |
| ENTRY LOBBY near sitting area | DEVELOPER STORY establish history and credibility | Pemtom has 25 years of building successful condominium and common interest communities in twin cities<br><br>Pemtom introduced first condominiums to area and has won national recognition for design and performance<br><br>This is the newest community—a joint venture with a major union pension trust fund | "Have you visited other Pemtom communities?" |

**FIGURE 7.7   Sales Presentation Guide (continued)**

| | | | |
|---|---|---|---|
| **Community:** Minnesota Valley Country Club Condominiums | | | **Date** 7-6-89 |
| *Station* | *Major Topic* | *Key Value Points* | *Qualifiers* |
| CENTRAL LOBBY<br>water fountain | BUILDING DESIGN<br>benefits of concept | Three levels—three private wings | "Are you familiar with the benefits of condominium living?" |
| | | Five neighbors in each private wing—like living on a cul-de-sac | |
| | | Central lobby and social areas on each floor—convenient access to each wing and to recreation areas | |
| | | Security system begins at entry with access only by residents' control | "How soon had you contemplated making a move to a new residence?" |
| | | Central mailboxes on main floor lobby convenient to the entry | |
| ELEVATOR TO<br>SECOND FLOOR | BUILDING DESIGN<br>benefits of lifestyle | Living here is like being on vacation every day! | "How many would be living in the home?" |
| | | Access to each floor by both elevator and large adjacent stairwells | |
| SECOND FLOOR<br>LOBBY AND<br>SOCIAL AREAS | BUILDING DESIGN<br>AND AMENITIES<br>view of golf course | Highly rated golf course . . . recently redesigned by Arnold Palmer | "How does our building compare with condominiums you have seen?" |
| | | Library and private reading areas | |
| | | Note the numerous places within the building that extend your living space | |
| FIRST MODEL<br>DESIGN<br>next to sales<br>office. | MODEL HOME<br>DESIGN<br>primary demonstration<br>of construction<br>benefits—features | Private recessed entry door and foyer | "What size home do you currently own?" |
| | | Spaciousness of the design | |
| | | Quality finish in details of design | "How long have you lived there?" |

**FIGURE 7.7   Sales Presentation Guide (continued)**

| Community: Minnesota Valley Country Club Condominiums | | | Date 7-6-89 |
|---|---|---|---|
| Station | Major Topic | Key Value Points | Qualifiers |
| FIRST MODEL kitchen and dining areas | KITCHEN DESIGN Pemtom features and design benefits | Sound engineering—with special floor-to-floor sound buffers<br><br>Cheerful lighting fixtures<br><br>Abundance of solid paneled cabinets<br><br>Quality appliances (demonstrate)<br><br>Open design allows you to communicate with guests while in the kitchen . . . yet it is visibly separated. | *"How does this design appeal to you?"*<br><br>Note:  Begin your trial interest questions to determine how the model and building fit into the criteria. |
| SUN ROOM IN FIRST MODEL | DESIGN BENEFITS Pemtom features and benefits | Value of the sun room, which is an exclusive Pemtom feature in each home<br><br>Demonstrate the Thermopane windows and the heavy insulated door treatment to patio deck<br><br>Accent the value of the outdoor sun deck | *"How does this compare to what you have seen?"* |
| MASTER SUITE baths and service area | DESIGN BENEFITS Pemtom features and benefits | Convenient service area with side-by-side washer and dryer<br><br>Bathroom fixtures and features<br><br>Privacy and views from master suites | *"How do you feel about this plan?"*<br><br>Note:  This is a decision point in the showing process. If not interested . . . or qualified . . . presentation can be politely terminated with a quick trip to sales office for literature.<br><br>If justified . . . presentation continues: |

**FIGURE 7.7   Sales Presentation Guide (continued)**

| Community: Minnesota Valley Country Club Condominiums | | Date 7-6-89 |
|---|---|---|
| Station | Major Topic | Key Value Points | Qualifiers |
| SALES OFFICE Next door to model. Go to site table. | MASTER PLAN OF THE COMMUNITY | Value of the location of this building:<br><br>  convenient to club house<br>  convenient to starting point for golfers<br><br>Emphasize view-orientations and access to recreation and pathways.<br><br>Reemphasize the protected environment. | "How is your time schedule today? Would you like more details and a complete tour of our building?" |
| SALES OFFICE AMENITIES DISPLAY WALL | THE COMPLETE LEISURE AMENITIES OF MINN. VALLEY C.C. | Six social areas throughout the building<br>Private owners' club room with kitchen and bar facilities<br>Large indoor all-season swimming pool<br>Men's and Women's saunas<br>Hobby room<br>Guest lodging facilities, etc. | "Have you ever belonged to a country club? When you live here you have our complete recreational and social facilities as part of your home!" |
| (elective) TO THIRD FLOOR LOBBY AND SOCIAL AREA | BUILDING DESIGN AND AMENITIES | Billiard table and playing area<br><br>Card-playing and social area<br><br>Emphasize the detailing and finish as you transit from one area to other. | "Do you play pool? Cards?" |
| (elective) TO MODEL(S) | MODELS AS NEEDED | Note:  Show only those models that meet interests of prospects and demonstrate as needed to build maximum perceived values. | |
| LOWER LEVEL RECREATION CENTER | BUILDING DESIGN AND AMENITIES | Easy access to social recreation area and to outdoor decks, paths.<br><br>History of Minnesota Valley C.C. | "Do you entertain very often?"<br><br>"Your guests will really enjoy our pool and club rooms!" . . . |

**FIGURE 7.7   Sales Presentation Guide (continued)**

**Community:** Minnesota Valley Country Club Condominiums    **Date** 7-6-89

| Station | Major Topic | Key Value Points | Qualifiers |
|---------|-------------|------------------|------------|
| LOWER LEVEL CLUB ROOM— SOCIAL AREA | BUILDING DESIGN AND AMENITIES | Spaciousness and elegance of the owners' club room<br><br>Complete kitchen and serving facilities<br><br>Charter-member wall and comments about the profile of the residents | "What plans have you made, if any, for the sale of your present home?"<br><br>"How do you feel about the quality of our recreation and social room?" |
| LOWER LEVEL SWIMMING POOL AND DECK AREA | BUILDING DESIGN AND AMENITIES | Year-round heated pool and "fun room"<br><br>Views you enjoy of the golf course area and outside patios while swimming and relaxing<br><br>Adjacent saunas, showers, etc. | "Do you (both) enjoy swimming?"<br><br>"Our owners tell us they appreciate having this beautiful pool so close to their condominium . . . and the fact that they do not have to go outside to have the benefit of the facilities!" |
| GARAGE AREA | BUILDING DESIGN AND AMENITIES | Private stalls—secured access for residents' cars<br><br>Car wash facility<br><br>Adjacent hobby room and direct access from garage for moving large equipment and supplies | "Do you have covered parking where you are now?"<br><br>"You will really appreciate not having to worry about starting cold engines and scraping ice when you have the benefit of this secure, underground garage!" |

**FIGURE 7.7  Sales Presentation Guide (concluded)**

| | Community: Minnesota Valley Country Club Condominiums | | Date 7-6-89 |
|---|---|---|---|
| Station | Major Topic | Key Value Points | Qualifiers |
| RETURN TO SALES OFFICE Counselling room | OWNERSHIP ALTERNATIVES Financing (if required) Financial analysis | It is easy to own one of our Minnesota Valley C.C. Condominiums<br><br>Financing/equity/etc.<br><br>Note: Prior to this point you must have selected a specific condominium site | *"How much of your savings (equity) have you anticipated investing?"*<br><br>*"What size initial investment would be comfortable for you?"*<br><br>*"How would this financing plan work for you?"* |
| | COMMUNITY SERVICES AND FEES | List of the services performed by the association<br><br>Budget breakdown of monthly amount per service item | Note: The closing and involvement questions must be tailored to the interests, abilities and needs of the specific prospective buyer.<br><br>This is the area where closing requires skill . . . and persistence. |

**FIGURE 7.8    Sales Brochures—Aids or Obstacles?**

## BROCHURES—SALES AIDS OR OBSTACLES?

New home brochures are an integral part of marketing campaigns for most new home sales organizations. They vary dramatically in size, format, content, quality and use. Most salespeople and marketers would agree they are helpful tools in the new home marketing process. However, views conflict on the value and use of these collateral support materials.

In our files at the Stone Institute, we have hundreds of brochures collected throughout the years from all parts of the United States and some foreign countries. We have participated in planning sessions when brochures were being designed for the communities and projects our clients developed. We have also interviewed numerous salespeople about their own feelings about the way brochures are designed and used. We will explore the concepts that seem to be most effective in new home brochure design and their application in sales environments.

## PRIMARY FUNCTIONS OF A BROCHURE

The brochure in new home marketing serves multiple purposes. These include the following:

- image statement for the community and builder
- on-site presentation guide to models and products
- silent sales aid that provides information a salesperson might not have the opportunity to communicate in a limited presentation
- sales-control piece that allows salespeople to hold the customers' attention
- follow-up piece for mail or delivery to prospects, either before or after visiting the site
- sales-reinforcement tool used as part of the package given to buyers at the time of signing the purchase agreement
- institutional marketing tool for favorably influencing lenders, investors, corporations and others
- prospect-generator when recipients show them to others or brochures are left in places where they can be picked up and perused

All of these uses are valid. Brochures that are well designed and efficiently distributed can be extremely valuable aids for marketing housing. On the other hand, we believe they can also have a negative influence on your marketing objectives if they are poorly designed and misused!

### The Brochure Versus the Sales Agent's Objectives

When a brochure is so complete that it answers all questions a prospect might raise, it has potentially eliminated the role of the sales representative. Any brochure quickly given to customers when they enter the sales office takes away from moments of control that could otherwise have been gained. The design and use of the brochure should always be done with a view to providing salespeople with a better opportunity to become involved with their prospects and to give them some measure of control over the sales process.

The typical on-site presentation includes giving the prospect a brochure shortly after arrival at the sales office. Most salespeople use the brochure as a crutch. When a copy is handed to the customer, it relieves the agent from having to explain the housing environment. It also satisfies the buyer's need to have something in hand to study when touring the property. A standard opening question for tract-sitters is: "Would you like a brochure?"

With a brochure in hand, the customer does not need the salesperson. Often, the immediate reaction is to open the pages of the brochure and begin reading the information—especially if a price list is included. The prospect may then indicate that he just wants to inspect the models and proceed in the direction of the show homes if they are evident.

You cannot sell if you cannot communicate! It takes time to qualify a prospect, provide controlled information in a logical sequence and break the ice so that a foundation of trust and confidence exists between you and the customer. If you lose the opportunity to perform these critical sales functions because you introduced the brochure prematurely, the entire objective of staffing the sales center has been lost!

*Control* is a primary objective of the sales process. Anything that causes you to lessen your ability to control the sequence of events has to be viewed as an obstacle to your fundamental sales function.

## WHAT SHOULD THE BROCHURE CONTAIN?

It is amazing how many different concepts can be expressed in the graphic arts interpretation of housing brochures. Many brochures have a simple, straightforward approach. The cover depicts the name of the community or builder with varying degrees of individuality. The inside cover most often has a brief description of the community or the history of the builder. Then come several pages of either inserts or affixed sheets that identify individual floor plans, features, site maps, options and prices. The fancier brochures have pages devoted to selling lifestyle benefits with photos of homes, recreational amenities and environmental scenes. Some of the brochures have formatted tab cuts that allow each insert to be easily identified. The back cover of the brochure frequently contains a general location map or institutional message. The most common size is some variation of the 8½ × 11 vertical notebook form.

Most of the elements contained in these brochures seem to be logical inclusions. They cover the basic facts about the project and the properties that buyers might want to know. However, from the position of the sales representatives who must use them, the majority of the brochures are poorly designed and inadequately organized. Much of the information provided to the consumer does not do justice to the homes or to those who created them. The size of the renderings and floor plans often decrease perceived values of the designs. Plot plans, feature lists, price lists and inventory data are potential negatives for the sales agent who is trying to influence and control the

**FIGURE 7.9   Display Center Guide**

# DISPLAY CENTER GUIDE

**The Orleans**
**Plan 9**
Classic 2-story with center foyer plan is displayed in our 4-bedroom version but also is available in a 3-bedroom plan, both with 2½ baths, sunken living room, dining room, large family room, and breakfast room bay.

**The Chateau**
**Plan 1**
Displayed as a 3-bedroom plan with den, this gracious ranch (also available in a basic 3-bedroom plan and a 4-bedroom version) has 2 full baths, sunken living room, kitchen, breakfast room bay and dining room. Note the luxury features available including sundeck and coffered ceilings.

**The Richleau**
**Plan 7**
This split foyer plan offers maximum space for your money on two exciting levels. Displayed as a 3-bedroom home with master bedroom lounge area, this home is available in a basic 3-bedroom plan and a 4-bedroom plan, each with 3 baths and indoor garden area.

**The Monte Carlo**
**Plan 11**
Spacious ranch style is displayed as a 3-bedroom plan with optional dining room (also available in 4-bedroom plan), 2 full baths, kitchen with separate breakfast room, family room and living room. Ask your Rolwes New Home Consultant about the many affordable, luxury additions available for this popular plan.

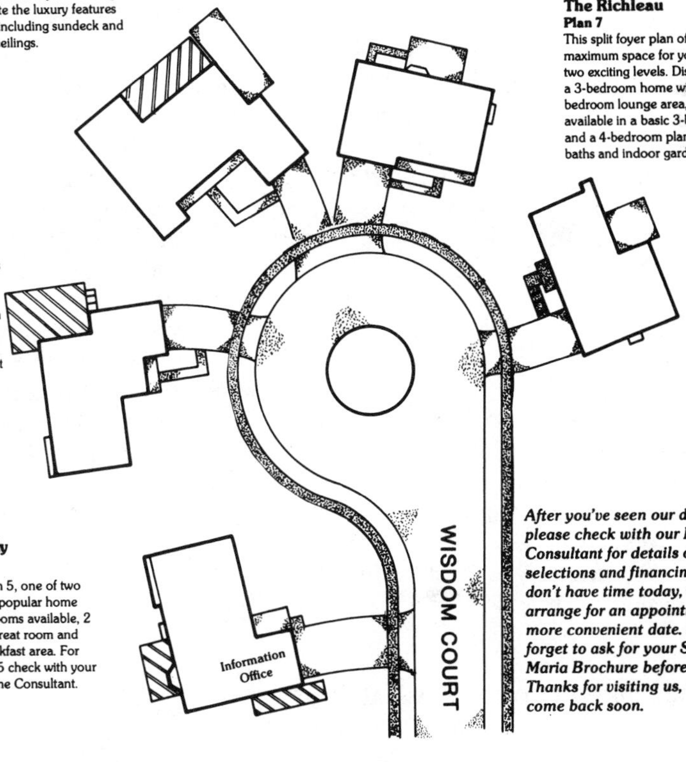

**The Burgandy**
**Plans 5 & 15**
On display is Plan 5, one of two variations of this popular home with 3 or 4 bedrooms available, 2 full baths, large great room and kitchen with breakfast area. For details on Plan 15 check with your Rolwes New Home Consultant.

Information Office

WISDOM COURT

*After you've seen our displays, please check with our New Home Consultant for details on prices, selections and financing. If you don't have time today, we can arrange for an appointment at a more convenient date. Don't forget to ask for your Sancta Maria Brochure before you leave. Thanks for visiting us, and please come back soon.*

# Sancta Maria

Display Center — 225-8544

**MOVE UP TO**
**ROLWES**

Decorative accessories, including all furnishings, special light fixtures and mirrors, are for display purposes only. Check with your Rolwes New Home Consultant for details on optional additions and prices.

sales process toward a positive decision. Let us examine the criteria for designing the format and content of a builder's brochure from the viewpoint of maximizing the salesperson's opportunities.

## Flexibility of Use Should Be an Objective

When a brochure is created, its adaptibility to the changing needs of the project should be a primary consideration. Floor-plan designs printed in the permanent brochure can become obstacles to sales when specific plans are sold out, changed or not available due to the phasing of the project. Suppose you have five floor plans featured in your community and one of them is no longer available for one of the above reasons. Every time a brochure is given to a prospect, the agent either has to explain the nonavailability of that plan, put an X or SOLD OUT stamp on it or wait to react to the buyer's request for information on the plan. The public always seems to be most interested in that which you do not have. There is absolutely no reason to ever have to defend your inventory of available homes against prepublished information you give to the buyers. The solution is simple: design insert sheets for all items which might change or which you do not want to emphasize at a particular time. This includes not only floor plans but also feature lists, options, site plans and price lists. Likewise, avoid using alphanumeric systems for identifying your floor plans. If the plans are lettered A, B, C, D, E, etc., and you sell out of plan C and/or do not want to build more, you are forced to explain that to a buyer who notices the absence of the C plan from the schedule. The same is true if you deal with plans numbered 1 to 5. Model names are far more appropriate. Some salespeople object to having brochures that they must assemble with the appropriate insert pieces, but, compared to the risks you take in providing information that works against your sales objectives, the time to assemble and control the brochures is a minor item. In many communities and building operations, the number of floor plans available is also an element of potential confusion and decreased urgency. Whenever more than five floor plans are featured, you should seriously consider personalizing the brochures to specifically meet the needs of each prospect rather than deluge with choices that will only complicate the selling process.

## Tiered or Tabbed Formats Are Not Practical

When brochure designers elect to have the floor-plan inserts (and the other support pages) indexed by different-length papers to achieve a tiered or tabbed effect, they create a special challenge for sales people as well as for prospects. Invariably, one or two of the inserts fails to get replaced properly when it is removed. This destroys any semblance of order that might have been originally conceived. It also forces the salesperson to include all inserts, even when they should be eliminated for reasons of product control. The prospect will take the brochure apart and usually not put it back the way it was delivered. This type of design serves no practical purpose and actually defeats the objective of coordinated inserts that meet today's needs.

## Brochures Within Brochures

One of the best ways of giving the prospects only the information they need when first inspecting the community, and at the same time being able to add what may be desirable from the salesperson's viewpoint, is to design brochures that can fit inside a master brochure.

A general introduction to the community that sells the benefits of the environment, the housing and the developer's credibility message can serve as the first element of the package. Individually folded inserts for each floor plan can serve as miniature presentation elements for the separate designs and be incorporated in the larger brochure at the discretion of the sales agent. This also has the effect of saving money for the marketing functions by not having to give out the deluxe brochure to everyone who comes to the sales office. This concept of using brochures within brochures is one of the better ways to meet multiple objectives and retain control over the literature that the prospects receive.

## Quality of Paper and Printing Reflect on the Product

Many brochures in my collection look like they were designed for low-cost doll houses—not expensive homes! The paper that is chosen for the brochure has a subtle reflection on the image values of the homes represented. Paper is not the major expense in printing a brochure, and one should never economize in areas where perceived values will be adversely affected. The same is true of typeset printing. Camera-ready art and copy should be of the style and size that will best communicate the quality of the housing. A few extra dollars invested in these areas of design can translate into far greater results when the customers' reactions are taken into consideration.

## Size and Format

Odd-size brochures, fancy box-shaped designs, triangles, oblong pieces of art, etc., do not sell more real estate. In fact, they tend to complicate the use of the brochure. The brochures that we hand to people are most easily used, referenced, added to and retained if they are the shape and size of a standard letter. The slightly oversized 8½″ × 11″ size is the most practical shape in my opinion. We can insert personalized letters, make additions for prices, options and special features, without having to design pieces that are out of the ordinary. It is the quality of the design and the messages the brochure contains that are the keys to a successful brochure. Playing games with the shape only complicates the long-range effectiveness of the brochure.

## Summary

A well-designed brochure takes into consideration the sales functions it must serve. The brochure cannot achieve its objectives if it confuses prospects, removes control from the salesperson, raises issues that must be resolved and lessens the perceived value of the homes and environment. It is unfortunate that so many brochures are designed by people who have never had to sell a new home and who do not know what the sales process really is like. Sales managers and salespeople should have some direct influence on this sales tool!

## CREATE OTHER SALES AIDS THAT FACILITATE SALES OBJECTIVES

A variety of sales-support tools are commonly used to assist marketing, presentation and closing. What is needed or advisable depends upon the nature of the project, the stage at which sales occur, the number of issues that must be resolved to overcome sales resistance and the selling techniques preferred by the representatives. Many of these will take the form of handouts or insertions with the brochure package. Others will be direct-mail pieces that can be used by salespeople to reinforce selling functions. A few are one-of-a-kind creations to be used only by sales representatives with their personal sales presentations. We are providing a few examples of selected types of sales aids for your review. As a reference guide for those who are evaluating what aids might be appropriate for particular marketing operations, we have assembled the following list with our notations about values and uses.

### General-Purpose Exhibits and Aids

- *Comparative value-index charts*. Hand out a one-page list of primary features that distinguish your homes and environment from the competition. Columns are usually provided for prospects to check other developments to compare feature against feature. No one else will have all of your benefits because you prepared the list!
- *Picture postcards*. One of the most effective direct-mail and handout items, photo postcards can be used in a variety of supporting roles. One or more selected pictures are taken of the community, individual housing styles, amenities or entry identities and converted to typical resort-type postcards. They are best used for follow-up notes to prospects and buyers. A secondary use is to encourage owners to send their change-of-address notices and other messages to friends on these cards. They advertise the community and the homes for you—and even mail carriers read them!
- *Community information literature*. It is always appropriate to have general literature about the area. Frequently, this is available free of charge from chambers of commerce, tourist bureaus and other sources. Occasionally, it is justified to publish your own summary of the benefits of living in your region of the country or city.
- *Newsletters published on a regular schedule*. A favorite sales tool, newsletters also serve multiple functions. They reinforce the interests of residents and pending purchasers. They provide progress reports on the status of development and local news about the people who live in the community. They also

---

**FIGURE 7.10   Picture Postcard**

SOURCE: Courtesy of Fonville Morisey Co., Raleigh, NC.

can help to reinforce salespeople by occasionally printing publicity pieces about them and their accomplishments.

- *Construction-feature lists and illustrations.* When you have special construction information of interest to some buyers, such as depicting dual-wall construction for sound engineering and safety or checklisting all of your energy-saving features, it may be appropriate to prepare special handouts that document and illustrate these value points. In some cases they merit physical display in the sales office, such as a cutaway wall section or an energy chart.

**FIGURE 7.11    Front Page of a Typical Newsletter**

# Millpond Messenger

Published by the Arvida Corporation

Summer, 1981   Volume I, Number 1

## City approves expansion of Millpond

The community of Millpond is growing up.

Fast gaining a reputation as the Boca Raton area's premier family-oriented neighborhood, Millpond recently received approval from the Boca Raton City Council to move ahead with new construction in the community located in the western portion of the city.

The new development will encompass 100 single-family homesites with expanded recreational facilities covering more than 10 acres of the site. A variety of home designs, built by independent builders, will be available in the expansion area.

"The new area will be very much a family community and will be integrated with the present Millpond development," said Frank Weed, Director-Boca Raton Builder's Program for Arvida.

The expansion of Millpond will be built on 60 acres with access from St. Andrews Boulevard on the west and bordered by the College of Boca Raton on the east. The development is a mile north of Glades Road.

Weed said Millpond will continue to stress the same family atmosphere — including the extensive use of open space for recreational activities — that has proven attractive to its residents.

"Millpond has established itself as a family community," Weed said. "Prospective buyers can see the care in planning that has given Millpond a reputation as an attractive community catering to a neighborhood concept. Millpond offers an environment the public desires."

A total of 3.5 acres will be set aside as a recreational area with an open field suitable for a variety of sports such as soccer, softball and touch football. A bike path will meander around this area, which will include a "tot lot" playground for youngsters. A 7.2-acre lake will be located in the middle of this new area for recreation.

Homes in the community will start at $140,000.

For further information, visit the Millpond sales center off St. Andrews Boulevard. It is open daily from 9 a.m. to 5:30 p.m. The office telephone number is 368-9383.

*This luxurious 4-bedroom, 2½ bath built by Concept Home Builders, Inc., is typical of homes in Millpond and its expansion.*

## Western picnic marks Grand Opening

Residents of the Village of Millpond, City of Boca Raton officials and the South Palm Beach broker community celebrated the Grand Opening of the expansion of the community in a gala picnic Saturday, May 30.

Based on a Country-and-Western theme, a full afternoon of activities were planned for the event, which was held at Millpond's Belle Park and hosted by the Arvida Corporation.

Guests, who were dressed in concert with picnic's theme, were greeted by hostesses decked out in full Western attire. A buffet spread including barbecue chicken, barbecue ribs, hot dogs, baked beans, cole slaw, muffins, brownies, lemonade, iced tea, beer and wine was served at tables draped in red-and-white checked tablecloths.

The Country-Western band, Golden Grass, played throughout the four-hour event and a clogging demonstration

was presented by a local dance troupe.

The Arvida hot-air balloon also was on hand to provide rides for guests.

The event was topped off by the awarding of a grand prize, a weekend trip for two to River Ranch, a family-oriented dude ranch in Central Florida.

### Inside the Messenger...

*Millpond solved a problem for the Johnsons, who were searching for a family neighborhood. Page 2.*

*The Millpond Bears are anxiously looking forward to their 1981 Challenge. Page 3.*

*Review Board offers a means for control. Page 4.*

## FIGURE 7.12    Construction Features

# Energy Saving Features

**The innovative homes by Hansen and Horn approach the costs of heating and air conditioning in three distinct and effective ways:**

- Design and construction features to greatly reduce the need for heating or cooling energy
- Supplement the basic heating and cooling energy source with passive solar techniques
- Installation of an efficient, energy-saving heating and air conditioning system

### Energy Saving Features:

- Double studded 2 x 4 exterior wall (R-33), composed of two (2) Pink Fiberglas® insulated batts, one 3½" (R-11), one 6¼" (R-19). Balance of wall components equal to R-3 creating a total "R" factor of R-33
- R-38 insulated ceilings
- Energy roof truss to allow full depth insulation at all exterior walls
- Steel insulated exterior entry door
- Double glazed, thermo break windows
- 2" Styrofoam® brand insulation below slab perimeter

The following items and features, efficiently and effectively working together, can heat and air condition a home for as little as $199.00* a year.

*Based on family of four using energy in specific patterns with weather profiles considered typical. Actual energy used may differ depending upon individual family patterns and weather conditions.

- Continuous polyethylene vapor barrier in ceiling, on all exterior walls and under foundation slab
- Reduction of air infiltration through maximum caulking and weather stripping
- Energy saving heating and cooling with a heat pump
- Energy saving insulated water heater
- Patio location on south to increase radiation reflection

Another community by Hansen & Horn

## TYPICAL DOUBLE WALL CONSTRUCTION

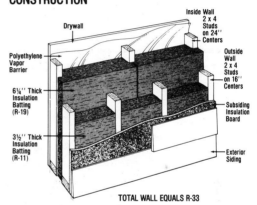

TOTAL WALL EQUALS R-33

## TYPICAL CORNICE DETAIL

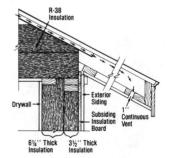

SOURCE: Courtesy of Hanson & Horn, Indianapolis, IN.

- *Photo albums and scrapbooks*. These are always appropriate. Since they serve so many valuable sales reinforcing roles. Pictures of people who have purchased, social and recreational events within the community, construction photos, examples of completed homes built by your company in other neighborhoods and personality profiles are just a few of the consumer-interest subjects that merit use. One of the most practical functions is to capture the history of the development from the initial ground breaking to the completion of the last home. Such an historical record provides an interesting exhibit that can be casually reviewed while guests are waiting in lobbies or formally introduced as part of the sales presentation.
- *Thank-you notes and personalized stationery*. As part of the basic identity package, thank-you notes and general stationery are often created to reinforce community or builder images. In some communities, it is appropriate to provide personalized stationery for buyers with subtle use of the community logo along with their names and new addresses.

---

**FIGURE 7.13   Example of Photo Album**

SOURCE: Courtesy of Trapp Family Guest Houses, Stowe, VT.

---

**FIGURE 7.14    Example of a Thank-You Note**

Thank you for visiting Guard Hill Manor on the grounds of the former Glass Estate. The sponsors have, we believe, constructed the townhouses here in the same tradition and quality of the original mansion house, yet tailored to contemporary living. Please do not hesitate to call me or our marketing staff if we may be of further assistance.

Sincerely,

---

# GUARD HILL MANOR

1006 Kensington Way, Mount Kisco, New York 10549    (914) 241-1117
*Created by Eagle River Builders, Inc.*

SOURCE: Courtesy of Eagle River Builders, Mount Kisco, NY.

---

- *Trail maps and nature articles.* Whenever you are selling a major community that has trails and interesting places to walk, trail maps are appropriate. When coupled with background information about the flora, fauna and natural environment, they can provide a special element of romantic interest. This is a primary sales tool in recreational resorts.
- *Historic pictures and articles.* History and romance sell real estate! Capitalizing on the legends of prior eras can make real estate ownership more attractive. Researching old photos, articles and information that can then be assembled into a history pamphlet is a good way to bring the past into today's sales presentations.

**FIGURE 7.15   Example of Historical Ad**

# Historical Facts on Tinton Falls

Founded in 1667 by James Grover, Tinton Falls was originally known as the "Falls of Shrewsbury". It was in this area that began the first mining of iron ore in New Jersey.

The plantation of James Grover was purchased in 1673 by Colonel Lewis Morris and named Tintern Manor after the family estate in Monmouthshire, Wales.

Known in the 18th and 19th centuries for the therapeutic qualities of its mineral springs, the area attracted visitors to the community in

general and in particular to the Mineral Springs Hotel, which was then located at the southeast corner of Tinton Avenue and Sycamore Avenue, in what was then Shrewsbury Township.

In 1950, the district of Tinton Falls and Wayside left the ancient township of Shrewsbury and formed the Borough of New Shrewsbury until the General Election of 1975 when the voters approved renaming their town the "Borough of Tinton Falls".

It is in this historical area that the lovely new homes of Shadow Woods at Tinton Falls are located.

SOURCE: Courtesy of Weichert Realtors®, Morristown, NJ.

## Preconstruction Marketing Tools

- *Full-size fold-out blueprints and floor plans.* In the pioneer marketing phases of a new community, when there are no completed production homes or models to inspect, the use of large fold-out or roll-up plans is an impressive way to illustrate the spaces and features that are hard to visualize from smaller reproductions. Some builders give their buyers actual blueprints with red-line notes to maintain a high degree of involvement during planning and preconstruction phases.
- *Artistic renditions of future amenities.* Any amenity not yet in place deserves to be illustrated and promoted during preconstruction periods. Separate handouts may be appropriate, especially if the design concepts are preliminary and not ready for inclusion in brochures.
- *Founders' club certificates and rosters.* One of the more effective ways to win the support of early-bird purchasers is to make them feel very special! The Founders' Club or Charter Owners' Club is one of the best ways to accomplish that objective. Those who must wait for everything to happen deserve special recognition. Charter certificates, rosters of club members, publicity photos of Founders Day parties, etc., are often employed to strengthen these relationships.
- *Portable presentation binders.* Very often our initial sales of a new development must be made away from the construction site. Staffing one community while trying to presell another or working from a general brokerage office necessitates portable presentations. The well-organized binder with protective vinyl sheets is the standard method of assembling this off-site marketing material. The use of photos, publicity stories, sketches, and feature lists along with site maps helps to control the visual presentation to prospective customers.

## Lot-Sales Programs (Not Necessarily Involving Home Sales)

- *Individual homesite presentation folders.* The most effective homesite sales programs recognize the need to give romance to the vacant land. A superior method of achieving this is to prepare separate file folders for each lot and include an enlarged plat of the site with appropriate topographical and engineering information. These are then used in one-on-one presentations to focus attention on the merits of each site without confusing prospective buyers with the entire plat.
- *Architects' and land planners' notations.* Selected comments taken from the notes of architects, planners, landscape specialists, etc., can make interesting additions to presentation information about individual homesites. Sometimes it is appropriate to use the sketch-pad approach and show the site in a variety of ways to depict potential home construction.
- *Topographical master-plan site maps.* Full-size handouts of the master-plan topo can be effective involvement aids in lot-sales programs. These are particularly important where preservation of the environment is a concern or where major changes have to be made to accommodate development.

## FIGURE 7.16   Example of a Floor Plan

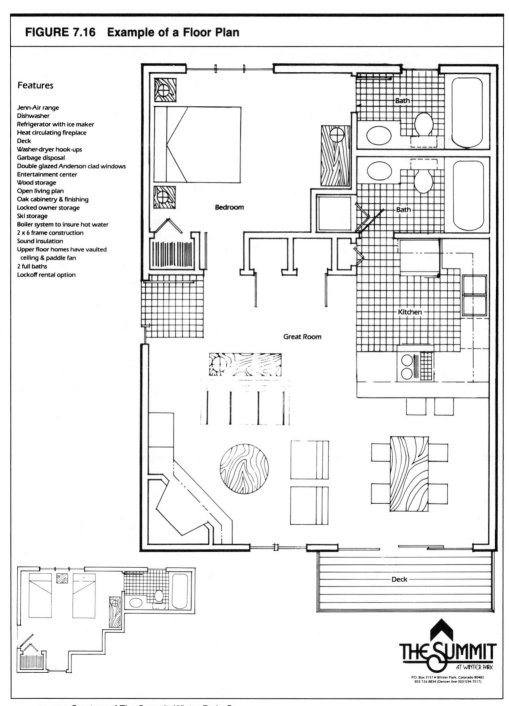

Features

Jenn-Air range
Dishwasher
Refrigerator with ice maker
Heat circulating fireplace
Deck
Washer-dryer hook-ups
Garbage disposal
Double glazed Anderson clad windows
Entertainment center
Wood storage
Open living plan
Oak cabinetry & finishing
Locked owner storage
Ski storage
Boiler system to insure hot water
2 x 6 frame construction
Sound insulation
Upper floor homes have vaulted
  ceiling & paddle fan
2 full baths
Lockoff rental option

SOURCE: Courtesy of The Summit, Winter Park, Co.

## FIGURE 7.17    Master Plan Site Map

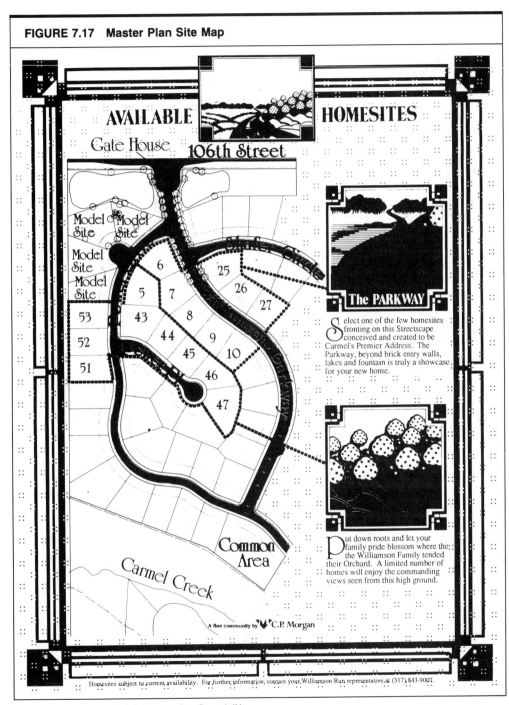

- *Photographs of each site from different perspectives*. One of the least expensive sales tools for lot-sales campaigns are photos of the individual sites shot from a variety of perspectives. Giving these photos to potential buyers helps to keep them picturing future ownership benefits. Where changing seasons affect values, it is wise to display shots of each site with its seasonal values, such as when the trees and meadows are green, in autumn when leaves are changing and perhaps in the winter. Whatever cannot be seen should be translated in a way that helps to overcome sales resistance to the unknown.

## Custom Housing and Build-On-Your-Lot Programs

- *Biographies and references of the builder*. A fundamental handout for custom builders is a simple biographical piece that humanizes the individual or team. The objective is to give potential customers the confidence to believe they are dealing with professionals who care about the people for whom they work. Sometimes these incorporate philosophy statements by the builder or architects involved in the design of the homes. Pictures of better homes constructed for others are also practical additions. The best bios are simple, credible and personal. Photos of the builder or his team taken in working environments can be very effective.
- *Guide to selecting a homesite and a builder*. A general article or pamphlet on the steps to take in looking for a builder or a custom homesite is frequently used by better builders to convey subtle messages that reinforce the reasons to work with their organizations. It also poses and answers the most frequently asked questions for those who are debating where and how to build their dream home.
- *Builder presentation album*. The individual custom builder more than any other contractor needs the sales power of a loose-leaf presentation album kept up to date with photos and information about new homes and programs. Many of these sales are made in the living rooms of potential customers who must sell one home to buy another. Painting the dream and building confidence in the building enterprise requires visual reinforcement.
- *Plan portfolios organized by type*. Another essential for the custom builder are plan portfolios. The better ones are hard bound with detailed plans and sketches organized by type of home. They should be portable, since presentations must be taken to the prospects.

## Condominiums and Major Planned-Unit Developments or Resorts

- *Calendar of events*. Whenever you are marketing a community or project that features social and recreational amenities, you should organize and promote the calendar of events, preferably a minimum of once per quarter for each season of the year. The social heart of a condominium or cluster-housing environment must be beating and healthy! This is often an item included in regularly published newsletters.

**FIGURE 7.18   Builder Profile**

## QUALITY BACKED BY EXPERIENCE

It takes more than know-how to build an adult community with the easy lifestyle, conveniences and craftsmanship you will discover at Homestead at Mansfield.

The builders, Mike Laino and Bud Quigley, have spent their entire professional careers in the construction business. In almost 30 years of building and designing homes, health care facilities, shopping centers and apartment houses, they have earned a reputation for excellence and integrity. Together they have built over 1,000 homes in Burlington County, where they are residents themselves.

Mike and Bud are family men. A home, to them, is a very special place, and that thought is uppermost in their minds when they build their homes for other people.

Their goal has always been to produce a better product: to refine it; redesign it; to take those extra measures that assure the highest caliber of craftsmanship.

Homestead at Mansfield is the culmination of that dream. All their years of know-how, planning, and hopes have come together in an inspired effort to create the ultimate in pleasurable living for a very special group of people — people like yourself, who have earned the best.

SOURCE: Courtesy of Weichert New Homes & Land Co., Morristown, NJ.

- *Feature articles and booklets about recreation.* Where there are major recreational amenities such as golf courses, marinas, tennis courts, jogging trails, etc., these value-adding features justify special literature that focuses on their benefits to owners and guests. For example, a golf course might have a booklet that explains hole-by-hole how each is designed and with players' or architects' comments about how to play them. A joggering trail with exercise stations could have a booklet that explained various ways to use the course and suggestions for exercises to be practiced at each designated station. Such literature enhances interest in the amenities and helps salespeople to create more value for the housing opportunities.
- *Homeowner association kits or booklets.* Condominium and other homeowner associations are topics of interest and concern for prospective buyers. Lack of credible information can lose sales. The positive aspects of professionally managed and protected owner environments need to be emphasized to offset concerns for monthly fees, the structure of the management company and the unknowns about living in a community where others can vote to change the rules. Articles or booklets that are effectively written and illustrated can be valuable reinforcers for salespeople.
- *Questions and answers about the community.* Another approach to the objective of communicating information in positive ways is to create a list of the most frequently asked questions about the community and provide succinct but benefit-oriented answers. This does not need to be an expensive production. Even a word-processed computer printout will do the job.
- *Condominium association fees and budgets.* A principal concern of potential condominium buyers is the nature and size of association fees. Horror stories about projects that were underestimated (possibly on purpose) and later experienced substantial assessments have been publicized in many parts of the country. Allaying fears is part of professional marketing objectives. A certified copy of the budget together with an analysis by line-item can overcome resistance of detail-minded prospects. A spreadsheet that shows how the budget relates to each unit helps to reduce perceptions of over- or undercharging for services.

## Move-Up Buyers Who Have Homes to Sell Before Purchasing

- *How-to-sell-your-home booklets or articles.* The issues involved in buying one home while trying to sell another one are often so frustrating that many potential move-up buyers elect to postpone the challenge as long as possible. If your homes are targeted to existing owners in your region, you should have some literature or checklists that will take some of the confusion and fear out of the process. REALTORS® have prepared articles and pamphlets that can be used as is or modified to meet specific needs.
- *Checklist or article on values of new versus older homes.* An excellent selling tool for handling hesitant resale prospects is a value-indexed checklist or article that emphasizes the benefits of a new home contrasted with living

in an older one not built to today's specifications or located in value-increasing new communities.

- *Explanations of the guaranteed-sales or equity plan.* Some builders and REALTORS® offer equity insurance in the form of agreements to purchase homes if not sold within specified time periods or to provide equity advances toward the completion of purchase until sold. REALTORS® involved may have their own literature and prepared summaries of procedures. If not, this is another sales tool that might be tailored to the marketing needs of an individual builder or community.
- *Direct-mail cards or letters aimed at existing owners.* To generate interest among move-up prospects, certain direct-mail pieces have proven very effective. These include a brief version of the checklist of value differences between new and old, testimonials from those who have made the move and once lived in the targeted neighborhoods, and feature/benefit emphasis of the advantages your specific homes offer compared to the specific tract housing in which the targeted customers currently reside.

### First-Time Buyer Markets

- *Tax-benefit-of-ownership charts.* A standard handout in presentation material used by most professionals who are targeting the starter market is the true-net-costs-of-home-ownership summary. This is a major motivator for beginners who are unaware of what they are missing in tax savings by not owning their own homes.
- *Complete checklist or articles on the benefits of ownership.* Beyond tax benefits, there is a long list of reasons why anyone who can afford to own should, rather than keeping the landlord rich! We have long employed a basic checklist and supporting literature that identifies a minimum of fifteen reasons to own.
- *Testimonial letters from other first-time buyers.* A unique technique for stimulating renters is to have prepared letters, from the buyers you sold, addressed to residents of the apartments from which they moved. Personalized stories and testimonials are among the very best sales aids you can use in a presentation or mailing campaign.

### Modular Housing and Pre-Engineered Homes

- *Modular-housing fact sheet.* The representation of manufactured housing in its various forms including modular designs requires special fact sheets that identify the many benefits of this preengineered and controlled production plan. Misconceptions must be countered and documentation is essential. This includes information about both structural and design integrity.
- *Photographs of the plant and process.* Again, photo albums can help. Video-tapes and slide programs are also recommended. A picture is worth a thousand words, and it is also worth many additional sales.

- *Testimonials and references.* Because misconceptions are common in this type of housing, testimonials are even more valuable and should be employed whenever possible. A list of quotes by those who own or inspect them is appropriate.

## Cooperative Broker Marketing Programs

- *Broker promotion kits.* Where other real estate brokers are important to the general marketing plan, it is helpful to prepare professionally organized kits or binders that contain all of the information they need to represent your properties effectively. Items typically included in these promotional packages are a letter inviting cooperation, a list of properties available with feature data, rules for cooperation and customer protection and contest or incentives currently applicable.
- *Broker newsletter.* Special newsletters designed just for cooperating brokers are an excellent support tool for encouraging REALTOR® interest. They need not be fancy. They can be informative and fun with emphasis on recognizing those most successful in selling your new homes.
- *Portable presentation binders.* For brokers very active in working your new homes, there may be value in creating a limited number of well-organized presentation binders that they can use in their own offices.
- *Satellite displays in brokers' offices.* Sometimes you can obtain the agreement of key brokers to assign a window or office display promoting your new homes within their sales offices. The minimum could be deluxe photographs displayed in their windows. The ultimate might be a backlit display with professionally prepared graphics.

## After-Purchase and Move-In Materials

- *Welcome-to-the-community letters and kits.* Reinforcing messages of welcome from executives of the development company are appropriate when you have closed a sale. The more extensive version is a welcome kit that contains a variety of support materials, including gift certificates from local merchants and suppliers.
- *What-to-expect-next checklists and pamphlets.* One recommended tool for confirming a sale and preventing buyers' remorse or overexpectation of the time it will take to complete a transaction is a checklist or article that details what must occur and what to expect from all involved.
- *Community services guide.* This is an alphabetical listing by category of the commercial, social, financial and recreational services available within the general community. It can be included in a welcome kit or used independently.
- *Postcards depicting phases of processing and delivery.* The creation of a series of postcards that illustrate in cartoon form the stages of processing and construction helps keep buyers involved from point of sale until final closing. Topics illustrated include:

  Your financing is approved.
  Your home has been started.

Inspect your home before it is framed.
It's time to select colors and accessories.
We are just about done.
We made it!

- *Premove-in kits.* This is a supplemental kit given to new buyers about midway in the process. It typically contains such items as furniture inventory and moving lists, packing and shipping labels, tips on moving, information about the coming settlement date and how to make arrangements for utilities. Many of these items can be obtained free of charge from moving van and storage companies as part of their business development services.
- *Change-of-address postcards.* These are items that might be included in premove-in kits or given separately. While you can use the ones furnished free of charge by the post office, wise marketers tie this owner notification process to the promotion of the community. As mentioned earlier, picture postcards are one of the most versatile means of promoting the community and work well for this purpose.
- *Warranties and customer-service documentation.* An essential part of the marketing program is the customer-service system. The representations made by salespeople about the warranties, customer follow-up and service after delivery need to be documented for use with consumers at the point of sale. If you have a more comprehensive orientation kit, these elements become a key part of that package.
- *Owner's manual (preferably personalized to each buyer).* The most professional approach to handling the introduction to a new home is to prepare a regular binder (preferably with logo and community colors) that has dividers for each section of the prepared materials it contains. Beginning with a congratulations-on-your-new-home letter, the binder covers care and feeding of the home, emergency procedures, warranties on all appliances, etc., the builder's warranties, a copy of the protective covenants and related information. Some builders add the ultimate touch of embossing the owners' names on the covers and spines.
- *Surveys and interview forms used after possession.* It is always appropriate to use some type of follow-up system after buyers take possession of their new homes. Professional third-party companies provide this service, and their involvement assures consistent and well-managed supervision of postsales relationships. If done in-house, follow-up should be carefully structured to reinforce the builder's interest in maintaining customer satisfaction and goodwill.
- *Personalized photo albums for each homeowner.* In some communities, marketers have used the photo album as one of the key postsales functions. They give buyers an album starting with a photo taken the day of the purchase, and they add pictures progressively as the home is built, capping it with a welcome-to-the-community party at which the buyers are the featured VIPs!
- *Bumper stickers and other identity items for purchasers and owners.* Bumper stickers, key chains, security gate passes and other owner-identity items are appropriate ways to deepen the involvement with the community.

# HOW TO MAXIMIZE RESULTS DURING HIGH-TRAFFIC PERIODS

In the world of new home sales there is often that unique challenge of trying to handle a large number of prospects who arrive all at the same time. Every experienced new home specialist knows the scenario: It is Sunday about 2 P.M. You are alone in the on-site sales office or model home. Only two or three prospects are hovering around, and then 16 couples show up at one time! They all want information, brochures and directions to models! Who is a prospect and who is a suspect? How do you get enough time to qualify, present your message, record information, set appointments or sell? You often feel like a mosquito in a nudist colony—you know the subject but not where to start!

Having discussed this subject with hundreds of real estate professionals, we have made a list of the best ideas these experts have discovered work for them. We summarize these findings and hope that their suggestions may be of benefit to you when you have a similar zoo environment with which to contend. We have subdivided the suggestions into ten categories, from organizing in advance to be ready for high traffic periods to what to do with the previously sold customers who interrupt you on busy Sundays.

## How to Get Ready for Those High-Impact Times

If your new home community is likely to have peak periods of prospect activity that stretch the capacity of a limited sales staff, it is logical that steps be taken in advance. Here is a list of suggestions gathered from the pros:

1.  Employ greeters who are available for these high-traffic days. It is often better to use residents (people who live in that neighborhood) and who can be available on short notice. The fact that they live in the community is a plus, since they can knowledgeably talk about the living benefits of the area.
2.  Have brochures and price lists ready for easy distribution, but do not leave them out for pickup by prospects unless you have no other choice.
3.  Attach registration cards to each brochure or price sheet so that when you hand one to a customer it is ready for registration use.
4.  Have coffee, soft drinks, etc., that can be served in an appropriate area so you can put prospects into holding patterns and have them feel comfortable about waiting for an agent to help them.
5.  Have a place for kids to play, or things for them to look at or do so that parents will be able to see your homes without additional frustration.
6.  Use an audio-visual presentation (such as a videotape) to allow prospects to get an overview of the community while waiting for a salesperson to help them.
7.  Use a personal tape recorder (small dictation-type) to quickly record observations following each interview to be able to capture all pertinent data before it is forgotten. Play it back in quiet hours and transfer to prospect cards.

8. Organize your site map so that it targets those properties you want to accent that day. Use of yellow flags or special messages can help this objective.

9. Use a blackboard or easel that has a special message for the day like: "Welcome to Pleasant Acres! We want you to feel at home. Have a cup of coffee, visit our models, and see why we have sold 15 homes this week! We will be with you as quickly as possible . . ."

10. To show activity and create a sense of urgency (which causes people to wait) have contracts, sales files, etc., visible to show you are doing business, and people are buying! One salesperson likes to have checks in a glass jar on her desk (sometimes one or two props) just to indicate the amount of activity she is experiencing.

11. Have your daily appointment calendar open on your desk, filled with appointments and ready for use to set one for another prospect. This adds credibility to the appointment process and the urgency to act.

12. Use silent salespeople or information notices in each model to be sure the customers receive key messages about the values you offer.

13. Hire a parking lot attendant who will help direct and control traffic. In some areas, a valet parking service is justified.

14. Provide sitting areas for waiting people. In warmer seasons, use outdoor furniture, umbrella tables, etc., to give the people one or more pleasant outdoor areas to enjoy while waiting for service.

15. Prepare kits of information to be given at the end of the visit in order to have a moment to debrief and chat with the customer. Anything you give away that is of interest to a buyer can be used as a holding tool.

### Greeting and Quick Qualifying Techniques

One of the keys to the successful handling of large crowds and heavy-traffic periods is to know how to make every word and motion count for you. It is essential to make people feel welcome and quickly involve them so that you can ascertain a portion of their motivations, abilities, and needs. On that subject, here are some of the recommendations of the professionals.

1. Always greet each group or individual on a personal basis even if only for a moment. It is important to make people feel important.

2. Use knock-out questions that will tend to separate the buyers from the suspects. A knock-out question is usually asked in a direct but friendly manner.

    "How soon would you like to be in a new home?"
    "Are you seriously looking for a new home?"
    "Did you bring your check book?" (with a smile)
    "Our homes are priced from $70,000 to $80,000. Is that the range you had in mind?"

3.  Have each registration-survey card attached to a miniature clipboard (a good quantity prepared in advance) so that the guests can register without having to congest the reception area.
4.  Use the prospect-survey card as the method of sorting the traffic into a sequenced flow that is somewhat spaced in time. It will take a few moments for each person to register. This means they will be returning from the models in a less congested manner. You also can then use the survey card to continue the qualifying on the way back from the models.
5.  Use the brochure or price list as a qualifier. As you hand it to a prospect, quote the range and ask two or three questions related to financial ability.
6.  Limit the initial qualifying to three areas: urgency, need and financial ability.
7.  Use the VHF (very-high-frequency) approach with each prospect. Turn up your eye contact, use pleasant but incisive questions, and give 100 percent attention for the few moments you are with each one. Do not try to qualify the group—qualify individually by the way you direct your questions and use body language.
8.  Use back-door qualifying rather than front-door whenever the traffic builds to an uncontrollable point. This means introduction, one or two knock-outs and a key point or two; then release them to the models. The balance of qualifying is done when they return, with concentration on those who show greatest degree of qualified potential.
9.  Use greeters to meet, query and introduce prospects to property. The agents then are clued by the greeters for targeting returning prospects.
10. On really high-traffic projects, try color-coding your handout literature in unobtrusive ways. The hostess who asks the quick qualifiers gives each prospect the color-coded sheet that indicates the qualification level. Sales agents then concentrate on just those prospects carrying the right-colored sheets.

## How to Use Group Presentations Effectively

Although most salespeople will tell you that they do not want to make group presentations and will avoid them if at all possible, sometimes they are necessary, simply due to the number of people in the sales facility at the same time. Here are some suggestions for handling these group situations:

1.  Cover only key points about the community, developer and housing opportunities when with the group. Then give each of them something to do (like touring models or filling out survey forms, etc.) so that you can spend a few private moments with individual prospects.
2.  Be sure to make eye contact and smile at each individual, even though the group is with you in one place.
3.  After model inspections (which may not be by group), narrow the group down to those interested in seeing the homesites and take that smaller group

on the tour. During this walking (or riding) event, ask each in turn a few key questions as you move among them.

4.  Use guides to give tours to those obviously not in the market now or who cannot qualify so that you can concentrate on the few valid prospects.

5.  As you tour or handle the groups returning from models, ascertain who can arrange to return and make specific appointments for them. Those who cannot, should be given as much time as possible for individual treatment.

## Create Some Involvement with the Property to Assure Return Visits

Studies seem to verify that prospects are far more likely to return to a community in which they became involved with specific homes and homesites the first time out than those who do not. That is one of the primary reasons for spending enough time with prospects at the first inspection to be sure they have something to return to. Getting them involved with a floor plan, model and homesite or two is part of the objective. On busy days, it is much harder to do this, because this type of involvement requires time. Here are some tips to help deepen the impressions of the first visit and increase the size of the be-back business:

1.  Use urgent phrases and information with the groups to point out the limited number of homes or homesites of particular types available that day. Urgency tends to increase the desire to know more and to return sooner.

2.  Carry a clipboard with you as you walk around talking to people and making key points. Use it to make notes about your prospects and to write things for them to take with them as momentos of the visit.

3.  Write special notes on the prospects' brochures or literature that will personalize the information you provide. This includes plan numbers, one or two lots that are available now, summary of key points, etc.

4.  Have the prospects carry a brief survey card with them that asks for opinions about the models. Their notes will increase the sense of involvement. It is appropriate to have inexpensive company-image pens or pencils with note paper for this purpose.

5.  Involve the children in the process, especially if they are old enough to make notes for their parents. In some communities, coloring books are used with each model depicted for the children to color their new home.

6.  Encourage people to inspect sites or production inventory even if you cannot be with them. Give them something they have to return (like oversized site maps or keys) to be sure you can talk to them when they return to the office.

7.  Always ask each customer before they depart, "Which model or plan did you like best?" Get them to express opinions that will help you reinforce (and record notes) about the one they prefered.

8.  If at all possible, try to get the prospects to specify production inventory of homesites, even if you have to do it by group tours.

## Sell Appointments and Confirm Them for Follow-Up

On a busy day, objectives often focus more on selling appointments than selling property. This is especially true if the traffic is totally unmanageable. Here are ideas about ways to get the appointments.

1.  Sell the idea of having quality time to be with the prospects for their benefit.
2.  Always have your calendar open and ready to record appointments. Be sure the days are fairly full of appointments in advance of the opening that Sunday. You can always make adjustments, but you need people to know you are busy and successful. That breeds a sense of urgency to return.
3.  Use your business card to record the appointment time and give to the customers as a reminder.
4.  Give the customer something to take with them and complete so that the return visit will be more productive. This can be something as simple as a questionnaire that asks a limited number of questions about the size and type of home desired, etc., to completion of a financial analysis.
5.  If more than one salesperson is in the sales office, obtain a commitment for the other one to be available during the time you need for your prospects when they return. This tends to deepen the obligation to return.
6.  Have some special events scheduled that the prospects would find interesting to attend. This can be wine-and-cheese parties or special showings of films on the housing environment.
7.  Most important, ask for the appointment. You don't get them if you don't ask.

## Obtain a Partial Buying Decision of Some Type

All master closers agree that you do not let anyone go who is a qualified prospect without trying for a close of some type. A number of partial closes can be used to get the prospect to take that first step that usually leads to the final step. On really busy days, it is difficult to do this as comfortably as those days when you can spend enough time with people, but the mere activity can be a stimulant to get prospects to take some form of action. Any of the following can be considered a partial close— backed up by an appointment to finish the details at a later time:

1.  a lot hold with a deposit check
2.  a reservation on a specific site
3.  a first right-of-refusal good for limited time
4.  a check to be held until the prospect returns

Added to these partial closes is the basic rule of having the customers do something to help reinforce the commitment. Have them put their names on the plat map, the sold button on the lot, the sign on the site. The more things the prospect does to indicate purchase, the more likely that the final commitment will be made.

## What Do You Do with the Hot Prospect on a Busy Sunday When You Have Other Prospective Buyers in the Office?

When we interview salespeople on this subject, we get a variety of responses. The master closers as a group tend to favor writing the contract even at the expense of the rest of the prospects. Many of them feel that the writing tends to increase the interest of the others who get caught up in the excitement of the sales activity.

Others contend that they would rather take a lot hold or a check but save the paperwork and all the time-consuming details for a later date. A few say that real buyers will return once they have made the emotional commitment.

We feel that each agent has to weigh this one based on the amount of traffic and his or her personal ability to capitalize upon the opportunities he or she is presented. A bird in the hand may well be worth two in a bush, but if you only write one when you could have written five, the price may be too expensive.

### Risks of Being Understaffed

Management has a responsibility on behalf of project objectives to be certain that there are enough qualified salespeople on hand to service the traffic rather than being totally dependent upon the services of one or two overworked agents. Once a salesperson is writing in excess of one or two sales a week, experience dictates that another salesperson staffing that location is probably in order. Commissions can be improved to accommodate more agents as a less expensive cost to management than losing valuable sales.

### Some Other Tips to Consider

Educate the people you have already sold not to use your busy weekends as the time to return and ask more questions. A polite way of handling this topic is to say something like:

> *"Mary and Bill, I know you will have questions you will want to ask and things that concern you as the home is being constructed in the next few weeks. I will stay in touch with you and want you to feel free to call me during the week. Please recognize, however, that the weekends, and particularly Sundays, are my time to find you the new neighbors you and we need to complete the community. The sooner we sell out of this area, the sooner you will have a completed neighborhood and our construction crew will be out of your way. If you come by on Sunday, I will wave at you, but if I'm busy, please look at the home on your own and then leave me a note or call during the week."*

You do not need to take valuable weekend time to try to handle old business.

If possible, try to get your hot prospects to come back the same day, but at a later and more convenient time. Perhaps send them to lunch and set an appointment later in the day. Some agents use the ploy of having the prospects bring them a hamburger or something else to eat, and to insure the return they give them $5. Most people will come back when this type of obligation has been created.

Avoid doing any more paperwork on busy days than absolutely necessary. Get others to help you if at all possible.

It is very important that you keep your own perspective and remain in control of your emotions and actions. You can get flustered, tired and become ineffective if you do not manage your own mental attitudes well!

## SUMMARY: THE BEST SALES PROGRAMS ARE THE RESULT OF ADVANCE PLANNING AND SUPERIOR EXECUTION

The number of variables that can adversely influence sales objectives dictates that we do whatever is practical to minimize risks. These risks include salespeople who do not prepare themselves before showing new housing and aggressive competition that elects to give away profits to increase market penetration! Part of the necessary marketing insurance is the creation of well-organized sales presentations and the supporting tools that help sales representatives overcome obstacles. Communicating values in positive ways so that potential buyers become enthusiastic about acting now rests with front-line salespeople—but is greatly assisted by all of the promotional tools we provide them to reinforce the emotional process. Advance planning must incorporate an appreciation for the sales presentation criteria and the support systems we should produce to facilitate sales. In final analysis, it is in the execution that we can judge the results. The basic rule is to constantly monitor the sales process and make whatever adjustments are required until you know you have the right people doing the right things—consistently well!

# 8: Marketing Programs That Generate Qualified Prospects

Homes must be shown to be sold! If that seems obvious, it nevertheless emphasizes a fundamental principle for developing an effective sales plan. Planned exposure to the right prospects must be the central objective of any real estate marketing campaign. Creating and implementing programs that assure sufficient exposure to qualified consumers at a reasonable cost per customer is the primary responsibility of the director of marketing. Unless profiled prospects are attracted in adequate numbers to the new housing environment, projected sales will not occur.

How much exposure is necessary or desirable? How many people need to see your new homes or come to your sales office(s) in order to meet sales projections? If you have only one home to sell, all you need is one qualified and motivated buyer who likes your product. If you have 100 to sell, you certainly need a minimum of 100 customers. However, since it is highly unlikely that you could expect a 100 percent closing ratio, your marketing plan must be targeted to a much larger number of potential buyers. The best sales staff in the industry will not sell to 100 percent of the people who see their housing. A 50-percent return is also unrealistic. The national average of exposures to conversions is less than five percent!

## PROSPECT GENERATION BEGINS WITH RESEARCH

As emphasized in chapter 2, research is the security blanket for all decision-making, especially that affecting the development of pragmatic marketing plans. The original research studies should clearly define profiled buyers and estimate the percentages of the total market that may be qualified and interested in the housing you are featuring. You certainly cannot generate more prospects than the marketplace contains! It is also unlikely that you can afford to reach every potential customer within that region or be certain they will respond to your promotional efforts. Penetration objectives should be realistic. For most of us, experience has indicated that trying to capture more than 10 percent of a market is extremely difficult, and 25 percent is a rarity for which we can only hope if we have an exclusive product in a high-demand area in which there is little or no competition.

Let's look at the variables in marketing plans as related to the limitations of a potential capture rate. Suppose your initial research indicates there are about 1,000 buyers for your kind of housing this year in your general market area. First, we must rule out the possibility of all 1,000 learning about and seeing your offerings. You might draw 25 percent to the site(s) or sales office(s) if all the right ingredients are in place to carry your value messages to the targeted groups. That would mean 250 exposures to qualified buyers. Others who are not profiled customers would undoubtedly investigate the homes, and they will increase the exposure numbers—but not necessarily the sales volume. Of the 250, a professional sales staff of superior closers might convert 25 percent, but it is far more likely that the rate will be under 10 percent. This means that, at optimum performance level, you might net about 60 sales and, with an average staff, only 25 or fewer. These are big differences, and they can play havoc with profit figures if you need more than 25 to reach a better than break-even crossover point.

Most marketers develop lead-generation campaigns based on a total number of buying units (qualified or unqualified) and shoot for reasonable conversion rates of *total traffic*. They feel that if they can produce 100 prospects through all forms of marketing and promotion—and the products have reasonable appeal, a minimum conversion of one to five percent can be budgeted into the pro formas. That means at least one to five sales for every 100 exposures. In some markets where competition is aggressive and buyers shop intensely, conversion rates can fall below one percent. In others, where product, staffing and marketing are well-positioned, rates of conversion to total traffic can rise above five percent. It is a mistake to base the marketing budget and prospecting programs on optimum numbers and superior sales performance. Sound strategy is to budget for a pessimistic to realistic level of prospect conversions and to devote the dollars needed to assure that these numbers are met!

Aggressive marketing campaigns can increase the number of qualified prospects provided sufficient total numbers exist within the market region to widen penetration opportunities. However, we must always take into consideration that spending more money does not necessarily produce proportionate increases in prospects. For example, if in the market there are only 1,000 people who could ever be interested in your housing this year, spending substantial sums to try to reach all of them could cause your per-head cost to far exceed the percentage of sales price you can reasonably budget for promotion and still make an adequate profit. On the other hand, if research indicates that the depth of the market exceeds 10,000 prospects this year for your type of housing in that region and you only have 100 to sell, you need only a one percent conversion rate of the total market to meet your objectives. Probably with a modest campaign you can attract 10 percent (1,000) and with fairly competent sales representatives close between five to ten percent of all qualified customers, thus netting between 50 and 100 sales.

Exposure in the housing business is a numbers game! The law of numbers and the law of averages must both be evaluated and strategically exploited. Any marketing plan that requires a high penetration rate of the projected total absorption capacity for a specific category of housing should be carefully analyzed before it is implemented. The fewer people you need to attract to meet your sales objectives, the less the risk in dollars and in net results. The converse is equally true: the more people you must draw to your sales environment to make the numbers work, the greater the risk and financial commitment required.

## THEORY OF EQUITABLE MARKETING STRATEGIES

If all of your prospects must be secured through expensive newspaper advertising, direct mail and broadcast media, the cost per delivered prospect can be very high. If, on the other hand, you could secure all of your buyers by word of mouth and personal referrals, you would have little or no cost for outside advertising and promotion. Few builders have such excellent reputations that they are able to live off of referrals alone. For them, marketing is simply a matter of protecting their reputations and letting their owners do the prospecting for them. Not many can boast that level of customer support.

Another element is vital in most markets: cooperating real estate brokers who bring their customers to the builder's product. Although compensated well for their efforts, they represent one of the more important ingredients in the total prospecting plan in those market areas where such cooperation is customary and consistently encouraged. Our research indicates that cooperating brokers and their associated agents account for more than 40 percent of all new home sales in America, despite the fact that some states and markets have very little cooperation between on-site specialists and the general brokerage community.

The theory of equitable marketing is to balance some of the more costly forms of prospect generation against those that have a very low dollar investment, so that the net result is a plan that will produce enough qualified buyers to lower the average cost per customer.

One broad approach to this concept is to divide prospecting into three general classifications and estimate the percentages to be derived from each source:

1. Street traffic generated from advertising, signage and on-site marketing activities
2. Broker cooperative sales produced by off-site agents
3. Referrals, publicity and personal prospecting

For example, if you budgeted one third of your prospects and sales from each source, the extra fees paid for off-site agent business can be offset by the nominal expense for cultivating referrals along with the self-prospecting activities of on-site specialists. For the sake of our illustration, assume that you have established an approximate budget of 1.5 percent of gross sales price for all promotional programs to generate your customers and closed buyers. If cooperative-broker sales represent an average of three percent (usually split 50–50 between broker and sales associate) and referrals have almost no costs involved, these two balance each other representing a net cost of 1.5 percent overall. We are assuming that on-site staff or account representatives are compensated for all sales made on a separate fee structure.

There is obvious synergy of marketing activities, one reinforcing the other. For example, REALTORS® will be influenced by the advertising dollars you invest in newspapers, housing guides and signage. They will be forced to discuss your homes with prospects who have seen your media messages. Housing guides, in particular, have dual efficiency: they reach the public through general distribution, and they are used by brokers to locate and index properties they plan to show to customers.

When preparing marketing budgets, always distinguish between sales commissions and promotional marketing expenses designed to produce prospective customers. The marketing plan for each specific project should take into consideration the logical distribution of prospect sources with allowances then made for relative differences in costs that must be built into the budget.

## CAN YOU HAVE TOO MUCH EXPOSURE?

The immediate answer to this question might seem to be NO! After all, the more people who see and talk about your new housing, the greater the chance of increasing current sales and enhancing your reputation in the marketplace. In the majority of cases, that would be the right response. However, situations exist where a carefully orchestrated strategy that limits exposure merits consideration. One of these is during the preconstruction phase of a new housing program. If the promotion is too widely

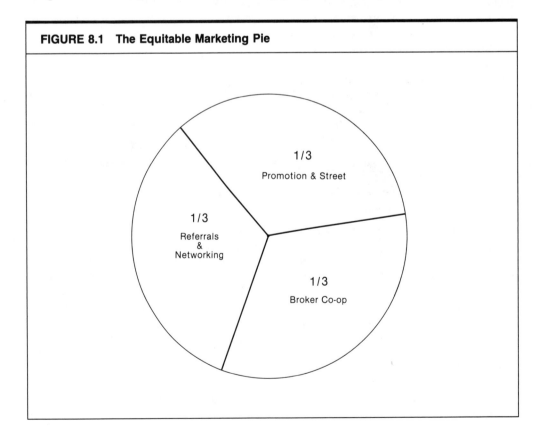

**FIGURE 8.1    The Equitable Marketing Pie**

1/3
Promotion & Street

1/3
Referrals
&
Networking

1/3
Broker Co-op

heralded during the pioneer period when there is very little to see or excite potential buyers, a distinct risk exists that the traffic will not be there when you need it during the grand-opening phase. In this case, overexposure to the market can result in loss of interest later because the community or program has become commonplace. Prospects who cannot visualize a home before it is finished and will not purchase until they can touch and feel the merchandise may be drawn to the site by the early promotional efforts but uninspired to act. Later, when you try again to win the attention of the same people, they may ignore your promotion because they have been there already. If first impressions were unfavorable, you may never get a second chance at the same group of buyers. Building the tempo of the marketing campaign to a crescendo timed to meet the optimum marketing conditions requires controlled exposure to a well-defined audience prior to launching major promotions and events. (See phasing strategies in chapter 3.)

Another case for controlling exposure is the luxury-housing community or product line exclusively designed for upscale buyers. Extensive exposure may be counter-productive when dealing with this price range. Private showings to a select few may produce far better results than allowing everyone to see the homes without prequalifying. The invitational approach, with carefully prepared presentations to targeted prospects, produces added prestige that enhances the entire marketing concept.

One other situation can be detrimental to sales objectives: too much exposure to too many people at one time! If you have a grand opening and more prospects arrive than you can even service, the promotion may be counterproductive. If customers cannot see the homes or get their questions answered because of wall-to-wall congestion, the mass marketing can be very inefficient. Plan ways to handle the expected traffic, even if it means putting some people into a holding pattern so that a limited number can inspect the models before another group is released.

Generally, it is better to err on the side of overexposure than underexposure! If costs for producing the traffic can be justified against the budgeted marketing plan, the larger number will decrease the risks and increase potential rewards. A vital profit-oriented consideration is the ability to maintain a reasonable cost per closed sale for all traffic generation activities. If you spend substantial sums to produce hundreds of customers and you only sell one or two homes, the relative cost per sale will be astronomical! Conversion rates must be taken into consideration when establishing your prospect-generation campaigns. This is one reason why many professionals test customer-acceptance levels for new products and validate the presentation and closing skills of the sales representatives before investing big dollars in nonrecoverable marketing expenses.

## HOW TO EVALUATE THE COST EFFECTIVENESS OF PROSPECTING PROGRAMS

Efficient marketers always measure the costs of marketing activities against actual results experienced on the front line. Past results provide a basis for making future projections. Unless you know how many people see your houses, why they came and what media or efforts produced the best results, you are in no position to plan efficiently the expenditure of your marketing dollars. Builders and developers who have assigned marketing to outside brokerage companies may feel they have less need to know these facts than those who use controlled, on-site personnel with full responsibility for their own marketing costs. In our opinion, the seller needs to be well informed about the relative effectiveness of all marketing activities to understand what works well and what does not. If the percentage of owner referrals is small, that could mean the builder is neglecting the customer-service functions on which referrals depend.

If cooperative-broker sales are less than local expectations, it might be traced to lack of confidence in the values being presented or the way the product is being promoted. Five basic methods are used to calculate the economic efficiency of prospect-producing activities:

1.  Total marketing expenditures (exclusive of sales commissions) are divided by the number of net closed sales. This gives you your average cost for securing each closed transaction based on your gross expenses including models, signage, literature, advertising, cooperative brokers, etc.
2.  Separate the marketing expenses directly related to prospect-generation functions from all other costs for general marketing, and divide this figure by the number of net closed sales. This is the average cost per sale based upon your advertising and promotion budget.
3.  Use this same figure divided by the total number of prospects generated from all sources. This reveals what it costs on average to produce individual customers. When that dollar number is compared with item two above, you can see the relative dollars invested for the conversion rates you are experiencing.
4.  Identify the dollars spent for each prospect development activity, and then divide the number of prospects produced from each source into these respective amounts. This gives you an efficiency measurement of targeted dollars to number of resulting prospects.
5.  Use the figures in number four above divided by the net closed sales resulting from each respective source. This is the bottom line for interpreting the true effectiveness of your invested marketing dollars measured against individual prospecting activities.

    For example: If you have determined that the buyers you secured from an ad in a housing magazine or digest cost you only $250 per head, versus $900 for every one secured from a newspaper ad, you would have justification for modifying your expenditures in the newspapers or increasing them in the housing guides!

## KEEP PROSPECT RECORDS

One of the biggest challenges for marketers and advertising agencies is obtaining accurate information about sources and profiles of prospects resulting from marketing efforts. The ultimate responsibility for data rests with front-line sales personnel, and they are usually reluctant to gather and share customer statistics. Sales management must educate, motivate and administrate to win this game. If agents can be made to appreciate how valuable this consumer information is to the investment of marketing dollars, they may be more diligent in providing facts. Prospect registration cards, weekly traffic-report summaries and complete buyer profiles are the three primary documents on which marketers depend for their research needs.

## WHAT IS A REASONABLE COST PER PROSPECT AND PER CLOSED SALE?

No exact answer can be given to this question. Each market area will have its own local criteria, as will each developer or builder. Occasionally, a new community will sell out without any advertising expenditures because pent-up demand has produced prospects by word of mouth! Others required expenditures of small fortunes before they were finally closed. The actual range in costs as a percentage of gross sales prices can be as little as .05 percent to as much as ten percent! A fairly typical range for merchant builders (those sustaining a volume of sales on a consistent basis) is between one percent and three percent with two percent being an acceptable average. (These figures exclude costs for salespeople or sales management.)

Where a brokerage company or outside marketing agency has a contract to represent the builder's homes for a gross percentage that includes all marketing expenses, the determination of available dollars for promotional activities is calculated by subtracting the percentages paid to listing and selling agents and then allocating a minimum of 20 percent to a high of 50 percent of the balance to advertising and promotion. Many brokers set aside a fixed percentage for new home marketing (like one percent of the gross sales price) before calculating commissions. Obviously, the motivations and interests of all parties must be considered when establishing marketing budgets. When an outside sales and marketing entity is involved, it is often in the best interest of all concerned to have a separate marketing budget funded by the builder or developer without confusing it with sales and management fees.

## SEVEN MAJOR EVALUATORS FOR PREPARING A PROSPECTING PLAN

To develop a well-conceived, efficient prospecting plan, experts in this profession recommend thorough evaluation of the following seven factors in this order of priority before committing time or money to implementation:

1. prospect profiles
2. location factors including signage
3. competition's impact on your strategies
4. referral base and cross-selling potential
5. cooperative broker support
6. media choices, costs and values
7. publicity, public relations and personal prospecting

Each of these deserves thoughtful review and a rating that will help to establish priorities of action. Let's explore them in greater detail from the vantage point of a marketer with a modest budget and an absolute necessity of moving the assigned merchandise within a specific time frame.

## ANTICIPATE AND INTERPRET PROSPECT PROFILES

The foundation for decision making in all areas of marketing is understanding the profiles of anticipated buyers. It is where research begins during the design stage and it reaches the critical point in the establishment of the prospecting plan. You cannot know too much about the people you hope to attract and sell. If you are extending an ongoing marketing program, it is simply a matter of reviewing whom you have and have not sold to date and interpreting the whys. If you are starting a totally new marketing operation with no base from which to draw conclusions, your investigation and projections must be very thoroughly tested. Everything you plan to do in reaching and convincing people to inspect and purchase your homes depends upon how well you have interpreted who they are and what will motivate them to act. Four major factors will dictate prospecting efficiencies:

1.  *Where do they live now and what do they own or rent?* Predicting where your profiled prospects currently reside and the nature of the housing they occupy is a vital factor in making your judgment calls on how to reach them and what to promote to gain their attention. How many customers will be currently residing within the county or city you are serving versus transferees and relocated families? Are they homeowners or renters? If owners, will most of them have to sell before they purchase and, if so, how easily will it be for them to dispose of their existing residences in the current market? What sizes and types of homes, condominiums or apartments will they typically occupy? If owners, what is the approximate price range of their present housing? Will they be moving up or down in price and size? (Note: if they are moving up, most studies show that the average improvement over existing housing prices is in the range of 20–35 percent maximum. If stepping down, particularly the empty-nester groups, they are most likely to be cash buyers with large equities seeking more convenience and comfort.) Most important, what discontent factors in their present environments (housing and neighborhoods) might trigger a desire to move? Since a primary objective of advertising and promotion is to breed discontent, it is essential to interpret correctly what you have to offer that will be perceived as an improvement by your targeted groups.

2.  *Where are your prospects currently employed and what industries or professions are high-target candidates?* Employment centers dictate housing locations. There is a limit to how far most people will drive to go to and from work each day. Newly located industries stimulate opportunities and motivations to relocate. Existing employment centers provide the key to housing decisions their employees will carefully weigh. In evaluating this

factor, try to isolate the professions, major employers, commercial enterprises and industrial or business complexes that will be important to profiled customers. Do particular groups such as doctors and medical assistants deserve special attention because you are near the major hospitals and clinics, or teachers because you are close to the university?

If transferees are important to you, you need a targeted approach to reach them before they make housing decisions. Often, that means cultivating the dominant relocation brokerage organizations as well as establishing direct contact with personnel offices of major employers. Anticipating where you will want signs and billboards relates to commuter patterns and employment locations.

3. *What are the lifestyles and social interests of your buyers.* How do your prospects live? What do they do for entertainment and recreation? What clubs, churches, business affiliations and social centers are important to them? Where do they congregate when they are not at home? What are their dominant interests in life? If you are appealing to a family-oriented market, the needs and interests of their offspring will be important to your marketing messages. Schools are the main factor, followed by social and recreational influences. Understanding what your prospects are most trying to improve or duplicate in their housing environments will provide clues for your promotional thrust.

4. *What media will most effectively reach your prospects?* As you evaluate investments in marketing messages, you need to interpret the relative values of various communication media in their ability to reach large segments of your potential buyers with cost-effective results. Start your evaluation with the more obvious means of exposure and work through the checklist to media that may only apply to a vary narrow segment of the population. The objective is to determine which vehicles will have the strongest influence on your profiled groups. What do your prospects read? Listen to? Watch? Whom and what do they trust? What types of messages and media win favorable attention?

Beginning with print media, your checklist should include a review of the following:

- Local newspapers
  Classified
  Display
  Sections most frequently read
  Which newspapers reach most prospects?
  Which days of the week have the highest readership?
- Real estate/housing periodicals
  New home magazines or catalogues
  General real estate periodicals
- Radio broadcasting
  Stations most listened to by your prospects
  Time of day for highest audience response

Radio personalities with most credibility to your audience

Types of programs that provide best listening formats

Validate ratings (Arbitron rating system)

- Television

  Channels most watched by prospects

  Cable channels versus commercial stations

  Prime time versus other viewing periods

  Validate ratings (Nielsen rating system)

- Billboards

  What are the most frequently travelled routes for your target groups?

  How much eye competition do they experience along these routes?

  What is the availability of billboard space in corridors with the greatest exposure?

  What are the competitive housing messages?

- Direct-mail campaigns

  Can you pinpoint names and addresses of profiled prospects?

  What are they currently receiving by direct mail from competitive programs?

  What mail pieces gain their attention and are most likely to be opened and read?

- Literature-distribution points

  Do your prospects pick up free literature about the community, housing or business?

  What distribution points work for you or your competitors?

  What types of free literature have the greatest appeal and the widest distribution?

  Are there companies or individuals in your market that provide a distribution service?

  Does the local chamber of commerce, visitors' information center or tourist bureau provide housing information to the public, especially transferees?

- Special events

  What special events related to housing interests currently attract consumers? Are there home and garden shows, housing fairs, county fairs, annual parade of homes, "street of dreams," or similar promotions worth consideration?

  What is the potential of bringing some of your prospects to an educational event such as how-to-buy-a-home seminar or real estate investment seminar?

  Are there ongoing educational programs that merit support?

- Satellite displays

  Where do potential buyers shop? Are these locations worth investment in satellite displays, booths or offices?

  If business travelers and transferees are target candidates for new housing, is the local airport an efficient means of reaching them?

  Are there cooperating lenders, REALTORS® and others whose offices would provide exposure opportunities?

- Telephone canvassing

    Can you pinpoint the addresses and phone numbers of your profiled prospects?

    How effective are others in using the telephone to prospect for new business?

    What hours of the days are most likely to find your prospects at home?

    What messages can you create that will capture and hold attention long enough to be effective on the telephone?

## Special Attention Should Be Devoted to Search-Corridor Media

When prospects are searching for housing, they have a more intensive interest in specific information sources than when they are on the sidelines only casually observing advertising programs. Classified ads, housing digests, new home supplements and directional signage are important elements in the search-corridor phenomenon. Thus, it may not be as important to know what your profiled prospects watch and read in their day-to-day activities as it is to pinpoint what they will seek when researching housing information because of a desire to relocate. The specific search-corridor media they select and the degree to which they use them are vital factors in choosing the placement of your advertising dollars. Knowing the normal media habits of your prospects is useful for placing intrusive advertising designed to stimulate interest where none was previously manifested. However, consumers who are in the market now are more important to your cause than those who might be encouraged to investigate after an intensive media intrusion into their consciousness. Your marketing dollars should be weighted toward activities that will reach the people already searching for new housing opportunities. That obviously includes influencing brokers who are working with a very high percentage of these active customers.

## EVALUATE THE LOCATION AND ITS EXPOSURE POTENTIAL

Once you have defined and analyzed your housing candidates, the next step is to review carefully the advantages and disadvantages of the location(s) you are marketing as prospect-recruiting tools. The least expensive of all lead-generation sources, other than personal referrals, is to use the location as the principal drawing card. For example, if your new community has the benefit of natural exposure to your profiled prospects because they drive by it every day, you might survive without running a single ad in the newspaper or spending dollars on any other form of marketing except for models and on-site sales facilities! Properly signed, flagged and well-lit show homes can become their own billboards. I have experienced many successful sales programs that derived almost all of their business from street traffic without any outside advertising expenditures. Their locations were their reasons for acceptance and success. On the other hand, if the housing location has very limited exposure to local traffic or to profiled buyers, you must compensate for that disadvantage and invest in off-site marketing systems.

The initial phase of extending your marketing message to reach customers begins with a thorough evaluation of signage needs and opportunities. Historically in the housing business, signs account for a very high percentage of closed sales. National averages range from 20 to 30 percent. In many markets, signs on major thoroughfares are far more important than ads in the newspaper. In the order of importance and working from the least expensive to the most costly, the types of signage we explore are:

1. On-site identification signs that capture maximum attention from passing or arriving traffic.

2. Portable directional signage that can be installed and removed as needed to direct traffic along major access streets. Sometimes these are known as bandits, bootlegs, or temporary signs. They vary in size from telephone-pole width to A-frames positioned on major corners or in medians. They are not legal in many cities, but we use them with discretion to accomplish objectives. Often they are installed on Friday night and removed on Monday morning just to meet the needs of weekend drive-bys. Some builders pay the fines imposed by the municipalities rather than forgo the exposure advantages of bootleg signage.

3. Semi permanent directional signage, typically of wood or fabricated materials that will stand some extended wear. Normal sizes range from four by seven feet to five by ten feet. Some leasing expenses may be incurred with these semi-portable directionals.

4. Major directional signage at key locations and with substantial structural quality and larger dimensions. These are more expensive installations and usually have to be elevated on tall supports to gain the height needed for maximum visibility. Professional sign companies are almost always required to handle these billboard-quality installations. Sizes range from eight by 16 feet to 20 by 40 feet or more. Leasing expenses are almost always involved.

5. Billboards installed and managed by outdoor advertising companies. These are the most expensive of all the signage campaigns and should be carefully studied before making the investment. Rotating billboards or negotiating for fixed locations for specific time frames must be weighed against other uses of available marketing dollars. Some of these boards can cost as much as $5,000 to $10,000 a month. However, if you are involved with a major project that needs to capture the attention of primary expressway traffic and your only means of effectively reaching prospects is to purchase one or more primary outdoor advertising display boards, the allocation of funds may be essential to your success. The use of an advertising agency is recommended if you elect to become involved with this medium of exposure.

To help you decide, it is best to take a local or regional street map and physically mark all locations for signage that seem appropriate to meet your objectives. Then someone should drive these streets and highways noting all existing signs and those that may be available. Study your competitor's signage program and evaluate its influences on your marketing strategies. The process of negotiating for sign locations is time consuming. That is why most marketing directors assign this function to either a professional sign company or a sales agent with an interest in seeing the community succeed. The person in charge of marketing should never abdicate the responsibility of personally inspecting the sites that are recommended prior to completion of the signage system.

When securing adequate signage is difficult due to regulations or restricted usage, always look at some of the creative solutions others have applied, such as:

- trailers or other vehicles with attached signs strategically parked in legal locations
- bus benches or sitting areas you provide with painted ads
- rent the end or side of an old barn and paint your sign on the building
- human billboards on weekends. Kids hired to hold or carry signs at strategic corners
- high-flying flags (or balloons) over the sales office
- riders on existing signs (with permission of owners)
- purchase signs on buses or taxis that cover your area

## CRITERIA FOR SIGNS THAT CREATE MAXIMUM INTEREST

Outdoor advertising has its own criteria that should not be confused with elements that influence brochures, print media or model home signage. Major signs on busy highways must be carefully designed to be read in four seconds or less. They must quickly capture visual attention against the backdrop of the sky, green trees, white snow and brown hills, often amidst eye pollution caused by multiple signage within a congested streetscape.

The first item to be rated in the design stage is how effective it will be against typical landscapes in which it will be located. The second is how readable it will be for occupants of automobiles moving at normal speeds. The third is what messages must appear and in what priority of position and size. The true test is to build a sample, set it in a typical location and have it inspected by a number of people. The name of the community, the housing types, the price range and brief directions may be all you can effectively display.

The Outdoor Advertising Institute recommends that no more than six words be used on a typical billboard. Instantly recognizable graphics able to communicate a motivating message should do what you cannot accomplish with words. It is best to use one key message and supplement it with your logo and a distinctive graphic. Driving directions, arrows and turn indicators can be placed on aprons or riders. As for the most effective colors, experts suggest the following guidelines:

- Black on yellow is easiest to read for roadside identification—but it lacks class.
- Earth tones depict quality but tend to bleed together and lose character.
- White on brown is a strong reader. Dark backgrounds with white or light reverses for messages stand out from a distance.
- Blues and greens are excellent colors for real estate developments, but caution must be exercised to avoid visual loss against blue skies and green backgrounds.
- Red or orange can be a very effective attention getter.

- White backgrounds often fade into the sky. Study the amount of light and the nature of the surroundings before choosing white as a dominant schematic.
- When colors blend or fail to pop, use drop-shadow letters with a black block effect.
- Cut outs that rise above the normal frame will create added visual interest.

## Signs Need to Reflect Activity and Success

Always design your signage program with the objective of keeping it fresh and keyed to the tempo of your community. Provide for ways to use riders or snipes for promoting special events like new openings, special financing, limited availability, etc. Be sure to provide for a sign-maintenance program that assures they will be clean, erect, fresh and effective. When signs begin to deteriorate, so will sales! Success is reflected in the images we visually portray.

The use of flags and other elements to create movement can measurably add to the attention gaining ability of any key billboard or directional. Regularly inspect your signage locations and note condition, visibility, readability, and competitive positioning.

## DEVELOP STRATEGIES THAT CAPITALIZE ON DIFFERENCES WITH YOUR COMPETITION

It is rare to have a community or housing product line that has no competition! If that ever occurs, you can ignore most of the advice we give you in this book, because the homes and location will probably sell themselves! Competitive housing is a factor in almost every marketing scenario. Your prospects are going to shop—and so should you! Unless you thoroughly know your competition and have developed positioning strategies to enhance your marketing effectiveness, you are at a distinct disadvantage. When assembling specifics that will influence your decisions, you need to study consumers' reactions to other offerings in your region and relate those findings to your communication criteria. What products are in direct competition for the same profiled buyers? Which are complementary, since they are above or below your price range and social-economic profiles? Which sites draw the most traffic and why? Can you use their traffic to help sell your products?

One of the better strategies (and certainly a cost-effective approach) is to place your signage where it will be highly visible to prospects inspecting your competition's housing, alerting them to the merits of seeing what you have to offer before they purchase. There are advantages to being in an area where multiple builders are providing housing products open to public inspection. When the public knows they can see a number of comparisons at the same time, they are more inclined to visit that location. The challenge and opportunity is to position your merchandise so it will benefit from the shopping experience.

Suppose you are building in a major subdivision or master-planned community and you are only one of several builders offering housing choices within its boundaries. How can you benefit from the traffic drawn to the general community? If the developer has accepted the responsibility of promoting the community for the benefit of all concerned, concentrate your prospecting dollars within the immediate area, particularly on your model showcase. If you have a primary location exposed to most arriving traffic, you can ignore your competition, providing you have superior on-site presentation elements. On the other hand, if your consumers are stopping at the other builders' homes first and you are located away from primary access routes, you need to develop strategies (including signage) that will gain consumers' attention. Sometimes that strategy must focus on the central sales organization that represents all builders in the community. Time and attention spent with agents to emphasize your values may be more important than anything else you can do to position your products correctly.

A primary objective of effective marketing is to establish clearly the unique selling points that distinguish your homes and environment from everyone else. Messages must be hard-hitting, easy to understand and motivating! You cannot effectively prospect for business without understanding what it will take to bring your customers to your front door!

## REVIEW THE POTENTIAL FOR CROSS-SELLING AND REFERRALS

If you have a building program with an established base of satisfied homeowners, part of your prospecting plan should focus on ways to capture the internal business opportunities available at your fingertips. Builders with a long history of quality construction in the same housing region normally experience a substantial percentage of new sales as a result of their previous involvement with purchasers. Trading up (or down) with the same builder is a potential if buyers believe they have been treated well by that organization and its representatives. Without a solid after-sales service plan, such referrals are seldom attained. This subject is addressed in greater detail later. For the moment, concentrate on prospecting and identifying ways to produce extra sales from the platform already in existence.

Suppose you currently have two or three projects or neighborhoods with model homes and sales operations. If you open another one within reasonable distance of these existing subdivisions, cross-selling potential exists. This is especially true if price ranges or products are distinctly different. People who are not qualified or interested in one category of housing can be directed or taken to another type and location more suited to their needs. When opening a new area, a practical way to keep marketing costs at a minimum and begin an early pioneering sales campaign is to use a nearby model or sales center as the base from which to presell the new one until it is ready for staffing.

Brokerage companies representing more than one builder can also use cross-selling techniques effectively as long as they do not subvert their primary responsibility to represent professionally and sell first the builder's homes to which prospects are drawn. Varying prices, styles and locations provide justification for guiding customers from one builder to another. Incentives should be in place for cross referrals when this is an objective of the marketing strategy. Salespeople on one site should benefit from keeping business within the family, but not necessarily to the same degree as they would from selling their assigned product lines.

## EVALUATE EXPECTED SUPPORT FROM COOPERATIVE BROKERS AND OTHER REAL ESTATE OFFICES

As previously noted, cooperating real estate agents working with on-site specialists or key agents within brokerage companies account for nearly 40 percent of all new housing sales in this country. The small-volume builder (under 25 homes a year) is far more dependent upon this source of buyers than are large-volume merchant builders. In most cases, the smaller builders do not have sites that justify full-time staffing, so most of their sales result from prospects delivered to them by either their listing agents or others who cooperate with them. Where on-site sales professionals have the primary responsibility for selling the builders' homes, the cooperation is accomplished by encouraging them to cultivate the brokers in their market area and develop productive working relationships. To assure maximum cooperation, most progressive marketers compensate their on-site specialists for every sale made by an outside agency. This promotes goodwill and provides incentives for the builders' representatives to assist the general agents and to follow through with all of the after-sales servicing activities.

Since new home sales commissions are often less than those paid to resale agents, there can be less motivation to show new homes than older ones. Sometimes it is wise to raise the new home cooperating rate to a level equal to or even slightly more than that for used home sales. The amount of support you can expect is directly related to the financial incentives provided to the outside sales representatives. When you have an on-site sales staff and are seeking outside-broker cooperation, it is best to treat dollars paid to brokerage firms as prospect-generation fees and not as sales commissions. Your specialists will still have to do most of the sales work and after-sale coordination. The fees paid to REALTORS® who deliver qualified customers to your front door and influence them to purchase are comparable to the dollars you spend for other forms of prospecting such as newspaper ads or billboards, but with a much greater return, since the fee is only due if a sale is closed. On-site representatives need to understand that concept. They tend to resent that outside salespeople receive more than they do and with less commitment to the sales process. If it is explained to them that these fees are for producing prospects and not for closing sales, they may be somewhat less inclined to depreciate the value of the cooperating brokers' roles.

How much support can you expect? That depends upon local market customs, money available to compensate general agents, the nature of the property and the type of buyers you are seeking. For example, transferees are far more likely to seek the services of real estate brokers than are first-time buyers. Single-family home buyers are more likely to use real estate brokers than are those seeking condominiums. One guideline is to check your competition and measure the amount of cooperative sales they are experiencing versus your own projects. Builders who aggressively cultivate brokers invariably realize a higher percentage of sales from this source than do those who ignore them.

There is also the matter of being consistent. It is unreasonable to expect support from brokers if you only involve them when you are in a cleanup role or in a difficult sales situation. To assure maximum support when you really need it, be consistent and maintain a cooperative marketing plan at all times. Major concerns expressed by general real estate agents who are asked to cooperate with on-site sales specialists include the following:

- *Client-protection policies.* Are they clear, and is the cooperating agent assured of protection if customers return and purchase from on-site personnel? To avoid misunderstandings, rules should be printed and distributed to all brokers.
- *Delays in payment of commissions.* Building a new home takes time and commissions are postponed until settlement. Will they be promptly paid and are they secure? To encourage support, some builders advance a portion of the broker's fee upon mortgage approval and the balance at closing.
- *Loss of referrals and future business.* Where on-site personnel are in regular contact with the customers introduced to them by cooperating agents, the relationships may be confused. The pros in real estate selling make it a practice to cultivate future referral business, and they want reassurance they have not lost those benefits because they sell new homes instead of resales.
- *Lack of information about the new homes and the details regarding what is included, optional, etc.* Warranties and related ownership factors are different than in resales, and agents are uncomfortable representing properties they do not fully understand.

### Ideas for Stimulating Cooperative-Broker Programs

Many ideas can be employed to win the cooperation of real estate brokers and their sales associates. Here is a partial list.

1.  Conduct regular on-site orientation sessions for preferred brokers, and notify agents in advance of each session. Make the sessions informative and fun. Serve refreshments, and take time to become personally acquainted with each salesperson.
2.  Assign one or more on-site specialists to service selected brokerage companies in your market area. Encourage these representatives to visit each office, meet the brokers and sales associates, participate in sales meetings and maintain regular contact by phone and mail.
3.  Register all brokers and agents who inspect your homes, and send thank-you notes for their support. Whenever they show your homes, always say thank you in special ways. Be certain to reinforce them in the presence of their customers.
4.  Publish a broker newsletter and mail it regularly to all individuals on your cooperating list. Use the letter both to promote current properties and to recognize agents who have shown and sold homes for you.
5.  Establish a broker-recognition program with appropriate awards for achievement. Cooperating agent or broker-of-the-month recognition culminating in company- and/or agent-of-the-year awards can provide additional stimulus to those who win as well as others who want to emulate their success.
6.  Refer listings and cooperative leads to agents who achieve the best results for you. This is a fringe benefit that on-site specialists can use to advantage in cultivating outside support.

7. Prepare presentation binders for use by outside agents. These visualizer kits can help to communicate your values in off-site selling environments.

8. Prepare a slide show or videotape that you can use to educate brokers and their people in their own offices.

9. Conduct special parties and events for brokers to bring everyone together for fun and recognition: annual picnics, Christmas parties, awards banquets, educational events, etc. A REALTOR® breakfast meeting is one of the more popular means of promoting a new community or recognizing performers. Broker recreation events also prove effective. If your community has amenities such as a golf course or swimming pool, you might reserve their use for a day and sponsor an event that will expose brokers to your environment under ideal conditions.

10. Design your contests and special incentives based on current marketing objectives. Provide cash bonuses for selling spec homes, vacation trips to selected resorts for attaining a prescribed number of sales. Gift certificates to restaurants, or choice of gifts from a catalogue are appropriate incentives based on accumulated points.

11. Feature the pictures of top cooperating agents in your offices.

12. Attend broker functions, such as multiple-listing meetings, and use these occasions to promote your homes as well as establish better working relationships with the leading brokers.

13. Print special flyers to alert cooperating agents about inventory, contests, etc., and circulate to every salesperson on the master list. If you are not a member of a multiple-listing service, you might elect to provide a quasi-MLS promotion by printing your own product work sheets complete with photographs of every home or homesite you have for sale.

14. Recognize cooperating REALTORS® in your own advertising. For example, you might feature a list of all participating brokers who have shown or sold your homes in the past few months. This could be just a strip across the bottom of a regular ad that does not detract from the primary function of the layout.

The following is an example of an information sheet and code of understanding published by a builder for the benefit of cooperative brokers.

## FIGURE 8.2  Broker Code of Mutual Understanding

We cordially welcome the participation of brokers in the representation of our new homes. We are publishing these procedures to promote mutual cooperation and assure the smooth and efficient processing of sales transactions. In the absence of a written agreement between a Broker and an Officer of our company, these guidelines will prevail over the spoken word. The intent is to encourage the Broker to show homes built by our company and receive a commission of three percent of the selling price for a Broker-generated sale. Sales generated by our own sales force will not involve commissions to brokers. The following guidelines will apply:

The broker, or salesperson, must personally take his/her client to our sales office and introduce the prospect to our on-site specialist(s). It will be his/her responsibility to register the client on the appropriate broker-registration card and present it to our representative. This card shall be dated, and the real estate office shall be due a commission, provided that the sales contract is originated within sixty (60) days from the date of the visit. It is understood that a visit constitutes a registration, even though such registration is done by the selling agent and the prospective buyer does not physically sign an instrument of registration. The broker or the agent is expected to assist our representative in showing the property and obtaining a sales agreement. Our representative shall be responsible for providing current information regarding sales prices, options, financing, available inventory and construction details.

We will honor the real estate broker's commission providing the following rules are followed:

1. The broker or his/her representative accompanies the client on the initial visit to our sales office.
2. The broker (agent) leaves written notice on the appropriate registration card indicating the pertinent information about the client.
3. The client purchases from our company within sixty (60) days of the initial visit or any authorized extension of that time period. The broker may extend the registration protection period for an additional thirty (30) days by written notice, mailed or delivered to our sales offices before expiration of the first 60 days.

Our Broker Code of Mutual Understanding also includes the following points:

1. No broker will be allowed to advertise our homes without our written permission.
2. We will maintain a single price policy: Whether we sell the new home or whether it is sold by a cooperating broker, the price will be the same. The selling price will always include the commission.
3. The broker will always use our purchase agreement.
4. The title company to be used and the place of closing will be solely at the discretion of our company unless otherwise agreed upon in writing by all parties.
5. The commission rate to the cooperating broker shall be three percent (3%) of the purchase price as it appears on page 1 of our Agreement for Sale and Purchase.
6. All commissions will be paid at closing by the title company or attorney.
7. While our company attempts to mark all optional extras in our models, the agent should ascertain which items are not included in the basic selling price by obtaining that information from one of our authorized representatives.
8. Any representations made by selling agent to buyer are not binding on our company unless incorporated in the contract by an addendum acknowledged by an officer of our organization.

(continued)

---

**FIGURE 8.2   Broker code of mutual understanding (concluded)**

---

9. No commission is earned by broker, nor any obligation incurred by our company, until the actual act of closing the sale occurs.

10. Mortgage processing will normally be the responsibility of our representatives. However, instances may occur when the broker will be required to assist and facilitate the mortgage approval process.

11. Registration in one of our subdivisions applies only to that specific location to which the broker has personally escorted and registered the client. Other projects must be separately visited and registered to qualify for commission protection.

12. Disbursement of commissions will be made from closing proceeds by the title company or attorney.

13. The published prices on all our homes are closely monitored and represent a fair reflection of market value at all times. Therefore, we do not accept offers that are less than full price nor negotiate sales prices.

14. Whenever you have a problem or a question, we encourage you to contact one of our sales consultants or our sales manager. We solicit your support and want to be sure we are providing you with the information and cooperation you need to effectively sell our homes.

Dated:_____ Real Estate Broker:_____

---

## EVALUATE THE COST EFFECTIVENESS OF ALL MEDIA

Your media choices, with the exception of billboards, can be classified into two broad categories: print and broadcast. Historically in our industry, print media capture the majority of our promotional dollars, and only a nominal amount is spent on electronic communication. Most of the print dollars will be spent with one or two leading newspapers and the balance in a select number of real estate-oriented periodicals, such as magazines that feature available housing in that region. In too many cases, our decisions to spend available marketing dollars are based on a follow-the-leader pattern. Because we see other builders and real estate organizations using a particular newspaper, we presume everyone else has done our research for us. Smart marketers do their own homework and validate their decisions by monitoring the cost effectiveness of media placement against the actual results realized on the sales line. You can employ advertising agencies or other media consultants to make recommendations, but you should also have a working knowledge of the relative costs and coverage of the media selected. Distribution patterns, audience profiles and readership totals are available from every newspaper or periodical. The same type of information about radio and television stations can be secured from independent monitoring organizations. Once you invest in a particular advertising vehicle, measuring the quantity and quality of responses serves as the best safeguard for making the wisest use of your dollars.

## WHAT SHOULD PRINT MEDIA ACCOMPLISH?

A primary objective of well-targeted advertising is to produce prospective buyers in sufficient numbers so that a substantial percentage of them will become new home owners. The degree to which that can be accomplished depends upon the readership value of the ads and the number of potential prospects in the market at the time they are featured. It is unreasonable to expect an ad to do what salespeople are employed to accomplish. Ads do not sell the homes. If they produce qualified traffic or make the phones ring, they have done their job. Advertising will not solve the problem of overpriced properties, compensate for bad designs or sell locations where people do not want to live! It is also unreasonable to expect your ads totally to prequalify your buyers. They can be targeted to arouse the interest of a select audience, but the coverage will spill over into other readership groups.

At a very minimum level of effectiveness, newspaper ads should arouse some degree of curiosity about your new housing neighborhoods. They should help establish and reinforce your image in the marketplace with residual benefits to all of your business objectives. Consumers as well as others in the business community can follow your progress through the advertising messages they review. A subtle but positive effect happens to the morale of your salespeople and purchasers from the placement of well-designed advertising. Many marketers believe that one of the primary objectives of newspaper promotion is to reinforce other forms of marketing such as billboards and directional signage. The ad plants a memory link, and the billboard triggers recall and results in a reinforcing action. Each was necessary to synergize the total marketing system.

Effective print media advertising should have the following characteristics:

1. A dominant, attention-winning theme that captures immediate interest of profiled readers.
2. Emotionally appealing graphics that complement the theme and the body copy.
3. Well-written copy that provides enough information to trigger further interest but still leaves things to be discovered upon arrival.
4. A continuity in the graphic representations of the community, the developer/ builder and the housing so that repetition will build sustained marketing images.
5. A sense of urgency to act now rather than delay inspection or a phone call.
6. Easy-to-interpret instructions (most often in the form of a map) to direct people to the sales facilities.
7. A design format that stands out from competitive advertising and favorably impresses the readers.
8. A good balance between selling housing products and lifestyles.
9. A clean, uncluttered appearance that does not lose the focus of the advertising theme.
10. Inclusion of all necessary disclaimers, truth-in-lending and equal-housing information. Always include phone numbers and office hours.

---

**FIGURE 8.3   Print Media Ad Examples**

---

Advertising Campaign
Shea Homes
*(Northern California Division)*

*Campaign Theme:*
It's the little things that make it a Shea.

This campaign was prompted by a desire to provide Shea Homes with ad designs that stood out from the usual clutter in local real estate sections; to break away from the long-established habit of trying to sell homes based on exterior designs, and create more interest in what it would be like to live INSIDE a Shea home.

To accomplish this, the campaign focused for the most part on details inside each home that could be seen as desirable, luxurious, or out of the ordinary. They were then visualized through realistic, elegant style illustrations with stark, simplistic headlines such as The Bath, The Hearth, The Solarium, etc. Each illustration was an actual representation of a feature in one of the homes. To then create the feeling of living in the home, people representative of the target profiles for each community became important elements in the illustrations.

The overall theme for the ads, "It's the little things that make it a Shea," captured the feeling of the careful planning and craftsmanship that goes into each home which create the value. Consequently, "value" became the umbrella word for the combo ad.

The campaign was extended very easily as new projects with new design features came along. The ads continued to appear fresh after running in print for three years, providing continuity to the desired image that Shea Homes is a home builder of consistent quality with products that encompass innovative living designs.

Throughout the three years of the campaign, traffic and sales have increased steadily at almost every community. In fact, at several communities the success was overwhelming with immediate sellouts of each new release regardless of price range. Also, during this period several comprehensive research projects were undertaken that further verified the validity of the advertising approach. The one notable exception was a community where the research indicated that the *location* had limited appeal to the target market and the advertising struggled to overcome this difficulty. The same product in a different location enjoyed an excellent sales success using a similar advertising approach.

Courtesy of Coakley, Heagerty Advertising Agency, Santa Clara, CA

**FIGURE 8.3    Print Media Ad Examples (continued)**

**FIGURE 8.3    Print Media Ad Examples (continued)**

**FIGURE 8.3 Print Media Ad Examples (continued)**

**FIGURE 8.3    Print Media Ad Examples (continued)**

THE BATH

Step inside the bath at Campton Chase. Notice how the sunken tub is surrounded by shiny ceramic tile? And how the sunlight brightly shines through the overhead windows? Over here are hardwood cabinets and a separate dressing area.

When Shea sets out to build a home, they carefully consider every detail, even down to the size and color of the tub. The result is a home that's not only a pleasure to see, but one that's a pleasure in which to live.

You see it here in the bath. And you'll see it throughout every Campton Chase home.

Three- and four-bedroom homes priced from the upper $200,000's.

Take Highway 17 to Camden Avenue. Turn left on Coleman; right on Almaden and follow the signs to the models. Open daily, 10 a.m. to 6 p.m. Call (408) 997-7636.

CAMPTON CHASE

Prices, terms, specifications and availabilities subject to change without notice.    *It's the little things that make it a Shea.*    Shea HOMES

**FIGURE 8.3   Print Media Ad Examples (continued)**

Ad Title: ''All Homes Are Not Created Equal''
Community: StoneRise
Developer: HOWCO RESIDENTIAL COMMUNITY, INC.
Location: Lawrenceville, New Jersey
Product: 72 Twin/Townhomes priced from $169,990
Comments:

Over 200 ads are running locally in the newspaper. Most of the ads are what you would typically see on the real estate page. To catch the eye of the reader (which is the first objective of any advertising), we developed the headline and visual. Once it attracts the attention of the reader, the ad tries to motivate qualified prospects to action. Traffic was excellent and excellent sales resulted.

SOURCE: Courtesy of Group Two, Philadelphia, PA.

---

**FIGURE 8.3   Print Media Ad Examples (continued)**

Ad Title: "Give These Homes the Boot"
Community: The Woods of North Ridge
Developer: Dominion Homes
Location: Raleigh, North Carolina
Product: Single family homes from $86,900
Comments:

This community of single family homes was in a preconstruction phase. However, one model was built for a parade of homes. The competition was offering similar product at moderately lower prices. Traffic was quite low and interest was poor.

How do we increase the traffic and over come price difference? We developed a strategy of creating a sense of urgency by creating an ad which would explain to potential prospects that they can save substantial dollars by coming out now. Preconstruction is traditionally associated with site activity and muddy shoes. We have used the appropriate visual and provocative headline to create this impression.

The community experienced 40-percent increase in traffic.

SOURCE: Courtesy of Group Two, Philadelphia, PA.

FIGURE 8.3    Print Media Ad Examples (continued)

Ad Title: "This Kitchen Cooks"
Community: Southern Oaks
Developer: Kettler Forlines Homes
Location: Fairfax County, Virginia
Product: 59 Townhomes in a Wooded Setting from the $140,000's
Target Market: Young professional couples mainly without children and, in addition, some professional singles.
Ad Rationale:

Many builders in this market were using very straightforward product advertising showing exteriors of their homes. The buyer profile identified this prospect as a busy professional who might be a weekend chef but also may be using the functional kitchen as a place for dining on take-out or for preparing foods for entertainment purposes.

Placing the photograph of the kitchen in the ad on an angle was the method used to attract attention to the copy of the ad as well as was the headline "This Kitchen Cooks," and subhead "Even if you don't." This is the reference to having a functional kitchen for entertainment or nightly cooking use. The formatted corporate border treatment is used in all Kettler Forline's ads as an immediate identifier of the Kettler Forlines Community. The corporate logo, the map and the community logo along with the phone number and directions are always kept in or near the same position in each of this builder's ads.

Traffic at this community increased 25 percent from the previous advertising and the additional prospects were better qualified than before.

SOURCE: Courtesy of Group Two, Philadelphia, PA.

## CREATIVITY AND THE MEDIA PLAN

Advertising is in many ways an art form—the art of persuasion. To persuade effectively, one must understand the motivations of human beings and be able to perceive how humans will react to various stimuli. Marketing is more than presentation, and persuasion is more than advertising. Successful advertisers believe that products exist for people—not people for products! All products must be positioned to fulfill human motivations and needs. All advertising messages must be provocative and attention holding! They must do so in a positive, professional and stimulating manner. They should also convey an image compatible with the consumer's values and the objectives of the company. The best ads not only convey a positive message, they motivate people to act! Headlines or graphics must capture attention, and then the copy must trigger one or more dominant motivations that cause readers to respond. Some sense of urgency is also essential to compensate for normal resistance to change.

Creative advertisers study the media and the competition to effectively position their clients' products in ways that contrast with what everyone else is doing! Formats, headlines, graphics, body copy and accent elements like typeface and tone contrast must aim for reader interest. The following is a checklist of recommended design and content criteria furnished to us by several agencies and marketing organizations nationally recognized as authorities in real estate advertising.

- Develop and consistently use a basic advertising format. One format will help your readers recognize your advertisements and impute such qualities as integrity, quality, stability and commitment.
- Always get your key message into the headlines. It should tell the story in brief, including brand name and the consumer benefit. Avoid headlines that do not convey consumer-oriented messages.
- Target the key headline to the interest of your profiled prospect. You can select your audience by appealing to the interests of your specific group.
- Make your headlines newsworthy. Whenever you have anything new to talk about, promote it. News and new things interest consumers.
- Don't shy from long headlines. Research indicates that, on the average, headlines with more information are more effective than shorter ones!
- Photographs are better than drawings if they reproduce well. Research verifies that photography increases memory recall an average of 26 percent over art work.
- Keep layouts simple. One dominant picture is better than a number of smaller ones.
- Always caption your photographs. Readership of photo captions is twice as great as that of body copy.
- Testimonials add to credibility. Endorsements of real people are more memorable and powerful than what you say about your own products.
- Review your ads in their editorial environment. Ask your agency or media manager to permit you to see your ads pasted into the newspaper or magazine in which they will be featured. You can be deceived by beautifully mounted, glossy finished ads that will never appear the same way when reproduced.

- Use white space and framing to create distinctive ad formats.
- All typeface, composition elements and white space balance should convey dignity and professionalism.
- Photography should be technically excellent. Graphics should be emotionally consistent with the primary message of the advertisement.
- Always position photography, art, logos, maps, headlines, and copy to communicate a clear, concise message. Do not try to tell everything in one ad.
- Seek page dominance by size, format or design. For example, if you design your ad to run above the fold in the paper (a minimum of 5 columns by 12 inches), you have a better chance of controlling the page than would a smaller ad.
- Avoid skinny ads that fall into the gutter, like those that are one column by 12 inches or two columns by full-page height.
- Since most people scan newspapers from right to left, try to design and position your ads to take advantage of this phenomenon.
- Consistency and cohesiveness should be maintained in ad design, format, and general appearance in collateral material. They should also be consistent from one media form to another so that all messages interrelate and increase the power of the marketing dollar.
- Consider using color for special promotions. Although it is typically 50 percent more expensive, the added attention value can often be justified. One of the values of housing digests and new home magazines is the reproduction capacity for 4-color ads that have maximum clarity in contrast to newspaper print methods.
- Make sure your messages are credible. Avoid exaggerations and generalizations. Include facts to back up your claims. Today's buyers are knowledgeable—and suspicious!
- Every ad should be written with a person in mind and read as though it might be talking one-to-one with the prospect.
- Use romantic words and phrases that articulate the benefits of the product, price, location and lifestyles. Empathy, understanding and respect for the reader should be conveyed in the language and style.

## GUIDELINES FOR PLACEMENT AND FREQUENCY

Since advertising should reach as many potential prospects as possible in a cost-efficient manner, the size, location and number of insertions are important considerations. Featuring larger ads just to obtain a sense of dominance is not necessarily cost effective. You do not increase readership proportionate to the increase in space! The same dollars you might spend for one full-page ad could well be divided between two half-page insertions located in different sections of the newspaper. Or you can repeat the smaller ad twice as often on different days of the week. Dominance for readership attention can be accomplished as much by the design and message of the ad as it can be by purchasing more space. Study the advertising used by others and try to be distinctly different and more dramatic so that readers' eyes automatically gravitate to your ads as they scan the pages. You seldom need to purchase a total page to accomplish visual dominance!

How often should you feature the same ad in the same medium? The rule is essentially: "if it is working—don't fix it!" Well-designed ads that continue to draw qualified traffic deserve repetition for two reasons:

1. Those in the market continue to review the newspaper ads until they are out of the market. This is an average decision time of 90 to 120 days for most new home buyers. Seeing the same ad several times is more likely to trigger interest than seeing it only once!
2. The total market of home buyers is not a standing audience. It is a passing parade! New prospects enter the market every day, and they will read and respond to the ads that are new to them even if they are stale to the advertiser!

However, another consideration is frequently overlooked by those who design and place ads. If you are trying to appeal to different market segments that have separate motivations, do not attempt to accomplish all of your objectives in one advertisement. For example, if your community or product line is designed to accommodate both the first-time buyer and the prestige move-up customer, you will have conflicting messages that are not well focused if you attempt to hit both groups with the same copy. In this situation, you should design two distinctly different themes (headlines and copy) while maintaining a similarity of format appearance. The headline for the starter group might read:

*"Your Landlord Will Not Appreciate This Ad!"*

while the move-up group may be more responsive to something like:

*"Your Friends Will Know You Have Arrived When You Move to Walden!"*

Each ad should have a central message that focuses on the motivations of a particular target group. When you have multiple market segments to reach, use a series of well-designed messages in similar formats separately placed to draw the attention of different buyers. Where budget considerations dictate economy, rotate ads on alternating days or weeks so that you maintain a visible presence for each of your target segments.

What about the merits of using umbrella ads versus individually featured messages about multiple properties? No clear cut answer can be given. Both advertising concepts have benefits and liabilities. Umbrella ads (those that feature a number of homes or individual locations under one theme heading) have the advantage of conserving dollars. These ads also establish a greater presence for the builder or real estate company through page dominance and thus make a greater impact than can be accomplished with smaller, scattered advertising. The disadvantage of group advertising is the loss of identity and focus for a particular housing type or neighborhood. When bundled together, the separate messages are subordinated to the "institutional theme." That can be a problem for certain product lines that need more emphasis to gain the attention of profiled prospects. One solution to this dilemma is to alternate umbrella ads with a rotated group of individual features from one week to the next. For example, you might combine all of your locations and products in one ad once a month and use the other weeks to concentrate on areas and homes that deserve the most attention.

## UNDERSTANDING REACH AND FREQUENCY VARIABLES

When selecting any medium, it is important to understand its capacity to reach your targeted audience. *Reach* refers to the number of different homes or individuals exposed to at least one message over a given period of time. Effective reach is based on the assumption that all frequency levels are not of equal importance. For example, if a frequency level of three-plus has been established for a specific campaign, the effective reach would then be the percentage of the population exposed to the message three or more times during the media schedule.

The *frequency measurement* is the average number of times a home or individual is exposed to the message. *Frequency distribution* is an analysis of how the average frequency actually spreads over the population. Some homes receive one message, some two, etc. The maximum is always the total number of advertisements that have been featured.

Since memories are short (most of us forget 60 percent of what we learn within 12 hours), the more repetition—the better the retention. When you attempt to reach a diverse audience at the expense of sufficient frequency, much of your advertising dollar is wasted. Do not shoot for a broad market with a small budget. Reduce the reach objective and aim for a smaller, better-qualified audience with greater frequency if funds are limited. This often means advertising in vehicles that reach a precisely defined group of people. For maximum retention, the message must have continuity as well as frequency.

One way to maximize dollars and obtain penetration of your target audience is by concentrating your advertising into short bursts followed by a brief pause. It is better to be in the market at meaningful levels for brief, concentrated periods (like four three-week periods) than to have fewer weekly insertions for a longer time. Sometimes the best approach is referred to as *pulsing*: continuous advertising plus periodic bursts to accommodate seasonality, special openings and promotional needs.

## DAILY NEWSPAPERS ARE ONLY PART OF THE PRINT MEDIA SCENE

Most builders and agencies think of mainline newspapers as the first line of attack in a print media campaign. The truth is that many alternatives exist, and some are less costly and more productive than the large-circulation dailies. High on the list in metropolitan markets are housing digests, new homes magazines and real estate-oriented periodicals. Housing guides often register very high on prospect source lists. They are organized by geographic areas, product types and price ranges. They act as miniature multiple-listing systems for new homes. In this context, a builder's ad has an opportunity to influence the public and REALTORS® who use these digests to schedule showings.

Suburban shopper newspapers, special-interest print media like military papers, and industry publications are also worth investigating. In resort markets, tourist guides and a multitude of free literature are given out by business enterprises hoping to capture some of the visitors' money. Before investing big dollars in any of these specialty publications, try a small test or check the results others are realizing. Cheap does not necessarily mean effective!

## WHAT SECTIONS OF THE NEWSPAPER SHOULD YOU EXPLORE?

Larger metropolitan newspapers are segmented into a number of sections to accommodate the interests of their readers. People who habitually read some sections also ignore others until they have an interest in that subject. The classified section is normally perused only when a special interest exists in shopping for something that might be listed there. New home sections (typically designed for weekend publication) have high readership by people in the housing market, but they will also be ignored by the majority not contemplating a move in the near future.

How do you reach your prospects? Logically your focus should be on people in the market or at least thinking about new housing. You cannot afford to miss that motivated group. Beyond that, however, are people who might be stimulated to action if they were exposed to your message. Apartment dwellers are a case in point. Many do not know they can afford to own homes, and others are complacent with their present arrangements. To reach them, you may want to run an ad in one of the other sections such as living, entertainment or sports. If you have a prestige product or an appeal to investors, the financial and social sections can be productive. One advantage you will enjoy when you move away from the general real estate columns is the ability to separate yourself from your competition. They have the herd instinct and will stay together trying to compete for the attention of the same buyers!

## THE QUALITY OF REPRODUCTIONS IS CRITICAL

The quality of reproduction systems varies greatly from one newspaper to the next. Some papers are conscientious about maintaining high standards of finished appearance, while others are less than proficient in this area. Since you cannot change the way newspapers operate, your only option is to design your advertising elements to fit their systems. Most newspapers maintain liaison personnel who will work with you to try to meet the challenges of their reproduction and printing systems. Study the ads, photos, renderings and composition of the real estate section and then decide how best to accomplish your objectives. For example, if photographs are blurred, dark or not well defined, you may elect to use artist renderings, which tend to be cleaner when reproduced. Some newspapers are very careless in the care and use of veloxes. Replacement of your often-used art work may be necessary simply to maintain the quality you desire. Graphic specialists and advertising agencies can be very helpful in guiding you through the processes that work best for the local media. Always start with good photos or clean-lined art work. You know that what comes out in the paper will be of lesser quality than what was submitted!

## MEMORY-LINK THE PROSPECT AT THE POINT OF SALE

Some of our clients have discovered the power of linking their media advertising to the point-of-sale environments. They know that the messages they communicate in newspapers (and other media forms) can be measurably reinforced when displayed in their sales offices where salespeople can use them to advantage. It is surprising to us that only a minority of builders have adopted the policy of having every new ad campaign mounted and prominently displayed in their sales arenas! When you consider the substantial media investments in newspapers and periodicals to promote specific housing products and relate that to on-site presentations where no evidence of these promotions is visible to prospective buyers, one must question the wisdom of those responsible for the marketing programs.

Three major advantages result from having your advertising campaigns dramatically featured in the sales offices or models where salespeople interview, qualify, demonstrate and attempt to close potential buyers. Any one of these is sufficiently important to justify featuring current advertising campaigns in the on-site displays.

1. *They provide a qualifying tool for the sales representatives.* If you have a glossy copy or slick of this week's newspaper ad mounted on an easel board or prominently featured in a panel display where the sales personnel or hostesses can easily refer to it as they greet new customers, it will give them a chance to measure how effective your advertising is in drawing people to your sales center. Marketers always complain that they do not have enough feedback from sales representatives about the effectiveness of advertising dollars. What better way to pinpoint that information than by showing a prospect an ad and asking if they have seen it?

   *"Did you see this ad featuring Heather Ridge in Saturday's real estate section?"*

   Whether the answer is yes or no, the representative can use the ad copy to emphasize salient points that distinguish your homes from others and lead naturally into the qualifying and demonstration sequence. Equally important, they can record the responses on either prospect cards or traffic control records so that the marketers will have tabulated results from which to measure the efficiency of the marketing dollar's impact.

2. *They provide visual memory links that reinforce values.* A major advantage in having on-site displays of current advertising messages is the reinforcement it provides to prospective buyers who have previously seen elements of the campaign in whatever media you are using. Repetitive message transmission is a primary objective of marketing programs. The more times you expose your message to your audience, the greater its potential for achieving

a retention level that works to your benefit. The point of sale is the one place where you really want to bring those messages home! Having seen an ad in a newspaper or in a home-buying guide and then spotting it in the sales center triggers recall and desirable emotional stimuli. It makes the salesperson's task easier, since it professionally conveys many points that he or she will want to make if given the time and opportunity.

3. *They serve as silent salespeople when agents are not present.* Sometimes salespeople are either not available to make complete value-enhancing presentations, or they forget (or neglect) to cover the points you need emphasized in the sales setting. Attractively displayed advertising provides another opportunity to tell your story at the decision-influencing point, whether or not the ads were previously seen in the media you selected. Why not get the most bang for your buck?

Do you devise and change advertising campaigns to hit the messages that will most likely stimulate your profiled prospects? If those messages are valuable off-site . . . they are certainly equally as valuable on-site!

## ESTABLISH A ROUTINE PROCEDURE FOR HAVING ALL ADS PREPARED FOR POINT-OF-SALE USE

Unless you tell your advertising agency, newspaper representative or marketing department that you want extra copies of the slicks or prints of your ads, they will not be produced. It costs little or nothing to have several copies of each ad run from camera-ready art when it is prepared by the graphics specialists. The best procedure is to have one person in your company responsible for seeing that ads are replicated (enlarged if needed), mounted and posted in appropriate locations in your sales offices and model homes. You will see a measurable improvement in the feedback from consumers about the effectiveness of your promotional efforts and in the power of these tools to help sales associates increase the interest level of your potential buyers. If you are not doing this today, start next week. It works!

## RADIO

The unique value of radio is in its power to stir the imagination. Those of us born before television can remember listening to "I Love a Mystery" or "The Green Hornet," and recall the vivid mental pictures we received from the sounds we heard from our radios. There are more radios than people in the United States. Another advantage of radio is its audience segmentation. Radio permits you to select your audience. It is also a very flexible medium. You can adjust your advertising schedule by time of day, season or weather. It might also be classified as a very personal medium. It talks to the listeners and realizes a higher degree of involvement than print or television.

One of the difficulties of this medium is the diversity of stations and the number you might have to cover to reach sufficient households to produce results. Experts suggest that the use of radio should incorporate the following guidelines:

- It should capitalize on the listener's imagination.
- It should employ memorable sounds.
- Convey one idea only; do not complicate the message.
- Identify your company name and product early in the commercial.
- Address your particular audience segment at the outset. If you are looking for renters, state that fact at the opening of the advertisement.
- Select your times carefully. Commuting times are high-yield and also in high demand. Drivers are more attentive than listeners at home. Prime time (6 AM to 10 AM) usually costs more but is worth what it costs.
- When possible, use the power of radio personalities to help endorse and sell your homes for you.
- Radio is always high-frequency, and you need more than one commercial to create audience interest. Develop a series of commercials for each campaign.
- Radio is most effective as an adjunct to special promotions such as grand openings and on-site events.
- Link your radio spots to newspaper advertising: "See this Sunday's ad in the *Herald Express* . . ."
- Repeat vital points—such as your unique selling propositions—a number of times. Repetition is essential when you depend upon the ear rather than the eye to receive the message.
- Only judge your commercials in the context of a taped presentation. Radio copy does not translate well until it is combined with voice, music and other imagery elements.
- Radio is one medium where the *burst theory* works well. A short, intensive campaign with high saturation will have a sustained carry-over period when you are off the air before you need to come back with another burst.
- Look for *packages*. Last-minute broadcast packages at much lower prices are very often available by merely shopping for them. Radio station owners are interested in selling the time before it is gone!

## TELEVISION ADVERTISING IS USED SPARINGLY IN MOST MARKETS

Home builders seldom have marketing budgets large enough to permit them to purchase adequate TV time and still achieve their other media objectives. Exceptions are major developers, national builders and merchant builders with high volume operating in relatively low-cost television markets.

Some builders have had good success with late-night programming when rates are low and audiences tend to be young. Television time can also be purchased *run of station* at a lower price than prime-time programming. ROS offers the lowest cost per spot in television's mixed bag. However, it also goes with lower audience ratings. Some tips in selecting and using TV as a promotional medium include:

- The picture must tell the story. This is the prime rule. Television is a visual medium and the pictures hold the viewers—not the sounds. When reviewing a proposed TV campaign, cover the copy and just look at the visuals. If the storyboard does not sell the message effectively, the sounds won't help.
- Always look for the key visual. One key visual must dominate the message. Busy, crowded and fast-moving commercials are hard to understand. The television screen is not a movie theater. The use and repetition of a key visual to tell the story and memory link the message is essential.
- The commercial must grab the viewer's attention within five seconds. If not, the rest is meaningless. The opening is the grabber that must compete with the high-intensity programming that has preceded and will follow the commercial.
- Professional production is essential. Homespun commercials are usually a disaster. If you cannot afford to do a quality production job in a TV studio with experts supervising the process, do not invest in TV advertising.
- Be brief and direct. A good commercial is uncomplicated. It never asks the viewer to do a lot of mental work.
- The basic commercial length in the United States is 30 seconds. The objectives of those few seconds must be: *name, claim, demonstrate*. This means you must name the product, state your consumer benefits and give the consumer a reason to believe you.
- Emphasize and register securely the name of your product. For example, if your company is Ruby Homes and that is what you want people to remember, state it early and repeat it as you demonstrate the benefits.
- TV is most appropriate in housing campaigns as a part of *burst* strategy when launching a new community or product line.
- Cable TV offers some opportunities in certain markets that feature housing shows. Some real estate brokers participate in or control housing information programs where builders' homes can be featured if represented by the sponsor.

## PUBLICITY, PUBLIC RELATIONS, DIRECT-MAIL AND PERSONAL PROSPECTING

Some of the most effective prospect-generating activities are also the least expensive. They are, however, people-intensive! They require the time and attention of individuals normally busy doing other things that have seemingly higher priorities. Publicity and public relations are closely related functions that demand the attention of top management. We know from experience that free publicity is usually far more effective than paid advertising in gaining the attention of prospective homebuyers. Articles by independent parties extolling our new housing environments add credibility we cannot attain through paid commercials. The image of being interested in the general welfare of the city in which we operate does not happen by accident. It comes from active participation in socially responsive groups such as economic development commissions, school boards, chambers of commerce, planning commissions, etc. It also is the direct result of having someone assigned the responsibility of obtaining as much positive publicity as possible from personal attention to those who place it. Unless someone in the company or in a professional consulting organization takes advantage of it, the free press available to us will be wasted. Some publicity articles are relatively simple to secure, such as those linked to your purchase of newspaper advertising. Announcements of new products, grand openings, award-winning designs and special events at your communities are newsworthy quid pro quo features. In exchange for regular advertising commitments to the news media, you are entitled to some reciprocal publicity. However, do not expect the newspapers to write them for you. They must be prepared by experts who know what is news and what is not. If you do not have a person on your staff (and few builders do) who can write solid, newsworthy articles and cultivate those who place them, you should employ agencies, public-relations specialists or freelancers. The few dollars you invest in consultants will be more than offset by the dollar value of the free publicity.

In a company with a number of people who can individually contribute to public-relations goals, it is wise to make a list of every organization and center of influence that needs to be cultivated. Prioritize them and make assignments to those who are best suited to exploit them. Do not duplicate efforts by having two people attend the same social functions or belong to the same influencing groups. Spread the power of your staff from management to sales to reach as far into the fabric of the community as is practical. Visible participation in social functions that guide the future of your area is both good public relations and self-enlightened protection of your own interests.

## TIPS ON HOW TO PLAN AND SECURE GOOD PUBLICITY

- Always consider publicity an alternative form of advertising. It can frequently be more effective than anything else you do. It also reduces the cost of your paid advertising.
- Cultivate the real estate editors of your local newspapers and be sure they know you are a professional interested in more than just free publicity. Concern for the community and the news needs of the editors will help to win free press.
- Do not be late with your stories. They are not news when they are old. Also, if you miss deadlines, you will find it difficult to get support in the future.
- Write all stories from the viewpoint of the readers. It must be news—not a commercial. If it is a blatant advertisement, it will probably not be featured.
- Always use a professional photographer to take any photographs that will accompany the story.
- Type stories on plain paper with the original (not the copy) sent to the newspaper. If is is an exclusive, be sure to emphasize that point. Editors prefer exclusives.
- Always provide a release date. Preferably designate it "for immediate release" and date it.
- Be credible in everything you say. Avoid puff and broad claims not supported with facts. Use documented figures and statistics, etc., whenever possible.

- Newsworthy publicity events include:
  announcement of new venture
  ground-breaking ceremonies
  grand openings and new product releases
  appointment or promotions of personnel
  top salesperson of the month, year, etc.
  success stories on sales made and completions
  opening of new amenities
  winning of awards, peer-group acknowledgments
  sponsorship of community events
  participation in charity events
  stories about individual purchasers of note
  professional achievement within home builder's association, local association of REALTORS®, etc.

- Public relations extends beyond publicity. Everyone in the organization should be concerned with maintaining a solid PR posture with the industry, the community and all of the resident owners. Publicity will result when you do things worth noticing, providing someone is paying attention to the PR opportunities!

## PROMOTION CHECKLIST FOR GRAND-OPENING PRESS PARTY

### Purpose

The formal opening of a design center, subdivision or model home is a newsworthy event. It can be very effectively exposed to your marketplace. A good deal of publicity can result if held in conjunction with a press party. Anyone can hold a press party—any builder of any size.

### The Four W's of Press Parties

1. The *Why* of holding a press party should be obvious: to gain as much exposure as possible for you and your homes. To aid you in planning and conducting your press party, the *Who, What* and *When* will be covered in this section. This section also includes a planning timetable and calendar for conducting the party.

2. *Who* should you invite to your press party?

   Women's page editors
   Home or real estate section editors
   Business editors
   Editors of local business or trade publications
   News directors of local radio and TV stations
   Representatives of local utilities
   Representatives of local and county governments

Representatives of your local chamber of commerce
Your principal building material suppliers
Your supervisors and principal employees
Who else you can think of?

Make sure you spell each name correctly and use proper titles and correct addresses when sending out invitations and releases. Send personalized invitations to home addresses; it is a more personal touch (they may bring a guest, spouse or friend).

3. *What* do you serve at a press party and how do you organize it? There are several alternatives, but it is best to keep it simple. The cocktail/buffet is probably the easiest to arrange. Include:

Wine/cheese stations—if you have more than one model, you can have someone serving a different wine and cheese in each home.
cocktails
hot or cold hors d'oeuvres

Plan the food for the latter part of your press party. This will insure the best coverage for you with the least distraction. You may call a good local caterer to handle the details of food and refreshments. Use your personnel to help serve and answer questions for individual members of the press. Make sure you and your staff meet every guest present.

The builder could make a short welcoming speech at the beginning of your party and use the rest of the time for socializing and answering questions. A slide show may be developed to promote you, your company and your homes.

4. *When* should you hold a press party? The best time is two or three days prior to public opening. This will make the press feel your party is a special event, and you will have a better chance of getting publicity prior to your public opening.

Send printed invitations, or type the invitations individually.
You may include a release with your invitations, or hand them out during the party.
You may want to include photos with captions with your release.

## Before Your Party

Make sure you have name tags for all of the guests—and extra ones for drop-ins. Make sure you have an adequate supply of releases, photos and photo captions if you plan to distribute them during the party. Use the planning calendar to make sure every detail is handled.

## After the Party

Send a note to all who attended, thanking them for coming. Send a short note to those who were unable to attend saying you're sorry they couldn't be there. Be sure to include copies of your release, photos and captions with this mailing.

---

**FIGURE 8.4   Press Party Planning Calendar**

Press party date: _____

Four weeks before party:                                                    Date

   1.  Notify all participants:

      A.  construction foreman          _____
      B.  landscaper                    _____
      C.  decorating consultant         _____
      D.  local utility representatives _____
      E.  county and municipal gov't. reps _____

   2.  Make arrangements for:

      A.  photographer                  _____
      B.  catering services             _____
      C.  any transportation needed     _____

Three weeks before party:

   1.  Prepare guest list:

      A.  real estate editors           _____
      B.  women's page editors          _____
      C.  business editors              _____
      D.  editors of local business publications _____
      E.  radio news directors          _____
      F.  TV news directors             _____

   2.  Check guest list for accuracy of spelling and titles.  _____

Two weeks before party:

   1.  prepare invitations             _____
   2.  print invitations               _____
   3.  mail invitations                _____

One week before party:

   1.  prepare and duplicate releases   _____
   2.  prepare and duplicate photos to be handed out (including captions)  _____
   3.  check with caterer               _____
   4.  confirm arrangements with participants  _____
   5.  make name tags for participants and guests  _____

After the party:

   1.  fulfill special requests for exclusive photos or stories  _____
   2.  arrange radio or TV interviews for decorator, architect, landscape, etc.  _____
   3.  arrange tours, clinics or activities within your design center, model home or subdivision  _____
   4.  send thank-you notes to all party attendees  _____
   5.  send releases and photos to those who could not attend party  _____

## DIRECT-MAIL ADVERTISING

Direct-mail advertising has some unique prospecting benefits not accomplished by other mediums. For one thing, it can be mailed to a select list of prospects, thus conserving on the dollars spent to broadside a market in other advertising systems. You can control the message and include more information than is practical in newspaper advertising. It is a very practical and personal tool when controlled by salespeople who can follow up with phone calls or reinforce face-to-face visits. A major key to effective direct-mail programs is to start with well-defined, highly qualified lists. If you cannot afford the services of a mailing house, prepare the list from street directories, cross directories or by personal inspection of the apartments or homes you want to target. You can employ young people at a nominal cost to assemble current lists. Another rule is always test-market the pieces you design before investing large sums in major campaigns. For example, mail 500 or 1,000 and measure the returns before mailing 5,000 or 10,000 pieces. It is a good idea to design and try more than one piece. Set up a control group to monitor the effectiveness of one versus the other. You will never know how effective the campaign might be unless you validate initial results and make necessary adjustments.

Some experts recommend staggering your mailings so you can both measure results and improve the messages as you progress through the targeted list. You might mail 1,000 one week, a second 1,000 the next week and continue on that basis until you have covered your entire list. Then you can begin again with either the same or an improved version of the piece hitting the identical market segment within three to six weeks. Mailing houses recommend a minimum of three mailings to the same audience within a fairly short time to realize maximum results. Studies seem to verify that the third mailing of a well-designed campaign produces the greatest returns.

All sales managers agree that the real key to a high return from direct mail is follow-up! Salespeople need to be involved and dedicated to the prospecting objectives by devoting enough time each day to follow up the mailings that have been made in the previous period. That is one reason for limiting the number of pieces mailed and for staggering the mailing sequence. Another way to increase yield is to offer some type of incentive to recipients such as a free booklet on home buying, a miniature calculator for visiting the models, or a chance to win something by dropping their mail card into a special box at the sales office. One builder had outstanding success by offering a $50 bill to each prospect who came to the sales office with a copy of their W-2 form showing a minimum qualifying income. His mailing to apartment dwellers produced hundreds of prospects and a high percentage of converted buyers. The money given to nonpurchasers who took the tours and did not act was more than offset by those who did purchase.

What is a reasonable rate of return from direct-mail advertising? National averages for the direct-mail industry reveal that a one-percent return is acceptable and a five-percent return exceptional. If you target your direct-mail programs to just those who have previously visited your community or sales offices, your return should be higher than five percent. If you are mailing to individuals not previously exposed to your products, a two- to three-percent return is reasonably good. The biggest challenge in direct mail is getting people to read what you mail before they discard it! That is why design is so critical. Anything that looks personal in nature or like it may have a check enclosed will be opened. Junk mail is so abused today that residents are immune to gimmicks. You must be different—and the best way to be different in direct-mail is to personalize the messages from envelope to the enclosures. Handwritten notes and postcards will be read before commercial looking flyers and business letters. My favorite direct-mail program is still the picture postcard or some variation of that theme. It does not require an envelope, everyone who sees it will look at it and it is very graphic! Cartoons on postcards can have the same impact. Brief, funny and hard-hitting!

If you invest in direct mail, be sure that what you send has a chance of capturing immediate attention and is worth reading!

## PERSONAL PROSPECTING CAN MAKE THE DIFFERENCE

When not enough prospects flow from other sources, the difference between success and failure can hinge on the quality and amount of personal prospecting. Included in this category are direct-mail programs aimed at specific neighborhoods or market segments, telephone canvassing, center-of-influence marketing and networking.

In the housing industry, salespeople and managers tend to depend mainly on street traffic as the principal source of new prospects. When the volume of business generated from media-drawn buyers is great enough to meet all sales and production goals, one might well ask: "Why expend time and energy pursuing other customer sources?" The answer to this question is that it pays to create additional prospect sources because:

1.  You can substantially reduce marketing costs by cultivating prospects from these other, less expensive activities.
2.  It is good business insurance to have multiple prospecting programs in place so as not to become dependent upon any one of them in case market conditions change.

In addition, there is also the professional satisfaction of the salesperson who knows he or she has developed a fair percentage of closed sales from personal prospecting efforts. Alert marketers and creative salespeople do not allow themselves to fall into the comfort trap of depending upon model attraction activities. They explore their own marketing opportunities to reach qualified customers who may not come to their offices as a result of advertising or normal signage. In working with these creative people, we have discovered that they do the little things that average sales representatives overlook or are unwilling to try.

### Start with Your Prospects and Buyers

The obvious place to begin building additional business is with the people you meet and sell. Referrals generated from customers and owners has to be the primary source for obtaining more qualified prospects. A series of little things can create referrals from these prime contacts.

1. Make it a policy to ask each new home buyer for the names of others they know who might be interested in your housing. The best time to do this is when they have just signed the purchase agreement and are still in a state of excitement. They are far more inclined to help you then than they may be after the newness of the event wears off!

2. Ask prospects you have not yet sold for names of friends and acquaintances who might be in the housing market. This also provides a good reason for an extra call back to follow-up customers who have not returned.

3. Give owners special invitation cards for their friends and associates who will be interested in knowing about the new homes. Ask for the privilege of mailing information to these people on behalf of the owners.

4. Provide referral incentive programs that reward owners for giving you names of prospects. These can range from the use of a wish book for selecting one of a variety of appropriate gifts to additional items for the new homes.

5. Give the owners literature (brochures, etc.) they can deliver to places of employment and other appropriate locations.

6. Hold welcome-to-the-community parties for all new owners on a regular basis, and have them invite friends and associates so that you can meet them and perhaps interest them in your housing.

7. Talk to owners regularly as you walk the neighborhood, and always ask for additional leads.

8. Enlist children of the community to help you promote homes by taking literature to school and giving you names of friends they know whose parents might be interested. Involvement in youth-oriented activities like Little League, Boy Scouts, Camp Fire Girls, etc., is a good way to strengthen these relationships.

9. Maintain a community-activity board in your sales office and post owner photos, public-relations stories, pictures of special events, etc. This will allow you to use the owners in your selling and prospecting efforts—even when they are not present. A scrapbook with pictures and testimonials is another way of involving residents of the community.

10. Provide identity elements that will help owners promote the community wherever they go. Some of the items used are:

    bumper stickers
    car license plate attachments
    special key chains with community I.D.
    clothing: T-shirts, caps, etc.
    membership cards and club I.D. elements

The key to obtaining referrals is asking for them consistently. Salespeople should set minimum contact goals, such as at least five owner referrals per week. When you have specific objectives and are disciplined to reach them, results are usually automatic.

## Cultivate Cooperative Brokers

Cooperative brokers are usually as important to our prospecting efforts as owner referral programs. In some cases, this is the largest source of buyers, particularly when dealing with the move-up market or with transferees in a broker-oriented environment. We have previously identified many ways to successfully cultivate these outside agents. A brief summary of the most important ideas include:

11. Select target brokers and individuals who service your profiled prospects, and invite them to inspect your homes. Hold open-house events aimed at these brokers, and provide incentives to inspect and show your homes.
12. Have an assigned sales representative visit each target broker office and meet with the people in their own environment. Hold sales meetings and bring new information.
13. Produce a newsletter and other hot sheets that alert your preferred brokers to all the information they need to know about your homes and community. Mail it on a regular basis.
14. Hold contests and special incentive programs for agents who show and sell the most new homes. Treat them as part of your own sales team.
15. Hold broker-orientation days on-site and use them to update experienced people and especially meet and educate new associates in these target offices.
16. Send a welcome-to-the-industry letter to every new licensee in your area—along with an invitation to learn about how easy it is to make their first commission by selling one of your new homes. You might include a $500 bonus certificate for their first sale as a way of getting them started right!
17. Attend multiple-listing meetings and promote your homes to the entire group of brokers and associates in attendance.
18. Always send thank-you notes and other appropriate forms of recognition to those who bring customers to your sales offices.

Properly administered, this phase of prospecting can generate at least one-third of your total business. Remember that whatever fee you pay to an outside broker is not so much a commission for selling as it is a marketing expense for producing a qualified buyer.

## Cooperate with Noncompetitive Builders and Agents

In many markets, one of the better ways to develop extra business is to establish a network with builders and sales agents who are working with housing that is not competitive in price ranges or types.

19. Identify builders and products in your general market area that are noncompetitive and make plans to meet the sales representatives.
20. Set up a referral program to cross-feed buyers who do not meet your profile in exchange for similar cooperation.
21. Follow up your own prospects who buy from competition. Send them special notes that show interest in their having solved their housing needs.

Build a working relationship. You can sometimes get referrals from the people you did not sell. Remember that all sales that are started do not close. You might rekindle business from those who place deposits on other builders' products.

## Enlist the Support of Employees, Subcontractors, etc.

Many people have an interest in seeing you succeed. They are either directly or indirectly involved with the building and sales programs. By making a list of these people and finding a way to encourage their active support, you can often secure extra business. Sometimes they are so close to us we forget to ask them for business. Referrals should come from those who have the most to gain or lose from your operations.

22. Meet all subcontractors on the job (with the approval of your builder). Ask for their cooperation in promoting the community. Provide them with referral cards and literature. Maintain regular contact. Invite them to talk to the sales staff at sales meetings about their particular functions and how they help to build values you can incorporate in your sales presentations.

23. Index the outside services used in processing sales and financing. Establish a plan for enlisting their support. These include lending institutions, title and escrow companies, attorneys, appraisers, decorators, architects, engineers, insurance companies, etc.

## Contact the People and Merchants in the Area

People in the immediate neighborhood have a genuine interest in your new housing programs. The homes you are building will affect their values and lifestyles—hopefully in a positive way. They should be your friends and supporters, but they can become a negative influence if neglected or poorly handled. You have more than one reason for cultivating these individuals. If they get on your team they can help you sell more homes by referring people to you and, sometimes, by trading up (or down) themselves. Businesses in the area are a very valuable source of leads. They have a financial interest in what you are doing, and you should recognize the mutual advantages of promoting each other.

24. Identify all small businesses (particularly retailers) within a reasonable distance of your new housing operations. Contact them on a planned basis to advise them about your homes and use the occasion to index information that you can include in a community fact sheet to be given to your new buyers. This helps promote the entrepreneurs and gives them an incentive for supporting you. Invite them to open-house events and keep them on your mailing list. In some cases, you can gain permission to have literature stands kept in their stores and shops.

25. Prepare a list of all neighbors within a one-mile radius. Make particular note of those communities that abut your housing. Send invitations to owners and tenants to visit your new models or office. Have a special

party for them prior to any grand-opening event. Ask them for names of people they know who might want to be among the first to take advantage of the new offering. Keep them on your mailing list for updated information. If you have a newsletter, mail it to them regularly. Use the telephone to call a select group of them each week.

## Contact the Social and Community Leaders

One of the best ways to gain community support for your new housing neighborhoods is by cultivating those who are the centers of influence in the educational and social leadership circles of that area. As you gather the information you need for your community fact book and your on-site sales presentation, it is logical that you begin your prospecting for additional leads from these valuable sources.

26.  Contact the principals or counselors of schools that will serve the needs of your residents. This includes preschools, grammar schools, junior high schools, high schools and colleges. Do not overlook private schools. When you visit them, ask questions that you need answered to be prepared for prospective buyers, but also ask for support in seeing and talking about your homes. Leave literature and establish a prospecting network with the key people you meet. An overlooked resource is school teachers and admissions officers who counsel children and parents. Housing in their school district that meets the needs of their applicants will be of interest to them.

27.  Contact churches in the area, particularly those that represent the major interests of your profiled prospects. Ministers are interested in the needs of their parishioners and they can influence them when it is appropriate. Invite these counselors to your open homes and put them on your communication list.

28.  The chamber of commerce is a source of information that many seek when thinking of moving to a new city. Having your literature available in these public-information offices is helpful to everyone. Cultivating the people in the chamber who advise tourists and prospective residents can produce extra leads. Often there is an open file of names and addresses of people who have written to the chamber prior to considering a move. You can copy that list and mail your information (or call) to gain an advantage over others who neglect this resource.

## Contact Major Industries and Relocation Specialists

Major employers are interested in the quality of housing available to their employees. They are often involved in providing advice to their personnel about availability of housing near their plants and offices. This is especially true if they relocate people from one city to another. Even if they are not moving people around, they can play a support role by their interest in local housing opportunities. When opening a new project, major industries should be identified as they fit the profile of prospective buyers and then contacted on a planned basis. Here are prospecting ideas for this employer group:

29. Prepare an information package or kit and hand deliver it to each key industry. Try to reach the person in the role of providing housing advice to employees. Set up a communication system with these people and invite them to special events on site. If the companies have recruiters, offer to furnish special information kits that can be included in the housing packages they give to prospective candidates.

30. Identify leading REALTORS® who maintain relocation departments and specialists that call on industry. Make a special point of meeting these people and getting a cooperative program established if possible. REALTORS® usually have a distinct advantage over individual builders in servicing transferees, since they are able to show all types of property and provide a total orientation to the city.

31. Keep track the employers of all the people you sell. Those working for companies you are interested in cultivating should be given special attention in order to gain access to their enterprises. They can carry your message and obtain information about new transferees that you might not be able to obtain from the directors of housing or personnel. Provide incentives for their support.

32. Ask for permission to take the salespeople on a tour of the target company and use it as an occasion to improve your knowledge about that enterprise. This is an excellent way to create good relationships with these companies and learn about them on a first-hand basis, which strengthens your on-site presentation.

### Select Target Neighborhoods for Direct-Mail and Off-Site Canvassing

A practical way to develop more prospects is to pinpoint neighborhoods where your profiled prospects now live and find creative ways to reach them with your housing messages. Whether selling the first-time buyer, the move-up buyer or the move-down buyer, this is a time-proven prospecting method. Here are some ways to tap this resource:

33. Research real estate values or rent ranges by studying multiple-listing sales, talking to real estate brokers, or physically touring the market area. Note the streets and numbers where the homes or apartments are located. Identify them on a master street map. Then secure either a directory, telephone cross directory, property microfiche or recorded title records. Set up a direct-mail campaign aimed at these specific owners or tenants. Use the telephone to add power to the mail campaign.

34. For move-up prospects, select homes where owners have at least three or more years of equity. A simple method of gaining this data is by comparing a recent city directory with one three or four years older. Call or write only those listed in both directories.

35. Offer a free booklet on housing facts, a tax guide (currently very appropriate) or other incentive for visiting the community.
36. Hold special on-site events just for residents of a specific area. "A Special Day at Walden—for the Residents of _____ ." Get a few sponsors in that neighborhood to help you organize these events.
37. With the permission of the people you have just sold, mail an announcement card to the neighbors in the community (or apartment building) from which they are moving: "Did you know that your neighbors have moved (or are moving) to beautiful Heather Ridge? Perhaps you should discover what they have found!" This is a creative way of using each sale as a way to make an impression on the people who still remain in the older neighborhoods.
38. Hold a housewarming party on-site for new owners and invite their immediate neighbors from the old area. This has real value in breeding discontent with the older neighborhood and allows you to meet people in the same social economic bracket as your new buyers.

## Use a Literature Distribution System in Key Locations

Satellite displays and literature distribution systems are effective means of reaching prospects who may not see your ads or signs. Major communities find this method of marketing essential to their objectives. Smaller builders may not be able to justify the literature costs. However, some locations deserve evaluation when you are establishing a prospecting campaign. While a number of very effective housing magazines serve larger markets, your ads in these publications are in competition with everyone else promoting housing. Special handout literature is often merited. Here are some locations our clients have found productive:

39. *Hotels.* Identify hotels where businessmen and your local prospects stay or visit regularly. They often have literature distribution racks for promoting local events and services. Housing literature is of interest to their guests, and you can often convince management that they should provide this added service. The person servicing this account can also make it a point to win the friendship of front-desk people, bellmen and others in a position to pass on information about housing opportunities to their guests.
40. *Beauty parlors, barber shops and health spas.* When people go to beauticians, barbers or gyms, they have spare time to read and relax. If your literature is there, it may hit a prospect! In addition, owners of these establishments are often very good bird dogs, since they talk to people as a normal part of their daily activities.
41. *Commercial and executive airports.* If you are serving transferees, airports can be excellent literature distribution centers. If they have places for placing literature or promoting housing, this may be worth investigating.
42. *Shopping malls and professional centers.* Wherever you have hundreds of shoppers, you have an opportunity to reach housing prospects. Satellite displays in such locations can produce results. Kiosks, news distribution centers, bulletin board areas, etc., are all possibilities worth exploring.

43. *Car washes and gas stations.* Gas stations and car-wash areas near your projects that serve your class of buyer can be worthwhile distribution spots. As people wait for service, they will pick up and read literature if it is accessible. Gas-station attendants are often asked directions to housing areas, and key locations on the path to your community may be important places to provide information to those in charge.

44. *Banks and savings and loan associations.* Although they can be stuffy and uncooperative, lenders who have an interest in your success may be willing to display literature on counters or in appropriate reading areas. No harm in asking. We have clients who have made this one work for them.

This is just a brief list of places where housing literature can be effective. If a regular distribution system is established, it will give the one making that run the opportunity to talk to the businesspeople and others with the objective of prospecting for new buyers!

## Keep a List of All Past Owners

If you are really building a product image and a personal reputation for quality housing and service, you should maintain a complete list of all past owners of your homes and use this as a special referral base. When you move from one neighborhood to another and open new housing models, do not forget the people you left behind. We have clients who build their entire marketing campaigns on just keeping previous buyers informed and involved. When they open a new community, the first party held is for their former owners. Often, the referrals they receive, along with the move-ups, will provide all the buyers they need. A California builder in San Jose has annually sold from 50–75 homes without ever running an ad! The buyers all come from word of mouth and, principally, from the previous owners. Here are some prospecting ideas for your older group:

45. Keep a computer list of all your buyers with all pertinent data. Invite them to every new event. Send newsletters and keep them informed. Send requests for referrals when new models and areas are opened. Provide incentives and recognition.

46. Create a Founders' Club or a Builders' Club that has special recognition. The first buyers in a community must wait for things to happen and deserve some attention. When you make them part of a special club and give them recognition, they tend to support your marketing efforts. You can add to the marketing value if you produce a roster of club members and post it in your sales offices to help convince others of the value of your homes.

## Call Buyers Who Have Previously Cancelled

An overlooked source is one that we have already had: the people you sold who did not complete their transactions for one or more reasons. Often, the reason for noncompletion was financial. A few months later, conditions may have changed.

47.  Maintain records on all cancellations, noting the reasons for the lost sales. Check back with these people several months (or even a year or so) later to see if they have bought elsewhere. If the conditions that prevented them from completing before have been resolved, they may be candidates for the new areas.

## Review Newspapers and Periodicals for Clues

The reasons behind housing moves are almost always tied to changing events in the lives of your prospective buyers. One way to uncover new opportunities is to review the news sources and watch for items that indicates a housing change may be imminent. Here are some newsworthy events that can produce prospects if you contact the people in an appropriate manner:

48.  *Openings of new businesses in your area.* Watch for news about new businesses of all types that may be opening in the near future in your immediate housing area. Whenever a company or store moves to the area, you have people associated with it who may prefer to live closer to work. Sometimes this will also signal transferees who must relocate. One Stone Institute client in Denver a few years ago sold 16 homes in a new community that was near a major new regional shopping center. By merely researching the names of the shops to be included in the mall and talking with the managers, they got the names of employees and made special appointments to give them an early-bird incentive for buying in the adjacent village they were creating. Newspaper articles, local commercial news and bird dogs can produce these valuable clues.

     Whenever a new shop opens in the immediate area, send a congratulations card or letter and follow it with a personal contact. This is an ideal time to get to know the people who may be centers of influence for you—and also possible prospects.

49.  *Promotions and publicity stories.* News articles can tell you who is being promoted to new positions of responsibility in the business community. If your target market is move-up housing, especially custom housing, these clues can be helpful to generating additional business. An appropriate congratulations card with an introduction to your housing opportunities can be the prelude to a personal contact. People who climb the economic ladder usually want the corresponding material rewards.

50.  *Marriages and divorces.* New family formations mean new housing needs. Divorces create a need for one, if not two, new residential arrangements. By watching these columns, you may spot people you know and be able to follow up good leads. While you must be cautious in divorce situations not to seem uncaring, there is a no reason why you should not assist in helping to resolve basic housing needs.

51.  *Birth announcements.* When children come along, there is usually a need for more space, unless one already lives in a large home. Shortly after such announcements, a congratulations card that includes a friendly invitation to explore future housing requirements can lead to new clients.

52. *Major urban construction events*. When civic improvements are announced such as new freeways, urban renewal, demolition of older buildings, it means that some people are going to have to relocate. While these may not be your profiled prospects, it is worth keeping in mind whenever the affected neighborhoods do represent your target markets.

## Study Multiple-Listing Records to Gain Leads

Within the limited time you have to participate in community activities, there are some groups and service organizations that can be very profitable, as well as satisfying to serve. Additional business can be gained by becoming directly involved in one or more such groups or programs. Here are some possibilities:

53. Participate in a charity or political group that provides services to your community. Become acquainted with the people whose contacts and positions can be helpful to your prospecting efforts. Use this base to create additional leads.

54. Volunteer to speak before social and civic groups at luncheons, etc. If you have any speaking skills, this is an excellent way to carry a message about real estate to a wider audience, win friends and discover business opportunities. Slide shows about trends in housing or in the community are very appropriate and can provide a platform for sales exposure.

## Hold Special On-Site Events

One of the ways to attract new prospects to your community is to hold special events that will serve as catalysts for present residents and guest prospects to meet. There are a long list of events that could be held. A few major ones are:

56. Special events for prospects and buyers:

> holiday parties and open houses
> barbecues and picnics
> welcome-to-the-community events
> decorating and design consultation events
> recreational parties like pool openings, tennis matches, etc., when
> appropriate

## Use Educational Events to Attract Prospects

One way to reach prospects who may not come directly to a real estate sales office or a new home community is to promote an educational event that they perceive as beneficial to their interests. Here are two examples:

57. *Home buying seminars*. For first-time homebuyers, one of the more effective educational events is a seminar on how to buy your first home. Many have held these with varying degrees of success. They should be well-organized, held away from the real estate operations, and provide

several experts presenting different aspects of the program. Appointments are made to follow up with those who have specific interests.

58. *New tax law seminars.* One of the more effective topics to attract customers are seminars on the impact of tax laws on housing and real estate. With the help of tax experts, arrange programs that appeal to present owners, prospects and the general public. Prepare a content summary in advance and mail to prospects.

## Create Opportunities

Prospecting is not limited to working hours. Salespeople should think of uncovering new business regardless of time or location. People are interested in real estate subjects and their personal estates. These conversations occur easily if you are always prepared and not bashful! Here are logical places to talk about housing:

59. *Shopping areas*

> gas stations
> grocery stores
> retail shops
> hardware stores

60. *People who call to sell services and supplies*

> insurance agents
> beauty aid salespeople
> soft-water services
> repairmen

61. *People seen in social and group settings*

> clubs
> churches
> schools
> day-care centers
> political meetings

62. *Build a stable of bird dogs and stay in touch.* The creative prospector is always looking for ways to multiply his or her effectiveness. The easiest way is to enlist as many people as possible to become part of your stable of *bird dogs.* These are people who lead you to additional opportunities because of their contacts and their interest in your objectives. Anyone you know can be a bird dog, but those with high-yield exposure are the most important people to cultivate.

We have listed a wide variety of possibilities in this chapter. There are many others. The key is simply in keeping a well-organized center-of-influence list and seeing that everyone who is important to your marketing efforts is contacted on a regular basis. As the great fisherman once said, "If you want to catch the most fish . . . you have to keep fishing!"

## THE CASE FOR USING AN ADVERTISING AGENCY

Advertising creativity is not a talent one usually finds within a typical home building company. Even professional real estate brokers have difficulty in producing effective in-house advertising programs. A few brokers and builders have on their staffs people reasonably proficient in creating and placing advertising, but there is always the risk of becoming stale without the advantage of fresh ideas from outside consultants. A well-organized advertising agency has both the creative talent and the support systems needed to translate ideas into effective marketing campaigns. Whether you establish a retainer relationship or just a spot-need service arrangement, situations arise when investment in agency services is well justified. Opening a new community, changing or improving your image in the marketplace, designing a fresh campaign to stimulate slow sales or trying to keep pace with aggressive competitors are valid times for seeking the assistance of marketing professionals.

How do you choose the right agency for your needs? How do you know you will achieve the results you expect? The best way to reduce risk is to go with proven performers. That is true in every category of services and especially in advertising creativity. Experimenting with unknowns can be a very costly venture. You seldom have the opportunity to restart your building process or make up for lost sales needed at the beginning of the project to maintain tempo and profits! Be careful about picking agencies inexperienced in real estate development. The fact that they can sell coffee or perfume does not mean they can sell housing with equal effectiveness. An agency must experience an educational curve in our industry before it is able to translate our needs into high-yielding campaigns. Before making a decision, check on what the agency has done for others in this industry. Ask to see their portfolios. Ask independent experts in the marketplace who can be objective, like researchers, graphic artists, newspaper editors and public-relations personnel. Real estate developers and builders are not the most popular accounts for many advertising firms. We are very demanding. We are typically small-volume accounts and we are constantly changing our advertising to accommodate our marketing needs. We also have a history of being risky and slow paying. We are seldom well-organized and prepared to work with agencies on a planned basis. We basically tend to be reactive instead of pro-active. Thus, we do not always receive prime attention from the agencies who have better-paying and more reasonable clients.

Agencies that specialize in the home building industry have learned to talk our language and live with our idiosyncracies. They can draw upon their experiences to help formulate campaigns that resolve specific marketing issues. Our experience is that smaller or medium-sized agencies are more effective in our business than the giants or the freelancers.

Since the selection of any agency can have a major financial impact on your success in securing prospects and closing sales, we recommend that candidate firms be given adequate presentation time before you determine the finalists. Here is a checklist for screening advertising agents:

1. Obtain an agency profile with specific information about key participants in the organization. Evaluate their credits and areas of expertise.

2.  Secure and review a list of all current clients. Check with a few selected clients to determine their satisfaction with their choice.
3.  Ask for an in-depth review of all real estate accounts they have handled in the past few years. Study the advertising, the graphics, brochures and other creative productions they have developed.
4.  Ask the agencies you have screened to inspect your housing operations, models, sales offices and previous advertising. Request a written summary of observations and broad-based recommendations. (It is unfair to expect them to give you all of their creative ideas until they are under contract)
5.  List your specific objectives for future marketing programs and ask the finalists to propose how they would meet them.
6.  Be sure each company tells you specifically how it will handle your account. Who will be in charge of research? Who will serve as account executive? How often will they meet with you? How frequently will they visit your sites and homes? What do they require from your people in order to be most effective in their roles?
7.  The companies that qualify justify your taking the time to visit their offices, meet with their key people and develop an understanding of how well they function internally.

Once you have chosen an agency, give it a chance to show you what it can do. Agree on the budget and target objectives, but allow freedom for the creative talent to explore ways to communicate your messages that are different from those used by competitors. Together, identify the unique marketing advantages you offer and help the agency to understand what your prospects need to hear and see. Hold a thorough orientation and planning session with all agency personnel involved in your account. They need the same information that your sales personnel require to prepare ads, brochures, direct-mail prices and collateral sales tools. The value-index system used to build a quality sales presentation is the same one needed in organizing an effective marketing campaign. Be sure to involve your front-line salespeople in some of these sessions. They are the ones who best understand what prospects and buyers are experiencing!

## THE CASE FOR FREELANCERS AND OTHER SUBCONTRACTORS

When no local advertising agency is capable of handling your account, or the economics do not justify the additional costs for a complete service agency, one alternative is to develop a support team of freelancers and related subcontracting specialists. Most market areas have talented people who offer creative services in various facets of advertising, graphics and merchandising on an independent basis. Graphic studios, copywriters, photographers and display specialists can be called upon to fulfill specific assignments as needed. Often, these are the same people who work for agencies, newspapers and others as part of their support team. You can usually find them by asking printers, architects, newspapers and educators whom they would recommend.

When you work with independent freelancers, it is important to give them a clear sense of direction and to coordinate all of their activities through one person on your team. They will seldom have the scope of understanding to give you the kind of representation you expect from a full-service agency. They will usually be less expensive and often more responsive to your needs. Many directors of marketing in our industry find it to their advantage to have a reservoir of creative talent upon which to draw as needed rather than to depend upon a single agency to meet all their requirements. In that role, freelancers become extensions of the in-house capacities of marketing management.

## STRENGTHS AND WEAKNESSES OF ADVERTISING MEDIA

We close this chapter with a list that condenses and summarizes our earlier discussion of the advantages and disadvantages of advertising in various media.

### Newspapers

#### *Strengths*

- rapid audience accumulation
- timeliness and immediacy of news environment
- flexibility in scheduling and space units
- short lead-time for closing dates
- excellent local-market penetration
- good merchandising and promotion vehicles—coupons and inserts
- editorial support sometimes available

#### *Weaknesses*

- high out-of-pocket cost
- cluttered environment
- poor reproduction quality
- lacks intrusiveness
- lack of standard newspaper formats
- lacks audience selectivity

### Housing Digests

#### *Strengths*

- selective audience who are mostly searching for housing
- high-quality four-color reproductions on glossy stock—excellent representation of housing
- used by brokers as well as buyers in selection process
- provides maps, orientation information and decision-influencing support data
- cost-effective compared to broadside advertising

- reinforces brochures and collaterals with use of same or equivalent production pieces
- provides a competitive shopping environment using geographical maps depicting all projects in the area

## Weaknesses

- circulation dependent upon distributors' locations
- direct comparison to competition not always in your best interests
- positioning to contrast competition limited by size of pages and predetermined format
- release dates and lead-time—less flexibility of scheduling

# Radio

## Strengths

- both mass and selective audiences
- high frequency
- audience selectivity
- low unit cost
- local personalities available
- local-market flexibility
- flexibility of scheduling to meet seasonal or regional needs
- flexibility in commercial length
- audio replay of television soundtrack
- advertise in key markets
- merchandising

## Weaknesses

- nonintrusive background medium
- commercial clutter
- lacks impact of TV
- small audience per announcement
- high out-of-pocket cost to achieve presence
- audience fractionalization

# Television

## Strengths

- dramatic presentation—sight, sound and motion
- high impact—ratings/intrusiveness
- high regional-reach potential

- in or adjacent to prestigious programs or personalities
- instantaneous audience accumulation
- audience selectivity/efficiency
- flexibility of scheduling to meet seasonal or regional needs
- fast awareness
- efficient reach of mass audiences

### Weaknesses

- frequent unavailability of desired time periods
- commercial clutter
- high cost of achieving presence
- limited audience selectivity
- skew toward lower-income, less-educated audiences

## Magazines

### Strengths

- audience selectivity
- compatibility of editorial environment
- efficiency in reaching selective audiences (particularly upscale, better-educated audiences)
- long life of advertising
- excellent color reproduction
- merchandising and promotion support—coupons, reprints

### Weaknesses

- long lead-time for commitment and copy
- slow accumulation of audience
- uneven patterns of circulation (market by market)
- lacks intrusiveness of TV
- limited positioning available
- banking of advertising in geographic and demographic editions
- clutter

## Direct Mail

### Strengths

- selectivity (targeted audience, message and offer)
- accountability (cost per inquiry and cost per sale)
- flexibility (seasonal, regional, message length/offer)
- testability (easier and less expensive to test offers, message, audience)

## Weaknesses

- high cost per unit (paper, postage, etc.)
- high cost per thousand prospects
- low intrusiveness/impact; high clutter (only seconds to attract attention)
- high cost per unit and per thousand prospects
- needs very controlled measurement/testing (measuring very small differences)

# 9: Customer Satisfaction and a Quality Delivery System

Buying a new home should be an exciting and memorable event. The reward of owning a brand-new residence that you can decorate and personalize to your own distinctive tastes should compensate for the details and irritants inherent in the purchasing process. Creating and maintaining a positive psychological climate and a strong bond of communication during the delivery process should be the objective of the management team and the sales staff. However, our experiences in working with hundreds of communities and thousands of home buyers indicate that the smooth and uncomplicated transaction is the exception not the norm for this industry. Murphy's law seems to work overtime in the housing profession: What can go wrong will go wrong! The sale and delivery of a new home is a potentially complicated and frustrating process. Unlike many other big-ticket items that can be enjoyed the same day they are purchased, closing a transaction for a new home brings little, if any, instant satisfaction. It takes time to process paperwork, obtain financing, build or finish the home, and make arrangements for all of the personal details that must be consummated in order to complete a move from one residence to another. Buyers are seldom prepared for events that typically transpire from the point of sale to the final settlement and move-in. Unexpected construction delays, changes in the mortgage market, complications with change orders and decor selections, and communication of all of the details to those involved can add to the stress and confusion in any relocation process. No single function in the home buying process can destroy the confidence and goodwill of a new home buyer more quickly than the failure of management to keep its commitments to service the home before and after possession. It is amazing to us that builders invest thousands of dollars in model homes, advertising and merchandising and then are willing to risk the credibility of their enterprises on inefficient procedures for servicing customers after purchase!

In this chapter, we will review programs proven effective in reducing the frustrations of the after-sale processing period. Many of the issues can only be resolved if executive management is committed to a policy of excellence. Loss of customer support can be very expensive! Referrals should account for at least 30 percent or more of all sales made, but our studies indicate that it is less than ten percent for all but a minority of building companies. Poor customer-service inevitably results in the collapse of consumer confidence and trust. At its worst it leads to anger, involvement of attorneys and never-ending call-back lists! Seven major areas of discontent trigger most adverse consumer relations:

1.  Overexpectation and a lack of understanding at the point of sale about what will happen, what is included, the responsibilities of the builder for service and maintenance, and the time required to complete the home.
2.  Delivery of a new home that is not complete and has defects at time of possession. Buyers have difficult understanding why a new home is not finished correctly at the time they are asked to close and move in!
3.  Lack of communication with salespeople and others about what is transpiring once the sale is made. Many have the feeling they were dumped when the purchase agreements were signed.
4.  Absence of an organized process for home buyers to communicate concerns to the builder's organization.
5.  Uncertainties about scheduling and completion of service items perceived to be the builder's responsibility.
6.  Absence of an adequate monitoring system that checks on work done by subcontractors and the builder's laborers.
7.  Failure to respond promptly to service requests that the buyers believe are covered by warranty.

## QUALITY AND EFFECTIVENESS OF CUSTOMER RELATIONS BEGIN WITH SALES REPRESENTATIVES

The framework for establishment of a meaningful customer-relations program begins at the time the sale is made. The understandings achieved at that point will affect all future relationships. As everyone in new home sales can readily testify, writing a purchase agreement is no assurance of a closed sale. Numerous things can go wrong. Lost or cancelled sales are common experiences. Even if we are successful in completing most of the transactions we write, we can still have dissatisfied residents who can work against our sales objectives. To avoid problems and maintain a positive environment of satisfied owners, everyone in sales and management must make a commitment to the quality delivery ethic! At the very beginning of the process, sales representatives need to communicate clearly and concisely the information buyers need to understand about the home building procedures. Written warranties coupled with an effective customer-communication system that specifies quality standards, optional selections and plan-review dates, and helps to guide buyers through the chain of events from purchase to move-in dates. The sales representative should keep in mind these five broad objectives:

1.  Keep customers informed, involved and happy.
2.  Anticipate problems and hit them before they hit you.
3.  Create a sense of community for all owners.
4.  Cushion the move-in with the welcome mat.
5.  Communicate and coordinate customer-service procedures.

This prescription for establishing good customer relations from the salesperson's position will only be effective if the other team members are equally committed to the same objectives. If sales representatives assure customers that the company will execute its service obligations in a professional and timely manner and then the construction department fails to keep those commitments, the agent can do little to offset buyers' frustrations and disappointments. Everyone gets blamed when things go wrong. The salesperson is also the most vulnerable target! Conversely, if the sales representative makes statements or promises that cannot be met or elects just to ignore matters that should have been covered, the building organization will suffer along with the agent.

## DOCUMENT YOUR CUSTOMER-SERVICE PROCEDURES

One of the best sales tools a representative can use to help alleviate home buyers' concerns about the builder's commitment to performance is a published customer-service manual along with documented warranty procedures. When reduced to writing and incorporated into the basic customer-orientation program at the point of sale, this provides a basis for customer confidence and a means of avoiding misunderstandings that occur when everything is left to personal conversation. Construction and sales should always work toward the same consumer-satisfaction objectives. If the various entities involved in sales, administration, construction and service are not synchronized to communicate and execute a consistent policy of quality delivery and customer service, the entire marketing system will suffer.

The best-organized companies use both administrative manuals for employees, dealing with the subject of customer-service procedures, and printed summaries that sales personnel give to their buyers at the point of sale. These policy manuals identify all systems and service responsibilities of the various personnel in the building enterprise, including the communication procedures for handling complaints and call-backs. The customer booklet is designed to explain and promote service policies in ways that will strengthen prospective buyers' conviction they are purchasing from a builder they can trust. At their optimum, these elements are combined into a major sales presentation display in the main sales arena and used with every visitor as part of the basic value-building message.

The most credible philosophy for any home builder to maintain is that the homes they deliver will reflect exactly what their customers expected and that quality control will ensure elimination of any defects before the customers take possession. That is a very strong position to take in an industry known for its undisciplined delivery procedures! However, when implemented, it is a powerful sales tool and an unbeatable way to assure referrals. Such a philosophy demands rigorous attention to quality-control procedures throughout the building process. We have clients who have adopted this ethic of delivering homes that are defect-free and who have incorporated it into their compensation systems for superintendents and service personnel as added incentives to maintain this high performance standard. While it is admittedly a demanding policy to fulfill consistently, the results for those who have adopted it have been outstanding! Marketing costs have been lowered because referrals have escalated.

Values have increased and the resulting prices have added to bottom-line profits. Call-back expenses are reduced because problems were caught in advance and solved before the new owners become involved. This kind of commitment to excellence is rare in the industry, but it certainly merits consideration by anyone trying to build a solid business based on consumer satisfaction.

## THE PREMOVE-IN AND INTRODUCTORY WALK-THROUGH ARE VITAL CUSTOMER-RELATIONS EVENTS

The method of introducing the new home to the buyer is a pivotal point in customer relations. It provides the official opportunity for the building company to review the home with the new purchasers and to communicate genuine interest in the buyers' future enjoyment of the home and the community. Regardless of what has preceded this event, the person(s) conducting the orientation can capitalize upon the innate excitement of moving into a new home. If delays and unexpected problems have occurred to this point, the blows can be softened by the treatment the customer receives during the inspection and indoctrination program. If the home is truly ready for occupancy, free of visible defects, cleaned and in a welcome mode, the experience should be very positive for all concerned. On the other hand, if it is not quite ready but must be delivered because of other timing factors, it is essential that the items that need to be fixed prior to possession have been indexed on management's control sheets before the inspection is conducted. Some builders like to leave an item or two for the buyers to discover so they will feel they are in a measure of control, while other builders believe it is best to have anticipated every question and issue that might arise. The key factor is how the buyers are treated at this point. Their commitment and money provide the opportunities for everyone else. They should be made to feel like important, welcome and valued members of the new community.

This is the time to demonstrate the features of the home and explain the warranty and service procedures so they are understood and accepted. The purpose of the walk-through is not to find what is wrong about the home but rather to focus on all the great things the new owners will enjoy by living in it. Items that should be demonstrated both for operation and maintenance include:

- heating and air-conditioning systems
- ventilating systems
- energy-efficiency systems
- electrical panel breakers and ground-fault interrupters
- smoke detectors
- alarm or security systems (if applicable)
- doors—locking systems
- plumbing fixtures
- access to ceilings, foundation areas, sewer drains and storage areas
- water heaters
- water shut-off valves

- gas cut-off valves
- major appliances: ranges, dishwashers, microwave ovens
- location and use of spare tiles, bricks, paint samples, carpet, etc.
- explaination of normal owner-maintenance responsibilities as differentiated from builder services
- landscaping opportunities and concerns including site drainage and easements

If it has not been presented during in a prior meeting, this is an appropriate time to hand the new owners their official move-in kit, including copies of all warranties and instructions on the care of their new home.

Items discovered or indexed during the premove-in inspection should be fixed immediately. If problems are solved before the new owners take possession, most customer-service issues will disappear. The speed and manner in which these adjustments are resolved make an impression (favorable or unfavorable) on the customers—and set the tone for future relationships.

## KEEP YOUR CUSTOMERS INFORMED, INVOLVED AND HAPPY

Once a sale has been written, the critical path to the delivery date begins. That involves myriad details and potential hurdles. We have to track four major processes, often at the same time:

1. Processing the financing package to stages of preliminary and final approval.
2. Selecting options, colors and decorator choices.
3. Monitoring construction-activity schedules from foundation to move-in dates.
4. Removing contingencies (such as selling another home) and arranging for the equity transfer.

Each of these procedural functions confronts buyers with issues they may question or not understand. It is easy to become frustrated with the amount of paperwork involved in buying and financing a home. The dates for moving become critical to the buyers' planning process, and uncertainties regarding completion and possession can be traumatic. After-buying blues are a common malady for new home buyers unacquainted with the process!

To prevent misunderstandings and overexpectations, you need a well-organized communication plan. Buyers must be kept informed, involved and reasonably happy throughout the lengthy process. The major portion of this burden falls on the originating sales representatives. If they do not educate and communicate with genuine concern for the emotional needs of their customers, the level of discontent can quickly rise to a point where it is out of control. The time to gain command of this process and to set the stage for an efficient delivery system is when the sale is consummated. Unless buyers are told what to expect and given encouragement to endure the vagaries of home-building environments, relationships can rapidly deteriorate.

As part of the closing process, at least seven things should be done before the customers leave the closing table.

1. Congratulate the buyers on making the right decision, and reinforce the picture of future ownership.
2. Explain the steps involved in procuring financing and tell them what to expect when they meet with lending representatives.
3. Review the sequence of events involved in construction and anticipated delivery dates. Keep the dates flexible for the unexpected and unknown. Be realistic.
4. Provide buyers with written checklists of things to do as they prepare for the upcoming move.
5. Make appointments for return visits, for decorators, etc.
6. Introduce the buyers to others they will need to know when they return for processing activities.
7. Most important of all: explain how you will communicate with the buyers and how they should communicate with you!

If you give your customers the necessary reassurances and information when they are still in positive moods, they are more likely to accept the realities of the procedures required to reach their dream homes. It is far wiser to prepare buyers for the worst, than to ignore those risks and later have to explain conditions difficult to accept. Only a fool would lead a housing customer to believe that everything is going to be smooth and uncomplicated! Credibility and trust are at stake. Overexpectation almost always leads to disappointments!

## WELCOME-TO-YOUR-NEW-HOME PACKAGE AND PREMOVE-IN KITS

Some of the most effective tools for reinforcing customer relationships and setting the stage for a pleasant home buying experience are the welcome packages and the premove-in kits that a number of progressive home builders use. These serve as information packets to help welcome and orient new buyers to the home, the community and the people who will be assisting them in completing the move. These are usually preassembled collections of items of interest to newcomers, although some companies prefer to personalize each kit based on specific interests and needs of individual buyers. When possession dates are months away, there is value in organizing this information into a number of smaller information kits that can be scheduled for delivery to buyers at appropriate times during the construction and delivery process. By having a number of items to distribute, sales personnel have the opportunity to maintain positive contacts while keeping their customers informed and involved. Here are some items that might be included in these initial orientation sets:

- a letter of welcome and congratulations letter from the builder or the building company
- an introduction to all the people and departments the buyers may encounter —often in the form of brief biographies, descriptions of functions, and accompanying photos
- an explanation of the building process and a checklist of steps that will be completed before the move-in date

- a checklist of things for the buyer to do in preparation for the move
- guidelines for obtaining a mortgage
- tips on selling present homes
- school-registration information
- summary of cultural activities in the area
- list of all service organizations with meeting locations and times
- for out-of-state buyers, information about securing a new driver's and automobile license
- change-of-address cards
- furniture-inventory booklets or lists
- packing labels
- photos of the new home to mail to friends
- community newsletter and activity calendar
- personalized community stationery
- community directory listing businesses and available services
- information about utility services and how to establish credit and hook-ups
- for pet owners, copies of ordinances pertaining to pets
- certificates and coupons from local merchants for discounts and gifts. You can often arrange for a special new home buyers' package for your people by direct negotiation.
- landscaping information: what grows and how to care for it
- lists of handymen, baby-sitters and maid services
- subscription to the local newspaper for next six months
- roster of owners in the new community

## INVOLVE BUYERS IN SPECIAL ACTIVITIES AND EVENTS

One of the best ways to keep your customers in good spirits and feeling positive about the transition to the new neighborhood is to enlist them in events and activities that put fun into the process. For example, during preconstruction marketing, help them to feel that they are more than spectators. Create a founders' club and have a founders' day party. Pass out hard hats whenever they want to inspect the site and have fun with them during the confusion of early construction activity. Take pictures of them with their homes during construction, and encourage them to build photo albums portraying the sequence of events from date of purchase through construction to move-in day. Send them cartoon cards or letters that depict the stages of processing and construction in humorous ways.

Another way to achieve this sense of participation is to give buyers mementos to keep or use that remind them and others of their new housing environment. In an earlier chapter, we reviewed the value of videotapes as one of those reinforcing tools. Here are some other examples:

- license plate attachments or bumper stickers identifying the new community
- photo albums
- t-shirts featuring the name of the community or builder
- personalized key chains

**FIGURE 9.1   Examples of Cartoon Letters**

Hi,

Can you believe it, it's been almost a month since you bought your new home.

Your loan is being processed and everything is running smoothly.

Now it's time to send in your second deposit. You can either put it in the mail or drop it by my office.

If you need any additional information or know someone else considering a new home, please call.

**FIGURE 9.1    Examples of Cartoon Letters (continued)**

Congratulations,

I wanted to be the first to let you know that we have put your home on our START SCHEDULE. It should take about 10 days to 2 weeks before you see something happening. During this time we will be ordering permits, engineering and staking out your foundation.

In the meantime, get your camera ready! You'll want to have a scrapbook to look back on someday.

If you have any questions or know someone interested in a new home, please call.

**FIGURE 9.1** Examples of Cartoon Letters (concluded)

Hi,

It's me again, your friendly sales representative! I'm writing to let you know that your home is in the final stages of construction. This week your home went into the drywall and trim phase, which is about 30 days before completion.

Soon you will be receiving a letter from our office that will give you presettlement and settlement dates. After that, Happy New Home!

- security or member's passes to the community facilities
- paperweights, coasters or pens with community name
- caps or joggers' headbands
- document holder
- matchbooks
- wall plaques

## ANTICIPATE PROBLEMS BEFORE THEY OCCUR

A home buyer who receives a last-minute notice about an unexpected delay in construction when he or she has already made firm plans to move is not a happy home buyer! When mortgage commitments at lower rates expire because the construction process is slow and buyers must then accept higher interest payments, they tend to blame the people who sold them the property regardless of explanations received. If the moving van is on the way from a distant city to deliver furniture next Tuesday and escrow papers have been delayed in processing for reasons the buyers cannot understand, frustration levels rise to the boiling point. These scenarios are common happenings in many building operations, and the consequences are always unpleasant for all concerned. Many of them are unpreventable for reasons beyond our control. The way we anticipate and handle them is within our control. A few flash points always occur along the critical path to the completion date, and these need to be carefully monitored with an awareness of what might go wrong. When you get even the slightest indication that things may not work out as planned, the salespeople need to be notified, and they, in turn, should communicate the new information to their buyers. Salespeople need open lines of communication with construction superintendents, mortgage-processors and administrators to find out the facts that can influence their relationships with customers. It is the responsibility of salespersons to seek the information they need to be on top of items that are important to their buyers. This includes personal inspection of construction sites and making visual observations of things they need to report to clients.

Surveys of thousands of new home buyers reveal that the three things that bothered them most about new home salespeople were:

1. They did not tell them the truth about possession dates.
2. They were mislead about financing rates, terms and procedures.
3. They promised things the builder did not include or do.

We do not mean to imply that most buyers felt this way. We are referring to those who were not satisfied with their sales representatives; although they were a minority, they still represented a significant number (over 20 percent of those surveyed). Remember that regardless of who is at fault in providing information about possession, financing or what is included with the home, the salesperson will always bear the brunt of blame for not communicating the facts!

Here is a checklist of suggestions from top sales professionals to help reduce misunderstandings with new home buyers.

- Prepare buyers for the loan-processing scenario. Tell them what questions they will be asked, the documents they need and the rationale for these procedures. Be sure to clarify mortgage terms and variables for possible rate changes.
- Do not estimate settlement dates so specifically that there is little room to adjust if construction does not move as rapidly as desired. Give yourself a margin for error and let your customers know you will be monitoring this factor on a regular basis.
- Obtain the total amount needed for closing and make sure the buyers are aware their commitment is final. Do not imply by what you do or say that they can easily cancel the transaction.
- If problems of any kind seem imminent, anticipate them and take action to head them off. Inspect your buyers' home while it is under construction to be sure the options and extras they ordered are correctly installed and construction errors corrected. If the buyers discover mistakes before you do, you are forced into a defensive role that risks loss of goodwill and possibly the sale.
- Maintain open lines of communication with construction superintendants and those who control the building process.
- If the buyers have a home to be sold, stay in touch with the broker or listing agent to maintain accurate knowledge of how well the home is being marketed. Keep the agent on your side by reinforcing the new home decision when he or she is communicating with the sellers.
- Keep complete notes in each transaction file so you will not have to trust your memory about what you have done. When there is a dispute, your records can reserve your credibility with your employers!

## CREATE A SENSE OF COMMUNITY FOR ALL YOUR OWNERS

Newcomers blues are a reality for people who do not quickly adjust to new environments, strangers and unexpected events. The uprooting and replanting experience carries with it fear of the unknown. Will we like it here? What type of neighbors will we have? How will our children adjust?, etc. One of our marketing goals should be to stimulate and sustain a vibrant sense of community that will help to reduce the insecurities of the new residents. Group events may be appropriate, but it takes more than social affairs to make a happy neighborhood. Most people want to feel they belong. Helping them to achieve that participatory attitude within their newly chosen housing environments is a subtle but vital aspect of effective marketing.

Introducing new owners to the established groups is one of the more effective ways to build a strong sense of community for everyone. Keeping profiles of every purchaser and searching for matching interests can help you provide catalysts for new friendships. Holding welcome-to-the-community parties for new arrivals and publishing the list of newcomers for circulation to all residents can be very productive. If home owner's associations are involved, you can use those to plan events both social and educational in nature. Whenever you have group events, be sure to have someone photograph those in attendance. These pictures have multiple uses, not the least of which is displaying them in the sales office for residents and future buyers to see. People love to look at pictures of themselves and their friends! Photograph albums kept in social settings serve as conversation-starters while humanizing the people who live there.

## SPECIAL EVENTS FOR NEW HOME COMMUNITIES

The following list of events for new home and condominium communities has been prepared to help our readers plan social and competitive programs that inspire resident involvement. Not all of the ideas will be applicable to any one community. Some are definitely resort-oriented and require environments that make them practical. Others can be sponsored even in small neighborhoods without amenities. The objective is to cultivate a social heart for the community that improves resident satisfaction while assisting the marketing objectives of building referrals and involving potential new buyers.

### Welcome-to-the-Community Parties

- Sponsor evening open-house events or weekend parties to welcome all new residents. These wine-and-cheese or light-snack parties can be held as often as once a month and may also be used to introduce residents to the Home Owners' Association.
- Prepare a roster or scroll placed on an easel that lists the new residents. (Obtain permission first. You do not want to violate privacy laws.)
- Send special invitations to the present senior-residents and to the newly involved ones. Invite prospects so they can sense the positive involvement and satisfaction of the owners.

### Block or Building Parties

- Any event can serve as the occasion for a block party or a condominium building party. They are excellent for encouraging get-acquainted activities.
- Barbecues and pot-luck events are particularly appropriate. Street dances and musical programs lend themselves to these social affairs.
- The organization of the block party must involve the residents, but it can be stimulated and sponsored by marketing personnel.

### Booster Clubs for Spectator Sport Events

- Where there is a strong local following of professional baseball, football, basketball or hockey teams, organized booster clubs are very popular. There is value in organizing booster clubs.
- Special caravans or bus parties can be provided to transport residents to the events. Tailgate parties are well-attended.

## Active Sporting Events

- tennis matches
- swim meets
- softball tournaments
- bicycle races
- jogging races
- volleyball meets
- skiing contests
- horseback-riding competitions
- sailing regattas
- golf touraments

## Passive Sporting Events

- card parties (all types)
- bingo parties
- fishing derbies
- horseshoe matches
- shuffleboard matches
- lawn-bowling competitions

## Special Holiday Parties and Social Events

There are the obvious celebrations, New Year's Day, and the Fourth of July. Any day, though, might serve as a special occasion. Successful events include:

- spring, summer, autumn or winter festivals
- western barbecues
- hayrides and sleighrides
- picnics
- beach parties

## Children's Events

It is important to have programs and activities for children and teenagers when they are part of the resident population. These include:

- swim parties/beach parties/picnics/campouts/hiking
- nature hikes
- pumpkin-carving contests (Halloween)
- supervised games and classes
- dance parties
- little-league baseball teams
- father-son events
- mother-daughter events

### Arts, Educational or Cultural Events

Among the best events for involving all of the resident population as well as outsiders are cultural offerings. They include:

- art festivals
- music festivals
- shakespearian theatre festivals
- gourmet-cooking classes
- art classes
- handicraft classes
- dance classes

### Physical-Fitness Programs

Numerous resort and major communities sponsor one or more physical fitness programs. Among the most popular are:

- exercise or aerobics classes
- therapy sessions
- jogging groups

### Promote and Publicize Your Social Events

The social-event calendar can be one of your more effective marketing tools if properly promoted. Set up a community-activity display board in your sales office, owners club room, or other appropriate places and keep it up-to-date with items of interest to the owners. The calendar can show several months of scheduling in advance. It should at least have photos and news clippings, etc., of recent events. This is a valuable reinforcement tool for new prospects. If you publish a community newsletter, the calendar of events should be a vital part of the news stories. Reports on recent activities and publicity on forthcoming events provide items of tremendous local interest. These involvement programs help to encourage resident support for marketing objectives.

## CUSHION THE MOVE-IN WITH THE WELCOME MAT

The actual moving day is a big event for new home buyers! This is not something they experience very often. While it is typically hectic and pressure-packed, it is also a great time to extend a genuine welcome on behalf of the building company and the sales organization. Alert salespeople who have their eyes on future referrals make it a point to do personal things for the new arrivals. Some arrange to deliver a picnic lunch, since they know that cooking is out of the question. Others provide maids or baby-sitters to help ease the workload of unpacking, dishwashing, etc. At the very least, salespeople should stop by and officially welcome newcomers to the new neighborhood. Marketers seize this opportunity to cement goodwill on behalf of the developer, builder and sales staff. In our opinion, every builder should include in his promotional package a small budget for spreading the welcome mat for new residents. Delivering something unexpected as a gift from the development company can help to soften other frustrations.

## MAKE YOUR OWNERS FEEL THEY ARE VERY SPECIAL

We would have very few problems with most of our consumers if they felt we sincerely cared about them and their personal needs. When people feel that others believe they are important, their self-images are enhanced and their insecurities reduced. Everyone on your team, from sales representatives to executive management, should recognize how vital it is to help prospects and residents feel they are appreciated. We know that there will always be a small minority of individuals you cannot satisfy no matter what you do. You cannot remake people. Those who are emotionally unstable bring their problems with them no matter where they reside. These, fortunately, are the exception. Most people respond favorably to those who give them their vitamin A's: attention, acceptance, appreciation and approval!

Taking the time to tell new owners how much you admire the landscaping design they have installed; sending a house-warming gift; saying hello to them as you walk down the street and see them working in their yards; paying attention to the interests of their children and sending thank-you notes for referrals they provide—these are small actions that can produce big results!

## SURVEY OWNERS AFTER POSSESSION

Developers and builders who invest in resident surveys know how valuable they can be. They accomplish several marketing objectives. They certainly evince to owners that the companies from whom they purchased care enough to ask for their opinions about the process and products. These questionnaires are valuable tools for marketing departments. They pinpoint motivations, issues and recommendations that can improve the effectiveness of the marketing effort. Builders will gain insight into design features that elicited the most favorable response as well as things owners would like to see improved. The entire process of investigating attitudes and observations after move-in serves the purpose of building a stronger bond of communication between buyers and the housing enterprise.

When you survey owners, be prepared for negatives! They do occur. It is better that they are vented in this manner than in more costly ways. Sometimes what you discover will help focus management's attention on issues previously overlooked, such as the quality of performance in servicing customer complaints.

Independent companies can play this survey role for you with more effectiveness than you can achieve on your own. Buyers are hesitant to tell the builder's staff what they want to say for fear it may hamper their ability to have the things fixed or the

---

**FIGURE 9.2    Homeowner's Satisfaction Survey**

Subdivision: _____    Survey date:_____

Type of Home:_____    Date sold: _____

Good evening, I'm _____ with _____
and we are conducting a survey of our recent home buyers. May I ask you a few questions?
(When would be a more convenient time to contact you?)

--------------------------------------------------------------------------------

1.  What were the reasons for choosing your _____ home?

    Location:        _____
    Price:           _____
    Quality:         _____
    Architecture:    _____
    Layout:          _____
    Other:           _____
    _____
    _____
    _____
    _____

2.  What type of home did you leave?

    Single family:   _____
    Apartment:       _____
    Condominium:     _____

3.  What features do you like best in your new home?

    _____
    _____
    _____
    _____
    _____

4.  What are your thoughts on the floor plan now that you have lived with it?

    _____
    _____
    _____
    _____
    _____
    _____
    _____
    _____
    _____

**FIGURE 9.2   Homeowner's Satisfaction Survey (continued)**

5.  Has anything in your home disappointed you?

    _____

    _____

    _____

    _____

    _____

    _____

    _____

    _____

6.  What changes would you make if you were building again?

    _____

    _____

    _____

    _____

    _____

    _____

    _____

    _____

7.  Did you use our service department? If yes, were your service requests taken care of promptly?

    _____

    _____

    _____

8.  Why did you begin looking for a new home?

    Employment transfer:      _____

    Wanted: _____ larger, _____ smaller home

    Less upkeep:              _____

    Better schools:           _____

    Nearer to employment:  _____

    Other:                    _____

    _____

    _____

    _____

**FIGURE 9.2   Homeowner's Satisfaction Survey (concluded)**

9.  How did you learn about the _____ home in which you now live?

Newspaper: _____

Friends: _____

Road signs: _____

Broker: _____

Other: _____

_____

_____

10.  What other communities did you consider?

_____

_____

11.  How would you evaluate the _____ sales team that worked with you?

Excellent: _____

Good: _____

Fair: _____

Why?: _____

_____

_____

_____

_____

12.  Would you recommend a _____ home to your friends?

Yes: _____

No: _____

Why?: _____

_____

_____

_____

_____

We thank you very much for your time and comments.

Interviewer comments:

_____

_____

_____

_____

_____

_____

problems solved. That is one reason for using an outside research service that is at least arms' length from your supervision.

## REFERRALS AND EFFICIENT CUSTOMER SERVICE GO HAND IN HAND

Always remember that your foundation for future business opportunities is the people you have already sold! Think of them first when creating marketing plans. Be sure that they are the first ones notified when you plan to open new sections of the community, introduce a new model or design, or hold a preview party or grand opening! We have clients who have built their entire sales strategy on cultivating their previous owners! The very first ones to learn of anything new and to be made part of the building family's progress are residents who live in the builders' homes. This is true even if the communities are scattered over a wide region. By maintaining a permanent roster and mailing list of owners and former owners, these marketing-wise builders have a gold mine of people who feel they are members of their builder's private club! That is the ultimate mark of success for customer relations and a quality delivery system!

# 10: Managing and Monitoring the Marketing Functions

When do we find time to monitor and manage the variables that affect our marketing systems? Some builders only become concerned when sales figures reflect little or no action. Small-volume builders often live with an awareness that they have one or two unsold specs, or that no contracts for build orders have been written this month. They evince panic symptoms when cash flow turns negative and construction loan payments make demands upon available reserves. A few phone calls to their REALTORS® or a face-to-face meeting with the assigned agent may produce some action, but there are no guarantees.

Salespeople, especially those who have the freedom to concentrate on the opportunities they choose, have plenty of excuses for why certain homes are not selling. They have not had customers for that style of home. The competition is offering more square-footage for comparable dollars. The market is soft at the moment. A better financing package is needed to induce purchaser interest. That plan does not appeal to most of their current prospects! How does the builder or developer know what or whom to believe? When their properties are not moving, some type of crisis-marketing is bound to occur. Lower the prices. That is a favorite remedy prescribed by sales agents. Any home will sell if the price is low enough!

In the other scenario, you have marketing periods when everything seems to be going well. Sales are ahead of construction. You have 15 reservations in a presale phase. Prospects are coming out to inspect your homes in record numbers. Based on this information you elect to start 25 spec homes. Then, suddenly, you discover that the reservations were not firm sales. Half of them cancel because of a slight rumble in the newspaper about a potential layoff of 500 people by one of the major local employers. Meanwhile, your competition opens a new neighborhood down the street and starts with a product that is ten percent under your prices for virtually similar styles. Now you are faced with a backlog of starts and a declining number of prospective buyers! Why did it happen? Could it have been prevented? What do you do now to adjust to the new realities of the marketplace?

The risks and rewards in this business are substantial. Margins of profit for most builders are not great enough to permit them to slash prices by ten percent and still survive. If a builder elects to work only on build orders to prequalified buyers, the risks will be reduced but so will the opportunities. The transferee is seldom prepared to wait four months for a home to be completed when others are available now that can be occupied in 30 to 60 days. Builders who speculate in order to have product ahead of sales can pick up extra volume from customers who prefer to see what they are buying and brokers who want to receive commissions without waiting four to six months. Conversely, the spec homes may sit while people choose to have homes designed and built to their specifications. Trying to operate in markets composed of builders willing to trade time for small dollars is a real challenge for any builder who needs to maintain a consistent volume and adequate margins to meet overhead and profit objectives. That is why it is essential that the variables of sales and marketing be anticipated and monitored constantly.

## SMART MARKETERS ARE ACTIVE NOT REACTIVE

As we identified in chapter 3, the better marketers in the housing industry make it a habit to study every facet of the process from the perspective of what might go wrong before they develop their sales and marketing strategies. Anticipating issues that can adversely affect their sales goals, they look for ways to minimize risk while aggressively pursuing courses of action that will optimize results. An active manager is one who does not wait for things to go wrong before taking corrective actions! The realistic approach is to index from experience or intuition the items that need the most planning and attention and then develop strategies that will reasonably protect the marketing systems. By being active, they provide business insurance for their employers. Since the marketing disciplines encompass every aspect of the development and home building enterprise, those in charge of these functions need to be involved in decision-influencing meetings from land acquisition to clean-up stages. While a team effort is required, those responsible for producing the sales that unlock all of the projected profits deserve a chance to play active roles instead of reacting to decisions they cannot change.

During my years of managing sales and marketing for a real estate development company and then as a consultant to other developers and builders, I have encountered literally hundreds of situations where the problems we were asked to solve could have been prevented or lessened if only someone knowledgeable in marketing had been involved from the beginning. Most frequently, the fundamental issue was the absence of market research prior to the execution of the development decisions. As we emphasized in chapter 2, research is your best security blanket. But beyond research is the ability to anticipate and project what has not yet occurred. Protecting product values and profits by speculating about possible future scenarios is a hallmark of a superior marketer. The active marketing manager uses personal knowledge, competitive research and constant monitoring to stay on top of factors that can influence the success or failure of marketing strategies.

Key areas of involvement in which those skills are needed are:

- land planning
- product design

- positioning (image projection)
- pricing (including financing)
- presentation
- phasing (inventory control)
- promotion
- sales management

In all of these vital functions, the decisions made can have profound impact on sales results. Although perfection is not attainable, we should try to prevent bad decisions and improve the odds of achieving our goals by using the checklisted road maps we or others have previously explored.

## THE VALUE OF CRITICAL-PATH MANAGEMENT SYSTEMS

Critical-path planning has been used by American industry since World War II, and it is a fundamental tool for most land development and home-building operations. However, its use by the marketing disciplines is less common than for development and construction functions. The concept is a simple one: you index all items that must be completed to achieve a specific goal. You then place them on a time-line control chart and establish dates by which each individual function must be completed to assure that all of them will be accomplished on schedule. Since the completion of one assignment will affect the timing of another one, it is essential that realistic estimates be made for the separate times needed for each function. Foundation functions that must be performed first before anything else can happen usually are starred, separately colored or given bold-face type identification so they will stand out from supporting details. For example, ordering renderings of floor plans and exterior elevations to use in brochures, displays and ads cannot occur until the decisions are made and blueprints received of the actual architectural plans to be featured. Thus, finalizing floor plans and architecture automatically becomes a key function on which a variety of related marketing decisions and actions are premised.

The use of some type of critical-path planning system reduces the risk of overlooking important items that must be accomplished to reach predetermined objectives. It also helps to keep everyone aware of the interrelationships of various functions and their combined impact on the ultimate success of the project. All individuals involved in the fulfillment of marketing goals should have copies of the CPM along with regular updates as often as needed.

Some managers like to maintain a working environment in which the time-line charts are constantly visible to themselves and their associates. Enlarged versions of the printed forms can be placed on walls or display panels in central planning rooms where managers and assistants can quickly see the status of all the functions and relate their responsibilities for keeping things on schedule. This type of war-room management is particularly helpful when you have several major developments to track at one time. You might be in an early lot-development phase on one community, beginning presales on another, preparing for a grand opening of a third one and in the clean-up phase of the last few homes in a fourth. Trying to mentally juggle all of these

**FIGURE 10.1   Critical-Path Marketing (CPM) System**

DEVELOPMENT SCHEDULE

PROJECT NAME _____

YEAR _____

| Res. | Month | 1 | 15 | 30 | 1 | 15 | 30 | 1 | 15 | 30 | 1 | 15 | 30 | 1 | 15 | 30 | 1 | 15 | 30 | 1 | 15 | 30 | 1 | 15 | 30 |
|---|---|---|---|---|---|---|---|---|---|---|---|---|---|---|---|---|---|---|---|---|---|---|---|---|---|---|
| | **DEVELOPMENT TEAM SELECTION** | | | | | | | | | | | | | | | | | | | | | | | | | |
| | MARKETING & DESIGN CONSULTANTS | | | | | | | | | | | | | | | | | | | | | | | | | |
| | COMPLETE MARKETING CONTRACT | | | | | | | | | | | | | | | | | | | | | | | | | |
| | Set marketing budget | | | | | | | | | | | | | | | | | | | | | | | | | |
| | Complete market survey/buyer profile | | | | | | | | | | | | | | | | | | | | | | | | | |
| | Select P/R Agency | | | | | | | | | | | | | | | | | | | | | | | | | |
| | Select advertising agency | | | | | | | | | | | | | | | | | | | | | | | | | |
| | COMMISSION ARCHITECTS | | | | | | | | | | | | | | | | | | | | | | | | | |
| | Set architectural budget | | | | | | | | | | | | | | | | | | | | | | | | | |
| | Set architectural criteria | | | | | | | | | | | | | | | | | | | | | | | | | |
| | Design land plan | | | | | | | | | | | | | | | | | | | | | | | | | |
| | Establish target price | | | | | | | | | | | | | | | | | | | | | | | | | |
| | SELECT PROPERTY MANAGEMENT CO. | | | | | | | | | | | | | | | | | | | | | | | | | |
| | Complete mgmt. contract | | | | | | | | | | | | | | | | | | | | | | | | | |
| | Develop CA budget | | | | | | | | | | | | | | | | | | | | | | | | | |
| | Determine housing req. | | | | | | | | | | | | | | | | | | | | | | | | | |

SOURCE Courtesy of The Codman Co., Boston, MA.

**FIGURE 10.1   Critical-Path Marketing (CPM) System (continued)**

DEVELOPMENT SCHEDULE

PROJECT NAME _____     YEAR _____

| Res. | Month | 1 | 15 | 30 | 1 | 15 | 30 | 1 | 15 | 30 | 1 | 15 | 30 | 1 | 15 | 30 | 1 | 15 | 30 | 1 | 15 | 30 |
|---|---|---|---|---|---|---|---|---|---|---|---|---|---|---|---|---|---|---|---|---|---|---|
| | **ARCHITECTURAL**<br>**FINAL FLOOR PLANS** | | | | | | | | | | | | | | | | | | | | | |
| | Hard line drawing/graphics | | | | | | | | | | | | | | | | | | | | | |
| | Scale site model | | | | | | | | | | | | | | | | | | | | | |
| | Select exterior material | | | | | | | | | | | | | | | | | | | | | |
| | Select exterior colors | | | | | | | | | | | | | | | | | | | | | |
| | Select interior finishes | | | | | | | | | | | | | | | | | | | | | |
| | Select options and upgrades | | | | | | | | | | | | | | | | | | | | | |
| | Entry design | | | | | | | | | | | | | | | | | | | | | |
| | Landscaping plan | | | | | | | | | | | | | | | | | | | | | |
| | Entry signage | | | | | | | | | | | | | | | | | | | | | |
| | Estimate start of models | | | | | | | | | | | | | | | | | | | | | |
| | Estimate start of production | | | | | | | | | | | | | | | | | | | | | |
| | Estimate completion of models | | | | | | | | | | | | | | | | | | | | | |
| | Develop standard spec | | | | | | | | | | | | | | | | | | | | | |
| | R factors for insulation | | | | | | | | | | | | | | | | | | | | | |
| | Selection of suppliers for interior finishes | | | | | | | | | | | | | | | | | | | | | |

**FIGURE 10.1   Critical-Path Marketing (CPM) System (continued)**

DEVELOPMENT SCHEDULE

PROJECT NAME _____                                    YEAR _____

| Res. | Month | 1 | 15 | 30 | 1 | 15 | 30 | 1 | 15 | 30 | 1 | 15 | 30 | 1 | 15 | 30 | 1 | 15 | 30 | 1 | 15 | 30 | 1 | 15 | 30 |
|---|---|---|---|---|---|---|---|---|---|---|---|---|---|---|---|---|---|---|---|---|---|---|---|---|---|
| | **CLOSINGS** | | | | | | | | | | | | | | | | | | | | | | | | |
| | SELECT END LOAN LENDER | | | | | | | | | | | | | | | | | | | | | | | | |
| | ATTORNEY TO REPRESENT SELLER | | | | | | | | | | | | | | | | | | | | | | | | |
| | FNMA REQUIREMENTS | | | | | | | | | | | | | | | | | | | | | | | | |
| | Appraisal | | | | | | | | | | | | | | | | | | | | | | | | |
| | Insurance | | | | | | | | | | | | | | | | | | | | | | | | |
| | Property management | | | | | | | | | | | | | | | | | | | | | | | | |
| | Legal opinion re: document presentation | | | | | | | | | | | | | | | | | | | | | | | | |
| | Application submitted | | | | | | | | | | | | | | | | | | | | | | | | |
| | CONDITIONAL APPROVAL | | | | | | | | | | | | | | | | | | | | | | | | |
| | FINAL APPROVAL | | | | | | | | | | | | | | | | | | | | | | | | |
| | AS-BUILT DRAWING | | | | | | | | | | | | | | | | | | | | | | | | |
| | SITE PLAN | | | | | | | | | | | | | | | | | | | | | | | | |
| | DOCUMENTS TO BE RECORDED | | | | | | | | | | | | | | | | | | | | | | | | |
| | Certificate of occupancy | | | | | | | | | | | | | | | | | | | | | | | | |
| | 6-D certificates | | | | | | | | | | | | | | | | | | | | | | | | |
| | Insurance certificates | | | | | | | | | | | | | | | | | | | | | | | | |
| | WALK-THROUGH PROCEDURES | | | | | | | | | | | | | | | | | | | | | | | | |

**FIGURE 10.1 Critical-Path Marketing (CPM) System (continued)**

PROJECT NAME _____

DEVELOPMENT SCHEDULE

YEAR _____

| Res. | Month | 1 | 15 | 30 | 1 | 15 | 30 | 1 | 15 | 30 | 1 | 15 | 30 | 1 | 15 | 30 | 1 | 15 | 30 | 1 | 15 | 30 | 1 | 15 | 30 |
|---|---|---|---|---|---|---|---|---|---|---|---|---|---|---|---|---|---|---|---|---|---|---|---|---|---|---|
| | **TEMPORARY SALES CENTER** | | | | | | | | | | | | | | | | | | | | | | | | | |
| | LEASE/PURCHASE TRAILER | | | | | | | | | | | | | | | | | | | | | | | | | |
| | INSTALLATION OF TRAILER | | | | | | | | | | | | | | | | | | | | | | | | | |
| | Order telephones | | | | | | | | | | | | | | | | | | | | | | | | | |
| | Lease furniture | | | | | | | | | | | | | | | | | | | | | | | | | |
| | Delivery of furniture | | | | | | | | | | | | | | | | | | | | | | | | | |
| | Interior design | | | | | | | | | | | | | | | | | | | | | | | | | |
| | Graphic design | | | | | | | | | | | | | | | | | | | | | | | | | |
| | Construction for graphic displays | | | | | | | | | | | | | | | | | | | | | | | | | |
| | Installation of graphics | | | | | | | | | | | | | | | | | | | | | | | | | |
| | Order displays of interior finish samples | | | | | | | | | | | | | | | | | | | | | | | | | |
| | PROCEDURES | | | | | | | | | | | | | | | | | | | | | | | | | |
| | Set up community control book | | | | | | | | | | | | | | | | | | | | | | | | | |
| | Set up files per policy book | | | | | | | | | | | | | | | | | | | | | | | | | |
| | Establish sales office hours | | | | | | | | | | | | | | | | | | | | | | | | | |
| | ORDER OFFICE EQUIPMENT | | | | | | | | | | | | | | | | | | | | | | | | | |
| | Office supplies—Codman form | | | | | | | | | | | | | | | | | | | | | | | | | |
| | Report forms—Codman | | | | | | | | | | | | | | | | | | | | | | | | | |
| | Print sales forms | | | | | | | | | | | | | | | | | | | | | | | | | |
| | Legal documents | | | | | | | | | | | | | | | | | | | | | | | | | |
| | Hire support staff | | | | | | | | | | | | | | | | | | | | | | | | | |

**FIGURE 10.1   Critical-Path Marketing (CPM) System (continued)**

DEVELOPMENT SCHEDULE

PROJECT NAME _____    YEAR _____

| Res. | Month | 1 | 15 | 30 | 1 | 15 | 30 | 1 | 15 | 30 | 1 | 15 | 30 | 1 | 15 | 30 | 1 | 15 | 30 | 1 | 15 | 30 | 1 | 15 | 30 |
|---|---|---|---|---|---|---|---|---|---|---|---|---|---|---|---|---|---|---|---|---|---|---|---|---|---|
| | **COLLATERAL AND PROMOTIONAL PIECES** | | | | | | | | | | | | | | | | | | | | | | | | |
| | NAME AND LOGO DESIGN | | | | | | | | | | | | | | | | | | | | | | | | |
| | BROCHURE | | | | | | | | | | | | | | | | | | | | | | | | |
| | Concept meeting | | | | | | | | | | | | | | | | | | | | | | | | |
| | Copy approval | | | | | | | | | | | | | | | | | | | | | | | | |
| | Layout approval | | | | | | | | | | | | | | | | | | | | | | | | |
| | Final printing received | | | | | | | | | | | | | | | | | | | | | | | | |
| | Print extra covers for legal presentation | | | | | | | | | | | | | | | | | | | | | | | | |
| | Floor plans | | | | | | | | | | | | | | | | | | | | | | | | |
| | STATIONARY/BUSINESS CARDS | | | | | | | | | | | | | | | | | | | | | | | | |
| | Design | | | | | | | | | | | | | | | | | | | | | | | | |
| | Printing | | | | | | | | | | | | | | | | | | | | | | | | |
| | DIRECT-MAIL PIECE | | | | | | | | | | | | | | | | | | | | | | | | |
| | Design | | | | | | | | | | | | | | | | | | | | | | | | |
| | Printing | | | | | | | | | | | | | | | | | | | | | | | | |
| | PHOTOGRAPHY | | | | | | | | | | | | | | | | | | | | | | | | |
| | AUDIO-VISUAL | | | | | | | | | | | | | | | | | | | | | | | | |
| | Concept meeting | | | | | | | | | | | | | | | | | | | | | | | | |
| | Approval | | | | | | | | | | | | | | | | | | | | | | | | |
| | Completion | | | | | | | | | | | | | | | | | | | | | | | | |
| | NAMES FOR UNIT TYPES | | | | | | | | | | | | | | | | | | | | | | | | |
| | SITE SIGNAGE | | | | | | | | | | | | | | | | | | | | | | | | |

**FIGURE 10.1   Critical-Path Marketing (CPM) System (continued)**

PROJECT NAME _____                                              YEAR _____

**DEVELOPMENT SCHEDULE**

| Res. | Month | 1 | 15 | 30 | 1 | 15 | 30 | 1 | 15 | 30 | 1 | 15 | 30 | 1 | 15 | 30 | 1 | 15 | 30 | 1 | 15 | 30 | 1 | 15 | 30 |
|---|---|---|---|---|---|---|---|---|---|---|---|---|---|---|---|---|---|---|---|---|---|---|---|---|---|
| | **ADVERTISING**<br>MEDIA SCHEDULE AND SOURCES | | | | | | | | | | | | | | | | | | | | | | | | |
| | Ad production | | | | | | | | | | | | | | | | | | | | | | | | |
| | Establish ad campaign | | | | | | | | | | | | | | | | | | | | | | | | |

**FIGURE 10.1    Critical-Path Marketing (CPM) System (continued)**

**DEVELOPMENT SCHEDULE**

PROJECT NAME _____    YEAR _____

| Res. | Month | 1 | 15 | 30 | 1 | 15 | 30 | 1 | 15 | 30 | 1 | 15 | 30 | 1 | 15 | 30 | 1 | 15 | 30 | 1 | 15 | 30 | 1 | 15 | 30 |
|---|---|---|---|---|---|---|---|---|---|---|---|---|---|---|---|---|---|---|---|---|---|---|---|---|---|---|
| | **LEGAL** | | | | | | | | | | | | | | | | | | | | | | | | |
| | DESIGN SALES FORMS | | | | | | | | | | | | | | | | | | | | | | | | |
| | Reservation | | | | | | | | | | | | | | | | | | | | | | | | |
| | P & S | | | | | | | | | | | | | | | | | | | | | | | | |
| | Priority reservation | | | | | | | | | | | | | | | | | | | | | | | | |
| | Define special conditions to be disclosed | | | | | | | | | | | | | | | | | | | | | | | | |
| | Design color selection form | | | | | | | | | | | | | | | | | | | | | | | | |
| | Limited warranty | | | | | | | | | | | | | | | | | | | | | | | | |
| | COMPLETE LEGAL PRESENTATION | | | | | | | | | | | | | | | | | | | | | | | | |
| | Survey of land | | | | | | | | | | | | | | | | | | | | | | | | |
| | Phasing of development | | | | | | | | | | | | | | | | | | | | | | | | |
| | COMPLETE STANDARD SPECS | | | | | | | | | | | | | | | | | | | | | | | | |
| | Complete options and upgrades | | | | | | | | | | | | | | | | | | | | | | | | |
| | ESTABLISH PRICES/PAYMENT PROCEDURE | | | | | | | | | | | | | | | | | | | | | | | | |
| | Determine % of interest | | | | | | | | | | | | | | | | | | | | | | | | |
| | Determine monthly CA charge | | | | | | | | | | | | | | | | | | | | | | | | |

**FIGURE 10.1   Critical-Path Marketing (CPM) System (continued)**

DEVELOPMENT SCHEDULE

PROJECT NAME _____        YEAR _____

| Res. | Month | 1 | 15 | 30 | 1 | 15 | 30 | 1 | 15 | 30 | 1 | 15 | 30 | 1 | 15 | 30 | 1 | 15 | 30 | 1 | 15 | 30 | 1 | 15 | 30 |
|---|---|---|---|---|---|---|---|---|---|---|---|---|---|---|---|---|---|---|---|---|---|---|---|---|---|
| | **PREOPENING SPECIAL EVENT** | | | | | | | | | | | | | | | | | | | | | | | | |
| | DETERMINE GUEST LIST | | | | | | | | | | | | | | | | | | | | | | | | |
| | Special list of public officials | | | | | | | | | | | | | | | | | | | | | | | | |
| | Hire photographers for press photos | | | | | | | | | | | | | | | | | | | | | | | | |
| | Develop press list | | | | | | | | | | | | | | | | | | | | | | | | |
| | Develop press kits | | | | | | | | | | | | | | | | | | | | | | | | |
| | ESTABLISH LOCATION | | | | | | | | | | | | | | | | | | | | | | | | |
| | Hire caterer | | | | | | | | | | | | | | | | | | | | | | | | |
| | DETERMINE SALES PROCEDURES | | | | | | | | | | | | | | | | | | | | | | | | |
| | Approve invitation copy | | | | | | | | | | | | | | | | | | | | | | | | |
| | Print invitation | | | | | | | | | | | | | | | | | | | | | | | | |
| | Approve caterer | | | | | | | | | | | | | | | | | | | | | | | | |
| | Mail invitations | | | | | | | | | | | | | | | | | | | | | | | | |
| | Order flowers | | | | | | | | | | | | | | | | | | | | | | | | |
| | Name tags | | | | | | | | | | | | | | | | | | | | | | | | |
| | Music | | | | | | | | | | | | | | | | | | | | | | | | |
| | Liquor | | | | | | | | | | | | | | | | | | | | | | | | |

**FIGURE 10.1   Critical-Path Marketing (CPM) System (continued)**

**DEVELOPMENT SCHEDULE**

PROJECT NAME _____     YEAR _____

| Month | 1 | 15 | 30 | 1 | 15 | 30 | 1 | 15 | 30 | 1 | 15 | 30 | 1 | 15 | 30 | 1 | 15 | 30 | 1 | 15 | 30 | 1 | 15 | 30 |
|---|---|---|---|---|---|---|---|---|---|---|---|---|---|---|---|---|---|---|---|---|---|---|---|---|
| Res. | | | | | | | | | | | | | | | | | | | | | | | | |
| **PERMANENT SALES CENTER** CONTRACT WITH INTERIOR DESIGNER | | | | | | | | | | | | | | | | | | | | | | | | |
| Furniture layout and purchase | | | | | | | | | | | | | | | | | | | | | | | | |
| Delivery of furniture | | | | | | | | | | | | | | | | | | | | | | | | |
| Install wall treatments | | | | | | | | | | | | | | | | | | | | | | | | |
| Install window treatments | | | | | | | | | | | | | | | | | | | | | | | | |
| GRAPHICS DISPLAY—(if not transferrable from temporary office) | | | | | | | | | | | | | | | | | | | | | | | | |
| Logo graphic | | | | | | | | | | | | | | | | | | | | | | | | |
| Floor plan | | | | | | | | | | | | | | | | | | | | | | | | |
| Site plan | | | | | | | | | | | | | | | | | | | | | | | | |
| Lifestyle photos | | | | | | | | | | | | | | | | | | | | | | | | |
| Development team photo | | | | | | | | | | | | | | | | | | | | | | | | |
| Area location map | | | | | | | | | | | | | | | | | | | | | | | | |
| SCHEDULE MOVE FROM TEMP. OFFICE | | | | | | | | | | | | | | | | | | | | | | | | |
| Order telephone installed | | | | | | | | | | | | | | | | | | | | | | | | |
| Arrange for cleaning | | | | | | | | | | | | | | | | | | | | | | | | |
| Contract for plant and maintenance | | | | | | | | | | | | | | | | | | | | | | | | |
| Print homeowner's manual | | | | | | | | | | | | | | | | | | | | | | | | |
| Order music for models | | | | | | | | | | | | | | | | | | | | | | | | |

**FIGURE 10.1  Critical-Path Marketing (CPM) System (continued)**

**DEVELOPMENT SCHEDULE**

PROJECT NAME _____                                                                      YEAR _____

| Res. | Month | 1 | 15 | 30 | 1 | 15 | 30 | 1 | 15 | 30 | 1 | 15 | 30 | 1 | 15 | 30 | 1 | 15 | 30 | 1 | 15 | 30 | 1 | 15 | 30 |
|---|---|---|---|---|---|---|---|---|---|---|---|---|---|---|---|---|---|---|---|---|---|---|---|---|---|
| | **MODELS** <br> DETERMINE BUDGET | | | | | | | | | | | | | | | | | | | | | | | | |
| | Determine date for completion | | | | | | | | | | | | | | | | | | | | | | | | |
| | Select decorator | | | | | | | | | | | | | | | | | | | | | | | | |
| | DETERMINE DECORATING STYLE | | | | | | | | | | | | | | | | | | | | | | | | |
| | Approve color scheme | | | | | | | | | | | | | | | | | | | | | | | | |
| | Approve special effects (to be included in model—built-ins, etc.) | | | | | | | | | | | | | | | | | | | | | | | | |
| | INSTALLATION OF SPECIAL EFFECTS | | | | | | | | | | | | | | | | | | | | | | | | |
| | BUILT-INS | | | | | | | | | | | | | | | | | | | | | | | | |
| | Wall treatment | | | | | | | | | | | | | | | | | | | | | | | | |
| | Window treatment | | | | | | | | | | | | | | | | | | | | | | | | |
| | Furniture delivery | | | | | | | | | | | | | | | | | | | | | | | | |
| | ORDER DISCLAIMER SIGN— FOR NONSTANDARD ITEMS | | | | | | | | | | | | | | | | | | | | | | | | |
| | PLANTS | | | | | | | | | | | | | | | | | | | | | | | | |
| | MAINTENANCE CONTRACT | | | | | | | | | | | | | | | | | | | | | | | | |
| | CLEANING | | | | | | | | | | | | | | | | | | | | | | | | |
| | | | | | | | | | | | | | | | | | | | | | | | | | |
| | | | | | | | | | | | | | | | | | | | | | | | | | |

**FIGURE 10.1    Critical-Path Marketing (CPM) System (continued)**

DEVELOPMENT SCHEDULE

PROJECT NAME _____    YEAR _____

| Res. | Month | 1 | 15 | 30 | 1 | 15 | 30 | 1 | 15 | 30 | 1 | 15 | 30 | 1 | 15 | 30 | 1 | 15 | 30 | 1 | 15 | 30 | 1 | 15 | 30 |
|---|---|---|---|---|---|---|---|---|---|---|---|---|---|---|---|---|---|---|---|---|---|---|---|---|---|
| | **GRAND OPENING**<br>DETERMINE BUDGET | | | | | | | | | | | | | | | | | | | | | | | | |
| | Caterer—Approve menu | | | | | | | | | | | | | | | | | | | | | | | | |
| | Approve invitation list | | | | | | | | | | | | | | | | | | | | | | | | |
| | Prepare press kit | | | | | | | | | | | | | | | | | | | | | | | | |
| | Hire photographer | | | | | | | | | | | | | | | | | | | | | | | | |
| | Special invitation to town & local officials (special tour) | | | | | | | | | | | | | | | | | | | | | | | | |
| | Supply bathroom facilities | | | | | | | | | | | | | | | | | | | | | | | | |
| | Plan parking/traffic control | | | | | | | | | | | | | | | | | | | | | | | | |
| | Order flowers | | | | | | | | | | | | | | | | | | | | | | | | |
| | Name tags | | | | | | | | | | | | | | | | | | | | | | | | |
| | Tent | | | | | | | | | | | | | | | | | | | | | | | | |
| | Background music | | | | | | | | | | | | | | | | | | | | | | | | |
| | Liquor service | | | | | | | | | | | | | | | | | | | | | | | | |
| | Address envelopes | | | | | | | | | | | | | | | | | | | | | | | | |
| | Mail invitations | | | | | | | | | | | | | | | | | | | | | | | | |

**FIGURE 10.1 Critical-Path Marketing (CPM) System (concluded)**

**DEVELOPMENT SCHEDULE**

PROJECT NAME _____        YEAR _____

| Res. | Month | 1 | 15 | 30 | 1 | 15 | 30 | 1 | 15 | 30 | 1 | 15 | 30 | 1 | 15 | 30 | 1 | 15 | 30 | 1 | 15 | 30 | 1 | 15 | 30 | 1 | 15 | 30 |
|---|---|---|---|---|---|---|---|---|---|---|---|---|---|---|---|---|---|---|---|---|---|---|---|---|---|---|---|---|---|
| | **FINAL OPENING CHECK LIST** | | | | | | | | | | | | | | | | | | | | | | | | | | | |
| | NEWSPAPER COPY | | | | | | | | | | | | | | | | | | | | | | | | | | | |
| | MEDIA SCHEDULE | | | | | | | | | | | | | | | | | | | | | | | | | | | |
| | SCHEDULE MOVE TO PERMANENT OFFICE | | | | | | | | | | | | | | | | | | | | | | | | | | | |
| | CHECK FOR ALL SUPPLIES | | | | | | | | | | | | | | | | | | | | | | | | | | | |
| | RECEIVE PRODUCTION AND COMPLETION DATES | | | | | | | | | | | | | | | | | | | | | | | | | | | |
| | ARRANGE INTERIOR OPTION | | | | | | | | | | | | | | | | | | | | | | | | | | | |
| | DISPLAYS | | | | | | | | | | | | | | | | | | | | | | | | | | | |
| | CHECK FOR ALL DISCLAIMER SIGNS | | | | | | | | | | | | | | | | | | | | | | | | | | | |
| | TEAM DINNER SALES MEETING WITH DEVELOPER FOR MOTIVATION, LAST-MINUTE PEP TALK AND DISCUSSION OF PROCEDURES | | | | | | | | | | | | | | | | | | | | | | | | | | | |

assignments or burying them in your files is inviting disaster. Something important is likely to be overlooked that will adversely affect the marketing pro formas. By visually placing all of these time-lined functions where they will be seen on a daily basis by everyone who must implement them, you minimize the chances for error while maintaining psychological pressure on the team to keep the balls rolling to the finish line.

## MASTER SITE MAPS AND INVENTORY-CONTROL SYSTEMS

Another fundamental management tool is the use of master site plans (typically engineering maps) to control information about the status of current inventory. Never confuse the inventory tools used by salespeople with their customers and those we need for accurate management of all homesites in all phases of development. What is released to sales personnel for representation with prospective buyers has to be limited to absorption rates, construction-sequencing, on-site marketing needs and current phasing strategies. As we emphasized in chapter 3, inventory control with consumers is a fundamental and essential aspect of maintaining a sense of urgency while reducing confusion and protecting values. The bigger picture on which all planning is premised must be portrayed visually for those in decision-influencing roles. The recommended approach is to mount individually each master site map in a prominent place (probably the same war room where CPM's are maintained), color-code all land development phases and identify each homesite or unit with appropriate notations about sales status, product, pricing, sequencing and construction. Sales management needs this visual reminder of what remains to be sold as well as what is unclosed to effectively communicate issues and objectives to the sales force.

Marketers must anticipate what to emphasize as they look ahead to promotional campaigns that need several weeks of advance planning. The one thing we can all be sure of is that inventory status will change or we are not needed! Every time something is sold, it changes the mix of what is left to sell. I have seen marketers maintain ads featuring homes or models that were either no longer available or were in short supply while ignoring the bulk of merchandise that needed to be sold! All advertising should be aimed at the remaining inventory, not the limited editions that will not make or break the profit picture!

Portable versions of these maps can be placed in control binders and taken to meetings with the advertising agency, used with salespeople and reviewed at planning sessions when the larger maps are not available.

Inventory-control systems should also incorporate some type of listing form that summarizes all essential information about each property currently for sale along with those that have been sold. The most practical way to achieve this objective is to use an inventory spread-sheet. At the beginning of a new project, begin a spread-sheet listing in numerical order or by phases all homesites or condominium units that have been released to sales. All unsold parcels remain blank except for lot or unit number until sales are originated. Each sale is logged as it occurs and is tracked across the spread-sheet, noting the dates of completion of each vital step until it is finally closed and disbursed. Since some sales will be canceled for one or more reasons, the form must either allow removal of the inserted information or be run on a copier for permanent record and replaced with an updated version.

Computer technology provides the most efficient means of managing inventory spread-sheets, and an increasing percentage of marketing managers are now using computer software programs to maintain constant control of inventory and sales data. Another way to list inventory for priority of attention is by age. Homes or sites that have been on the market the longest are listed first in an aging sequence from oldest to newest. This is a good management tool to force concentration of efforts on the properties that have the greatest carrying costs and that may represent reduction in profits if not sold soon.

Real estate brokers like to have their listings organized by price and type, so you may need more than one summary. This is one of the more important sales management tools for planned encounters with sales personnel. A weekly review of every case in process, along with a discussion of what has not yet been sold, is the best way for the sales manager to educate and motivate sales agents to maintain high standards of performance.

## PREPARING AND MONITORING THE MARKETING PRO FORMAS

As emphasized in chapter 3, development of a realistic marketing budget or pro forma is the first step in creating and implementing your marketing strategies. It begins with the determination of the number of units to be sold with estimated gross dollar volumes and available funds to pay marketing expenses. A pro forma that is unrealistic is worse than none at all! Basing your decisions to expend dollars for models, decor, signs, brochures, advertising, etc., on figures difficult to achieve is operating in a fool's paradise. All budgets should be based on what is most likely to happen and then analyzed from worst-case to best-case scenarios. They should also provide for prioritizing all marketing decisions that will affect the bottom line, so that everyone in management is fully cognizant of the consequences of not meeting minimum projections.

For example, many marketing decisions are variables that can be adjusted as required to meet the realities of market activity, such as advertising, holding major events and ordering more brochures. Others are fixed expenditures once committed, and the consequences of erring in these judgments cannot be easily adjusted. If you decide to build three furnished model homes, establish a major sales facility with all of the professional displays envisioned as necessary to communicate values effectively, these commitments require making a certain number of sales to amortize expenditures and still maintain reasonable profit margins. If you fail to hit those numbers, the costs will erode or destroy profits. That is why it is so important for the marketing team to validate the feasibility analysis on which the sales pro forma will be based.

Another variable in the picture is knowing for any project where the crossover point occurs between being in the red or the black. If it takes 19 sales closed in phase one of the new lot development project to break even on land and development costs, then the pro forma needs to reflect both the investment costs to reach that point and the safeguards that are programmed to assure that it occurs on schedule.

**FIGURE 10.2   Sales Process/Inventory Spread-Sheets**

| Lot | Plan | Buyer | Telephone No.'s (H)(W) | Purchase Date | Sales Price | Loan Type | Lender | Loan Amount | Loan Pkg. In | Escrow Inst. Signed | Vesting | Carpet Selection | Processing Complete | Loan Approved | Ecr's Install | Move-In Letter | Contingency | Contingency Removed | Unit Finaled | Ins. At Escrow | Docs. Signed | Carpet Instal | Walk-Thru | Unit Ready | Offer to Purc Close of Escr | Move-In Date | Broker Referr In/Ob | Date: _____ By: _____ Notes |
|---|---|---|---|---|---|---|---|---|---|---|---|---|---|---|---|---|---|---|---|---|---|---|---|---|---|---|---|---|
| | | | | | | | | | | | | | | | | | | | | | | | | | | | | |
| | | | | | | | | | | | | | | | | | | | | | | | | | | | | |
| | | | | | | | | | | | | | | | | | | | | | | | | | | | | |
| | | | | | | | | | | | | | | | | | | | | | | | | | | | | |
| | | | | | | | | | | | | | | | | | | | | | | | | | | | | |

Project _____
Phase _____
Escrow Co. _____

## FIGURE 10.2    Sales Process/Inventory Spread-Sheets (continued)

### INVENTORY CONTROL FORM
(PRICE LIST)

PROJECT NAME_____ DATE_____

| Lot # | Plan # | Address | Base price | Lot premium and/or option price | Total price |
|-------|--------|---------|------------|--------------------------------|-------------|
|       |        |         |            |                                |             |
|       |        |         |            |                                |             |
|       |        |         |            |                                |             |
|       |        |         |            |                                |             |
|       |        |         |            |                                |             |
|       |        |         |            |                                |             |
|       |        |         |            |                                |             |
|       |        |         |            |                                |             |
|       |        |         |            |                                |             |
|       |        |         |            |                                |             |
|       |        |         |            |                                |             |
|       |        |         |            |                                |             |
|       |        |         |            |                                |             |
|       |        |         |            |                                |             |
|       |        |         |            |                                |             |
|       |        |         |            |                                |             |
|       |        |         |            |                                |             |
|       |        |         |            |                                |             |
|       |        |         |            |                                |             |
|       |        |         |            |                                |             |

APPROVED BY_____ DATE _____

**FIGURE 10.2   Sales Process/Inventory Spread-Sheets (concluded)**

**Community Status Report**

Builder _____

Community _____

Sales Manager _____

**New Homes and Land Division**   Date _____

| STATUS | LOT | BUYER | BROKER | MODEL | SALES PRICE | CONTRACT DATE | OFFICE USE |
|--------|-----|-------|--------|-------|-------------|---------------|------------|
|        |     |       |        |       |             |               |            |
|        |     |       |        |       |             |               |            |
|        |     |       |        |       |             |               |            |
|        |     |       |        |       |             |               |            |
|        |     |       |        |       |             |               |            |
|        |     |       |        |       |             |               |            |
|        |     |       |        |       |             |               |            |
|        |     |       |        |       |             |               |            |
|        |     |       |        |       |             |               |            |
|        |     |       |        |       |             |               |            |
|        |     |       |        |       |             |               |            |
|        |     |       |        |       |             |               |            |
|        |     |       |        |       |             |               |            |
|        |     |       |        |       |             |               |            |
|        |     |       |        |       |             |               |            |
|        |     |       |        |       |             |               |            |
|        |     |       |        |       |             |               |            |
|        |     |       |        |       |             |               |            |
|        |     |       |        |       |             |               |            |
|        |     |       |        |       |             |               |            |

Spending extra dollars to pick up momentum at the beginning may be a wiser investment rather than trying to get by on minimum budgets until a limited number of sales have been made. The entire process of planning the marketing pro formas and monitoring the variables that affect bottom-line performance is a balancing act that should not be left to amateurs.

Once the budget has been established, it must be kept up-to-date and adjusted based on actual performance data. I have often been asked to review a marketing plan along with its originating pro formas, only to discover that no one had made any adjustment to the figures even though sales were behind projections and costs were in excess of estimates. This is like driving in the dark without lights or a map! How can you make reasonable judgments if you do not know the consequences of what has already been implemented? Someone must be assigned the responsibility (preferably weekly) of maintaining the records on which management decisions will be based. Whether that is done by the accounting department that gathers information from sales and construction or the marketing department (broker) that is in charge of sales is unimportant. It must be done regularly and interpreted at least once a month if not more often. When sales management is in the dark about costs of marketing and the potential consequences of the decisions they make, the predictable confusion will adversely affect all disciplines in the enterprise.

Following are examples of typical pro formas and monitoring systems used by marketing professionals in the housing industry.

**FIGURE 10.3 Project Sales Analysis Form**

CLIENT: ______________________

DEVELOPMENT: ______________________

SALES STARTED: ______________________

| | Month Ending___ | Month Totals | Month Ending___ | Month Totals | Month Ending___ | Month Totals | QUARTERLY TOTALS | TOTALS SINCE OPENING |
|---|---|---|---|---|---|---|---|---|
| 1. Traffic (Sun./wkly.) | | | | | | | | |
| 2. Sales (gross) | | | | | | | | |
| 3. Cancellations | | | | | | | | |
| 4. Sales (net) | | pro. / act. | | pro. / act. | | pro. / act. | pro. / act. | pro. / act. |
| 5. Conversion ratio (net) | | | | | | | | |
| 6. Escrow closings | | pro. / act. | | pro. / act. | | pro. / act. | pro. / act. | pro. / act. |
| 7. Advertising a. media | | | | | | | | |
| b. publicity | | | | | | | | |
| 8. Price increase | | | | | | | | |
| 9. New unit open | | | | | | | | |
| 10. Plans mix | | cans. / net sales | | cans. / net sales | | cans. / net sales | cans. / net sales | cans. / net sales |
| | | | | | | | | |
| | | | | | | | | |
| | | | | | | | | |
| | | | | | | | | |
| | | | | | | | | |
| | | | | | | | | |
| | | | | | | | | |

**FIGURE. 10.4   Marketing Analysis Worksheet**

Division: _____
Building Partnership: _____
Prepared by: _____

Tract: _____
No. of Houses: _____
Date: _____

| | | | | | Projected Total Cost* |
|---|---|---|---|---|---|
| Model Home Complex Costs | | | | | |
| Model Home Land Acquisition, Carrying and Improvement | | | | | |
| Model Home Hard Construction Costs | | | | | |
| Model Home Job Overhead | | | | | |
| Model Home Landscaping | | | | | |
| Model Home Decorating Fee | | | | | |
| Alterations Before Selling Models | | | | | |
| Total Model Homes | | | | | |
| Less: Sales Price—Gross | | | | | |
| Add: Sales Commission | | | | | |
| Closing Costs | | | | | |
| Discount and Loan Expense | | | | | |
| Subtotal | | | | | |
| Furniture for Models | | | | | |
| Less Resale | | | | | |
| Subtotal | | | | | |

**FIGURE. 10.4  Marketing Analysis Worksheet (continued)**

Division: _____

Building Partnership: _____

Prepared by: _____

Tract: _____

No. of Houses: _____

Date: _____

| | | | | | | Projected Total Cost* |
|---|---|---|---|---|---|---|
| Sales Office Hard Construction Costs | | | | | | |
| Less Resale | | | | | | |
| Subtotal | | | | | | |
| Construction and Land Improvement | | | | | | |
| Loan Exp | | | | | | |
| Loan Interest Furnishings | | | | | | |
| Marketing Allocation—Models | | | | | | |
| Administrative Allocation—Models | | | | | | |
| Customer Service Allocation—Models | | | | | | |
| Total Model Home Complex Costs | | | | | | |
| Marketing Expenses | | | | | | |
| Salaries, Commissions and Related | | | | | | |
| Payoff Costs | | | | | | |
| Advertising | | | | | | |
| Promotion | | | | | | |
| Sales Office Expense | | | | | | |
| Model Home Expense | | | | | | |

**FIGURE. 10.4  Marketing Analysis Worksheet (concluded)**

Division: _____
Building Partnership: _____
Prepared by: _____

Tract: _____
No. of Houses: _____
Date: _____

| | | | | | Projected Total Cost* |
|---|---|---|---|---|---|
| Closing Costs | | | | | |
| Transportation, Entertainment and Subsistence | | | | | |
| Professional Fees | | | | | |
| Miscellaneous | | | | | |
| Total Marketing Expenses | | | | | |
| Grand Total Tract Model Home Complex Costs and Marketing Expeneses | | | | | |

$$\text{Average Per House} = \frac{\text{Grand Total}}{\text{No. of Houses in Tract}} = \underline{\hspace{2cm}}$$

*For projected total costs, derive from Project Marketing Report. If not available, derive from Marketing Budget.

## COORDINATION PROCEDURES BETWEEN SALES AND CONSTRUCTION

The absence of a solid working relationship between those in charge of construction and those in charge of sales can produce havoc for any building enterprise. A natural tendency seems to exist for these two disciplines to distrust each other. People in construction sometimes express contempt for the sales agents who sit in comfortable offices and seem to do little to justify their existence. Sales agents complain that production personnel are insensitive to buyers and not cooperative when it comes to making changes or meeting deadlines. Each tends to see the other from a vantage point that distorts the reality of their mutual importance to each other. Sales and marketing managers have the obligation to try to provide a forum for these separate functions that will minimize differences and concentrate on the attainment of mutual objectives. That is difficult to achieve if the executives of the company do not understand and respect the contributions each discipline is making to the enterprise.

Strong sales managers realize they cannot afford to sit back and let communication issues complicate the sales process. If the clients for whom they work do not provide the leadership to bring these forces into harmony, they step in and find ways to achieve coordination on their own. It must first be recognized that it is not a question of whether sales agents or construction people are more important, because the truth is none of them would have jobs if the real boss ignored them: the consumer! Everyone in the system needs to remember who is ultimately dictating their survival and success: the home buyers who either choose to buy from their company or from someone elses! Here is a checklist of some ideas that progressive, team-oriented developers, builders and marketers use to maintain effective working relationships between sales, construction and all of the supporting functions on which both are dependent:

1. Provide written policies that clarify procedures for handling all coordination elements efficiently, from originating a start order through options, change orders, and move-ins.

2. Hold a team meeting with all participants present at the launching of a new project. The principals express their appreciation for the roles each person and department plays in the total picture, and set the tone for a cooperative effort.

3. Publish a communication chart that correctly reflects the positions and authority of each person in the system. Some companies include photos, biographies and notes of achievement for each individual player so that everyone will appreciate the talent in the system.

4. Encourage the superintendent to stop at the sales office at least once a day (preferably early in the morning) to update construction status and pick up information about sales activity. While authority lines are still maintained by those in charge of sales and production, the communication channels should be kept open at the front line so a spirit of cooperation is fostered.

5. Hold once-a-week administrative meetings attended by heads of production, sales, development, processing, etc. A review of all sales, starts, closings, move-ins and unsold inventory is part of the ongoing agenda. This

provides an opportunity for each department to clarify its concerns and explore ways to improve efficiency.

6. Publish an in-house news bulletin or letter that summarizes accomplishments, recognizes performers in all departments, and builds morale by humanizing the enterprise.

7. Prior to a grand opening or preview of new models, hold a special party for those in construction, sales and management. This is often a barbecue or pot-luck affair held on site with members of the team and sometimes their families. Management thanks everyone for what he or she has accomplished in getting the site ready for sales, and sets the tone for continued cooperation.

8. Have sales managers encourage their salespeople to say thank you to people in production whenever they do special things that help the sales effort. Occasionally, a spontaneous party on Friday afternoon might be given by the sales staff for the construction personnel as a special way of thanking them for meeting deadlines, handling an unusual number of move-ins in a short time or meeting some other goal.

9. Sponsor a contest that involves both sales and production personnel. Too often, contests are solely aimed at salespeople and do not take into consideration the other functions. By including construction (and other departments) in the goal-oriented program, the spirit of cooperation between the disciplines is usually enhanced. If the goals are met, everyone shares in the rewards.

10. Institute an employee-of-the-month award that recognizes the person who has contributed most to the company's goals that month. This should naturally rotate over a period of time from one department to another, thus building the morale of all associated with the organization.

11. Encourage salespeople to introduce superintendents or production personnel to their buyers whenever appropriate. The personalization of relationships between buyers and members of the team can reinforce the buyers' confidence in the company. Caution must be exercised to avoid buyers believing they can go directly to superintendents and construction people to obtain information or request service. The responsibility for that rests with sales personnel.

12. Take team photos of construction and other departments. Display them on the activity panels in the sales office or in the photo albums available for review by prospective buyers.

13. Hold an annual banquet for the entire company (possibly including cooperating REALTORS®) at which awards are given to individuals in each department who have met company goals for the year. Peer-group recognition goes a long way toward building morale.

14. When buyers move into their new home, arrange a photo session that includes the sales agent, the on-site superintendent and anyone else who was a key participant in the fulfillment of the buyers' dream! Give a copy to the new owners for their album and keep an extra one for use by the sales organization.

15. Use the after-move-in survey form to evaluate performance of all departments and personnel in a constructive manner. It provides an opportunity to compliment and instruct both production and sales personnel with the objective of strengthening the commitment to excellence.

## EASY-TO-USE FORMS AND SYSTEMS FOR INTERDEPARTMENTAL COMMUNICATION

The source of most problems in any company can be traced to the quality of the communication systems. When misunderstandings arise, it is invariably because of failure to communicate effectively and to document agreements. Between sales and production, the confusions stem from three critical factors:

1. Failure of the salesperson to obtain agreement from buyers on what will be included with the home at authorized prices (materials, options, upgrades, colors, etc.) and communicate them in writing in time to have them implemented by construction.
2. Failure of construction personnel promptly to review and initiate authorized work orders according to approved specifications.
3. Failure of management or construction to notify sales about realistic dates of delivery when conditions change that affect projected completion schedules.

While a variety of other challenges arise in the processing of contracts between sales and construction, the majority of complaints surround the initiation of the work orders and the subsequent additions (or deletions) that occur during the construction schedule. Salespeople are notoriously careless with paperwork. Construction personnel, especially subcontractors, like to build according to plan and resent any changes that will complicate the construction schedule or the way they prefer to build. That is why it takes strong supervision on both sides to keep these two disciplines working together for the builder's profit and the buyer's satisfaction.

The way the work order is initiated is critical to the efficiency of the entire system. Unless it is properly priced, documented with the right specifications and distributed promptly to all who will be involved in implementing construction, problems are bound to result. On the following pages we provide you with examples of some of the best forms and procedures used by our clients in handling the processing of construction work orders and related modifications.

---

**FIGURE 10.5   New Home Closing Forms**

**Preliminary Closing Statement**

Buyer:_____ Proposed Closing Date: _____
Seller:_____
New Home Address:_____
_____

| Description | Debit | Credit |
|---|---|---|
| Purchase Price | $ _____ | |
| Earnest Money | | $ _____ |
| Additional Deposits | | $ _____ |
| New Mortgage | | $ _____ |
| Contract for Deed | | $ _____ |
| Mortgage Application Costs | | |
| • Appraisal Fee | $ _____ | |
| • Credit Report | $ _____ | |
| • Other:_____ | $ _____ | |
| _____ | $ _____ | |
| Closing Costs | | |
| • Mortgage Insurance | $ _____ | |
| • Mortgage Discount Points | $ _____ | |
| • Mortgagee Title Insurance | $ _____ | |
| • Owners Title Insurance | $ _____ | |
| • Special Assessment Search | $ _____ | |
| • Plat Drawing | $ _____ | |
| • Real Estate Taxes_____ | $ _____ | |
| • Recording Fees | $ _____ | |
| • Mortgage Registration | $ _____ | |
| • Closing Fee | $ _____ | |
| • Other:_____ | $ _____ | |
| _____ | $ _____ | |
| Prepayable and Escrow Costs | | |
| _____ months Hazard Ins. Escrow | $ _____ | |
| _____ months Tax Escrow | $ _____ | |
| _____ days Mortgage Interest | $ _____ | |
| Other:_____ | $ _____ | |
| Other:_____ | $ _____ | $ _____ |
| _____ | $ _____ | $ _____ |
| _____ | $ _____ | $ _____ |
| Required Cash at Closing from Buyer | | $ _____ |
| Total Proceeds | $ _____ | $ _____ |
| Buyers Monthly Payment | | |
| • Principle and Interest | $ _____ | |
| • Mortgage Insurance | $ _____ | |
| • Hazard Insurance Escrow | $ _____ | |
| • Real Estate Tax Escrow | $ _____ | |
| Total Monthly Payment | $ _____ | |

It is understood by the Buyers there may be slight differences between the costs identified in this Statement and the final costs at the closing.

**Accepted by:**
Buyer:_____ Date:_____
Buyer:_____ Date:_____
Prepared by:_____ Date:_____
Approved by:_____ Date:_____

**FIGURE 10.5   New Home Closing Forms (continued)**

**Addendum to Purchase Agreement**

Buyer's Name:_____

New Home Address:_____

_____

Project:_____

Model/House Plan:_____

| | |
|---|---|
| **Price of Base Home*** | $_____ |
| **Lot Price/Premlum** | $_____ |
| **Selected Optional Features** | |
| _____ | $_____ |
| _____ | $_____ |
| _____ | $_____ |
| _____ | $_____ |
| _____ | $_____ |
| _____ | $_____ |
| _____ | $_____ |
| _____ | $_____ |
| _____ | $_____ |
| _____ | $_____ |
| **Total Optional Features** | $_____ |
| **Total Purchase Price** | $_____ |

*   The features included in base home are defined in the Standard and Optional Feature
    Specifications which have been reviewed by Buyer(s).

Buyer's Signature_____ Date_____

Buyer's Signature_____ Date_____

Accepted:_____ Date_____
(Builder)

---

**FIGURE 10.5   New Home Closing Forms (continued)**

---

**New Home Closing Checklist**

Buyer:_____

New Home Address:_____

_____

Closing scheduled at: _____ am/pm     Date:_____

Location:_____

_____

_____

You must bring to the closing of your new home:

• Certified or cashiers check in the amount of $_____, payable to:

_____

• Receipt showing payment of one year's premium for hazard insurance on the property with coverage in an amount at least equal to the mortgage amount.

• Personal check for any minor differences in projected closing costs.

• As described in the mortgage commitment letter, you must supply evidence of:_____

_____

_____

• Other:_____

_____

_____

The closing of your home is the formal point at which you will take legal title to your new home and you must be sure to bring with you all the required documents. Also, unless arrangements have been made otherwise, all persons taking legal title to the new home of signing the mortgage documents must attend the closing.

**Acknowledged by:**

Buyer:_____ Date:_____

Buyer:_____ Date:_____

Prepared by:_____ Date:_____

Approved by:_____ Date:_____

## FIGURE 10.5   New Home Closing Forms (concluded)

_____

(Date)

_____

_____

| DESCRIPTION | TENTATIVE SCHEDULE | ACTUAL DATE | DESCRIPTION | TENTATIVE SCHEDULE | ACTUAL DATE |
|---|---|---|---|---|---|
| Mortgage Loan Applications | 5 | | Porch Finish | 2-3 | |
| Color Selection | 5 | | Insulation | 1 | |
| Material Selection | 5 | | Sheetrock | 8-9 | |
| Loan Approval | 30 | | Brick | 1-8 | |
| Site Plan | 3 | | Exterior Paint | 2-3 | |
| Preconstruction Meeting | 1 | | Guttering | 1 | |
| No-Start Survey | 1 | | Trim | 6-7 | |
| Building Permit | 1 | | Kitchen Cabinets | 1-2 | |
| Excavation | 1-2 | | Paint and Stain Interior | 5-6 | |
| Order Windows and Doors | 1 | | Ceramic Tile | 4 | |
| Basement Walls | 1-2 | | Install Appliances | 1 | |
| Order Trusses | 1 | | Plumbing Final | 1-2 | |
| Basement Plumbing | 1-2 | | Electric Final | 1-2 | |
| Basement Floor | 1 | | Heat and Air Final | 1 | |
| Backfill/Waterproofing | 1-2 | | Carpeting | 2 | |
| Exterior Flat Work | 2-3 | | Signature Quality Check | 1 | |
| Framing | 6-8 | | Finish Grade | 1 | |
| Roofing Material and Labor | 3 | | Final Inspection | 1 | |
| Install Ext. Doors and Windows | 1-2 | | Buyer Walk-Through | 1 | |
| Rough-in Plumbing | 3 | | Preclosing Review | 1 | |
| Order Sewer/Water Service | 1 | | Closing | 1 | |
| Rough-in Heat and Air | 3 | | 30 Day Warranty Letter | 30 | |
| Rough-in Electric | 2 | | 5 Month Warranty Letter | 150 | |
| Siding | 5-6 | | 11 Month Warranty Sign-Off | 330 | |

## ESTABLISH AND MONITOR PERFORMANCE STANDARDS

When you have clearly defined minimum (and maximum) performance standards for each of the key factors affecting the efficiency of sales and marketing, you are in a solid position to manage the salespeople, the marketing support personnel, the subcontractors and anyone else whose activities influence the success of your operations. We have discussed in chapter 6 the value of having sales-oriented performance standards. This same concept should extend to all marketing systems. Written guidelines (or checklists) that specify the criteria by which you will measure each category of your total marketing program provide you with the management tool to secure improved performance. The following key areas of marketing deserve their own written performance standards:

- company image identification—graphic representation
- sales representatives' responsibilities
- sales-office organization
- model home decor and maintenance
- on-site signage, landscaping and general appearance
- cooperative broker supervision
- off-site signage
- advertising
- public relations and publicity
- production models and spec inventory
- amenity management
- collateral materials and sales aids
- sales-processing procedures
- quality-delivery and customer-service program

Checklists that specify acceptable performance for each of these categories can become a primary management instrument for monitoring and improving the system. On the following pages we provide you with a few of the performance checklists used by others in our industry along with inspection-evaluation forms for measuring compliance.

---

**FIGURE 10.6  Performance Checklist and Monitoring Forms**

---

### MODEL HOME CHECKLIST

/_____  1. Unlock all model homes as scheduled and check for any unfavorable showing conditions.

/_____  2. Turn on lights in all rooms and replace any burned-out bulbs.

/_____  3. Adjust heat or air conditioning to assure proper temperature level.

/_____  4. Use air sprays to eliminate unpleasant odors.

/_____  5. Adjust bedspreads, lamps, ornaments, pictures and any other items out of place or in disarray.

/_____  6. See that display signs, directionals and cigarette containers are in proper location and condition.

/_____  7. Note any items needing repair or touch-up and report them to the sales manager for immediate attention. Model homes should always be in showcase condition for inspection.

/_____  8. Note condition of the yards, walks, signs and all other exterior factors and report any needed improvements to the sales manager.

/_____  9. Although a regular janitorial team will be employed to care for all models and the sales centers, sales associates must assist in keeping these vital facilities in top condition. Observe efficiency of the janitorial service and report observations to the sales manager.

/_____  10. At night when locking up the models, careful inspection must be made to be sure that no one remains inside. All windows and doors must be locked to prevent entry, most lights must be turned off, and any unusual conditions reported or corrected. The security guard must be called at _____ and advised to place the model under night surveillance.

/_____  11. The physical status of model signs, "for sale" and "sold" signs must be inspected.

Other Notes:_____

_____

_____

_____

_____

_____

_____

_____

_____

_____

_____

_____

_____

_____

_____

_____

_____

**FIGURE 10.6   Performances Checklist and Monitoring Forms (continued)**

## MODEL AND INVENTORY CONDITION REPORT FORM

COMMUNITY/PROJECT_____ DATE _____

SALES ASSOCIATE_____

Condition of Sales Office_____

_____

Model/Lot # _____ _____

_____

Model/Lot # _____ _____

_____

Model/Lot # _____ _____

_____

Model/Lot # _____ _____

_____

Model/Lot # _____ _____

_____

Model/Lot # _____ _____

_____

Model/Lot # _____ _____

_____

Model/Lot # _____ _____

_____

GENERAL OBSERVATIONS:_____

_____

_____

If other comments are needed please turn this form over and write them on the back.

# FIGURE 10.6  Performances Checklist and Monitoring Forms (continued)

**CUSTOMER FOLLOW UP REPORT**

_____
(COMMUNITY)

_____
(DATE)

_____
(SALESPERSON)

| NAME | HOME/LOT | WEEK 1 | | WEEK II | | WEEK III | | WEEK IV | |
|---|---|---|---|---|---|---|---|---|---|
| 1. | | ☐ MAIL | ☐ PHONE | ☐ MAIL | ☐ PHONE | ☐ MAIL | ☐ PHONE | ☐MAIL | ☐ PHONE |
| 2. | | ☐ MAIL | ☐ PHONE | ☐ MAIL | ☐ PHONE | ☐ MAIL | ☐ PHONE | ☐ MAIL | ☐ PHONE |
| 3. | | ☐ MAIL | ☐ PHONE | ☐ MAIL | ☐ PHONE | ☐ MAIL | ☐ PHONE | ☐ MAIL | ☐ PHONE |
| 4. | | ☐ MAIL | ☐ PHONE | ☐ MAIL | ☐ PHONE | ☐ MAIL | ☐ PHONE | ☐ MAIL | ☐ PHONE |
| 5. | | ☐ MAIL | ☐ PHONE | ☐ MAIL | ☐ PHONE | ☐ MAIL | ☐ PHONE | ☐ MAIL | ☐ PHONE |
| 6. | | ☐ MAIL | ☐ PHONE | ☐ MAIL | ☐ PHONE | ☐ MAIL | ☐ PHONE | ☐ MAIL | ☐ PHONE |
| 7. | | ☐ MAIL | ☐ PHONE | ☐ MAIL | ☐ PHONE | ☐ MAIL | ☐ PHONE | ☐ MAIL | ☐ PHONE |
| 8. | | ☐ MAIL | ☐ PHONE | ☐ MAIL | ☐ PHONE | ☐ MAIL | ☐ PHONE | ☐ MAIL | ☐ PHONE |
| 9. | | ☐ MAIL | ☐ PHONE | ☐ MAIL | ☐ PHONE | ☐ MAIL | ☐ PHONE | ☐ MAIL | ☐ PHONE |
| 10. | | ☐ MAIL | ☐ PHONE | ☐ MAIL | ☐ PHONE | ☐ MAIL | ☐ PHONE | ☐ MAIL | ☐ PHONE |

---

**FIGURE 10.6   Performances Checklist and Monitoring Forms (continued)**

**Community Audit**

Community_____ Date_____

City_____ Sales/Div. Mgr._____

Sales Representative_____

Type Homes_____

Price Range_____

Legend:   (1) Acceptable; (2) Unacceptable; (3) Date to Complete

| | 1 | 2 | 3 | Comments |
|---|---|---|---|---|
| A. *Signage* | | | | |
| 1. Graphic Standards | ( ) | ( ) | (____) | _____ |
| 2. Conformance to Marketing Specifications Manual | ( ) | ( ) | (____) | _____ |
| 3. Maintenance | ( ) | ( ) | (____) | _____ |
| 4. Directional Signs to Community | ( ) | ( ) | (____) | _____ |
| 5. Directional Sign Schedule | ( ) | ( ) | (____) | _____ |
| 6. Entrance Signage | ( ) | ( ) | (____) | _____ |
| a. Appearance | ( ) | ( ) | (____) | _____ |
| b. Information Correct | ( ) | ( ) | (____) | _____ |
| B. *Production Area* | | | | |
| 1. Production Office | ( ) | ( ) | (____) | _____ |
| 2. Appearance of Construction Site | ( ) | ( ) | (____) | _____ |
| 3. Vacant Homesites | ( ) | ( ) | (____) | _____ |
| 4. Inventory Homes Marked With "For Sale" Signs (Selected Homes) | ( ) | ( ) | (____) | _____ |
| 5. "Available" Signs (Selected Homesites) | ( ) | ( ) | (____) | _____ |
| 6. Sold Homes Marked With "Sold" Signs | ( ) | ( ) | (____) | _____ |
| 7. Appearance of Inventory Homes | ( ) | ( ) | (____) | _____ |
| a. Exterior | ( ) | ( ) | (____) | _____ |
| b. Interior | ( ) | ( ) | (____) | _____ |
| C. *Model Area* | | | | |
| 1. Approach Impression | ( ) | ( ) | (____) | _____ |
| 2. Overall Appearance—Designed for Market | ( ) | ( ) | (____) | _____ |
| 3. Cleanliness | ( ) | ( ) | (____) | _____ |

---

**FIGURE 10.6   Performances Checklist and Monitoring Forms (continued)**

Legend:   (1) Acceptable; (2) Unacceptable; (3) Date to Complete

|  | 1 | 2 | 3 | Comments |
|---|---|---|---|---|
| 4. Maintenance | ( ) | ( ) | (_____) | _____ |
| 5. Model Signage | ( ) | ( ) | (_____) | _____ |
| 6. Landscaping | ( ) | ( ) | (_____) | _____ |
|   a. Grass | ( ) | ( ) | (_____) | _____ |
|   b. Plant Material | ( ) | ( ) | (_____) | _____ |
|   c. Mulch | ( ) | ( ) | (_____) | _____ |
|   d. Flowers | ( ) | ( ) | (_____) | _____ |
|   e. Patios, Walks and Decks | ( ) | ( ) | (_____) | _____ |

**D. *Sales Office***

|  | 1 | 2 | 3 | Comments |
|---|---|---|---|---|
| 1. Overall Appearance | ( ) | ( ) | (_____) | _____ |
| 2. Sales Desk | ( ) | ( ) | (_____) | _____ |
| 3. Maintenance | ( ) | ( ) | (_____) | _____ |
| 4. Displays | ( ) | ( ) | (_____) | _____ |
|   a. Accuracy | ( ) | ( ) | (_____) | _____ |
|   b. Appearance | ( ) | ( ) | (_____) | _____ |
|   c. Traffic Flow | ( ) | ( ) | (_____) | _____ |
|   d. Complete | ( ) | ( ) | (_____) | _____ |
|   e. Equal Housing Opportunities Display | ( ) | ( ) | (_____) | _____ |
|   f. H.O.W. Plaque | ( ) | ( ) | (_____) | _____ |
| 5. Site Plan Table Current | ( ) | ( ) | (_____) | _____ |
| 6. Contract Files | ( ) | ( ) | (_____) | _____ |
| 7. Creation of a Sense of Urgency | ( ) | ( ) | (_____) | _____ |

**E. *Sales Aids***

|  | 1 | 2 | 3 | Comments |
|---|---|---|---|---|
| 1. Training of Hostess/Host | ( ) | ( ) | (_____) | _____ |
| 2. Community Book (Articles about the Community, Home Buying and Economy | ( ) | ( ) | (_____) | _____ |
| 3. Availability List | ( ) | ( ) | (_____) | _____ |
| 4. Satisfied Customer Book | ( ) | ( ) | (_____) | _____ |
| 5. Construction Delivery Dates of Unsold Units | ( ) | ( ) | (_____) | _____ |
| 6. Product and Warranty Books | ( ) | ( ) | (_____) | _____ |

---

**FIGURE 10.6   Performances Checklist and Monitoring Forms (concluded)**

Legend:   (1) Acceptable; (2) Unacceptable; (3) Date to Complete

|  |  | 1 | 2 | 3 | Comments |
|---|---|---|---|---|---|
| 7. | Cleanliness of Car | ( ) | ( ) | (____) | _____ |
| 8. | Competitive Analysis | ( ) | ( ) | (____) | _____ |
|  | a. New Homes | ( ) | ( ) | (____) | _____ |
|  | b. Resale Homes | ( ) | ( ) | (____) | _____ |
| 9. | Policies and Procedures | ( ) | ( ) | (____) | _____ |
| 10. | Financing Handouts | ( ) | ( ) | (____) | _____ |
| 11. | HOW Information | ( ) | ( ) | (____) | _____ |
| 12. | Other Handouts | ( ) | ( ) | (____) | _____ |

F. *Models*

|  |  | 1 | 2 | 3 | Comments |
|---|---|---|---|---|---|
| 1. | Overall Appearance | ( ) | ( ) | (____) | _____ |
| 2. | Interior Decorating | ( ) | ( ) | (____) | _____ |
| 3. | Furniture Placement | ( ) | ( ) | (____) | _____ |
| 4. | Maintenance | ( ) | ( ) | (____) | _____ |
| 5. | Interior Signage | ( ) | ( ) | (____) | _____ |
| 6. | Evidence of Punchlist | ( ) | ( ) | (____) | _____ |
| 7. | Interior Lighting | ( ) | ( ) | (____) | _____ |
| 8. | Maintenance of Light Bulbs | ( ) | ( ) | (____) | _____ |
| 9. | Maintenance of Interior Plants | ( ) | ( ) | (____) | _____ |
| 10. | Cleanliness | ( ) | ( ) | (____) | _____ |
| 11. | Touch-up | ( ) | ( ) | (____) | _____ |

Additional Comments_____
_____
_____
_____
_____
_____
_____
_____
_____
_____

Overall Performance Rating_____
(1—Unacceptable, to 10—Excellent)

Date of Next Community Audit_____

## ESTABLISH WRITTEN POLICIES AND
## PROCEDURES FOR SALES AND MARKETING

One of the best ways to prevent confusion and ease the strain on management time required for indoctrination and monitoring is to put your policies and procedures in writing. Managing by exception is one of the principles of efficient supervision. The rule is: if it is something that has to be explained or handled more than once, establish a policy or procedure to which those concerned can refer when necessary. If managers have to coach each new recruit on company policies, or have to offer frequent refresher instruction when an employee's memory fails, the organization is not effectively utilizing its most valued resource: the time and knowledge of its executives. Written policies have the added value of providing confidence to candidates you are attempting to bring on board. Well-run companies have documented systems for doing business, and most of us prefer to work for those which are well-organized than to suffer through impulsive and undisciplined management styles.

Well-organized companies in this industry have policy-and-procedures manuals for all departments and functions. Sales and marketing compose just one section of the comprehensive management system. However, with or without a general operations manual, those responsible for sales always need a manual for their sales representatives. In the absence of firm guidelines, other departments will suffer.

Where outside agents are involved along with captive on-site specialists, the need for the written manual is even more critical. Forms and processing systems must be documented. Staffing and presentation guidelines need to be established. Builders' authorized representations of warranties and service procedures are essential. These and other topics should be committed to writing and published for all sales personnel to read and sales management to enforce. If you are dealing with independent contractors instead of employees, you should couch your language in terminology that will not be interpreted as violating independent-contractor status.

---

**FIGURE 10.7   Policies and Procedures**

---

POLICIES and PROCEDURES

TABLE OF CONTENTS

SECTION 1.0: **ORGANIZATION OF THE COMPANY**

   1.1   Organization
   1.2   Departments of the Company
   1.3   Current Roster of People and Positions
   1.4   Administration of Marketing and Sales Activities
   1.5   Position Description for Sales Associates
   1.6   Goals and Objectives


   1.6a—Daily Planning Guide
   1.6b—Sales Associate's Monthly Goal-Planning Memorandum
   1.6c—Sales Associate's Annual Goal-Planning Memorandum


SECTION 2.0:  **EMPLOYMENT AND COMPENSATION**

   2.1   Employment Policies
   2.2   Basic Compensation Plan for the Marketing Department
   2.3   Accounting Procedures
   2.4   Draws and Advances
   2.5   Reimbursable Expenses
   2.6   Contingent or Guaranteed Sales Referrals
   2.7   Inter project Referrals
   2.8   Forfeitures and Cancelled Transactions
   2.9   Commission Arbitrations
   2.10  Limitations of Recommendations and Referrals for Subcontractors, Suppliers, Etc.
   2.11  Termination and Compensation Agreements

   2.1a—Sales Associate's Employment Agreement
   2.2a—Compensation Addendum to Employment Agreement
   2.3a—Sales Commission Form
   2.3b—Sales Associate's Commission Activity Form
   2.4a—Referral-Control Form
   2.5a—Termination/Transfer Form


SECTION 3.0:  **STAFFING ASSIGNMENTS AND RESPONSIBILITIES**

   3.1   Staffing Assignment Procedure
   3.2   Community and Product Indoctrination
   3.3   Competitive Analysis and the Development Profile Form
   3.4   Staffing Hours and Days Off
   3.5   Use of Telephones

---

**FIGURE 10.7   Policies and Procedures (continued)**

---

3.6    Brochures, Sales Literature and Office Supplies
3.7    Standard On-Site Sales Office Operation Procedures
3.8    Weekly Traffic and Sales Reporting System
3.9    Model-Home Control
3.10   Inventory Control
3.11   Advertising and Promotion
3.12   Vehicles and Customer Presentation

   3.2a—Community Services Guide
   3.2b—Community Training Guide
   3.3a—Development Profile
   3.5a—Long-Distance Telephone Log
   3.6a—Sales Office Inventory and Supply Request Form
   3.8a—Weekly Traffic and Sales Control Form
   3.9a—Model-Home Checklist
   3.9b—Vandalism/Thievery Report Form
   3.9c—Model and Inventory Condition Report Form
   3.10a—Inventory Control Form

SECTION 4.0:   **ORIGINATING AND PROCESSING PURCHASE AGREEMENTS**

4.1    Prospect Registration System
4.2    Prospect Control and Follow-Up Procedures
4.3    Product Presentations
4.4    Home Estimate Sheet
4.5    Standard Purchase Contract and Receipt for Deposit
4.6    Deposit Monies and Receipts
4.7    Buyer Profile Form
4.8    Processing and Acceptance Procedure
4.9    Mortgage-Processing
4.10   Change Orders, Options and Extras
4.11   Color and Decorator Procedures
4.12   Production Scheduling Dates
4.13   Cancellations and Noncompletions
4.14   Contingent Sale of Purchaser's Existing Property

   4.2a—Prospect Card
   4.4a—Home Estimate Sheet
   4.5a—Purchase Agreement
   4.5b—Addendum to Sales Agreement
   4.6a—Receipt
   4.6b—Processing Checklist
   4.7a—Buyer Profile Form
   4.8a—Standard Letter
   4.9a—Mortgage Qualifications Prescreening Form

---

**FIGURE 10.7    Policies and Procedures (continued)**

---

4.14    Contingent Sale of Purchaser's Existing Property (*continued*)

  4.9b—Loan Application Form
  4.14a—Notice of Cancellation
  4.14c—Standard Letter
  4.15a—Application for Guarantee
  4.15b—Contingency Addendum
  4.15c—Contingency/Exchange Roster

SECTION 5.0:  **CONSTRUCTION COORDINATION, MOVE-IN PROCEDURES AND CUSTOMER SERVICE**

  5.1    Coordination Between Sales Department and the Client
  5.2    Pre-Move-In Inspection Procedures
  5.3    Key Release Procedures
  5.4    Move-In and Utility Connection Procedures
  5.5    Rental Agreements
  5.6    Home Owners Warranty Package
  5.7    Customer-Service Procedure
  5.8    New Resident Activities

  5.2a—Customer-Service Walk-Through Inspection
  5.3a—Key Slip
  5.4a—Checklist to Organize Your Move
  5.5a—Rental Agreement
  5.5b—Agreement to Store Furniture

SECTION 6.0:  **PERSONNEL POLICIES AND PROCEDURES**

  6.1    Policies and Procedures
  6.2    Company Fringe Benefits
  6.3    Dress Code
  6.4    Personal Habits
  6.5    Buying and Selling Real Estate
  6.6    Involvement with Referrals and Outside Real Estate Activities
  6.7    Vacations, Time-Off, Sick Leave, Etc.
  6.8    Automobiles and Insurance
  6.9    Recognized Holidays
  6.10   Sales Meetings
  6.11   Legal Matters
  6.12   Attitude and Conduct

SECTION 7.0:  **CURRENT BUILDER PRODUCT LINES AND PRICES**

SECTION 8.0:  **CURRENT BUILDER OPTIONS, ALTERNATES AND EXTRAS**

---

**FIGURE 10.7   Policies and Procedures (continued)**

---

**SECTION 1.0: ORGANIZATION OF THE COMPANY**

**1.1   Organization**

The Marketing Group was formed to develop, promote and operate the most professional firm specializing in the sales and marketing of new home developments.

Nowhere in the business world is the demand for the astute combination of marketing talent, experience and professionalism more acute than it is in the very fragmented business of home building and real estate development. There is no test laboratory such as that at Proctor and Gamble. There is no test track such as that available in Detroit for General Motors.

Our clients are the alchemists of the 1980s. The marketplace is their laboratory, and the test track in many cases will amount to a million-dollar display of model houses and merchandising aids. No matter how big or how small, they are all looking for the formula that combines land, architecture, finance, construction, marketing and sales into a profitable, ongoing business.

Our company was also formed because of the myriad of resale brokerage companies that were attemping to handle various builder sales programs.

Resale agents are a vital, integral part of the industry but cannot relate to representing the manufacturer of a product versus the consumer.

As you will learn during your association with our company, marketing new homes requires many different disciplines than is required in selling resale housing.

Our company takes as much pride in the success of our clients as in the success of our own employees and our organization.

We look for lasting and mutually profitable relationships with our clients.

**FIGURE 10.7    Policies and Procedures (continued)**

## 1.2  Departments of the Company

Organizational Chart

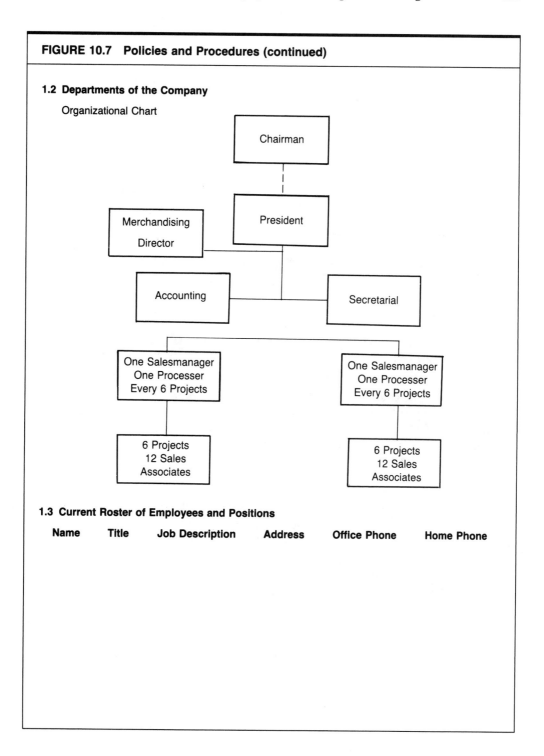

## 1.3  Current Roster of Employees and Positions

| Name | Title | Job Description | Address | Office Phone | Home Phone |
| --- | --- | --- | --- | --- | --- |

---

**FIGURE 10.7  Policies and Procedures (continued)**

---

### 1.4 Administration of Marketing and Sales Activities

Marketing and sales activities of the Marketing Group are supervised by the president. The president is responsible for hiring and supervision of all sales association. This duty may be delegated to a sales manager but final approval must come from the president.

The president expects sales associates to adhere to the policies and procedures set forth in this manual. The sale associates should conscientiously apply themselves to the proper execution of their assignments as outlined by management.

### 1.5  Position Description for Sales Associates

Sales associates are basically responsible for the following activities:

(A)   Total familiarity with the products and programs they represent on behalf of the company.

(B)   Seeing to it the sales office and model homes are open each day for the hours scheduled. All prospects should be greeted courteously, invited to inspect the model homes, and provided with the necessary information to help them make make a housing decision.

(C)   Monitoring the care and maintenance of all model homes as well as the sales office.

(D)   Maintain records on each transaction from date of sale to closing as set forth in this manual. This information should be made available for review or forwarded to the proper parties as indicated in this manual.

(E)   Regular inspection of competitive projects and reporting findings to the sales manager as requested.

(F)   Familiarity with all community services and programs that are important to our potential purchasers such as schools, churches, shopping, etc. Completion of Sales Training Guide Questionnaire is a required duty of each sales associate.

(G)   Participation in regular sales meetings held for the benefit of the entire sales team to maintain open communication between the various departmental operations.

(H)   Maintain good relations with the residents in the community to which assigned. The primary objectives are to build referrals for additional business and to assure maximum resident satisfaction.

(I)   To perform all services in a manner that will reflect a favorable image for Marketing Group.

---

**FIGURE 10.7    Policies and Procedures (concluded)**

---

**1.6  Goals and Objectives**

The company's primary objective is to make a reasonable profit by selling fine homes in well-planned residential communities. Each sales associate is expected to establish annual goals and objectives that are compatible with those of the company and to communicate such plans to their sales manager.

We have included a Daily Planning Guide (1.6a) and Sales Associate's Goal-Planning Memoranda (1.6b and 1.6c) at the end of this Section to help you schedule your daily activities. Very little is accomplished without a goal and a goal is never reached without definitive plans. The Sales Associate's Goal-Planning Memoranda should be used to identify desired achievements on a monthly and annual basis as designated on the forms.

---

## THE TIME-MANAGEMENT TRAP

The development and execution of results-oriented marketing strategies coupled with the demands of effective sales management requires efficient use of available time for those in charge of volume operations. Even in smaller companies where the builder may be doubling as part-time marketing manager, the challenge is comparable because of the pressure of supervising construction, land acquisition and financial affairs. We do not intend to devote much space in this book to the subject of time management, but we believe a few observations are worthwhile, especially as they apply to those wearing more than one hat in the building/marketing game. Our experience in working with numerous clients is that sales management is normally the first area to suffer when marketers get busy. The people who make the sales take second-place to what has to be done to design and decorate new models, arrange for advertising, negotiate with suppliers, and expedite sales in progress. Sometimes the result is having only a one- or two-hour sales meeting once a week. The rest of the time the salespeople never see or hear from their supervisors. The penalty for that misplaced judgment can be very expensive! Salespeople who are not cultivated, educated, motivated and supported through hands-on contact by knowledgeable coaches seldom perform as well as those who have leaders dedicated to the ''people'' side of the sales management equation.

The second area to suffer is having adequate time to anticipate the marketing needs of the future. Day-to-day operations have a way of postponing the very planning that protects tomorrow's investment. Unless adequate time is set aside for long-range planning, the consequences of local housing trends, changes in demographics, innovations others are making but you are not, and other variables that affect your business environment are ignored. Wise leaders assemble their managers and advisors periodically in a location removed from the business scene to evaluate the past and future. Such sessions provide a refreshing view of the company's issues and opportunities.

Meetings held in a resort environment, with healthy recreation and relaxation between sessions, usually provide greater creativity and renewed dedication to the bigger goals. Every planning session should address the four major topics that follows.

1.  Direction evaluation

    history of accomplishments
    number of objectives reached since last planning session
    realistic evaluation of current operations
    projections based on present business course

2.  Growth and opportunities

    rate of growth in all categories
    business growth objectives based on motivations of principals
    areas of opportunity for future exploration
    evaluation of all trends affecting business
    rating of priorities in terms of human and financial resources available
        to take advantage of potential opportunities

3.  Performance evaluation

    efficiency rating of each function or department
    evaluation of performance standards
    areas that need the most attention in next time period
    issues that need resolution to improve organizational efficiency

4.  Motivations, abilities and needs of the group

    each manager or participant states current motivations for self and business
    each is asked to rate his or her own abilities and discuss improvements
        he or she anticipates making in the next phase
    each is asked what is needed to help achieve individual goals and how
        the company can/might assist during the coming period

## CAUTION: DO NOT FALL INTO THE MEETING TRAP

While well-structured planning sessions are important to the long-range survival of a business enterprise, too many meetings can hinder progress. Some of our clients seem to spend all of their time in executive board rooms in closed-door meetings. They call a meeting for almost any excuse and bring everyone into it, even if their participation is unnecessary. Someone once defined a committee as ''a group of people who seem to do nothing but who do it better together.'' A lot of truth is in that saying. Limit meetings to those individuals essential to the subject and spend more time in the field with the players than in conference rooms with the theorists! All meetings should be planned, have prepared agenda sent to all participants before the session, include only those whose participation is essential, and be limited to the agenda at hand by a leader who knows how to keep control when people tend to wander. If it can be done face-to-face in a few moments or be covered by a memo, why hold a time-consuming meeting?

---

**FIGURE 10.8   Project Planning Worksheet**

PROJECT:_____

_____

_____

OBJECTIVES:_____

| Action Step | Target Date | Cost | | Assigned Responsibility |
|---|---|---|---|---|
| | | Dollars | Time | |
| | | | | |
| | | | | |
| | | | | |
| | | | | |
| | | | | |
| | | | | |
| | | | | |
| | | | | |
| | | | | |
| | | | | |
| | | | | |
| | | | | |
| | | | | |
| | | | | |
| | | | | |
| | | | | |
| | | | | |
| | | | | |
| | | | | |
| | | | | |
| | | | | |
| | | | | |
| | | | | |

## PLAN FOR PERSONAL GROWTH IN A RAPIDLY CHANGING INDUSTRY

Marketing is a subjective discipline. Personal feelings, intuitions and instincts influence the decisions we make. We ask ourselves questions like: How will that ad appeal to our buyers? How do I know I am getting the best that salesperson has to offer? Which decor will sell the design features of this model home? Why are we losing sales to Brand X? Since there are no right or wrong decisions (at least until we look backwards at what happened), those of us in the etheral world of influencing humans to purchase housing have to rely on accumulated experience and the advice we accept from others.

To stretch ourselves and move beyond our self-imposed limitations requires getting outside of our own marketing arenas to study what others are doing. A marketing manager who does not take two or three trips a year to other regions of the country to study what is happening elsewhere develops the same inbred marketing habits of local real estate experts. Competitors who travel and research ("caring enough to steal from the best"), return and introduce ideas you wish you had conceived and implemented. To be a leader means to advance, explore and try new ways to do things. You learn faster by observing new markets than you will by dissecting your own.

Membership and participation in the National Association of Home Builders and its educational arm, the Sales and Marketing Council, offers the opportunity to mix with and learn from other professionals in the industry. Attending conferences, reading books and listening to tapes are also valuable forms of self-improvement. Your personal plan for growth is an asset no one can steal from you. The more you learn, the more you appreciate how much you do not know!

# 11: Adjusting to Challenges and the Unexpected

Marketing managers are like doctors. They prescribe courses of action that should keep the patient healthy, but then the unexpected occurs. There is a loss of vitality. Things do not go as expected, and the marketing prescription has to be changed. No matter how well-planned and executed, every project has the potential of straying from its original plotted course. Some conditions we cannot control. Changes in interest rates, reversals in local or national economics, delays in construction and unanticipated construction costs can adversely affect even carefully devised marketing strategies. Periodic checkups are necessary just to keep the sales pro forma on track. If you wait until you have a crisis, it may be too late to correct the problems without serious economic consequences. Sometimes the costs of restoring or revitalizing a marketing program are prohibitive! When sales decline or stop, it is time to examine the fundamental elements of the marketing plan and test them against anticipated performance standards. Like a good doctor, you need to identify causes before you make recommendations to change the prescription.

The ability to spot the early warning signals that indicate market conditions are changing or are about to change is a valuable talent. It does not require special powers to foresee most of the broad-based changes that result from normal business cycles. Admittedly, some totally unpredictable events that can throw business into a tailspin erupt overnight. Actions by the federal government or international crises can precipitate traumatic market reactions. For those events, we can only hope we have been pragmatic in setting aside reserves for survival and have been reasonably flexible in programming our risk-taking ventures. Market periods precipitated by the oil embargo of 1974 and the sudden rise of the prime interest rate to over 20 percent in 1980 were both unpredictable and catastrophic for the real estate industry! Reaction to those challenges demanded more than just making minor adjustments to the marketing strategies.

Such dramatic changes will probably occur again, and when they do builders and their marketers will have to adapt quickly if they are to survive. We lost about 30 percent of all the players in our industry during the 1980-1982 housing depression. The toll was heavy because many were overstocked with spec homes they could only sell by taking severe losses, and others were locked into land development obligations that drained their cash reserves. Thousands of real estate agents left the business and never returned. However, during that same period some builders did well. They sold homes and made profits despite the high interest rates. Marketers resorted to creative financing programs and aggressive promotion to attract first-time buyers. Whether markets are rising or declining, there are housing companies that find their niches and prosper!

## HOW TO SPOT MARKET INDICATORS THAT PREDICT CHANGE

A number of primary indicators are precursors to changes in the housing market. By monitoring these, you may spot some early warning signals that permit you to make marketing adjustments before your risk factors have reached the danger zone. Here is a checklist for detecting market fluctuations:

1.  comparisons of reported sales to prior months and years
2.  major variations in the number of people inspecting new homes
3.  decrease in the number of be-backs or returning prospects
4.  changes in the prime interest rate
5.  substantial change in the number of resale listings on the market (multiple-listing statistics) relative to the percentage sold
6.  increase or decrease in the number of plotted lots available for development and construction in immediate future
7.  fluctuations in the number of housing starts reported
8.  modifications in the average turnover time for resale properties
9.  increase or decrease in rental vacancy factors
10. changes in the local employment picture and comparison of building permits to employment ratios
11. variations in the number of completed spec homes unsold
12. more incentives by competition to attract purchasers
13. moritoriums or pending governmental actions that limit land development
14. pending shortages of building materials or available construction labor

## YOUR PRESCRIPTION CHECKLIST WHEN
## SALES ARE NOT MEETING PROJECTIONS

Experienced new home marketers know that, with the exclusion of construction and development obstacles, only five basic factors influence the success or failure of a residential building program. When things are not going as planned, they thoroughly examine each of these to detect which ones account for variances in the projected game plan. These broad determinants of market reactions have many individual subtleties that may have to be explored in greater detail once the primary culprits have been identified. One of the issues that must be tested is whether the projections were realistic for the marketplace at the time they were prepared. Original feasibility studies may have been overly optimistic about the potential absorption rates, or the researchers may have overlooked some critical factor like the number of new communities and building sites coming on the market at the same time the subject property was being introduced.

The big five checkpoints start with market research as the first major testing point and proceed through the other controlling factors:

1. market research: current conditions
2. perceived values
3. prospect exposure
4. presentation effectiveness
5. performance of the sales representatives

Let's review the highlights of this marketing checkup guide.

### Test General Market Conditions for Clues

If you have consistently monitored local housing activity, you have a general awareness of the cyclical changes of starts, sales and closings. Keeping tabs on local real estate trends at least on a month-to-month basis is absolutely essential to strategic planning. The more informed you are about what is happening in your own back yard, the easier it is to anticipate and respond to changing conditions. If your current sales are not on target with those of previous months or have not come up to the levels predicted by advance research, the first clues might be found in the statistics about local housing activity. Has new home sales volume declined? How are your competitors doing? By observing traffic at the competition's model homes or sales offices, you can compare the relative number of prospects they are attracting with those at your own locations. What is the resale market experiencing? Once you have tested the marketplace and determined that the decline in sales is not representative of what is occuring in the rest of the housing market, you need to thoroughly examine your own products, promotion, presentation and people.

### Review the Consumers' Value Perceptions of Your Housing

When your homes are not selling, one of the most common culprits is the perceptions of consumers! Prospects have measured the merchandise and found it wanting in regard to what they expect for the price and terms featured. Perceived values are the principal determinant of the degree of acceptance or rejection experienced by one housing program relative to another. Customers have their own value-index system, and they do not necessarily relate to those established by developers and home builders. Cost does not equal value. Price is a function of consumer acceptance. When something is perceived to be worth more than the asking price, it sells quickly, and often with more people trying to acquire it than the supplier can accommodate. Conversely, if the product is perceived to be less valuable than the asking price, it is difficult to sell. In the home building business, value perceptions depend on five major consumer judgment factors:

1. *Location values.* Sometimes general location is the principal reason one new home community outsells another. People measure location from perspectives

of convenience, established values, accessibility, environmental benefits and quality of life, which includes quality of education, recreation and cultural activities.

2.  *Neighborhood values and development status.* The prices of surrounding homes as well as the general appearance of streetscapes, architecture, maintenance and amenities play a key part in the consumers' decision-making process. If the land plan is in the initial phase of development and many unknowns or uncertainties exist about whether or not the area will ever be completed as promoted, hesitant prospects postpone decisions or select alternative neighborhoods.

3.  *Housing design and included or available features.* The focal point of the decision rests with the floor plan, architecture and refinements included or available with a particular home. If the basic design does not meet either needs or expectations of the profiled prospective buyers for that price range, it can be a disaster. We have investigated some housing communities where the original homes were so out of sync with the motivations and perceptions of the consumers that they ultimately had to be leveled and new ones designed to replace them! Even if the floor plan is satisfactory, the issue may be the options or variables consumers expect for the prices asked.

4.  *The homesites: sizes, locations and amenities.* If you build a large home on a small lot in a price range that expects larger homesites, your value perceptions can be adversely affected. When the lots you are trying to sell abut an undesirable element such as a busy highway, ugly apartment buildings or the city dump, they will suffer value depreciation from those adjacent influences. Individual sites will be rated against competitive alternatives. Sometimes the absence of trees can make a big difference in what the public believes a homesite is worth.

5.  *Financing, the terms and costs of ownership.* Price alone does not determine value. How easy it is to own and maintain is an equally important consideration. If competition is offering financing at two percent less than you have available, that can swing the sales decision in their favor. In a community that has a home owners' association, the monthly or annual service fees can be a major decision factor for marginally qualified buyers. High taxes, expensive energy costs, extra payments required because of bond improvements—extra costs that competition does not experience—are all factors that can combine to lower perceived values.

## Not Enough Prospects Are Being Exposed to the Property

As we extensively reviewed in chapter 8, attracting the right prospects in sufficient numbers is a primary responsibility of marketing managers. You cannot make your sales numbers work unless a reasonable number of qualified prospects are exposed to your sales representatives for face-to-face selling opportunities. All other factors being equal, increased exposure means increased sales. When sales are not up to expectations, this traffic-generating key must be thoroughly evaluated and new strategies put into place that will improve the closing odds.

### Investigate the Quality of the Presentation Elements

The value of a specific home or community is not automatically accepted by prospective buyers. You can have an excellent value in terms of design, footage, amenities and housing sites from a direct comparison of facts and figures, and still not be effectively communicating those values to the public. That is why on-site presentation factors need to be carefully planned and executed. If the housing area is cluttered, difficult to inspect, shows little or no sign of becoming an attractive neighborhood with well-kept homes and yards, customers often translate those conditions into a reason to wait and see what the future will bring or to purchase in better-merchandised communities. The on-site presentation needs to compensate for what is not yet finished. Sample environments with one or more models or clean production housing help to offset the negatives of construction areas. Furnished models with the right decor and emotionally appealing surroundings have proven their effectiveness in projecting tomorrow's dreams today. Study every aspect of the physical setting to be sure that you have not permitted negatives to depreciate your values.

### Evaluate the Quality of Your Salespeople

If all of the other factors have been objectively evaluated and rated satisfactory, only one critical area is left on which to focus attention: your sales representatives!

Many builders are quick to blame salespeople when the results they expect are not occurring. That is not fair. The other four major influences need first to be placed in perspective. Sales agents are not miracle workers. If the public does not want what you are offering, the best salespeople in the business will not counter these reactions. Desire must precede commitment. However, our research and consulting activities over the years have led to the conclusion that deficiencies in stimulating new home sales are directly traceable to salespeople about 50 percent of the time. Poor salesmanship, unmotivated agents, untrained people and the absence of professional sales management are all too often the real deterrents to the attainment of optimum sales volume. If you are not sure how well or poorly your housing is being presented to the public and how effective the representatives are in qualifying, demonstrating and closing, it pays to have them professionally evaluated.

Mystery shoppers can be helpful in that role as can be sales managers and outside consultants. Selling is not a game that should be played with amateurs when you have the extensive financial risks that are inherent in the home building industry!

## A PRESCRIPTION CHECKLIST FOR MOVING STALLED INVENTORY

When you are faced with completed housing inventory that is not selling, actions must be taken that will rectify the situation. Speculative homes that have been around too long, clean-up phases in a production housing operation, scattered sites isolated from primary sales areas and homes that come back on the market because of cancelled transactions demand special attention. It is very costly to hold finished homes as unsold inventory. At a very minimum, a vacant, nonincome-producing new home costs one and a half percent of its gross sales value per month to maintain. When you consider interest costs (including the value of the equity dollars that are frozen), basic maintenance, management time to supervise the property and the repairs often required as a result of vandalism, this figure can be as much as two percent of value. In a period of three or four months, the building company has invested five to six percent, which equals a full real estate commission! This does not take into consideration psychological depreciation, which can adversely affect the attitudes of brokers and buyers. As one of my sales managers used to say to me: ''You have to sell what you have to sell!''

Over the years we have accumulated a checklist of potential solutions for moving stalled inventory. In any particular situation, only one or two of these may be applicable answers. When you are unsure of the course of action to pursue, review this summary of ideas and perhaps you will find an application that meets your needs.

1. *It is usually better to add to value than to reduce price.* To stimulate interest in unsold homes, builders frequently provide consumer incentives that add to the total value of the package. For example, the additions might be items that would normally be options or upgrades but are temporarily included in the basic price. They are often items like fencing, landscaping, decks, patios or interior upgrades like microwave ovens, paddle fans or more-expensive floor coverings. It is normally better to add to value than risk price reductions that can adversely affect customer relations with those who have already purchased and closed at higher prices. When you start lowering prices, you also trigger consumer fears about your products. They wonder why the houses have not sold at the published prices and what will happen to future values if they buy and you lower prices again. It is also less expensive for a builder to add something at his costs that has a greater retail value than to make equivalent cash reductions.

2. *Make it easier to own: improve the financing terms.* The easier it is to own a new home, the more people there will be who can afford to purchase it. Financing terms have been responsible for thousands of home sales. If you have a spec home or two that are not moving and they are profiled for the middle- to lower-income groups, try adjusting the terms of purchase. For example, you might buy down the interest rate for the mortgage and make it applicable to just these target homes. Sometimes it is wiser to take the dollars you had planned to use for reductions and apply them instead to financing. You can also apply these financing terms to the purchase of the older home that must be sold in order to close the new one. Equity accumulation plans, lease options and rent-to-own programs are all part of this easy-terms concept.

3. *Adjust lot values and balance the value perceptions.* When you have a number of homesites (or homes) yet to be sold and certain locations or types are proving less acceptable, a practical approach is to rebalance the total dollars involved in the underlying site pricing (not the costs of the improvements). For example, if you have three sites backing up to a less

desirable area that are not moving and other lots are proving more acceptable, you could lower the lot values on those three and raise an equal amount spread over the more desirable ones so that the gross dollars remain the same. This effectively reduces the gross price of these specific homes, but it can be easily justified as considerations for site locations and landscaping allowances. Another way to accomplish the same objective is to raise the prices of all lots except those on which the spec inventory is located.

4. *Provide bonus incentives to the sales representatives.* Money does motivate most salespeople. A $1,000 bonus paid to a selling agent will probably be more effective than $1,000 reduction in price. When cooperating brokers are an important part of your lead generation system, the "spiffs" offered on specific inventory can be an effective means of gaining their attention. When you try this approach, be sure to put a time limit on the incentive. If it does not work, resort to other creative approaches to solve the problem.

5. *Raise the prices of new models or phases and keep older merchandise at lower prices.* Even if you have not started another home like the one you are trying to sell or opened a new phase, you can publish the minimum starting price for that production when it occurs. Creating perceived value differences between existing inventory and the next generation to be released is a good way to help buyers understand that they are gaining equity dollars by purchasing now rather than delaying.

6. *Physically add something to one spec home not offered on a similar one.* The one-of-a-kind theory can be a very effective way to move standing inventory when you have a number of similar homes. By doing something special for one spec at a time, it can be shown to prospects after they see the basic properties that do not include this extra feature and offered as "just one that we are willing to sell at the same price as the others if you act now." Finished basements, extra decking, patios, outdoor barbecue gas grills, special window treatments are typical improvements. Showing the other homes first is the key to making this concept effective.

7. *Provide a landscaping allowance or a site-enhancement plan.* For single-family homes, one of the most effective techniques for moving stalled inventory is to offer a generous landscaping allowance for the specific homesites you want to move. It is easy to justify this incentive. For example: "This is a strategic homesite which we need to have attractively landscaped to help set the tone for the others. . . . " "We made special allowances for certain homesites to include landscaping plans, and this happens to be one of them. . . ." When you improve one site, it automatically helps the adjacent housing and the streetscape. Sometimes it is wise to actually install the landscaping before it is sold to offset the negative appearance of the property or its surroundings.

8. *Complete some spec homes with carpets and window coverings and maintain in spotless, move-in condition.* Homes that are carpeted, clean and ready for occupancy show and sell better than those in less-attractive condition. If you have several completed homes of the same type, you

might elect to carpet some and leave others so that purchasers can make their own floor-covering selections. Even if the number is limited, the bottom line is to evaluate the cost of changing carpets versus holding unsold inventory. Carpeting is the decor element that dominates the interior appearance of a home, and when you show customers a spec house without it compared to one that has it, they will most often favor the finished home.

9. *Furnish one of the unsold homes, sell it and furnish another.* Beyond carpeting, furnishings really bring a home to life. That is why we encourage builders to show at least one furnished model whenever economics permit. Where unsold speculative housing is concerned, it is sometimes justified to furnish all or part of one home or two until sold and then move the furnishings to the next target property that needs attention.

   Vignettes (limited furniture arrangements in focal areas of a home) are also a means of putting life into a cold, vacant house. Plants, spotlights, wall hangings, wallpaper and mirrors are elements that can be used to improve the appearance of a production house. Selecting the house that most needs to be dramatized while leaving others to be shown in normal condition will help tilt acceptance in favor of that property.

10. *Provide special fringe incentives related to amenities.* One of the more creative ways to stimulate sales is to offer a fringe benefit of some type that is not necessarily directly related to the home. For example, I know of one community successful in selling the last 11 homes by arranging with a nearby golf club for memberships (purchased on a group discount basis) that they gave with each sale, providing it was made by a specified date. Others prepaid a year's dues for swim clubs or physical-fitness facilities. Prepaying home owner association fees or adding benefits not normally included, such as greens fees, lessons from sport pros or a number of dinners at the club are fringe-benefit incentives that merit consideration. It is usually better to use them as closing tools rather than featuring them in advertising.

11. *For move-up buyers, provide allowances to help sell old homes.* If the target market for your standing inventory is the existing owner who must first sell a residence, the incentives can be directed at the used housing. Offering to provide equity loans, guarantee equities or pay for all or part of the sales costs are concepts used by builders suffering from stagnant market conditions. Be fair to all buyers and to provide allowances to those who do not need the move-up package in a way commensurate with what is being done for the others.

12. *Raise prices on the unsold homes and use the increases to pay for the special incentives.* Sometimes a price increase on the homes that are not selling is the best way to provide the dollars needed to make the necessary improvements or add the incentives while giving these properties the psychological benefit of greater value. I have some homesites backing up to railroads or a high-power-line easement raised above the levels of other homes in the same community and sold at these prices because they had

more privacy, deeper lots or a bigger landscaping package included in the price!

13. *Offer a guaranteed buy-back agreement as a closing tool.* In a really difficult market where buyers are concerned about future values, some builders have offered buy-back agreements to overcome the fears of hesitant prospects. It is most often used as a closing tool and limited to either specific homes that need to be sold or certain buyers (like those subject to transfer). The buy-back period is usually limited to a period of one to two years and covers only the initial investment, not the equity accumulation. Builders and developers using this tool must have the contingent funds available in case they are called upon to make good their guarantees.

14. *Make sure that homes that need to be sold are always shown first!* Housing that salespeople avoid showing because of personal prejudices will never be sold. There is a buyer for every property! Sales representatives need incentives and guidance in showing first the homes that most need to be sold before they work on the easy ones! This requires management's attention to training and motivation. Every prospect qualified to see a particular category of housing should be exposed to the target properties that are on the inventory hot sheet. If customers are allowed to ignore them, the problems will only become more severe.

15. *Feature individual spec homes in small classified ads.* Instead of using display advertising to sell clean-up phases or to focus on the remaining housing, try small classified ads that read like for-sale-by-owner advertising. Select one house and write the ad as it would be featured for a resale property. This allows you to attract people who are searching for specific homes in the classified section and not necessarily looking for a new one. The phone call generated by the ad is often the first contact, just as it is in the typical brokerage office.

16. *Define the profiled buyer and cold-call those who fit that profile.* When you thoroughly evaluate a specific house or type of home, you can usually pinpoint the logical prospective buyer. It is a matter of aggressively seeking those candidates once they have been profiled. Do not try to broadside the market with general advertising when you need to move limited inventory. For example, I recall a townhome community we were marketing in which one particular floor plan was not selling well to our basic traffic. We were selling the other designs but not this one. It had only one bedroom and a loft and was the smallest of the group. We analyzed the two or three sales we had made of that plan and discovered that single women (two being nurses at a nearby hospital) had been our only buyers. We had seven to sell, which were beginning to age. We used the nurses that had purchased as our base and got them to introduce us to others at the same hospital. With persistent follow-through, we sold six of the seven to other nurses and medical students in the same hospital!

17. *In a soft market, it may pay to rent a few homes until the market and values improve.* While it is seldom the desirable approach and often

economically impossible, renting selected inventory until market conditions change is far better occasionally than keeping units vacant. This may require taking out permanent mortgages or making special arrangements with your lending institutions. This is more practical for starter housing than move-up housing in most cases. If indications that local market factors adversely affecting sales will improve in the near future, this interim move can reduce holding costs and perhaps provide a base of potential buyers at the same time.

18.   *Reduce prices and promote the reductions.* While it is seldom desirable or recommended, sometimes the only remaining avenue to explore is an outright price reduction. Like the car industry, we can have close-out sales, model-home sales, year-end inventory sales, etc. They are risky. The people we have sold in the same neighborhood who paid the higher prices will not be happy with the perceived value reductions. It can have an adverse impact on new phases you plan to open in the near future. If you elect to reduce prices, it is preferable to do it on select inventory. Never feature it as applicable to all remaining homes.

19.   *Involve the owners who already live in the new community.* Vacant, unsold housing depreciates the value of all the homes in a neighborhood. Other than the builder/developer, the people who have the most to lose or gain are the owners of the homes in the immediate area, especially those on the same street. By actively enlisting their support to help find prospective buyers, you can sometimes accomplish what your marketing is unable to achieve on its own. In certain distress situations, I have brought the local residents together with the builder and convinced them they were now partners in the business. If they failed to lend their enthusiastic support, the values of their equities were going to decline, and the community would suffer psychological and physical depreciation. If any of them were anticipating trying to sell in the near future, it was going to be difficult for them to secure the dollars they hoped to gain unless these remaining new homes were successfully taken off the market. With the realization of this economic reality, they accepted part of the responsibility for seeking prospects and promoting the community to those they knew. We have closed out neighborhoods just from that kind of owner participation in our marketing efforts!

20.   *Secure adjustments from your lenders and suppliers.* When you are really in trouble and the enterprise is in danger of not being able to provide future opportunities for all of those who have depended upon you in the past, you may be able to secure some support and relief from the suppliers, subcontractors and lenders who have a vital interest in your success or failure. Interest moratoriums on the standing inventory, special financing packages, rebates or contributions of additional work to finish inventory by subs who want to see you survive are remote possibilities. They are usually available only to those builders and developers who have a long history of being trustworthy and who have carefully protected supplier relationships.

21. *Bulk sales or investment packaging may be the final recourse.* When everything else fails and there is still equity with which to work, investment packaging may provide the way out. Most builders do not have enough margin to allow them to wholesale their homes to a third party. The exceptions are those who had purchased the land at such a price that the developed lots have appreciated enough to provide a margin for discounting. Taking a loss on a few homes to preserve the rest of the operation may be a practical move for long-range survival. It usually takes a professional to know how to package and wholesale a series of homes. One of the kickers to help preserve a reasonable price level is the agreement to repurchase the homes at a future take-out price in a specified period of time if the investors have not sold them to others in the interim.

Whenever you have inventory that is not moving, it needs to be analyzed and given concentrated attention. Moving those properties should receive top priority. If you procrastinate, it will only become more expensive. These problems do not go away by themselves, so do not ignore them. Assign one person to concentrate full time to promoting and selling these homes, so that they are not left to general agents who gravitate to the homes they like. Do not be tempted to chase the new projects you enjoy while leaving behind capital-intensive investments of past efforts. Those most successful in this business know that the two most critical aspects of making and preserving a profit are in planning and buttoning-up what has been started.

## MINIMIZE THE IMPACT OF CLEAN-UP PHASES BY ADVANCE PLANNING

Trying to unload the last few homes in a subdivision after all of the best lots have been sold can be a costly experience. Left to their own instincts, salespeople will gravitate to the better lots first because they are easier to sell. Customers will choose the better lots if they are permitted to do so. The time to prevent tail-end clean-up blues is at the beginning of the project. By planning ahead and anticipating possible inventory difficulties before they occur, you can minimize the economic consequences of having a number of less-desirable properties to sell at the conclusion of the project.

The best way to avoid those problems is to provide incentives of one kind or another that will help to remove these potential negatives before they can accumulate to haunt you at the conclusion of the development. Here are techniques employed by many alert marketers in their attempts to prevent these inventory problems:

- Start the community with the less-desirable sites first and work toward the better lots as the community progresses. This is not always possible, but it is a proven strategy that decreases the risks of inventory imbalance. Since it is best to keep opening prices low and plan for increases as you proceed from one phase to the next, selling first those sites that permit lower pricing adds to the value of remaining properties, thus building the perceived values right to the end of the community.

- If you cannot start with the less-expensive lots, at least attempt to balance the inventory as you proceed, so that you have some of each kind always available. Be sure to place premiums on the choice sites to create value differences that will force the sales of less-attractive locations.
- If you are selling homes on build contracts and limiting your speculative housing, consider building specs on the less-desirable sites early in the game. When you put a home on a vacant lot you diminish the visual impact of adverse elements, and you also have a better chance of selling the site to someone who needs earlier occupancy than permitted by your normal building schedule. Transferees often represent the target market for such housing opportunities.
- Budget for clean-up at the beginning of the project. Build in a small amount per house that can be accumulated and applied to those last few properties that may need special attention or incentives. This can be a swing bonus given to the salespeople if they move everything in balance and on time. Or it can be applied to any costs to move properties not sold with the normal marketing plan.
- Pay special attention to difficult sites before selecting the plans to be offered. Small adjustments are sometimes required to position the homes to compensate for environmental factors that might otherwise detract from perceived values. Occasionally we have to create one-of-a-kind floor plans designed for individual homesites simply to meet the physical challenges of those locations.
- Put bonus incentives on lots that need to be sold, or hold contests that reward those who show and sell them.

## HOW TO COUNTER A COMPETITIVE CHALLENGE

Sometimes we are faced with aggressive competition that forces us into some very difficult marketing positions. Some builders will give away profits to increase market share. Others do not know their true bottom-line costs of operation; they underprice their homes without realizing that they will have to pay the piper some day. Others are just good merchandisers who know how to attract traffic and increase sales by using incentives that are appealing to home buyers. When we share the markets with these competitors and are losing customers to them, we must make appropriate responses or risk the results of decreased sales volume. Each situation needs specific analysis and the plan of attack should be one that does not defeat broader objectives such as maintaining the reputation and image of a successful community or company. The thrust of your response (if any) will probably focus on one or more of the following possibilities.

### Value-Indexing Your Product/Price Comparisons

The first area to explore is the real or perceived difference in values between what you offer versus your competitor's products. The competitive value-index system to which we referred in other chapters of this book is your fundamental tool for making a realistic comparison that can be translated into sales and marketing aids designed to overcome consumer resistance. When you study the competition carefully, you can usually identify those advantages you possess that they do not. The key is in building a solid case for your homes that will outweigh arguments for choosing the other housing. The comparison index can then be used as a sales tool with each consumer who is judging the benefits of one environment over the other. If you are truly at a price disadvantage, you must then decide whether you should try to meet it or sell around it. Often the key to selling around it is in communicating the long-range benefits of a better home, superior neighborhood and resale values that are being protected by professional planning and dedicated attention to details. A quality-delivery system coupled with a top-flight consumer protection plan can compensate for less-expensive housing that does not incorporate an equal commitment.

## Incentives to Stimulate Immediate Action

If your competitors are dangling incentives like free microwave ovens, upgraded carpeting, washers and dryers or other options included with their homes, and you suffer by comparison because you do not have these items in your package, your choice comes down either to emphasizing alternative benefits developed from your value-index checklist or meeting the response with similar inclusions. In many cases, the best method for countering this gimmick is to effectively reduce the costs of those items to the small dollars they represent and then show prospects what they are losing by not having all of the superior features you include.

The other approach is to offer and promote a different set of inclusions that collectively represent a much better value than those used by your competitors. This gets down to the issue of whether to feature a base-priced home with the options as add-ons or to establish an all-inclusive price that provides the normal options most of your profiled buyers can afford and want. The decision must be based on the perceptions and financial qualifications of your targeted customers. If it is justified, an ad that reads, ''All of our homes come with the extras others omit,'' can frequently attract the interest of value-conscious home buyers.

## Merchandising Differences Can Be the Heart of the Challenge

If your competitors have invested more dollars to landscape, decorate and furnish model homes than you have, direct comparison can be detrimental unless it is properly addressed. Prospects are automatically drawn to well-presented model sales areas. They like to look at furnished homes. On the other hand, many builders cannot afford to compete with the investments made by merchant-developers in their expensive on-site presentations. While it is important to have a clean and well-maintained sales environment, you can justify the lack of the Hollywood approach to models by simply emphasizing the quality of what you build. In fact, one reverse psychology approach that works well for many small builders is to promote the fact that they do not furnish model homes as a statement of superior value and performance. For example, an unfurnished model might display a sales message that declares:

*We do not furnish our models because we do not want to hide the quality of our construction or deny you the privilege of using your own imagination. When you inspect our award-winning homes, please note the superior craftsmanship on which we have built our reputation. We take pride in our commitment to excellence, and want you to know that what you see here is what you can expect in your own Thomas-built home!*

If you are using fully decorated models, study them from the vantage point of prospective customers who are shopping your competition before they make a decision. Are your houses furnished to the profile and budget of your target market? Do the furnishings help to sell the homes, or detract from the space and features that must be fully appreciated to justify the price? Are the homes colorful and exciting? Sometimes a few minor adjustments will correct presentation errors. Sometimes it is necessary to completely redecorate a model because it did not fulfill the objective of visually translating the values to visiting prospects.

Effective merchandising includes all on-site conditions that can affect buying attitudes. Poor condition of unsold inventory, vacant sites that are not well-maintained, cluttered streets, absence of any sense of community because of scattered building programs, or no evidence of sales and move-ins can combine to give the competition the advantage if they have addressed these issues and you have not!

It is also important to train your salespeople to use what you have to advantage and to anticipate objections or value differences that might prevent prospects from fully appreciating the merits of your homes.

## Promotion Strategies Should Be Designed to Emphasize Unique Differences

It is usually a mistake to play the game called "me too!" If you copy your competition just to follow the leader, you will depreciate the power of your personal marketing advantages. Always work from a position of strength, not weakness. Do not worry about meeting competition. Concentrate on doing best what you know how to do, and then be sure to package and promote it in ways that will win favorable consumer response. Values are created in the minds of prospective customers, and it is the job of marketers to find effective ways to communicate the positive aspects of any offering for which they are responsible. The use of testimonials and documented benefits can be one of the most effective ways to offset aggressive competition that does not have the same values you provide. Brainstorm with salespeople and other experts about challenges as they arise, and draw upon their opinions before finalizing a specific course of action. In the process, always be careful to evaluate what you have done right rather than allow yourself to be panicked into unwarranted marketing tactics that can depreciate the base from which you have been successfully working.

## The Confidence Level of the Consumer in Your Performance

A subtle but very real factor in the consumers' decision-making process is the degree of confidence they have in one developer or builder over another to successfully complete and care for a community. If one community has already established a successful tempo and achieved both sales and move-ins at a rate dramatically exceeding that of another project, the prospects will be drawn to the winner by what we call the herd instinct. Success breeds success. If one developer is doing well and another is not, the consumers may not know why but their fears of being involved in the wrong venture will drive them toward the performer. Word of mouth and bad publicity have killed more than one housing project! A subdivision that gets off to a slow start must contend with the free advice that REALTORS® will give their customers as well as their compatriots in the business: "That community isn't selling well!" or, "I'm not sure why, but they seem to be having some problems getting their homes built!" The rumor mill can effectively shut down sales when there is no plan to counter adverse comments.

If your community or company has suffered any unfavorable publicity, you should employ experts to mount campaigns that will lessen its potential negative impact on sales. Going directly to the brokers and having on-site orientation sessions that present a favorable picture may be the appropriate response. Forthrightly addressing the questions and issues that have arisen is sound policy. Unknowns and lack of action usually produce more of the same!

Study your housing neighborhood with a critical eye. See what prospects see! Does it have the feeling of success or failure? Do the lots or undeveloped acreage present a negative picture of the future? No one wants to live in a community that is going to take forever to sell out or complete. People do not want to invest in an area where values are not assured of being enhanced as rapidly as possible. The sales pace, the visual impact of unfinished areas, the image and track record of the developers and builders and the exterior quality of housing under construction will have an affect on consumers' level of confidence.

## UNLOCKING EQUITIES AND APPEALING TO THE MOVE-UP MARKET

The greatest market opportunity for most single-family builders is the move-up segment. We are a nation of home owners! More than 60 percent of the heads of households in this country own their own residences. That means that the best buyer for a new home is the person who already owns an older one! To be successful in the move-up market you need more than good housing. You need salespeople who know how to counsel and motivate existing owners in ways that will help them over the emotional hurdles of selling one home in order to to buy another. You also need to breed discontent with existing housing by the enhancements you incorporate in your designs and amenities that these prospects do not currently enjoy.

Smart marketers aggressively pursue owners of older homes as a primary method of increasing new home sales. Some REALTORS® who work with home builders have introduced the guaranteed-sales plan (more appropriately called the guaranteed-equity plan) to insure the net value of older homes that must be sold in order to complete new home transactions. Such professionally managed equity-release systems and contingency-purchase plans account for a substantial number of new construction sales every year. The financial risks attendant with the guaranteed-equity plans prevent most REALTORS® and builders from being directly involved in the underwriting process. Alternative solutions have less risk but still achieve the objectives: *make it easy for the buyer to do business with you, and remove the fear of owning two homes with double payments!*

The primary solution used by most progressive marketers is the well-managed contingent-purchase agreement. A new home sale is made subject to the sale of the buyer's present residence within a prescribed time period, such as 30, 60 or 90 days. If the builder cannot afford to start the new house without assurance of a closed transaction, the buyer is usually given a guaranteed price on the new home but with the understanding that it will not be started until the contingency is released—and that must be accomplished within a relatively short time frame. An improvement on this plan is the addition of a release clause that can be exercised at the builder's option whenever another purchaser for the same home or lot is secured. This contingency clause typically provides for 24- to 72-hour advance notice to the first buyer, during which time he or she can remove the contingency (whether or not the existing house has been sold) and thus move forward on the transaction. If he or she does not act within that time, the agreement is terminated and the new buyer steps in. However, in practice, what often happens is the first buyer releases that homesite and moves forward in the subdivision area to another location where the process is renewed until the existing home is successfully sold. Prices may adjust upwards during this transition if the originally guaranteed dates for performance were not met.

This plan, or some variation of it, results in thousands of new home sales every year! When the market is hot and everyone wants to purchase, builders tend not to offer any contingency marketing plan. When sales are more difficult to secure and competition for the resale buyer becomes more intensive, you see builders and realtors doing everything from guaranteeing equities to making direct trades! The risks in underwriting older homes are substantial. It requires both capital and an aggressive marketing system that will move existing inventory to justify direct involvement with these equity-unlocking concepts.

Regardless of the degree of financial involvement you elect to take in the equity-transfer process, always have some method of promoting the ease of ownership when your profiled buyers are local owners moving up or down from their present housing environments. The minimum approach is to provide guidance on how to sell the older properties and to communicate with them throughout the entire process. It is not necessary to institute a trade-in plan or provide financial assistance to increase your share of the resident-owner market. Simple but effective strategies can be employed to penetrate this vital market segment.

If you have an on-site sales facility or model home that attracts unescorted customers, you need to visually and verbally convey messages that will help to reduce resistance to the pain of selling and moving. A display that explains how you help owners to move up to a better life is appropriate in the primary sales office or show home. Do not assume that those who have homes to sell will readily share that information with you or your sales representatives. They may just look at the your new housing, pick up brochures and return to their established nests where they can debate the potential risks and frustrations of the decision to move. To trigger extra sales from this target group, use displays that anticipate their concerns:

- *Home owners welcome! Ask our sales counselors about our equity-assistance plan. It is easy to move up to a better life at Pheasant Run!*

- *Move up to the wonderful life at the Colony! We can help you sell your old house and move your equity to your dream home on one of our exclusive golf-course sites!*
- *Ask for your free booklet that helps you sell your present house the easy way! Our counselors are professionally prepared to assist you in unlocking your equity so you can enjoy all of the benefits of life at Woodlake!*

The objective is to stimulate positive response from hesitant owners who may resist purchasing new homes because of the complexities of trying to sell older homes. One of the major keys to selling the existing-owner market is to provide peace of mind in all those areas that tend to complicate the relocation process. When you make it easy for people to do business with you, you tend to do more business!

## ESTABLISH POLICIES AND PROCEDURES FOR HANDLING CONTINGENCIES

Fulfilling the needs of the move-up market almost always requires the involvement of residential brokers who specialize in resale housing in the specific neighborhoods from which the buyers are moving. Residential resale agents are usually only effective in the immediate market areas in which they list and sell. To be effective, an agent must know the local market. An agent unfamiliar with the neighborhood will have a difficult time attracting prospective buyers, and won't be able to do an adequate job representing the sellers. If you have on-site specialists selling your new homes to a profiled move-up market segment, they should identify the brokers in those neighborhoods who historically are effective in selling older homes. You may not want to recommend a particular agent or company for a variety of reasons, but you can offer a list of all of the companies in that area, based on records you secure from sources such as the multiple-listing system or private researchers. You can review this list with prospective buyers.

Reciprocal marketing agreements are effective. Selected offices enter into agreements with you to represent your homes to their prospects, and, in turn, you promise to refer listing leads that are related to your move-up buyers' needs. It is best to have written policies for both your sales staff and outside brokers that explain how you will handle contingency transactions. Circulating those policies to all the brokers in the area will reduce the risks of being misrepresented or accused of being unfair.

## PREPARE LITERATURE FOR PROSPECTS WHO HAVE HOMES TO SELL

One of the better marketing aids to assist your objectives of tapping more move-up buyers is the move-up kit. This is a brochure or package of materials that provides existing owners with the information they need to make an easy transition to your new homes. Some of these kits are very elaborate. Others are just a single-page summary of basic information that can be given to prospects along with other inserts assembled by the new home sales representative. Much of the material you use can be obtained free of charge from REALTORS®, real estate boards, and private networks that have prepared them for their normal marketing activities. By assembling them in your own marketing jacket, you add the professional touch that sets your company apart from competitors who leave this complex process to the home owners' imaginations. Here is a list of items that you might include in a move-up kit:

- A letter of explanation from the builder or marketer about the benefits of selling and moving to the new community. This should outline the steps involved in easy-to-understand language.
- How to select a broker, with emphasis on the value of professional marketing and experience. This should discourage customers from trying to sell their own homes, since the odds of their success are very low and, consequently, the risks to the builder in taking a home off the market are substantially greater.
- Tips on preparing a home to be sold. Excellent leaflets and checklists are available from real estate associations. Here are some typical topics covered:

  The value of giving brokers complete privacy for each showing appointment.

  The importance of keeping the home neat and clean for all showings. Special attention to impact areas, like baths and kitchens.

  Checklist of repairs and touch-up areas that usually need special attention.

  How to approach the establishment of market value and the pricing range.

  Suggestions on ways to put color and warmth into a home by using fresh flowers, air fresheners, etc.

  Tips on landscaping, with emphasis on streetscape appearance and first impressions.

It is well worth the time to prepare your own letter and personalized checklists on your own stationery. The more that your prospects perceive that you are doing things for them that others do not offer, the greater will be their confidence in you and your housing programs.


## DIRECT-MAIL TARGETED TO MOVE-UP NEIGHBORHOODS CAN ACHIEVE RESULTS

When it is possible from market research to pinpoint neighborhoods from which your move-up customers are most likely to be drawn, use of a tailored direct-mail program can be an effective means of securing additional business. Direct-mail is always most effective when combined with a telephone follow-up plan. The mail package might consist of a general letter introducing the new home opportunity and a brief description of current choices and prices. Included should be a reference to your contingency program, whatever it is. A variation on this theme is to mail cards or letters to the neighbors in the homes surrounding those from which you are drawing buyers, announcing the recent sales you have made from their area.

*Mr. and Mrs. Bill Johnson, who formerly lived at 236 Highlands Drive, are now happily settled in their exciting new home at Walden! They invite you to discover what they have found: life is better at Walden! They made their move the easy way with our special equity-assistance plan, which allowed them to market their older house while we built their new dream home. Let us show you how pleasant and easy it is to move up to the better life at Walden. Call or visit our offices. . . .*

You must have the written permission of your buyers to use their names in this direct-mail program, but that may not be difficult to achieve when you have happy owners who sincerely believe they made the right decision. All you have to do is ask! Personal testimonials are still one of the best ways of reinforcing your marketing presentations. To increase the return from this campaign, we recommend that you limit your mailings to those who have at least three to five years' equity. This can be obtained by researching tax records or comparing older city directories with newer ones.

## CLOSE COORDINATION WITH LISTING AGENTS RESULTS IN MORE CONVERSIONS

One of the obvious keys to increasing conversion ratios from contingency marketing programs is to assure yourself that the subject properties are being effectively promoted. Pricing is the most important element in the marketing plan, and you need to know that the sellers (your buyers) have realistically valued the homes to which your sales are tied. That is why it is vital to establish a direct communication link with the sales representatives who are the listing agents for these houses. Here is a recommended checklist for on-site sales personnel to use in the management of contingency transactions:

1.  Give new buyers the checklist of things to do, which includes instructions on selecting their broker and notifying you about their choice.
2.  Contact the broker and review the details of the new home purchase, the possession-scheduling and the other factors that the broker should know to be effective in representing the seller. Ask for a copy of the listing agreement for your files. Inquire about the market range, current turnover rates and time periods and the number of competitive properties on the market. If expectations are unrealistic, perhaps you should review the need to bring the price into line with the market and not depend upon the broker alone to achieve that objective.
3.  Ask the listing broker to keep you informed at least once a month (if not more often) about the activity the property is receiving along with any recommendations he or she has made to the owners. If the agent does not call you, call the agent.
4.  If the property is not receiving sufficient exposure, discuss with both the broker and the owners the marketing adjustments that might be appropriate to assure an early sale.

5. Once a sale is secured, ask the broker to notify you with the details. Some on-site agents like to receive a copy of the purchase agreement for their own files. Pay careful attention to those factors that can affect your new home closing such as settlement dates, other contingencies and the amount of equity to be transferred.

6. When the transaction is successfully completed, send a thank-you note to the cooperating broker. This courtesy can lead to continued support for you and your housing.

7. Stay informed about what is happening in the general resale market, so you can knowledgeably discuss market conditions with brokers and buyers and anticipate adjustments you may have to make to remain competitive and profitable!

## WHAT TO DO WHEN RESALES ARE ADVERSELY AFFECTING NEW HOME SALES

Older homes always compete for some of the new home business because buyers do shop, compare and judge the advantages of purchasing new residences relative to purchasing existing ones. It is normal in most markets for resale housing to be somewhat less expensive for comparable sizes and features. After all, they have depreciated to some degree and seldom have all of the benefits offered in a newly constructed home built to today's standards. Land values tend to be the major variable. Older areas may have distinct location values that cannot be duplicated by neighborhoods in outlying suburbs, where available land and growth patterns have forced development of new housing communities. However, today's new housing neighborhoods often include amenities such as parks, ponds, pools, and trails that were not incorporated into subdivisions of earlier decades. In most cases, the ongoing competition against established neighborhoods and older homes is not a major concern for new home marketers.

The problem becomes far more challenging when the resales with which you are competing are the homes your company constructed in the same immediate neighborhoods. This always happens when you have a major development that cannot absorb all of the housing you build within a two- to three-year time period. Normal relocation factors will bring onto the market a limited number of newer resales within three years, and the turnover rate thereafter tends to stay in the 15–25 percent range, based on the characteristics of that category of housing within the local market area. A major complication can arise if your marketing attracts investors in the early phases and they elect to try for quick profits by putting the units back on the market in large numbers while you still have a number of homes (or lots) to sell in subsequent phases. The marketing issues in these highly visible new home sales arenas are very different than mere competition of older homes against newer ones. These are often the same designs you have been selling for some period of time and may be still offering to visiting prospects. If your prices are substantially greater than listings of comparable homes only three or four years older, your new buyers will be tempted to opt for the resales, which by now are landscaped, decorated and ready for living!

Even more important can be the assumable financing that is in place on the preowned homes. If the resales of your previous models have financing that is more favorable than current terms, their appeal is measurably enhanced. How should you address these issues, and equally important, how can you anticipate and minimize the challenges before they arise?

## PLAN TO PREVENT UNNECESSARY RESALE COMPETITION

If your building activity is concentrated in one neighborhood or major project and the absorption time exceeds two years, you should carefully consider implementing strategies that reduce the impact of potential resales. The checklist of variables includes the following:

1. Avoid selling nonoccupant investors in the early phases unless absolutely essential to meet your sales projections. For example, in a condominium project that may appeal to both users and investors, your risks of both excessive resales and future-owner resistance because of the high percentage of renters are increased if you aim your marketing at the investor group first. You can discourage this involvement by requiring personal possession of the condominium, limiting one unit per customer, requiring substantial down payments on investor purchases and publishing guidelines for the community with the emphasis on owner occupancy and participation. In some communities, you can even limit the right to rent housing units by requiring notification and approval of the board of trustees.

2. Incorporate protective covenants that strictly limit the use of "for sale" signs. Even with normal turnover, the number of resale signs on a street can discourage new buyers. Questions are raised as to why so many homes are for sale, and if there is something happening in the neighborhood causing people to sell prematurely! That psychology can be very detrimental to the sales efforts of the representatives staffing the new inventory.

3. Plan to introduce new models with fresh design concepts in any area where your absorption capacity exceeds two years. The best insurance against direct comparisons and lost sales to previous models is to breed discontent by offering architectural concepts not previously seen. Improving key areas of a winning plan is another way to accomplish this objective. You may not want to eliminate a best-seller from your selection, but you can add features to master bathrooms, kitchens and living centers that will create obsolescence for the older designs. Staying with the same old plans too long is a sure way to risk losing momentum as well as profits. You can charge more for new ideas than for older ones!

4. Avoid scatter-building. When new and resale housing have to compete side by side, the comparison is even more obvious than when they are separated by previously completed phases. Building in sequence and finishing neighborhoods as you progress to new areas achieves a number of positive marketing goals. Established streetscapes help to sustain values so that older

homes appreciate, and that keeps prices up so sellers do not undercut the market. These nesting areas also serve as good examples of the quality your company exercises in the building process. People like to live in attractive, fully developed neighborhoods rather than among vacant lots and open fields that are unattended for long periods of time.

5.  Reserve prime homesites or future models where you can control neighborhoods, traffic patterns and the presentation of your designs. If you fail to think ahead to model needs in the latter phases, you may force buyers to drive down streets or areas you prefer they did not see before they are with your sales representatives. Losing control of the front gate or the premier location for demonstrating your housing environment can be a costly mistake.

6.  If you have a brokerage division or the capacity to handle resales, create a marketing plan promoted to all the owners that help them see the benefits of protecting the community and their equities. Sometimes it is wise to appoint a specialist to work just the resale properties and keep that marketing effort totally separate from the new home sales programs. In some cases, it may be wise to post resale offerings on a bulletin board or special listing sheet in the main new home sales center with the understanding that you will help your previous owners achieve their objectives while maintaining values for everyone concerned.

7.  If you are in a multiple-builder community as one of the preferred builders in the program, it may be in your best interests to suggest to the developers and the other builders that they adopt policies and procedures that will limit the problem of resales using the above checklist along with additional ideas.

## EDUCATE AND MOTIVATE OWNERS TO WORK TOGETHER TO PROTECT EQUITIES

Whenever the number of resales in a new community begins to exceed the ability of the marketplace to absorb the amount of product being offered, it is appropriate to initiate a forum for interested owners and recommend collective strategies that will relieve the pressure. We have participated in some of these crisis-intervention sessions and experienced reasonable success in communicating issues and achieving cooperation. Minimum goals normally involve the following:

- Convincing owners who do not need to sell now that they will gain more by waiting until the community is further along or the market has improved. Withdrawing excess inventory is not easy to accomplish, but can be done in some cases, particularly when the sellers are investors rather than people who must move.

- Establishing a plan for removing excessive "for sale" signs. One method is to rotate signs by days or weekends so that every owner gets some sign exposure, but the streets do not look like a desperation bail out! REALTORS®

have to be convinced that this is in their best interests, since they are historically dependent on signs to draw more buyers and listings.

- Agreeing to a central sales-information program that represents all resale owners equally in exchange for removal of signs and cooperation in maintaining prices.
- Enlisting all owners in the prospecting programs to bring more buyers to the area—not just to their individual homes. Group events are occasionally a good method for accomplishing this goal.
- Making certain that everyone appreciates the real values of the community and is enlisted as a supporter instead of a detractor. Values are psychologically depreciated when residents bad-mouth the developer, builder and neighborhood. They must first appreciate that they are taking money out of their own pockets as well as their neighbors' by maintaining a negative posture. Peer-group pressure can accomplish what you may not be able to do alone!

## EDUCATE SALESPEOPLE TO SELL THE BENEFITS OF NEWER HOMES VERSUS OLDER RESALES

Finally, the game plan comes down to the salespeople on the front line. They must be convinced that the new homes they represent are worth more than the older ones and they must be able to communicate that message with confidence to all prospective buyers they meet. If they have doubts, they will be transmitted to the visiting public. Sales management has the responsibility of reinforcing the messages salespeople should use and of maintaining a positive attitude that filters down to those who must convince others to act. Comparative checklists for new versus old homes are part of the training materials that should be used when resales begin to cut into the sales volume needed to sustain building programs.

## STAY ALERT AND FLEXIBLE IF YOU WANT TO SURVIVE THE CURVES

We cannot predict with any certainty what will happen to the housing markets of tomorrow. There are too many variables! The economics are influenced by national and international events over which we have no control. Local market conditions may be somewhat more predictable, but they can quickly change when someone deals an unexpected blow to the job market or the rules by which you acquire, develop and build new projects. The keys to survival are alertness and flexibility! Do not become complacent when things are going well, because they are bound to change and often for the worse. Don't become so involved in your own activities that you fail to observe what is happening to other builders and the marketplace in general. In all of your planning, build in alternative courses of action in case Plan A does not work. Keep your inventory releases and the neighborhoods under tight control—and as small as possible so you can switch game plans without disrupting what you have already started. Most important, recognize that housing curves have been with us as long as we have had a building industry, and they broadcast advance warning signals predicting changes in direction. Still, you must have your antennae in position to receive and interpret them!

# 12: Creative Marketing Programs in Action

In this final chapter of *New Home Marketing*, we decided to present a selection of case histories submitted to us by professional marketers. We chose these examples because they illustrated practical concepts. Several emphasize the value of trying something different rather than the routine marketing approaches employed by the majority of builders and brokers. We also had the objective of demonstrating how small-volume builders and developers can effectively compete with larger organizations without spending fortunes.

The essence of marketing is in its alternatives. When you realistically evaluate market opportunities for a specific parcel of real estate, land plan, housing concept and product line, you always discover a variety of choices. Some conditions cannot be altered; others can. As you decide to develop the land with certain yield objectives and begin to narrow design selections to fit both land and market opportunities, your marketing strategies should already be reasonably well-defined. You do not market at the *end* of the process! Marketing *is* the process! Every choice you make affects public acceptance, sales rates and profit margins. Essentially, it is a matter of packaging and presentation. How do you assemble the right ingredients and create a housing environment readily accepted by profiled prospects? How do you communicate that package to potential customers? The goal is to achieve your marketing objectives while protecting your profits!

Each marketing adventure begins with a discovery process. You prepare yourself by first assembling all facts needed to make informed choices. Find out the nature and depth of the market. Evaluate the competition. Consider the political and economic climates in which you will be doing business. Most important, understand the value perceptions in which your housing products will be measured. When you have identified the principles that should guide your development strategies, create the road map for reaching your consumers. Where are they? What will attract them? How important is off-site marketing (including cooperative broker plans) to attaining your sales goals? What roles will the on-site presentation package and sales staff play (if any)? What is needed to achieve exposure levels necessary for a reasonable sales conversion ratio? Whom do you need to close the customers who are attracted to the sales environment? Finally, how much will it cost?

One challenging aspect of the marketing director's role is to inexpensively create and implement pragmatic sales and marketing strategies. Most builders are concerned about spending dollars for intangibles like merchandising and marketing. Brokers who represent builders have fixed percentages of their gross commissions to devote to marketing activities if they are responsible for advertising and promotion. Working within limited budgets while achieving optimum results tests the creative skills of most new home sales and marketing experts. The ideas presented in this chapter were very cost effective. They produced results without exceeding reasonable budgets. This is easier to accomplish if you have a clearly defined target. Very often, a campaign worked because it communicated a motivating message to the right prospects in a creative manner.

As you review these case studies and brief scenarios, keep in mind that the marketers were working in environments they understood. Every market region has its own peculiarities. What may be applicable in dynamic southern California may not be appropriate in Syracuse, New York! Some areas are dominated by high-volume merchant builders, and others are still the provinces of modest-volume builders. Annual absorption rates and consumer profiles are always local in nature. Pricing strategies and value perceptions differ dramatically. For example, as of 1988, a typical three-bedroom, two-bath home, with 1,500 to 1,800 square feet of living space on a single family homesite, ranged from a high of over $500,000 in Stamford, Connecticut, to as little as $63,000 in Bowling Green, Kentucky. Know your market before you attempt to introduce any new marketing concept. Do not generalize! Appreciate the thought processes and creativity involved in these marketing applications, but always prepare your own plans based on the demands and needs of your company in your market!

## CASE STUDY: ELDAN MEADOW

Eldan Meadow is a multiple-builder community in Cicero, a suburb of Syracuse. Dan Barnaba, as both developer and builder, had been experiencing a decrease in the sales rate and an increase in inventory of production homes for sale—both his own and those of other builders in the project. This community should produce a minimum of one sale per week, but the rate had declined to half of that. Previous advertising emphasized Eldan Meadow as "a special place to call home." The marketing team recommended a more direct and product-oriented program. The opening ad in the new campaign was titled: "Special Home Tour Today" and it featured seven completed homes as models available for inspection. Although none was furnished, the concept of a special tour of finished homes was very effective. The results speak for themselves:

- Sales traffic increased 100 percent.
- Four of the seven homes sold that week.
- All seven plus several others sold within three weeks.

This is a case of making a vice into a virtue. Standing inventory became the basis for a model tour. On-site sales personnel were able to create excitement from the increased traffic and a sense of urgency was added to their sales presentations.

**FIGURE 12.1   Home Tour Ad**

## A DAN BARNABA COMMUNITY
# SPECIAL HOME TOUR TODAY!

Come to Eldan Meadow today, and tour some of our finest new homes. You'll have the opportunity to see the custom designs and quality craftsmanship that have made Eldan Meadow so special. Stop at our first model, on Farm Gate Path, and we'll take you on the tour.

**Farm Gate Path, Lot 31.** Your first stop is this value-priced traditional colonial with all the extras included, but just $115,000.

**Hardwood Lane, Lot 56.** Next, we'll go to Hardwood Lane and stop at this luxurious 4-bedrm., 2½-bath colonial, priced at $145,000.

**Hardwood Lane, Lot 61.** Across the street, you'll find this distinctive Cape Cod with 4 bedrms., 3 baths, and fantastic floor plan, for $144,900.

**Hardwood Lane, Lot 63.** Like contemporary? Don't miss this exciting 3-bedrm., 2½-bath home with skylights, Jacuzzi, for $134,900.

**Hardwood Lane, Lot 53.** Distinctly different, and set on a gorgeous wooded lot, is this handsome 3-bedrm., 2½-bath contemporary colonial, at $139,900.

**Hardwood Lane, Lot 66.** Just down the street is a contemporary, 3-bedrm., 2½-bath home with an exciting, yet functional floor plan. Quality workmanship throughout, for $139,900.

**Hardwood Lane, Lot 41.** Travel around the corner to a ranch-lover's dream home—this 3-bedrm., 2-bath beauty with space and style galore, for $129,900.

## Open Sunday 1–4 PM

Take Rt. 81 north to the Cicero exit, Exit 30. Take Rt. 31 east, then first left onto Lakeshore Rd., 1½ miles on Lakeshore to the Eldan Meadow entrance.

For more information, call Frank D'Agostino, broker, at 458-9100.

**Central New York's**
**#1 Residential Real Estate Company**

## CASE STUDY: CHICKERING

Chickering (in Atlanta, Georgia) was the result of a major land acquisition by a developer not known in the local Atlanta market. One marketing concern was the establishment of corporate name recognition, community identity and the initiation of REALTOR® loyalty for an out-of-town developer. To facilitate the first phase of the marketing program, a three-tier, direct-mail piece was designed and circulated to local REALTORS®. The intent was to create a collateral piece that would ensure project recall by its design and presentation. A call to action was purposely avoided in the original direct-mail program. It served as a teaser statement to generate REALTOR® interest and a desire to see the community once it was officially announced. The three pieces chosen emphasized the potential commission earnings offered by the new developer to entice support from cooperating agents. The second objective was to design the mailers to clearly differentiate them from other correspondence and promotional literature with which agents are bombarded. To achieve this, the mailers were designed with pop-up art in the centerfolds. Each piece was also adaptable to multiple communities in various markets, thus permitting the developers to amortize production costs over a number of projects.

The six-month teaser campaign culminated with an on-site broker luncheon and a grand opening that attracted over 600 REALTORS® and their guests during a two-and-one-half-hour period. The campaign generated more than $1.5 million in cooperative broker sales during the predevelopment opening and following three weeks.

## CASE STUDY: SHEPHERD'S VINEYARD

Shepherd's Vineyard is presented because it illustrates how builders of differing product lines and production capacities can achieve superior results when their developer follows a well-conceived marketing plan. Located in Apex, a suburb of Raleigh, North Carolina, the land parcel required thoughtful planning to create a distinctive community bordered by Highway 64 and Old Apex-Macedonia Road. The planning team recognized the importance of creating separate neighborhoods within the total community to provide product and pricing differentiation. Chimney Hill was designed to fill the moderate-price range and Carriage Ridge the more prestigious custom-home enclave. Each was divided into logical phases that could be adjusted in size to maintain inventory control and a sense of urgency based on actual absorption rates.

Prior to the launching of Shepherd's Vineyard, the Raleigh–Durham market had been dominated by a developer's philosophy of creating all the lots that builders would buy and letting the builders make all decisions on product, pricing and marketing. The usual plan was to bring in as many builders as possible and let the competitive climate determine the winners. This often resulted in too much inventory being on the market, speculative homes standing unsold and sales being negotiated at less-than-desired profit margins. Fonville-Morisey & Company made the decision to limit the builders to a carefully selected preferred group, not to exceed six for the entire project. To qualify, the candidates had to have solid track records, proven

**FIGURE 12.2    A Shepherd's Vineyard Ad**

# SHEPHERD'S VINEYARD UNVEILS
# SIX FULLY FURNISHED MODEL HOMES.

No other community has ever offered this incredible opportunity! Six fully furnished model homes in one easy-to-visit location.

Imagine, door-to-door exciting decorating ideas in six different, professionally landscaped, beautifully crafted homes built by five of the area's most preferred builders.

Plus, there will be thirty exciting floor plan designs for your consideration.

And right now, special prices are being offered. Chimney Hills homes start at $104,500. Carriage Ridge homes at $143,150.

**Shepherd's Vineyard.**
**The Good Life Starts Here.**

Convenient to Raleigh, Durham, Chapel Hill, Cary and the Research Triangle Park, Shepherd's Vineyard has everything your family requires. Excellent schools, dining, entertainment, shopping and recreational facilities are all nearby.

Within the community careful attention has been given to preserve the natural environment.

A thirty acre greenway system with jogging trail winds through the entire community, bordering each neighborhood, creating a sense of seclusion and privacy.

And while you're here notice nestled in the heart of this special community the Swim & Racquet Club, one of the most beautiful, full-facility swim clubs you'll find anywhere.

**Shepherd's Vineyard.**
**The Opportunity Won't Last Long.**

Shepherd's Vineyard has just opened, but a large percentage of Phase One has already sold out.

So if you want to share in what is fast becoming the most talked about and sought after residential community in the Triangle, visit or call today. Sales Center and furnished models are open from 1–6 daily. Or phone 362-1462.

**Shepherd's**
**Vineyard**

DIRECTIONS: *Take US 1 South to 64 West exit. Right 1½ miles past MacGregor Downs.*

*Sales by Fonville Morisey*

capacity to deliver and a willingness to subscribe to a total marketing plan. This included a requirement that each participant build and furnish one model home and maintain at least one similar replication of the show home in the available inventory. A builder's manual was drafted and presented to all candidates for approval. It incorporated plan-protection policies, inventory-control guidelines and uniform community signage regulations. Five building companies were selected, with one of them to have models in both neighborhoods. The largest builder was a volume operator selling more than 150 homes a year in multiple locations. The smallest sold an average of 15–20 homes a year.

A key marketing element in the Shepherd's Vineyard plan was use of a central sales facility for all builders. The developers designed, furnished and maintained a home for the sales office, modifying it so that all of the rooms served sales functions (see chapter four). Each builder was prominently featured in the builder's showcase room.

The presale campaign began in the spring of 1986 with a teaser promotion that urged the public to rediscover Shepherd's Vineyard. The campaign recounted the rich and romantic history of the land, which had been settled in 1820 by a Reverend Patrick Dowd. A temporary sales trailer was moved on site until the sales office and models were ready. During this pioneer period, interest was piqued by carefully engineered marketing messages. By the time REALTORS® and the public were formally introduced to the preconstruction program, a solid backlog of interest quickly produced a number of pioneer sales. By grand-opening time, the completed sales facility, model homes and public awareness resulted in hundreds of people seeing the community and a rapid sales pace. All of the builders enjoyed success, although some did better than others. That is to be expected in a competitive situation. However, they all did better than they expected, and the protected values added opportunities for protected profits.

The advertising and promotional materials created by Everett Boyd and Associates, a creative Raleigh-based advertising organization, captured the theme of a community with a heritage and a place for the good life.

## CASE STUDY: BEACON HILL

For Steve Critchfield and Wichita, Kansas, the Beacon Hill development was a departure from conventional wisdom. Located in an area bordering multifamily housing and an older low-end tract-housing project, it was not considered the ideal place for a planned community. The 241-acre parcel had been passed over by the major developers in town. The young marketing team of Critchfield, Inc., decided to tackle what others had rejected. The planning team recognized the need to buffer the site from potentially adverse influences and to create an environment that would attract young families and people making their first or second move up from other locations. They designed a land plan that incorporated a man-made lake system, walking trails, parks and play areas. In addition, the community was to be enclosed by attractive masonry walls and architecturally pleasing fencing.

---

**FIGURE 12.3   Teaser Promotion Ad**

# A LOVE AFFAIR THAT BEGAN IN 1820 IS YOURS TO CONTINUE TODAY.

They loved this land the moment they saw it. And not even a war could dampen their dreams of happiness. They knew this would be their place for the good life.

Today you can discover Shepherd's Vineyard for yourself. Find out about the history of this land and the exceptional pre-construction prices on single family homes now being offered. Chimney Hill homes from $100,000. Carriage Ridge from $140,000.

Open 1–6 daily. Or call 362-1462.

*Shepherd's Vineyard*

*US 1 South to 64 West exit. Right 1½ miles past McGregor Downs.*

*Sales by Fonville Morisey*

---

Accepting the advice of marketing consultants, Steve Critchfield elected to begin the sales program with the least desirable sites at the rear of the community, in order to mask the properties at the back line and create an attractive future streetscape for arriving traffic once the initial neighborhood was established. This also permitted him to start with lower initial prices and preserve his better lakeside sites and entry-gate locations for later marketing when they would command more of a premium than was possible the first year.

The lot-release program for the first phase of The Courts at Beacon Hill was limited to 18 sites, plus four furnished models in a separate, landscaped cul-de-sac. Absorption was predicted at two to three net sales per month. The preconstruction sales campaign had to be held off-site, since the city denied him the right to install a sales trailer. Prospective buyers responded to on-site signage and were brought to the central offices of the corporation for an orientation and a planned tour of the emerging community. To get to the first homes under construction required driving through the multifamily apartment project and approaching Beacon Hill from the rear, since the entry bridge across the waterway would take several months to complete. Despite these disadvantages, 12 of the first 18 homesites sold before models were finished— all from off-site marketing efforts. When the official opening was held in the fall of 1987, the credibility of the early sales helped to pick up the momentum. A key ingredient to the acceptance of Beacon Hill was the developer's ability to create a sense of community for the owners. Prior to the grand opening, he held a ''Founder's-Day'' party that included all of the early purchasers. This was promoted in the local newspaper, resulting in additional sales from those who had previously questioned the viability of the project.

The starting prices in the $70,000's increased to an average of $103,000 within 12 months, and the sales pace maintained an average of three per month or better. Today, Beacon Hill has custom home builders successfully competing for the move-up market against subdivisions that were considered the place to be based on Wichita standards. The Critchfield Company broadened its product line while selling sites to others who specialize in larger personalized housing. The marketing philosophy of creating and protecting future values by the careful control of the early sales environment is a lesson every developer and builder should heed!

## CASE STUDY: BRADFORD HEIGHTS

This is the case of a low-volume builder who prefers a modest but steady pace of sales, not more than one per month or 12 per year. Luber Homes, Inc., of DeWitt, New York, builds large colonials and contemporary designs for discriminating buyers. The Luber name is well known in DeWitt and is associated with quality craftsmanship and hands-on supervision of the homes he builds. His target is the high-end, move-up market (both local and transferees).

The Bradford Heights project did not have a furnished model. Instead, a production home was used to illustrate design concepts and workmanship. The site was held open only on weekends and managed by a key agent who answered phone calls and gave showings from an off-site location during the week. An interesting marketing lesson in this case history is the value of pinpointing your market and

FIGURE 12.4    Bradford Heights Ad

targeting your advertising to reach them. The Bradford Heights location is near the major hospitals and Syracuse University. Doctors and other professionals who want to reside close to employment were prime targets. Nearly 50 percent of the sales were to doctors! The theme of the ad aims specifically at their motivations:

*"A World Apart, Just Five Minutes Away!"*

This low-cost marketing budget achieves results because it is aimed at specific profiles and motivations!

## CASE STUDY: COUNTRY CLUB OF THE SOUTH

The Country Club of the South is a prestigious and very successful golf-course community in Atlanta, Georgia, planned and developed by the Jack Nicklaus Development Corporation. Despite its current success and the outstanding amenities it offers, it presented a unique challenge to the marketers during its early phases. A key factor in the Atlanta region is the high impact of the REALTOR® community on new home sales, especially in the prestige price ranges for which Country Club of The South was designed. REALTORS® account for more than 80 percent of all sales in the $300,000-plus price categories.

When the development was first released to cooperating brokers, the company elected to maintain tight control over access to the facilities with emphasis on the guarded-gate security system through which all traffic must enter. All visitors, including brokers, were required to go to the sales office first where they registered and met an on-site specialist for initial orientation and an escorted tour of the community. An unexpected consequence of this requirement was the resistance of the local REALTORS® to show the Country Club of The South, because they felt forced to yield control of their clients. This perceived threat to their customer relationships caused them to bypass this project unless their clients insisted on seeing it.

Realizing the importance of REALTOR® support to the total marketing objectives, the management team instituted a unique program to counter the problem. They designed a Gold Gate Card, together with a color brochure that became a driving tour map of the community, which was distributed to the top 200 agents in the Atlanta market. This prestige card gave these selected REALTORS® access through the guarded gate without stopping at the sales center, and it also allowed them to charge lunch for their customers at the award-winning clubhouse. The only requirement the REALTOR® had to meet to retain these privileges was to register his or her clients at the sales center before leaving the Country Club of The South. The Nicklaus agents were trained to treat the REALTORS® with the respect they deserved, and they always assemble and personalize marketing materials needed for any specific client.

In concert with this promotion, the developer established a REALTOR®-of-the-Year program, which included top prizes of a trip to Pebble Beach or Britannia for one week for the agent and a guest. To further ensure that the developer's image became synonymous with support for the real estate community, a "pick-a-stick" prize was awarded each selling agent after a closing. The on-site representative who had worked with the selling broker visits the REALTOR's® office during their weekly sales meeting with a golf bag filled with clubs. Tied to each club was a card listing a prize from either the pro shop or the clubhouse. The selling agent was given the opportunity of picking a stick during the meeting and winning whatever prize is noted.

As an added incentive to win REALTOR® support, the Jack Nicklaus Development Company invited local brokers to hold one of their weekly meetings at the impressive clubhouse as guests of the developer. During the meeting, a catered buffet was served, followed by a tour of the newest homes in the community. The response to the program was exceptional and led to a modification of the promotion to broaden its effectiveness. Agents are now allowed to earn a Gold Card by showing a minimum of four prospects during a 12-month period. The Country Club of The South averaged over $1 million per month in sales following institution of the cooperative-broker promotion, and more than 90 percent of this volume came from REALTOR®-originated transactions!

## SOME MARKETING TIPS FROM NICKI JOY

Nicki Joy, of Nicki Joy and Associates in Washington, DC (a firm specializing in marketing services), submitted the following information on some of her clients. Ruxton Homes, a small-volume builder in northern Virginia, decided to generate some preconstruction interest in a partially cleared site even before a sales trailer was installed. Chip Benson, the director of marketing, responded well to the idea of holding an informal barbecue for those in the immediate neighborhood and people passing the site during pleasant summer weekends. The "preview Barbeque plan" was initiated. A few flags and balloons were used to attract attention, along with a sign inviting the public to a free lunch. We set up some grills and served hot dogs, cold drinks and chips. It was amazing how many people stopped, had a picnic and became involved in the plan for future development. The tab for one weekend was typically $400, and the result was three early sales!

Ashley Homes in Norfolk, Virginia targets the entry-level buyer, and the marketer realizes that many prospects do not know how or when to buy a new home. These beginners are often confused and embarrassed to ask about the process. Ashley addresses their fears and concerns with an informative leaflet entitled: "Are You Really Ready to Buy a New Home?" It details the factors involved in the decision to take that first ownership step and includes a budget analysis along with a tax-savings guide that motivates the potential buyers to ask the sales counselor for more information. By being simple and direct, this introductory literature helps to set the stage for the salespeople and encourages hesitant neophytes to enter the marketplace. Response to this educational service has been exceptional, according to the principals of the company. Other builders whose prospects are first-time buyers might well borrow Ashley's marketing book!

A new trend in on-site merchandising and promotion of model homes is the use of professionally prepared audiotapes that really portray the sounds of living in a home with positive messages. For example, as prospects enter the dining room of a model, instead of hearing standard background music, they hear the sounds of a family enjoying Thanksgiving dinner. In the family room are sounds of family events, games and Monday-night football. The bathroom tape plays sounds of childrens' squeals of laughter playing in the tub, and on the deck or patio you hear crickets chirping and a dialogue by imagined owners like: "What a day, Honey . . . living here would really be the great life!" Tapes for each model are produced to fit the lifestyles of the profiled prospects. When you add these real-life sounds to other emotionally stimulating merchandising, like fragrances that match the rooms, you have the ultimate in mood-setting! Equally important, people remember and give your homes the cheapest form of advertising: word of mouth!

## AUDIO DIRECT-MAIL

A blank envelope with an enclosed audiotape created one of the most unique and effective target-marketing programs in the Atlanta market in 1986. It was so effective that it won the Home Builder's Silver Award for the most innovative marketing idea of the year. The condominium project for which this audio-mail program was created had experienced a drastic decline in sales because of a decrease in interest rates and the affordability of single-family homes, which diverted previous condominium buyers. The developer decided to become radically aggressive in his attempt to sell the 70 remaining units within a 90-day period. His first step was to secure a very attractive financing package that made the condominiums more appealing to budget-conscious prospects. To do so, he had to buy down the rate, and this required use of most of the funds that might otherwise have been budgeted for advertising. It was then necessary to develop a less-expensive, more targeted approach to marketing. A key ingredient in this campaign was the audio direct-mail concept. It consisted of three separate tapes directed at three different buyer profiles: one for managers of local businesses, another for local real estate brokers and a third for apartment-renters within the immediate target market area. The objective was to be sure each tape was played by the targeted customer. Delivery was done by hand. In the case of the apartment dwellers, delivery was made by college students between midnight and 2 A.M. Each tape was placed in a white envelope with the word "personal" handwritten on the outside of the envelope. The envelopes were then placed under the windshield wipers of the cars parked in the selected apartment projects.

The intent of the program was to avoid apartment management discovering and removing the tape material before it was played (a problem typical of housing literature distributed to renters). The most important consideration was to be sure the recipients listened to the messages. It was predicted that once a treatment reached the car and saw an envelope marked "personal" with an unmarked tape enclosed, he or she would certainly play the tape on the way to work. The message on the cassette was very simple and to the point. It merely advised listeners that an opportunity existed for home ownership within a few minutes of their apartment with the cost of ownership being virtually equivalent to their rent payments. The tape explained the creative financing package that had a time limit for action, and then described the amenities concluding with directions to the community from a central location in the immediate area.

The tapes directed to REALTORS® were slightly different, but the intent was the same. These tapes were delivered to individual sales agents in their offices by the on-site sales staff. The response to these audio messages was extraordinary. The program, in concert with an aggressive cooperative-broker plan, enabled the builder to sell all of the inventory in less than 90 days, and at a fraction of the cost that normal promotions would have required.

## CHANGE YOUR FOCUS

Dave Olson, of the Olson Marketing Group in Denver, Colorado, was asked to find a marketing solution for 32 completed townhomes in Gillette, Wyoming, which had been standing unsold for nearly a year. During his two-day audit of the local market, he concluded that little or no demand existed for these homes from the established housing market of single-family owners or apartment dwellers. As he was driving through the city and its environs, he noticed a number of mobile-home parks. On returning to the project office, he asked the builder's sales representatives if they had ever had any inquiries from people living in mobile homes. The answer was: "Oh, those people. Why, we must have 20 or 30 a month asking us if we could take their mobile homes in trade!" Dave then asked the builder whether he would rather continue to hold the fixed location asset of the townhomes or consider accepting mobile homes, which can be financed and shipped to other markets if they could not be sold locally. The local mobile-home market was soft, but it was more dynamic in areas like Denver and Salt Lake City. Mobile homes have many alternative uses: as temporary sales offices, bank branches and construction trailers! The result was an aggressive direct-mail and newspaper campaign targeted to trailer-park residents that successfully closed all 32 townhomes in 60 days. By using wholesale and retail sources, the mobile homes were liquidated within six months, permitting the builder to survive and concentrate on more-profitable ventures!

## CASE STUDY: SULLY STATION

Robert C. Kettler, president of Kettler & Scott of Centreville, Virginia, recognized the development opportunities of the Route 28 and Interstate 66 Dulles corridor in the early 1980s and began a major assemblage of nearly 45 contiguous parcels that were ultimately rezoned into a 1,200-acre master-planned community in 1985. The planning process identified three major issues that needed special attention by those in charge of marketing strategies:

1. *No proven market.* Prior to the introduction of this project. Centreville was an area of small working farms and a few scattered subdivisions of modest homes built in the 1950s and 1960s. In the early 1980's, some adventurous builders pioneered a few projects that ultimately failed because of economic conditions of that time, casting doubt over the future marketability of new housing environments. Marketing would have to address the issue of consumer acceptance in creative ways.
2. *No direct access from any major highway.* Although very well located in relation to general transportation corridors, this community did not have a front door or easy access to one of the major highways. Prospects would have to meander through an emerging 20-million-square-foot office park.

Kettler & Scott worked closely with the neighboring commercial developer to coordinate entrance-feature designs and streetscaping that would create a unified theme and park-like setting for both projects.

3. *Potential competition from smaller communities.* The Kettler & Scott organization was not alone in recognizing potential future demand, as several smaller communities were put into motion with market entry scheduled for approximately 12 months later. This added impetus to the need to establish this master-planned project as the premier community where buyers would realize optimum values.

As the master plan developed, the theme of Sully Station was defined and implemented to position the community of 3,200 single-family homes, townhomes, multifamily and adult housing units as "a good place to raise a family." Researchers identified the primary market profile as 25-45-year-old professional couples with annual incomes exceeding $60,000. These suburban yuppies would include both beginners and move-up buyers seeking improved lifestyles for themselves and their offspring in a secure community with its own private golf course, lake, two clubhouses, swimming pools, tennis courts, jogging trails and open-space parks.

A teaser advertising campaign was created to introduce Sully Station in the spring of 1986. A sequential series of newspaper ads with the headlines "Get Ready," "Get Set," and "Go" was featured over the three-week period before a public preview opening. The developer established maximum credibility prior to launching the campaign by having in place a landscaped sales park with facaded trailers, first-phase installation of roads, parkways and paths, and an elaborate identity signage program. The signage campaign was so successful it subsequently won the coveted MAME award from the Home Builders Association.

The subsequent "preview opening" campaign emphasized to prospective buyers the message: "Your timing is perfect." It ran for 13 weeks and drew more than 2,800 prospects. The cooperating builders, working without models, sold 79 homes during this launching phase. In the following weeks, schedules for models were accelerated and homes were deliberately sited where they would create a sense of community and attractive streetscapes for the early residents. Sully Station looked successful and thriving from the day it first opened for business, and the media campaign reinforced the tempo.

The advertising in the fall of 1986 extolled the extensive amenities and wide choice of homes. Traffic averaged 175 per week, and the sales pace held at about 10 per month. By the winter of 1987, the ads capitalized on the MAME award as community of the year, along with testimonials of the families who now made Sully Station their home. This theme was expanded and maintained through the spring of 1987 and sales grew to more than 25 per month from traffic counts of 200 per week. The competition was now in full swing, but with the weakness of "me too" marketing messages.

A radio campaign was initiated featuring a well-known tune from the 1940s, "Chattanooga Choo-Choo" ("Pardon me boy, is this the Pennsylvania Station?"), with new words about Sully Station. It was purposely recorded in the original big-band style for authenticity and maximum memory-linking. The entire message was in the lyrics. No announcer was involved. The basic idea was to relate a familiar and

---

**FIGURE 12.5    Sully Station Advertisement**

---

# If you're ready to live in Fairfax County's most beautiful new community, your timing is perfect.

**Long Homes of Virginia**
Colonial homes from the low $200's. 631-6813

The model homes are open, the fall colors are beautiful, and the buyers are coming in record numbers.

Welcome to Sully Station, your next stop on your way up. Here in the heart of western Fairfax County's new "boom" area, we're creating one of the most thoughtfully planned, carefully protected, painstakingly designed luxury communities in Northern Virginia. And we're creating it specifically for people like you.

It may well be the only community of its kind in this growing area. And ulti-

**Van Metre Companies**
Colonial homes from the low $200's. 830-5488

mately the most coveted. That's because we've done more than make it a comfortable, convenient community. We've also made it a

beautiful one.

More than 40 percent of the land around the homes — about 134 acres in all — is preserved as woodlands, parks and streams. And amid the tall trees and meadows, you'll find ball fields, tot lots, multi-purpose courts, and 4½ miles of jogging paths. Plus the community recreation center — featuring a two story

**Fairfield Homes**
Victorian and colonial design homes from the $190's. 378-0050

clubhouse, Olympic-size swimming pool and tennis courts. And there's one more community amenity you'll enjoy every day. Your own shopping center. Beautifully designed as a charming 19th-century English country train station. Featuring one of the new super Safeway stores with a pharmacy and bakery, plus a dry cleaner, and other convenience shops.

All of this will be yours,

**NVHomes**
Colonial homes from the low $170's. Sold out

in a private residential enclave of luxurious traditional and colonial homes, sited along landscaped winding lanes and cul-de-sacs.

Your neighbor to the west is the

**Glenberry by**
**William L. Berry & Co., Inc.**
Luxury Townhomes from the low $130's
Models now open 631-3363

Chantilly National Golf and Country Club. To the north is Westfields, the heralded office campus which leads to Dulles Airport, a short drive away. To the south is E. C. Lawrence Memorial Park, one of the largest in Fairfax County. And just down Sully Road (Rt. 28) is convenient commuting along Route 50 or I-66. Or drive a short way to the new Vienna Metro and ride from there.

Everything you'd expect in a luxury community is here. Recreation. Convenience. An elementary school. A real neighborhood feeling. The beauty of the

countryside. And the beautiful homes. It's all yours here at Sully Station. Your next stop on your way up.

Sales offices and model homes open daily, 11-6. The sooner you get here, the

**Signature Communities**
Traditional three level townhomes from the $120's. 830-3969

better your choice of homes, lots and prices. And the sooner you'll be moving in.

Directions: Take I-66 west, approximately 4½ miles past Fair Oaks Mall to exit for Sully Road (Rt. 28) north. Continue north on Sully Rd. approxi-

## MODEL HOMES NOW OPEN

mately 2 miles to signs and entrance to Sully Station on left. Turn left onto entrance road, follow signs ½ mile to sales park on your right.

Developed by
KETTLER & SCOTT

# SULLY STATION

---

**FIGURE 12.6   Sully Station Advertisement**

---

# Homebuyers at Sully Station are like kids in a candy store.

It's been called "the most beautiful new community in Fairfax County."

Ever since it opened last year, it has attracted more homebuyers week after week than any comparable community in Northern Virginia.

Even other homebuilders are impressed. Recently they named it the "Community of the Year" for metropolitan Washington.

No wonder your face will light up the moment you drive in.

### 8 of Virginia's most popular builders have exciting homes to show you.

Sully Station is a winner. Because if there's anything your heart desires in your neighborhood,

Long Homes of Virginia

you'll probably find it here. And you can have it now.

Acres of woodlands, parks and streams. Miles of bike paths,

Glenberry by
William L. Berry & Co., Inc.

jogging trails and nature walks. Ballfields, tot lots, multi-purpose courts — and of course, schools. The community center has

EQUAL HOUSING
**OPPORTUNITY**

its own 2 story clubhouse, Olympic-size pool, sundeck and tennis club. There is even

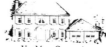

**Van Metre Companies**
Colonial homes from the low $200's $30-5448

your own neighborhood shopping center, designed after a 19th century English train station. With the Safeway, bakery, pharmacy, dry cleaners and other convenience stores.

**Signature Communities**
Traditional three level townhomes from the $120's $130-1969

And someday soon, these winding lanes and quiet cul-de-sacs will seem even more convenient. Because commuters will be able to ride a Metro express bus from Sully Station to the Vienna Metro station.

But Sully Station is more than

a great place to live. It's also a great place to buy.

Eight of Virginia's most popular builders are here. With finished homes, model homes

**Fairfield Homes**

and exciting plans to show you. And their names are enough to make a homebuyer's mouth water:

Fairfield Homes. Long Homes of Virginia. Van Metre Companies. William L. Berry & Co., Inc.

### New owners like you are moving in. Models are open today.

Signature Communities. The Milton Company. The Christopher Companies. And even apartments from America's leader — The Trammell Crow Company.

Everything's open this weekend. So come on. The candy store's open.

Sales office and model homes open daily, 11-6. Directions: Take I-66 west, approximately 4½ miles past Fair Oaks Mall to exit for Sully Road (Rt. 28) north. Continue north on Sully Rd. approximately 2 miles to signs and entrance to Sully Station on left. Turn left onto entrance road, follow signs ½ mile to sales park on your right. Or call 631-4910.

**SULLY STATION**
A Kettler & Scott Community.

**FIGURE 12.7    Sully Station Advertisement**

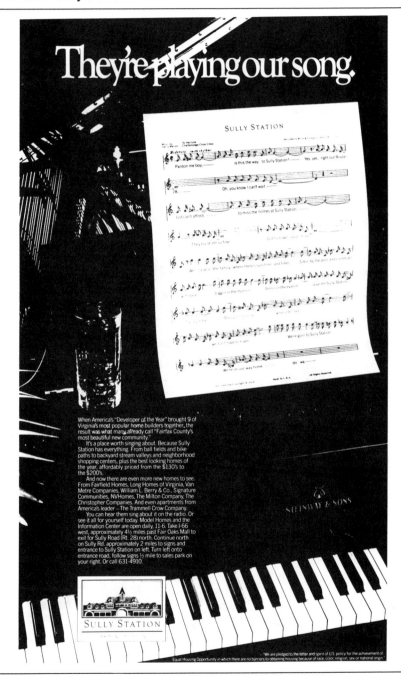

**FIGURE 12.8    Sully Station Advertisement**

# A Sully Station resident talks about commuting:

Sully Station has been Northern Virginia's favorite new community from the day it opened. A beautiful, established neighborhood covering 2 square miles, stretching from Sully Road south to Lee Highway, it is bordered by the golf course on the north, and vast public

## 31 DIFFERENT TOWNHOMES AND HOUSES FROM 12 GREAT BUILDERS, FROM THE $140's. TO THE $220's.

parklands on the south and west.

"It's right here in the neighborhood" is a familiar comment for Sully Station residents, because they have their own shopping centers, schools, swim clubs, tennis courts, community centers and ballfields, more than 12 miles of biking and jogging paths, and nearly 300 acres of their own parks, playgrounds and open spaces.

In its first year, Sully Station was named "Community of the Year" by area homebuilders. Today, eleven of them are building their finest townhomes and single family homes here for this year's new residents.

The new Visitor Center and model homes are open 12-6 daily. Take I-66 west past Fair

## IT'S ALL RIGHT HERE IN THE NEIGHBORHOOD.

Oaks Mall to exit for Sully Rd. (Rt. 28) north. Up Sully Rd. 2 miles to entrance on left. Follow into Sully Station to Visitor Center signs. Or call 631-4910.

*Getting to school on my own is easy, 'cause there are bike paths all over our neighborhood. My mom also lets me ride to the store for her, since the shopping center is just up the street. And when I go to the pool or Bobby's house, I can even walk by myself.*
*My mom says she likes that everything is right here, so she doesn't have to drive me everywhere, and she can meet her friends at the tennis club.*
*My dad even uses the jogging path by our house once in a while, but mainly he just rides the Metro to work.*
*I guess we're all glad we moved to Sully Station.*

**SULLY STATION**

A Kettler & Scott Community

memorable song to the Sully Station name. Companion newspaper advertising repeated the same song lyrics. This campaign did wonders! Traffic increased and sales leaped forward once again.

In early 1988, the campaign focused on the many reasons why Sully Station was the most popular new planned community in the region. It promised success that buyers could see and share. Sales were now averaging more than 35 per month. By the spring of 1988, a fresh campaign was introduced that addressed major buyer concerns, such as commuting and recreational facilities, through the eyes and words of children who now lived in Sully Station. This proved to be a very credible campaign delivered by the most convincing residents in the community.

This case study illustrates the importance of understanding your market, tailoring your advertising to fit the targeted audience, building credibility through on-site environments, and consistently reinforcing the benefits of the housing by concentrating on the motivations of profiled consumers. Excitement, urgency and values become the synergistic messages linked to an evolving Sully Station story!

## MARKETING PRINCIPLES FOR DECISION-MAKING

We have explored a variety of new housing scenarios in this book and have provided readers with reference materials that can be individually adapted to local marketing needs and opportunities. Developers and home builders are always on the cutting edge of the entrepreneurial spirit! They are risk-takers, but they are also creators who take raw, undeveloped parcels of land and mold them into housing neighborhoods that shape long-range values. The more sensitive they are to the motivations, abilities and needs of their customers, the more effective they are in producing environments that attract new residents. Value creation and enhancement are physically demonstrated in the communities they produce.

The marketing disciplines cannot be separated from those that guide sound business practices. They are an integral part of the total process. Unless you produce a product that satisfies basic interests of your anticipated customers at prices they can afford, the enterprise will fail. Once you have designed and prepared your products for the marketplace, you must find cost-effective ways to expose them to enough prospective candidates thereby enabling your sales representatives to convert a reasonable percentage into homeowners. Timing is critical in the housing game. If a builder enters the market at the wrong time with the wrong product, misses the season or holds speculative housing months after completion, the financial consequences can be disastrous. In the complex world of real estate development, there is always a multitude of uncertainties. Even the most experienced and successful player should be hesitant to make a commitment for land acquisition and construction, unless he or she has first used proven marketing guidelines to measure the venture.

I hope that this book has reinforced these foundation principles of successful new home marketing, and provided a ready reference to those who are already involved in the home building industry, as well as others who are exploring its potentials for the first time. In closing this final chapter, permit me to summarize the key messages we have attempted to communicate.

## Profits Usually Result from Efficient Planning and Disciplined Execution

It has often been said that people do not plan to fail, they just fail to plan! The complexities of land development and home building demand thoughtful planning and disciplined supervision of the many steps involved in converting raw land into completed neighborhoods occupied by happy residents. My personal experiences have validated to my satisfaction that most of the profits in this challenging game are made before the first spade of dirt is turned! They are made (or lost) at the beginning. Whenever you pay too much for the land or fail to estimate the real costs of development, building, marketing and delivering your housing, the result will be lost profits and, often, lost investment capital. If you do not design housing environments that are competitive and appealing to your profiled prospects, you will lose the game. The use of critical-path planning charts and comprehensive checklists are safety measures that help you avoid costly wrong decisions and potential failure. At the risk of missing a market, it is usually better to extend your planning time and put more thought into the creation of values that will meet consumer demand than to rush into the game unprepared and without knowing the consequences of your actions! Once the project is launched, the profits are best protected by disciplined supervision of all phases of development, construction, marketing and sales. An appropriate motto to follow is: "Inspect what you expect!"

## Support Marketing Decisions with Solid Research

The security blanket for decision-making in this industry is well-documented research! Most failures can be traced to a fundamental flaw in the input phase of the planning process. When you make decisions in a vacuum, you are playing Russian roulette! You cannot know too much about the marketplace. The more you know and have documented, the more confident you can be about the results. The most essential factor in research is the ability to correctly interpret gathered data. Facts alone mean little. They must serve as the basis for asking the right questions and projecting the right answers.

## Marketing Tempo Is Influenced by Inventory Creation, Release and Price

In chapter 3, we examined a number of fundamental marketing concepts advocated by leaders in our industry. Topping that list is the principle of phasing and releasing sites and housing units to the marketplace in a pattern that avoids oversupply, decreased urgency, confusion and depreciation of values. Whenever prospective customers perceive that the supply is great enough to permit them to delay their housing decisions, you lose momentum and risk failure. Equally important, value perception is influenced by the pace at which homes are built and sold. Few people are willing to risk buying in neighborhoods where everything is for sale and future values are uncertain. Value perceptions are subtle. They are often highly emotional. The old saying that success breeds success and that failure breeds failure is literally true in the home building business. Managing the way housing opportunities are introduced to the marketplace is a key consideration in protecting values.

## On-Site Merchandising Directly Affects Sales

When prospective buyers arrive at a housing site, they are influenced more by visual impressions than by what salespeople tell them! Emotions and sensory experiences tend to be more important than logic in buying a home. That is why it is essential to prepare the on-site sales environment with effective merchandising tools designed to maximize value perceptions. This does not necessarily mean furnished models or elaborate sales centers. A single homesite or home under construction can be the only location available for demonstration of a builder's product line. Good merchandising can be as simple as having a fairly clean construction site with one graphic element, such as a sign that describes the housing in motivating language. When economics permit, it is always better to provide a finished (and preferably furnished) model to involve consumers and communicate unique features.

## Recruit Salespeople Who Can Counsel and Close

All salespeople are not equal! It is also true that selling new homes is distinctly different than selling older resale properties. Specialists in builder sales invariably produce greater results for their clients than generalists who have never mastered the knowledge and skills of new construction marketing. Those responsible for choosing sales representatives should have a genuine concern for the quality of the people they select. Whether outside brokerage offices or controlled in-house sales staffs are involved, it takes closers to realize optimum results! In chapter 4, we reviewed criteria used by professionals in recruiting and selecting the salespeople who perform. Whenever you are not achieving projected sales, evaluate your front-line representatives. Often the problem can be solved by putting the right salespeople on the job!

## Training and Motivating Sales Personnel

Superior results are usually realized when dedicated professionals consistently perform their assignments with confidence and enthusiasm. Sales personnel in particular need attention and guidance from managers they respect in order to maintain peak sales levels. That is why sales management is so important to the total marketing picture. In chapter 6, we provided orientation checklists along with valuable tips from leading sales managers on how to effectively train and motivate new home sales personnel. Monetary incentives are important, but they are not the only factors involved. Marketing creates sales tools, provides model-home environments, advertises and promotes property and is primarily responsible for bringing qualified prospects to sales offices. However, all of these functions are depreciated if sales representatives are not motivated to perform their closing roles.

## Organized Sales Presentations

New home marketers are responsible for designing all graphic elements necessary to effectively communicate sales messages to customers once they are in sales environments or face-to-face with sales counselors. They are also responsible for creating collateral sales aids such as brochures and presentation literature. The quality of these visual sales tools and the way they are organized and used in the sales facilities directly affects the selling process. As we illustrated in chapter 7, there is a logical qualifying sequence of messages and stations of involvement when on-site representatives are demonstrating housing values. Regardless of the size of the marketing budget, some of these tools must be professionally prepared and used even if other elements of the marketing plan are sacrificed. They are most important when you are attempting to paint the dream of future housing neighborhoods without benefit of furnished models or established values. Every factor that may affect a potential home buyer's favorable decision should be converted into a graphically effective tool that can be introduced at the appropriate moment in the sales process.

## Generate Qualified Customers With Multiple Prospecting Programs

An effective marketing plan considers the relative importance of every potential prospecting source and allocates appropriate percentages of total marketing dollars to access them efficiently. While print media campaigns are a dominant ingredient, they may only account for a nominal percentage of the closed buyers. The role of cooperative brokers, signage, owner referrals, street traffic, and publicity must be objectively evaluated along with promotional events and direct-mail programs before the budget is weighted in favor of any particular medium. Synergistically link of all your marketing efforts so that every dollar spent helps to multiply the effectiveness of companion programs. If you create and communicate consistent images and messages clearly targeted to profiled customers over extended periods of time, the repetitive impressions help to position your product and your values competitively.

## Customer Service

Today's home buyers shop and compare with genuine concern for both the value of their new housing and the service they expect after purchase. A quality delivery system supported with warranties and customer-oriented follow-up procedures influences the initial degree of consumer acceptance and the amount of referral business that can be generated after occupancy. It should be more than just giving a customer a printed sheet or a rehearsed sales pitch. Marketing programs that do not consider the value of building a solid owner base are ultimately far more expensive than those that do! Word-of-mouth advertising is the most effective and least costly means of obtaining new prospects. The total marketing plan should consider from the outset issues that may adversely affect consumer confidence before and after purchase. These factors should then be addressed by developing and implementing service-oriented programs. Builders and developers who go out of their way, creating friendly neighborhoods and doing the little things that help residents to feel part of the sales team, win the long-term relationships that keep them in business when others are suffering from declining markets.

## Monitor Your Marketing Efforts and Objectives

It is extremely rare for any of us to create a marketing plan that works exactly as programmed without needing adjustments. Even if we were that lucky, it would be foolish to presume we could overlook the day-to-day monitoring process that helps us measure our effectiveness. Sales personnel play a major part in helping to determine what is working and what needs improvement. Unless feedback comes from the front line, it is extremely difficult to make the right marketing calls. Sales managers and marketing executives need to be closely linked by mutual interests of producing traffic and closing sales. Traffic reports, prospect profile cards, buyer profiles and owner surveys are necessary ingredients in a total monitoring plan. When no other way exists to get needed information, personal interviews should be employed.

In addition to monitoring the sources and results of prospect generation programs, marketing managers, in concert with the other members of the team, must keep everything on schedule to meet deadlines for launching projects and strategic campaigns. Myriad details require controlled orchestration in the marketing game, and the challenge is to keep them all on course without losing sight of larger objectives. That is why marketing managers need to use critical-path checklists, project-control systems and prioritized time-management procedures.

## Innovate When Necessary

Yesterday's well-travelled path may not be the right one to follow. At times, the marketing manager has to leave the established routes and explore trails others have overlooked. Creativity is a basic characteristic of superior marketers. They are willing to look at alternatives and to brainstorm for fresh concepts with compatriots in their profession when old ones fail to produce results. It is impossible to anticipate all conditions that can suddenly affect existing marketing programs. Competition does not share in advance plans to reduce prices, offer special incentives or introduce newer designs. Financial markets are notorious for their unpredictability. When interest rates start to rise, the marketing strategies have to be reviewed to either take advantage of the increased urgency or counter the concerns of prospects who find it harder to qualify. Local political and economic conditions can change and drive customers into a retreat psychology. Alert marketing strategists find solutions to the problems they encounter. They are paid for their creative talents and are expected to find answers, not make excuses. From preconstruction marketing through clean-up phases, the objective is to expose qualified prospects to the merchandise so that salespeople can convert a reasonable percentage into owners. In chapter 11 we reviewed the guidelines for reading the marketplace and provided potential solutions for the variables we may encounter.

## Marketing Alternatives

As I conclude this compendium of marketing concepts, I feel it is appropriate to summarize my observations with this thought: The essence of marketing is in its many possibilities. No course of action will work in all situations, nor is there only one way to sell the housing products assigned to the marketing team. Alternatives always exist! Many of them have not yet been explored, and that is why they are not included in this book! We have not given you any magic answers guaranteed to work in every case. Marketing is a creative discipline, and it flourishes with the freedom to explore the unlimited potentials of creative thought before narrowing the conclusions to specific action plans. Willingness to examine new ideas and challenge old ways is the hallmark of the leadership of our industry.

We opened this book by asking, "Who is in charge of marketing?" The observation was made that everyone from the land developer to the salesperson on the front line plays an essential part in developing and executing marketing decisions, whether or not he or she realizes it! Marketing alternatives and the consequences of each decision along the way should consciously influence the choices made. Land planners are in the marketing game. The choices they make begin to define and limit the alternatives. Those who design the homes and price the homesites are deeply involved in marketing. They make choices that will certainly shape the marketing images and value perceptions. The individuals who decide which products, options and extras will be offered have contributed to the marketing package in a very specific way that determines how the housing will be measured by the public. Model merchandisers, landscape architects, sign painters, printers, copywriters and graphic artists all add or detract from the effectiveness of the total program. The real estate broker who delivers a customer to the building site is also a key influencer whose attitudes, knowledge and skills will certainly affect the most important person of all: the prospective home buyer!

The essence of marketing is in its many alternatives, but its effectiveness lies with the ability to interpret and communicate new housing values in ways that motivate prospects to step forward to enjoy the benefits of newly created environments!

# Appendix: Research and Exhibit Contributors

**A**

Aist, Herb—Los Angeles, CA
Anderson, Leland—Minneapolis, MN
Arkae Development, Inc.—Winter Park, CO
Arvida Corporation—Miami, FL

**B**

Baritell, David—Syracuse, NY
Barrow, Rick—Washington, DC
Beal Locke & Associates—Shreveport, LA
Becker, William—Teasneck, NJ
Blackhawk Realty—Danville, CA
Brandermill Group, Inc.—Midlothian, VA
Brightwater Marketing Associates—Missouri City, TX
Brown Realty Co.—Thousand Oaks, CA
    Joe Brown, President
Browning, Charles—Brookeville, MD
Brownson, James—St. Paul, MN
Bryan, Richard—Columbia, MD
Buckhead Brokers—Atlanta, GA
Builder Magazine—Washington, DC
Builder Marketing Services—Mt. Prospect, IL
Builder Marketing Society—
    340 University Ave., Ste. F,
    Los Gatos, CA 95030
    (408) 356-6050
Butera, Karen—Palo Alto, CA

**C**

Calia Development Corp.—Barrington, IL
Callawassie Island—Ridgeland, SC
Camelot Homes—Orland Park, IL
Centex Homes, Inc.—Chicago, IL
Chamberlain, Randy—Tempe, AZ
Clark, Carol—Atlanta, GA

Clarke, Charles—Jacksonville, FL
Coakley Heagerty Companies, Ltd.—Santa Clara, CA
Codman Company—Boston, MA
Connor, Jim—Louisville, KY
Continental Homes—Scottsdale, AZ
Coover, Russ—Morristown, NJ
C.P. Morgan Homes—Carmel, IN
Crawford, Richard—Grosse Pointe Shores, MI
Critchfield, Inc.—Wichita, KS

**D**

D & S Development Co.—Sylmar, CA
Dartmouth Corp.—Portland, ME
DeShetler Homes—Chesterfield, MO
Design One—Los Angeles, CA
Developers Marketing Group—Las Vegas, NV
Development Directions, Inc.—Rochester, MN
Dinkel, John—Stockton, CA
Domber, Steven—Poughkeepsie, NY
Dumser, Fred—Columbia, MD

**E**

Eagle River Builders—Carmel, NY
Eastern Properties—Princeton, NJ
Elkman, Richard—Philadelphia, PA
Elliott, Gary—Edina, MN
Emerald Homes—Phoenix, AZ
ERA–Serls Realty—LaGrangeville, NY
Everett Boyd & Associates—Raleigh, NC
Exhibits, Inc.—Denver, CO

**F**

F & G Construction, Inc.—Drexel Hill, PA
Farber, Ed and Steve—St. Louis, MO
Fiehn, Roger—Houston, TX
Fieldstone Co.—Brea, CA

Fisher, Nancy—Albuquerque, NM
Fonville-Morisey Realtors—Raleigh, NC
Fonville, Tommy—Raleigh, NC
Fulton, George—Fairfax, VA
Fulton Research, Inc.—Fairfax, VA

**G**

Gallinger Real Estate, Inc.—Syracuse, NY
Gans, George—Louisville, KY
Gilligan, Frank—Tampa, FL
Goodkin, Sanford—La Jolla, CA
Goodman, Lester—Irvine, CA
Gornall, John—Millsboro, DE
Griffin Homes—Calabasas, CA
Grossman, Jay—Boston, MA
Group Two Advertising Agency—Philadelphia, PA
Grupe Development Co.—Stockton, CA
Grupe, Fritz (Greenlaw)—Stockton, CA

**H**

Habitat, Inc.—Tempe, AZ
Hale, Jim—Raleigh, NC
Halter, Pete—Atlanta, GA
Hansen & Horn Contractors—Indianapolis, IN
Hart, Robert—Claremont, CA
Heagerty, David—Saratoga, CA
Henderson, Jim—Atlanta, GA
Herbart Aist & Associates—Los Angeles, CA
Herbert Horita Realty, Inc.—Honolulu, HI
Herbst, Daniel—Bloomington, MN
Hidden Valley Resort—Somerset, PA
Hixson, Michael—Irvine, AC
Horowitz, Larry—Denver, CO
Housing Digest Association—Washington DC

**J**

Jack Nicklaus Development Corp.—Tampa, FL
Jagoe Homes, Inc.—Owensboro, KY
Jim Mitchell Bros., Contractors—Birmingham, AL
Johnson, Thomas—Wichita, KS

**K**

Karen Butera, Inc.—Palo Alto, CA
Kemp Homes—St. Louis, MO
Kettler Brothers, Inc.—Gaithersburg, MD
Kettler & Scott—Vienna, VA

**L**

Levitt Properties—Santa Barbara, CA
Loeb & Hanan—Montgomery, AL
Long & Foster, Realtors—Fairfax, VA

**M**

Marketing Forum, Inc.—
  340 University Ave. Ste. F
  Los Gatos, CA 95030
  (408) 354-9040
McMillin Development Co.—Bonita, CA
Meritor Development Corp.—Bloomington, MN
Minnesota Mutual Life Insurance Co.—St. Paul, MN
Mission Viejo Co.—Highlands Ranch, CO
Mitchell Co.—Calabasas, CA
Mitchell, Mike—Camarillo, CA
Morisey, Johnny—Raleigh, NC
Morris-Casper Creative Marketing—Washington, DC
Morris, Mark—Washington, DC
Multi-Housing News—New York, NY
Myerscough Development Co.—Riverside, CA

**N**

National Association of Home Builders—
  15th & M Streets, NW
  Washington, DC 20005
  (800) 368-5242
National Association of REALTORS®—
  430 N. Michigan Ave.
  Chicago, IL 60611
  (312) 329-8200
Nicki Joy and Associates—Brookeville, MD
Northside Realty Associates—Atlanta, GA

**O**

O'Brien, Keith—St. Paul, MN
Olson Marketing Group—Englewood, CO
Olson, David—Englewood, CO
Orleans, Inc.—Huntington Valley, PA
Otis Crowell & Co.—Augusta, GA
O'Sullivan, Danny—Fairfax, VA

**P**

Pace Advertising Agency, Inc.—New York City, NY
Pacific Scene—San Diego, CA
Paul Semonin Company—Louisville, KY
Peachtree City Marketing Group—Peachtree City, GA
Pemtom Co.—Minneapolis, MN
Personnel Profiles—Huntington Beach, CA
Piney Creek Development Co.—Denver, CO
Pond, Ed—Houston, TX
Porten-Sullivan—Bethesda, MD
Price, Robert—Morristown, NJ
Probert, Bill—San Diego, CA
Probert, Gary—Simi Valley, CA
Professional Builder Magazine—Denver, CO
Pulte Home Corp.—Santa Clara, CA
Putman, Marc and Tierney—Rochester, MN

**Q–R**

Quincy Johnson & Associates, Inc.—Boca Raton, FL
Redwood Shores—Redwood City, CA
Richey Resources, Inc.—
    1700 W. Loop South #800
    Houston, TX 77027
    (703) 622-0877
Richey, Tom—Houston, TX
Robuck Homes—Raleigh, NC
Rosenberg, Allan—Dallas, TX
Rowles Co.—Florissant, MO
Rowles, Larry—St. Louis, MO
Ryland Group, Inc.—Columbia, MD
Ryness Co.—Danville, CA
Ryness, Gary—Danville, CA
Ryno, Craig—Morristown, NJ

**S**

Schatz, Manny—Danville, CA
Schlosser, Richard—Peachtree City, GA
Scotko Sign & Display, Inc.—Gibbsboro, NJ
Secured Communities, Inc.—Atlanta, GA
Siegel, Robert—New Orleans, LA
Signature Homes, Inc.—Wichita, KS
Sims, John D.—Morristown, NJ
Stanford Research Institute—Palo Alto, CA
Stratton Corp.—Stratton Mountain, VT
Suarez Housing—Tampa, FL
Suddath, Lovick—Hilton Head Island, SC

Sugarloaf Homes—Carrabassett Valley, ME
Summit, The—Winter Park, CO

**T**

Thompson, Patricia—Vienna, VA
Trammell Crow Company—Residential—Atlanta, GA
Trapp Family Lodge—Stowe, VT

**U**

Unruh, Douglas—Stockton, CA
Urban Land Institute—
    1090 Vermont Ave., NW
    Washington, D.C. 20005
    (202) 728-5918
U.S. Homes Corp.—Dallas, TX

**V–W–Y**

Vail Associates—Avon, CO
Warmington Homes—Costa Mesa, CA
Weekly Homes, Inc.—Houston, TX
Weichert New Homes & Land Co.—Morristown, NJ
William E. Becker Organization—Hackensack, NJ
Wolfe Resources Group—Annapolis, MD
Wood Brothers—Denver, CO
Woodland, John—St. Paul, MN
Woodland, O'Brien & Associates—St. Paul, MN
Woodlands Corp.—The Woodlands, TX
Words & Co.—Washington, D.C.
Yung, William—Wichita, KS

# Bibliography and Recommended References

**A**

*Action Selling*. Jim Mills. National Association of Home Builders, 1978.

*Aggressive Selling in a Defensive Market* (video film). Thomas Richey. Washington, DC: National Association of Home Builders, 1984.

*American Houses*. Phillip Langdon. Washington, DC: Stewart, Tabori and Chang, 1987.

*Analysing Real Estate Opportunities*. Messner, Boyce, Trimble and Ward. Chicago: REALTORS® National Marketing Institute, 1977.

*Anatomy of a Successful Salesman*. Arthur Mortell. Rockville Centre, NY: Farnsworth, 1973.

*The Art of Argument*. Giles St. Aubyn. New York: Emerson Books, 1962.

*The Art of Negotiation*. Gerard I. Nierenberg. New York: Hawthorne Books, 1968.

**B**

*Be Good to Be Great* (video film). William Smolkin. Washington, DC: National Association of Home Builders, 1980.

*Big League Sales Closing Techniques*. Dane. West Nyack, NY: Parker Publishing, 1975.

*Builders Guide to Merchandising* (booklet). Carol Ann Cardella. Washington, DC: National Association of Home Builders, 1978.

*Building a House* (slide show). Washington, DC: National Association of Home Builders, 1980.

*Building Better Ads: Real Estate Advertising Problems, Solutions and Results* (booklet). Richard Elkman. Washington, DC: National Association of Home Builders, 1987.

*Building Sales through People Motivation* (booklet). Tom Richey. Washington, DC: National Association of Homebuilders, 1980.

*The Business of Business*. Robert Beadle. New York: Harcourt Brace Jovanovich, 1981.

**C**

*Classified Information: Practical Guide to Successful Real Estate Newspaper Advertising* (booklet). Richard Elkman. Washington, DC: National Association of Home Builders, 1984.

*The Closers*. Pickens. New York: William & Steven, 1984.

*Color It Home*. Beverly Trupp. Boston: CBI Publishing, 1986.

*Community Applications of Density, Design and Cost* (booklet). David Jensen. Washington, DC: National Association of Home Builders, 1983.

*Community Control Manual* (manual). David Stone. Los Gatos, CA: The Marketing Forum, 1987.

*Community Design Guidelines: Responding to a Changing Market* (booklet). David Jensen. Washington, DC: National Association of Home Builders, 1944.

*Complete Book of Closing Sales*. Sal T. Massimino. New York: Amacom, 1982.

*Comprehensive Guide to Real Estate Finance*. Jeff Elias. Richardson, TX: Jeff Elias Publications, 1988.

*Cost Effective Site Planning: Single-Family Development*. Washington, DC: National Association of Home Builders, 1986.

*Condominium and Homeowner Associations That Work*. David B. Wolfe. Washington, DC: Urban Land Institute and Community Association Institute, 1978.

*Creating a Community Association: The Developer's Role in Condominium and Homeowner Associations* (booklet). C. James Dowden. Washington, DC: Urban Land Institute and the Community Association Institute, 1986.

*Creative Real Estate Financing* (audiotape series). David Stone. Los Gatos, CA: The Marketing Forum, 1980.

*Customer Service for Home Builders* (booklet). Washington, DC: National Association of Home Builders, 1988.

**D**

*Designing Sales: The Builder/Merchandiser Handbook*. Karen Butera. Washington, DC: National Association of Home Builders, 1987.

*Design with Nature*. Ian L. McHarg. Garden City, NY: The Natural History Press, 1969.

*Do It Yourself Marketing for the Small Volume Home Builder*. Charles Clark and David Parker. Washington, DC: National Association of Home Builders, 1986.

**E**

*Essential Dictionary of Real Estate Terminology*. Hemphill and Hemphill. Englewood Cliffs, NJ: Prentice-Hall, 1984.

*Essentials of Marketing*, 9th ed. E. Jerome McCarthy. Homewood, IL: Richard D. Irwin, 1987.

*Establishing a Builder/Realtor® Cooperative Program* (video film). Thomas Richey. Washington, DC: National Association of Home Builders, 1986.

*Eupsychian Management*. Abraham H. Maslow. Homewood, IL: Richard D. Irwin, 1965.

**F**

*Financial Management of Condominiums and Homeowners' Associations*. Washington, D.C.: Urban Land Institute and Community Associations Institute, 1985.

*Five Great Rules of Selling*. Percy Whitehead. New York: McGraw Hill, 1957.

**G**

*Get Ready to Manage* (video film). Dave Stone and Tom Richey. Washington, DC: National Association of Home Builders, 1986.

*Getting to Yes*. Roger Fisher and William Ury. Boston: Houghton Mifflin, 1981.

*Gold Series in Real Estate Sales* (videotape series). David Stone. Barrington, IL: John Krause & Associates, 1984.

*Guaranteed Sales Plan*. David Stone. Washington, DC: National Association of Home Builders, 1966.

*Guideposts for Effective Salesmanship*. Robert R. Blake and Jane Srygley Mouton. New York: Jove—The Berkley Group, 1984.

**H**

*Higher Density Housing: Planning, Design, Marketing*. Washington, DC: National Association of Home Builders, 1986.

*Hiring, Training and Motivating Real Estate Salespeople* (audiotape series). David Stone. Los Gatos, CA: The Marketing Forum, 1974.

*History of Housing in the United States*. Mason. Washington, DC: National Association of Home Builders, 1979.

*Homebuilders and New Home Training Series* (videotapes). David Stone. Denver: American Salesmasters, 1979.

*Home Builders Publicity Manual: A Step-by-Step Guide for Successful Public Relations* (booklet). Deborah Johnson. Washington, DC: National Association of Home Builders, 1984.

*Homes and Homebuilding 1988*. Washington, DC: National Association of Home Builders, 1988.

*House*. Tracy Kidder. New York: Houghton Mifflin, 1981.

*Housing America: The Challenges Ahead*. Washington, DC: National Association of Home Builders, 1985.

*How to Become a Successful New Home Sales Manager* (manual and audiotape series). David Stone and Thomas Richey. Washington, DC: National Association of Homebuilders, 1985. Distributed by The Marketing Forum, Los Gatos, CA.

*How to Demonstrate a Model Home* (video film). Clark Rector. Washington, DC: National Association of Home Builders, 1978.

*How to Get More Business by Telephone*. Dan Schwartz. New York: The Business Course, 1965.

*How to Increase Sales and Put Yourself Across by Telephone*. Mona Ling. Englewood Cliffs, NJ: Prentice-Hall, 1963.

*How to Master the Art of Selling*. Tom Hopkins. New York: Warner Books, 1980.

*How to Measure and Evaluate Salesmen's Performance*. Waylon A. Tonning. Englewood Cliffs, NJ: Prentice-Hall, 1967.

*How to Operate a Real Estate Trade-in Program*. David Stone. Englewood Cliffs, NJ: Prentice-Hall, 1959.

*How to Organize Your Work and Your Life*. Robert Moskowitz. Garden City, NY: Doubleday, 1981.

*How to Sell New Homes and Condominiums*. David Stone. New York: McGraw-Hill, 1975.

*How to Show and Tell to Up the Sell: A Guide for Home Builders*. Briggs Napier and Joyce Hovelsrud. Minneapolis: Shepard Marketing, Inc., 1979.

**I**

*In Search of Excellence.* Thomas J. Peters and Robert H. Waterman, Jr. New York: Warner Books, 1982.

*Integrity Selling.* Willingham. New York: Doubleday, 1982.

**K**

*Kuesel on Closing Sales.* Harry N. Kuesel. Englewood Cliffs, NJ: Prentice-Hall, 1978.

**L**

*Land Buying Checklist* (booklet). Washington, DC: National Association of Home Builders, 1985.

*Land Development.* Washington, DC: National Association of Home Builders, 1987.

*Land in America.* Peter Wolf. New York: Pantheon, 1981.

*The Language of Real Estate.* John Reilly. Chicago: Longman Group,

*Les Dane's Master Sales Guide.* Les Dane. West Nyack, NY: Parker Publishing, 1980.

*Lloyd Purves on Closing Sales.* Lloyd Purves. West Nyack, NY: Parker Publishing, 1980.

**M**

*Management Manual for the Small Volume Home Builder.* Washington, DC: National Association of Home Builders, 1979.

*The Management of Sales Training.* Jared F. Harrison, ed. Reading, MA: Addison-Wesley, 1977.

*The Management of Time.* James T. McCay. Englewood Cliffs, NJ: Prentice-Hall, 1959.

*Management: Tasks, Responsibilities and Practices.* Peter F. Drucker. New York: Harper & Row, 1974.

*Managing the Move-in* (video film). Frank Basile. Washington, DC: National Association of Home Builders, 1984.

*Marketing Checklist for the Development of a Single Family Residential Community* (booklet). William E. Becker. Washington, DC: National Association of Home Builders, 1985.

*Marketing Imagination.* Levitt. Chicago: The Free Press, 1980.

*MaxiMarketing.* Stan Rapp and Tom Collins. New York: McGraw Hill, 1987.

*Megatrends.* John Naisbitt. New York: Warner Books, 1978.

*Money Making Models: Selling Through Design* (video film). Sara Olesker and Nancy Sublette. Washington, DC: National Association of Home Builders, 1986.

**N**

*New Home Sales.* David Stone. Chicago: Longman Group, 1982.

*New Home Sales* (videotape series). David Stone. Burbank, CA: Lumbleau Stone Productions, 1983.

*New Horizons in Real Estate* (videotape series). David Stone. Denver: American Salesmasters, 1979.

*New House Planning and Idea Book* (booklet). Toronto: Home and Community Design Branch of Alberta Agriculture Brick House Publishing, 1983.

*New Rules.* Yankelovich. New York: Random House, 1981.

*No Bull Sales Management*. Trishler. New York: Business and Finance Publications, 1985.

**O**

*Ogilvy on Advertising*. David Ogilvy. New York: Vintage Books—Random House, 1983.

*One Hundred and Twenty Seven Sales Closes That Work*. Gary O'Brien. New York: Hawthorne Books, 1979.

*The Organized Executive*. Stephanie Winston. New York: W W Norton, 1983.

**P**

*A Passion for Excellence*. Tom Peters and Nancy Austin. New York: Warner, 1986.

*Personal Power Through Creative Selling*. Elmer G. Letterman. New York: Harper & Brothers, 1955.

*Planning and Design of Townhouses and Condominiums*. Robert Engstrom and Marc Putman. Washington, DC: Urban Land Institute, 1980.

*Planning for Housing: Development Alternatives for Better Environment*. Washington, DC: National Association of Home Builders, 1980.

*Policies and Procedures Manual for New Home Sales*. David Stone. Los Gatos, CA: The Marketing Forum, 1984.

*Professional·Approach to Selling Real Estate*. (book and audiotapes) David Stone. Los Gatos, CA: The Marketing Forum, 1968.

*Proven Sales Ideas for Home Builders: How to Maintain Control in Your Marketplace*. (audio cassette series). Briggs Napier. Washington, DC: National Association of Home Builders, 1981.

*Psychology of Motivation and Selling in Real Estate*. John Cyr. Englewood Cliffs, NJ: Prentice-Hall, 1974.

*PUDS in Practice* (booklet). Collen Grogan Moore. Washington, DC: Urban Land Institute, 1985.

**Q**

*Quality Is Free* Philip B. Crosby. New York: Mentor—New American Library, 1979.

**R**

*Radio Commercials that Work for the Building Industry* (audio cassette). Richard Elkman. Washington, DC: National Association of Home Builders, 1985.

*Real Estate Office Administration*. David Stone, et al. California Association of Realtors, 1963.

*Rental Housing*. W. Paul O'Mara and Cecil E. Sears. Washington, DC: Urban Land Institute, 1984.

*Renting is Selling* (video film). Frank Basile. Washington, DC: National Association of Home Builders, 1983.

*Road to Success in Real Estate* (videotape series). David Stone. Denver: American Salesmasters, 1976.

*Role of the Sales Manager* (video film). Dave Stone and Tom Richey. Washington, DC: National Association of Home Builders, 1986.

**S**

*Sales Closing Power*. Edwards. Washington, DC: National Toll Free Marketing, 1983.

*Sales Closing Techniques*. Dane. West Nyack, NY: Parker Publishing Co., 1982.

*Sales Management and Motivation*. Henry and Callahan. New York: Franklin Watts, 1980.

*Sales Manager as a Trainer*. Harrison. New York: Addison-Wesley, 1983.

*Secrets of Closing Sales*. Charles B. Roth. Englewood Cliffs, NJ: Prentice-Hall, 1978.

*Selection and Recruitment of Sales Personnel* (video film). Dave Stone and Thomas Richey. Washington, DC.: National Association of Home Builders, 1986.

*Selling Personality: Persuasion Strategy*. Walter Gorman. New York: Random House, 1979.

*Service America*. Albrecht and Zemke. Homewood, IL: Dow Jones—Irwin, 1986.

*Seven Basics of Selling New Homes* (video film). David Stone. Washington, DC: National Association of Home Builders, 1982.

*Shut Up and Sell*. Don Sheehan. New York: Amacom, 1981.

*Signage that Sells*. Washington, DC: National Association of Home Builders and the Urban Land Institute, 1988.

*Surefire Sales Closing Techniques*. Les Dane. West Nyack, NY: Parker Publishing, 1978.

*Synergogy*. James Srygley Mouton and Robert R. Blake. San Francisco: Jossey-Bass, 1984.


**T**

*A Technique For Producing Ideas*. James Webb Young. Chicago: Crain Communications, 1979.

*Telephone Techniques that Sell*. Charles Bury. New York: Warner Books, 1980.

*There Is a Better Way to Sell*. Sidney Edlund. New York: Amacon, 1980.

*Thirty-Six Biggest Mistakes Salesmen Make and How to Correct Them*. George N. Kahn. Englewood Cliffs, NJ: Prentice-Hall, 1982.

*Training and Supervising Salesmen*. Charles L. Lapp. Englewood Cliffs, NJ: Prentice-Hall, 1960.

*Training Manual for Real Estate Salespeople*. David Stone. Englewood Cliffs, NJ: Prentice-Hall, 1965.

*Training Sales People and Prospecting* (video film). Dave Stone and Thomas Richey. Washington, DC: National Association of Home Builders, 1986.


**U**

*Unlimited Power*. Anthony Robbins. New York: Ballantine, 1986.

*Using a Host/Hostess in the Sales Office* (video film). Nicki Joy. Washington, DC: National Association of Home Builders, 1983.


**W**

*Winning Moves*. Ken Delman. Burbank, CA: Warner Communications, 1984.


**Y**

*Your Blueprint for Selling Success* (audio tape series). Thomas Richey. Houston: Richey Resources, 1986.

*Your Changing World of Real Estate* (audio tape series). David Stone. Los Gatos, CA: The Marketing Forum, 1962.

## Z
*Zig Ziglar's Secrets of Closing Sales*. Zig Ziglar. Dallas: Resell Publications, 1979.

# Index